THE OXFORD HANDBOOK OF

JAPANESE LINGUISTICS

Edited by

SHIGERU MIYAGAWA
AND MAMORU SAITO

OXFORD
UNIVERSITY PRESS

OXFORD
UNIVERSITY PRESS

Oxford University Press is a department of the University of Oxford.
It furthers the University's objective of excellence in research, scholarship,
and education by publishing worldwide.

Oxford   New York
Auckland   Cape Town   Dar es Salaam   Hong Kong   Karachi
Kuala Lumpur   Madrid   Melbourne   Mexico City   Nairobi
New Delhi   Shanghai   Taipei   Toronto

With offices in
Argentina   Austria   Brazil   Chile   Czech Republic   France   Greece
Guatemala   Hungary   Italy   Japan   Poland   Portugal   Singapore
South Korea   Switzerland   Thailand   Turkey   Ukraine   Vietnam

Oxford is a registered trade mark of Oxford University Press
in the UK and certain other countries.

Published in the United States of America by
Oxford University Press
198 Madison Avenue, New York, NY 10016

© Oxford University Press 2008

First issued as an Oxford University Press paperback, 2012.

All rights reserved. No part of this publication may be reproduced, stored in a retrieval system, or transmitted,
in any form or by any means, without the prior permission in writing of Oxford University Press,
or as expressly permitted by law, by license, or under terms agreed with the appropriate
reproduction rights organization. Inquiries concerning reproduction outside the scope of the above
should be sent to the Rights Department, Oxford University Press, at the address above.

You must not circulate this work in any other form
and you must impose this same condition on any acquirer.

Library of Congress Cataloging-in-Publication Data
The Oxford handbook of Japanese linguistics / Edited by Shigeru Miyagawa
and Mamoru Saito.
p. cm.
Includes index.
ISBN 978-0-19-530734-4 (hardcover); 978-0-19-983007-7 (paperback)
1. Japanese language—Grammar.   I. Miyagawa, Shigeru.   II. Saito, Mamoru.
PL533.O94   2008
495.6'5—dc22   2007041899

Printed in the United States of America
on acid-free paper

THE OXFORD HANDBOOK OF
JAPANESE LINGUISTICS

Contents

Contributors, vii

1. Introduction, 3
   Shigeru Miyagawa and Mamoru Saito

2. On the Causative Construction, 20
   Heidi Harley

3. Japanese -*Wa*, -*Ga*, and Information Structure, 54
   Caroline Heycock

4. Lexical Classes in Phonology, 84
   Junko Ito and Armin Mester

5. On Verb Raising, 107
   Hideki Kishimoto

6. Nominative Object, 141
   Masatoshi Koizumi

7. Japanese Accent, 165
   Haruo Kubozono

8. *Ga/No* Conversion, 192
   Hideki Maki and Asako Uchibori

9. Processing Sentences in Japanese, 217
   Edson T. Miyamoto

10. The Acquisition of Japanese Syntax, 250
    Keiko Murasugi and Koji Sugisaki

11. The Syntax and Semantics of Floating Numeral Quantifiers, 287
    Kimiko Nakanishi

12. V-V Compounds, 320
    Kunio Nishiyama

13. *Wh*-Questions, 348
    Norvin Richards

14. Indeterminate Pronouns, 372
    Junko Shimoyama

15. Noun Phrase Ellipsis, 394
    Daiko Takahashi

16. Ditransitive Constructions, 423
    Yuji Takano

17. Prominence Marking in the Japanese Intonation System, 456
    Jennifer J. Venditti, Kikuo Maekawa, and Mary E. Beckman

18. The Structure of DP, 513
    Akira Watanabe

Author Index, 541

Subject Index, 549

Contributors

Mary E. Beckman
Ohio State University, mbeckman@ling.osu.edu
Language-specific and language-universal aspects of lingual obstruent productions in Japanese-acquiring children. (with Kiyoko Yoneyama and Jan Edwards) *Journal of the Phonetic Society of Japan* 7:18–28. (2003)
The ontogeny of phonological categories and the primacy of lexical learning in linguistic development. (with Jan Edwards) *Child Development* 71:240–249. (2000)
Japanese tone structure. (with Janet B. Pierrehumbert) Cambridge, Mass.: MIT Press. (1988)

Heidi Harley
University of Arizona, hharley@email.arizona.edu
On obligatory obligation: The composition of Italian causatives. (with Raffaella Folli) *Linguistic Inquiry* 38(2):197–238. (2007)
How do verbs get their names? Denominal verbs, Manner Incorporation, and the ontology of verb roots in English. In *The syntax of aspect*, ed. Nomi Erteschik-Shir and Tova Rapoport, 42–64. Oxford: Oxford University Press. (2005)

Caroline Heycock
University of Edinburgh, c.heycock@ed.ac.uk
On the interaction of adjectival modifiers and relative clauses. *Natural Language Semantics* 13(4):359–382. (2005)
Categorical Subjects. (with Edit Doron) *Gengo Kenkyu* 123:95–135. (2003)
Layers of predication: The non-lexical syntax of clauses. New York: Garland. (1994)

Junko Ito
University of California, Santa Cruz, ito@ucsc.edu
Japanese morphophonemics: Markedness and word structure. (with Armin Mester) Cambridge, Mass.: MIT Press. (2003)
Japanese phonology. (with Armin Mester) In *The handbook of phonological theory*, ed. J. Goldsmith, 817–838. Oxford: Blackwell. (1995)
A prosodic theory of epenthesis. *Natural Language & Linguistic Theory* 7:217–260. (1989)

Hideki Kishimoto
Kobe University, kishimot@lit.kobe-u.ac.jp
Wh-in-situ and movement in Sinhala questions. *Natural Language & Linguistic Theory* 23:1–51. (2005)
Binding of indeterminate pronouns and clause structure in Japanese. *Linguistic Inquiry* 32:597–633. (2001)
Split intransitivity in Japanese and the unaccusative hypothesis. *Language* 72:248–286. (1996)

Masatoshi Koizumi
Tohoku University, koizumi@sal.tohoku.ac.jp
Cognitive processing of Japanese sentences with ditransitive verbs. (with Katsuo Tamaoka) *Gengo Kenkyu* 125:173–190. (2004)
The split VP hypothesis: Evidence from language acquisition. In *Language universals and variation*, ed. Mengistu Amberber and Peter Collins, 61–81. Westport, Conn.: Praeger. (2002)
String vacuous overt verb raising. *Journal of East Asian Linguistics* 9:227–285. (2000)

Haruo Kubozono
Kobe University, kubozono@lit.kobe-u.ac.jp
Temporal neutralization in Japanese. In *Papers in laboratory phonology 7*, ed. Carlos Gussenhoven and Natasha Warner, 171–201. Berlin: Mouton de Gruyter. (2002)
The organization of Japanese prosody. Tokyo: Kurosio. (1993)
The mora and syllable structure in Japanese: Evidence from speech errors. *Language and Speech* 32(3):249–278. (1989)

Kikuo Maekawa
The National Institute for Japanese Language, kikuo@kokken.go.jp
Corpus-based analysis of vowel devoicing in spontaneous Japanese. (with Hideaki Kikuchi) In *Voicing in Japanese*, ed. Jeroen van de Weijer, Kensuke Nanjo, and Tetsuo Nishihara, 205–228. (2005)
Statistical tests for the study of vowel merger. *Quantitative Linguistics* 39:200–219. (1989)

Hideki Maki
Gifu University, makijp@gifu-u.ac.jp
Two notes on *wh*-movement in Modern Irish: Subject/object asymmetries and superiority. (with Dónall P. Ó Baoill) *Gengo Kenkyu* 128:1–31. (2005)
Embedded topicalization in English and Japanese. (with Lizanne Kaiser and Masao Ochi) *Lingua* 109:1–14. (1999)
Implications of embedded topicalization. (with Lizanne Kaiser) *English Linguistics* 15:290–300. (1998)

Armin Mester
University of California, Santa Cruz, mester@ucsc.edu
Japanese morphophonemics: Markedness and word structure. (with Junko Ito)
    Cambridge, Mass.: MIT Press. (2003)
The phonological lexicon. (with Junko Ito) In *The handbook of Japanese linguistics*,
    ed. Natsuko Tsujimura, 62–100. Oxford: Blackwell. (1999)
The quantitative trochee in Latin. *Natural Language & Linguistic Theory* 12:1–61.
    (1994)

Shigeru Miyagawa
Massachusetts Institute of Technology, miyagawa@mit.edu
On the "undoing" property of scrambling: A response to Bošković. *Linguistic
    Inquiry* 37:607–624. (2006)
Argument structure and ditransitive verbs in Japanese. (with Takae Tsujioka)
    Journal of East Asian Linguistics 13:1–38. (2004)
Structure and Case marking in Japanese. San Diego, Calif.: Academic Press. (1989)

Edson T. Miyamoto
University of Tsukuba, miyamoto@alum.mit.edu
Factors in the incremental processing of NPs in Japanese. In *Proceedings of the
    7th Tokyo Conference on Psycholinguistics*, ed. Yukio Otsu, 1–24. Tokyo: Hituzi
    Syobo. (2006)
Unscrambling some misconceptions: A comment on Koizumi and Tamaoka 2004.
    (with Michiko Nakamura) *Gengo Kenkyu* 128:113–129. (2005)

Keiko Murasugi
Nanzan University, murasugi@nanzan-u.ac.jp
VP-shell analysis for the acquisition of Japanese intransitive verbs, transitive
    verbs, and causatives. (with Tomoko Hashimoto and Chisato Fuji) *Linguistics*
    43:615–651. (2007)
An antisymmetry analysis of Japanese relative clauses. In *The syntax of relative
    clauses*, ed. Artemis Alexiadou, Paul Law, André Meinunger, and Chris Wilder,
    231–263. Amsterdam: John Benjamins. (2000)
N′-deletion in Japanese: A preliminary study. (with Mamoru Saito) *Japanese and
    Korean linguistics*, ed. Hajime Hoji, 285–301. Stanford, Calif.: CSLI Publica-
    tions. (1990)

Kimiko Nakanishi
University of Calgary, k.nakanishi@ucalgary.ca
Formal properties of measurement constructions. Berlin: Mouton de Gruyter. (2007)
Measurement in the nominal and verbal domains. *Linguistics and Philosophy*
    30:235–276. (2007)
Japanese plurals are exceptional. (with Satoshi Tomioka) *Journal of East Asian
    Linguistics* 13(1):113–140. (2004)

Kunio Nishiyama
Ibaraki University, kn20@mx.ibaraki.ac.jp
Verbs, adjectives, and Pred: Review of Mark C. Baker, *Lexical categories*. *English Linguistics* 22:133–161. (2005)
Adjectives and the copulas in Japanese. *Journal of East Asian Linguistics* 8:183–222. (1999)
V-V compounds as serialization. *Journal of East Asian Linguistics* 7:175–217. (1998)

Norvin Richards
Massachusetts Institute of Technology, norvin@mit.edu
Phase edge and extraction: A Tagalog case study. (with Andrea Rackowski) *Linguistic Inquiry* 36:565–599. (2005)
Movement in language: Interactions and architectures. Oxford: Oxford University Press. (2001)
An island effect in Japanese. *Journal of East Asian Linguistics* 9:187–205. (2000)

Mamoru Saito
Nanzan University, saito@nanzan-u.ac.jp
Expletive replacement reconsidered: Evidence from expletive verbs in Japanese. In *Form, structure, and grammar: A festschrift presented to Günther Grewendorf on occasion of his 60th birthday*, ed. Patrick Brandt and Eric Fuss, 255–273. Berlin: Akademie Verlag. (2006)
Subjects of complex predicates: A preliminary study. *SBOPL 1: Intensionality and sentential competition*, ed. Tomoko Kawamura, Yunju Suh, and Richard K. Larson, 172–188. Stony Brook, N.Y.: Stony Brook University. (2006)
Ellipsis and pronominal reference in Japanese clefts. *Studies in Modern Grammar* 36:1–44. (2004)

Junko Shimoyama
McGill University, junko.shimoyama@mcgill.ca
Indeterminate phrase quantification in Japanese. *Natural Language Semantics* 14:139–173. (2006)
Indeterminate pronouns: The view from Japanese. (with Angelika Kratzer) In *The proceedings of the 3rd Tokyo Conference on Psycholinguistics (TCP 2002)*, ed. Yukio Otsu, 1–25. Tokyo: Hituzi Syobo. (2002)
Internally headed relative clauses in Japanese and E-type anaphora. *Journal of East Asian Linguistics* 8:147–182. (1999)

Koji Sugisaki
Mie University, sugisaki@human.mie-u.ac.jp
The parameter of preposition stranding: A view from child English. (with William Snyder) *Language Acquisition* 13:349–361. (2006)
Early acquisition of basic word order: New evidence from Japanese. In *Proceedings of the 29th annual Boston University Conference on Language Development,*

ed. Alejna Brugos, Manuella R. Clark-Cotton, and Seungwan Ha, 582–591. Somerville, Mass.: Cascadilla Press. (2005)

Preposition stranding and the compounding parameter: A developmental perspective. (with William Snyder) In *Proceedings of the 26th annual Boston University Conference on Language Development*, ed. Anna H.-J. Do, Laura Dominguez, and Aimee Johansen, 677–688. Somerville, Mass.: Cascadilla Press. (2002)

Daiko Takahashi
Tohoku University, daiko@m.tains.tohoku.ac.jp
Apparent parasitic gaps and null arguments in Japanese. *Journal of East Asian Linguistics* 15:1–35. (2006)
Determiner raising and scope shift. *Linguistic Inquiry* 33:575–615. (2002)
Move-F and raising of lexical and empty DPs. In *Step by step: Essays on minimalist syntax in honor of Howard Lasnik*, ed. Roger Martin, David Michaels, and Juan Uriagereka, 297–317. Cambridge, Mass.: MIT Press. (2000)

Yuji Takano
Kinjo Gakuin University, ytakano@kinjo-u.ac.jp
Object shift and scrambling. *Natural Language & Linguistic Theory* 16:817–889. (1998)
Symmetry in syntax: Merge and Demerge. (with Naoki Fukui) *Journal of East Asian Linguistics* 7:27–86. (1998)
Predicate fronting and internal subjects. *Linguistic Inquiry* 26:327–340. (1995)

Asako Uchibori
Nihon University, uchibori@cit.nihon-u.ac.jp
Pseudoraising. (with Daiko Takahashi) *Gengo Kenkyu* 123:299–329. (2003)
Raising out of CP and C-T relations. In *MITWPL 41: Proceedings of FAJL3*, ed. María Cristina Cuervo, Daniel Harbour, Ken Hiraiwa, and Shinichiro Ishihara, 145–162. Cambridge, Mass.: MIT Working Papers in Linguistics. (2002)
Opacity and subjunctive complements in Japanese. In *Japanese and Korean linguistics 6*, ed. Ho-Min Sohn and John Haig, 399–414. Stanford, Calif.: CSLI Publications. (1997)

Jennifer J. Venditti
San Jose State University, jen.venditti@mac.com
Prosody in sentence processing. In *Handbook of East Asian psycholinguistics: Vol. 2*, ed. Reiko Mazuka, Mineharu Nakayama, and Yasuhiro Shirai, 208–217. Cambridge: Cambridge University Press. (2006)
The J_ToBI model of Japanese intonation. In *Prosodic typology: The phonology of intonation and phrasing*, ed. Sun-Ah Jun, 172–200. Oxford: Oxford University Press. (2005)

Akira Watanabe

University of Tokyo, akirawat@l.u-tokyo.ac.jp

The genesis of negative concord: Syntax and morphology of negative doubling. *Linguistic Inquiry* 35:559–612. (2004)

Case absorption and wh-*agreement*. Dordrecht: Kluwer. (1996)

Subjacency and S-structure movement of *wh*-in-situ. *Journal of East Asian Linguistics* 1:255–291. (1992)

THE OXFORD HANDBOOK OF

JAPANESE LINGUISTICS

CHAPTER 1

INTRODUCTION

SHIGERU MIYAGAWA AND MAMORU SAITO

In his 1977 keynote address to the Japanese linguistics community gathered for the LSA Linguistic Institute in Honolulu, Susumu Kuno congratulated the field for the enormous body of work produced on Japanese, which, as he observed, gave the Japanese language the distinction of being the most studied language within the generative tradition next to English (Hinds and Howard 1978:213). Today, the sheer number of linguists working on Japanese and the immense volume of research that continues to be published serve as witnesses to the fact that the Japanese language continues to engender high-quality work in vast amounts. Susumu Kuno's congratulatory comment in 1977, if repeated today, would be just as apt.

For this *Handbook of Japanese Linguistics*, we selected topics that capture this excitement of the field over the past fifteen years or so. In making the selections, we made two decisions. First, we wanted this handbook to have an overall coherence in approach. For this reason we decided to focus our coverage on "formal" studies of Japanese—syntax, semantics, morphology, phonetics, phonology, acquisition, sentence processing, and information structure. The chapters relate to each other across the different subdisciplines not only in the general approach taken but also at times even in the particular phenomenon being studied. For example, we find issues of word order taken up in syntax, acquisition, processing, and information structure. Moreover, although the topics we chose center on some aspect of Japanese, they also contribute to linguistic theory in general. As we discuss in this introduction, many works that have appeared in the last fifteen years or so have this characteristic: not only do they provide new and exciting analyses of aspects of Japanese, but also they make a direct and important contribution to our understanding of human language. Each chapter indicates precisely in what way the study of a particular topic has a bearing on the general linguistic theory. Due to this focus on "formal" approaches to Japanese linguistics, we did not attempt to cover other areas such as discourse analysis and sociolinguistics. This is not to say that there have not been important contributions beyond Japanese in these research domains—for example, in the area of "politeness" there are a number of important achievements that have contributed to our overall understanding of this topic. Nevertheless, we feel that, because of fundamental differences in approach, it would take away from the coherence of the *Handbook* to try to include works from these areas.

Our second decision concerns how we present the various topics. Going back for a moment to Susumu Kuno's 1977 address, it is suggestive of the field at that time that his remarks are included in Hinds and Howard's *Problems in Japanese Syntax and Semantics* (1978). Among the large number of subfields of Japanese linguistics, syntax and semantics represented the largest body of work then, and, we believe, also over the past fifteen years. Consequently, we chose a variety of topics in syntax-semantics and requested contributions from a number of linguists. We also included morphology, which is relatively new in generative studies of Japanese, and chose a topic that has a direct bearing not only on morphological theory but on syntactic theory as well. To round out the volume, we decided to include state-of-the-art chapters on phonetics, phonology, acquisition, sentence processing, and information structure. The chapters on syntax-semantics-morphology cover a variety of topics, are written by linguists who have directly contributed to the understanding of the particular topics, and are relatively short. The state-of-the-art chapters, some of which are considerably longer, are also written by leading scholars of the subfield.

1.1 SYNTAX AND SEMANTICS

S.-Y. Kuroda's 1965 doctoral dissertation, *Generative Grammatical Studies in the Japanese Language*, marked the beginning of the generative studies of Japanese. The vast amount of research that Susumu Kuno celebrated in 1977 was spawned by Kuroda's work to a large extent, all in the spirit of pioneering a new way to look at Japanese. Given that there was no prior work of this nature, the focus, necessarily, was on the analysis of Japanese through application of contemporary linguistic theory, although Kuroda himself was clearly using Japanese to gain insights into the nature of human language and provided important theoretical innovations such as the attachment transformation. In one way or another, most works in the 1970s and early 1980s asked the question: What can linguistic theory say about the Japanese language?

The main enterprise of this era was to seek empirical generalizations within Japanese that made it possible to describe some significant aspect of Japanese grammar in a formal and insightful fashion. In other words, the focus was principally on Japanese independent of other languages, and linguistic theory was a tool by which one could gain insights into the language. It is important to point out that this singular focus on the analysis of a specific language reflected the linguistic theory of the time—the standard theory developed by Chomsky and his colleagues and students in the 1950s and 1960s. Transformational-generative grammar, as it was known, set out a framework that tended to steer researchers to look deeply into a single language as opposed to seek generalizations across languages. Exemplary works in this enterprise include Kuno 1973, Inoue 1976, and Shibatani 1976, among many others.

In the 1980s, alongside the "Japanese-specific" research agenda of earlier years, a fundamentally new research direction in Japanese linguistics arose. This new direction is captured in the following question, which echoes the title of a WCCFL paper Kuroda gave in 1983: What can Japanese say about linguistic theory?

That is, works began to appear in vast numbers that used Japanese as the basis for making a direct contribution to linguistic theory. In most cases these works also embodied the spirit of the earlier era in presenting an extensive analysis of some aspect of Japanese grammar. The difference is that the analysis of Japanese is not an end in itself, but it is used to make a direct contribution to our knowledge of human language. It is no accident that this new trend in Japanese linguistics coincided with a fundamental shift in linguistic theory, from the rule-based transformational-generative grammar to what has come to be known as the principles-and-parameters approach to human language.

The principles-and-parameters approach postulates that the core of all human languages is defined by a uniform set of principles. The differences among languages arise from the fact that these principles are parameterized; the job of the language learner is to set the parameter of each principle according to the language encountered in the environment (Chomsky 1981). To give a couple of examples, there is a principle that requires that every phrase be headed; this principle is parameterized for head initial (e.g., Indonesian) or head final (e.g., Turkish). (See also Stowell 1981.) In another work, Rizzi (1982) observed that English and Italian have different parametric settings for bounding nodes for Subjacency: the bounding nodes S (present-day TP or IP) and NP (DP) are what are set for English, but in Italian they are set for S' (CP) and NP (DP). This allows extraction out of some *wh*-islands in Italian, for example. The principles-and-parameters theory set a new research agenda that sought to identify the universal principles and the nature of the parameter associated with them. To carry out this agenda, it often became necessary to pursue cross-linguistic analysis as opposed to simply looking deeply into one language.

An early work in this period that used an analysis of Japanese to shed light on linguistic theory is Saito and Hoji 1983.[1] They challenged Ken Hale's (1980, 1982) Configurationality Parameter, which had emerged as a highly influential theory of human language within the principles-and-parameters approach. Hale suggested a parameter that partitioned the languages of the world into two groups: configurational and nonconfigurational.

(1)   Configurational   Nonconfigurational

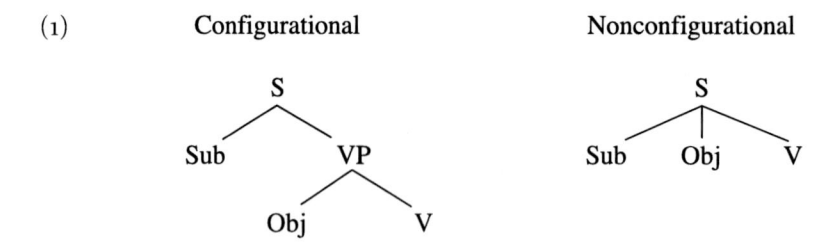

```
           S                              S
         /   \                         / | \
       Sub    VP                     Sub Obj V
             /  \
           Obj   V
```

Unlike configurational languages, which have the typical hierarchical structure of the subject separated from the VP, nonconfigurational languages lack the VP node, so that they are associated with a flat structure, with all phrases being dominated directly by the S node. A reflex of this nonconfigurational property of flat structure is free word order: because all phrases have a symmetrical (mutual c-command) relation with the verb, they are free to occur in any order without disturbing the meaning of the sentence. Because Japanese is a free-word-order language, Hale (1980) suggested that it belongs to the nonconfigurational group of languages.

In response to this, Saito and Hoji (1983) used arguments based on weak crossover, condition C effects, and other phenomena to show that Japanese is just as configurational as English. Although their empirical work focused by and large on the Japanese language, the principal message that the field took away from it is that there is no such thing as a nonconfigurational language. Thus, to the question, what can Japanese say about linguistic theory? Saito and Hoji's work had a clear message: every language is configurational. Although the "flat" structure has been rejected, it is important to point out that linguists in recent years have "rediscovered" Hale's proposal and have incorporated parts of it in dealing with free word order and related issues (e.g., Bošković and Takahashi 1998; Miyagawa 1997, 2001; Oku 1998; Saito 2003).

Other works of this nature—using Japanese to shed light on linguistic theory—include Miyagawa 1989, which, based on earlier works by Haig (1980) and Kuroda (1980, 1983), showed that the distribution of numeral quantifiers in Japanese gave evidence for NP trace, a theoretical notion whose existence has been questioned throughout the history of generative grammar (see also Ueda 1986). In another work, Watanabe (1992) analyzed *wh*-questions in Japanese as involving overt movement of a phonetically empty operator, in a fashion that parallels overt *wh*-movement languages. He concluded that in a *wh*-question, some element of the *wh*-phrase must move overtly, and that this is a universal requirement. This laid the groundwork for the notion of "strong" (and, by implication, "weak") features in the early period of the Minimalist Program (Chomsky 1993).

The last fifteen years have seen theoretically oriented works on Japanese syntax and semantics in vast numbers. The topics discussed cover a wide range of phenomena: ellipsis, compounds, quantifiers and numerals, and operator binding, just to name a few. Whenever there is an important theoretical issue, it is now almost always possible to find relevant works on Japanese. It is this sense of excitement that we wish to convey in this *Handbook*, and we have included articles on various topics in syntax and semantics for this reason.

We cannot close out the section on syntax and semantics without a mention of scrambling. No other topic has attracted as much attention among those who work on Japanese, and the interest has only grown as we have attained a deeper understanding of the phenomenon. One reason why scrambling has intrigued so many linguists is that at any given point, there are at least two theories competing for the correct analysis of it. In the 1970s and 1980s, the issue was whether scrambling resulted from movement or if the various word orders were base generated. Harada (1977) was the first to take a clear position on scrambling as movement. Shortly thereafter, Hale (1980, 1982) proposed the configurationality parameter and suggested that Japanese belongs to the nonconfigurational family of languages, with the result that scrambling is a function of the flat phrase structure, thus base generated. As we noted earlier, Saito and Hoji (1983) responded to Hale's characterization of Japanese as being a nonconfigurational language by showing that Japanese is associated with a configurational syntactic structure.

Saito and Hoji's characterization naturally led to the view that scrambling is due to movement. But now, a question arises: What motivates this movement? This is a hotly debated issue today. One view, held by the majority of linguists working on scrambling, is that the movement responsible for scrambling is purely optional, and no motivation is necessary (e.g., Fukui 1993; Kuroda 1988; Saito 1992, 2005; Saito and Fukui 1998). An early work that represents this view of scrambling is Saito 1989, which argued that scrambling—he was making use of long-distance scrambling—is semantically vacuous and must be radically reconstructed at LF. The semantic vacuity of scrambling provides the crucial argument for those who wish to view scrambling as purely optional: if it has no semantic import, it makes sense for it to be optional. The other view of scrambling is that it must be motivated by some factor. One of the earliest analyses to adopt this view is from Kitahara (1994), who suggests that scrambling is subject to what we would now call Closest Attract, a notion that requires a triggering feature for the movement. In a series of works, Miyagawa (1994, 1997, 2001, 2003, 2005a, 2005b, 2006) develops a study of scrambling that requires some motivation—either a formal requirement such as the EPP or, in the case of optional scrambling, the idea that it must lead to a new interpretation not possible without the movement (see Fox 2000). Other works that assume some sort of motivation include Grewendorf and Sabel 1999, Kawamura 2004, Kawashima and Kitahara 2003, and Sabel 2001, among others. In a slightly different vein, Bošković and Takahashi (1998) argue that the minimalist notion of "last resort" applies to scrambling. Two books devoted to scrambling and related issues have recently appeared (Karimi 2003, Sabel and Saito 2005), and in this *Handbook*, we decided not to take it up beyond what we just described, because so much has recently been written and it would be difficult to do justice to the phenomenon in one chapter. That is not to say that we completely ignore the issue. Miyamoto's chapter on sentence processing, and Murasugi and Sugisaki's chapter on acquisition, treat scrambling among other constructions from the perspectives particular to these chapters.

1.2 PHONOLOGY

Largely parallel to research in syntax and semantics, work in Japanese phonology has undergone a reorientation from focusing on the analysis of the language to focusing on the conclusions to be drawn from such analysis for general phonological theory; the relation between phonology, morphology, and syntax; and the structure of the lexicon.[2] Although this perspective was not absent from leading works of the earlier period, such as McCawley 1968 and Haraguchi 1977, it has taken center stage since the mid-1980s.

Work on the prosodic morphology of Japanese (Ito 1990; Ito and Mester 2003; Kubozono 1995; Mester 1990; Poser 1984a, 1990) revealed the overwhelming importance of the bimoraic foot—a unit realized as a single heavy syllable or as a sequence of two light syllables—in many kinds of word formation where canonical patterns play a role, such as nicknames, truncations, and the like. The fact that such higher level organization into feet asserts itself in Japanese, a language lacking an intensity-based system of prominence ("stress"; see Beckman 1986), was instrumental in establishing the view that prosodic structure—and most prominently, foot structure—is a general kind of rhythmic skeleton present in all languages, not just in those where foot heads are marked with phonetic stress. In a different vein, Ito and Mester (1986, 2004; Mester and Ito 1989) used some of the central morphophonemic alternations of Japanese to argue for specific properties of autosegmental representation and feature specification and, more recently, for a specific version of markedness principles operating in tandem with constraints on word structure in Optimality Theory.

The modern understanding of pitch accent systems is to a significant extent based on studies devoted to Japanese, such as Poser 1984b, Kubozono 1993, Pierrehumbert and Beckman 1988, and Selkirk and Tateishi 1988, which have established the general result that such systems involve only a few tonal landmarks (boundary tones and accentual tones) assigned at well-defined locations within an articulated prosodic constituent structure. As a last example, the segregation of the Japanese lexicon into separate layers governed by somewhat different principles (native, Sino-Japanese, Western loans) served as an empirical model for different variants of a universal theory of the phonological lexicon in Optimality Theory that can adequately represent such internal variation (Fukazawa, Kitahara, and Ota 1998; Ito and Mester 1995a, 1995b, 1999, 2001, 2002).

In one of the phonology chapters, "Lexical Classes in Phonology," Junko Ito and Armin Mester explore loanword phonology from the perspective of substructures that are known to exist in the Japanese lexicon. In another, "Japanese

Accent," Haruo Kubozono reexamines the Tokyo Japanese accent and develops a much simplified analysis. In "Prominence Marking in the Japanese Intonation System," Jennifer J. Venditti, Kikuo Maekawa, and Mary E. Beckman show that Japanese employs a variety of prosodic mechanisms to mark focal prominence, although, crucially, this does not include manipulation of accent.

1.3 ACQUISITION

Acquisition research on Japanese has a long history of its own, comparable to syntax and phonology. One of the main topics has been word-order variation as in syntax. Given that both SOV and OSV orders are available in adult grammar, with S and O carrying morphological nominative and accusative case markers, respectively, the question often addressed has been at what age children can correctly comprehend the "scrambled" OSV order (e.g., Hayashibe 1975, Sano 1977). The early works noted that young children had difficulty with the OSV order, mistaking it as SOV, which suggests that in early stages word order plays a prominent role, and it is the "neutral" SOV order that they assume. However, Otsu (1994) questioned this result by showing that children had no problem with the scrambled OSV order if a proper context introduced the sentence, thus showing that scrambling occurs earlier than previously believed. This result was reinforced by Murasugi and Kawamura (2005), who demonstrated that even three-year-olds were able to comprehend OSV sentences and, further, had knowledge of the reconstruction properties of scrambling.

Although it has been shown that many grammatical properties are acquired quite early, it has also been noted that the acquisition of others may be delayed. One candidate for late acquisition is A-chain. Here, the relevant theoretical proposal is Borer and Wexler's (1987) A-Chain Deficit Hypothesis, which states that maturation is required for the formation of A-chains. A number of works have appeared, for example, on Japanese passives and unaccusatives to examine this hypothesis, and a definite conclusion is yet to be attained. Whereas Miyamoto et al. (1999) argue for the hypothesis, Sano (2000) and Sano, Endo, and Yamakoshi (2001) argue against it, both on the basis of acquisition data on unaccusatives. Sugisaki (1999) and Minai (2000) take the late acquisition of passive as evidence for the hypothesis. Machida, Wexler, and Miyagawa (2004) concur with them, offering an alternative interpretation for the unaccusative data. But Murasugi and Kawamura (2005) suggest that the late acquisition of passive may be due to factors independent of A-chain maturation. The debate is yet to be settled.

In their chapter on acquisition, "The Acquisition of Japanese Syntax," Keiko Murasugi and Koji Sugisaki explore a number of issues concerning parameter setting and developmental factors in language acquisition. They consider those cases that fall under Wexler's (1998) Very Early Parameter Setting (VEPS) hypothesis and those that apparently involve delayed parameter setting. They discuss some data that pertain to A-chain maturation as well as to the gradual process of the acquisition of lexical items.

1.4 PROCESSING

Paralleling its study in syntax and semantics and also acquisition, scrambling is a prominent topic of research in Japanese sentence processing. The question is, is there a difference in processing load between SOV and OSV word orders? There is an important theoretical implication. By Hale's (1980, 1982) configurationality parameter, languages with flexible word order are nonconfigurational. According to this characterization, different word orders such as SOV and OSV are base generated. No movement is involved, so that, from the viewpoint of processing, there should be no difference in the processing load across different orders. However, the "scrambling" analysis (Harada 1977, Saito 1985) could predict a difference. SOV is the "base" order, and OSV involves movement of the object over the subject, thus increasing complexity and processing load. As Edson T. Miyamoto discusses in his chapter on sentence processing, "Processing Sentences in Japanese," the results of experiments on this topic have been mixed.

Another area that has attracted attention is the relative clause. Given that Japanese is head final, including the head of the relative clause, researchers wonder how speakers process relative clauses. Here, too, there are consequences for the general theory of sentence processing. What Miyamoto in his chapter calls a "head-driven" model predicts that Japanese is processed nonincrementally. Everything must be kept in working memory until the pertinent head appears and assigns each phrase an appropriate role. This makes Japanese sentence processing fundamentally different from the processing of head-initial languages. That claim, in fact, has been made (e.g., Mazuka and Lust 1990; see Hasegawa 1990 in the same volume for comments). Moreover, the nonincremental processing places a huge burden on memory. Miyamoto summarizes the research on Japanese relative-clause processing, including discussion of alternatives to this language-specific model.

1.5 INFORMATION STRUCTURE

Kuroda's 1965 doctoral dissertation includes a discussion on -*wa* and -*ga*, where he proposes that they represent distinct judgment forms. Although he has developed this analysis over the years, equally influential on this and other topics in the analysis of Japanese was Kuno's (1973) *The Structure of the Japanese Language*. That book laid the groundwork for a number of important research topics, and one of its vital achievements is the analysis of -*wa* and -*ga* in what we would now call information structure.

In her chapter, "Japanese -*Wa*, -*Ga*, and Information Structure," Caroline Heycock revisits the important descriptive observations in Kuno 1973 and develops a view of -*wa* and -*ga* based on modern theories of information structure. This is a continuation of the project she initiated in Heycock 1993, where she provided an explanation for what Kuno (1973:49–59) called "exhaustive-listing *ga*" in the mapping from syntactic structure to information structure. As Heycock shows, the information-structure analysis of -*wa* and -*ga* not only can successfully account for their complex properties but also may help to clarify aspects of the theory of information structure itself. Moreover, there may very well be contributions to be made to the analysis of other languages (e.g., verb-second).

1.6 BRIEF SUMMARY OF THE CHAPTERS

1.6.1 Phonetics and Phonology

In "Lexical Classes in Phonology," Junko Ito and Armin Mester explore class distinctions, such as Germanic versus Latinate in English, which occur in virtually all languages.[3] The synchronic status of such lexical strata is controversial in linguistics, and Japanese plays a prominent role in the discussion, partially because lexical class distinctions are so clearly visible, even in the writing system. With the shift in phonology from a rule-based derivational framework to a system of ranked and violable constraints that came with Optimality Theory, a new perspective on this topic has developed. This chapter takes up some of the conceptual issues connected with the theoretical shift and its empirical predictions and problems.

In "Japanese Accent," Haruo Kubozono demonstrates the simplicity of (Tokyo) Japanese accent through a review of the recent studies. He specifically argues for the following two points. First, word accent is only sparsely specified in the lexicon; that is, only certain classes of words in the whole vocabulary are lexically specified with their accent patterns, whereas a majority of words are literally unmarked in the lexicon. Second, major accent rules previously proposed as independent rules in Tokyo Japanese—such as the loanword accent rule, compound accent rules, and the accent rule for verbs and adjectives—can all be generalized.

In "Prominence Marking in the Japanese Intonation System," Jennifer J. Venditti, Kikuo Maekawa, and Mary E. Beckman show that Japanese uses a variety of prosodic mechanisms to mark focal prominence, including local pitch range expansion, prosodic restructuring to set off the focal constituent, postfocal subordination, and prominence-lending boundary pitch movements, but (notably) *not* manipulation of accent. In this chapter, they describe the Japanese intonation system within the Autosegmental-Metrical model of intonational phonology and review these prosodic mechanisms that have been shown to mark focal prominence. They point out potentials for ambiguity in the prosodic parse and discuss their larger implications for the development of a tenable general theory of prosody and its role in the marking of discourse structure.

1.6.2 Acquisition, Sentence Processing, Information Structure, and Syntax-Semantics-Morphology

In "On the Causative Construction," Heidi Harley shows that the analysis of the affixal Japanese causative morpheme -(s)ase requires an explicit treatment of the morphology-syntax interface, because it exhibits syntactic characteristics typical of both monoclausal and biclausal constructions, despite forming a single phonological word in combination with the verb stem to which it attaches. The arguments bearing on both lexicalist and syntacticocentric approaches are considered, and an articulated syntax-based treatment is presented. Additionally, the relationship between the lexical causatives and the productive causatives of Japanese is discussed in detail, and Harley argues that the allomorphic properties of the former support a Late Insertion approach to the syntax-phonology interface.

In "Japanese -Wa, -Ga, and Information Structure," Caroline Heycock discusses two of the most long-standing interrelated issues in the synchronic study of Japanese: the interpretation of the "topic marker" *wa* and the "nominative/subject/focus marker" *ga*. Descriptively, it appears that the former can have both contrastive and noncontrastive interpretations, and that the latter sometimes, but not always, expresses narrow focus. Similar patterns have been observed in languages where topic and focus are not marked morphologically; Japanese then may hold the key to a better understanding of these very contentious notions and, in particular, to the questions of how and why the different interpretations arise.

In "On Verb Raising," Hideki Kishimoto discusses issues and controversies surrounding verb raising in Japanese by looking at the null-object construction, unusual coordination, and emphatic verbal sequences. In the null-object construction, overt verb raising is argued to take place alongside VP-ellipsis (Otani and Whitman 1991), and the unusual coordination is claimed to involve overt verb raising (Koizumi 1995, 2000). By contrast, it is claimed that the emphatic verbal construction signals the absence of overt verb raising (Sakai 1998, Aoyagi 1998). A number of counterarguments as well as some alternative views are advanced in the literature in response to these arguments, so the claims still remain highly controversial.

In "Nominative Object," Masatoshi Koizumi presents a study of sentences in which the object is marked with the nominative case-marker *ga* (the nominative object construction). Such sentences contrast with prototypical transitive sentences where the subject and the object bear nominative and accusative cases, respectively. The nominative marking of objects is found in many languages of the world and has raised a number of important questions such as: (1) Is the nominative object really an object rather than a subject? (2) When does it occur? (3) Why does the nominative object tend to have wider scope compared with the accusative object?

In "*Ga/No* Conversion," Hideki Maki and Asako Uchibori examine the two major approaches to the Japanese *ga/no* (nominative/genitive) conversion phenomenon: the DP approach by Miyagawa (1993) and Ochi (2001), and the non-DP approach by Hiraiwa (2001a). They compare the strengths and weaknesses of each approach and then suggest a refined analysis that incorporates ideas from both approaches. In the suggested analysis, D licenses the genitive Case as in the DP approach, but movement into Spec,DP is not involved in genitive Case licensing, as in the non-DP approach.

In "Processing Sentences in Japanese," Edson T. Miyamoto discusses many of the major topics in sentence processing, including incremental processing of head-final constructions, clause-boundary ambiguities, implicit prosodic contours, relative clauses (attachment ambiguities, relativized position), *wh*-phrases, word order, and center embedding. A recurring theme is that the mechanisms and strategies used in processing are language independent (although some potential counterexamples are also discussed), so one crucial goal is to determine how seemingly distinct phenomena in typologically diverse languages can be subsumed under a unified account.

In "The Acquisition of Japanese Syntax," Keiko Murasugi and Koji Sugisaki begin by noting that the theory of language acquisition attempts to answer the foundational question of how innate linguistic knowledge, or Universal Grammar (UG), interacts with linguistic experience to yield a particular grammar in the actual time course. They review some representative studies on the acquisition of Japanese that attempt to answer this question and hence have a direct bearing on the construction of the theory of language acquisition. These studies are discussed along the following theoretical dimensions: (1) early emergence of UG principles, (2) parameter (re)setting, (3) A-chain maturation, and (4) the acquisition of lexical items.

In "The Syntax and Semantics of Floating Numeral Quantifiers," Kimiko Nakanishi looks at two competing views on floating numeral quantifiers (FNQs)—that is, numerals that appear away from their host NPs. One view holds that FNQs are transformationally derived from their nonfloating counterparts, whereas the other view assumes no transformational relation. The chapter compares the two by investigating how they fare with various syntactic and semantic properties of FNQs. In particular, at issue are distributional restrictions, such as why the object cannot intervene between the subject and its FNQ, and semantic restrictions, such as why FNQs permit distributive but not collective readings.

In "V-V Compounds," Kunio Nishiyama discusses V-V compounds as a construction that has inspired the lexicon versus syntax debate for the place of morphology. Some major lexical and syntactic analyses are reviewed, and Nishiyama examines how they fare empirically with the main properties of V-V compounds. Basically, transitive-transitive combinations are rather easy to capture, but complications arise when one of the verbs is intransitive. To accommodate some idiosyncrasies of V-V compounds within the syntactic approach, principles of Distributed Morphology are invoked—in particular, the root-as-categorially-neutral hypothesis. The goal of the chapter is to examine the implications of V-V compounds for the organization of grammar.

In "*Wh*-Questions," Norvin Richards considers some approaches to the syntax of Japanese *wh*-in-situ, contrasting movement with nonmovement accounts. The representative nonmovement account is Shimoyama's (2001), which gives Japanese *wh*-words a semantics that allows them to be interpreted in situ. The discussion of covert-movement approaches centers on the type first proposed by Nishigauchi (1986), with covert pied-piping of islands; the approach is modified, following von Stechow (1996), to allow subsequent reconstruction of the island. Data are drawn from conditions on the placement of *ittai*, quantifier intervention effects, multiple-*wh* questions, additional-*wh* effects, the distribution of *mo*, and semantic conditions on interpretation of pied-piped structures.

In "Indeterminate Pronouns," Junko Shimoyama provides a survey on issues surrounding the so-called indeterminate pronouns in Japanese such as *dare* 'who' and *nani* 'what', of which similar counterparts are found cross-linguistically. It focuses on two contexts, interrogative and universal, which easily allow apparently long-distance association of indeterminates with the particles *ka* and *mo*. The chapter examines two major types of analyses for the association, the movement and nonmovement analyses, in light of questions concerning (1) what the semantics of indeterminates are, and how the appropriate sentential meaning can be derived from the syntactic structure; and (2) how the intriguing locality pattern found in the association should be dealt with.

In "Noun Phrase Ellipsis," Daiko Takahashi presents an overview of the analysis of null arguments in Japanese in terms of ellipsis. The idea of "noun phrase ellipsis" was put forth in part to overcome certain difficulties faced by the traditional analysis based on empty pronouns. There are two main varieties of ellipsis analysis: one employs VP-ellipsis (Otani and Whitman 1991) and the other, more directly, NP-ellipsis (Oku 1998, Kim 1999). Although the former proposal is quite ingenious, this chapter shows that there are fairly strong arguments in favor of the latter. The NP-ellipsis analysis also has the possibility of relating the presence of null arguments to the free-word-order phenomenon (Oku 1998), which sheds a new light on the issue of (non-)configurationality.

In "Ditransitive Constructions," Yuji Takano looks at the syntactic properties of the two objects in Japanese ditransitive constructions. One major issue he takes up is whether or not word-order alternation between the two objects is to be attributed to movement (scrambling). It is shown that various arguments have been presented in the literature in favor of both approaches. Given this, Takano suggests a possible way to unify the two approaches.

In "The Structure of DP," Akira Watanabe looks at two peculiarities of Japanese nominals—namely, multiple possibilities for numeral placement and the existence of an indeterminate system. The internal structure of DP is explored by investigating the parametric sources of these two interesting characteristics. The possibility that emerges is that Japanese has more agreement relations within DP than has English and that the movement operations fed by these agreement relations produce the diversity of numeral placement. The indeterminate system is also shown to depend on agreement. Additionally, the behavior of nonnumeral quantifiers is taken up and compared with that of numerals.

Acknowledgments

Earlier versions of many of the chapters were presented at the Workshop on Linguistic Theory and the Japanese Language at the 2005 MIT–Harvard LSA Summer Institute. We thank the audience for numerous useful suggestions. We are grateful to the Japan Foundation, the MIT School of Humanities, Arts, and Social Science, as well as MIT Foreign Languages and Literatures for providing financial support for the workshop. We also wish to express our gratitude to the anonymous reviewers whose critical comments helped to strengthen the arguments in each of the chapters. This volume follows in the footsteps of *The Handbook of Japanese Linguistics* (1999) edited by Natsuko Tsujimura; the way we conceived this volume was greatly informed by the earlier work. Finally, we would like to thank the OUP editors for their enormous help, and Eli Laurençot for coordinating this complex project and providing expert copyediting for the entire volume, which made our editorial work enormously easier.

Notes for Chapter 1

1. The configurational analysis of Japanese is further developed in Saito 1985 and Hoji 1985.
2. We thank Junko Ito and Armin Mester for extensive assistance with this section on phonology.
3. The summaries of the chapters presented here are based on the abstracts written by the authors. Please see the reference sections of the individual chapters for the works cited in these summaries.

References

Beckman, Mary. 1986. *Stress and non-stress accent*. Dordrecht: Foris.
Borer, Hagit, and Kenneth Wexler. 1987. The maturation of syntax. In *Parameter setting*, ed. Thomas Roeper and Edwin Williams, 123–172. Dordrecht: Reidel.

Bošković, Željko, and Daiko Takahashi. 1998. Scrambling and Last Resort. *Linguistic Inquiry* 29:347–366.
Chomsky, Noam. 1981. *Lectures on government and binding.* Dordrecht: Foris.
Chomsky, Noam. 1993. A Minimalist Program for linguistic theory. In *The view from Building 20*, ed. Kenneth Hale and Samuel Jay Keyser, 1–52. Cambridge, Mass.: MIT Press.
Fox, Danny. 2000. *Economy and semantic interpretation.* Cambridge, Mass.: MIT Press.
Fukazawa, Haruka, Mafuyu Kitahara, and Mitsuhiko Ota. 1998. Lexical stratification and ranking invariance in constraint-based grammars. Ms., University of Maryland, College Park, Indiana University, Bloomington, and Georgetown University, Washington, DC.
Fukui, Naoki. 1993. Parameters and optionality. *Linguistic Inquiry* 24:399–420.
Grewendorf, Günther, and Joachim Sabel. 1999. Scrambling in German and Japanese: Adjunction versus multiple specifiers. *Natural Language & Linguistic Theory* 17:1–65.
Haig, John H. 1980. Some observations on quantifier floating in Japanese. *Linguistics* 18:1065–1083.
Hale, Kenneth. 1980. Remarks on Japanese phrase structure: Comments on the papers on Japanese syntax. In *MITWPL 2: Theoretical issues in Japanese linguistics*, ed. Yukio Otsu and Ann Farmer, 185–203. Cambridge, Mass.: MIT Working Papers in Linguistics.
Hale, Kenneth. 1982. Preliminary remarks on configurationality. In *Proceedings of NELS 12*, ed. James Pustejovsky and Peter Sells, 86–96. Amherst, Mass.: GLSA Publications.
Harada, Shin-Ichi. 1977. Nihongo-ni henkei-wa hitsuyou-da [Japanese grammar requires transformational rules]. *Gengo* [Language] 6(10):88–95, 6(11):96–103.
Haraguchi, Shosuke. 1977. *The tone pattern of Japanese: An autosegmental theory of tonology.* Tokyo: Kaitakusha.
Hasegawa, Nobuko. 1990. Comments on Mazuka and Lust's paper. In *Language processing and language acquisition*, ed. Lyn Frazier and Jill de Villiers, 207–223. Dordrecht: Kluwer.
Hayashibe, Hideo. 1975. Word order and particles: A developmental study in Japanese. *Descriptive and Applied Linguistics* 8:1–18.
Heycock, Caroline. 1993. Focus projection in Japanese. In *Proceedings of NELS 24*, ed. M. Gonzàlez, 159–187. Amherst, Mass.: GLSA Publications.
Hinds, John, and Irwin Howard, eds. 1978. *Problems in Japanese syntax and semantics.* Tokyo: Kaitakusha.
Hoji, Hajime. 1985. Logical Form constraints and configurational structures in Japanese. Doctoral dissertation, University of Washington, Seattle.
Inoue, Kazuko. 1976. *Henkei punpoo to nihongo* [Transformational grammar and the Japanese language]. Tokyo: Taishukan.
Ito, Junko. 1990. Prosodic minimality in Japanese. In *Proceedings of CLS 26: Parasession on the syllable in phonetics and phonology*, 213–239. Chicago: Chicago Linguistic Society.
Ito, Junko, and Armin Mester. 1986. The phonology of voicing in Japanese: Theoretical consequences for morphological accessibility. *Linguistic Inquiry* 17:49–73.
Ito, Junko, and Armin Mester. 1995a. Japanese phonology. In *Handbook of phonological theory*, ed. John Goldsmith, 817–838. Oxford: Blackwell.
Ito, Junko, and Armin Mester. 1995b. The core-periphery structure of the lexicon and constraints on reranking. *UMOP 18: Papers in Optimality Theory*, ed. Jill Beckman, Laura Walsh Dickey, and Suzanne Urbanczyk, 181–210. Amherst, Mass.: GLSA Publications.

Ito, Junko, and Armin Mester. 1999. The phonological lexicon. In *A handbook of Japanese linguistics*, ed. Natsuko Tsujimura, 62–100. Oxford: Blackwell.
Ito, Junko, and Armin Mester. 2001. Covert generalizations in optimality theory: The role of stratal faithfulness constraints. In *Proceedings of the 2001 International Conference on Phonology and Morphology*, 3–33. Seoul: Korea Research Foundation.
Ito, Junko, and Armin Mester. 2002. One phonology or many? The role of stratal faithfulness constraints. *Phonological Studies* 5:121–126.
Ito, Junko, and Armin Mester. 2003. Weak layering and word binarity. In *A new century of phonology and phonological theory: A festschrift for Professor Shosuke Haraguchi on the occasion of his 60th birthday*, ed. Takeru Honma, Masao Okazaki, Toshiyuki Tabata, and Shin-ichi Tanaka, 26–65. Tokyo: Kaitakusha.
Ito, Junko, and Armin Mester. 2004. *Japanese morphophonemics: Markedness and word structure*. Cambridge, Mass.: MIT Press.
Karimi, Simin, ed. 2003. *Word order and scrambling*. Oxford: Blackwell.
Kawamura, Tomoko. 2004. A feature-checking analysis of Japanese scrambling. *Journal of Linguistics* 40:45–68.
Kawashima, Ruriko, and Hisatsugu Kitahara. 2003. Phonological content and syntactic visibility. *Gengo Kenkyu* [Language Research] 123:137–170.
Kitahara, Hisatsugu. 1994. Restricting ambiguous rule-application: A unified analysis of movement. In *MITWPL 24: Proceedings of FAJL 1*, ed. Masatoshi Koizumi and Hiroyuki Ura, 179–209. Cambridge, Mass.: MIT Working Papers in Linguistics.
Kubozono, Haruo. 1993. *The organization of Japanese prosody*. Tokyo: Kurosio.
Kubozono, Haruo. 1995. *Gokeisei to on'in-kouzou* [Word formation and phonological structure]. Tokyo: Kurosio.
Kuno, Susumu. 1973. *The structure of the Japanese language*. Cambridge, Mass.: MIT Press.
Kuroda, S.-Y. 1965. Generative grammatical studies in the Japanese language. Doctoral dissertation, MIT, Cambridge, Mass.
Kuroda, S.-Y. 1980. Bun kouzou no hikaku [The comparison of sentence structures]. In *Niti-eigo hikaku kouza 2: Bunpou* [Lectures on Japanese-English comparative studies 2: Grammar], ed. Tetsuya Kunihiro, 23–61. Tokyo: Taishukan.
Kuroda, S.-Y. 1983. What can Japanese say about government and binding? In *Proceedings of WCCFL 2*, ed. Michael Barlow, Daniel P. Flickinger, and Michael T. Wescoat, 153–164. Stanford, Calif.: Stanford Linguistics Association.
Kuroda, S.-Y. 1988. Whether we agree or not. *Linguisticae Investigationes* 12:1–47.
Machida, Nanako, Ken Wexler, and Shigeru Miyagawa. 2004. A-chain maturation reexamined: A response to Sano et al. In *MITWPL 48: Plato's problem: Problems in language acquisition*, ed. Aniko Csirmaz, Andrea Gualmini, and Andrew Nevins, 91–112. Cambridge, Mass.: MIT Working Papers in Linguistics.
Mazuka, Reiko, and Barbara Lust. 1990. On parameter setting and parsing: Predictions for cross-linguistic differences in adult and child processing. In *Language processing and language acquisition*, ed. Lyn Frazier and Jill de Villiers, 163–205. Dordrecht: Kluwer.
McCawley, James D. 1968. *The phonological component of a grammar of Japanese*. The Hague: Mouton.
Mester, Armin. 1990. Patterns of truncation. *Linguistic Inquiry* 21:475–485.
Mester, Armin, and Junko Ito. 1989. Feature predictability and underspecification: Palatal prosody in Japanese mimetics. *Language* 65:258–293.
Minai, Utako. 2000. The acquisition of Japanese passives. *Japanese/Korean Linguistics* 9:339–350.

Miyagawa, Shigeru. 1989. *Structure and case marking in Japanese* (Syntax and Semantics 22). San Diego, Calif.: Academic Press.

Miyagawa, Shigeru. 1994. Scrambling as an obligatory movement. In *Proceedings of Nanzan University International Symposium on Japanese Language Education and Japanese Language Studies*, 81–92. Nagoya, Japan: Nanzan University.

Miyagawa, Shigeru. 1997. Against optional scrambling. *Linguistic Inquiry* 28:1–26.

Miyagawa, Shigeru. 2001. The EPP, scrambling, and *wh*-in-situ. In *Ken Hale: A life in language*, ed. Michael Kenstowicz, 293–338. Cambridge, Mass.: MIT Press.

Miyagawa, Shigeru. 2003. A-movement scrambling and options without optionality. In *Word order and scrambling*, ed. Simin Karimi, 177–200. Oxford: Blackwell.

Miyagawa, Shigeru. 2005a. On the EPP. In *MITWPL 49: Perspectives on phases*, ed. Martha McGinnis and Norvin Richards, 201–235. Cambridge, Mass.: MIT Working Papers in Linguistics.

Miyagawa, Shigeru. 2005b. EPP and semantically vacuous scrambling. In *The free word order phenomenon*, ed. Joachim Sabel and Mamoru Saito, 181–220. Berlin: Mouton de Gruyter.

Miyagawa, Shigeru. 2006. On the "undoing" property of scrambling: A response to Bošković. *Linguistic Inquiry* 37:607–624.

Miyamoto, Edson T., Kenneth Wexler, Takako Aikawa, and Shigeru Miyagawa. 1999. Case-dropping and unaccusatives in Japanese acquisition. In *Proceedings of BUCLD 23*, ed. Annabel Greenhill, Heather Littlefield, and Cheryl Tano, 443–452. Somerville, Mass.: Cascadilla Press.

Murasugi, Keiko, and Tomoko Kawamura. 2005. On the acquisition of scrambling in Japanese. In *The free word order phenomenon*, ed. Joachim Sabel and Mamoru Saito, 221–242. Berlin: Mouton de Gruyter.

Ochi, Masao. 2001. Move F and *ga/no* conversion in Japanese. *Journal of East Asian Linguistics* 10:247–286.

Oku, Satoshi. 1998. A theory of selection and reconstruction in the minimalist perspective. Doctoral dissertation, University of Connecticut, Storrs.

Otsu, Yukio. 1994. Early acquisition of scrambling in Japanese. In *Language acquisition studies in generative grammar*, ed. Teun Hoekstra and Bonnie D. Schwartz, 253–264. Amsterdam: John Benjamins.

Pierrehumbert, Janet, and Mary Beckman. 1988. *Japanese tone structure*. Cambridge, Mass.: MIT Press.

Poser, William J. 1984a. Hypocoristic formation in Japanese. In *Proceedings of WCCFL 3*, ed. Mark Cobler, Susannah MacKaye, and Michael T. Wescoat, 218–229. Stanford, Calif.: Stanford Linguistics Association.

Poser, William J. 1984b. The phonetics and phonology of tone and intonation in Japanese. Doctoral dissertation, MIT, Cambridge, Mass.

Poser, William J. 1990. Evidence for foot structure in Japanese. *Language* 66:78–105.

Rizzi, Luigi. 1982. *Issues in Italian syntax*. Dordrecht: Foris.

Sabel, Joachim. 2001. *Wh*-questions in Japanese: Scrambling, reconstruction, and *wh*-movement. *Linguistic Analysis* 31:1–41.

Sabel, Joachim, and Mamoru Saito, eds. 2005. *The free word order phenomenon*. Berlin: Mouton de Gruyter.

Saito, Mamoru. 1985. Some asymmetries in Japanese and their theoretical implications. Doctoral dissertation, MIT, Cambridge, Mass.

Saito, Mamoru. 1989. Scrambling as semantically vacuous A'-movement. In *Alternative conceptions of phrase structure*, ed. Mark Baltin and Anthony Kroch, 182–200. Chicago: University of Chicago Press.

Saito, Mamoru. 1992. Long-distance scrambling in Japanese. *Journal of East Asian Linguistics* 1:69–118.

Saito, Mamoru. 2003. On the role of selection in the application of merge. In *Proceedings of NELS 33*, ed. Makoto Kadowaki and Shigeto Kawahara, 323–345. Amherst, Mass.: GLSA Publications.

Saito, Mamoru. 2005. Further notes on the interpretation of scrambling chains. In *The free word order phenomenon*, ed. Joachim Sabel and Mamoru Saito, 335–376. Berlin: Mouton de Gruyter.

Saito, Mamoru, and Hajime Hoji. 1983. Weak crossover and move-α in Japanese. *Natural Language & Linguistic Theory* 1:245–259.

Saito, Mamoru, and Naoki Fukui. 1998. Order in phrase structure and movement. *Linguistic Inquiry* 29:439–474.

Sano, Keiko. 1977. An experimental study on the acquisition of Japanese simple sentences and cleft sentences. *Descriptive and Applied Linguistics* 10:213–233.

Sano, Tetsuya. 2000. Issues on unaccusatives and passives in the acquisition of Japanese. In *Proceedings of the Tokyo Conference on Psycholinguistics 1*, ed. Yukio Otsu, 1–21. Tokyo: Hituzi Shobo.

Sano, Tetsuya, Mika Endo, and Kyoko Yamakoshi. 2001. Developmental issues in the acquisition of Japanese unaccusatives and passives. In *Proceedings of BUCLD 25*, ed. Anna H.-J. Do, Laura Domínguez, and Aimee Johansen, 668–683. Somerville, Mass.: Cascadilla Press.

Selkirk, Elisabeth, and Koichi Tateishi. 1988. Constraints on minor phrase formation in Japanese. In *Proceedings of CLS 24*, ed. Lynn MacLeod, Gary Larson, and Diane Brentari, 316–336. Chicago: Chicago Linguistic Society.

Shibatani, Masayoshi. 1976. *Japanese generative grammar* (Syntax and Semantics 5). San Diego, Calif.: Academic Press.

Shimoyama, Junko. 2001. *Wh*-constructions in Japanese. Doctoral dissertation, University of Massachusetts, Amherst.

Stechow, Arnim von. 1996. Against LF pied-piping. *Natural language Semantics* 4:57–110.

Stowell, Tim. 1981. Origins of phrase structure. Doctoral dissertation, MIT, Cambridge, Mass.

Sugisaki, Koji. 1999. Japanese passives in acquisition. *UConnWPL 11: The syntax-semantics interface*, 145–156. Cambridge, Mass.: MIT Working Papers in Linguistics.

Tsujimura, Natsuko, ed. 1999. *The handbook of Japanese linguistics*. Oxford: Blackwell.

Ueda, Masanobu. 1986. Quantifier float in Japanese. In *UMOP 11: Oriental linguistics*, ed. Nobuko Hasegawa and Yoshihisa Kitagawa, 269–309. Amherst, Mass.: GLSA Publications.

Watanabe, Akira. 1992. Subjacency and S-structure movement of *wh*-in-situ. *Journal of East Asian Linguistics* 1:255–291.

Wexler, Kenneth. 1998. Very early parameter setting and the unique checking constraint: A new explanation of the optional infinitive stage. *Lingua* 106:23–79.

CHAPTER 2

ON THE CAUSATIVE CONSTRUCTION

HEIDI HARLEY

What is remarkable about the Japanese causative forms is that, unlike many languages, intransitive verbs also form causatives even when there are corresponding transitive verbs with a causative meaning...shar[ing] a great many semantic properties. These competing forms provide a rare opportunity for the examination of the differences between lexical word formation and syntactic word formation.

(Shibatani 1990:380)

2.1 AFFIXAL CAUSATIVES AND ARCHITECTURES

Japanese was the first language with morphological affixation of causative morphemes to receive serious attention from generative grammarians (perhaps because it is the first language of several important early generative theoreticians, such as Saito, Kuroda, and Kuno). The typological differences between Japanese and English represented the first exploration of the Universal Grammar hypothesis, which predicted the existence of important similarities in the grammatical structure of languages from unrelated language families. Consequently, its impact on generative linguistic theories in general and on principles-and-parameters approaches specifically has been very significant.

The Japanese causative represents in a very pure form the problem of the morphology/syntax interface. Consequently, the causative construction is one of the most theoretically significant aspects of Japanese grammar, its three subtypes having attracted more attention and inspired more theoretical proposals than almost any other construction. Analyses of the causative have had a major influence on many foundational aspects of syntactic theory, including control, case marking, clause structure, θ-theory and argument structure, and the morphology-syntax interface.

All of these issues have received extensive treatment in the literature, and this chapter touches on many of them. However, I focus on the importance for linguistic theory of a single problem posed by the construction: In what component of the grammar are the various causatives constructed? It turns out that the answers to many of the other syntactic questions posed by causatives depend on the theoretical choices made in answering this one. In fact, it is not unreasonable to say that the entire architecture of a given linguistic theory can be deduced from the answer given to this one question. The best analysis, we presume, provides a theoretically satisfying, cross-linguistically consistent, and most important, *unified* treatment of the causative morpheme -(s)ase. I endeavor to show that such an analysis exists and that it demands a certain type of theoretical framework; indeed, such a unified analysis could not exist in a framework configured differently in any significant way.

2.1.1 The Empirical Base

To create a causative expression in Japanese, the bisyllabic morpheme -(s)ase is attached to what would be the embedded verb in an equivalent English causative construction, as illustrated in the example in (1).

(1) Taroo-ga   Hanako-o   ik-ase-ta.
     Taroo-NOM   Hanako-ACC   go-*ase*-PST
     'Taroo made Hanako go.'

The Causer (here, *Taroo*) is the nominative-marked subject of the whole sentence. The logical subject of the root verb, referred to below as the Causee, is marked with accusative or dative case (here, *Hanako*, using the accusative variant).

All V+*sase* combinations exhibit similar morphophonological properties, indicating the indivisible nature of the single phonological word constructed by -*sase* affixation. These are listed in (2), many of them taken from Manning, Sag, and Iida (1999).

(2) Properties of all -*sase*- causatives
    a. V+*sase* behaves as a single phonological word with respect to stress assignment and other phonological processes sensitive to word-sized domains (Kitagawa 1986, 1994)
    b. -*sase* is subject to phonological allomorphy depending on the last segment of V (if it is a vowel, then -*sase*, if consonant, then -*ase*; Kuroda 1965a)

c. V+*sase* may feed productive nominalization with -*kata*, 'way of'
d. -*sase*- is a bound morpheme; by itself it may not behave as a lexical verb (stem):[1]
   i. It may not be reduplicated by itself to express repetition.
   ii. It may not bear focus intonation by itself.
   iii. It may not be inflected for subject honorification by itself.
   iv. It may not stand alone as an answer to a *yes/no*-question.

Despite their morphophonological similarity, however, certain subtypes of V+*sase* combinations may be distinguished. The literature has, over time, identified two main classes of V-(s)*ase* sequences in Japanese: the "lexical" (unproductive) causative in (3) (see Miyagawa 1980, 1984; Jacobsen 1981, 1992; Matsumoto 2000) and the "syntactic" (productive) causative in (4) (see Kuroda 1965a, 1965b; Kuno 1973). These two V+(s)*ase* combinations have been shown to have distinct syntactic and semantic properties, although they are morphophonologically very similar. Within the class of syntactic causatives, two further subtypes have been identified: the 'make', -*o*-causative (see (4a)), and the 'let', -*ni*-causative (see (4b)).

(3) (A subset of) Lexical causatives
Taroo-ga   zisyoku-o   niow-ase-ta.
Taroo-NOM resignation-ACC smell-*ase*-PST
'Taroo hinted at resignation.' (Lit. 'Taroo made resignation smell.')

(4) *Productive causatives*
a. Make-*causatives*
Hanako-wa   Yoshi-o   ik-ase-ta.
Hanako-TOP Yoshi-ACC go-*ase*-PST
'Hanako made Yoshi go.'
b. Let-*causatives*
Hanako-wa   Yoshi-ni   ik-ase-ta.
Hanako-TOP Yoshi-DAT go-*ase*-PST
'Hanako allowed Yoshi to go/Hanako had Yoshi go.'

The key problem of the causative construction has to do with a conflict between its morphophonological status and its semantic status, which leads to significant problems in its syntactic analysis. As noted in (2a), the V+*sase* combination, together with any other verbal suffixes that are attached to it, constitutes a single phonological word. On the assumption that phonological words are (syntactically simplex) terminal nodes—the "leaves" of syntactic trees—the derived V+*sase* verb should head a single syntactic verb phrase, and clauses containing such a verb phrase should behave in all respects like a monoclausal construction.

For the lexical causatives, this does not lead to any serious difficulties. Lexical causatives are monoclausal with respect to all relevant syntactic tests (see discussion below). Further, they can undergo semantic drift, acquiring idiomatic readings in combination with particular argument NPs (as illustrated by the example in (3), and discussed by Miyagawa 1980, 1984 and Zenno 1985). Speakers have a sense that these V+*sase* combinations are "listed" and nonproductive. Lexical V+*sase* combinations feed nonproductive nominalization processes that can then independently undergo semantic drift (Volpe 2005). The arguments of a lexical causative are case-marked like the arguments of a single clause—only a single nominative case is possible, assigned to the Causer subject. Finally, many lexical causative verbs (in fact, most such verbs) are formed with some lexical causative morpheme other than -*sase*; choice of the causative allomorph is a listed, arbitrary property for a given lexical causative verb root (Jacobsen 1981). In short, lexical causatives behave syntactically, semantically, and morphophonologically like single "words"—single verbs that head a single verb phrase.

Productive causatives, however, exhibit a number of biclausal properties, most obviously, semantically: A productive V+*sase* combination refers to an event in which an external Causer, X, acts to induce someone else, a Causee, to bring another event or situation about, as described by the V^0. The best translation equivalent of a productive causative in English involves embedding a clause headed by a bare infinitive verb under a causative matrix verb (usually *make* but sometimes *let* or *have*). Besides that intuitive biclausality, however, productive causatives like those in (4) exhibit several other biclausal properties, listed in (5)–(8).

(5) Scopally, VP-modifying adverbials can be interpreted as modifying the caused event or the causing event. Similarly, quantifiers on the object of the root verb can take scope over just the caused event, or both the causing and caused events (see Shibatani 1990:314).

(6) Subject-control adjuncts formed with the -*te* suffix can be controlled either by the external argument of the causative verb (Causer) or the external argument of the embedded verb (Causee). (This latter possibility is particularly notable because the Causee is a surface *object*, with accusative or dative, rather than nominative, case.) (See, among others, Terada 1991, Dubinsky 1994.)

(7) The subject-oriented anaphor *zibun* can be anteceded by either the Causer or the Causee, which again suggests that the subject argument of the embedded verb is a true subject, although it is a surface object (see Oshima 1979:433).

(8) Two separate events can be conjoined using the disjunct -*ka* 'or' underneath a single causative morpheme (see Kuroda 2003:455).

All of these properties—together with full productivity and compositionality—suggest that these constructions are biclausal and that the V+*sase* combination is assembled in the syntactic component.

Productive causatives do exhibit several features that are typical of single clauses, however. Besides being a single morphophonological word, a productive causative clause is clearly a single case-marking domain, licensing only a single nominative argument. Further, productive causatives obey the Double-*o* Constraint (Harada 1973): causatives of intransitive Vs may show accusative case on the Causee argument, as illustrated in (1), but causatives of transitive Vs, which require an accusative case for the object of the V, require the Causee to receive the dative -*ni* marker, given that within a single clause only a single accusative argument is possible.[2,3] Similarly, a productive causative is only a single tense domain. No independent tense marking is possible to distinguish the time of the caused event from the time of the causing: the single tense morpheme on the end of the complex verb must cover both. Finally, productive causative clauses behave as a single domain for clausemate negative polarity item licensing.

The main distinguishing properties of these two types of causatives are summarized here:

(9) a. *Lexical causative*
Monoclausal by all tests
Can have idiomatic interpretations
Exhibits allomorphy with other lexical causative affixes
Strong speaker sense of "listedness," nonproductivity
May feed (nonproductive) nominalization
b. *Productive causative*
Biclausal by tests involving scope, adverbial control, binding, and disjunction
Monoclausal by tests involving negative polarity and tense
(*Make*-causative) monoclausal by tests involving case.
Causee must be animate/agentive
Productive

There is also an interesting acquisition difference between lexical -*sase* and syntactic -*sase* (Murasugi, Hashimoto, and Kato 2004): lexical -*sase* appears first in the speech of children, before productive -*sase* (but not as early as zero-derived lexical causative *uses* of verbs show up).

Within the set of causatives classified as "productive," two subtypes have been identified (Kuroda 1965a, 1965b; Kuno 1973), where a difference in reading affects the case-marking possibilities on the Causee of an intransitive verb. When the causative has a 'make' reading—forcible or direct causation—the case marker on the Causee of an intransitive verb is accusative, as noted in (4). When it has a reading more similar to 'let'—permission or indirect causation—the Causee receives dative -*ni*, even if the verb is intransitive and the Double-*o* Constraint is not in effect (see (4)). Although this distinction has received considerable attention in the literature, I do not discuss it here. For extensive discussion of the 'make/let' distinction, see Dubinsky 1994, Miyagawa 1999, and citations therein.

Examples illustrating each individual property described in (9) are not provided here for space reasons and because similar summaries have been provided in multiple publications elsewhere. For useful summaries exemplifying most of these properties, see Kitagawa 1986, 1994 and Manning, Sag, and Iida 1999. For surveys of many previous analyses, see Cipollone 2001 and Kuroda 2003.

2.1.2 Theoretical Approaches

This constellation of properties really forces one to face one's theoretical priorities. The productive V+*sase* forms pose serious architectural issues, even without considering the lexical causatives. How should a theoretical framework be configured to allow it to accommodate a construction that appears to be headed by a single morphological verb and is monoclausal with respect to case, tense, and NPI licensing, but appears to be biclausal with respect to binding, scope, control, and disjunction? Resolving these issues usually involves radical replumbing of grammatical architectures. Consequently, the influence of Japanese causatives on linguistic theory could not be bigger.[4]

2.1.2.1 *Lexicalist treatments of V+sase: HPSG*

Lexicalist frameworks take it as axiomatic that single morphophonological words correspond to terminal nodes in the syntax. It follows that productive causatives must be treated as syntactically monoclausal: only one morphophonological verb, therefore only one clause.

Consequently, the apparent multiclausal properties of causative constructions *must* arise from the productive operation that affixes the causative morpheme in the lexicon and produces a complex word. It then follows that binding relations, adverbial scope, quantifier scope, and adverbial control are phenomena that depend on lexical operations, not syntactic structure—in other words, these phenomena are not properly "syntactic" phenomena at all. This position is thoroughly presented in the proposal of Manning, Sag, and Iida 1999, which treats causatives within the Head-driven Phrase Structure Grammar (HPSG) framework. There, the key replumbing of the architecture is the inclusion of adjunction and quantifier scope as lexical operations. Syntactic constituency is no longer at issue in treating these phenomena in HPSG.

The most serious challenge to this approach to causatives, within the terms of HPSG, comes from the availability of disjunction of two VPs under a single causative morpheme, as discussed by Kuroda (2003:455).[5] Kuroda's examples showing disjunction of VPs under -*sase* are given in (10).

(10) a. Hanako-ga   [[Masao-ni   uti-o   soozisuru]-ka
       Hanako-NOM [[Masao-DAT house-ACC clean]-OR
       [heya-dai-o   haraw]]-aseru koto ni   sita.
       [room-rent-ACC pay]]-*sase* that DAT   do
       'Hanako decided to make Masao clean the house or pay room rent.'
       Reading: *sase* scopes over OR; Masao has a choice.

b. Hanako-ga [[Masao-ni   uti-o   soozis-aseru]-ka
   Hanako-NOM Masao-DAT house-ACC clean-*sase*-OR
   [heya-dai-o   haraw-aseru]] koto ni   sita.
   room-rent-ACC pay-*sase*   that DAT   do
   'Hanako decided to make Masao clean the house or she decided to make him pay room rent.'
   Reading: OR scopes over *sase*; Masao does not have a choice.

The availability of disjunction of the verb phrase without the -*sase* affix is a significant challenge to the lexicalist treatment of -*sase*, because in the phrase-structure grammars employed for the syntactic component by these frameworks, disjunction is treated syntactically, not lexically.[6] Treating the adjunction of adverbs as lexical, as well, raises issues concerning how to capture syntactic adjunct/argument asymmetries within HPSG, as discussed by Cipollone (2001): if both argument structure-altering operations and adjunction operations are lexically implemented, it is not clear how their different behaviors with respect to extraction and other phenomena may be captured.

2.1.2.2 *Principles and parameters: Logical Form from syntax*

In principles and parameters (P&P) approaches, however, a different set of priorities are in force. The ultimate syntactic representation of a clause is taken to be (isomorphic to) its Logical Form. Semantic properties such as scope assignment of quantifiers must therefore be syntactically represented. Further, the notion "subject" is famously a configurational one in P&P; consequently, the assignment of antecedents for subject-oriented reflexives or of controllers for adjoined -*te* phrases must be (at least partially) syntactically determined. The consequence of these assumptions, then, is that the causative morpheme and the verb to which it is affixed must each head a separate syntactic projection, which creates different constituents that can independently be used to construct scopal or subject properties. To account for the ways in which causatives have syntactically monoclausal properties, then, P&P frameworks propose that the embedded clausal structure is deficient in some way—not a full CP or TP but some reduced yet thematically complete clause is embedded by the causative morpheme. The absent intermediate projections account for the monoclausal behavior in the relevant domains.

The inescapable conclusion given this set of priorities is that morphological and phonological words are not in a one-to-one relationship with syntactic terminal nodes. The biggest problems to be faced by the P&P approach, then, are the following: Where are words made—before or after syntax, or both? What is the constituent structure of the embedded phrase?

There have been many proposals in the literature within these broad lines. They are outlined in (11) in roughly chronological order, followed by their key analytical property and the locus of word formation in the model:

(11) a. Predicate raising (e.g., Kuno 1973). Biclausal D-structure collapses to monoclausal S-structure; syntax feeds word formation.

b. Parallel monoclausal and biclausal trees. Word formation feeds syntax (e.g., Miyagawa 1984).
c. LF-excorporation and projection. Word formation feeds syntax, which then deconstructs complex words to project (covert) biclausal structure (Kitagawa 1986, 1994). (This proposal could be understood as a variant of Chomsky's [1993] lexicalist checking theory and prefigures in some ways Brody's [2000] Mirror Theory.)
d. Incorporation (Baker 1988). Syntax manipulates morphemes, feeds word formation.

Baker's Incorporation account became the most familiar P&P analysis and still represents the core idea behind most current approaches in the literature. It itself was an updated version of Kuno's predicate-raising approach. The updating involved understanding how the "collapse" of the biclausal structure is only apparent: the V that heads the lower VP simply head-moves to adjoin to the -*sase* morpheme, which is a V in its own right, projecting the matrix VP. On this approach, syntactic terminal nodes are not initially headed by fully formed morphophonological words but rather individual morphemes. Productive morphology is affixed to its host by syntactic operations such as head-movement. Because head-movement leaves a trace, there is no collapse of the lower clause when this happens; rather, the entire structure remains present and interpreted at LF—it is merely unpronounced. An illustration of this account is provided in (12).

(12) Derivation of *Hanako-ga Taroo-ni piza-o tabe-sase-ta* in a Baker-style Incorporation account:[7]
Input to the syntax: {Hanako$_N$, Taroo$_N$, piza$_N$, -ga$_K$, -ni$_K$, -o$_K$, tabe$_V$, -sase$_V$, -ta$_I$}

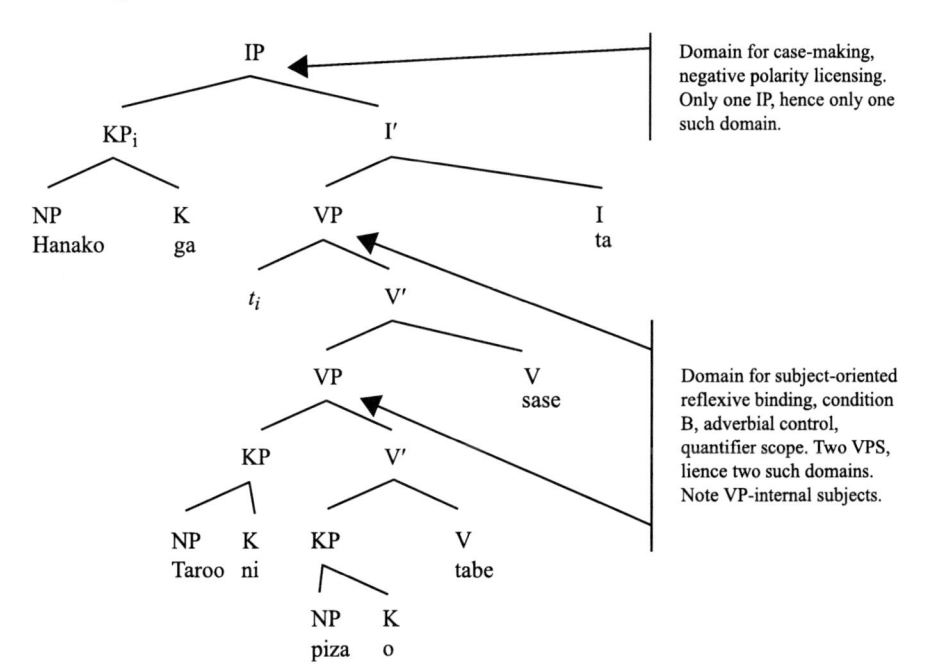

Domain for case-making, negative polarity licensing. Only one IP, hence only one such domain.

Domain for subject-oriented reflexive binding, condition B, adverbial control, quantifier scope. Two VPS, lience two such domains. Note VP-internal subjects.

Several ingredients are needed to make an Incorporation account of productive causatives work, and each has major theoretical consequences for the rest of the framework.

Given that it is ungrammatical to attach a separate tense or complementizer morpheme to the verb stem before affixing -*sase*, the proposal is that the constituent embedded under -*sase* is VP rather than IP (TP) or CP. This accounts for the absence of separate tense domains for the two clauses. The theory can then explain the availability of negative polarity items (NPIs) in the embedded VP by assuming that the clausemate condition on Japanese NPI licensing is sensitive to the TP domain, not the VP domain: because there is only one TP in a productive causative, NPIs in the embedded VP meet the clausemate requirement.

The VP-internal subject hypothesis is then also necessary, so that the embedded subject argument can be introduced in the lower VP, which allows for the presence of the Causee in the structure without an embedded TP.

It must also be the case that clausal conditions on case assignment like the Double-*o* Constraint are sensitive to the TP domain, rather than VP. To capture this, a theory of abstract Case checking is needed in which clausal Case domains are bounded by a TP projection—a Dependent Case case theory of the Marantz 1991 type (see, e.g., Miyagawa 1999). Such an account predicts that the transitivity of the embedded VP can affect the morphological case realized in the whole clause.

Similarly, it is necessary to have in place a theory of scope that allows quantifiers to scope at the VP level as well as the CP level, to account for lower-clause quantifier scope.

Finally, and most important, the approach entails a partial rejection of the Lexicalist Hypothesis: the account only works if the syntax manipulates bound morphemes, as well as free ones.[8] In other words, productive inflectional and derivational affixes must be considered to be input to the syntax. Rather than being presyntactically attached to their host stems in the lexicon, such affixes are attached to their hosts either in or following the syntactic component.

What of the lexical causatives? Recall that they are irregular, stem specific, semantically idiosyncratic, and nonproductive. Nonproductive affixes are *not* input to the syntax in this approach; they come preattached to their stems in a presyntactic morphological component (the locus of irregularity). This explains (a) their nonproductivity, given that syntax is understood as the domain of productivity; and (b) the uniformly monoclausal behavior of lexical causatives: one V in the numeration, one VP in the derivation.

The end result is a type of hybrid account, where productive causatives are combined with their verbs in the syntax, but lexical causatives are treated in a separate, presyntactic part of the grammar.[9] The remainder of this chapter makes an argument that something is wrong with this picture and explores the implications for linguistic theory.

2.2 LEXICAL CAUSATIVES

Like many languages, Japanese is rich in semantically related inchoative/causative pairs of verbs, with overt causativizing (and/or inchoativizing) morphology attached to a common root. These pairs have been extensively documented by Jacobsen (1992); the first two examples of each class of pairs he identifies are given in table 2.1. (None of these pairs involve -*sase*).

Table 2.1 Semantically related inchoative/causative verb pairs in Japanese

Class/#[a]	Root	Intransitive	Transitive	Rough root gloss
I: e/Ø 30 pairs	hag hirak	hag-e-ru hirak-e-ru	hag-Ø-u hirak-Ø-u	'peel off' 'open'[b]
II: Ø/e 44 pairs	ak hikkom	ak-Ø-u hikkom-Ø-u	ak-e-ru hikkom-e-ru	'open' 'draw back'
III: ar/e 71 pairs	ag aratam	ag-ar-u aratam-ar-u	ag-e-ru aratam-e-ru	'rise' 'improve'
IV: ar/Ø 8 pairs	hasam husag	hasam-ar-u husag-ar-u	hasam-Ø-u husag-Ø-u	'catch between' 'obstruct (clog, jam?)'
V: r/s 27 pairs	ama hita	ama-r-u hita-r-u	ama-s-u hita-s-u	'remain' 'soak'
VI: re/s 18 pairs	arawa hana	arawa-re-ru hana-re-ru	arawa-s-u hana-s-u	'show (up)' 'separate from'
VII: ri/s 2 pairs	ka ta	ka-ri-ru ta-ri-ru	ka-s-u ta-s-u	'borrow/(lend)' 'suffice/(supplement)'
VIII: Ø/as 38 pairs	hekom her	hekom-Ø-u her-Ø-u	hekom-as-u her-as-u	'dent' 'decrease'
IX: e/as 45 pairs	bak bar	bak-e-ru bar-e-ru	bak-as-u bar-as-u	'turn into/bewitch' 'come/bring to light'
X: i/as 8 pairs	ak dek	ak-i-ru dek-i-ru	ak-as-u dek-as-u	'tire' 'come/bring into existence'
XI: i/os 6 pairs	horob ok	horob-i-ru ok-i-ru	horob-os-u ok-os-u	'(fall to) ruin' 'get up'
XII: Ø/se 6 pairs	abi ki	abi-Ø-ru ki-Ø-ru	abi-se-ru kise-ru	'pour over (self/other)' 'put on (self/other)'
XIII: e/akas 4 pairs	obi hagur	obi-e-ru hagur-e-ru	obi-(y)akas-u hagur-akas-u	'take fright/frighten' 'stray/evade'
XIV: or/e 2 pairs	kom nukum	kom-or-u nukum-or-u	kom-e-ru nukum-e-ru	'be fully present/fill' 'warm'
XV: are/e 3 pairs	sut wak	sut-are-ru wak-are-ru	sut-e-ru wak-e-ru	'fall into disuse/discard' 'divide'
XVI: Misc 25 pairs	nigiwa nob	nigiwa-Ø-u nob-i-ru	nigiwa-s-u nob-e-ru	'(make) prosper' 'extend'

[a] The number of pairs does not include other pairs derived from a root already on the list even when these are not semantically related; the number of listemes on each list, then, is likely larger.
[b] Mamoru Saito and Yosuke Sato (pers.comm.) inform me that the forms meaning 'open' here, *hirakeru~hiraku*, are not used (the pair from class II, *aku~akeru*, is the appropriate one). Some other items in Jacobsen's lists also seem to not currently be in use; for example, *bakasu*, *dekasu*, and *nukumeru*.

2.2.1 Syntactic and Semantic Properties of Non-*Sase* Lexical Causatives

The causative member of these pairs has one more argument than its intransitive counterpart and bears a roughly causative reading with respect to it (sometimes one or the other member of the pair having undergone some semantic drift) but shows no obvious symptoms of a multiclausal syntactic structure. For example, compare the available controllers for a -*te*- phrase in a syntactic versus a lexical causative.

(13) *Basic intransitive verb and its syntactic causative*
    a. Hanako-wa   arui-te   it-ta.
       Hanako-TOP walk-*te* go-PST
       'Hanako, walking, went.'
    b. Taroo-wa   arui-te Hanako-o   ik-ase-ta.
       Taroo-TOP walk-*te* Hanako-ACC walk-*sase*-PST
       Readings: 'Taroo made Hanako go, walking.'
                  'Taroo, walking, made Hanako go.'

In the syntactic causative in (13b), the phrase *arui-te*, 'walking', can be controlled either by *Hanako*, the Causee subject of the embedded verb (who is the controller in the noncausative sentence in (13a)) or by *Taroo*, the Causer subject of the causative -*sase*. An identical pair of sentences is given for a lexical causative formed with the suffix -*as*- in (14).

(14) *Inchoative intransitive and its lexical causative*
    a. Hanako-wa   nure-te   hi-e-ta.
       Hanako-TOP   wet-*te*   cool-INCH-PST
       'Hanako('s body), getting wet, cooled.'
    b. Taroo-wa   nure-te   Hanako-o   hi-(y)as-ita.
       Taroo-TOP   wet-*te*   Hanako-ACC cool-CAUS-PST
       Reading: 'Taroo, getting wet, cooled Hanako.'
       Impossible: 'Taroo cooled Hanako, (Hanako) getting wet.'

Even though the notion of someone becoming cool by getting wet is semantically sensible (as shown by the inchoative (14a)), the only available controller of the -*te* phrase *nure-te* 'getting wet' in (14b) is the Causer, *Taroo*, rather than the Causee who is becoming cool, *Hanako*. Lexical causatives, like underived transitive verbs, are monoclausal with respect to this and all the other tests for biclausality listed above.

    As shown by Miyagawa (1980, 1984, 1989, 1994, 1998) and Zenno (1985), lexical causatives share another property with underived transitive verbs: they may form part of an idiom. Sometimes their inchoative counterpart also participates (i.e., the idiom alternates), as in (16), sometimes not, as in (15). (These examples are from Miyagawa 1989:126–127; they are given as V+object only, not in sentential uses.)

(15) *Lexical causatives in idioms by themselves*
    a. kama-o   kake-   (intr. *kak-ar* does not
       sickle-ACC splash on   participate in this idiom)
       'trick into confessing'
    b. zibara-o   kir- (intr. *kire* not in this idiom)
       my.stomach-ACC cut
       'pay out of one's own pocket'
    c. tenoura-o kaes-   (intr. *kaer* not in this idiom)
       palm-ACC return
       'change one's attitude suddenly'

(16) *Lexical causatives in alternating idioms*
    a. te-ga   kuwawar-   te-o   kuwae-
       hand-NOM join   hand-ACC add
       'be altered'   'alter'
    b. hone-ga   ore-   hone-o   or-
       bone-NOM break$_{intr}$ bone-ACC break$_{tr}$
       'require hard work'   'exert oneself'
    c. mune-ga itam-   mune-o itame-
       heart-NOM ache   heart-ACC hurt
       'be worried'   'worry (oneself)'

Another test, developed by Oerhle and Nishio (1981), showed that lexical causatives can participate in "adversity" readings, like simple transitive verbs and unlike productive causatives (example in (17) taken from Miyagawa 1989:130).

(17) a. *Simple transitive with adversity reading*
       Taroo-ga   ie-o   yai-ta.
       Taroo-NOM house-ACC burn-PST
       'Taroo burned his house.'
       'Taroo's house burned, and he was adversely affected (he didn't cause it.)'
    b. *Lexical causative with adversity reading*
       Boku-wa booru-o   gake kara   ot-os-ita.
       I-TOP   ball-ACC   cliff from drop-CAUS-PST
       'I dropped the ball from the cliff.'
       'The ball dropped from the cliff, and I was adversely affected.'

2.2.2 V+*Sase*: The Same Properties as Lexical Causatives or Not?

The examples in the previous section applied these tests to unambiguously lexical causatives, formed with causative affixes other than -*sase*. As noted in section 1, Miyagawa argues that some V+*sase* combinations behave like the other lexical causatives discussed earlier.[10] They participate in idioms, sometimes with (see (18c,d)) and sometimes without (see (18a,b)) their intransitive counterpart:

(18) *Lexical V+sase causatives in idioms*
    a. tikara-o   aw-ase-
       power-ACC together-*sase*-
       'pull together'
    b. mimi-o sum-ase-
       ear-ACC clear-*sase*
       'listen carefully'
    c. hana-ga   saku-   hana-o   sak-ase-
       flower-NOM bloom   flower-ACC bloom-*sase*
       'be done heatedly'   'engage in heatedly'
    d. hara-ga   her-   hara-o   her-ase-
       stomach-NOM lessen   stomach-ACC lessen-*sase*
       'get hungry'   'fast/wait for a meal'

Some such V+*sase* forms also allow adversity causative interpretations (examples from Miyagawa 1989:129):

(19) *V+sase forms in adversity causatives*[11]
    a. Taroo-ga   yasai-o   kusar-ase-ta.
       Taroo-NOM vegetable-ACC rot-*sase*-PST
       'Taroo spoiled the vegetables.'
       'The vegetables rotted, and Taroo was adversely affected.'
    b. Taroo-ga   kaisya-o   toosans-ase-ta.
       Taroo-NOM company-ACC bankrupt-*sase*-PST
       'Taroo bankrupted the company.'
       'The company went bankrupt, and Taroo was adversely affected.'

But most V+*sase* combinations do not exhibit these properties—most V+*sase* combinations are productive, not lexical. For instance, no adversity causative interpretation is available for the V+*sase* forms here (Miyagawa 1989:130):[12]

(20) a. Boku-wa booru-o   gake kara oti-sase-ta.
       I-TOP   ball-ACC cliff from drop-*sase*-PST
       'I caused the ball to drop from the cliff.'
       Impossible: 'The ball dropped from the cliff, and I was adversely affected.'
    b. Kotosi-wa   dekinai gakusei-o   hue-sase-ta.
       this.year-TOP poor   students-ACC increase-*sase*-PST
       'This year, we caused (the number of) poor students to increase.'
       Impossible: 'This year, the number of poor students increased, and we were adversely affected.'
    c. Taroo-wa   niku-o   koge-sase-ta.
       Taroo-TOP   meat-ACC scorch-*sase*-PST
       'Taroo caused the meat to scorch.'   (Pylkkänen 2002)
       Impossible: 'The meat scorched, and Taroo was adversely affected.'

Similarly, given an intransitive verb that participates in an idiom, like the examples in (18c,d), a V+*sase* combination formed on the intransitive is not guaranteed to also participate in the idiom (Miyagawa 1989:126):

(21) a. kiai-ga   hair-   *kiai-o   hair-ase-
        spirit-NOM   enter   spirit-ACC   enter-*sase*
        'be full of spirit'   'inspire/put spirit into'
    b. hakusya-ga   kakar-   *hakusya-o   kakar-ase-
        spur-NOM   splash.on   spur-ACC   splash.on.*sase*
        'spur on$_{intr}$'   'spur on$_{tr}$'

These verbs have lexical causative forms with non-*sase* causative affixes, *ir-e-ru* and *kak-e-ru* (they are members of Jacobsen's class III alternators). The difference between the verbs in (21), which do not allow an idiomatic interpretation with -*sase*, and the verbs in (18c,d), which do allow such an interpretation, is that the verbs in (18) have no other lexical causative form. This is Miyagawa's central observation—the only verbs that show lexical causative behavior with -*sase* are the verbs that have no other idiosyncratic lexical causative suffix of their own. In other words, lexical behavior of -*sase* is only possible in cases where it is not blocked by a more specific causative suffix.

2.2.3 The Blocking Effect

The hybrid P&P account outlined in section 2.0 simply divided V+*sase* combinations into productive, regular, compositional forms (created in the syntax) and nonproductive, noncompositional forms (listed in the lexicon). This captures the distinctions between the two types of forms, but it does not predict that there should be any systematic relationship within the lexicon between lexical V+*sase* and the other lexical causative forms, or that there should be any systematic relationship between lexical V+*sase* and syntactic V+*sase*. If there is any such systematic relationship, then the hybrid account is flawed.

In fact, such a systematic relationship does exist. As noted above, Miyagawa (1980 et seq.) and Zenno (1985) show that there is a simple way to predict when a V+*sase* combination can behave like other lexical causatives and when it may only behave as an productive causative, with no noncompositional interpretation and no adversity causative: *Only intransitive roots with no other transitive form can behave lexically with -sase.*

That is, lexical interpretations of -*sase* are possible only if the root to which it is attached does not have a transitive form derived in another way.

2.2.4 Miyagawa's (1984) Treatment: Paradigmatic Structure

The sensitivity of lexical V+*sase* to the (non)availability of another derived form with the same meaning is a classic example of morphological *blocking*, seen crosslinguistically in both derivational and inflectional morphology. A simple case is the

English past tense. Some verbs do not have a past tense formed with -ed: *runned, *writed, *feeled, *hitted. The reason is that they have an independently formed, irregular past tense, which blocks the regular form: ran, wrote, felt, hit.[13]

The same phenomenon is argued to occur in derivational morphology. Many English adjectives have a negative form in un-, but some do not: *unpossible, *unconsiderate, *uncoherent. These are blocked by the irregular negative forms: impossible, inconsiderate, incoherent.

The grammatical mechanism that is responsible for blocking effects in many theories of morphology (for instance, Paradigm-Function Morphology, as described in, e.g., Stump 2001) is the n-dimensional grammatical space of a paradigm. For English verbs, for example, blocking is captured in the following way. Every verbal word form is understood to be attached to a paradigm space, defined by the inflectional features of English verbs: past and present participle, 1, 2, 3, SG, PL. Some verbs come with their paradigm space partially filled in, "lexically" as it were— for instance, in the past-tense space for write, the form wrote is already entered—but empty slots are available for filling in by default affixes. In the case of the empty progressive participle slot, this will result in write+ing.[14]

(22) *Paradigm in the lexicon for* write

V: WRITE	write
Infinitive	
Present ppl.	
Past ppl.	written

Before lexical items are sent off to the syntax, empty paradigm spaces are filled in by default morphology (bolded in the tables).

(23) *Paradigm in the lexicon for* write

V: WRITE	write
Infinitive	**write**
Present ppl.	**writing**
Past ppl.	written

To apply such an analysis to derivational morphology, one has to allow derivational features to define a paradigm space, such as [±negative] for the *impossible/*unpossible* pairs or [±nominal] for their nominalizations. Words with special negative or nominal forms will have their relevant paradigm slots already filled in, blocking the productive insertion of the default form un- in the negative slot, or the default form -ness in the nominalization slot, illustrated in (24).

(24) *Paradigms in the lexicon for* possible, likely, happy

A: POSSIBLE	*possible*
Negative	*impossible*
Nominal	*possibility*

A: LIKELY	*likely*
Negative	**unlikely**
Nominal	*likelihood*

A: HAPPY	*happy*
Negative	**unhappy**
Nominal	**happiness**

Miyagawa (1980, 1984, 1989) treated the blocking effect in Japanese causatives with such a derivational paradigmatic structure, defined by a feature [±transitive]; without it, the blocking effect could not be captured. In terms of its position and function in the model, Miyagawa's level of Paradigmatic Structure is the same level of structure that paradigm-function morphologists work with, although Miyagawa used it independently of that framework.

He proposed a paradigm space defined by intransitive, transitive, and ditransitive features. For many verb stems, an irregular form already occupied the "transitive" or "ditransitive" slot in the paradigm. Only if an irregular form did not occupy that slot could a default -*sase* form be constructed to fill the gap.

(25) *Paradigm in the lexicon for the root* ag

V: √AG	*agar* 'rise'
Intransitive	*agar-*
Transitive	*age-*
Ditransitive	

(26) *Paradigm in the lexicon for the root* sak

V: √SAK	*sak-* 'bloom'
Intransitive	*sak-*
Transitive	**sak-ase**
Ditransitive	

To account for the systematicity of the lexical V+*sase* forms, then, Miyagawa proposed to adopt an extra layer of lexical structure. However, his theory went beyond the lexical causatives to include the syntactic causatives as well.

Miyagawa argued that it cannot be a coincidence that these default V+*sase* combinations are morphophonologically indistinguishable from productive causatives. That is, according to their morphophonological properties, a lexical causative formed with -*sase* is exactly the same as a productive causative formed with -*sase*. He reasoned that syntactic causatives are spelled out as -*sase* because -*sase* is just the Elsewhere, default form for a causative meaning: the lexical causative suffix -*sase* and the productive causative suffix -*sase* are the same suffix. If lexical causatives had nothing to do with syntactic causatives, there would be no reason for the same morpheme to be involved in both.

Consequently, Miyagawa (1984) concluded that syntactic causatives had to be created in the lexicon, in the paradigmatic structure, as well. However, all of the questions discussed earlier concerning how to capture the biclausal properties of the productive causatives within a lexicalist approach then became problematic within his analysis. This led to his proposal that causatives are associated with parallel monoclausal and biclausal structures. The theory became ever more complex.

2.2.5 Theoretical Options

We now are in a position to summarize the state of affairs systematically. V+*sase* combinations can be lexical or productive. If productive, they behave biclausally with respect to binding, control, scope, and idiom interpretation. If lexical, they behave monoclausally. The lexical V+*sase* combination is in complementary distribution with the other lexical causative morphemes discussed by Jacobsen, such as V+*e*, V+*s*, V+*os*, and so on, with -*sase* acting as the default suffix for lexical causative formation when no other form exists. The default lexical -*sase* is morphophonologically identical to the productive -*sase*.

Three possible analytical approaches seem open at this point:

1. Treat the lexical and syntactic causatives completely separately. On this approach, the V+*sase* lexical causatives would be relegated to the lexicon with the rest of the lexical causatives. The morphological identity between the default lexical causative morpheme and the syntactic causative morpheme would be irrelevant. That is, Jacobsen just missed class XVII: Ø/-*sase*.
2. Unify the lexical and syntactic causatives by treating them both in the lexicon. On this approach, something other than "in the lexicon" has to distinguish the syntactic and lexical causatives.
3. Unify the lexical and syntactic causatives by treating them both in the syntax. On this approach, a theory of postsyntactic morphology would be needed. Again, something other than "in the syntax" has to distinguish the two types.

Enter Distributed Morphology, Hale and Keyser's v^0, and minimalism.

2.3 Late Insertion, the Elsewhere Condition, vPs, and Phases

In this section, I describe how independently motivated theoretical proposals in distinct domains of research turn out to naturally provide a unified account of lexical and syntactic Japanese causatives.[15] First I introduce the distinct proposals, and then I show how they fit together.

2.3.1 Distributed Morphology, Late Insertion, and the Elsewhere Principle

In Baker's Incorporation account and later work inspired by it, the syntax manipulates and combines the lexical entries of complete morphemes, fully specified for phonological, morphological, syntactic, and semantic properties. In this section, I show how adopting a Late Insertion approach, according to which phonological information is only inserted to realize syntactic terminal nodes later in the derivation, allows the capture of paradigmatic blocking effects without the use of paradigms.

In Distributed Morphology (Halle and Marantz 1993 et seq.), the syntax manipulates and combines abstract feature bundles, selected by the grammar of the individual language learner from an inventory provided by UG on the basis of positive evidence. These feature bundles are the input to, and terminal nodes of, a syntactic derivation.

After the syntax has completed its derivation, (via the Agree, Merge, and Copy operations, per minimalist theory) and Spell-Out is reached, the syntactic structure, with (possibly slightly changed) feature bundles in its terminal nodes, is sent off to PF/LF for interpretation.

An early step on the PF side is Lexical Insertion, at which the abstract bundles are given phonological "clothing" prefatory to pronunciation. Vocabulary Items (VIs)— phonological strings identified as expressing certain features—compete to realize the terminal nodes that the syntactic derivation has made available. At each terminal node, there may be many VIs whose feature specification is compatible with the feature content of the terminal node. The VI with the most compatible features (but no incompatible ones) realizes that node—it wins the competition and blocks the other compatible VIs from occupying the node. When no other VI is available, the default VI is inserted—the Elsewhere VI. A system that chooses a morpheme based on feature specification this way is said to obey the Elsewhere Principle.

Here is a (syntactically very simplified) example derivation. Imagine an initial Numeration consisting of feature bundles such as those listed in (27).

(27) {[$_D$ +1, +PL, +NOM], [$_T$ +PAST, +NOM], [$_D$ +PL, +ACC], [$_V$KEEP, +ACC]}

The syntax merges and moves these feature bundles to create a syntactic tree, in which all the necessary feature-checking has been accomplished. After the syntax is done with it, the (simplified) tree in (28) is handed off to Spell-Out. The VIs *I, we, it, kep-, keep, -ed,* and *them* are all compatible with the available positions, but only the most highly specified VI at each slot succeeds in actually realizing the terminal node. The competition is illustrated at the bottom of the tree.

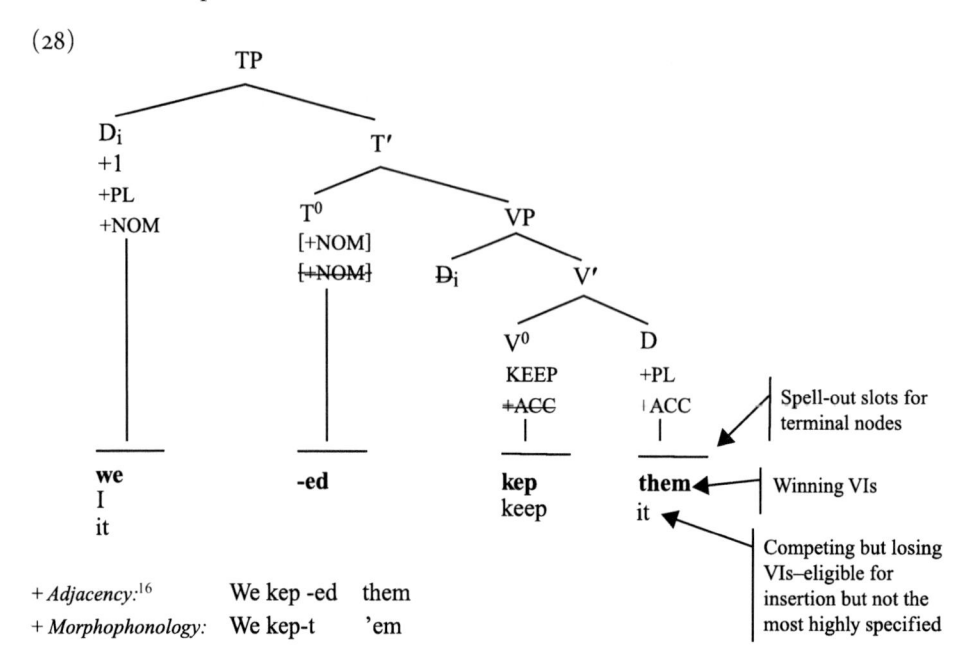

(28)

```
                            TP
                ┌───────────┴───────────┐
              Dᵢ                        T'
              +1              ┌─────────┴─────────┐
              +PL            T⁰                   VP
              +NOM         [+NOM]        ┌─────────┴─────────┐
                           [+NOM]       Dᵢ                   V'
                                                   ┌─────────┴─────────┐
                                                  V⁰                   D
                                                 KEEP                 +PL
                                                 +ACC                  ACC
                                                  │                    │
           ─────────           ─────            ─────                ─────      Spell-out slots for
                                                                                terminal nodes

             we                 -ed              kep                  them      Winning VIs
             I                                   keep                 it
             it
                                                                                Competing but losing
                                                                                VIs–eligible for
  + Adjacency:¹⁶        We kep -ed  them                                        insertion but not the
  + Morphophonology:    We kep-t    'em                                         most highly specified
```

The theoretical attraction of such an approach is that it allows a natural account of mirror principle effects, provides a straightforward relationship between syntax and morphology and, most important, calls for only a single generative engine—it requires no generative mechanisms in the lexicon. That is, there is no need for a separate level of paradigmatic structure to generate inflected and/or derived word forms, or to capture the blocking effect. The equivalent of a single slot of paradigmatic space is provided by the syntactic terminal node and its feature specification. The blocking effect is captured by the process of competition of compatible VIs into the terminal node. The default, Elsewhere VI wins the competition only if no more specific VI is compatible with that slot.

2.3.2 (Modified) Hale and Keyser (1993, 2002)–type vPs for Causative/Inchoative Alternations

In the Distributed Morphology (DM) conception of blocking, the VIs in a given competition must be competing to realize a slot that corresponds to a terminal node in a syntactic tree. With respect to the lexical causative/inchoative pairs, which behave syntactically like monomorphemic simplex verbs, there had been no previous suggestion in the literature that their syntactic representation should be any more complex than simply V⁰. However, given DM assumptions, if the causative morphemes in lexical causatives are competing with each other, there must be a syntactic terminal node within the root+suffix complex for the suffix alone—that is, the syntactic representation of the lexical causative verb must involve one verbal projection for the root and a separate projection for the suffix.

Hale and Keyser (1993, 2002) proposed that all transitive verbs—even morphologically simplex ones—are made up of two separate heads: The main V⁰ introduces the internal arguments of the verb and projects to VP, and the external argument is introduced in the specifier of a v⁰ taking the VP as its complement. In a slight revision to their account, Harley 1995a and Marantz 1997 proposed that a v⁰ was also present in inchoative constructions but that it was a distinct v⁰ that selected no external argument.[17] The lower root √ head-moves to attach to its c-commanding v⁰ head, creating a syntactically complex head-adjunction structure with two terminal nodes. The two resulting structures for inchoative (unaccusative intransitive) verbs and causative, agentive, transitive verbs are given in (29).

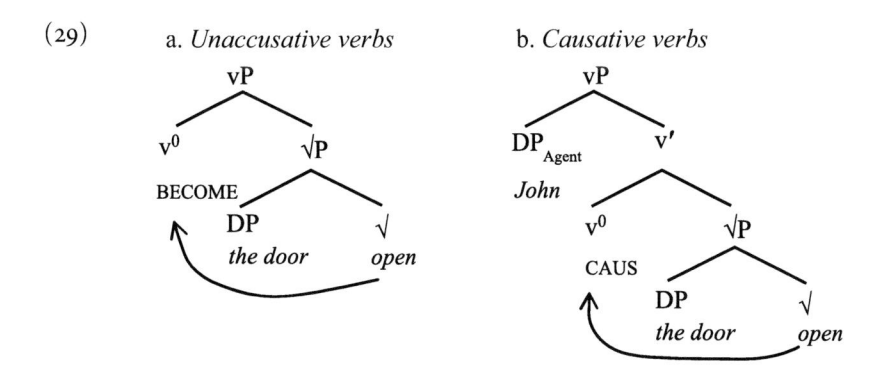

(29)   a. *Unaccusative verbs*   b. *Causative verbs*

```
        vP                                  vP
       /  \                                /  \
      v⁰   √P                            DP    v'
   BECOME /  \                         Agent  /  \
         DP   √                         John v⁰   √P
       the door open                        CAUS /  \
                                                DP   √
                                             the door open
```

The relevance to the problem of where in the syntax to locate the inchoative/causative suffixal morphology of Japanese, documented so extensively by Jacobsen, is clear. That morphology is a realization of the two types of v⁰ head illustrated above.

2.3.3 Late Insertion and Lexical Causatives

The treatment of the blocking phenomenon in lexical causatives suggested by this set of assumptions should now be clear. In a derivation that contains a "lexical" causative,[18] all the various causative morphemes compete to realize the v_{CAUS} head in the syntactic tree.[19] Depending on the class membership of the causative root, one particular causative morpheme wins—the one specified for co-occurrence with roots of that particular class. If no class is specified for a given root—the Elsewhere case—then the default -*sase* morpheme steps in to fill the gap. The list of morphemes competing to realize v_{CAUS} is given in (30); for completeness the list of morphemes competing in the inchoative case to realize v_{BECOME} is given in (31).

(30) *Morphemes competing to realize v_{CAUS} in Japanese*

-Ø- ↔ CAUS / [$\sqrt{}_{I+IV}$ ___v]	(38 Jacobsen roots on the list for -Ø-)
-e- ↔ CAUS / [$\sqrt{}_{II+III+XIV+XV}$ ___v]	(120 roots on list)
-s- ↔ CAUS / [$\sqrt{}_{V+VI+VII}$ ___v]	(47 roots on list)
-as- ↔ CAUS / [$\sqrt{}_{VII+IX+X}$ ___v]	(91 roots on list)
-os- ↔ CAUS / [$\sqrt{}_{XI}$ ___v]	(6 roots on list)
-se- ↔ CAUS / [$\sqrt{}_{XII}$ ___v]	(6 roots on list)
-akas- ↔ CAUS / [$\sqrt{}_{XIII}$ ___v]	(4 roots on list)
sase ↔ CAUS / Elsewhere	(no roots on list) Blocking effect!

(31) *Morphemes competing to realize v_{BECOME} in Japanese*

-e- ↔ BECOME / [$\sqrt{}_{I+IX+XII}$ ___v]	(79 Jacobsen roots on the list)
-ar- ↔ BECOME / [$\sqrt{}_{III+IV}$ ___v]	(79 roots on list)
-r- ↔ BECOME / [$\sqrt{}_{V}$ ___v]	(27 roots on list)
-re- ↔ BECOME / [$\sqrt{}_{VI}$ ___v]	(18 roots on list)
-ri- ↔ BECOME / [$\sqrt{}_{VII}$ ___v]	(2 roots on list)
-i- ↔ BECOME / [$\sqrt{}_{X+XI}$ ___v]	(14 roots on list)
-or- ↔ BECOME / [$\sqrt{}_{XIV}$ ___v]	(2 roots on list)
-are- ↔ BECOME / [$\sqrt{}_{XV}$ ___v]	(3 roots on list) (Elsewhere? See n. 20)
-Ø- ↔ BECOME / [$\sqrt{}_{II+VII+XII}$ ___v]	(88 roots on list) (Elsewhere?)

So, it is possible to treat the lexical causative as subject to syntactic decomposition and thus capture the blocking effect. How does this help with the productive causative? And how are the other distinctions between the two causatives to be captured in this all-syntax approach?

2.3.4 Implications for Syntactic Causatives

If -*sase*- is simply an Elsewhere form of the agent-introducing v_{CAUS}, and if all syntactic causatives are realized with -*sase*-, then syntactic causatives are also a realization of the agent-introducing v_{CAUS}. The syntactic version of this v_{CAUS}, however, does not take a $\sqrt{}$P headed by a verb root as its complement but rather a complement that has a thematically complete argument structure—another vP, with its own independent agent argument. This is illustrated for a productive causative of the simple transitive verb *tabe-* 'eat' in (32). Like all agentive transitive verbs in Hale and Keyser's approach, *tabe-* is itself a realization of a root plus an external-argument introducing v⁰ head. In the case of *tabe-*, we assume that the v⁰ that introduces its external argument is realized by a null morpheme. (In a syntactic causative of a lexically causative verb, that lower v⁰ slot is filled by whatever causative morpheme is appropriate to the lexical causative root, of course, as in, e.g., *kow-as-ase*, [[break-CAUS]_{vP₁}-CAUS]_{vP₂}, 'cause (someone) to break (something)'.)[20]

(32) a.

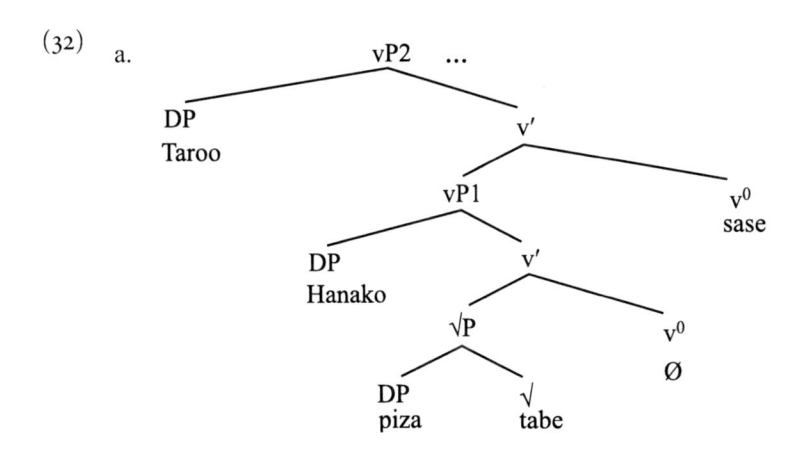

```
                    vP2  ...
                   /    \
              DP          v'
              Taroo      / \
                     vP1    v⁰
                    /   \   sase
                DP       v'
                Hanako  / \
                      √P   v⁰
                     /  \   ∅
                   DP    √
                   piza  tabe
```

b. Taroo-ga   Hanako-ni   piza-o   tabe-sase-ta.
   Taroo-NOM Hanako-DAT pizza-ACC eat-CAUS-PST
   'Taroo made Hanako eat pizza.'

In a syntactic causative, the matrix CAUS v⁰ does not meet the structural description for any special root-conditioned allomorphs of CAUS, because it is not structurally adjacent to any root. The matrix CAUS is insulated from the root by one layer of bracketing—it is separated from the root by the embedded v⁰.[21] Consequently, in productive causatives, the prediction is always that the default realization of the v_{CAUS} morpheme will win the competition—productive causatives will always be spelled out by the VI *-sase-*.

(33) Matrix v⁰ after head-to-head movement: [[√TABE ___v] ___v]

We are now in a position to propose clear definitional criteria for distinguishing lexical and productive V+*sase* combinations in this framework:

(34) a. "Lexical" causative: A CAUS v⁰ that is immediately adjacent to a root.
     b. "Productive" causative: A CAUS v⁰ that is not adjacent to a root (i.e., one that embeds a vP).

Compare the lexical and syntactic causative structures in (35).

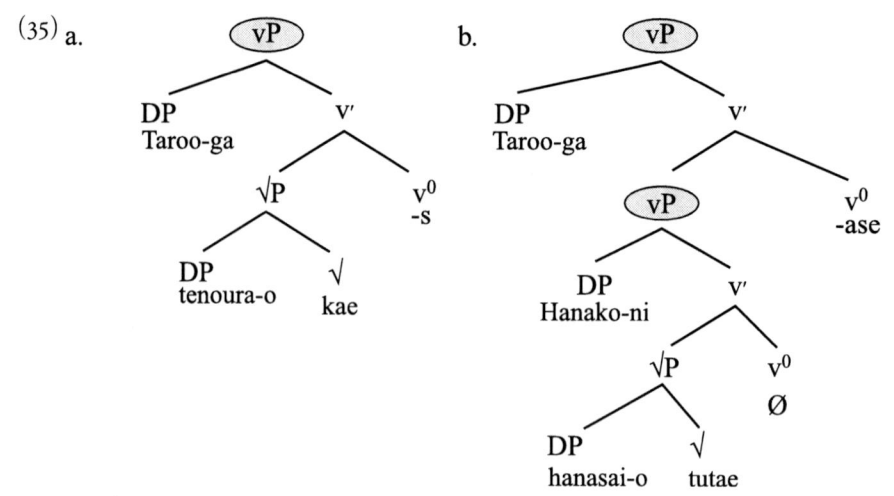

(35) a.
```
        vP
       /  \
      DP   v'
   Taroo-ga / \
          √P   v⁰
         /  \   -s
        DP   √
    tenoura-o kae
```

b.
```
        vP
       /  \
      DP   v'
   Taroo-ga / \
           vP  v⁰
          /  \ -ase
         DP   v'
      Hanako-ni / \
              √P   v⁰
             /  \   ∅
            DP   √
        hanasai-o tutae
```

a'. Taroo-ga tenoura-o kae-s....
    Taroo-NOM palm-ACC return-CAUS
    'Taroo changed his attitude suddenly.' (cf. (15c))

b'. Taroo-wa Hanako-ni hanasi-o tutae-sase-ta.
    Taroo-TOP Hanako-DAT story-ACC convey-CAUS-PST
    'Taroo made Hanako convey a story.'

To distinguish between the syntactic properties of lexical and productive causatives, then, it suffices to identify vP as the locus of the relevant syntactic properties that suggest a biclausal approach. First, it has long been assumed that vP is a locus for successive-cyclic A'-movement, and hence a possible target constituent for quantifier scope. Second, given that vP introduces the external argument, it is natural to associate subject-oriented binding preferences with vP, as well as subject control into adverbials, perhaps supplemented with a c-command restriction. Finally, because vP is the modern equivalent of the former simple VP projection, it is natural to think of VP adverbials as having two loci for scope in productive causatives but only one in lexical causatives. In short, by ascribing these properties to a particular functional projection, we are able to appeal to the same type of explanation for their absence in the lexical causative as we appealed to in explaining the single-clause effects on case assignment and NPI licensing in the productive causative. The culprit is the absence of two instances of the relevant syntactic projection in each case—TP in case of case assignment and NPI licensing in productive causatives, and vP in case of subject control, adverbial modification, quantification and binding in lexical causatives.[22]

2.3.5 Why Not a v$_{\text{BECOME}}$ Layer in Lexical Causatives?

Miyagawa (1994, 1998) proposes that there is also an inchoative v⁰ embedded under the causative v⁰ of a lexical causative, adopting a structure like that given in (36).

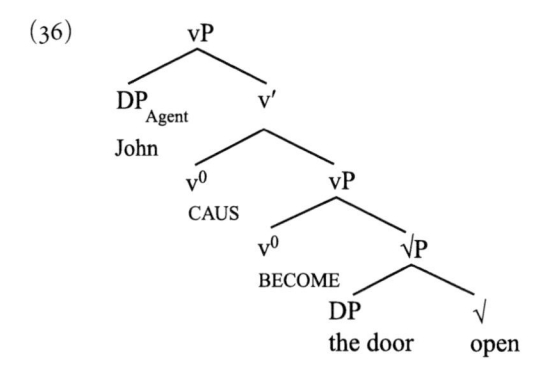

(36)
```
            vP
           /  \
         DP    v'
        Agent /  \
        John v⁰   vP
             CAUS/  \
                v⁰   √P
              BECOME/  \
                   DP    √
                the door open
```

To capture the fact that inchoative morphology disappears in the lexical causative member of the causative/inchoative pair for the vast majority of cases, Miyagawa proposes that the lexical causative morphemes realize a complex segment, the $v_{CAUS}+v_{BECOME}$ heads together. To accomplish this, the v_{CAUS} and v_{BECOME} morphemes must fuse into a single terminal node prior to insertion. In one case where he discusses the lexical causative meaning 'bother', *iya-gar-sase*, it appears as if inchoative morphology, *-gar-*, is indeed embedded under the lexical causative morpheme *-sase*; Miyagawa assumes that Fusion must then have failed in this one case, justifying the account.

On the present approach, where the lexical causative v^0 and the inchoative v^0 are interchangeable, rather than simultaneously present, we would have to assume that *-gar* is not the Spell-Out of the inchoative v^0 head but some other morpheme. This is necessary given the logic of the analysis above. If lexical causatives embedded an inchoative v^0 rather than a bare $\sqrt{P}$, it would become impossible to distinguish between syntactic causatives of inchoatives and lexical causatives. Compare the structures, under the inchoative-inside-lexical-causatives hypothesis, for the following two sentences (from Miyagawa 1989:130 [43a,b]). The availability of the adversity reading for (37a), as well as the irregular causativizer *-os-*, indicates that *ot-os-* is a lexical causative; the absence of the adversity reading in (37b), along with the default causativizer *-sase-*, indicates that *ot-i-sase* is a productive causative.

(37) a. *Lexical*
Boku-wa booru-o gake kara ot-os-ita.
I-TOP ball-ACC cliff-from drop-CAUS-PST
'I dropped the ball from the cliff.'
'The ball dropped from the cliff, and I was adversely affected.'
b. *Productive*
Boku-wa booru-o gake-kara ot-i-sase-ta.
I-TOP ball-ACC cliff from drop-BECOME-CAUS-PST
'I caused the ball to drop from the cliff.'
#'The ball dropped from the cliff, and I was adversely affected.'

On Miyagawa's (1994, 1998) structures, where the lexical causative embeds the inchoative, these two sentences would be represented as in (38).

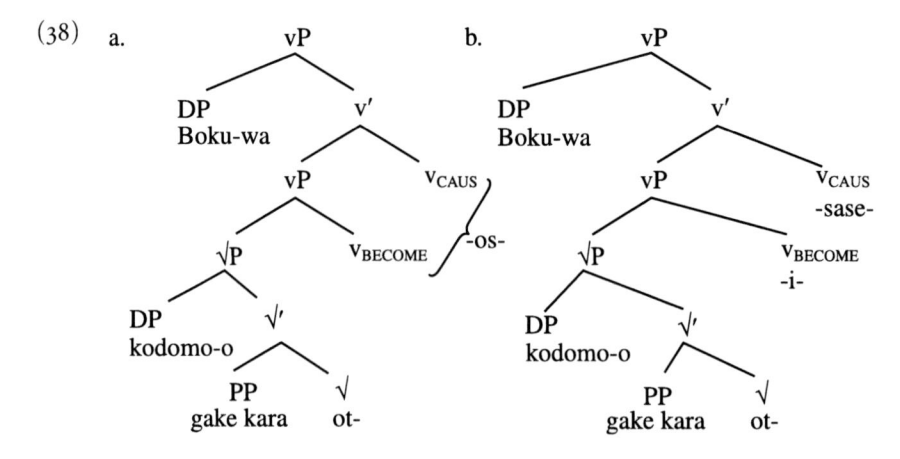

(38) a.
```
              vP
             /  \
           DP    v'
        Boku-wa  / \
                vP  v_CAUS
               /  \    \
              √P   v_BECOME  -os-
             / \
           DP   √'
        kodomo-o / \
                PP  √
             gake kara ot-
```
b.
```
              vP
             /  \
           DP    v'
        Boku-wa  / \
                vP  v_CAUS
               /  \   -sase-
              √P   v_BECOME
             / \    -i-
           DP   √'
        kodomo-o / \
                PP  √
             gake kara ot-
```

If the lexical causative *ot-os* includes a v_{BECOME} in its structure, then the only difference between the lexical causative and the productive causative is whether Fusion (a postsyntactic operation) has applied to the v_{BECOME} and v_{CAUS} roots to ensure that they are spelled out by the single *-os-* morpheme. This type of postsyntactic operation cannot account for the syntactic distinctions observed between lexical and productive causatives in terms of adverbial scope, control possibilities, availability of adversative readings, and so on. The lexical/productive distinction must be more categorical than a mere postsyntactic morphological diacritic, especially because it has such strong consequences for meaning. The distinction must be represented at LF. Consequently, it is preferable to treat the lexical causative as directly embedding the √P, hence lacking the intervening vPBECOME.

The notion that *-gar* in *iya-gar-sase* 'bother' is not the inchoative but some other type of morpheme is supported by the fact that it seems to appear in psychological predicates only, such as *kuyasi-garu* 'dumb-gar' (lit. 'regret'), *samu-garu* 'cold-gar' (lit. 'feel cold'), *atsu-garu* 'hot-gar' (lit. 'feel hot'), *hoshi-garu* 'want-gar' (lit. 'feel like'), and *kowa-garu* 'fear-gar' (lit. 'fear') (Yosuke Sato, pers. comm.). Indeed, Miyagawa (1989:157) notes that *-gar-* affixation only appears with these adjectives when they have a non-first-person subject—in the first person, the *-gar-* affix is not needed. This suggests perhaps some connection of *-gar-* to evidentiality rather than to the BECOME v^0 predicate, because presumably the event/argument structure of experiencing these emotions is identical no matter what the person feature of the subject DP is.

2.3.6 Correlations with Other Proposals in the Literature

One significant distinction between the lexical and syntactic causatives that I have not discussed much yet is the possibility of idiomatization in the former and the impossibility of it in the latter. In fact, this pattern fits well with independent proposals in the literature by Kratzer (1996) and Marantz (1997), according to which the agent-selecting vP is the boundary of a domain for special meaning specification—no projection outside a vP can participate in an idiomatic specification that depends on the root. This proposal was introduced to account for a pattern of facts first observed in Marantz 1984: idiomatic meanings for verbs are often conditioned by the object of a transitive verb ('kill the afternoon', 'kill the bottle', 'kill an audience') but are seldom or never conditioned by the subject associated with a transitive verb. The assumption that agent-introducing v^0 is an interpretive boundary of this type can account for those facts and also predicts the pattern of facts about idiomatization observed here: lexical causatives, with nothing intervening between the causative head and the root, often idiomatize, whereas productive causatives, with a vP between the causative head and the root, never do.

Another proposal has to do with the conditioning of allomorphy by the root only. So far, nothing I have said prevents a particular root in combination with a particular v^0 from conditioning causative allomorphy for a productive causative that takes that vP as its complement. However, that does not seem to occur: productive causatives are always realized with the default causative morpheme -*sase*.

Arad (2003) has claimed, based on evidence from Hebrew, that the domain for special meanings—that is, the vP—is also a boundary domain for allomorphic conditioning of this type: roots can only condition specific allomorphs of morphemes that are syntactically directly adjacent to them. If this is true, it also predicts that Japanese productive causatives could never be allomorphically conditioned by the roots with which they occur.[23]

Both the proposal concerning vP as boundary for idiomatic semantic interpretation and the proposal taking vP to be a boundary for allomorphic conditioning correlate well with Chomsky's (2001) claim that vP is a phase edge—a boundary in the syntactic derivation at which the v^0 complement is sent for interpretation to LF and PF and which is subsequently impenetrable to later syntactic operations. Given that in lexical causatives the complement to v^0 consists of a $\sqrt{}$ and its selected object, this constituent corresponds exactly to the V+Obj sequence that Marantz's generalization claims is the locus of idiomatization. The notion of interpretation by phase, then, can provide a theoretical basis for the claim that $\sqrt{}$+Obj may idomatize whereas agent+$\sqrt{}$ (without Obj) may not.

2.3.7 The Beginning of the High/Low Attachment Analysis

The analysis of Japanese causatives described above was one of the first proposals in a very fruitful line of inquiry that I call "high/low attachment analyses." Since then, many analyses have appealed to the idea that attachment of a morpheme to a higher functional projection results in regular morphology and compositional meaning, whereas attachment of the same morpheme to a lower projection (often the $\sqrt{}$) results in some allomorphy and potential meaning drift. Other early examples of such an analysis are the approach to English *of*-ing and *acc*-ing gerunds presented in Kratzer 1996 and the approach to Chichewa statives and passives sketched in Marantz 1997. Since then, such approaches have been extremely fruitful in looking at all kinds of morphology on the derivational/inflectional, unproductive/productive cusp in many unrelated languages: Travis (2000) used such an approach to treat Malagasy lexical and syntactic causatives, in very much the same spirit as outlined here for Japanese. Embick (2004) adopts the idea to treat the distinction between stative, resultative, and passive participle formation in English. Fortin (2004) applies it to Minnangkabu causatives. Jackson (2005) shows it applies to statives and resultatives in Pima. Alexiadou and Anagnostopoulou (2005) use it to treat adjectival participles in Greek. Svenonius (2005) continues the trend, discussing high/low treatments for causatives in several languages.

2.4 CONCLUSION

I hope to have shown in this chapter that Japanese causatives have been extremely influential in shaping developments in syntactic theory, indeed, in many syntactic theories. Japanese causatives—even omitting the "lexical" ones—either force one to do more syntax in the lexicon (Manning, Sag, and Iida 1999) or more morphology in the syntax (Baker 1988).

I have argued that a careful examination of lexical causatives forces one to figure out a way to unify traditional idiosyncratic, irregular word formation with regular, compositional syntax and yet maintain a principled distinction between the two. A postsyntactic morphology—a Late Insertion approach—with recursive vPs, allows a simple, unified treatment of all three types of lexical causatives, with a principled understanding of the nature of the distinction between lexical and syntactic causatives.

The analysis in general can be taken as additional evidence for the phasal status of vP, and for successive-cyclic QR through vP, among other things.

NOTES FOR CHAPTER 2

I wish to express my gratitude to the workshop organizers, Shigeru Miyagawa and Mamoru Saito, for inviting me to present at the Workshop on Linguistic Theory and the Japanese Language in July 2005 at Harvard University, and for their valuable feedback, as well as that of the audience there. Thanks also to Yosuke Sato and Kunio Nishiyama for their detailed comments, which have improved the manuscript greatly. Caroline Heycock and Akira Watanabe also provided important comments. Takaomi Kato, Yosuke Sato, Hironobu Kasai, and Kazutoshi Ohno helped me with some of the Japanese example sentences herein. Finally, many thanks to Mark Volpe for providing me with the introductory quotation from Shibatani. Any and all remaining shortcomings and mistakes are, of course, my responsibility entirely.

1. Kuroda 1981, 1990 (as cited in Kuroda 2003) presents some examples from negation and intervening particles to suggest that -*sase*- does have an independent existence as a verbal morpheme; Miyagawa (1989:115f.) and Kitagawa (1994:184f.), followed by Manning, Sag, and Iida (1999:47), argue that in fact these are examples of the -*ase*- allomorph suffixed to light verb *s*-, 'do'. Kuroda (2003, n. 14) disagrees, ascribing Kitagawa's position to grammaticality judgment differences.

2. In the case of the *make*-reading of a causative of a transitive verb, it seems that the dative -*ni* on the Causee is the structural case marker -*ni*, not postpositional -*ni* (Sadakane and Koizumi 1995). In *let*-reading causatives, with both transitive and intransitive root verbs, the -*ni* on the Causee seems to be P -*ni*.

3. An interesting piece of evidence showing the monoclausal nature of the case marking of productive causatives is noted by Manning, Sag, and Iida (1999): when a productive causative is suffixed with the potential/abilitative morpheme -*e*-, the embedded accusative argument may be optionally marked with nominative case, rather than accusative—just like the accusative arguments of monoclausal, morphologically simple transitive verbs suffixed with the same morpheme. Example (i) illustrates this phenomenon.

(i) Sensei-ga   Taroo-ni   tsukue-ga/o   soujis-ase-re-naka-tta
    teacher-NOM   Taroo-DAT   desk-NOM/ACC   clean-CAUSE-ABL-NEG-PAST
    (koto).
    (fact)
    'The teacher was not able to make Taroo clean his desk.'

4. See Nishiyama, this volume, for discussion of this problem with respect to other types of morphologically complex words in Japanese.

5. Akira Watanabe (pers. comm.) notes that this same problem for lexicalist treatments of complex predicates arises with the affixal light-verb constructions in Japanese.

6. Interestingly, it seems that this structure is not available for examples involving true coordination, rather than disjunction (thanks to Takaomi Kato for these examples and discussion):

(ii) *Ken-wa   [Naomi-ni   [kesa   hurui   huku-o
     Ken-TOP   [Naomi-DAT   [this.morning   old   clothes-ACC
     sute]   [sakuban   kuroozetto-o   soozi]]-sase-ta.
     throw.away [last.night   closet-ACC   cleaning]]-*sase*-PST
     'Ken made Naomi throw away her old clothes this morning and clean out the closet last night.'

(iii) *Yamada kyoozyu-wa   [betubetu-no   gakusei-ni   [toogoron-no
      Yamada professor-TOP [different-GEN   student-DAT   [syntax-GEN
      ronbun-o yomi]   [oninron-no   ronbun-o   kak]]-ase-ta.
      paper-ACC read]   [phonology-GEN   paper-ACC   write]]-*sase*-PST
      'Prof. Yamada made different students read a paper on syntax and write a paper on phonology.'

In (ii), temporal modifiers are included that make the first VP temporally follow the second; in (iii), *betubetu* 'different' is attached to the Causee argument. Both of these controls are intended to enforce a true coordination structure, and the sentences are ungrammatical. (See Takano 2004 on relevance of *betubetu* for ensuring that a given sentence with a bare V-stem VP contains a true coordination structure rather than an adjoined, VP-modifier position for the first VP). Similar examples without the temporal modifiers or *betebetu* seem clearly to involve adjunction, as argued by Manning, Sag, and Iida (1999); they get a sequential 'After Xing, Y' or 'X, then Y' reading. Interestingly, the same is true in Korean, which, unlike Japanese, has an overt coordination particle. It is quite mysterious why coordination is not allowed under *-sase* but disjunction is—especially because, as Takano shows, coordination in Japanese can apply to bare verb stems (i.e., under a single tense morpheme).

7. Given that I have said that such an approach should treat all productive morphology (especially inflectional morphology) as syntactically attached, I have adopted a "KaseP" hypothesis for Japanese case particles in this tree. For discussion of how these case morphemes can be licensed by particular case-marking heads, see Miyagawa 1999.

8. Because productive causatives can undergo nominalization, this theory has to allow the syntax to derive *-kata* 'way of' nominals, too.

9. This basic picture, once established, leaves many questions to be solved concerning the *make/let* distinction; the role of unergativity, unaccusativity, and agentivity; psych-predicate causatives, restructuring effects, and more. See the survey literature cited above and references therein.

10. See also Matsumoto 2000.

11. The adversity interpretation is not available for these examples for at least some speakers (Yosuke Sato, pers. comm.).

12. Kunio Nishiyamia (pers. comm.) notes that some clearly monoclausal (and hence lexical) causatives nonetheless do not have an adversity interpretation, such as *sir-ase-ru* 'inform' (lit. 'know-cause'). The idiomatization and adversity causative implications are thus unidirectional: If a causative has an idiomatic interpretation or an adversative interpretation, it is lexical; if it does not, the predicate's lexical or syntactic status is still underdetermined. Tests involving the full constellation of monoclausal/biclausal properties are necessary to establish lexical versus syntactic status in many individual cases. The testing situation is complicated in cases where a root and the unaccusative/inchoative form of the verb are phonologically identical, however, given that both the lexical reading (embedding the root) and the syntactic reading (embedding the inchoative vP) may be available.

13. Another clear example of blocking arises in the case of verb-specific honorific morphology in Japanese, as for *tabe* 'eat'. It cannot be marked with the productive honorific **o-tabe-ni naru*. Rather its irregular honorific form must be used: *mesiagaru* 'eat.HON'. For discussion, see Volpe 2005.

14. In such theories, there is an important distinction between the root lexeme itself, which is the "real" lexical entry, and its word forms, which merely occupy the slots of its paradigm. In theories that allow paradigms to attach derivational morphology, like Miyagawa's, the word forms that fill the slots in a derivational paradigm are also themselves lexemes that have their own *inflectional* paradigms attached—paradigms within paradigms, as it were.

15. Most of the following is a mildly revised version of Miyagawa's (1994, 1998) analysis, which appeared in Harley 1995a. It has been updated to take recent minimalist terminology into account, but the crucial mechanisms remain the same.

16. But see Takano 2004.

17. In the Distributed Morphology account of Harley 1995a and Marantz 1997, there is no constituent V^0, and hence no VP: a verb is created in the syntax by combining a $\sqrt{}$ and a v^0 head. The distinction between a light verb and a main verb, then, comes down to whether the v^0 element has had a $\sqrt{}$ element combined with it: main verbs are $v^0 + \sqrt{}$ combinations; light verbs like *-sase-* are pure v^0. The question of whether any given verb in a language is a realization of just v^0 or of $v^0 + \sqrt{}$, then, is an empirical question. For instance, English *make* might be a v^0, like *-sase-*, or a $v^0 + \sqrt{}$ (=V) combination, like *coerce* or *permit*. See also note 20.

18. Despite the terminology, in the analysis presented below, the class of causatives I have been calling "lexical" are formed in the syntax, and no presyntactic word-forming lexical component is assumed. This is the major conceptual advantage of the analysis. For terminological consistency, however, I continue referring to these monoclausal causatives as "lexical."

19. To make the accounts of the English and Japanese lexical causatives as parallel as possible, let us assume that the v^0 head has had the $\sqrt{}$ node adjoined to it by head-movement. Because Japanese is head-final, however, the head-movement is not necessary to get all the morphemes in the correct order; they could remain in situ but simply merge under adjacency.

20. Sometimes, of course, the appropriate v^0 causative morpheme in a lexical causative is itself the null v^0 morpheme, as for Jacobsen's classes I and IV (e.g., *ak-Ø-U* 'open.TR'). The question of why the root $\sqrt{ak}$ 'open' may also be embedded under v^0_{BECOME} (allomorph *-e-*) but the root $\sqrt{tabe}$ 'eat' apparently may not, despite also taking the Ø allomorph of the external-argument-selecting v^0, can be answered in one of two ways. If *-rare-*, the passive morpheme, is the Elsewhere form of v^0_{BECOME}, then it is perhaps the case that $\sqrt{tabe}$ does alternate, with its passive form *tabe-rare* involving replacing the Ø v^0_{CAUS} morpheme for a v^0_{BECOME}, *-rare-*, thus explaining the suppression of the external argument, similar to the analysis of Persian light verbs presented in Folli, Harley, and Karimi 2005. Alternatively (if the productive passive is assumed to involve embedding vP, rather than $\sqrt{}$P, like the productive causative), the failure of $\sqrt{tabe}$ to alternate can be taken as an indication that the immediate licensing environment for $\sqrt{tabe}$ insertion does not allow a v^0_{BECOME}; for discussion on how to restrict the productivity of inchoative/causative alternations in a syntactic approach to verb-formation, see Harley and Noyer 2000.

21. This is the case no matter whether the $\sqrt{}^0$ and embedded v^0 head move to the matrix v^0, or if they are attached just by virtue of their head-final adjacency in Japanese. In either case, the same remarks obtain: a productive causative v^0 is never adjacent to a root but always is separated from it by another v^0, the one that comes lexically with that $\sqrt{}$.

22. There are still generalizations about the various causatives that remain uncaptured on this analysis. For instance, why does lexical *-sase-* always alternate with an inchoative form whose inchoative suffix is Ø? In principle, a root could be on a special list for an unaccusative morpheme like *-r-* or *-e-*, but not for a causative morpheme, and hence *-r-* or *-e-* could in principle alternate with *-sase-*, yet this does not seem to occur. See Miyagawa 1998 for a proposal. Similarly, the haplological restriction on multiple occurrences of *-sase-* are unexplained—one would expect that infinite recursion should be possible—as with *John made Mary make Joe make Sue eat pizza*—but more than one syntactic *-sase-* embedding is ungrammatical (though Kuroda 1994 shows that a lexical *-sase-* may combine with one syntactic *-sase-*).

23. There are interesting reasons to question this precise formulation of both of these claims, brought up by Volpe (2005). Lexical causatives can be the input to nominalization, with nominalizing morphemes conditioned by the particular lexical causative

involved, and subject to subsequent meaning drift. For example, the lexical causative *chiras-u* 'to scatter', when suffixed by nominalizing *-i* (*chirashi*), refers idiomatically to 'leaflets', not to any scattered item. Yet this idiomatic nominalization clearly includes the causative suffix *-as-*, which should have been a barrier to special meaning assignment, under the Marantz/Arad hypothesis. Pylkkänen (2002) proposes that the causative head and agent-introducing heads are distinct, with the latter selecting the former as its complement, and that only the agent-introducing head is the boundary for special meaning. It is possible that her approach could resolve the conflict between Volpe's idiomatic nominalization facts (including v_{CAUS} but not the agent head) and Miyagawa's verbal idiomatization facts (assuming the productive causative embeds the agent-introducing phrase, not just $v_{CAUS}P$).

REFERENCES

Alexiadou, Artemis, and Elena Anagnostopoulou. 2005. On the syntax and morphology of Greek participles. Talk presented at the Workshop on the Morphosyntax of Modern Greek, LSA Institute, July.

Arad, Maya. 2003. Locality constraints on the interpretation of roots: The case of Hebrew denominal verbs. *Natural Language & Linguistic Theory* 21:737–778.

Baker, Mark. 1988. *Incorporation*. Chicago: University of Chicago Press.

Brody, Michael. 2000. Mirror Theory: Syntactic representation in perfect syntax. *Linguistic Inquiry* 31:29–56.

Chomsky, Noam. 1993. A Minimalist Program for linguistic theory. In *The view from Building 20: Essays in linguistics in honor of Sylvain Bromberger*, ed. Kenneth Hale and Samuel Jay Keyser, 1–52. Cambridge, Mass.: MIT Press.

Chomsky, Noam. 2001. Derivation by phase. In *Ken Hale: A life in language*, ed. Michael Kenstowicz, 1–52. Cambridge, Mass.: MIT Press.

Cipollone, Domenic. 2001. Morphologically complex predicates in Japanese and what they tell us about grammar architecture. In *OSU Working Papers in Linguistics* 56, ed. Michael Daniels, David Dowty, Anna Feldman, and Vanessa Metcalf, 1–52. Columbus: Ohio State University, Department of Linguistics.

Dubinsky, Stan. 1994. Predicate union and the syntax of Japanese causatives. *Journal of Linguistics* 30:43–79.

Embick, David. 2004. On the structure of resultative participles in English. *Linguistic Inquiry* 35(3):355–392.

Folli, Rafaella, Heidi Harley, and Simin Karimi. 2005. Determinants of event structure in Persian complex predicates. *Lingua* 115(10):1365–1401.

Fortin, Catherine R. 2004. Minangkabau causatives: Evidence for the l-syntax/s-syntax division. Talk presented at AFLA 2004, ZAS Berlin, April.

Hale, Kenneth, and Samuel Jay Keyser. 1993. On argument structure and the lexical expression of syntactic relations. In *The view from Building 20: Essays in linguistics in honor of Sylvain Bromberger*, ed. Kenneth Hale and Samuel Jay Keyser, 53–108. Cambridge, Mass.: MIT Press.

Hale, Kenneth, and Samuel Jay Keyser. 2002. *Prolegomena to a theory of argument structure*. Cambridge, Mass.: MIT Press.

Halle, Morris, and Alec Marantz. 2003. Distributed Morphology and the pieces of inflection. In *The view from Building 20: Essays in linguistics in honor of Sylvain Bromberger*, ed. Kenneth Hale and Samuel Jay Keyser, 111–176. Cambridge, Mass.: MIT Press.

Harada, S. I. 1973. Counter equi NP deletion. *Annual Bulletin* 7:113–147. Research Institute of Logopedics and Phoniatrics, Tokyo University.

Harley, Heidi. 1995a. Subjects, events, and licensing. Doctoral dissertation, MIT, Cambridge, Mass.

Harley, Heidi. 1995b. *Sase* bizarre: The structure of Japanese causatives. In *Proceedings of the Canadian Linguistic Society Meeting*, ed. Päivi Koskinen, 221–232. Toronto: Toronto Working Papers in Linguistics.

Harley, Heidi, and Rolf Noyer. 2000. Licensing in the non-lexicalist lexicon. In *The lexicon/encyclopedia interface*, ed. B. Peeters, 349–374. Amsterdam: Elsevier Press.

Jackson, Eric. 2005. Derived statives in Pima. Paper presented at the SSILA Annual Meeting, January. http://www.linguistics.ucla.edu/people/grads/ejackson/SSILA05 PimaDerivedStatives.pdf.

Jacobsen, Wesley. M. 1981. Transitivity in the Japanese verbal system. Doctoral dissertation, University of Chicago.

Jacobsen, Wesley. M. 1992. The transitive structure of events in Japanese. *Studies in Japanese Linguistics I*. Tokyo: Kurosio.

Kitagawa, Yoshihisa. 1986. Subjects in Japanese and English. Doctoral dissertation, University of Massachusetts, Amherst.

Kitagawa, Yoshihisa. 1994. *Subjects in Japanese and English*. New York: Garland.

Kratzer, Angelika. 1996. Severing the external argument from its verb. In *Phrase structure and the lexicon*, ed. Johan Rooryck and Laurie Zaring, 109–137. Dordrecht: Kluwer.

Kuno, Susumu. 1973. *The structure of the Japanese language*. Cambridge, Mass.: MIT Press.

Kuroda, S.-Y., 1965a. Causative forms in Japanese. *Foundations of Language* 1:30–50.

Kuroda, S.-Y. 1965b. Generative grammatical studies in the Japanese language. Doctoral dissertation, MIT, Cambridge, Mass.

Kuroda, S.-Y. 1981. Some recent issues in linguistic theory and Japanese syntax. *Coyote Papers* 2:103–122.

Kuroda, S.-Y. 1990. Shieki no jodoshi no jiritsu-sei ni tsuite [On the independence of causative auxiliaries]. In *Bunpo to imi no aida: Kunihiro Tetsuya kyoju kanreki taikan kinen ronbunshu* [Between grammar and meaning: A collection of papers in honor of Professor Tetsuya Kunihiro on the occasion of his retirement], 93–104. Tokyo: Kurosio.

Kuroda, S.-Y. 1994. Lexical and productive causatives in Japanese: An examination of the theory of paradigmatic structure. *Journal of Japanese Linguistics* 14:1–83.

Kuroda, S.-Y. 2003. Complex predicates and predicate raising. In *Formal Japanese syntax and Universal Grammar: The past 20 years*, ed. Naoki Fukui, *Lingua* 113(4–6):447–480.

Manning, Christopher, Ivan Sag, and Masayo Iida. 1999. The lexical integrity of Japanese causatives. In *Studies in contemporary phrase structure grammar*, ed. Robert D. Levine and Georgia Green, 39–79. Cambridge: Cambridge University Press.

Marantz, Alec. 1984. *On the nature of grammatical relations*. Cambridge, Mass.: MIT Press.

Marantz, Alec. 1991. Case and licensing. In *ESCOL '91: Proceedings of the 8th Eastern States Conference on Linguistics*, ed. German Westphal, Benjamin Ao, and Hee-Rahk Chae, 234–253. Somerville, Mass.: CLC Publications.

Marantz, Alec. 1997. No escape from syntax: Don't try a morphological analysis in the privacy of your own lexicon. In *UPenn Working Papers in Linguistics 4.2, Proceedings of the 21st Annual Penn Linguistics Colloquium*, ed. Alexis Dimitriadis, Laura Siegel, Clarissa Surek-Clark, and Alexander Williams, 201–225. Philadelphia: University of Pennsylvania, Department of Linguistics.

Matsumoto, Yo. 2000. On the crosslinguistic parameterization of causative predicates: Implications from Japanese and other languages. In *Argument realization*, ed. Miriam Butt and Tracy Holloway King, 135–169. Stanford, Calif.: CSLI Publications.

Miyagawa, Shigeru. 1980. Complex verbs and the lexicon. Ph.D. dissertation, University of Arizona, Tucson.

Miyagawa, Shigeru. 1984. Blocking and Japanese causatives. *Lingua* 64:177–207.

Miyagawa, Shigeru. 1989. *Structure and Case marking in Japanese*. New York: Academic Press.

Miyagawa, Shigeru. 1994. (S)ase as an Elsewhere causative. *Program of the Conference on Theoretical Linguistics and Japanese Language Teaching*, 61–76. Tsuda University, Tokyo.

Miyagawa, Shigeru. 1998. (S)ase as an Elsewhere causative and the syntactic nature of words. *Journal of Japanese Linguistics* 16:67–110.

Miyagawa, Shigeru. 1999. Causatives. In *The handbook of Japanese linguistics*, ed. Natsuko Tsujimura, 236–268. Oxford: Blackwell.

Murasugi, Keiko, Tomoko Hashimoto, and Sachiko Kato. 2004. On the acquisition of causatives in Japanese. *BU Conference on Language Development 28 Proceedings Supplement*. http://www.bu.edu/linguistics/APPLIED/BUCLD/supp.html.

Oehrle, Richard, T., and Hiroko Nishio. 1981. Adversity. In *Coyote Papers 2: Proceedings of the Arizona Conference on Japanese Linguistics*, ed. Ann K. Farmer and Chisato Kitagawa, 163–187. Tucson: University of Arizona Linguistics Circle.

Oshima, Shin. 1979. Conditions on rules: Anaphora in Japanese. In *Exploration in linguistics: Papers in honor of Kazuko Inoue*, ed. George Bedell, Eichi Kobayashi, and Masatake Muraki, 423–448. Tokyo: Kenkyusha.

Pylkkänen, Liina. 2002. Introducing arguments. Doctoral dissertation, MIT, Cambridge, Mass.

Sadakane, Kumi, and Masatoshi Koizumi. 1995. On the nature of "dative" particle -ni in Japanese. *Linguistics* 33:5–33.

Shibatani, Masayoshi. 1990. *The languages in Japan*. Cambridge: Cambridge University Press.

Stump, Gregory T. 2001. *Inflectional morphology: A theory of paradigm structure* (Cambridge Studies in Linguistics 93). Cambridge: Cambridge University Press.

Svenonius, Peter. 2005. Two domains of causatives. Talk presented at CASTL, March 10. http://www.hum.uit.no/a/svenonius/papers/Svenonius05TwoDomains.pdf.

Takano, Yuji. 2004. Coordination of verbs and two types verbal inflection. *Linguistic Inquiry* 35(1):168–178.

Terada, Michiko. 1991. Incorporation and argument structure in Japanese. Doctoral dissertation, University of Massachusetts, Amherst.

Travis, Lisa. 2000. Event structure in syntax. In *Events as grammatical objects: The converging perspectives of lexical semantics and syntax*, ed. Carol Tenny and James Pustejovsky, 145–185. Stanford, Calif.: CSLI Publications.

Volpe, Mark. 2005. Japanese morphology and its theoretical consequences: Derivational morphology in Distributed Morphology. Doctoral dissertation, Stony Brook University, New York.

Zenno, Yasushi. 1985. Paradigmatic structure and Japanese idioms. Master's thesis, Ohio State University, Columbus.

CHAPTER 3

JAPANESE -*WA*, -*GA*, AND INFORMATION STRUCTURE

CAROLINE HEYCOCK

3.1 INTRODUCTION

The first nonintroductory chapter of Kuno 1973 opens with the statement, "The distinction in meaning between *wa* and *ga* is a problem that perpetually troubles both students and instructors of Japanese" (p. 37). To the list of those perpetually troubled by the distribution and interpretation of these two morphemes can be added theoretical linguists, who continue to grapple with the problem of accounting for them in the most convincing and elegant way. This issue has become of interest far beyond those who seek to understand the particular facts of Japanese, because it has become a truism that Japanese has an overt marker for topic (*wa*), a concept that is much appealed to in accounts of not only the pragmatics but also the syntax and semantics of a wide range of languages, in many of which however the evidence for the category "topic" is quite indirect. The hope then is that the properties of Japanese *wa* might constitute a leading light for the understanding of this concept.

3.2 Core Data

3.2.1 Thematic and Contrastive *Wa*

In Kuno 1973, which draws in this area heavily on the work of Kuroda (1965), two uses of *wa* and two of *ga* are distinguished as follows (p. 38):[1]

(1) a. *wa* for the theme of a sentence: "Speaking of..., talking about..."
John *wa* gakusei desu.
John WA student is
'Speaking of John, he is a student.'
b. *wa* for contrast: "X..., but..., as for X..."
John ga pai *wa* tabeta ga (keeki *wa* tabenakatta).
John GA pie WA ate but cake WA ate-NEG
'John ate (the) pie, but he didn't eat (the) cake.'
c. *ga* for neutral descriptions of actions or temporary states
Ame *ga* hutte imasu.
rain GA falling is
'It is raining.'
d. *ga* for exhaustive listing "X (and only X)..." "It is X that..."
John *ga* gakusei desu.
John GA student is
'(Of all the people under discussion) John (and only John) is a student. It is John who is a student.'

"Thematic" *wa* is so named because Kuno takes it to indicate the *theme* of the sentence, in the sense of the Prague School. In this use, *wa* does not encode any sense of contrast; with this in mind I use another common, less theory-specific term for this interpretation of *wa* and refer to it from now on as *noncontrastive wa*. The sentence in (1a) can be used to convey information about John, apparently without any implicature about the properties of any other individual, for example, as an answer to the question, *What do you know about John?* Contrastive *wa*, however, does generate implicatures concerning other entities in the discourse model, as illustrated by this example from Hara 2006a:

(2) a. Dare ga paatii ni kita ka?
who GA party to came Q
'Who came to the party?'
b. JOHN wa kita.
John WA came
'As for John, he came.' (Implicature: It is possible that it is not the case that John and Mary came. ≈ I don't know about other people.)
c. John ga kita.
John GA came
'John came.' (Complete answer.)

The capitalization of *john* in (2b) indicates stress; according to Kuno, the contrastive reading of *wa* is always associated with "prominent intonation," whereas this is absent from noncontrastive *wa*-phrases. There seems to be comparatively little literature on the contours associated with the different interpretations of *wa* (or *ga*), but see Nakanishi 2004 for some experimental and corpus evidence supporting Kuno's intuition.

As Kuno notes, in some cases there is ambiguity between these two uses, which may however be resolved by either stress or context, or both. Thus (2b), in another context and without the stress on John, can be interpreted as a case of noncontrastive *wa*. However, contrastive *wa* is freer than noncontrastive *wa* in its distribution, as will be shown, so that there is only partial overlap in the environments in which they occur.

3.2.1.1 *Clause types*

Most generally, noncontrastive *wa* is a "root phenomenon." That is, it does not appear in subordinate clauses, except in complements to certain verbs, such as *say* and *know*. Thus *Mori san* does not necessarily get a contrastive interpretation in (3a), where the embedding verb is *siru* (know), although it does in the minimally different (3b), where the embedding verb is *zannen-ni omou* (regret) (Kuroda 2005:19–20).

(3) a. John wa Mori san wa Toyota no syain de aru koto o sitte-iru.
John WA Mori san WA Toyota GEN employee be fact ACC knows
'John knows that Mori is an employee of Toyota.'
b. John wa Mori san wa Toyota no hira-syain de aru koto o
John WA Mori san WA Toyota GEN flat-employee be fact ACC
zannen-ni omotte iru.
regrets
'John regrets that Mori is a mere employee of Toyota.'

Kuroda's generalization is that noncontrastive *wa* can only occur in "statement-making contexts";[2] Hoji (1985) refers to the complements of "bridge verbs." There does not yet appear to be the kind of detailed listing of exactly what constitutes the kind of statement-making contexts or the types of verbs that allow noncontrastive *wa* that exists for embedded root phenomena such as verb-second order in the Germanic languages (see, e.g., Vikner 1995 and references therein). This issue, broached in Whitman 1991, could clearly be pursued further as a contribution to a theoretical understanding of embedded root phenomena (see Heycock 2006 for an overview of some of the issues).

Contrastive *wa*, however, can occur in a wider range of subordinate clauses, although apparently not all (for discussion of contexts where contrastive *wa* is excluded, see Hara 2006a, 2006b).

3.2.1.2 *Iteration*

According to Kuno (1973:48), noncontrastive *wa* does not iterate within a sentence, which can therefore contain at most one instance. Contrastive *wa*, though, can iterate. Further, whereas noncontrastive *wa* has to be sentence initial, contrastive *wa* can be clause internal. Thus in the following example only the first *wa*-phrase is noncontrastive:

(4) Watasi wa tabako   wa suimasu ga sake   wa nomimasen.
     I   WA cigarette WA smoke   but alcohol WA drink-NEG
     'I smoke, but I don't drink.'

However, there is some dispute as to whether noncontrastive *wa* really has to be unique. Tomioka (to appear a) describes multiple noncontrastive *wa*-phrases as "not totally prohibited but rather rare." Kuroda (1988) goes further, taking iterability to be a fundamental property of all *wa*-phrases. He gives the following example as involving two noncontrastive *wa*-phrases:

(5) Paris de wa Masao wa Eiffel too   to Notre Dame-no too   ni nobotta.
     Paris in WA Masao WA Eiffel tower and Notre Dame GEN tower in climbed
     'In Paris, Masao climbed up the Eiffel tower and the tower of Notre Dame.'

It is no coincidence that the *wa*-phrases here are a locative adjunct and a subject.[3] It is common to get a noncontrastive reading for a subject or a scene-setting adverbial, but *wa*-marking of other arguments strongly favors the contrastive reading, a fact that is well known but again not yet satisfactorily explained.[4]

3.2.1.3 *Movement*

Saito (1985) argues that sentences with initial nominal *wa*-phrases are ambiguous in their derivation and structure: the *wa*-phrase may have moved to the sentence-initial position, leaving a trace, or it may be generated in the initial position, binding an empty pronominal. Hoji (1985), building on this, argues that the difference correlates with interpretation: *wa*-phrases that show the hallmarks of movement (such as island sensitivity and reconstruction effects) receive only a contrastive interpretation, whereas sentence-initial *wa*-phrases that cannot have reached the initial position by movement are unambiguously noncontrastive.

3.2.2 Exhaustive and Descriptive *Ga*

3.2.2.1 *Correlation with predicate types*

As noted earlier, Kuroda (1965) points out that *ga* sometimes, but not always, gives a reading of "exhaustive listing" and that there is a correlation between these readings and the nature of the predicate: in a main clause, a *ga*-marked subject of a stage-level predicate gets either an exhaustive-listing or neutral reading, whereas a *ga*-marked subject of an individual-level predicate can only get the exhaustive-listing reading.

(6) a. John ga kita.
    John GA came
    'John came.' or 'JOHN came./It is John who came.'
   b. John ga gakusei desu.
    John GA student is
    'JOHN is a student./It is JOHN who is a student.'

This restriction is almost certainly stated too categorically; some qualifications are discussed in section 3.3.2.3.

3.2.2.2 *Clause type*

The pattern just noted is again, like the possibility of a noncontrastive interpretation of *wa*, a root phenomenon. To be more precise, it is only in clauses that are unambiguously nonsubordinate that the exhaustive-listing reading is forced on the subject of individual-level predicates; both in a clearly subordinate clause (such as the antecedent of a conditional, for example) and in the type of clause that optionally allows embedded root phenomena this reading is not forced but merely available.

3.3 QUESTIONS OF ANALYSIS

Given the kind of data discussed in the previous section, a number of questions immediately arise. First, the characterizations of the interpretations of *ga* and *wa* are both disjunctive. Is this an irreducible fact, or is there some underlying unity to the different uses or interpretations in each case? If so, what interactions give rise to the apparent diversity? Second, these characterizations have appealed to the notions of "exhaustive listing" and of "topic"; what definitions are being assumed?

3.3.1 *Ga* and Focus

It has become common[5] to assume that the exhaustive-listing reading of a *ga*-phrase should be considered to amount to *narrow focus* on that constituent (that is, focus that does not include any larger containing constituent). Unfortunately "focus" has an enormously wide range of meanings in the literature. Here it is used in a sense that belongs to the pragmatic tradition that goes back to the Prague School, where it means, very approximately, the informative, nonpresupposed, part of an utterance. In this sense it is often also referred to as the *rheme*. It is crucial to bear in mind that there is no requirement that the referents of focal constituents be textually new, so that there is no contradiction in analyzing *me* as the focus in (7B), even though the speaker and the hearer are generally taken to be linguistically salient in any conversation, and in this case the speaker has even been mentioned in the same sentence.

(7) A: Who did your parents contact?
B: My mother phoned ME, of course.

As in this last example, in a typical question-answer pair, the focus of the answer is the part that corresponds to the *wh*-phrase in the question.[6] In (8) the foci of the answers are indicated by bracketing.

(8) a. A: Why didn't you answer the phone?
B: [F I was reading a great novel by YOSHIMOTO].
b. A: What were you doing all afternoon?
B: I [F was reading a great novel by YOSHIMOTO].
c. A: What were you reading?
B: I was reading [F a great novel by YOSHIMOTO].
d. A: Who is the author of the novel you were reading?
B: I was reading a great novel by [F YOSHIMOTO].

The examples in (8) illustrate the well-known fact that in English focus (understood in informational terms) can "project" from the constituent bearing the pitch accent, so that only the context indicates whether the focus of B's sentence is the DP *Yoshimoto* or one of a number of larger constituents. However, projection of focus is not unconstrained: for example, there is no "wide focus" or "focus-projected" reading of an example like (9a), as shown by its infelicity as a response to the question in (9b), in contrast to (9c).[7]

(9) a. I was reading a [F LONG] novel.
b. A: What were you reading?
B: #I was reading a [F LONG] novel.
c. A: What kind of novel were you reading?
B: I was reading a [F LONG] novel.

A possible redescription of the distinction between the exhaustive-listing and neutral description *ga*, then, is that *ga* is a focus marker (the equivalent of an English "A" accent, indicated by small caps in the examples just given) and that the projection of focus is affected in some way by the nature of the predicate. Such a proposal was made by Diesing (1988), who observed that the distribution of the "neutral description" *ga* in Japanese appeared to mirror the distribution of focus projection from subjects in English, where it has been argued to be restricted to the subjects of unaccusative verbs and stage-level predicates. Thus, (10a,b) can only be interpreted with narrow focus on the subject, but (11a,b) can also be interpreted with wide focus, so that the entire sentence constitutes new information. That is, the sentences in (11), but not those in (10), have one focus structure that makes them acceptable answers to questions such as, What happened/was happening? and Why are the chefs running for the door?

(10) a. [F The EMPEROR] was playing pool.
b. [F BLOWFISH] are poisonous.

(11) a. [F [F The EMPEROR] arrived].
b. [F [F BLOWFISH] are available].

These examples, Diesing argued, exemplify the same phenomenon as Kuno's examples in (6), repeated here as (12).

(12) a. [F John ga] gakusei desu.
John GA student is
'JOHN is a student./It is JOHN who is a student.'
b. [F [F John ga] kita].
John GA came
'John came.' or 'JOHN came./It is John who came.'

Diesing's proposal was that focus cannot project from the external subject position (the position in which the subjects of unergative and transitive verbs and individual-level predicates originate); but the subjects of unaccusative verbs and stage-level predicates originate in a lower position inside the VP. Assuming that the trace of the subject is visible to focus projection, focus is able to project from the VP-internal traces in (11a,b) and (12b). This structural difference is then the explanation for the correlation of the different readings of *ga*-phrases with predicate types noticed by Kuroda and described in section 3.2.2.1.

One further advantage of assimilating the exhaustive-listing reading of *ga* to narrow focus is that the kind of explanations that have been developed to explain the readings of the latter—possibly encoded in different ways in different languages—can simply be extended to Japanese, as pointed out by Shibatani (1990:270–271).

Taking the exhaustive-listing reading of *ga* to be an instance of narrow focus does not, however, entail that *ga* is itself a focus marker (only that it is compatible with being contained in a focused constituent). Indeed, there are considerable and well-known problems with the analysis of *ga* as a focus marker.

First, as Shibatani observes, it does not occur freely on constituents other than the subject. For that reason, it is very widely assumed to be a case marker, entirely parallel to the accusative case marker *o*.[8] Second, although the correlation with predicate-type seems to mirror the pattern of focus projection in English, the correlation with clause-type (see section 3.2.2.2) does not. That is, whereas the *ga*-marked subject of an individual-level predicate in a subordinate clause is not necessarily interpreted with narrow focus, the embedded subject of such a predicate in English continues to disallow focus projection, so that there is an ambiguity in the scope of the focus in (13b) that is not evident in (13a).

(13) a. I only said that [F BLOWFISH] were poisonous.
    b. I only said that [F [F BLOWFISH] were available].

There is no natural extension of any theory of focus projection that can explain why or how there should be a main clause–subordinate clause asymmetry in Japanese in this respect, should *ga*-marking indeed encode focus in the way that the A accent does in English.

Heycock 1993 proposes a weaker link between *ga* marking and information structure. There it is argued that *ga* does not encode information status except in an indirect, negative sense; a *ga*-marked subject (like an *o*- or *ni*-marked constituent) is, by definition, not *wa*-marked. That paper then makes the following additional assumptions:

1. Nominals, but not predicates, that are topics must be marked with *wa*.
2. Every sentence, but not every clause, must have a topic (whether overt or null).
3. Topics and foci are necessarily disjoint (this follows from Vallduví's definition of topic/link and focus, discussed below).
4. Stage-level predicates, but not individual-level predicates, have a Davidsonian event argument that is available as a topic.

Given these assumptions, a sentence with a stage-level predicate such as (14) can have the Davidsonian event argument as the topic; the subject may therefore be the focus, but the focus could equally well be all the overt material.[9]

(14) [F [F John ga] kita].
    John GA came
    'JOHN came.'

When the predicate is stage-level, however, there is no Davidsonian argument available. In (15), therefore, the only available topic is the predicate (if the subject were topic, it would be marked with *wa*). This leaves the subject as the only possible focus, so that wide focus on the entire sentence is excluded.

(15) [F John ga] kasikoi.
    John GA smart
    'JOHN is smart.'

Finally, given that the requirement for a topic is a requirement on sentences, rather than clauses, it is possible for the clause in (15) to have an all-focus reading if it is embedded, since the requirement for a topic can now be satisfied by some other element in the sentence.[10]

This analysis also accounts for the observation that in a matrix clause with no *wa*-phrase and multiple nominatives, only the first nominative has to be interpreted as being in focus, whereas the others do not necessarily receive this interpretation.

(16) Nisi no hoo   ga ame ga taihen desu.
    west GEN alternative NOM rain NOM great is
    'It is in the west that the rain is a nuisance.'

Again, in the absence of a *wa*-phrase the predicate must be taken to be the topic. On the assumption that in Japanese a clause can be abstracted over to produce an (individual-level) sentential predicate (see Heycock and Doron 2003 for discussion), noninitial nominatives, although they cannot be topics themselves—else they would have to be marked with *wa*—can be included in a predicate that is the topic. But in this case at least the highest nominative must be excluded from the topic and therefore treated as focal, because the sentence requires not only a link/topic but also a focus.

Essentially the same assumptions are used by Tomioka (2000, to appear a) to explain the contrast between (17), which is ambiguous between a locative and a part-whole reading, and (18), which has only the locative reading unless *enzin ga* (engine GA) is read with narrow focus, and also to explain why this contrast does not obtain in subordinate clauses (where both readings are possible for both orders, without any particular focus assignment):

(17) Torakku ni enzin-ga aru.
 truck LOC engine-GA exist
 Locative: 'There is an engine in the/a truck (possibly on its bed).'
 Part-whole: 'The/a truck has an engine (as one of its essential parts).'

(18) Enzin ga torakku ni aru.
 engine GA truck LOC exist
 Locative: 'There is an engine in the truck (possibly on the truck's bed).'
 Part-whole: 'The/a truck has an engine (as one of its essential parts).'
 (Only possible with narrow focus on *enzin*.)

This account additionally exploits the fact that *wa* may optionally be omitted but that, when this is the case, the result is a bare PP or bare (non-case-marked) nominal, so *torakku ni* (in the/a truck) in (17) can be interpreted as a topic, but *enzin ga* (engine GA) in (18) cannot. The possibility of interpreting *torakku ni* in (17) as a topic immediately explains why it does not have to have a narrow focus reading, but the lack of this possibility for *enzin ga* in (18) is still not quite enough to explain why it has to have a narrow focus reading if the sentence is given a part-whole interpretation. After all, it seems that on the locative reading of (18) the sentence can get an "all focus" interpretation. Here the argument parallels that given in Heycock 1993 for examples like (15). As the part-whole relation is more or less permanent, it is not compatible with an event argument; this then is not an available topic for (18) with the part-whole interpretation. That leaves as the only possible topic the remainder of the sentence—*torakku-ni aru* (the truck has)—so that *enzin* is forced to constitute the focus. The locative reading, however, allows an event argument, which can function as the topic, allowing for an "all focus" reading of the overt material. The distinction between the two readings disappears in subordinate clauses because in such cases the topic of the sentence may be within the matrix, so that the lack of an event-topic in the subordinate clause no longer forces some other part of that clause to be the topic and the *ga*-phrase to constitute the focus.

To summarize: there is a fairly general consensus (modulo the dissent, mentioned previously, of Kuroda 2005 and Vermeulen 2005) that *ga* should not be singled out as carrying any semantic or pragmatic information; its alternation with *wa* is only privileged with respect to the alternation between, say, *o* (the accusative marker) and *wa* in the sense that it appears that subjects are an unmarked choice of topic.

3.3.2 *Wa* and Topic

If the range of definitions and uses of the word "focus" is wide, the situation is possibly even worse for "topic"; the discussion here is necessarily limited to a small subset of the definitions in the literature, which are discussed because of their relevance to the work on Japanese (and vice versa).

3.3.2.1 *Topic as anchor for information*

The notion of topic that is appealed to in Heycock 1993 and Tomioka 2000, to appear a, and to appear b is Vallduví's concept of *link*. For Vallduví, the participants in a discourse each maintain a knowledge store that is taken to be a Heimian collection of entity-denoting file cards, each card containing information relevant to the entity. The role of information packaging is to aid the hearer by giving instructions as to how to update this database. At the level of information structure, where these instructions are encoded, a sentence may be articulated into focus and ground, and the ground may itself be composed of a link and a tail. The link points to a specific file card where the (new) information carried by a given sentence is to be entered; the focus is that information; and the ground gives further information about where in the record the new information is to be entered. Note that for Vallduví the only one of these elements that is obligatory in every sentence is the focus (see McNally 1998b for discussion of the necessarily default nature of focus as an update instruction). Heycock's proposal, adopted also by Tomioka (to appear a), that every sentence must have a link, even if phonetically null, is a modification of Vallduví's framework.

Vallduví's notion of link embodies in a quite direct way the intuition that a sentence topic is what the sentence is "about." The proposal of Portner and Yabushita (1998, 2001) is similar to Vallduví's, as they state, in that they also take topics to be entities, with which information is associated. Rather than positing a distinct level of representation (Vallduví's Information Structure), however, they instead propose an enriched notion of the common ground of a discourse, defined as a set of infinite sequences of pairs, where each pair consists of an entity (the link) and a set of possible worlds (the information entered with respect to that link). Portner and Yabushita support this view of topics (at the least, of noncontrastive *wa*-marked phrases in Japanese) by sequences of sentences showing that discourse entities can most felicitously be picked out by information that was contributed while the entity in question was encoded as a topic. However, as they acknowledge, intuitions about these discourses are not clear cut. Portner and Yabushita also show that their adaptation of the file-card approach to topics can explain the obligatory wide scope for the *wa*-phrase in (19b), which contrasts with the minimally different (19a).[11]

(19) a. John dake ga kuru to omotteita.
John only GA come that thought
'I thought that only John would come.'
b. John dake wa kuru to omotteita.
John only TOP come that thought
'John is the only one who I thought would come.'

One further support for this way of approaching noncontrastive *wa* is that certain quantified expressions appear to be incompatible with noncontrastive *wa*. Kuno (1973) points this out for *oozei no X* 'many X' and *dareka* 'somebody', and Tomioka (to appear b) gives a longer list of what he calls anti-Topic Items (ATIs) and seeks to account for their incompatibility in terms of the properties of links.

3.3.2.2 *Topic as expressing an active mental representation*

Portner (2007) proposes a modified view of topics-as-entities, in which topicalization encodes an expressive meaning in the sense of Potts (2005):

(20) "(I report that) my/the speaker's mental representation of X is active."

This approach is consistent with (although it does not entail) a less structured linguistic representation of the common ground of a discourse; on this approach, the notion of "filing" information about an entity under a particular heading becomes a pragmatic effect that is achieved indirectly (as a perlocutionary, rather than illocutionary, act), through the explicit mention of the speaker's mental state. In relating sentence topics to the speaker's mental state, rather than to instructions to update the hearer's representation, Portner suggests a system that is potentially much more consistent with Kuroda's view of *wa*-phrases, discussed in section 3.3.3.1, although the motivations for this outlook appear to be quite different. Portner makes the interesting point that the possibility of topics in embedded contexts argues for a speaker-oriented account, given that not only verbs such as *tell* or *say* but also *think* allow embedded topics, as shown for Japanese *wa*-phrases by this example from Kuno, which allows an indirect speech interpretation:[12]

(21) John wa boku wa oobaka to omotte iru.
John WA I WA idiot that thinking is
'John thinks that I am a fool.'

The crucial point is that, whereas *tell* and *say* may introduce an addressee, this is not true of *think*; however, what they all do have in common is that they introduce the referent of the subject as a deictic center, as the speaker is the deictic center for an unembedded clause. Whether this approach could incorporate some aspects at least of Kuroda's view of the interpretation of *wa*-phrases as the subject of categorical judgments would depend largely on how the notion of the speaker's mental representation being active was cashed out.

3.3.2.3 *Topic as question (under discussion)*

An alternative view to topics as (pointers to) entities is that topics are anaphoric to *open questions*, typically modeled as sets of propositions (see Portner and Yabushita 1998, McNally 1998a for useful overviews). This approach is most associated with von Fintel 1994, Büring 1999, and Roberts 1996, 1998; this definition of topic seems also to some extent to correspond to Steedman's (2000a, 2000b) theme.

Researchers on Japanese have not as yet tended to adopt this view of topic as a way of explicating the distribution and interpretation of noncontrastive *wa*. The main exception is the proposal of Fiengo and McClure (2002); although they couch their analysis in terms of an Austinian theory of assertive speech act types, the dimension that is taken to explain the distribution of *wa* (not just noncontrastive *wa*: Fiengo and McClure, like Shibatani 1990, aim to give a unified account of both interpretations) is *direction of fit*, which distinguishes what is *given* from what is *produced*. The definition of these Austinian terms is not made very clear, but they propose exactly the question-answer heuristic: if the sentence *That bird is a nuthatch* is produced as an answer to *What do you call that bird?*, the predicate *is a nuthatch* is "produced" whereas the subject is "given." It thus seems that, at least as a first approximation, produced = focus/rheme, and given = ground (in Valldudí's terminology).[13] And their account of *wa* is then that *wa* is placed on an NP if and only if that NP refers to an item that is given (Fiengo and McClure 2002:13). Crucial to their account are the equivalent or close parallel of two assumptions explicitly made also in Heycock 1993: they assume that in performing an assertive speech act a speaker must not only "produce" something (every utterance must have a focus/rheme) but must also take another thing as given (cf. assumption 2 in section 3.3.1); and they note that a predicate, unlike an NP, can be "given" without being marked with *wa* (cf. assumption 1).

The lack of a clear definition for what is "given" makes it hard to see how this analysis handles the problem that what is *wa* marked in Japanese typically does not include all the ground (nonquestioned, presupposed, not-at-issue) material. For example, (22B) is a (pedantic) answer to the question in (22A); the variant in (22C) is, as Fiengo and McClure note, not a natural answer, and the *wa*-marked object can only be read as highly contrastive:

(22) A: Dare ga keeki o tabeta no?
　　　who GA cake ACC ate Q
　　　'Who ate (the) cake?'

B: John ga keeki o   tabeta.
   John GA cake ACC ate
   'John ate (the) cake.'
C: #John ga keeki wa tabeta.
   John GA cake WA ate
   'John ate (the) cake.'

The question here is why in the straightforward answer the object *keeki* 'cake' is not marked with *wa*, as it appears to be a part of the presupposition of the answer, just as much as the verb. Fiengo and McClure, however, state that although the cake is previously mentioned, it is not "given" in the Austinian sense, and they caution against reducing Austin's distinctions to others (p. 39). It is not obvious from their proposal, however, what definition of "given" makes the necessary cut here.

The lack of an obvious distinction between elements within the ground is thus one problem for a question-under-discussion theory of noncontrastive *wa*-phrases/topics. Another, pointed out in Portner and Yabushita 1998, is that noncontrastive *wa*-phrases can occur in questions. In the case of an example like (23), the question that is presupposed by the topic (or that the topic is anaphoric to) is identical to the question actually asked; this seems paradoxical.[14]

(23) John wa nani o   yatta no?
     John WA what ACC did Q
     'What did John do?'

Finally, Roberts's (1996, 1998) question-under-discussion analysis of Jackendoff's "B" intonation contour (Steedman's L+H* LH% "theme" tune) in English is suggested in McNally 1998a as a possible cross-linguistically valid account of topic-marking. In this account, a "contrastive topic" like *China* in (24), marked by the B accent, is in fact a focus, just like the A-accented element *April*, so that the second speaker indicates that the presupposed "superquestion" is in fact *Where is Bill going when?*.

(24) (No prior discourse, at least on a related subject).
     A: When is Bill going to China?
     B: Well, he's going to [B CHINA] in [A APRIL].

The additional function of the B accent on an argument is to indicate that the speaker is choosing first to pick from the alternative set corresponding to that argument in setting up a subquestion (here *When is Bill going to China?*) as part of a strategy to answer the superquestion. This account of "contrastive topics" in terms of a strategy of subquestions is, however, explicitly intended to account only for contrastive topics. It is therefore unclear how it could shed any light on the use of *wa* in situations where no such interpretation is at issue (I return to the question of contrastive topics in section 3.3.4).

However, it should perhaps be noted that although Heycock 1993 and Tomioka 2000, to appear a, and to appear b adopt Vallduví's theory of topics/links in their accounts, it is crucial for both that predicates can function as topics, given that this is the basis for the accounts of narrow focus on the subject in examples like (15) and (18), repeated here as (25a,b).

(25) a. [F John ga] kasikoi.
           John GA smart
           'JOHN is smart.'
       b. Enzin ga   torakku ni   aru.
          engine GA truck   LOC   exist
          Locative: 'There is an engine in a truck (possibly on the truck's bed).'
          Part-whole: 'The/a truck has an engine (as one of its essential parts).'
          (Only possible with narrow focus on *enzin*.)

It is not clear that this is really consistent with the entity view of topics (although, of course, properties can be anaphorically referred to in discourse and so at least are able to contribute discourse entities). Matsuda (1997) resolves this by proposing that in such sentences the predicate is actually a nominalized clause, as schematized in (26a)—in fact, the same headless relative (although a certain amount of syntactic/morphological detail must be dealt with) that occurs in the initial position in the specificational sentence in (26b).[15] (26b) is argued to be derived from the same basic structure as (26a) by overt topicalization of the headless relative (see den Dikken 2006 for a very similar derivation for specificational sentences in English). Because Matsuda adopts the common assumption that there is a structurally defined position for topics at the left periphery of CP, she further argues that (26a) involves LF-movement of the free relative to this position.

(26) a. John ga [CP Op$_i$ [IP [PrP t$_i$ kasikoi] no̶]].
           John GA   smart   NMZ
           'JOHN is smart.'
       b. Kasikoi no wa John da.
          smart   NMZ   John IND
          'The smart one is JOHN.'

However, in later work, Matsuda (2003) raises an interesting problem for this type of approach: namely, that it seems to predict that the two sentences in (27) should have identical Information Structures:

(27) a. Are, isya   wa Hiromi da.
           oh   doctor   WA Hiromi IND
           'Oh, the doctor is Hiromi.'
       b. #Are, Hiromi ga isya   da.
           oh   Hiromi GA doctor IND
           'Oh, HIROMI is the doctor.'

However, she argues that if two speakers are looking at a scene containing a baseball player, a policeman, and a doctor, and one of them suddenly realizes that the one in the white coat is their mutual friend Hiromi, (27a) is a felicitous response but (27b) is not.

This asymmetry is an interesting one and certainly a challenge for analysis.[16] However, it is debatable whether the effect should be attributed to the behavior of topics/*wa*-phrases. Copular sentences like (27a,b) raise notoriously thorny problems, despite their surface simplicity (see, e.g., Higgins 1979, Moro 1997, Heycock and Kroch 1999, Schlenker 2003, den Dikken 2006, and references therein), and it is far from clear that the two noun phrases have the same semantic status. In particular, the initial phrase alone carries a presupposition of existence; and this asymmetry persists even in subordinate clauses where *wa* marking is not an issue. For example, in the scenario set out in (28), there is a sharp difference in the acceptability of the two continuations: but note that in neither case is topichood at issue, given that the relevant clause is the antecedent of a conditional and its subject therefore not marked with *wa* (and not a topic, on any theory).

(28) Scenario: the speaker and the hearer both know that Ken has a single sister, and that her name is Kimiko, but they do not know whether she is younger or older than Ken. They are debating whether she would have been old enough to see the moon landing.

    a. Mosi Kimiko ga Ken no imooto datta to sitara,
        if   Kimiko GA Ken GEN little-sister was COMP make-COND
        nenrei-teki ni itte tuki-tyakuriku o miteta hazu
        age-wise to speak moonlanding ACC saw expectation
        ga nai.
        GA exists-NEG
        'If Kimiko is Ken's little sister, she couldn't have seen the moon landing.'
    b. #Mosi Ken no imooto ga Kimiko datta to sitara,
        if   Ken GEN little-sister GA Kimiko was COMP make-COND
        nenrei-teki ni itte tuki-tyakuriku o miteta hazu ga nai.
        age-wise to speak moonlanding ACC saw expectation GA exists-NEG
        'If Ken's little sister is Kimiko, she couldn't have seen the moon landing.'

This contrast shows that nonpresuppositional use of *Ken no imooto* 'Ken's little sister' is possible in the second position in the copular sentence but not in the subject position. It follows that the interpretation when the "same" phrase is topicalized from the two positions is not predicted to be equivalent. This alone is sufficient to predict that pairs like (27a,b) also may not be equivalent.

English, of course, shows exactly the same effect (the translation of (28b) is infelicitous in the given scenario and contrasts with that of (28a)). But note that the Japanese examples show that this fact does not have to do with the topic status of any element in the clause, given that it obtains also in this subordinate clause. Thus, whereas copular sentences containing only two noun phrases may seem to be the simplest, most minimal structures for investigating information structure, in fact they embody asymmetries that appear to be independent of whatever is encoded by *wa* (a fact of no little interest for those interested in the syntax of specificational sentences).

Returning to the possibility of nonnominal topics: the fact that predicates may (according to Heycock and Tomioka) be noncontrastive topics is perhaps reconcilable with a view of topics as entity denoting, given a sufficiently inclusive notion of "entity." Potentially more troubling are cases with a covert/null topic, such as this example from Tomioka (to appear a), who argues that the broad focus reading available for A's answer shows that there must be such a topic and seems to suggest that this topic must be sentential or propositional in nature:

(29) A: Motto anzen-ni ki-o tuketa-hoo-ga ii-desu-yo.
more safety-DAT attention-ACC pay-rather-GA good-COP-PART
'You'd better pay more attention to your safety.'
B: Soo-desu-ka?
SO-COP-Q
'Really?'
A: Ee. Tatoeba, kagi-ga toire-no mado-ni nai-de-syoo?
yes for example lock-GA toilet-GEN window-LOC NEG-COP-PART
Abunai-desu-yo.
dangerous-COP-PART
'Yes. For instance, the bathroom window doesn't have a lock, right? That's dangerous.'

It is, however, notable that examples with null topics show asymmetries that parallel cases with overt nominal topics. Thus, for example, the contrast between (30B) and (30B′)—where the nominative is possible in the former with a broad focus reading but can only yield a (disfavored in this context) narrow focus reading in the latter—seems to parallel the contrast that Kuno (1973) pointed out between (31a) and (31b).[17]

(30) A: Doosite sonna-ni hayaku kaeritai no?
why so early leave-want Q
'Why do you want to leave so early?'
B: [F Miti-ga abunai].
roads-GA dangerous
'The roads are dangerous.'
B1: ?#[F Newark ga] abunai.
Newark GA dangerous
'Newark's dangerous.'

(31) a. Kono kurasu wa dansei ga yoku dekiru.
this class WA males GA well can
'Speaking of this class, the boys do well.' [Not necessarily narrow focus on boys.]

b. Kono kurasu wa John ga yoku dekiru.
   this class   WA John GA well can
   'Speaking of this class, JOHN does well.' [Necessarily narrow focus on John.]

If the contrast between the definite and the proper name in subject position derives from the possibility of a null possessive coreferential with a topic in the former case only, this parallel could be taken as evidence in favor of an entity-type topic in examples like (30B) as well (suggesting that the topic in (31b) has a special status in not "counting" as the link for the sentence). However, in the absence of a worked-out account, this remains for now at the level of speculation.

3.3.3 *Wa* as the Marker of a Categorical Judgment

A notable critique of the assumption that the distribution and interpretation of *wa* are to be explained in terms of information structure (whether this is viewed as a distinct level of representation, as in Vallduví 1992, or as an articulation of the common ground, as in Portner and Yabushita 1998) has been enunciated over several decades by Kuroda (1965, 1972, 1990, 1992, 2005). Kuroda proposes that there are two types of judgments, which he describes as cognitive or mental acts (Kuroda 2005:15): categorical/predicational judgments and thetic/descriptive judgments. These judgments are expressed by utterances in which the speaker commits him- or herself to the truth of the propositions that they are said to represent, in a type of speech act. On the common assumption that speech acts are not generally the right type of object to combine with other linguistic objects, this means that judgments are generally not expressed in embedded clauses. In the most recent reworking of his ideas on judgment types, Kuroda maintains that sentences containing a noncontrastive *wa* (*wa*-topicalized sentences) invariably express categorical/predicational judgments. Sentences that do not may either express thetic/descriptive judgments (as must be the case when they appear as matrix clauses) or, in a context where a judgment is not made (as, for example, in an embedded clause), they may simply represent propositions.[18]

The notions of categorical/predicational and thetic/descriptive judgments are, in Kuroda's view, entirely independent of discourse notions of topic and focus. Note that this is not necessarily the case for other linguists who have appealed to these concepts since they were introduced into linguistic theory by Kuroda from the philosophical work of Franz Brentano and Anton Marty; thetic sentences are frequently assumed to be defined as "all focus" utterances. In Kuroda 2005, in particular, arguments are given in two directions against the equation of noncontrastive *wa*-phrases and information-structural concept of topic/link (these arguments would also apply to the kind of theory proposed in Fiengo and McClure 2002 as I understand it): Kuroda argues both that *wa*-phrases may constitute informationally defined foci, and that *ga*-phrases may constitute informationally defined topics. Further, he argues that the exhaustive-listing interpretation of *ga* is independent of focus—and a fortiori is not the result of a configuration of narrow focus.

Evidence against the hypothesis that *wa* is a topic marker is constituted by dialogues in which a *wa*-phrase in an answer corresponds to the *wh*-phrase in the question, the classic diagnostic for focus. Example (32) is one instance (Kuroda 2005:(5), (6)).

(32) A: Dare ga oo-ganemoti desu ka?
    who GA big-rich   is   Q
    'Who is very rich?'
  B: Microsoft no syatyoo no Gates-san wa/#ga ooganemoti desu.
    Microsoft GEN president GEN Gates-HON WA/GA big-rich   is
    'Mr. Gates, the president of Microsoft, is very rich.'

The force of this as a counterexample depends on *Microsoft no syatyoo no Gates-san wa* not being taken as a contrastive topic; Kuroda argues that it does not carry the implicatures that are characteristic of contrastive topics (p. 8), but this judgment appears to be a delicate one, not shared by all speakers.[19]

Evidence against the hypothesis that a *ga*-phrase cannot constitute a topic comes from examples such as (33) (Kuroda 2005:(18)), where *ano hito* 'that person' is given in the question and is the expected topic of the answer:

(33) A: Ano hito wa dare desu ka?
    that person WA who is Q
    'Who is that person?'
  B: Ano hito   wa/ga ano yuumeina Microsoft no syatyoo   no
    that person WA/GA that famous Microsoft GEN president GEN
    Gates-san   desu yo
    Gates-HON   is   EMPH
    'That person is that famous president of Microsoft, Mr. Gates.'

This last example is also used as evidence that the exhaustive-listing implicature is not the result of narrow focus, because if *ano hito ga* is not the focus of B's response but nevertheless gets an exhaustive-listing reading, this must mean that this reading is derived in some other way. However, Kuroda notes that the use of *ga* in such examples is only acceptable when the nature of the predicate (possibly together with world knowledge) entails that only one entity could satisfy it. This is, of course, true in (33) but false in (34), which therefore only allows for *wa* in (34C) (absent a particular context in which there is known to be only one office worker) (Kuroda 2005:11).

(34) A: Mori-san wa Toyota no dareka/hito desu.
    Mori-HON WA Toyota GEN someone/person is
    'Mori-san is someone from Toyota.'
  B: Mori-san wa Toyota no nan desu ka?
    Mori-HON WA Toyota GEN what is   Q
    'Who/what of Toyota is he?'
  C: Mori-san wa/#ga zimuin   desu.
    Mori-HON WA/GA office worker is
    'Mori-san is an office worker.'

Thus it appears from this description that *ga* when used on a topic carries a *presupposition* of uniqueness. This certainly does not follow from the information-structural view of how *ga* functions; it is not immediately clear whether it follows from Kuroda's basic assumptions or has to be stated as an independent principle. It should also be noted that if the name of an unfamiliar person (e.g., *Miller san to yuu hito* 'a person called Miller') is substituted for *Gates*, the use of *ga* in (33B) is strongly dispreferred (Satoshi Tomioka, pers. comm.), which suggests that the answer in (33B) with *ga* is possible only to the extent that *Gates* is taken to be the topic in some wider context.[20]

Kuroda's own proposal, as stated before, is that *wa* is used only to express the subject of a categorical judgment; *ga* is used either in the expression of a thetic/descriptive judgment or (the Elsewhere case) in a context where no assertion is being made, as in (most) subordinate clauses. Descriptive judgments are said to "affirm" either what is given in perception (this is the most commonly cited type of example of a thetic sentence) or what is "given in the conceptual understanding of a cognitive agent." This latter characterization is important because it is necessary for extending the notion of thetic/descriptive judgment to the responses to questions: in particular, to account for the use of *ga* on the subject of an individual level predicate in an example like R's answer in (35) (Kuroda 2005:33).

(35) Q: Dare ga Nihon iti no   sakka desu ka?
          who GA Japan one GEN author is   Q
         'Who is Japan's greatest writer?'
      R: Natsume Soseki ga Nihon iti no   sakka desu.
          Natsume Soseki GA Japan one GEN author is
         'Natsume Soseki is Japan's greatest writer.'

Kuroda's idea is that the inquiry "brings into R's awareness" the conceptual situation of Natsume Soseki being the greatest writer, and R responds by describing this "conceptually grasped" scene. Given that Kuroda notes that R might also respond as in (36), however, he further argues that an answer can also consist of the expression of a categorical judgment about an author.

(36) R: Nogami Yaeko wa, kaigai de sirarete imasen ga, Nihon iti no
         Nogami Yaeko WA abroad LOC known   is-NEG but Japan one GEN
         sakka desu.
         author is
         'Nogami Yaeko, though she is not known abroad, is Japan's greatest writer.'

The possibility of (36) as a response in the context of (35Q) is certainly problematic for the information-structural account of *wa*. Possibly the line that could be pursued by a defender of such an account is that this could be an instance of a hearer employing a set of "packaging instructions" for the answer that are not those suggested by the questioner. That something like this might be at issue is suggested also by Kuroda's other example (2005:10):

(37) A: Tokorode, dare ga Nihon iti no sakka desyoo?
by-the-way who GA Japan one GEN author be-would
'By the way, who would be Japan's greatest writer?'
B is silent for a while, pondering the question, then says:
B: Un, soo da, Nogami Yaeko wa Nihon iti no sakka desu yo.
yes so is Nogami Yaeko WA Japan one GEN author is EMPH
'Yes, that's right, Nogami Yaeko is Japan's greatest writer, I would say.'

B begins her or his answer by apparently agreeing with something: but it cannot be with the question. So, it seems that B is presenting her or his announcement as confirmation of something that the original questioner is asked to accommodate as having been under discussion.

Of course, if responses to questions are allowed freely to embody an information structure that is quite different from that suggested by the immediate context, an account in terms of information structure loses all predictive power. It seems to me at this stage that the pervasiveness of the problem posed by the kind of example that Kuroda adduces remains to be fully determined, and that some theoretically inspired corpus-based work could be very useful in this area.

As far as the exhaustive-listing reading is concerned, Kuroda maintains that it is an implicature that follows from a maximality constraint on descriptions that requires that "a description is to be chosen that makes the grasped situation a maximal fit" (2005:38). Thus the sentence in (38) implicates that Mori-san is the only office worker from Toyota in the context.

(38) Mori-san ga Toyota no zimuin desu.
Mori-san GA Toyota GEN office worker is
'Mori-san is an office worker at Toyota.'

This maximality constraint does have to be stipulated to apply to the subject argument only, given that there is no parallel exhaustiveness implicature from objects (or for that matter from the predicate itself). There does not seem to be any account of the difference between stage- and individual-level predicates with respect to this kind of implicature, however; in fact, it is stated that the maximality constraint applies equally in both cases (Kuroda 2005:39). What is to be made then of the intuition that there is a difference between sentences like (14) and (15), repeated here as (39a,b)?

(39) a. John ga kita.
John GA came
'JOHN came.'
b. John ga kasikoi.
John GA smart
'JOHN is smart.'

Kuroda's claim about examples like (39a) is that there *is* an exhaustiveness implicature with respect to the subject but that the hearer accommodates a restricted domain within which this exhaustiveness holds: "We take the relevant context of the utterance to be narrower: the perceived situation that is described contains only one person.... The hearer can understand that the speaker's visual perception is so narrowed as to make this situation a maximal fit" (p. 39). Just as was observed above with respect to weakening the analysis offered by the information-structural account, the risk here is that the analysis loses its predictive power. In particular, is there an account of why the "conceptually grasped" situation in an example like (39b) should not also be understood to be narrowed? Without such an account, the intuition that there is a difference between cases with stage- and individual-level predicates, to the extent that it is robust, is unexplained.

3.3.4 Contrastive *Wa*

Thus far, I have mainly restricted the discussion to noncontrastive *wa*. Treating noncontrastive and contrastive *wa* separately is a common strategy, but at least some authors have attempted to achieve a unified analysis of *wa*—see, in particular, Shibatani 1990 and Fiengo and McClure 2002. Before looking at the facts and analysis of Japanese, it is probably worth clarifying some important concepts.

3.3.4.1 *Contrastive themes and contrastive rhemes*

First, and most important, it is necessary to appreciate that contrast is a dimension that is, at least pretheoretically, orthogonal to the theme/rheme or topic/focus dimension(s). This point is made explicitly by Fiengo and McClure (2002:24–27) but is perhaps most clearly (if informally) set out in Vallduví and Vilkuna 1998 (see also Kiss 1996).[21] Vallduví and Vilkuna argue that much of the discussion of focus has been confused by the conflation of two different concepts: the notion of focus/rheme in the sense I have been using it here on the one hand, and a use that comes more from the semantics literature, where it refers to an operatorlike element that crucially ranges over a set of alternatives. Vallduví and Vilkuna propose that these two concepts should be clearly distinguished and that, in fact, operators ranging over alternative sets can be found associated both with thematic and with rhematic domains. They propose for such operator constructions the term *kontrast*. Kontrast in association with rhematicity results in "contrastive focus," or what has sometimes been called *identificational focus* or (Vallduví and Vilkuna's term) *identificational kontrast*; contrast in association with thematicity results in "contrastive topics."

One type of evidence for an independent category of kontrast comes from Finnish, where Vallduví and Vilkuna argue that there is a distinct CP-initial position for kontrast that does not distinguish between theme and rheme, as illustrated by these examples (Vallduví and Vilkuna 1998:90–91).[22]

(40) What things did Anna get for her birthday?
 Anna sai [R KUKKIA].
 'Anna got flowers.'

(41) What is it that Anna got for her birthday?
 [R KUKKIA] Anna sai.

(42) What about flowers? Did Anna have to buy some or did she get them for free?
[Context: the speaker knows that Anna got some of the decorations for free and that others she had to buy.]
Kukkia Anna [R SAI].

The claim is that in (41) *kukkia* is a contrastive focus, whereas in (42) it is a contrastive theme.[23]

3.3.4.2 *Contrastive wa as a contrastive theme*

With this background, it seems reasonably clear that Japanese contrastive *wa* marks elements that are both kontrastive and thematic; it does not mark contrastive rhemes.[24] Thus the question, *Which boy left, Ken or Tamio?* cannot be answered with (43) without generating the implicature that the speaker is not sure about Tamio, just as is the case for the use of the B accent in English in this context.

43. #Ken wa kaetta.
     Ken WA left
     'Ken left.'

This fact makes it attractive to look for an analysis that can unify the non-contrastive use of *wa* and this contrastive use. A further motivation is that at least sentence-initial contrastive *wa*-phrases appear to be able to satisfy the requirement that a sentence have a topic/link, given that (44) is well formed, and the *wa*-phrases have the typical contrastive interpretation.

(44) Mary-wa kasikoi ga John wa kasikoku nai.
     Mary WA smart but John WA smart NEG
     'Mary is smart but John is not.'

Finally, as noted by Watanabe (2003:549), the initial position in a German verb-second sentence shares with Japanese *wa* marking the property that subjects can occur there with no implication of contrast, whereas internal arguments seem to be interpreted as contrastive topics;[25] to the extent that this parallel is strong (detailed investigation remains to be done) this makes the postulation of simple ambiguity for Japanese *wa* less plausible, because it would then be a coincidence that a particular syntactic position in German induced just the same ambiguity.

As mentioned earlier, Fiengo and McClure attempt a unified analysis, against the background of a definition of *wa*-phrases in terms of an Austinian notion of givenness that appears to resemble Vallduví's notion of ground or the concept of an open question. Their proposal runs something as follows:

1. When making an assertive speech act, the speaker must produce something (provide a rheme) and take another thing as given.
2. The default/simplest mapping between syntactic structure and speech act maps the constituent in sentence-initial position to the given item.

3. Marking any other part of the sentence as referring to a given item, because it is not required by statement number 1 above, implicates a contrast with some other item, which, when combined with the rest of the sentence, would have resulted in a false statement (a predicate whose sense did not *match*—another Austinian term—the item referred to by the sentence-initial given constituent).

The first two assumptions are needed to explain why (matrix) sentence-initial *wa*-phrases do not generate implicatures of contrast. Note that the reference to syntactic structure is also necessary and does not follow from anything else: it is a stipulation about the syntax of givenness. Also notice that the third statement could equally well read, "Taking the referent of any other part of the sentence as referring to a given item (and therefore marking it with *wa*)...," because being given is a necessary and sufficient condition for being marked with *wa*. This is where we come back to the problem of understanding exactly what givenness amounts to; it cannot be the same as what is common to all the propositions that make up the open question.

If we give up on the attempt to provide a fully unified analysis, contrastive topics seem to be amenable to a treatment in terms of a question-under-discussion approach (a hypothesis also put forward in Tomioka 2000, and which is largely consistent with Vallduví and Vilkuna's description of the nature of +kontrast +theme elements, because the question-under-discussion approach assumes the kind of alternative semantics taken to be definitional of kontrast). For some recent work on this type of approach to contrastive topics in Japanese, see Hara 2006a, 2006b.

Let me offer a brief speculative comment about contrastive *wa* before concluding. It has been known at least since Kuno 1973 that contrast can "project" in Japanese. This is true of the sentence that Kuno gave to exemplify contrastive *wa*:

(45) Ame wa hutte imasu ga (taisita koto wa arimasen).
     rain-WA falling is   but important matter WA exists-NEG
     'It is raining, but it isn't much.'

He gives an even more striking example in a footnote, attributing it to Minoru Nakau:

(46) Ame wa hutte imasu ga kasa   wa motte ikimasen.
     rain-WA falling is   but umbrella WA take go-NEG
     'It is raining, but I'm not taking my umbrella with me.'

Although *wa* attaches to the noun *ame* 'rain', it is clear that this constituent is not contrasted with other elements in a set of alternatives; the contrast seems to be between situations. For English speakers, the following example is also striking, in that it is clear that in English the peak of the B accent is on the verb *came*, whereas in Japanese *wa* attaches to the quantified subject (locating the peak of the B accent on the corresponding element in the English sentence yields a highly infelicitous utterance), but it seems that a similar effect is achieved in the two languages:

(47) A: How was the party?
B: Minna   wa kita kedo tumaranakatta.
   everyone   WA came but   boring-PST
   'Everyone came but it was boring.'
C: Everyone [B CAME], but it was boring.
C′: #[B EVERYONE] came, but it was boring.

This phenomenon remains to be properly described and explained. But one could entertain the speculation that noncontrastive topics (always, recall, constituents that are in the highest position in the sentential tree) are simply contrastive topics where contrast has been able to project to a high enough position that it outscopes practically everything and contrasts only one proposition with another (this is perhaps similar to the proposal in Shibatani 1990). That is to say, although Fiengo and McClure, for example, start from noncontrastive *wa* and attempt to derive contrastive readings from it (by some kind of implicature), it is possible to attempt a move in the other direction—and given the appeal of recent work on contrastive topics in English and German, there is a strong attraction in attempting to reduce all cases to the contrastive one. Whether this reduction can be achieved is a question that remains open at present.

3.4 IMPLICATIONS

In recent years the study of information structure, once perceived as clearly the domain of a separate pragmatic module of language, has moved more and more into the mainstream of semantics. This has clearly been the case for the concepts of topic and focus. To make serious progress on the questions that arise around these concepts (including the question of what they might tell us about the boundaries of semantics and pragmatics), it is evident that there should be some degree of consensus as to how they are defined. Particularly in the case of topic, it seems clear that movement in this direction has been hampered by the fact that in English there is very little straightforward evidence for the utility of the concept at all. In Japanese, however, it is extremely common for syntacticians at least to refer to *wa* as a "topic marker" without feeling the need for further explication. One strategy that research on Japanese makes available, therefore, is to consider the distribution and interpretation of *wa*-phrases in light of the predictions of available theories of topic to determine whether the data from Japanese constitute a reason for choosing one over another (or rejecting all in favor of a new approach). The discussion in this chapter has attempted to indicate the implications of various aspects of the Japanese data in this light. It is clear that there is considerable scope for further research. In particular, a formal treatment of the relation between contrastive and noncontrastive *wa* is badly needed, both for a satisfactory description of Japanese and more generally for the light that it might shed on the concept of topic writ large.

NOTES FOR CHAPTER 3

I would like to record my gratitude to Yurie Hara, Kaori Miura, Satsuki Nakai, Mits Ota, Satoshi Tomioka, Yuki Watanabe, John Whitman, and Shuichi Yatabe for their help with various aspects of this chapter. They bear no responsibility for the use that I have made of their comments and judgments.

1. The example of contrastive *wa* is not that given by Kuno; I have substituted another (from Fiengo and McClure 2002) for reasons that are discussed in section 3.4.

Kuno, in fact, distinguishes three, not two, uses of *ga*. The third is the use of *ga* to mark what appear to be the internal arguments of stative transitive verbs. This use is essentially orthogonal to any issues discussed here, and so it is set aside.

2. Note that this phrasing should not be taken to exclude the possibility of *wa* occurring in questions, which it freely does (as long as it is not attached to the *wh*-phrase itself):

(i) Mitiko wa nani o   site   imasu ka?
    Mitiko WA what ACC doing is   Q
    'What is Mitiko doing?'

3. Hoji (1985) claimed that PP *wa* phrases are necessarily contrastive, and this claim is taken up by various authors since (e.g., Portner and Yabushita 1998), but the literature that deals explicitly with "scene-setting" adjuncts seems unanimous that PPs in this function may have a noncontrastive reading.

4. The same observation has been made of the initial position in the main clause of Germanic verb-second languages, also a position associated with "topics."

5. Common, but not universal. In particular, Kuroda (2005:41) argues that the "exhaustive listing" interpretation of *ga* phrases is not related to focus.

6. Note that the correspondence between the *wh*-phrase in a question and the focus in an appropriate answer is a useful heuristic but is not actually definitional. On the one hand, it is very generally assumed that all sentences must include a focus (see McNally 1998b for useful discussion), but not all are produced as the answers to overt questions; on the other hand, there are appropriate answers to questions whose information structure cannot be derived from the form of the overt question is such a simple way. A trivial example is (ii).

(ii) A: What did you buy today?
     B: I didn't GO shopping.

7. The question of how to account for exactly when focus can "project" is a far more complex subject than can be dealt with here; for two important but very different accounts, see Schwarzschild 1999 and Steedman 2000a. For the present purposes, the parallel between the interpretations of the English and Japanese examples is the most crucial point, regardless of exactly how they are derived.

8. But see Vermeulen 2005 for an analysis of *ga* as a marker for focus when attached to adjuncts in the "multiple nominative" construction.

9. Presumably the focus could also be the predicate alone, a possibility not discussed in Heycock 1993. In this case, the subject would have to be the *tail* in Vallduví's terminology.

10. It should be noted that, here as elsewhere, the concepts of stage- and individual-level predicates that are appealed to are not unproblematic. In particular, adjectives that express transient states can be the predicates of all-focus sentences like (14); this is also true of English. This is consistent with the discussion in the text if such adjectives are taken to be stage-level. At the same time, it is often proposed that stage-level predicates license a weak reading for bare plural subjects. So, we would expect that the same predicates that license the all-focus sentences also license weak (existential) readings for bare plurals. But, as noted in McNally 1998c, this is not the case, as shown by the absence of (pragmatically appropriate) existential readings in examples like (iii):

(iii) a. The diners complained because plates were dirty/greasy.
  b. Turn on the dryer again because shirts are still damp.

11. Given that *think* is the kind of verb that tends to allow embedded root phenomena, it is actually not clear why the topic should not just take the highest scope within the subordinate clause.

12. This example also allows the direct-quote interpretation *John thinks "I am a fool"*; this is irrelevant for the argument here.

13. As in all theories of topic as question-under-discussion, Fiengo and McClure note that the question heuristic is only a way to set up a context that (almost) guarantees that the utterance supplied as answer is a speech act of a certain type, but that the same speech act can occur in discourse without there being an overt question in the context.

14. One might try to salvage this by appealing to the notion of accommodation; but such a move risks weakening the proposal to the point of vacuity.

15. Matsuda uses the term *specificational* to refer to any sentence with obligatory narrow focus, in a similar vein to Declerck 1988; here I stick to the less inclusive definition where specificational sentences are a type of copular sentence.

16. To my ear, there is an effect in English as well, although it is weak.

17. Heycock 1993 notes a similar pattern with respect to focal stress on the subject in English in these contexts.

18. Kuroda generally limits his discussion of these judgment types to declaratives; it is not exactly clear how questions, for example, would fit into this categorization.

19. The # indicator of infelicity for the *ga* version is Kuroda's, which indicates that this choice implicates that Gates is the unique individual in the discourse context with the given property and that a context in which this would be the case is "marked."

20. Kuroda argues explicitly against such an interpretation of (33B), citing the fact that it could be followed by an explicit statement that A may not know who Gates is, such as *to wa ittemo, seken sirazu no anata no koto dakara, Gates-san to itte mo dare da ka siranai desyoo* 'but, as unconcerned about the real world as you are, you would not know who Mr. Gates is', but it needs to be shown that such a follow-up is not necessarily interpreted as a repair, indicating that B realizes that the presupposition of her/his statement (that A knows Gates's identity) may be incorrect.

21. Steedman (2000a, 2000b) also argues that there can be sets of alternatives associated with the theme as well as the rheme. He differs from Vallduví and Vilkuna, however, in taking the rheme alternative set to be an essential part of the definition of rhematicity, and thus in not distinguishing between two different types of rheme.

22. In these examples, the R subscript indicates rheme. Vallduví and Vilkuna note that in (40) and (41) there is only one perceived intonational peak but that in (42) there are two, just as there are in English cases with contrastive topics like (iv).

(iv) A: Where did you buy the decorations?
B: The FLOWERS I BOUGHT, the CANDLES I got from my MOTHER.

Unlike in English, however, Vallduví and Vilkuna state that there is no difference in intonation contour between the two intonation peaks in Finnish examples like (42).

23. Vallduví and Vilkuna further cite Japanese as providing evidence for the independence of focus, arguing that the possible co-occurrence of *wa* with *dake* 'only', widely assumed to be a "focus sensitive particle," in examples like (19b) above demonstrates that such "focus" sensitive elements actually associate with kontrast. A simple equation of *dake* and *only* is not possible however (Futagi 2004); how exactly *dake* interacts with *wa* and focus requires further research.

24. In this, Japanese *wa* may differ from Korean *nun*, which Han 1998 argues can be interpreted both as a contrastive topic and a contrastive focus. As an example of contrastive focus, Han states that (v) is a possible answer to the question *Who does John like?* if the speaker wishes to convey that John does not like other individuals in the context.

(v) John-i   Mary-nun coahanta.
John-NOM   Mary-NUN likes
'John likes Mary (but not others).'

The crucial question though is whether the interpretation of *nun* in (v) is distinct from that of *wa* in examples like (2b). Further arguments that Korean *nun* and Japanese *wa* are not functionally equivalent can be found in, for example, Choi 1997 and Shimojo and Choi 2000, but further research in on this question is still needed.

25. Although Watanabe does not mention this, scene-setting adverbials behave like subjects in both languages in not forcing a contrastive interpretation, as noted previously.

REFERENCES

Büring, Daniel. 1999. Topic. In *Focus: Linguistic, cognitive, and computational perspectives*, ed. Peter Bosch and Rob van der Sandt, 142–165. Cambridge: Cambridge University Press.

Choi, Hye-Won. 1997. Topic and focus in Korean: The information partition by phrase structure and morphology. In *Japanese/Korean Linguistics 6*, ed. Ho-Min Sohn and John Haig, 545–561. Stanford, Calif.: CSLI Publications.

Declerck, Renaat. 1988. *Studies on copular sentences, clefts, and pseudo-clefts*. Dordrecht: Leuven University Press.

den Dikken, Marcel. 2006 *Relators and linkers: The syntax of predication, predicate inversion, and copulas*. Cambridge, Mass.: MIT Press.

Diesing, Molly. 1988. Bare plural subjects and the stage/individual contrast. In *Genericity in natural language: Proceedings of the 1988 Tübingen Conference*, ed. Manfred Krifka. SNS-Bericht, 88–42, Universität Tübingen, Tübingen, Germany.

Fiengo, Robert, and William McClure. 2002. On how to use -wa. *Journal of East Asian Linguistics* 11:5–41.

Fintel, Kai von. 1994. Restrictions on quantifier domains. Doctoral dissertation, University of Massachusetts, Amherst.
Futagi, Yoko. 2004. Japanese focus particles at the syntax-semantics interface. Doctoral dissertation, Rutgers University, New Brunswick, N.J.
Han, Chung-hye. 1998. Asymmetry in the interpretation of -(n)un in Korean. In *Japanese/Korean Linguistics 7*, ed. Noriko Akatsuka, Hajime Hoji, Shoichi Iwasaki, Sung-Ock Sohn, and Susan Strauss, 1–15. Stanford, Calif.: CSLI Publications.
Hara, Yurie. 2006a. Implicature unsuspendable: Japanese contrastive *wa*. In *Proceedings of 2004 Texas Linguistics Society conference*, ed. Pascal Denis, Eric McCready, Alexis Palmer, and Brian Reese, 35–45. Somerville, Mass.: Cascadilla Proceedings Project.
Hara, Yurie. 2006b. Japanese discourse items at interfaces. Doctoral dissertation, University of Delaware, Newark.
Heycock, Caroline. 1993. Focus projection in Japanese. In *Proceedings of NELS 24*, ed. Mercè Gonzàlez, 159–187. Amherst, Mass.: GLSA Publications.
Heycock, Caroline. 2006. Embedded root phenomena. In *The Blackwell companion to syntax: Vol. 2*, ed. Martin Everaert and Henk van Riemsdijk, 174–209. Oxford: Blackwell.
Heycock, Caroline, and E. Doron. 2003. Categorical subjects. *Gengo Kenkyu* 123:95–135.
Heycock, Caroline, and Anthony Kroch. 1999. Pseudocleft connectedness: Implications for the LF interface level. *Linguistic Inquiry* 30(3):365–397.
Higgins, Francis Roger. 1979. *The pseudo-cleft construction in English*. New York: Garland. [Doctoral dissertation, MIT, Cambridge, Mass., 1973.]
Hoji, Hajime. 1985. Logical Form constraints and configurational structures in Japanese. Doctoral dissertation, University of Washington, Seattle.
Kiss, Katalin É. 1996. The focus operator and information focus. *Working papers in the theory of grammar* 3.2. Budapest: Research Institute for Linguistics, Hungarian Academy of Sciences.
Kuno, Susumo. 1973. *The structure of the Japanese language*. Cambridge, Mass.: MIT Press.
Kuroda, S.-Y. 1965. Generative grammatical studies in the Japanese language. Doctoral dissertation, MIT, Cambridge, Mass.
Kuroda, S.-Y. 1972. The categorical and the thetic judgment. *Foundations of Language* 9:153–183.
Kuroda, S.-Y. 1988. Whether we agree or not: A comparative syntax of English and Japanese. *Lingvisticae Investigationes* 12:1–47.
Kuroda, S.-Y. 1990. Cognitive and syntactic bases of topicalized and nontopicalized sentences in Japanese. In *Japanese/Korean Linguistics 1*, ed. Hajime Hoji, 1–26. Stanford, Calif.: CSLI Publications.
Kuroda, S.-Y. 1992. *Japanese syntax and semantics*. Dordrecht: Kluwer.
Kuroda, S.-Y. 2005. Focusing on the matter of topic: A study of *wa* and *ga* in Japanese. *Journal of East Asian Linguistics* 14:1–58.
Matsuda, Yuki. 1997. Representation of focus and presupposition in Japanese. Doctoral dissertation, University of Southern California, Los Angeles.
Matsuda, Yuki. 2003. Predication and discourse functions of focusing in Japanese. In *Japanese/Korean Linguistics 11*, ed. Patricia Clancy, 381–393. Stanford, Calif.: CSLI Publications.
McNally, Louise. 1998a. On recent formal analyses of topic. In *The Tbilisi Symposium on Language, Logic, and Computation: Selected papers*, ed. Jonathan Ginzburg, Zurab Khasidashvili, Carl Vogel, and Jean-Jacques Levy, 147–160. Stanford, Calif.: CSLI Publications.

McNally, Louise. 1998b. On the linguistic encoding of information packaging instructions. In *The limits of syntax* (Syntax and Semantics 29), ed. Peter Culicover and Louise McNally, 161–183. San Diego, Calif.: Academic Press.

McNally, Louise. 1998c. Stativity and theticity. In *Events and grammar*, ed. Susan Rothstein, 293–307. Dordrecht: Kluwer.

Moro, Andrea. 1997. *The raising of predicates: Predicative noun phrases and the theory of clause structure*. Cambridge: Cambridge University Press.

Nakanishi, K. 2004. Prosody and scope interpretations of the topic marker *wa* in Japanese. In *Topic and Focus: Cross-linguistic perspectives on intonation and meaning*, ed. Chungmin Lee, Matthew Gordon, and Daniel Büring, 177–193. Dordrecht: Springer.

Portner, Paul. 2007. Instructions for interpretation as separate performatives. In *On information structure, meaning, and form*, ed. Kerstin Schwabe and Susanne Winkler, 407–425. Amsterdam: John Benjamins.

Portner, Paul, and Katsuhiko Yabushita. 1998. The semantics and pragmatics of topic phrases. *Linguistics and Philosophy* 21:117–157.

Portner, Paul, and Katsuhiko Yabushita. 2001. Specific indefinites and the information structure theory of topics. *Journal of Semantics* 18:271–297.

Potts, Christopher. 2005. *The logic of conventional implicatures*. Oxford: Oxford University Press.

Roberts, Craige. 1996. Information structure in discourse: Towards an integrated formal theory of pragmatics. In *OSU working papers in linguistics 49: Papers in semantics*, ed. Jae-Hak Yoon and Andreas Kathol, 91–136. Columbus: The Ohio State University.

Roberts, Craige. 1998. Information structure in discourse: Towards an integrated formal theory of pragmatics. [Revised version of Roberts 1996.] http://semanticsarchive.net/.

Saito, Mamoru. 1985. Some asymmetries in Japanese and their theoretical consequences. Doctoral dissertation, MIT, Cambridge, Mass.

Schlenker, Phillipe. 2003. Clausal equations (a note on the connectivity problem). *Natural Language & Linguistic Theory* 21:157–214.

Schwarzschild, Roger. 1999. Givenness, AvoidF, and other constraints on the placement of Accent. *Natural Language Semantics* 7:141–177.

Shibatani, M. 1990. *The languages of Japan*. Cambridge: Cambridge University Press.

Shimojo, Mitsuaki, and Hye-Won Choi. 2000. On asymmetry in topic marking: The case of Japanese *wa* and Korean *nun*. In *Proceedings of the Chicago Linguistic Society 36.1: The main session*, ed. Arika Okrent and John Boyle, 455–467. Chicago: Chicago Linguistic Society.

Steedman, Mark. 2000a. Information structure and the syntax-phonology interface. *Linguistic Inquiry* 31(4):649–690.

Steedman, Mark. 2000b. *The syntactic process*. Cambridge, Mass.: MIT Press.

Tomioka, Satoshi. 2000. Information structure and disambiguation in Japanese. In *Proceedings of WCCFL 20*, ed. Karine Megerdoomian and Leora Anne Bar-el, 101–114. Somerville, Mass.: Cascadilla Press.

Tomioka, Satoshi. To appear (a). The Japanese existential possession: A case study of pragmatic disambiguation. *Lingua*.

Tomioka. Satoshi. To appear (b). Pragmatics of LF-intervention effects: Japanese and Korean *wh*-interrogatives. *Journal of Pragmatics*.

Vallduví, E. 1992. *The informational component*. New York: Garland.

Vallduví, E., and M. Vilkuna 1998. On rheme and kontrast. In *The limits of syntax* (Syntax and Semantics 29), ed. Peter Culicover and Louise McNally, 79–108. San Diego, Calif.: Academic Press.

Vermeulen, R. 2005. Possessive and adjunct multiple nominative constructions in Japanese. *Lingua* 115:1329–1363.
Vikner, Sten. 1995. *Verb movement and expletive subjects in the Germanic languages*. Oxford: Oxford University Press.
Watanabe, Akira. 2003. *Wh* and operator constructions in Japanese. *Lingua* 113:519–558.
Whitman, John. 1991. String vacuous V to Comp. Paper presented at GLOW, Leiden University, the Netherlands.

CHAPTER 4

LEXICAL CLASSES IN PHONOLOGY

JUNKO ITO AND
ARMIN MESTER

4.1 INTRODUCTION

Linguistic descriptions of natural languages routinely face the necessity to draw distinctions between different lexical classes—such as Latinate versus native roots in English, to which affixes like noun-forming *-ation* are sensitive ([$_{lat}$ *vari*]*ation*, but *[$_{nat}$ *buri*]*ation*, etc.; see Ito and Mester 1995b:818 for relevant examples from a variety of different languages). Details vary from language to language, but the basic observation is the same: Not all morphemes participate in the major morphological and phonological processes to the same degree.

The status of such morpheme classes, or lexical strata, in the synchronic grammar has long been a controversial issue in linguistics, and the Japanese language has played a key role in these discussions, partially because lexical class distinctions are so prominent here and so clearly visible, even in the writing system. The examples in (1) (from Ito and Mester 2003:122) illustrate the phenomenon with the perhaps most well-known case of this kind in Japanese, where native morphemes undergo a widespread morphophonemic process of compound voicing (*rendaku*), but nonnative morphemes (both Sino-Japanese items and Western loans) do not.[1]

(1)

Native morphemes: Compound voicing		Nonnative morphemes: No compound voicing	
a. kane 'money'	nise-gane 'counterfeit money'	kin 'money'	nise-kin 'counterfeit money'
b. tana 'shelf'	garasu-dana 'glass shelf'	keesu 'case'	garasu-keesu 'glass case'

With the shift in phonology from a rule-based derivational framework to a system of ranked and violable constraints that came with the rise of Optimality Theory (OT), a new perspective on this topic has developed in recent years. We here take up some of the issues connected with this change in theoretical focus, some of its theoretical consequences, and its empirical predictions and problems.

Ito and Mester 1995a, with further development in Fukazawa 1998 and Ito and Mester 1999, among others, argue that the distinguishing formal property of lexical strata in an optimality-theoretic grammar is stratum-specific faithfulness ranking, within an otherwise invariant hierarchy of markedness constraints (see Inkelas, Orgun, and Zoll 1997, Pater 2000, and Anttila 2002 for interesting alternative proposals sharing the same basic approach). The result is a containment hierarchy of inventories of the kind depicted in (2): The more markedness constraints are active on a given stratum (by dominating stratum-specific faithfulness), the more structures are ruled out, and the smaller the inventory associated with the stratum.

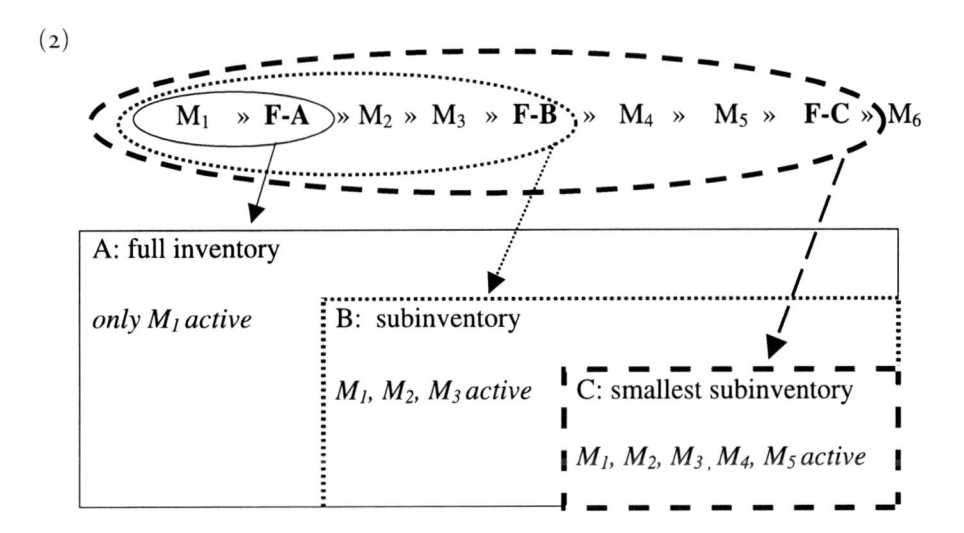

(2)

$M_1 \gg$ F-A $\gg M_2 \gg M_3 \gg$ F-B $\gg M_4 \gg M_5 \gg$ F-C $\gg M_6$

A: full inventory
only M_1 active

B: subinventory
M_1, M_2, M_3 active

C: smallest subinventory
M_1, M_2, M_3, M_4, M_5 active

The empirical interest of nested inventory structures as in (2) lies in the fact that they seem to provide good models for the vocabularies of natural languages, which can in many cases be shown to be organized in this way. This is shown in (3), which summarizes some of our main findings for the lexicon of Japanese: The Yamato (native) inventory is the most restrictive, observing all three constraints relating to voicing; Sino-Japanese items are exempt from the postnasal voicing requirement and fall into two subcategories, depending on whether they observe compound voicing; and the Foreign vocabulary is exempt from all three constraints.

(3)

	Foreign	Sino-Japanese A	Sino-Japanese B	Yamato	
a. OCP(VOI)	No	Yes	Yes	Yes	Observes multiple obstruent voicing ban
b. REALIZE-M(ORPHEME)	No	No	Yes	Yes	Here: realizes compound voicing morpheme
c. NO-NÇ	No	No	No	Yes	Observes postnasal voicing requirement
Containment relations between the inventories					

4.2 DESCRIPTION OF CORE DATA

Previewing our main results, grammars that give rise to such nested inventory structures have a stratally differentiated faithfulness component of the kind given in (4) for Japanese, where we write F for foreign, SJ for Sino-Japanese, CSJ for Common Sino-Japanese, and Y for Yamato or native.

(4) IDENT » OCP » IDENT » REALIZE »   IDENT » NO » IDENT » NO
     -F   (VOI)   -SJ   -MORPHEME -CSJ   -NÇ -Y   -VOIOBS

That OCP(VOI) is active on Y-morphemes and SJ-morphemes is shown in (5a,b),[2] whereas F-morphemes are free to have two voiced obstruents (5c).

(5) a. tako   'octopus' *dago
       toge   'splinter' *doge
       geta   'clog'   *geda
    b. getu   'month'   *gedzu
       geki   'theater' *gegi
       doku   'poison'   *dogu
       butu   'thing'   *budzu

c. daburu   'double'
   baggu   'bag'
   bebii   'baby'
   baabekyuu 'barbecue'

Although (5a,b) suggest that markedness is active—schematically, MARK»FAITH—this is contradicted by (5c). Stratal faithfulness means that, instead of a whole-scale deactivation of markedness (FAITH»MARK), we find only partial deactivation: FAITH-α»MARK»FAITH, with undifferentiated faithfulness remaining in its dominated position. This crucially requires the existence of a lexical class α (here, foreign items) that is recognizable for the learner by a combination of properties, including both phonotactics and morpheme combinatorics (native stems mostly combining with native suffixes, etc.). The extent to which the behavior of novel forms can be predicted on the basis of their shape alone is unclear (see Pierrehumbert 2006 for a case of statistical predictability involving velar softening in English; see also Pater 2005 for an explicit procedure for constructing such indexed constraints on the basis of universal constraints in the course of learning). For the present case, this means high-ranking faithfulness IDENT-F for F-items dominates OCP(VOI):

(6)   IDENT-F » OCP(VOI) » IDENT

This ranking allows for double voiced obstruency in F-indexed items such as *daburu* 'double', but for a hypothetical input /dogu/ not indexed for F (and ultimately, within the fully developed stratal system, indexed for SJ or Y) and hence subject to general faithfulness, the grammar takes corrective action and outputs a less marked structure (either *doku* or *togu*, depending on the verdict of other constraints).

(7) a. *daburu* 'double'

/daburu/_F	IDENT-F	OCP(VOI)	IDENT
▶ daburu		*	
taburu	*!		*

b. Hypothetical input /dogu/

/dogu/_Y/SJ	IDENT-F	OCP(VOI)	IDENT
dogu		*!	
▶ doku			*
▶ togu			*
toku			**!

The next constraint to consider is No-NÇ̥, which militates against sequences consisting of nasals followed by voiceless obstruents. As (8) shows, it is active on Y-items (8a) (No-NÇ̥ » IDENT—we take Y-items to be associated with unindexed IO-Faithfulness, unless there is a specific reason to introduce a specific IDENT-Y),[3] but not on SJ- or F-items (8b,c) (IDENT-F, IDENT-SJ » No-NÇ̥).

(8) a. tonbo 'dragonfly'   *tonpo
      kangae 'thought'   *kankae
      cf. voicing alternations such as:
        /yom+te/ → [yonde]   'read'-GERUND
        /yom+ta/ → [yonda]   'read'-PAST
        /yom+tara/ → [yondara]   'read'-CONDITIONAL
        /yom+tari/ → [yondari]   'read'-NONEXHAUSTIVE LISTING
  b. gen+ki   'health(y)'
      kan+koo   'sightseeing'
      den+pa   'electric wave'
      san+po   'walk'
      sen+soo   'war'
      han+too   'peninsula'
  c. panku   'puncture, flat tire'
      torankiraizaa 'tranquilizer'
      syanpuu   'shampoo'
      konpyuutaa   'computer'
      konsaato   'concert'
      sentaa   'center'
      bentyaa   'venture (firm)'

This means that a new species of stratified faithfulness, IDENT-SJ, has emerged out of general IDENT and lodges above No-NÇ̥, preserving the relations encoded in (6); that is, beneath OCP(VOI) (different from IDENT-F). The new subgrammar obtained is (9), where the box encloses the newly added constraints.

(9)   IDENT-F » OCP(VOI) » IDENT-SJ » No-NÇ̥ » IDENT

The tableaux in (10) illustrate how this grammar segregates Y-, SJ-, and F-items, respectively.

(10) a. *sinde* 'die-GERUND'

/sin-te/_Y	IDENT-F	IDENT-SJ	No-NÇ̥	IDENT
sinte			*!	
▶ sinde				*

b. *kankoo* 'sightseeing'

/kankoo/_SJ_	IDENT-F	IDENT-SJ	No-NÇ̬	IDENT
▶ kankoo			*	
kangoo		*!		*

c. *sentaa* 'center'

/sentaa/_F_	IDENT-F	IDENT-SJ	No-NÇ̬	IDENT
▶ sentaa			*	
sendaa	*!			*

It is often seen as a problem for lexical strata that their boundaries are fuzzy. Nativization of loanwords is a gradual affair, which makes it difficult to draw a clear line in the lexicon to separate native from nonnative items. In Japanese, a well-known problem of this kind arises in connection with the distribution of compound voicing, usually considered to be restricted to Yamato items. We here assume a basic analysis developed elsewhere (Ito and Mester 1986, 2003) that understands compound voicing as the manifestation of a grammatical linking morpheme (/ori+R[voi]+kami/ → [origami] 'paper folding', etc.) whose realization is governed by the constraint REALIZE-M(ORPHEME). Lack of compound voicing in SJ-items means that REALIZE-M is dominated by IDENT-SJ, as in (11), preventing a change in the voicing feature. Illustrative examples appear in (12).

(11) IDENT-F » OCP(VOI) » IDENT-SJ » REALIZE-M, No-NÇ̬ » IDENT

(12) a. *sinbun haitatu* 'newspaper delivery'

/sinbun +R+ haitatu/_SJ_	OCP(VOI)	IDENT-SJ	REALIZE-M	IDENT
▶ sinbun haitatu			*	
sinbun baitatu		*!		*

b. *ike bana* 'flower arrangement'

/ike +R+ hana/_Y_	OCP(VOI)	IDENT-SJ	REALIZE-M	IDENT
ike hana			*!	
▶ ike bana				*

The overall grammar developed so far has the ranking shown in (13).

(13) IDENT » OCP » IDENT » { REALIZE   No } » IDENT » No
     -F   (VOI) -SJ   { -MORPHEME, -NÇ }   -Y   -VOIOBS

That we are dealing here with aspects of the synchronic grammar as acquired by contemporary speakers, and not just with quasi-sedimentary layers of history visible in the vocabulary of the language, is shown by numerous cases where lexical class membership diverges from etymological origin. Some examples are given in (14). Takayama (1999) argues that such native look-alikes are phonotactically indistinguishable from Y-morphemes and have, in fact, changed stratal membership.

(14) Nonnative undergoers of compound voicing
   a. Older Western loans: *iroha garuta* 'syllabary playing cards' (*karuta*), *ama gappa* 'rain cape' (*kappa*)
   b. Loans from Chinese: *no giku* 'wild chrysanthemum' (*kiku*), *tya gasi* 'tea sweets' (*kasi*)
   c. Recent Western loans: *take zukii*[4] 'bamboo skis' (*sukii*)

But lexical distinctions are more fine-grained than whole-scale nativization, and it is an important test for any model whether it provides enough flexibility to draw all the necessary distinctions. The grammar in (13) makes a clear prediction: A further stratal distinction could in principle be made by faithfulness ranking between the (so far unranked) constraints REALIZE-MORPHEME and No-NÇ.

It is therefore of great interest that this is precisely what we find: a class of Sino-Japanese items in everyday use (some examples are given in (15)) that have become nativized enough to undergo compound voicing but are still special in other respects, as seen by the fact that they fail to conform to No-NÇ.

(15)
kenka	'quarrel'	oyako-genka	'parent-child quarrel'
tansu	'drawers'	yoohuku-dansu	'drawers for clothes'
kaisya	'company'	zidoosya-gaisya	'car company'
hootyoo	'carver'	deba-bootyoo	'pointed carver'
toohu	'tofu'	yu-doohu	'hot tofu'
husoku	'lack'	ne-busoku	'lack of sleep'
kotatu	'table warmer'	denki-gotatu	'electric table warmer'

Takayama (1999) argues that these items belong to a separate substratum, here referred to as Common Sino-Japanese (CSJ). The final version of the grammar is given in (16), where faithfulness is fully distributed over the markedness hierarchy.

(16)

| IDENT » | OCP » | IDENT » | REALIZE » | IDENT » | No | » | IDENT » | No |
| -F | (VOI) | -SJ | -M | -CSJ | -NÇ | | -Y | -VOIOBS |

Partial nativization phenomena and transitional strata therefore provide important support for this model.

4.3 Controversies Regarding Analysis

Recent work on lexical classes in phonology, spurred, in part, by the detailed analyses and proposals regarding the Japanese lexicon, has led to fresh questions and various types of inquiries. These range from the specific formal implementation within Optimality Theory to the implications of such a system in the broader arena of linguistic inquiry including psycholinguistic studies, language acquisition, and diachronic change. We here briefly take up some of the issues that have received most attention.

4.3.1 Indexed Faithfulness versus Co-grammars

The formal expression of lexical classes by means of indexed faithfulness, motivated in some detail in the previous section, is based on Correspondence Theory (McCarthy and Prince 1995). Lexical strata result from splitting up individual constraints into stratum-specific indexed versions (Fukazawa 1998; Ito and Mester 1999, 2003; Pater 2000, among others). Besides this correspondence-theoretic version, an alternative formal implementation within OT is the "co-grammar" approach advocated by a number of researchers including Anttila 2002, Inkelas, Orgun, and Zoll 1997, and Ito and Mester 1995b. In this view, lexical strata result from a class of slightly different stratum-specific grammars (co-grammars), with different rankings of constraints, which collectively form a family of grammars. This is illustrated in (17) for the body of data discussed in the previous section. Instead of a single grammar (see (16)) with multiple indexed faithfulness constraints, there are multiple co-grammars with a single but differently ranked faithfulness constraint.

(17)   Multiple co-grammars with a single faithfulness constraint:

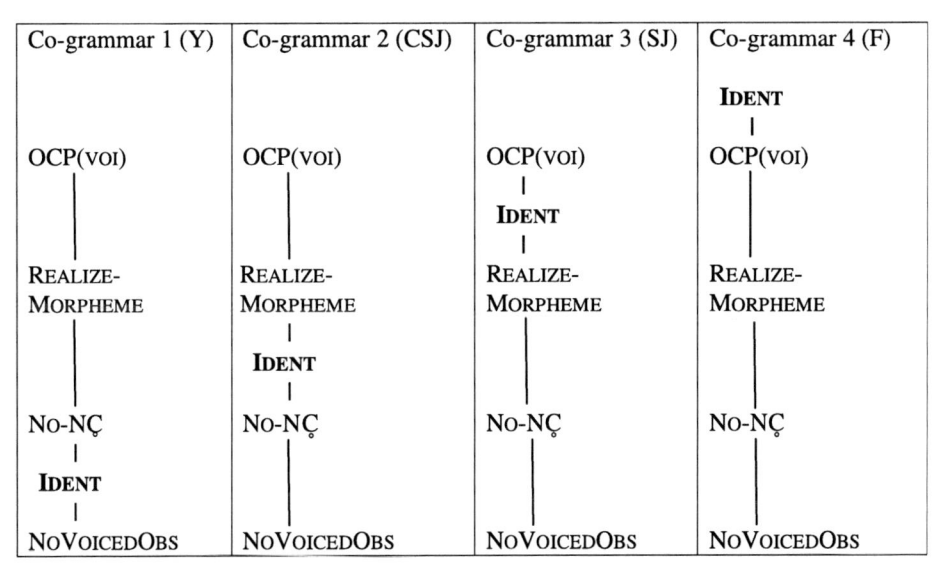

Co-grammar 1 (Y)	Co-grammar 2 (CSJ)	Co-grammar 3 (SJ)	Co-grammar 4 (F)
			IDENT |
OCP(voi) |	OCP(voi) |	OCP(voi) | IDENT |	OCP(voi) |
REALIZE- MORPHEME |	REALIZE- MORPHEME | IDENT |	REALIZE- MORPHEME |	REALIZE- MORPHEME |
NO-NÇ̬ | IDENT |	NO-NÇ̬ |	NO-NÇ̬ |	NO-NÇ̬ |
NOVOICEDOBS	NOVOICEDOBS	NOVOICEDOBS	NOVOICEDOBS

For a co-grammar approach to be a viable alternative to the single-grammar approach, it would be necessary to flesh out the theory in more detail so that questions regarding the extent to which co-phonologies differ and how they interact can be answered (for proposals along these lines, see Orgun 1996). Which constraints can be reranked? The co-grammars in (17) only rerank faithfulness constraints (a proposal first made in Ito and Mester 1995b on the basis of other facts in Japanese), but is this a necessity? How are forms composed of morphemes from different strata evaluated? Stratal organization of the lexicon does not mean stratal uniformity of morphological structures. For example, for a compound form like [supootu dayori] 'sports tidings', co-grammar 4 would have to deal with the first member from the Foreign stratum, and co-grammar 1 would have to deal with the second member from the Yamato stratum. Which co-grammar would deal with the accentuation of the entire compound? These are implementation questions that can no doubt be resolved, but it remains true that these complications do not arise in the single model grammar.

4.3.2 Indexed Faithfulness versus Indexed Markedness

Closely related questions arise in the single grammar model in connection with the concept of indexation itself, however. In the model presented in the previous section and argued for in more detail in Ito and Mester 2003 and earlier work based on Japanese phonology, indexation of constraints is restricted to faithfulness constraints, but it is an open question whether indexation is also an option for markedness constraints. Should indexation be available to both faithfulness and markedness or to only one or the other type of constraint? Restrictiveness demands that we consider this question carefully and not automatically adopt the most permissive approach without argument. Several researchers have taken the position that it is not always possible to capture all the facts with one type or the other. Thus Pater (2000) has argued that both types of indexed constraints are necessary to capture the details of secondary stresses in English (see also Anttila 2002 on Finnish and Anttila and Cho 1998 on English). However, if indexation is restricted to a certain type of constraint in some way, does the restriction follow from something else in the theory?

Stepping back from the pros and cons that arise from the—real or apparent—descriptive necessities raised by particular phenomena, we focus here on some of the basic implications of a stratal faithfulness approach versus a stratal markedness approach for the overall theory. To take a simple example, consider the well-known palatalization in Japanese of coronal plosives and fricatives before [i], which applies to native and nativized words (*mat-i-masu* → *matʃ-i-masu* 'wait, polite present') but not to recent loanwords (*paatii* → **paatʃii* 'party'). The constraints and rankings necessary for the two approaches are given in (18) and (19), using "Pal" as an informal abbreviation for the well-known constraint demanding palatalization of coronals before high front vowels.

(18) Indexed faithfulness:
 IDENT-loan » PAL » IDENT

(19) Indexed markedness:
 PAL-native » IDENT » PAL

In the indexed faithfulness approach (18), the general faithfulness constraint IDENT ranked below the markedness constraint PAL ensures palatalization in the (unmarked) native items, whereas the special (indexed) faithfulness constraint ranked above PAL prohibits palatalization for the loan items. However, in the indexed markedness approach (19), the special (indexed) markedness constraint PAL ranked above faithfulness ensures palatalization in native items, whereas the general markedness PAL ranked below faithfulness is unable to enforce palatalization outside of the native stratum. Although both approaches capture this simple palatalization case, some considerations militate against the idea of indexed markedness. First, faithfulness constraints have two arguments—an input and an output—so indexation to certain classes of inputs is a natural development. This is not so for markedness constraints, which apply strictly to outputs. Second, relativization of markedness to a specific domain raises the possibility of templatic constraints, such as NOCODA/REDUPLICANT, and thereby the specter of pathological backcopying (McCarthy and Prince 1999:258–267), with *mouse* reduplicated as *mou-mou* through a ranking such as NOCODA/RED, MAX-BR » MAX-IO » NOCODA (see Ito and Mester 1999:90–91 for a fuller development of these two points). Third, indexed markedness constraints resurrect the language-particular processes of rule-based phonology (McCawley 1968, Chomsky and Halle 1968, among others) where "palatalization" is earmarked to apply only to [+native] forms: t[+native] → tʃ / __i. Abolishment of language-particular processes is an important achievement of OT; their reintroduction as ranked constraints must raise theoretical concerns. Finally, indexed faithfulness treats ("native") palatalization before [i] as the general case, which contrasts with ("foreign") nonpalatalization as the special case. This is just the opposite of the special-general relation with indexed markedness, which singles out palatalization before [i] as the special case. The latter is odd because such palatalization is the unmarked situation, universally and in each individual language. Indexed markedness turns this state of affairs on its head.

4.3.3 Indexed Faithfulness and Default M»F Ranking

Stratification is one way of maintaining a version of the low (default, dominated) position of F even in the face of counterevidence—whenever it is possible to confine the counterevidence within a stratum α whose inhabitants have other things in common. Instead of immediately collapsing in the face of anti-M data (20a), stratification entails trying out option (20b).

(20) a. M » F → F » M
 b. M » F → F-α » M » F

This can be seen as an instance of the M » F ranking default (Smolensky 1996), available only when the members of stratum α have several characteristics in common, not just their identical behavior with respect to a single constraint. The latter point should follow from the economy considerations concerning the overall grammar, and it forestalls the possibility of pseudo-strata (such as *VoiObs-observing *pick* vs.*VoiObs-violating *pig* in English).

4.3.4 Indexed Faithfulness and Restrictiveness

It is sometimes said that limiting stratal indexation to faithfulness doesn't amount to much because most phonological effects result from interaction of markedness with faithfulness. The justification of this criticism is in a sense proportional to the power of the faithfulness component—in the extreme case, in a model of OT where faithfulness is as fine-grained as markedness, with Ident[+F] and Ident[−F] for every imaginable property F, it is indeed fully justified. But such models of OT stumble over their own feet for other reasons—a version of OT that reflects markedness in a shadow world of faithfulness constraints is redundant and problematic, a fallback to rule-based phonology with its structural descriptions ("markedness") and associated structural changes ("faithfulness"), with "A → B / C __ D" translated as "[M] *CAD » [F] *(A→B)".

In a theory with general and highly symmetric faithfulness constraints confronting highly diversified markedness constraints, one faithfulness constraint impinges on many markedness constraints (not just on "its associated M"). Here limiting indexation to faithfulness constraints is a genuine restriction because it severely limits the set of possible strata in a grammar. Theories with unconstrained faithfulness components, though, lead to the proliferation of stratal distinctions and are overly powerful on general grounds.

4.3.5 Loanword Adaptation and Perceptual Assimilation

This chapter has so far been concerned with questions regarding the formal theory of grammar: How does the computational system of an OT-grammar interact with a nonhomogeneous lexicon? Loan adaptation provided interesting data for the investigation of this question. We now consider some issues concerning the relation between the architecture of a (relatively) stable synchronic system of lexicon+grammar and the diverse factors involved in loanword adaptation. There has been a recent upsurge of work with a somewhat different focus that is concerned with the close empirical observation of concrete loanword adaptation processes. These kinds of investigations (see Dupoux et al. 1999; Jacobs and Gussenhoven 2000; Kang 2003; Kenstowicz 2003, 2004; Paradis 1995; Paradis and LaCharité 1997; Peperkamp and Dupoux 2003; Silverman 1992; Smith 2006, to appear; Yip 1993, 2002; among others) are of interest here for what they can tell us about the phonological component of the grammar and its relation to the perceptual system. This literature presents a wide variety of competing claims, from perception-only to phonology-only approaches, with various intermediate positions.

Of particular interest is a recent proposal developed by Peperkamp and Dupoux (2003) that regards all loanword adaptation as perception-based. Consider a typical case of loanword adaptation in Japanese—in particular, what has traditionally been analyzed as phonological epenthesis to break up illicit clusters and avoid illicit codas. A well-known case often cited in introductory linguistics textbooks is the disyllabic English word *Christmas* becoming pentasyllabic in the loanword [.ku.ri.su.ma.su.] in Japanese.

The perception-only approach claims that Japanese speakers literally hear three epenthetic vowels in *Christmas*—first, by mapping the acoustic input to a representation in terms of available native phonetic categories, which do not include [kr], [sm], and [s#] and instead substitute [kur], [sum], and [su#]; and second, by subsequently mapping this percept to a full-fledged underlying representation (UR), with all epenthetic vowels already in place. Under this view, there is no phonological process of epenthesis involved; the grammar needs no separate stratum for loanwords and no separate faithfulness constraints regulating the foreign stratum in the phonology—it's all in the ears of the beholder, so to speak.

It turns out, however, that this claim is not supported by the available evidence. It has long been known that native speakers' first language molds not only their production but also their perception of unfamiliar sounds and sound combinations in other languages (in the foundational work of modern phonology, Trubetzkoy [1939:47–50] already presents a detailed and insightful analysis of relevant examples). In recent psycholinguistic work, this has come to be known as "perceptual assimilation" (see Best, McRoberts, and Goodell 2001 and work cited there). Speakers of Japanese are no exception. For example, Japanese phonotactics does not admit VCCV sequences like *abza* (with a first C not a nasal place-assimilated to the second C), whereas French phonotactics does. Both languages admit VC[u]CV sequences like *ab[u]za*. Dupoux et al. (1999) have shown that Japanese listeners do much worse than French listeners in discriminating between VCCV stimuli and VC[u]CV stimuli. But it is a far cry from this fact to the idea in Peperkamp and Dupoux 2003 that the epenthetic vowels in a word like [kurisumasu] are literally part of the percept when hearing *Christmas* and become automatically part of the UR of the corresponding loanword.

First, if epenthetic vowels were perceptually given and hence indistinguishable from nonepenthetic vowels for speakers of Japanese, there would be no way they could be treated differently by the phonology for some purpose. However, they are treated differently in accent assignment, where we see clear evidence for the operation of a constraint of the HEADDEP variety (Alderete 1995, 1999) militating against accent falling on vowels without a correspondent in the source word (see Katayama 1995, 1998 and Kubozono 1996; their findings have been further confirmed in Shinohara 2000 with loan experiments on the basis of French inputs; see also Kenstowicz 2003 for discussion).

Second, if loanword epenthesis were purely perceptual, it should be inescapable as a repair for illicit codas in source words. Smith (2006, to appear) shows that this is by no means the case, adducing deletion/epenthesis doublets like [risurin] 'glycerine' next to epenthesizing [gurisurin], or [ausai] 'outside' next to [autosaido]. She goes on to distinguish between auditory and orthographic loans, arguing that it is precisely the deletion versions that constitute perceptual deletions and hence auditory loans, as opposed to the epenthesizing variants, which are orthography-based. Seen in this light, the attempt to anchor the epenthetic vowels of a word like *kurisumasu* in perception might have the story exactly backward.

Auditory-orthographic doublets like those cited by Smith 2006 can easily be multiplied. Thus an online dictionary gives two kana transcriptions for the English loanword "good": [guu] and [guddo], with slightly different meanings; [guu] is used as an exclamation ("good!"), whereas [guddo] is found mostly in nativized compounds such as [guddo aidea] 'good idea'.[5] Other common loanword exclamations tend to show deletions (all right → [o:rai], don't mind → [don mai] 'never mind', encouraging shouts in sports when a team member makes a mistake). For older loans, deletion seems in fact to be the norm. An NHK dialect survey notes a Taisho period (early twentieth century) loan for 'go ahead' [goo hee].[6] One of the most interesting linguistic testimonies of the first systematic contacts between speakers of Japanese and Westerners are the so-called *Yokohama kotoba*,[7] the vocabulary used by nineteenth-century Yokohama merchants to communicate with their American and European trading partners. Examples appear in (21).

(21) *Yokohama kotoba* (Kanagawa Prefecture Social Studies Research Council 1996)

	Yokohama loan	Modern loan
(ice) cream	kurin	kuriimu
five	fai	faibu
eight	ei	eito

The *Yokohama kotoba* in the column on the left should be compared with the currently used variants of these loanwords listed on the right. Where we find final epenthesis in the currently used loanword, the Yokohama version of 'cream' contains a final moraic nasal, and the codas for the numbers 'five' and 'eight' are simply deleted.

Why this difference? The syllable structure restrictions have not changed, and neither the perception-only approach nor the grammar-only approach can give a plausible answer. It seems difficult to argue that the perception of nineteenth-century Japanese speakers was radically different from that of twentieth-century Japanese speakers, in such a way that at some point the latter started hearing epenthetic vowels. In terms of the indexed faithfulness grammar, the difference can certainly be encoded in the relative ranking of MAX-segment (constraint against deletion) and DEP-segment (constraint against insertion), but such a change cannot be motivated in any other part of Japanese phonology.

A more illuminating interpretation takes up the idea that at least two different strategies for loanword adaptation are available to speakers: (i) perception loan adaptation, the main strategy of the Yokohama loans; and (ii) phonemic loan adaptation, which became the prevalent loanword strategy in Japanese and is based on a rationalization of English orthography, which diverges from both British and American pronunciation habits in several respects.

The goals of the two types of loanword adaptation are different. The *Yokohama kotoba* vocabulary is aimed at communicating with speakers of English and is therefore as close to the pronunciation of the source word as Japanese syllable structure would allow. But how do we measure closeness? From a segmental perspective, it is not clear which is more faithful to the source word—the deleting version has too few consonants, the epenthesizing version too many vowels. But in fact, the Yokohama loans have a crucial point in their favor: They are more faithful to the English source in their prosodic (syllabic) makeup—the source words *five* and *eight* in (21) are monosyllabic, and so are the consonant deletion versions [fai] and [ei]. However, the phonemic (and orthographic) form of the source word is hard to recover from these items. This, then, is a type of Output-Output prosodic correspondence, which reflects the fact that the nineteenth-century *Yokohama kotoba* are auditory loans.

The epenthesizing loanwords that populate the current Japanese language are mostly used to communicate with other speakers of Japanese, and they are strongly based on spelling, with well-defined strategies for placing the epenthetic vowels so that all source consonants are protected from deletion. There is no attempt to preserve the prosodic structure of the source words (epenthesis almost inevitably changes the number and shape of syllables). Instead, the phonemic (and orthographic) form of the source word is largely recoverable (apart from segmental neutralizations such as l, r>r).

Overall, there can be no question that the perception-based account is on the right track in certain areas of loanword phonology such as the cases illustrated in (21). The epenthesis strategy seen in the overwhelming number of Japanese loans, however, seems to involve more than just perceptual adaptation. Other areas where perception plays a direct role are not difficult to find. Consider the facts in (22).

(22) Palatalization of velars before original [æ]
  /_[æ]   cf.   /_[ˆ]
  [kʲatto] 'cat'   [katto] 'cut'
  [gʲamburu] 'gamble' [gamu] 'gum'

The English front low vowel [æ] triggers a significant degree of allophonic palatalization of preceding velars, which is perceived by speakers of Japanese and preserved in the Japanese loanword. The motivation here is clearly not contrast-based: If the reason for the palatalization was to distinguish 'cat' and 'cut' (*kyatto* vs. *katto*), then labials should also follow this pattern. But they do not, as shown in (23). Our interpretation here is that palatalization of labials before [æ] is negligible, and hence no perceptual effect is expected in the loanwords.

(23) No palatalization of labials before original [æ]

                    /_[æ]   /_[ˆ]
     [batto], *[bʲatto] 'bat'   [batto] 'but'
     [panda], *[pʲanda] 'panda' [pantʃi] 'punch'

4.4 IMPLICATIONS FOR THE GENERAL THEORY

The stratified grammar developed and argued for in section 4.2 (repeated here in (24)) identifies the relevant voicing-related markedness constraints and interleaved indexed faithfulness constraints.

(24) Stratified grammar (repeated from (16))
IDENT » **OCP** » IDENT » **REALIZE** » IDENT » **No** » IDENT » **No**
-F   (**VOI**)   -SJ   -M   -CSJ   -NÇ -Y   -VOIOBS

In this (partial) grammar, IDENT-F is ranked highest, which ensures that F-items can surface with violations of the voicing-related markedness constraints, such as OCP(VOI) and No-NÇ. The ranking in (24) does not exist in a vacuum, however, but is part of the overall grammar of Japanese. As is usual in OT, it is always possible for other aspects of the overall constraint system to lead to the selection of a different winner.

Here we take up two cases where new generalizations have emerged that are at first glance problematic for (24)—namely, cases where OCP(VOI) and No-NÇ appear to be observed in F-items, even though the model with high-ranking IDENT-F predicts otherwise. We show that the overall model not only successfully deals with these cases, but actually already predicts that they should be possible.

4.4.1 TETU I: Contextual Markedness

As a theory of ranked and violable constraints, OT makes a clear prediction: IDENT-F, even though highest ranked so far, can still be trumped by an even higher-ranking markedness constraint, which would manifest itself in a kind of Emergence-of-the-Unmarked effect (TETU; see McCarthy and Prince 1995) in the foreign stratum. A case in point is the novel finding by Nishimura (2001) regarding the constraint against voiced geminates (a constraint never violated in Y and SJ items). Starting with the observation in Ito and Mester 1995a, 1999 that this constraint is also responsible for the devoicing of geminates found in some assimilated F-items (such as *bakku* 'bag' and *betto* 'bed'), Nishimura surveyed recent loanword patterns through Google searches and found that geminate devoicing is especially frequent in one specific type of loanwords: those containing a second voiced obstruent besides the geminate voiced obstruent. This is schematically illustrated by the contrast shown in (25).

(25) hotto doggu ∼ hotto dokku 'hotdog'[8]
 hamu eggu ∼ *hamu ekku 'ham and eggs'

This finding is surprising because OCP(voi) should be inactive on such F-items, given the ranking IDENT-F » OCP(voi). The tendency to devoice in the context of additional obstruent voicing is confirmed in (26), which replicates Nishimura's search at a later date.

(26) Google hits on 7/23/05, 11:40 A.M. EST

		# of hits	%
Voiced	hotto **dog**gu	129,000	68
Devoiced	hotto **dok**ku	62,000	32

		# of hits	%
Voiced	hamu **eg**gu	27,100	99.9
Devoiced	hamu **ek**ku	25	0.1

To capture these facts, Nishimura (2001) proposes a contextual markedness constraint against voiced obstruent geminates in co-occurrence with another voiced obstruent.[9] This constraint, variably ranked with respect to IDENT-F, can force a violation of the latter and map /doggu/ to [dokku], with a devoicing geminate (and without an OCP(voi) violation). The result shows that even highly ranked indexed faithfulness can be trumped by a contextual version of a lower-ranking markedness constraint.

4.4.2 TETU II: Allomorphy and Faithfulness Neutralization

A second kind of TETU-effect occurs in situations where faithfulness, instead of being trumped by markedness, is neutralized in some other way. The result is that dominated markedness, otherwise muted, suddenly becomes decisive.

 A case in point is an interesting generalization first noted by Tateishi (2001, 2003) concerning the ways in which the English plural -s suffix appears in loanwords. Japanese does not have a regular plural marker, and English words that are usually pluralized are sometimes borrowed with the plural marker intact (*doonattsu* 'donuts', *piinattsu* 'peanuts'), a cross-linguistically common event (Campbell 1999:57–88), sometimes without (*surippaa* 'slippers', *koon fureeku* 'cornflakes'); in still other cases, both pluralized and nonpluralized forms are found (27). As a result, loanword Japanese has come to possess a quasi-suffix expressing some kind of plurality.

(27)

With plural suffix	*Without plural suffix*
[kyattsu] 'Cats' (title of musical)	[kyatto fuudo] 'cat food'
[handzu appu] 'hands up'	[hando kuriimu] 'hand cream'

Loanwords with *-su/zu*, with the expected epenthesis, are found among the growing F-items. Tateishi (2001, 2003) noted that the distribution of the two variants in the loanwords does not necessarily follow the distribution of the corresponding English elements—that is, voiced after voiced, and voiceless after voiceless. In particular, the voiceless variant is sometimes found in unexpected environments:

(28) English source word   Japanese loan word
      men's [z]   menzu ~ *mensu
      ladies' [z]   rediisu ~ rediizu

The results of a Google search for co-occurrences of the different versions, in katakana syllabary, of "men's/ladies'" and "Dragons/Tigers" (names of baseball teams) appear in (29) and (30).

(29) "men's, ladies'" Google search (7/23/2005, 2:18 P.M. EST)
      men-zu, redii-su   1,870,000   99.6701%
      men-zu, redii-zu   5,570   0.2969%
      men-su, redii-su   611   0.0326%
      men-su, redii-zu   8   0.0004%

(30) "Dragons, Tigers" Google search (7/23/2005, 2:35P.M. EST)
      doragon-zu, taigaa-su   48,600   97.6335%
      doragon-zu, taigaa-zu   807   1.6212%
      doragon-su, taigaa-su   361   0.7252%
      doragon-su, taigaa-zu   10   0.0201%

Here [-zu] occurs after nasal-final loanwords, and [-su] elsewhere—quite different from the allophonic rule in English. The generalization is not without exceptions but apparently solid enough to warrant a systematic explanation. Even though divergent from what is found in English, it might still reflect some phonetic property of the English models, similar to the way final vowel epenthesis in plosive-final English loans in Korean appears to correlate with the probability that the corresponding plosive is released in American English (see Kang 2003). In the present case, however, this mode of explanation seems less attractive: We are not aware of relevant empirical studies, but the idea that the postnasal -[z] of *Dragons* should be consistently more strongly voiced than the postvocalic -[z] of *Tigers* seems farfetched.

Setting aside the possibility of explaining the distribution as learned through diligent observation of American English pronunciation habits, we turn to another attractive mode of explanation—the constraints of universal phonology, as ranked in the grammar of Japanese. The *-su/zu* pattern obviously conforms to the postnasal voicing pattern familiar from the native stratum of Japanese (see (8)–(10) above). This suggests, and all recent analyses (Tateishi 2001, 2003; Fukazawa, Kitahara, and Ota 2002, and the one developed here[10]) agree on this point, that what we are dealing with is an *F*-item on which No-NÇ is in some way active. But in what way? This is where our hypothesis departs from the other two, who see this as a case of restratification, arguing that the foreign quasi-suffix has either joined the *Y*-items (Tateishi 2003) or is subject to lower-ranking affixal IDENT (Fukazawa, Kitahara, and Ota 2002). Either way, the IDENT responsible for /-su/ ranks below No-NÇ. These are certainly viable analyses, but there is some concern whether it is really correct to declare *-su/zu* a native suffix (in the face of speakers' intuitions declaring it to be distinctly "foreign"), and in general a proliferation of faithfulness constraints dealing with single elements should give us pause.

Is there a simpler alternative? We claim that there is: In English, the *-s* plural morpheme is realized as voiced or voiceless, depending on the environment. The crucial voiced/voiceless distinctions in the phonological environment are lost in Japanese because of epenthesis: (Boston) Pop[s] → *poppusu*, (Chicago) Cub[z] → *kabusu*. As a result, both allomorphs are borrowed as a lexically listed pair /-su, -zu/. But once this is the case, the ranking [IDENT-F » ... » No-NÇ » IDENT-Y » No-VoiObs], already firmly anchored in the grammar (see (24)), predicts the distribution that Tateishi discovered. Allomorph listing means that allomorph selection is purely phonologically conditioned. With faithfulness (i.e., IDENT-F) neutralized, as far as voicing is concerned, the subhierarchy [No-NÇ » IDENT-Y » No-VoiObs] means voiced after nasals (*doragon-zu*, (31)), otherwise voiceless (*taigaa-su* (32)).

(31)

/doragon/, /-zu, -su/	IDENT-F	No-NÇ	IDENT	No-VoiObs
▶ doragon zu				(*d *g) *z
doragon su		*!		(*d *g)

(32)

/taigaa/, /-zu, -su/	IDENT-F	No-NÇ	IDENT	No-VoiObs
taigaa zu				(*g) *z!
▶ taigaa su				(*g)

Exceptions are cases of straight borrowing of voiced [-zu], such as *syuu-zu* 'shoes'.[11] This avoids both construction-specific rules and unenlightening listing of allomorph environments and follows the OT analysis of allomorphy and lexical selection in many earlier studies, beginning with Mester 1994 for Latin (see Anttila 1997; Burzio 1994, 1997; Kager 1996; Mascaró 1996a, 1996b; Perlmutter 1998; Russell 1995; Tranel 1996a, 1996b, 1998; among others). This leads to a TETU-effect for such listed pairs of allomorphs (Mascaró 1996b)—here, postnasal voicing in tandem with default voicelessness—in thoroughly foreign territory, where IDENT-F otherwise prevents any changes in voicing. Similar TETU-effects with affixal elements in Japanese arise with Sino-Japanese counters (Ito and Mester 2003:138–141) and verbal suffixes (Ito and Mester 2004).

Overall, taking on phonological processes in their actual lexical complexity, including the patterning and lexical distribution of the various kinds of underapplication and overapplication, is a fruitful enterprise. It leads to a deeper understanding of the way phonology, as a computational system of ranked constraints, interacts with the lexicon. This interaction is mediated through indexed faithfulness constraints, which provides the phonology with the means to fold the nonuniformities of a historically grown stratified lexicon into a single coherent synchronic system. The architecture of OT allows us to understand why peripheral items like loanwords can be both more marked than native words in some respects and less marked in others (TETU-effects). Far from being a problem for the theory, these are in fact points in its favor in that new generalizations are found that would otherwise not have been discovered.

NOTES FOR CHAPTER 4

1. Here and throughout, unless otherwise noted, we use the broad transcription for Japanese proposed and explicated in detail in Ito Mester 2003 (pp. 6–11).

2. SJ-morphemes in fact observe an even stronger requirement: C2 cannot be a voiced obstruent.

3. But see Kawahara, Nishimura, and Ono 2003 for arguments that faithfulness constraints for Sino-Japanese are ranked lower than those for Yamato.

4. A Kanazawa dialect form, according to the NHK series *Furusato Nihon-no kotoba* (2000–2001). http://www.asahi-net.or.jp/~QM4H-IIM/ktb_frmd.htm/.

5. http://www.excite.co.jp/dictionary/japanese/.

6. http://www.asahi-net.or.jp/~QM4H-IIM/ktb_fr_a.htm.

7. http://www.search-japan.com/honmoku/rekisi/rekisi1.html#rekisi_7.

8. A familiar example is *burudokku tonkatu soosu*™ 'Bulldog *tonkatsu* sauce'.

9. See also Kawahara 2005 for an interesting faithfulness-based restatement of Nishimura's original observation.

10. First presented in class lectures at the 2005 LSA Linguistic Institute at MIT/Harvard University (July–August 2005).

11. There appear to be other moderately productive criteria. For example, postvocalic [zu] is more likely if there is no other voiced obstruent in the word—for example, *wookaa-zu* 'Walkers', (a 2007 NHK TV drama about the Shikoku 88-temple pilgrimage) versus *taigaa-su* 'Tigers' (a baseball team) with a word-internal voiced [g] triggering an OCP-like effect.

REFERENCES

Alderete, John. 1995. Faithfulness to prosodic heads. Rutgers Optimality Archive, ROA-94-0000. http://roa.rutgers.edu/.

Alderete, John. 1999. Head dependence in stress-epenthesis interaction. In *The derivational residue in phonological Optimality Theory*, ed. Ben Hermans and Marc van Oostendorp, 29–50. Amsterdam: John Benjamins.

Anttila, Arto. 1997. Deriving variation from grammar. In *Variation, change, and phonological Theory*, ed. Frans Hinskens, Roeland van Hout, and W. Leo Wetzels, 35–68. Amsterdam: John Benjamins.

Anttila, Arto. 2002. Morphologically conditioned phonological alternations. *Natural Language & Linguistic Theory* 20:1–42.

Anttila, Arto, and Young-Mee Yu Cho. 1998. Variation and change in optimality theory. *Lingua* 104:31–56.

Best, Catherine T., Gerald W. McRoberts, and Elizabeth Goodell. 2001. Discrimination of non-native consonant contrasts varying in perceptual assimilation to the listener's native phonological system. *Journal of the Acoustical Society of America* 109:775–794.

Burzio, Luigi. 1994. *Principles of English stress*. Cambridge: Cambridge University Press.

Burzio, Luigi. 1997. Cycles, non-derived-environment blocking, and correspondence. Ms., Johns Hopkins University, Baltimore, Md.

Campbell, Lyle. 1999. *Historical linguistics: An introduction*. Cambridge, Mass.: MIT Press.

Chomsky, Noam, and Morris Halle. 1968. *The sound pattern of English*. New York: Harper & Row.

Dupoux, Emmanuel, Kazuhiko Kakehi, Yuki Hirose, Christophe Pallier, and Jacques Mehler. 1999. Epenthetic vowels in Japanese: A perceptual illusion? *Journal of Experimental Psychology: Human Perception and Performance* 25:1568–1578.

Fukazawa, Haruka. 1998. Multiple input-output faithfulness relations in Japanese. Rutgers Optimality Archive, ROA-260-0698. http://roa.rutgers.edu/.

Fukazawa, Haruka, Mafuyu Kitahara, and Mitsuhiko Ota. 2002. Constraint-based modelling of split phonological systems. *Phonological Studies* 5:115–120.

Inkelas, Sharon, Orhan Orgun, and Cheryl Zoll. 1997. The implications of lexical exceptions for the nature of grammar. In *Derivations and constraints in phonology*, ed. Iggy Roca, 393–418. Oxford: Oxford University Press.

Ito, Junko, and Armin Mester. 1986. The phonology of voicing in Japanese: Theoretical consequences for morphological accessibility. *Linguistic Inquiry* 17:49–73.

Ito, Junko, and Armin Mester. 1995a. The core-periphery structure of the lexicon and constraints on reranking. In *Papers in Optimality Theory*, ed. Jill Beckman, Suzanne Urbanczyk, and Laura Walsh, 181–210. Amherst, Mass.: GLSA Publications.

Ito, Junko, and Armin Mester. 1995b. Japanese phonology. In *The handbook of phonological theory*, ed. John Goldsmith, 817–838. Oxford: Blackwell.

Ito, Junko, and Armin Mester. 1999. The phonological lexicon. In *The handbook of Japanese linguistics*, ed. Natsuko Tsujimura, 62–100. Oxford: Blackwell.

Ito, Junko, and Armin Mester. 2003. *Japanese morphophonemics: Markedness and word structure*. Linguistic Inquiry Monograph 41. Cambridge, Mass.: MIT Press.

Ito, Junko, and Armin Mester. 2004. Morphological contrast and merger: *Ranuki* in Japanese. *Journal of Japanese Linguistics* 20:1–18.

Jacobs, Haike, and Carlos Gussenhoven. 2000. Loan phonology: Perception, salience, the lexicon, and OT. In *Optimality Theory: Phonology, syntax, and acquisition*, ed. Jost Dekkers, Frank van der Leeuw, and Jeroen van de Weijer, 193–209. Oxford: Oxford University Press.

Kager, René. 1996. On affix allomorphy and syllable counting. Rutgers Optimality Archive, ROA-88. http://roa.rutgers.edu/.

Kanagawa Prefecture Social Studies Research Council. 1996. *Kanagawa-ken-no rekishisampo* [History walks through Kanagawa Prefecture]. Rekishisampo 14. Tokyo: Yamakawa Publishing.

Kang, Yoonjung. 2003. Perceptual similarity in loanword adaptation: English postvocalic word-final stops in Korean. *Phonology* 20:219–273.

Katayama, Motoko. 1995. Loanword accent and minimal reranking in Japanese. In *Phonology at Santa Cruz: Papers on stress, accent, and alignment*, ed. Rachel Walker, Ove Lorentz, and Haruo Kubozono, 1–12. Santa Cruz: Linguistics Research Center, University of California.

Katayama, Motoko. 1998. Optimality Theory and Japanese loanword phonology. Doctoral dissertation, University of California, Santa Cruz.

Kawahara, Shigeto. 2005. A faithfulness ranking projected from a perceptibility scale: The case of [+voice] in Japanese. Rutgers Optimality Archive, ROA 749-0605. http://roa.rutgers.edu/.

Kawahara, Shigeto, Kohei Nishimura, and Hajime Ono. 2003. Unveiling the unmarkedness of Sino-Japanese. In *Japanese/Korean Linguistics 12*, ed. William McLure, 140–151. Stanford, Calif.: CSLI Publications.

Kenstowicz, Michael. 2003. Salience and similarity in loanword adaptation: A case study from Fijian. Rutgers Optimality Archive, ROA-609. http://roa.rutgers.edu/.

Kenstowicz, Michael. 2004. Issues in loanword phonology. Paper presented at the Phonetic Society of Japan workshop, Tokyo University of Foreign Studies, December.

Kubozono, Haruo. 1996. Syllable and accent in Japanese: Evidence from loanword accentuation. *Bulletin of the Phonetic Society of Japan* 211:71–82.

Mascaró, Joan. 1996a. External allomorphy and contraction in Romance. *Probus* 8:181–205.

Mascaró, Joan. 1996b. External allomorphy as emergence of the unmarked. In *Current trends in phonology: Models and methods*, ed. Jacques Durand and Bernard Laks, 473–483. University of Salford, Manchester: European Studies Research Institute.

McCarthy, John J., and Alan S. Prince. 1995. Faithfulness and reduplicative identity. In *University of Massachusetts occasional papers in linguistics* 18, ed. Jill Beckman, Suzanne Urbanczyk, and Laura Walsh, 249–384. Amherst, Mass.: GLSA Publications.

McCarthy, John J., and Alan S. Prince. 1999. Faithfulness and identity in prosodic morphology. In *The prosody-morphology interface*, ed. Harry van der Hulst, René Kager, and Wim Zonneveld, 218–309. Cambridge: Cambridge University Press.

McCawley, James D. 1968. *The phonological component of a grammar of Japanese*. The Hague: Mouton.

Mester, Armin. 1994. The quantitative trochee in Latin. *Natural Language & Linguistic Theory* 12:1–61.

Nishimura, Kohei. 2001. Lyman's Law in Japanese loanwords. Paper presented at PAIK (Phonology Association in Kansai), Kobe University, Kobe, Japan, October.

Orgun, Orhan. 1996. Sign-based morphology and phonology, with special attention to Optimality Theory. Doctoral dissertation, University of California, Berkeley.

Paradis, Carole. 1995. Derivational constraints in phonology: Evidence from loanwords and implications. In *CLS 31*, ed. Audra Dainora, Rachel Hemphill, Barbara Luka, Barbara Need, and Sheri Pargman, 360–374. Chicago: Chicago Linguistic Society.

Paradis, Carole, and Darlene LaCharité. 1997. Preservation and minimality in loanword adaptation. *Journal of Linguistics* 33:379–430.

Pater, Joe. 2000. Nonuniformity in English secondary stress: The role of ranked and lexically specific constraints. *Phonology* 17:237–274.

Pater, Joe. 2005. The locus of exceptionality: Morpheme-specific phonology as constraint indexation. Ms., University of Massachusetts, Amherst.

Peperkamp, Sharon, and Emmanuel Dupoux. 2003. Reinterpreting loanword adaptations: The role of perception. *Proceedings of the International Congress of Phonetic Sciences* 15, 367–370. Barcelona, Spain: Universitat Autònoma de Barcelona.

Perlmutter, David M. 1998. Interfaces: Explanation of allomorphy and the architecture of grammars. In *Morphology and its relation to phonology and syntax*, ed. Steven G. Lapointe, Diane K. Brentari, and Patrick M. Farrell, 307–338. Stanford, Calif.: CSLI Publications.

Pierrehumbert, Janet. 2006. The statistical basis of an unnatural alternation. In *Laboratory phonology 8*, ed. Louis Goldstein, Douglas H. Whalen, and Catherine T. Best, 81–106. The Hague: Mouton de Gruyter.

Russell, Kevin. 1995. Morphemes and candidates in Optimality Theory. Rutgers Optimality Archive, ROA-44. http://roa.rutgers.edu/.

Shinohara, Shigeko. 2000. Default accentuation and foot structure in Japanese: Evidence from adaptations of French words. *Journal of East Asian Linguistics* 9:55–96.

Silverman, Daniel. 1992. Multiple scansions in loanword phonology: Evidence from Cantonese. *Phonology* 9:289–328.

Smith, Jennifer L. 2006. Loanword adaptation is not all perception: Evidence from Japanese loan doublets. In *Japanese/Korean Linguistics 14*, ed. Timothy J. Vance and Kimberly A. Jones, 63–74. Stanford, Calif.: CSLI Publications.

Smith, Jennifer L. To appear. Source similarity in loanword adaptation: Correspondence Theory and the posited source-language representation. In *Phonological argumentation: Essays on evidence and motivation*, ed. Steve Parker. London: Equinox.

Smolensky, Paul. 1996. The initial state and "Richness of the Base" in Optimality Theory. Rutgers Optimality Archive, ROA-154-1196. http://roa.rutgers.edu.

Takayama, Tomoaki. 1999. Shakuyoogo-no rendaku/koo'onka-ni-tsuite [On rendaku and fortition in loanwords]. In *Report of the Special Research Project for the Typological Investigation of Languages and Cultures of the East and West: Part 1*, 375–385. Tsukuba, Japan: Tsukuba University.

Tateishi, Koichi. 2001. On'in jisho kurasu seeyaku no bunpu ni tsuite [On the distribution of constraints for phonological sub-lexica]. Paper presented at the 26th meeting of the Kansai Linguistic Society, Ryukoku University, Kyoto, October.

Tateishi, Koichi. 2003. Phonological patterns and lexical strata. Paper presented at CIL XVII, Prague, July.

Tranel, Bernard. 1996a. French liaison and elision revisited: A unified account within Optimality Theory. In *Aspects of Romance linguistics*, ed. Claudia Parodi, Carlos Quicoli, Mario Saltarelli, and María-Luisa Zubizarreta, 433–455. Washington, D.C.: Georgetown University Press.

Tranel, Bernard. 1996b. Exceptionality in Optimality Theory and final consonants in French. In *Grammatical theory and Romance languages*, ed. Karen Zagona, 275–291. Amsterdam: John Benjamins.

Tranel, Bernard. 1998. Suppletion and OT: On the issue of the syntax/phonology interaction. In *Proceedings of the West Coast Conference on Formal Linguistics* 16, ed. Emily Curtis, James Lyle, and Gabriel Webster, 415–429. Stanford, Calif.: CSLI Publications.

Trubetzkoy, Nikolai Sergeevich. 1939. *Grundzüge der Phonologie*. Traveaux du Cercle Linguistique de Prague 7. (Reprinted by Vandenhoeck and Ruprecht, Göttingen, 1967.)

Yip, Moira. 1993. Cantonese loanword phonology and Optimality Theory. *Journal of East Asian Linguistics* 2:261–292.

Yip, Moira. 2002. Perceptual influences in Cantonese loanword phonology. *Journal of the Phonetic Society of Japan* 6:4–21.

CHAPTER 5

ON VERB RAISING

HIDEKI KISHIMOTO

5.1 Introduction

In the literature, there has been a lively debate as to whether Japanese has verb raising (V-to-T raising).[1] Japanese is a strict SOV language in which all verbal heads cluster together at the right periphery of the clause. Owing to this word-order property, overt verb raising—even if it exists—does not change surface string in Japanese, so that conventional heuristics for verb raising in Indo-European languages, that is, diagnostics to assess the verb's position relative to certain types of negative and adverbial expressions, are not available. The rigidly head-final character of the language makes it difficult to confirm the presence or absence of verb raising. Opinions are still divided between two extremes. Some researchers (e.g., Otani and Whitman 1991; Koizumi 1995, 2000) hold that Japanese has overt verb raising, but others (e.g., Sakai 1998; Aoyagi 1998; Fukui and Takano 1998; Fukui and Sakai 2003; Kishimoto 2001, 2005) maintain that it does not. In this chapter, I survey the major issues for verb raising in Japanese by looking closely at the constructions that are claimed to diagnose verb position.

5.2 The Core Data

In Japanese, the usual tools used to locate verb position in English and other Indo-European languages are not applicable. As a result, some familiar generalizations concerning head raising observed in European languages (e.g., Holmberg's generalization, the interplay of verb raising and object shift) cannot be easily verified in

Japanese.[2] Thus, we need to appeal to other measures to assess the presence or absence of overt verb raising. In this section, I look at three constructions that have been discussed in the Japanese linguistic literature and delineate how they might answer the question of whether overt verb raising takes place in Japanese.

First of all, Otani and Whitman (1991), who advocate an "overt verb raising" view, suggest that verb raising should be induced prior to LF in light of the interpretations available in a null-object construction like (1b) when (1a) serves as a preceding sentence.

(1) a. John$_i$-wa [zibun$_i$-no tegami-o] sute-ta.
John-TOP self-GEN letter-ACC discard-PAST
'John threw out self's letter.'
b. Mary-mo [e] sute-ta.
Mary-ALSO discard-PAST
'Mary also threw out.' (= Mary$_i$ also threw out her$_i$ letter/John's letter.)

The null-object construction (1b)—where the direct object is missing on the surface—has a bound variable (i.e., sloppy) reading in which the possessor of the null object refers to *Mary* as well as a strict reading in which the possessor refers to *John*. Otani and Whitman suggest that these strict and sloppy readings are equivalent to those obtained for the possessor of the null object in the English VP-ellipsis construction in (2b).

(2) a. John threw out his letters.
b. Mary did [$_{VP}$ [$_V$ e] [$_{NP}$ e]] too. (= Mary$_i$ threw out her$_i$ letters/John's letters.)

They argue that the parallelism in the interpretations between (1b) and (2b) can be neatly captured if (1b) involves VP-ellipsis, despite the fact that the verb is not elided. They suggest that the verb is extracted from the VP-ellipsis site, as a consequence of overt V-raising, as in (3).

(3) [Mary-mo [$_{VP}$ t$_i$] sute$_i$-ta]

In (3), the verb is located outside VP. Thus, even if VP-ellipsis takes place, the verb remains undeleted.

According to Otani and Whitman, the absence of a sloppy identity reading in (4b) lends support to their "overt verb raising" view.

(4) a. John$_i$-wa [NY Times-ga zibun$_i$-no kizi-o inyoosi-te i-ru
John-TOP NY Times-NOM self-GEN article-ACC quote be-PRES
to] kii-ta.
COMP hear-PAST
'John$_i$ heard that *The NY Times* is quoting self$_i$'s article.'
b. Bill-mo [NY Times-ga [e] inyoosi-te i-ru to] kii-ta.
Bill-also NY Times-NOM quote be-PRES COMP hear-PAST
'Bill$_i$ also heard that *The NY Times* is quoting (John's article/*his$_i$ article).'

ON VERB RAISING 109

When preceded by (4a), (4b) is not construed as having a sloppy identity reading, which suggests that a locality condition is imposed on sloppy identity. A parallelism between Japanese and English is also found here, because (5b)—unlike (5a)—does not have a sloppy identity reading, as noted by Williams (1977).

(5) a. John$_i$ thinks that Bill likes him$_i$ and Mary does [$_{VP}$ e] too.
    b. John$_i$ thinks that Bill likes him$_i$ and Mary thinks Bill does [$_{VP}$ e] too.

In Williams 1977, the interpretive effects of VP-ellipsis are accounted for by appealing to the Derived VP Rule and the (optional) Pronoun Rule. First, let us consider how the English example in (2b) is treated in Williams's framework. Abstracting away from some irrelevant details, the application of the Derived VP Rule to (2a) gives rise to (6a), and further, if the Pronoun Rule—which turns a pronoun into a variable—applies to (6a), (6b) is derived.

(6) a. John [$_{VP}$ λx(x throw out his letter)]
    b. John [$_{VP}$ λx(x throw out x's letter)]

If the VP structures in (6) are copied onto the gapped VP in (2b), we can derive the following representations.

(7) a. Mary did [$_{VP}$ λx(x throw out his letter)]
    b. Mary did [$_{VP}$ λx(x throw out x's letter)]

In (7a) the pronoun *his* refers to *John*, so that a strict reading obtains. In (7b) the variable x is bound by the lambda (λ) operator, which yields a sloppy reading in which the possessor of the letter refers to *Mary*. The two representations in (7) account for why both the sloppy and nonsloppy readings are possible in (2b).

Turning to (5a,b), the two possible representations of the first clause are given in (8), which are formed from the application of the Derived VP Rule and the optional Pronoun Rule.

(8) a. John [$_{VP}$ λx(x think that Bill [$_{VP}$ λy(y like him)])]
    b. John [$_{VP}$ λx(x think that Bill [$_{VP}$ λy(y like x)])]

If the matrix VP constituents in (8)—which exclude only the matrix subject—are copied onto the gap in the second clause in (5a), the following representations are derived.

(9) a. Mary does [$_{VP}$ λx(x think that Bill [$_{VP}$ λy(y like him)])] too.
    b. Mary does [$_{VP}$ λx(x think that Bill [$_{VP}$ λy(y like x)])] too.

In (9a), the pronoun *him* in the embedded verb refers to *John*, which leads to a nonsloppy reading. In (9b), the variable x in the position of the embedded object is bound by the lambda operator in the matrix clause, which gives rise to a sloppy identity reading in which the missing embedded object is taken to refer to *Mary*. This explains why both sloppy and nonsloppy readings are available in (5a).

In (5b), in contrast, a sloppy reading is absent. This can be explained as follows. First, the Derived VP Rule applies to the matrix VP in the second clause, deriving the representations in (10).

(10) Mary does [$_{VP}$ λz(z think that Bill does [$_{VP}$ e])] too.

After the representation in (10) is derived, the embedded VP material in (8)—either [λy(y like x)] (on the sloppy reading) or [λy(y like him)] (on the strict identity reading where *him* refers to *John*)—can be copied onto the gapped VP.

(11) a. *Mary does [$_{VP}$ λz(z think that Bill does [$_{VP}$ λy(y like x)])] too.
      b. Mary does [$_{VP}$ λz(z think that Bill does [$_{VP}$ λy(y like him)])] too.

The LF representation in (11a) is ill-formed, however, because the embedded VP contains the variable *x* that is left unbound. Thus, the only legitimate representation for (5b) is (11b), which entails that only the nonsloppy reading is available for (5b).

Otani and Whitman (1991) argue that analogous interpretive operations apply to the null-object construction in Japanese, the only substantial difference being that overt verb raising is induced. For instance, in (1a), the verb first moves out of VP, and then the Derived VP Rule and the optional Pronoun Rule apply to the verbless VP constituent, which yields the following representations.

(12) a. John-wa [$_{VP}$ λx(x zibun-no tegami-o t_V)] sute$_V$-ta.
      b. John-wa [$_{VP}$ λx(x x-no tegami-o t_V)] sute$_V$-ta.

If the VP structures in (12) are mapped onto the gap in (1b), where the verb is also raised out of VP, the following representations are derived.

(13) a. Mary-mo [$_{VP}$ λx(x zibun-no tegami-o t_V)] sute$_V$-ta.
      b. Mary-mo [$_{VP}$ λx(x x-no tegami-o t_V)] sute$_V$-ta.

Because these are well-formed representations, (1b) can have both the sloppy reading (where the possessor of the letter counts as *Mary*) and the nonsloppy reading (where the possessor refers to *John*). In this particular case, the verb position does not affect the possibility of interpretations, so legitimate representations for both readings could be derived even if the verb is not raised out of VP. Nevertheless, Otani and Whitman argue that overt verb raising is necessary, because the verb in the gapped clause does not have to be identical to the verb in its antecedent clause, as illustrated in (14).

(14) a. Jane$_i$-ga   [zibun$_i$-no   kodomo-o   taien-s-ase-ta]   node, ...
         Jane-NOM   self-GEN   child-ACC   withdraw-CAUSE-PAST   since
         'Since Jane$_i$ withdrew self$_i$'s child from kindergarten, ...'
      b. Mary-wa   [[e] nyuuen-s-ase-ta].
         Mary-TOP   enroll-CAUSE-PAST
         'Mary$_j$ enrolled self$_j$/Jane$_i$'s child in kindergarten.'

If the VP-gap does not contain the verb, it is naturally expected that a sloppy reading is possible under VP-ellipsis, even if the verb in (14b) is not identical to the one in the preceding sentence in (14a).

In a case like (4), the interpretive operations apply in the same manner as (5b), the only crucial difference being that the verb is overtly moved out of VP. First, the representations in (15) are derived from (4a) by applying overt verb raising, the Derived VP Rule, and the optional Pronoun Rule.[3]

(15) a. John-wa [$_{VP}$ λx(x[NYT-ga [$_{VP}$ λy(y zibun-no kizi-o t_V)] inyoosi-te-iru$_V$ to]) t_v] kii$_V$-ta]
      b. John-wa [$_{VP}$ λx(x[NYT-ga [$_{VP}$ λy(y x-no kizi-o t_V)] inyoosi-te-iru$_V$ to]) t_v] kii$_V$-ta]

Example (4b) contains a gap in the embedded clause. If the embedded VP constituents in (15) are copied onto the gap in (4b) after Derived VP Rule is applied to the matrix clause, the following representations are derived.

(16) a. Bill-mo [$_{VP}$ λz(z[NYT-ga [$_{VP}$ λy(y zibun-no kizi-o t_V)] inyoosi-te-iru$_V$ to]) t_v] kii$_V$-ta]
      b. *Bill-mo [$_{VP}$ λz(z[NYT-ga [$_{VP}$ λy(y x-no kizi-o t_V)] inyoosi-te-iru$_V$ to]) t_v] kii$_V$-ta]

The representation in (16b) is ruled out, however, on the grounds that an unbound variable occurs in the embedded VP. Given that (16a) is the sole legitimate representation, only the nonsloppy identity reading in which the missing object is understood to refer to *John's article* is permitted for (4b).

The crucial fact is that the main verb is overtly realized in the null-object construction in (1b), even though (1b) permits both sloppy and nonsloppy readings. Otani and Whitman (1991) claim that the facts of the null-object constructions lend empirical support to the overt verb-raising view, because their appropriate interpretation can be made only if the verb is raised out of VP before reaching the LF level where the elided VP material is restored.

Let us turn now to Koizumi's (1995, 2000) argument for overt verb raising. Koizumi presents an argument in favor of overt verb raising (up to C), in the light of unorthodox coordinate constructions such as (17).

(17) a. Mary-ga   [[John-ni ringo-o   2-tu] to [Bob-ni banana-o 3-bon]]
          Mary-NOM John-DAT apple-ACC 2-CL and Bob-DAT banana-ACC 3-CL
          age-ta.
          give-PAST
          'Mary gave two apples to John and three bananas to Bob.'
      b. [[Mary-ga   ringo-o   2-tu] to [Nancy-ga banana-o   3-bon]] tabe-ta.
          Mary-NOM apple-ACC 2-CL and Nancy-NOM banana-ACC 3-CL   eat-PAST
          'Mary ate two apples, and Nancy, three bananas.'

In (17a), the direct and indirect objects are coordinated, so Koizumi (2000) suggests that the verb is overtly raised to I (=T), as illustrated in (18).

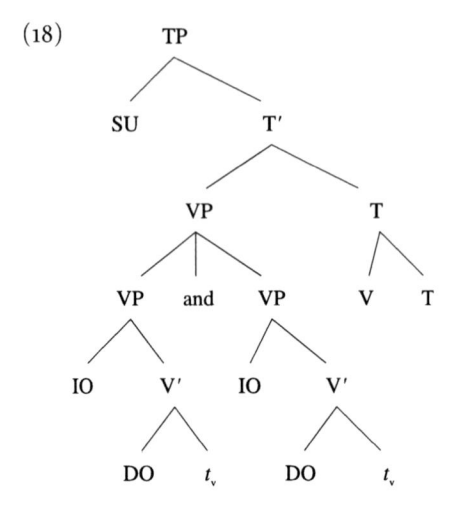

(18)

```
              TP
             /  \
           SU    T'
                /  \
              VP    T
             /  \  / \
           VP and VP V  T
          /  \   /  \
         IO   V' IO  V'
             /  \    / \
           DO   t_v DO  t_v
```

Notice that in the coordinate construction, the verb must be moved out of the two conjuncts in an "across-the-board" manner. The same type of coordinate structure obtains in (17b), in which the two conjuncts contain the subject as well as the object, but exclude the verb.[4] On the premise that subjects are overtly raised to Spec,TP (=IP), Koizumi suggests that (17b) involves TP-coordination and that the verb is overtly raised up to the C-head position.

It is easy to confirm that the verb does not constitute a part of the second conjunct in (17a,b). This can be checked, for instance, by way of scrambling the coordinate structure, as illustrated in (19).

(19) a. [[John-ni   ringo-o   2-tu] to [Bob-ni   banana-o   3-bon]]ᵢ
        John-DAT apple-ACC 2-CL and Bob-DAT banana-ACC 3-CL
        Mary-ga   tᵢ age-ta.
        Mary-NOM   give-PAST
        Lit. '[Two apples to John and three bananas to Bob] Mary gave.'
   b. [[Mary-ga   ringo-o   2-tu] to [Nancy-ga   banana-o   3-bon]]ᵢ
        Mary-NOM apple-ACC 2-CL and Nancy-NOM banana-ACC 3-CL
        Becky-ga   tᵢ tabe-ta   to   omot-te i-ru   (koto).
        Becky-NOM   eat-PAST COMP think   be-PRES   (fact)
        Lit. '[[Mary two apples] and [Nancy three bananas]] Becky believes that ate.'

In both examples in (19), the coordinate structure can be fronted while leaving the verb behind. If the verb were located inside the second conjunct, the conjoined constituents could not be moved to the front.

Koizumi (1995, 2000) presents essentially the same argument for overt verb raising up to C in light of cleft sentences that place a multiple number of phrases in focus position, which are exemplified in (20).

(20) a. Mary-ga   age-ta   no-wa [John-ni   ringo-o   3-tu] da.
       Mary-NOM give-PAST NL-TOP John-DAT apple-ACC 3-CL COP
       Lit. 'It is [three apples to John] that Mary gave.'
   b. Age-ta   no-wa [Mary-ga John-ni   ringo-o   3-tu] da.
       give-PAST NL-TOP Mary-NOM John-DAT apple-ACC 3-CL COP
       Lit. 'It is [Mary three apples to John] that gave.'

In (20a), the direct and indirect objects appear in focus position. According to Koizumi (2000), this is indicative of the fact that the VP constituent—out of which the verb is extracted—is clefted. In (20b), the moved constituent is the TP containing the subject in addition to the direct and indirect objects, so the verb should be raised to C.

Koizumi argues that the verb cannot be head-raised beyond a finite C, in light of the unacceptability of (21), in which the matrix clause is coordinated along with its complement clause.

(21) *[Mary-ga   [John-ga   ringo-o   2-tu]] to   [Nancy-ga   [Bob-ga
      Mary-NOM John-NOM apple-ACC 2-CL   and Nancy-NOM Bob-NOM
      banana-o   3-bon]]   kat-ta   to   omot-te   i-ru   (koto).
      banana-ACC 3-CL   buy-PAST COMP believe be-PRES (fact)
      'Mary believes that John bought two apples, and Nancy believes that Bob bought tree bananas.'

As shown in (21), the matrix argument cannot co-occur with the embedded arguments within a single conjunct. Likewise, (22), in which both matrix and embedded arguments are moved into the focus position, is deviant.

(22) *Kat-ta   to   it-ta   no-wa   [Mary-ga   Nancy-ni   [John-ga
      buy-PAST COMP say-PAST NL-TOP Mary-NOM Nancy-DAT John-NOM
      ringo-o   3-tu]] da.
      apple-ACC 3-CL   COP
      Lit. 'It is [Mary to Nancy John three apples] that said that bought.'

In (21) and (22), if the embedded verb is raised to the matrix C together with the embedded C, the entire verbal complex should be located outside the matrix TP constituent. If this is the case, the matrix TP constituent can be moved or coordinated, and (21) and (22) would be expected to be well formed. However, given that both examples are unacceptable, contrary to expectation, Koizumi concludes that a clausemate condition is imposed on verb raising and that the verb cannot be head-raised beyond a tensed clause boundary.

Finally, Sakai (1998) and Aoyagi (1998) argue against overt verb raising. Their arguments are primarily drawn from the differences in verbal morphology that arise depending on the presence or absence of an intervening adverbial particle.[5]

(23) a. John-ga   ringo-o   tabe-ta.
       John-NOM apple-ACC eat-PAST
       'John ate the apple.'

b. John-ga   ringo-o   tabe-mo/-sae/-dake si-ta.
   John-NOM   apple-ACC eat-also/-even/-only do-PAST
   'John also/even/only ate the apple.'

In arguing for the absence of overt verb raising, Sakai and Aoyagi both take up the question of whether a verbal complex—in this case, a verb+tense sequence—is formed via head raising or morphological merger. They claim that the adverbial particles occurring after the verb should be viewed as cliticlike elements adjoined to VP, rather than taking VP as a complement.[6]

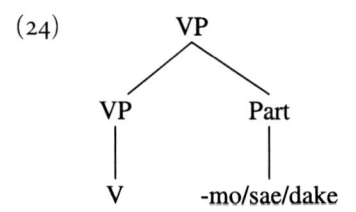

(24)
```
           VP
          /  \
        VP    Part
         |     |
         V    -mo/sae/dake
```

Sakai and Aoyagi maintain that overt head raising is constrained by the Head Movement Constraint (HMC) and that head movement of X to Y is blocked by an intervening head Z but not by a nonhead. (Note that an adverbial adjunct typically does not block head movement, as exemplified by a French example like *Jean embrasse₁ souvent t₁ Marie* 'John often kisses Mary'.) Given that Japanese does not have verbal strings where the verb occurs to the right of its associated adverbial particle, Sakai and Aoyagi claim that the verb+tense sequence in (23a) is formed via morphological merger without syntactic head raising (see Marantz 1989). In their analyses, the supporting verb *suru* in (23b) is inserted due to the disruption of linear adjacency by an intervening adverbial particle. Sakai remarks that if the verbal complex is formed via head raising, there is no need to resort to the supporting verb *suru* to produce a well-formed output.

This analysis crucially relies on the assumption that, in (23b), the focus particles are adjoined to VP. According to Sakai, this assumption is justified by the fact that a focus particle can be attached to various constituents such as NP and VP without changing the category of its host, as seen in (25).

(25) a. Takasi-ga   ringo-mo/-sae/-dake   tabe-ta.
        Takasi-NOM   apple-also/-even/-only eat-PAST
        'Takasi ate also/even/only an apple.'
     b. Takasi-ga   ringo-o   tabe-ta-to-mo/-sae/-dake
        Takasi-NOM   apple-ACC eat-PAST-COMP-also/-even/-only
        iw-are-ta.
        say-PASS-PAST
        'It is also/even/only said that Takashi ate an apple.'

As further support to the claim that the addition of adverbial particles involves adjunction, Sakai presents data on the distribution of negative forms like *mai/masen* 'not'.

(26) a. Takasi-wa ringo-o tabe-masen.
 Takasi-TOP apple-ACC eat-POLITE.NEG
 'Takasi does not eat apples.'
 b. Ringo-ga oisiku-*ari*-masen.
 apple-NOM delicious-be-POLITE.NEG
 'The apples are not delicious.'

The negative suffix *masen* can only take a verbal predicate as its complement. When *masen* occurs with an adjectival predicate, as in (26b), the insertion of the verb *aru* to support an adjective is necessary to satisfy the selectional requirement of *masen*. Notably, the verb *aru* is required even when a particle is added to an adjective, as seen in (27).

(27) Ringo-ga oisiku-mo/-sae/-dake-*ari*-masen.
 apple-NOM delicious-also/-even/-only-be-POLITE.NEG
 'The apples are not also/even/only delicious.'

When an adverbial particle is added after the verb in (26a), the required supporting verb is *suru* but not *aru*, as shown in (28).

(28) Takasi-wa ringo-o tabe-mo/-sae/-dake-*si*-masen.
 Takasi-TOP apple-ACC eat-also/-even/-only-do-POLITE.NEG
 'Takasi does not eat also/even/only apples.'

This would not be expected if the added particle had its own projection selecting its host as a complement. Sakai claims that because the choice of the supporting verb does not vary whether or not an adverbial particle is added, the adverbial particles in (23b) are modifiers adjoined to VP, and hence they do not determine the categorical status of their host.

In essence, Sakai and Aoyagi argue for a "non-raising verb" view, claiming that V and T are coalesced into a single verbal cluster V-T via morphological merger—that is, without syntactic head raising. Under their view, focus particles do not block overt head movement, and when an emphatic particle intervenes between V and T, dummy verb support takes place because it disrupts linear adjacency—a prerequisite to morphological merger.

5.3 Controversies Regarding Analysis

The previous section shows some of the core data used to argue for or against overt verb raising. In the Japanese linguistic literature, however, a number of counter-arguments and alternatives to the proposals have been put forth. In this section, I review some of the controversies.

Hoji (1998) presents arguments against Otani and Whitman's (1991) analysis. He argues that the "sloppy identity" reading available in the Japanese null-object construction is not the same as what obtains in English VP-ellipsis, so that Otani and Whitman's analysis of the null-object construction in terms of VP-ellipsis plus overt verb raising is not warranted. He suggests that the relevant null-object construction can be better analyzed as involving "a null object argument" rather than "VP-ellipsis."

Hoji presents a number of different arguments for his claim that the Japanese null-object construction should not involve VP-ellipsis. First, he argues that the null-object construction does not necessarily yield a sloppy identity reading in the same manner as English VP-ellipsis.

(29) a. John$_i$-wa zibun(zisin)$_i$-o nagusame-ta.
       John-TOP   self-ACC   console-PAST
       'John consoled himself.'
    b. Bill-mo e nagusame-ta.
       Bill-also console-PAST
       'Bill also consoled e too.'
    c. Bill$_i$-mo zibun(zisin)$_i$-o nagusame-ta.
       Bill-also self-ACC   console-PAST
       'Bill also consoled himself.'

When (29a) counts as a preceding sentence, (29b) is not construed as having a sloppy identity reading, so (29b) cannot mean what (29c) can mean. This is apparently due to the fact that the act of consoling is more likely to be directed toward someone other than the subject in an ordinary pragmatic context (see Hoji 1995). The English VP-ellipsis construction in (30b), by contrast, readily allows for a sloppy identity reading.

(30) a. John consoled himself.
    b. Bill did too. (= Bill consoled himself.)

This suggests that in English VP-ellipsis, sloppy identity readings are made possible syntactically. In the Japanese null-object construction, by contrast, the possibility of sloppy identity readings is affected by the choice of predicate. Hoji argues that this difference would not be expected under Otani and Whitman's analysis, which equates the Japanese null-object construction with the English VP-ellipsis construction.

Second, Hoji questions the validity of the generalization on the locality effect for sloppy identity in the Japanese null-object construction, in the light of the availability of a sloppy identity reading in (31b).

(31) a. John$_i$-wa zibun$_i$-no gakusei-o suisen-si-ta.
John-TOP self-GEN student-ACC recommend-PAST
'John recommended self's student.'
b. (Demo) Mary$_i$-wa [Bill-ga e suisen-si-ta to] omot-te i-ta.
but Mary-TOP Bill-NOM recommend-PAST COMP think be-PAST
(Dakara e$_i$ zibun-de-wa nani-mo si-nakat-ta.)
so self-with-TOP anything do-NEG-PAST
'(But) Mary$_i$ thought that Bill recommended her$_i$ student. (So she did not do anything herself.)'

According to Hoji, the sloppy identity reading on which *Mary* counts as the possessor of the missing object in (31b) is possible in the following context. John and Mary have been competing with each other in placing their students in good teaching positions. Whenever John recommends his students, Mary does it as well. Bill, who used to be her student, even recommends Mary's students on behalf of Mary. In (32), however, the sloppy reading is not possible even if the same pragmatic context is available.

(32) John recommended his student, but (since) Mary thought that Bill did, (she did not do anything about recommending her own student).

The two crucial properties of sloppy identity observed in English VP-ellipsis therefore do not obtain in the Japanese null-object construction. Hoji concludes then that the latter should not be analyzed on a par with the former.

Hoji further observes that the following two facts cannot be accommodated under Otani and Whitman's analysis. First, in (33b), a sloppy reading is available despite the fact that the object in the antecedent clause (33a) is a proper noun.

(33) a. John-ga John-o suisen-si-ta.
John-NOM John-ACC recommend-PAST
'John recommended John.'
b. Bill$_i$-mo e$_i$ suisen-si-ta.
Bill-also recommend-PAST
'Bill also recommended e.'

Second, there are cases in which a sloppy reading is available even if a pronoun in the preceding clause is not c-commanded by its antecedent. In (34b), for example, the gap in the object position of the verb *homeru* 'praise' can refer to *Bill*.

(34) a. [Mukasi John$_i$-o osie-ta] sensei-ga kare$_i$(-no koto)-o
years.ago John-ACC teach-PAST teacher-NOM he-GEN fact-ACC
home-te i-ru.
praise be-PRES
'[The teacher who taught John years ago] is praising him.'

b. [Mukasi Bill$_i$-o osie-ta] sensei-mo e$_i$ home-te i-ru.
   years.ago Bill-ACC teach-PAST teacher-also praise be-PRES
   '[The teacher who taught John years ago] too is praising e.'

In English, sloppy identity does not obtain when a pronoun is not c-commanded by its antecedent (see Reinhart 1983). Thus, the English sentence *John's sister scratched his arm, and Bill's sister did, too* has only the strict reading where the second clause means "Bill's sister scratched John's arm" (see Sag 1976). It is obvious then that the examples in (33) and (34) cannot be accounted for under the VP-ellipsis analysis, given that the preceding clause does not provide a necessary condition for the following clause to have sloppy identity under VP-deletion.

Hoji (1998) holds that in the Japanese null-object construction, a phonologically null argument appears in the direct object position—with no VP-ellipsis involved. In his analysis, the null argument is an invisible NP-like element, such as [$_{NP}$ Bill] or [$_{NP}$ car], whose reference can be supplied contextually. He suggests that what Otani and Whitman call "sloppy identity reading" is not a sloppy identity reading but a "sloppy-like reading," and that sloppy-like readings are derived from the nature of the null argument occupying the object position.

Hoji's main point is that the facts of the null-object construction are better analyzed by positing a null argument in the gap (see Takahashi, this volume, for discussion on some controversies regarding the interpretations of the null argument as well as other possible alternative analyses).[7] Hoji does not commit himself to the question of whether Japanese has overt verb raising, but he does suggest that there is no compelling reason why the null-object construction should be analyzed as involving VP-ellipsis plus overt verb raising, as claimed by Otani and Whitman (1991).

Let us now turn to the discussion of controversies concerning the peculiar cleft and coordinate constructions that Koizumi (1995, 2000) claims to show the existence of overt verb raising. Takano (2002) and Fukui and Sakai (2003) argue against Koizumi's analysis, and also question some of the theoretical consequences derived from his analysis.

Koizumi (2000) discusses some implications and consequences of his analysis. One such implication concerns the Proper Binding Condition (the PBC), which has often been assumed to apply at S-structure (see Saito 1989). To begin, note that the coordinate structure in (35) can be scrambled to the front, leaving the dative phrase *Mary-ni* 'to Mary' behind.

(35) [[Tom-ga t$_i$ ringo-o 2-tu] to [Bob-ga t$_i$ banana-o 3-bon]]$_j$
    Tom-NOM   apple-ACC 2-CL and Bob-NOM   banana-ACC 3-CL
    Mary-ni$_i$ t$_j$ age-ta.
    Mary-DAT   give-PAST
    'Tom gave two apples to Mary and Bob gave three bananas to Mary.'

In Koizumi's analysis, the surface configuration in (35) is derived as follows. First, the dative phrase is moved out of the two conjuncts in an across-the-board manner, as in (36a), and then the conjoined structure is scrambled to the front, as in (36b).

(36) a. [_TP DP-DAT_i [[DP-NOM t_i DP-ACC] and [DP-NOM t_i DP-ACC]] V]

b. [_TP [[DP-NOM t_i DP-ACC] and [DP-NOM t_i DP-ACC]]_j DP-DAT_i t_j V]

Example (35) is acceptable despite the fact that the conjuncts contain unbound traces. By contrast, (37) is unacceptable.

(37) *[Bill-ga t_i sunde i-ru to]_j sono-mura-ni_i John-ga t_j omotte
　　　Bill-NOM　 reside be-PRES COMP that-village-in John-NOM think
　　　i-ru　　　(koto).
　　　be-PRES　 (fact)
　　　'John thinks that Bill lives in that village.'

Example (37) involves a derivation similar to (35), in that the embedded clause is moved to the front of the sentence after the dative clause is scrambled out of the embedded clause. Saito (1989) attributes the unacceptability of (37) to be a violation of the PBC, because the fronted embedded clause contains an unbound trace at S-structure. In Koizumi's analysis, (35) contains unbound traces just in the same way that (37) does, but still, (35) is acceptable. Thus, Koizumi claims that the PBC—which is often claimed to apply at S-structure—does not exist (but he assumes that it applies at LF, as discussed below), and proposes to account for the contrast in acceptability between (35) and (37) by way of Müller's generalization on remnant movement given in (38) (see Müller 1996).

(38)　If α dominates a trace of β which has been created by a certain type of movement, α cannot undergo the same type of movement yielding the structure in which the trace of β in α is unbound.

In his proposal, the distinction between A- and A'-movement plays a crucial role in determining the contrast in acceptability, and his explanation does not make reference to S-structure configurations, as described below (see Saito 1992).

In (37), the long-distance movement of the dative phrase is construed as A'-movement, and the fronting of the embedded clause is middle-distance scrambling, which can be either A- or A'-movement. If the latter counts as A'-movement, the derivation violates Müller's generalization. If it is A-movement, it cannot be reconstructed into its trace position, which means that the derivation violates the PBC at LF. (Koizumi assumes that radical reconstruction is allowed only for A'-movement.) In either case, the derivation crashes, hence the unacceptability of (37).

In (35), however, the two instances of movement are middle-distance scrambling, which can be either A- or A'-movement. In this case, there is at least one legitimate derivation. To be concrete, if the coordinate structure is fronted via A'-movement and the dative phrase via A-movement, then Müller's generalization is not violated. Additionally, because the coordinate structure moved by A′-movement can be reconstructed into its premovement site at LF, no PBC violation is incurred. This derivation turns out to be legitimate, so (35) is acceptable.

Takano (2002), however, observes one empirical problem with his analysis, which concerns the well-formedness of (39).

(39) [[John-ga t_i ringo-o   3-tu] to   [Bill-ga t_i banana-o   2-hon]]$_j$
     John-NOM   apple-ACC 3-CL and   Bill-NOM   banana-ACC 2-CL
     zibun-zisin-ni$_i$ t_j kat-ta.
     self-DAT   buy-PAST
     'John bought three apples for himself and Bill bought two bananas for himself.'

Example (39) differs from (35), in that the anaphor *zibun-zisin* 'self', which can take *John* and *Bill* as its antecedents, occurs immediately before the verb. Takano argues that if the traces in the coordinate structure are to be properly bound by their antecedents, the coordinate structure must be reconstructed. Then, its fronting operation must be A′-movement. Note, however, that the anaphor comes to be bound by its antecedents once the coordinate structure is reconstructed into t_j. If the anaphor is located in A-position, its binding violates condition C of the binding theory. Then, the anaphor must be located in an A′-position. This means that the dative phrase should be subject to A′-movement when it is extracted from the coordinate structure. However, this derivation results in a violation of Müller's generalization, because the coordinate clause also involves A′-movement. Under Koizumi's account then, there is no convergent derivation for (39).

Takano (2002) claims that the peculiar coordination and clefting constructions should be explained in terms of "oblique" movement, which invokes adjunction of one nominal to another (see Saito 1994 and Sohn 1994).

(40) John-ga   age-ta   no-wa   hon-o   Mary-ni   da.
     John-NOM give-PAST NL-TOP book-ACC Mary-DAT COP
     Lit. 'It is a book to Mary that John gave.'

On Takano's proposal, the surface configuration in (40) is derived as follows. First, the accusative phrase is adjoined to the dative phrase by way of oblique movement, yielding a nominal-stacking structure like (41b).

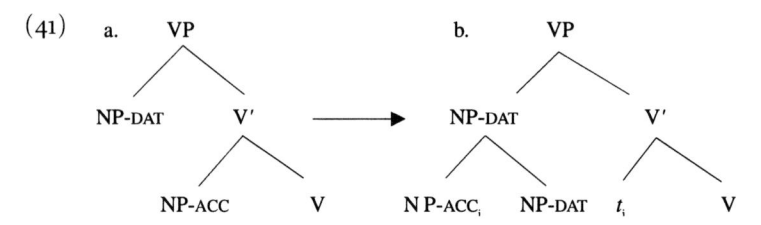

(41) a.   VP   b.   VP
             /   \   /   \
         NP-DAT   V'   NP-DAT   V'
         /   \   /   \   / \
      NP-ACC   V   NP-ACC$_i$ NP-DAT t_i V

The adjunction operation creates a nominal constituent comprising both the dative and accusative phrases.[8] Then, the cluster of the two phrases is moved to the focus position via pseudo-cleft movement. As a result of these syntactic operations, the "surprising constituent" in the focus position of the cleft sentence in (40) is derived.

Note here that some nonstandard syntactic operations are required in deriving a coordinate structure like (39) in Takano's "oblique movement" analysis. Takano proposes that the coordinate structure is formed in the following way. For the formation of the second conjunct, the object *banana-o 2-hon* is first scrambled to TP, and then the subject *Bill-ga* is moved and adjoined to the object in TP. These operations yield the structure (42).

(42) [$_{TP}$ [Bill-ga$_i$ [banana-o 2-hon]$_j$] [$_{TP}$ t_i t_j V]]

The first conjunct is constructed independently of the second conjunct. To form the first conjunct, *John-ga* is left-adjoined to *ringo-o 3-tu*, then the coordinator *to* 'and' is further adjoined to the resultant constituent, as in (43).

(43) [$_&$ [John-ga [ringo-o 3-tu]]-to]

If the conjunct (43) is left-adjoined to the conjunct (42), the formation of coordinate structure is complete, as shown in (44).

(44) [$_{TP}$ [$_&$ [John-ga [ringo-o 3-tu]]-to] [Bill-ga$_i$ [banana-o 2-hon]$_j$] [$_{TP}$ t_i t_j V]]

In (44), the two conjuncts form a constituent that may undergo a syntactic operation like scrambling. Here, the subject and the object in the first conjunct do not leave their traces in TP, as represented in (44), but it is assumed that they are associated with the existing subject and object traces in a loose way. Although Takano does not make any specific proposal to this effect, he claims that this assumption is justified by an English example like (45), in which the trace located in the fronted VP is somehow associated with the two subjects.

(45) It's given $t_{i/j}$ a raise that Betsy$_i$ should be and Julie$_j$ was.

If Universal Grammar (UG) provides a way of assigning a proper interpretation to (45), there is no reason why the same interpretive mechanism should not apply to (39). Crucially, in Takano's oblique movement analysis, neither Müller's generalization nor the PBC is violated in the derivation of (39). Moreover, in (44), the nominative phrases in the two conjuncts are associated with the trace t_i in TP, which would c-command the anaphor *zibun-zisin*. Thus, it comes as no surprise that (39) should be acceptable on the interpretation in which the two subjects in the coordinate structure serve as the antecedents of the anaphor.

Takano's oblique movement analysis is motivated by Sohn's (1994) observation on "saving effects" observed in *wh*-questions such as (46).

(46) a. ??Naze$_i$ sono-hito-o$_j$ John-wa [Mary-ga t_i t_j uttae-ta
         why   that-person-ACC John-TOP Mary-NOM   sue-PAST
         toyuu uwasa]-o   kii-ta   no?
         COMP rumor-ACC hear-PAST Q
         'Why did John hear the rumor that Mary sued that person?'

b. ??Sono-hito-o$_j$ naze$_i$ John-wa [Mary-ga t_i t_j uttae-ta
      that-person-ACC why   John-TOP Mary-NOM   sue-PAST
      toyuu uwasa]-o   kii-ta   no?
      COMP rumor-ACC   hear-PAST Q
      'Why did John hear the rumor that Mary sued that person?'

Both examples in (46) have the status of a Subjacency violation but not of an ECP violation, despite the extraction of the adjunct *naze* 'why' from a complex DP island. Sohn (1994) attributes the mild ungrammaticality of (46) to the extraction of the object to which *naze* 'why' is adjoined. (Because this extraction does not involve adjunct extraction per se, there is no reason why it should yield an ECP violation.[9]) Takano claims that Sohn's analysis implementing oblique movement should be extended to the analysis of unusual cleft and coordination structures.

This does not mean, however, that Koizumi (2000) has not taken into consideration the possibility of forming an unusual constituent via oblique movement; in fact, he rejects this type of analysis, on the basis of examples such as (47).

(47) a. Nani-o   naze John-wa katta   no?
         what-ACC why John-TOP bought   Q
         'Why did John buy what?'
      b. *Naze nani-o   John-wa katta   no?
         why what-ACC John-TOP bought   Q
         'What did John buy why?'

As shown in (47b), when *naze* 'why' is located higher than *nani* 'what', an ECP effect is not voided. In Sohn's version of adjunction analysis, left- and right-adjunction to a nominal is possible. If *naze* can be left-adjoined to a *wh*-phrase, (47b) should not show an ECP effect, as the argument *wh*-phrase that comprises *naze* could be moved in the same way as (47a). The presence of an ECP effect in (47b) leads Koizumi to reject Sohn's adjunction-to-argument analysis.

Koizumi's (2000) argument against Sohn's analysis draws on Watanabe's (1992) proposal that *naze* yields an ECP violation when it c-commands another *wh*-phrase (i.e., the so-called anti-superiority effect).[10] Takano (2002), however, notes that if only leftward adjunction is permitted in an adjunction-to-argument operation, and if it is assumed, following Kayne (1994), that an adjoined element asymmetrically c-commands the category to which it is adjoined, the desired results can be derived even in the oblique movement analysis.

Takano presents another argument against Koizumi's overt verb-raising analysis, building on Carlson's (1987) observation on the sentence-internal reading of the English words *same* and *different*, which concerns a comparison between the events denoted by the clause containing them. Note that the Japanese words *onazi* 'same' and *tigau* 'different', just like *same* and *different*, can have a sentence-internal reading when the sentence has a conjoined NP, as can be confirmed by (48).

(48) John-to   Bill-ga   *onazi/tigau*   eiga-o   mi-ta.
     John-and   Bill-NOM   same/different   movie-ACC   see-PAST
     'John and Bill saw the same movie/different movies.'

In (49) by contrast, *onazi* and *tigau* cannot have a sentence-internal reading, because the sentence does not have a conjoined NP indicating plurality.

(49) John-ga   *onazi/tigau*   eiga-o   mi-ta.
     John-NOM   same/different   movie-ACC   see-PAST
     'John saw the same movie/different movies.'

Notice here that *onazi* and *tigau* in (50) can also invoke a sentence-internal reading.

(50) [[John-ga   ringo-o   1-tu]   to   [Bill-ga   banana-o   1-pon]]
     John-NOM   apple-ACC   1-CL   and Bill-NOM   banana-ACC 1-CL
     onazi/tigau   hito-ni   age-ta.
     same/different   person-DAT   give-PAST
     'John gave an apple, and Bill gave a banana, to the same person/different persons.'

Takano claims that the availability of a sentence-internal reading for *onazi* and *tigau* in (50) cannot be captured by the overt verb-raising approach taking the dative phrase as originating from within the TP-conjuncts.

(51) [[$_{TP}$ John-ga t_i ringo-o 1-tu] to [$_{TP}$ Mary-ga t_i banana-o 1-pon]]
     [*onazi/tigau* hito-ni]$_i$ age-ta.

In this analysis, the dative phrase should be interpreted within each conjunct. To derive the desired sentence-internal reading for *onazi* and *tigau* in (50) then, it is necessary for each TP conjunct to denote a plural eventuality. However, given that *onazi* and *tigau* in (52) cannot have a sentence-internal reading, this cannot be the case.

(52) John-ga   *onazi/tigau*   hito-ni   ringo-o   1-tu   age-ta.
     John-NOM   same/different   person-DAT   apple-ACC   1-CL   give-PAST
     'John gave an apple to the same person/different persons.'

Under the oblique movement approach by contrast, (50) is expected to have a sentence-internal reading for *onazi* and *tigau*, because the conjoined structure does not coordinate two TPs but has only stacked nominals, as shown in (53).

(53) [$_{TP}$ [[$_{DP}$ John-ga [$_{DP}$ ringo-o 1-tu]] to [$_{DP}$ Mary-ga [$_{DP}$ banana-o 1-pon]]]
     onazi/tigau hito-ni age-ta]

The derivation by way of oblique movement does not involve remnant movement, and both the conjoined structure and the dative phrase are located within a single TP. The sentence in (50) therefore has a configuration that allows *onazi* and *tigau* to have a sentence-internal reading.

Takano (2002) further suggests that the clausemate condition that Koizumi (2000) has observed for the peculiar cleft construction should not be derived from a constraint on verb raising, given the contrast in acceptability between (54a) and (54b).

(54) a. *[[Bill-ga   ae-ru   to]   omot-te i-ru]   no-wa   John-ga
         Bill-NOM can.meet-PRES COMP think   be-PRES NL-TOP John-NOM
         Mary-ni   da.
         Mary-DAT   COP
         Lit. 'It is John Mary that thinks Bill can meet.'
    b. [[pro_i ae-ru   to]   omot-te i-ru]   no-wa   John_i-ga
                can.meet-PRES COMP think   be-PRES NL-TOP John-NOM
         Mary-ni   da.
         Mary-DAT   COP
         Lit. 'It is John Mary that thinks (he) can meet.'

The acceptability of (54b), which has a phonologically unrealized embedded subject coreferential with the matrix subject, is not expected if the clausemate condition comes from a constraint preventing the verb from crossing a clause boundary. Takano suggests that the cleft construction with two clausal constituents in (54a) is ruled out by two conflicting requirements imposed on clefting and oblique movement; that is, radical reconstruction is required of oblique movement (scrambling), which moves the embedded object *Mary-ni* long distance to form a two-clause constituent, but cleft movement forbids it. According to Takano, it is these two conflicting requirements that make the cleft sentence in (54a) illegitimate. Note that in Takano's analysis, it is necessary to assume that radical reconstruction is not required of the scrambled object in (54b) to account for its acceptability. In (54b), the embedded object *Mary-ni* is exempt from the reconstruction requirement because its oblique movement out of the embedded clause behaves like clause-internal scrambling.[11]

Fukui and Sakai (2003) also raise a number of criticisms against Koizumi's analysis. One such criticism is derived from the acceptability of (55).

(55) Taroo-ga   [Hanako-ni   ringo-o   3-tu]   to   [Kumiko-ni
     Taroo-NOM Hanako-DAT apple-ACC 3-CL and Kumiko-DAT
     banana-o   2-hon]   katte-kuru-yooni   (teinei-ni)   tanon-da.
     banana-ACC 2-CL   buy-bring-to   politely   ask-PAST
     Lit. 'Taroo (politely) asked Hanako to buy and bring three apples and Kumiko to buy and bring two bananas.'

In (55), each conjunct contains a dative phrase selected by the matrix verb and an accusative phrase selected by the embedded verb. To derive the unusual constituent in (55) under Koizumi's approach, the embedded verb in the infinitival complement must be raised to the matrix verb, as the verbal complex should be located outside the coordinate structure.[12] However, given that an adverbial like *teinei-ni* 'politely' can intervene between the matrix and embedded verbs, the overt verb raising at issue cannot take place. An additional problem noted by Fukui and Sakai concerns an example such as (56), in which the second conjunct is case-marked.

(56) Taroo-ga   [[Hanako-ni ringo 3-tu] to   [Kumiko-ni banana 2-hon]
     Taroo-NOM   Hanako-DAT   apple 3-CL   and Kumiko-DAT banana 2-CL
     (to)]-o   age-ta.
     and-ACC   give-PAST
     Lit. 'Taroo gave three apples to Hanako and two bananas to Kumiko.'

In the overt verb-raising analysis, the coordinate structure in (56) should fall into a VP category. However, given that the coordinate structure can bear the accusative case -o, which can be assigned to a nominal but not to a VP, it should belong to a nominal category that cannot be created by verb raising (see also Fukushima 2003). Fukui and Sakai claim that the facts of (55) and (56) are difficult to explain if the conjoined structure is formed by way of overt verb raising.

Fukui and Sakai observe yet another problem for Koizumi's proposal analyzing unusual constituents as involving overt verb raising. This has to do with the impossibility of forming a conjoined structure with the particle *mo* shown in (57a).

(57) a. *Taroo-ga   [[Hanako-ni ringo-o   3-tu] mo   [Kumiko-ni
        Taroo-NOM   Hanako-DAT   apple-ACC   3-CL   also Kumiko-DAT
        banana-o   2-hon] mo   age-ta.
        banana-ACC   2-CL   also give-PAST
        Lit. 'Taroo gave three apples to Hanako and two bananas to Kumiko.'
     b. Taroo-ga   [[Hanako-ni ringo-o   3-tu age] mo   [Kumiko-ni
        Taroo-NOM   Hanako-DAT   apple-ACC   3-CL give also Kumiko-DAT
        banana-o   2-hon age] mo   si-ta.
        banana-ACC 2-CL   give also do-PAST
        Lit. 'Taroo gave three apples to Hanako and two bananas to Kumiko.'

Example (57a) illustrates that the two constituents containing the dative and accusative phrases cannot be conjoined if the verb occurs outside the particle *mo*. As shown in (57b), however, when the verb is located inside *mo*, coordination is possible. (57b) shows that *mo* can be adjoined to VP, because it involves VP coordination where the verb stays in its original position. Fukui and Sakai argue that Koizumi's analysis confronts difficulty in accounting for the unacceptability of (57a), because (57a) should involve the addition of *mo* to VP, in the same way as (57b).

As an alternative to Koizumi's overt verb-raising analysis, Fukui and Sakai (2003) propose a PF reduction analysis, according to which an "unusual" constituent is formed by way of deleting the predicate in the first conjunct under identity with the one in the second at the PF level, as shown in (58).

(58) Taroo-ga [Hanako-ni ringo-o 3-tu ~~age~~] to [Kumiko-ni banana-o 2-hon age]-ta.

They claim that the PF reduction analysis has an advantage over Koizumi's analysis, given that (55) can be easily accommodated as an instance of PF predicate deletion in their analysis. Koizumi (2000) rejects this type of PF predicate reduction analysis because conjoined constituents can be scrambled altogether, as shown in (59).

(59) [[Mary-ga   ringo-o   2-tu] to [Nancy-ga   banana-o   3-bon]]$_i$
      Mary-NOM   apple-ACC   2-CL and Nancy-NOM banana-ACC 3-CL
      Becky-ga t$_i$ tabe-ta   to   it-ta   (koto).
      Becky-NOM   eat-PAST   COMP   say-PAST   (fact)
      Lit. '[[Mary two apples] and [Nancy three bananas]] Becky said that ate.'

Fukui and Sakai (2003) argue, however, that the PF reduction analysis is plausible in view of the recent development of the theory of scrambling. If scrambling can be a PF operation, as claimed by some researchers (e.g., Ueyama 2003), the elements fronted by scrambling need not form a constituent in narrow syntax. Fukui and Sakai propose that the discontinuous constituents in (59) are reanalyzed into a single constituent under string adjacency (without head raising) via "Phrase-Level Merger" in PF and that the reanalyzed constituent is fronted by way of PF scrambling. In their analysis, the resultant constituent created by way of PF merger belongs to a nominal category, so case marking is allowed to appear on the coordinate constituent in (56).

Furthermore, it is argued by Fukui and Sakai (2003) that the PF reduction analysis can explain the clausemate condition noted by Koizumi (2000), given that predication deletion can take place across a nonfinite, but not a finite, clause boundary, as illustrated by the pair of the English examples in (60).

(60) a. Mary forced Tom to go to Cambridge, and ~~forced~~ John ~~to go to~~ Oxford.
      b. *John thinks that Bill will see Susan, and Harry ~~thinks that Bill will see~~ Mary.

The PF reduction analysis is also claimed to provide a ready answer to the question of why *mo* cannot occur in the unusual constituent in (57a). The particle *mo*—unlike *to*—carries quantificational force, which means that *mo* must be present in LF as well as in narrow syntax.[13] Thus, Fukui and Sakai claim that an unusual constituent like one in (57a) must be formed in narrow syntax. Given that Phrase-Level Merger is a PF operation, they conclude that (57a) is unacceptable because there is no way of forming an unusual constituent in the syntax.[14]

Alternatively, one might argue that an unusual coordinate structure is formed by way of right-node raising, which extracts the verb from each conjunct. This analysis is denied by Koizumi, however. Drawing on McCawley's (1982, 1987) proposal that right-node-raised elements are located within the coordinate structure, Koizumi argues that the right-node-raising analysis is not plausible because it predicts that whenever an unusual constituent is scrambled, the verb should be moved as well. As we have already seen (e.g., (35)), the scrambling of an unusual constituent leaves the verb behind (and in fact, the verb cannot be moved along with it). Koizumi claims then that right-node raising cannot be involved in the formation of an unusual coordinate structure.

Although Koizumi's argument against the right-node-raising analysis hinges on McCawley's specific proposal, it is worth noting that we can still observe some difference between the right-node raising and unusual coordinate constructions. In the unusual coordinate construction, adverbial modifiers (adjectives) such as *sintyoo-ni* 'cautiously' appear to be excluded from the unusual conjuncts, whereas DPs and PPs (such as locative PPs) are permitted. Thus, (61), where adverbial modifiers are included in the peculiar conjuncts, is degraded.[15]

(61) ??[[Mary-ni   sintyoo-ni   hon-o   2-satu] to   [Bob-ni   subayaku
     Mary-DAT   cautiously   book-ACC   2-CL   and   Bob-DAT quickly
     zassi-o   1-satu]]$_i$ John-ga t_i watasi-ta   (koto).
     magazine-ACC 1-CL   John-NOM hand-PAST (fact)
     Lit. '[[Two books to Mary cautiously] and [a magazine to Bob quickly]] John handed.'

By contrast, in the right-node-raising construction—typically formed with *sosite* 'and'—no restriction is imposed on the types of expressions that occur inside the conjoined structure, as shown in (62) (see Kuno 1978).[16]

(62) [[John-ga   sintyoo-ni   hon-o]   sosite [Mary-ga   subayaku
     John-NOM   cautiously   book-ACC and   Mary-NOM   quickly
     zassi-o]]   yon-da.
     magazine-ACC read-PAST
     'John read the book cautiously, and Mary, the magazine quickly.'

The difference in acceptability between (61) and (62) shows that the unusual coordinate construction possesses properties that differ from those of the right-node-raising construction.

In regard to the coordinate and cleft structures of unusual constituents, three different analyses have been proposed. In Koizumi's analysis, unusual constituents are created by way of overt verb raising. In Takano's oblique movement analysis, these constituents involve stacked nominals. In Fukui and Sakai's analysis, unusual constituents are formed via PF predicate deletion plus PF Phrase-Level Merger.[17] The unusual coordinate and cleft constructions display some intriguing properties that cannot be treated in a simple, straightforward manner, however.

Finally, let us turn to the discussion of the pair of the verbal complexes found in (63) (= (23)), which is used by Sakai (1998) and Aoyagi (1998) to argue for the absence of overt verb raising.

(63) a. John-ga   ringo-o   tabe-ta.
       John-NOM apple-ACC eat-PAST
       'John ate the apple.'
    b. John-ga   ringo-o   tabe-mo/-sae/-dake si-ta.
       John-NOM apple-ACC eat-also/-even/-only do-PAST
       'John also/even/only ate the apple.'

Both Sakai and Aoyagi maintain that adverbial particles behave like adjuncts and do not block head raising. Under their view, the predicate+tense sequence—exemplified in (63a)—is formed by morphological merger (without verb raising). In (63b), the emphatic particles that disrupt linear adjacency occur to the right of the verb and, thus, the dummy verb *suru* is inserted to support tense.

The proposed analysis rests on the assumption that adverbial particles do not block head raising. However, Miyagawa (2001) makes a suggestion to the contrary. Although his main concern is the nature of the EPP in Japanese, his data are also pertinent to the issue of verb raising. He observes that if *zen'in* 'all' occurs in object position in a negative sentence, *zen'in* falls under the scope of negation.

(64) Taroo-ga   zen'in-o   home-nakat-ta.
     Taroo-NOM all-ACC   praise-NEG-PAST
     'Taroo did not praise all.'
     not>all, (*)all > not

If *zen'in* 'all' occurs in subject position, as in (65), it is interpreted outside the scope of negation.

(65) Zen'in-ga   sono-testuto-o   uke-nakat-ta.
     all-NOM   that-test-ACC   take-NEG-PAST
     'All did not take that test.'
     *not > all, all > not

Furthermore, the narrow scope interpretation of *zen'in* becomes possible if the object is scrambled to the front.

(66) Sono-tesuto-o_i zen'in-ga t_i uke-nakat-ta.
     that-test-ACC   all-NOM   take-NEG-PAST
     'That test, all did not take.'
     not > all (all > not)

Miyagawa argues that in (64) and (65), the subject is attracted to Spec,TP due to an EPP feature on T. By contrast in (66), the object is moved to Spec,TP via A-scrambling (i.e., A-movement), whereas the subject remains in situ. This suggests that the EPP requirement of T may be satisfied by the subject or object.

(67)

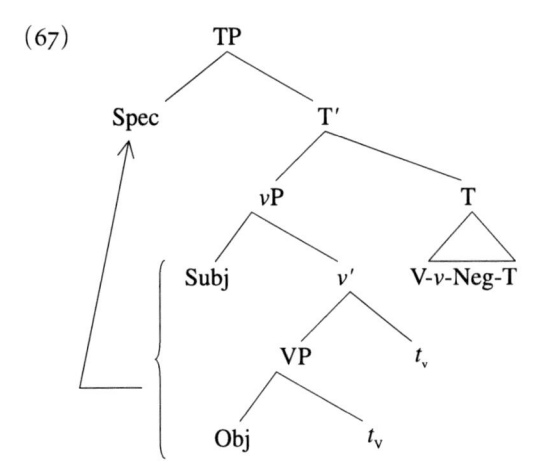

```
              TP
             /  \
          Spec   T'
           ↑    /  \
              vP    T
             /  \   /\
          Subj  v' V-v-Neg-T
               /  \
             VP    t_v
            /  \
          Obj   t_v
```

Miyagawa's argument here is that either the subject or object can be moved to Spec,TP in (67), because these two phrases become equidistant from T, as a consequence of overt V-to-T raising.[18] In his analysis, overt verb raising to T should take place in an unmarked case where no adverbial particle intervenes between the verb and tense—contrary to the proposal made by Sakai (1998) and Aoyagi (1998).[19]

Miyagawa also observes that *zen'in* takes scope over negation even when an object is scrambled to the clause-initial position in an emphatic construction in which the verb is separated from tense by an emphatic particle such as *mo*.

(68) Sensei-o_i   zen'in-ga t_i seme-mo   si-nakat-ta.
     teacher-ACC all-NOM   blame-even   do-NEG-PAST
     'The teacher, all did not even blame.'
     *not > all, all > not

He argues that in (68), the subject falls outside the scope of negation, because it undergoes A-movement to Spec,TP, whereas the object undergoes A'-scrambling rather than A-scrambling—just like a case in which an object is moved long distance.

(69) Syukudai-o_i   zen'in-ga [sensei-ga t_i das-u   to]
     homework-ACC all-NOM   teacher-NOM   assign-PRES COMP
     omowa-nakat-ta.
     think-NEG-PAST
     'Homework, all did not think that the teacher would assign.'
     *not > all, all > not

In Miyagawa's analysis, overt verb raising does not take place in (68), so the subject and the object are not equidistant from T. In this case, the subject located higher than the object must be raised to Spec,TP by A-movement. The scope fact in (68) suggests that head raising should be blocked by emphatic particles.

Kishimoto (2005, 2007) provides a different type of argument to the effect that overt raising of a predicate with an adverbial particle is not possible. His argument is based on the fact that whereas the main verb allows the suffixation of an adverbial particle, the sentential negator *nai* 'not' does not.[20]

(70) a. John-ga   hon-o   yoma-nakat-ta.
        John-NOM book-ACC read-NEG-PAST
        'John did not read books.'
    b. John-ga   hon-o   yomi-mo si-ta/si-nakat-ta.
        John-NOM book-ACC read-also do-PAST/do-NEG-PAST
        'John also read/did not read books.'
    c. *John-ga   hon-o   yoma-naku-mo   at-ta.
        John-NOM book-ACC read-NEG-also   be-PAST
        'John also did not read books.'

Assuming that an adverbial particle is head-adjoined to a lexical head on its right, he suggests that a particle cannot be embedded inside a complex lexical head, because it has the property of marking the right-boundary of a head. (71b) illustrates that a complex head containing an adverbial particle inside is unacceptable.

(71) a. kaigai-mo   b. *kaigai-mo-ryokoo
        overseas-also   overseas-also-travel
        'overseas also'   'overseas also travel'

Kishimoto (2005, 2007) maintains, just like Miyagawa (2001), that an adverbial particle cannot occur to the right of a moving head. The reasoning here is different, however, because it is viewed that the overt head raising of a head with an adverbial particle to a higher head ends up with an illegitimate complex head inside which the particle is embedded. The contrast in acceptability between (70a,b) and (70c) follows if the negative head *nai* undergoes overt head raising but a verbal head does not. Kishimoto claims then that whereas the "negative-tense" sequence in (70a) is created via overt head raising, the "verb-tense" sequence in (63a) is not, as illustrated in (72).

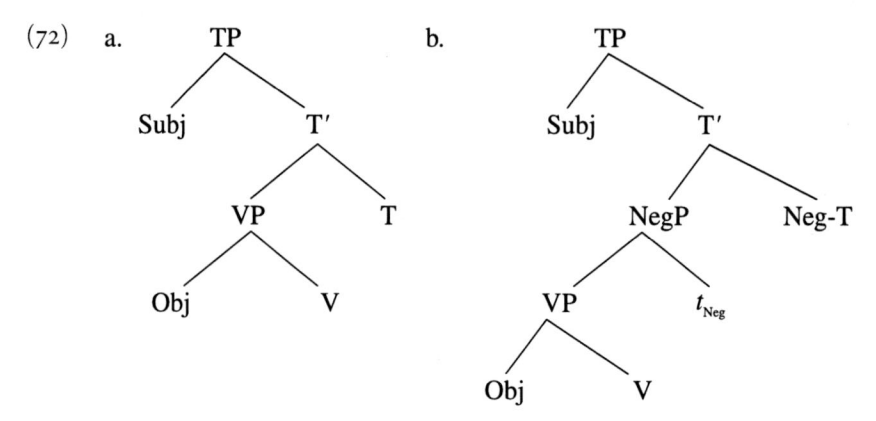

(72) a.   TP   b.   TP
            /   \   /   \
         Subj   T'   Subj   T'
                 /   \   /   \
               VP   T   NegP   Neg-T
              / \   /   \
            Obj   V   VP t_{Neg}
                                       / \
                                     Obj   V

In Kishimoto's analysis, the dummy verb support found in (63b) above is motivated for morphological reasons: The dummy verb *suru* is inserted to the front of tense in (63b) for supporting morphologically dependent tense separated from the main verb by an adverbial particle.

Kishimoto (2005, 2007) argues that the presence of negative head raising can be assessed by the extent of the scope of negation. In Japanese, negative scope extends over TP in an ordinary clause, so no subject-object asymmetry is observed in regard to NPI licensing, as exemplified in (73).

(73) a. Dare-mo hon-o yoma-nakat-ta.
 anyone book-ACC read-NEG-PAST
 'No one read the book.'
 b. John-ga nani-mo yoma-nakat-ta.
 John-NOM anything read-NEG-PAST
 'John did not read anything.'

The English negative element *not* does not undergo overt verb raising, and we observe a subject-object asymmetry in the licensing of NPI elements, as shown in (74).

(74) a. *Anyone did not read the book.
 b. John did not read anything.

Kishimoto suggests that the expansion of negative scope correlates with the possibility of overt head raising, in the light of the following examples, where the object NPI, but not the subject NPI, can be licensed by *nai*.

(75) a. John-ga dare-mo kyoositu-ni haire-naku si-ta.
 John-NOM anyone classroom-in enter-NEG do-PAST
 'John made anyone unable to enter the room.'
 b. *Dare-mo Mary-o kyoositu-ni haire-naku si-ta.
 anyone Mary-ACC classroom-in enter-NEG do-PAST
 'Anyone made Mary unable to enter the room.'

In the causative construction in (75), the scope of negation does not extend over the entire clause. In this type of construction, it is possible to add an adverbial particle to the right of *nai*.

(76) John-ga Mary-o kyoositu-ni haire-naku-mo si-ta.
 John-NOM Mary-ACC classroom-into enter-NEG-also do-PAST
 'John also made no one able to enter the room.'

The subject-object asymmetry in (75) can then be attributed to the absence of Neg-raising, which is derived from T's inability to attract the negative head *nai* (by virtue of the intervening verb *suru* 'make'). Kishimoto further suggests that the negative head *nai* undergoes overt raising in a sentence such as (70a), given that it counts as a light functional predicate (i.e., a sentential negator), in an analogous way to an English light verb *have*, which serves as an aspectual verb.

(77) a. John {has not been/*does not have been} to Paris.
b. John {did not have/*had not} his students examined by the doctor.

In English, a light verb, but not a main verb, is amenable to head raising. If this difference extends to Japanese, it is expected that in Japanese, just as in English, overt head raising should not apply to main verbs. In effect, the fact that main verbs tolerate the addition of an adverbial particle to their right suggests that they do not undergo overt verb raising.

Sakai (1998) and Aoyagi (1998) maintain that an adverbial particle does not block head raising and that the unmarked verbal sequence of "verb-tense" is formed via morphological merger without head raising. However, some different proposals on the formation of a "verb-tense" sequence are also available. Miyagawa (2001), assuming that an adverbial particle blocks head raising, claims that the "verb-tense" sequence is created via overt head raising to T. However, Kishimoto (2005, 2007) holds that the overt raising of a head plus adverbial particle results in unacceptability and suggests that because the verb allows an adverbial particle to be placed on its right, the ordinary "verb-tense" sequence should be formed without recourse to syntactic head raising.

Although much more work needs to be done to resolve the problem on how verbal complexes are formed, there is one piece of empirical evidence suggesting that the "verb-tense" sequence can be formed irrespective of whether syntactic verb raising takes place. To see this, consider (78), which comprises the idiomatic adjectival expression *warikire-nai* 'not satisfied', which takes either a dative-nominative or a nominative-nominative case pattern.[21]

(78) a. John(-ni)-wa   sono-kettei-ga   warikire-na-i.
       John-DAT-TOP that-decision-NOM satisfied-NEG-PRES
       'John is not satisfied with that decision.'
    b. John(-ni)-wa   sono-kettei-ga   warikire-naku-mo ar-u.
       John-DAT-TOP that-decision-NOM satisfied-NEG-also be-PRES
       'John is also not satisfied with that decision.'

Example (78b) shows that the negative expression *nai* in *warikire-nai* behaves just like an ordinary adjectival predicate, in that it allows an emphatic particle to be inserted to its right. Notably, in this case, negative *nai* does not extend its scope over the entire clause, as shown in (79).

(79) a. John(-ni)-wa   sono-kettei-ga   sukosimo/tittomo warikire-na-i.
       John-DAT-TOP that-decision-NOM at.all/in.the.least   satisfied-NEG-PRES
       'John is not satisfied with that decision at all/in the least.'
    b. ?*Dare-mo sono-kettei-ga   warikire-na-i.
       anyone   that-decision-NOM satisfied-NEG-PRES
       'Anyone is not satisfied with that decision.'

The NPI in subject position is not licensed, as shown in (79b), whereas the occurrence of NPI adverbs like *sukosimo/tittomo* is legitimate in (79a), which indicates that *nai* does not take scope over TP even though it bears syntactic scope. The scope fact here suggests then that the "negative-tense" sequence in (78a)—unlike the same "negative-tense" sequence in (70a)—is formed with no overt head raising.

The data in (79) imply that syntactic head raising is not a prerequisite for agglutinative morphology of verbal complexes and that the ordinary "verb-tense" sequence could be created with no syntactic verb raising. Note that in (63b), the verb tolerates the addition of an emphatic particle to its right. This fact suggests that overt verb raising should not be induced for the formation of the ordinary "verb-tense" sequence in (63a).

5.4 Implications for the General Theory

The central issue on verb raising in Japanese is the question of how verbal clusters are formed. Japanese is an agglutinative language, where discrete verbal heads are coalesced into a single complex predicate morphologically. This is one of the notable typological properties that distinguish Japanese from English. In the early days of Japanese generative grammar, it has commonly been assumed that syntactic verb raising is instantiated to produce agglutinative morphology of verbal complexes. More recently, however, this assumption is called into question—especially with the advent of Distributive Morphology, which does not posit a strict syntax-morphology correspondence by allowing late insertion of lexical items (see Halle and Marantz 1993). Some of the recent works on verb raising in Japanese reflect this trend and address the question of whether verbal clusters are formed via syntactic head raising. The empirical data that are taken to diagnose verb position do not necessarily point to the same conclusion. If, however, the suggestion made at the end of the previous section is correct—that is, the suggestion that morphological verbal complexes can be created without regard to syntactic verb raising—then we can say that the morphophonological organization of verbal complexes does not have to reflect their syntactic structure strictly. Furthermore, if verb raising has syntactic consequences, as discussed in a number of works mentioned in this chapter, it must constitute part of the grammar of syntax (despite some recent theoretical skepticisms raised on syntactic head raising). Although further research is necessary to find out the exact status of verb raising in Japanese, the verb raising dispute, once it is resolved, would provide us with a clue to the proper understanding of the mechanisms of verb raising implemented in Universal Grammar.

NOTES FOR CHAPTER 5

Part of the material in this chapter was presented at the Workshop on Linguistic Theory and the Japanese Language, held at Harvard University on July 29–30, 2005. I am grateful to Shigeru Miyagawa, Mamoru Saito, Heejeong Ko, Koichi Takezawa, Yusuke Kubota, Elizabeth Smith, Mark Campana, and anonymous reviewers for helpful comments and suggestions. Needless to say, I am solely responsible for any remaining inadequacies and errors.

1. On the split *v*P hypothesis, the existence of V-to-*v* raising is plausible, and there might be verb raising below *v*P. Nevertheless, the discussion in this chapter is limited to the issue pertaining to V-to-T raising (and further conceivable T-to-C raising). There is some issue concerning V-to-*v* raising, since Chomsky (1995, 2000, 2001) assumes that V-to-*v* raising is universally implemented, but Fukui and Takano (1998) argue that Japanese does not have V-to-*v* raising. In Japanese, there is also an issue concerning verbal noun constructions. Saito and Hoshi (2000) and Kishimoto (2001) suggest the possibility of covert raising of verbal nouns to the light verb *suru* (see also Kageyama 1999). Fukui and Sakai (2003) put forth an alternative view that dispenses with this covert raising.

2. For discussion on verb raising in European languages, see Pollock 1989, Chomsky 1991, Holmberg 1986, 1999, and others.

3. Otani and Whitman (1991) do not represent the embedded clause, but I follow Williams's representation more closely on this point.

4. Koizumi (1995, 2000) adds a numeral quantifier at the end of each conjunct to avoid attaching the coordinator *to* to a case marker directly, which is illicit for an independent reason.

5. Sakai (1998) and Aoyagi (1998) reach virtually the same conclusion independently.

6. Here, Aoyagi (1998) is more specific than Sakai (1998), in claiming that adverbial particles are nonprojected heads (clitics) in the sense of Chomsky (1995).

7. Hoji (1998) suggests that a comparative ellipsis such as (i) exhibits properties analogous to VP-ellipsis.

> (i) Iintyoo-wa   [subete-no nihonzin huuhu-ni   yori]-mo sakini
> chairperson-TOP all-GEN   Japanese couple-DAT than-also early
> subete-no amerikazin huuhu-ni   onazi gakusei-o
> all-GEN   American   couple-DAT same student-ACC
> suisen-s-ase-ta.
> recommend-CAUSE-PAST
> 'The chairperson made every American couple recommend the same student earlier than every Japanese couple.'

He argues that the comparative construction in (i) can have the same sloppy reading as does the English VP-ellipsis construction in (ii).

> (ii) Every Japanese couple recommended the same student; and every American couple did too.

He does not suggest that (i) involves VP-gapping, but (ii) shows that Japanese has a construction that behaves more like VP-ellipsis than the null object construction. For the details of the analysis, see Hoji 1998.

8. If the order of the two phrases is reversed, the dative phrase must be adjoined to the accusative phrase after the latter is scrambled to the front, because Takano (2002) allows only the left-adjunction to a nominal via oblique movement.

9. In (46), *naze* can be placed before or after the object *sono-hito-o* without incurring an ECP effect. According to Takano (2002), both orders can be derived in the following way. First, the object to which *naze* is adjoined is moved out of the island, which incurs only a Subjacency violation. If *naze* is scrambled out and adjoined to TP after this movement, the "*naze*-object" order is produced. Note that this scrambling operation is necessary because an adverbial can intervene between the two phrases. If the object is further scrambled across *naze*, the "object-*naze*" order is created.

10. For the present purposes, it is sufficient to say that if *naze* is not the closest potential binder to c-command its trace, an ECP violation ensues. It should be noted, however, that more articulated theoretical assumptions need to be introduced in order to fully explain why an ECP effect emerges when *naze* occurs to the left of the object in (47b). See Saito 1994.

11. Takano's analysis provides an account for the facts regarding (54) but leaves the unacceptability of the coordinate construction in (21) unaccounted for. If the judgment is as reported by Koizumi (2000), it is necessary to stipulate some conditions that make (21) unacceptable. Although Takano does not provide an account, he reports that (21) sounds better than (22), though degraded, and it becomes fully acceptable when the embedded subject is replaced with *pro*.

12. In effect, Koizumi (2000) claims that complex verb formation, which is highly productive in Japanese, takes place in overt syntax.

13. Obviously, one inherent problem with this analysis is that an unusual constituent can be formed with the particle *ka* 'or'.

(iii) Taroo-ga [[Hanako-ni ringo-o 3-tu] ka [Kumiko-ni banana-o
Taroo-NOM Hanako-DAT apple-ACC 3-CL or Kumiko-DAT banana-ACC
2-hon] (ka)] age-ta (koto).
2-CL or give-PAST (fact)
Lit. 'Taroo gave three apples to Hanako or two bananas to Kumiko.'

The particle *ka* carries quantificational force like *mo*. In Fukui and Sakai's analysis then, the coordinate structure in (iii) can never be formed in the syntax, and hence should be excluded in the same way as (57a). However, the fact of the matter is that (iii) is acceptable.

14. Notice that the pseudo-cleft construction involving an unusual constituent poses a problem on the PF reduction analysis, because PF merger should not apply to the formation of a cleft sentence such as (iv).

(iv) Taroo-ga yomu-yooni nessin-ni susume-ta-no-wa Hanako-ni
Taroo-NOM read-COMP earnestly recommend-PAST-NL-TOP Hanako-DAT
Russell-no hon-o (san-satu) da.
Russell-GEN book-ACC three-CL COP
Lit. 'It is Russell's (three) books to Hanako that Taroo earnestly recommended to read.'

Pseudo-clefting undoubtedly has an interpretive effect, because focus is separated from presupposition. This means that unusual cleft formation cannot be accounted for by appealing to the PF merger that takes place after PF predicate deletion. Fukui and Sakai (2003) argue, however, that the elements in the focus position of the pseudo-cleft construction need not be reanalyzed into a constituent, because the "apparent" unusual constituent in focus position is created by virtue of topicalization of a nominalized predicate, as illustrated in (v).

(v) [Ringo-o tabe-ta-no]$_i$-wa Taroo-mo t_i da.
    apple-ACC eat-PAST-NL-TOP Taroo-also COP
    'It was also Taroo that ate apples.'

In their analysis, the elements in the focus position do not undergo movement, so there is no reason why they should form a syntactic constituent. If they do not form a constituent, it is not surprising that the sentence is well formed even if PF merger cannot apply to the elements in the focus position. Fukui and Sakai's claim here is that two different analyses apply to the same type of phenomenon, but this seems undesirable. Their analysis predicts that the coordinate structure of unusual constituents will never be created in the focus position of a cleft sentence. However, this prediction is not borne out, as the following sentence is acceptable.

(vi) Taroo-ga age-ta no-wa [[Mary-ni banana-o 2-hon] to
     Taroo-NOM give-PAST NM-TOP Mary-DAT banana-ACC 2-CL and
     [Jane-ni ringo-o 3-ko]] da.
     Jane-DAT apple-ACC 3-CL COP
     Lit. 'It was [[to Mary, two bananas] and [to Jane, three apples]] that Taroo gave.'

According to Fukui and Sakai, clefting involves predicate nominalization, but as can be clearly seen in (vi), the moved material contains tense, which means that clefting should involve TP-nominalization (or sentential nominalization). If so, the unusual constituent in (vi) must somehow be moved out of the clause for the nominalized constituent to be fronted, contrary to their claim.

15. Heejeong Ko (pers. comm.) calls this fact to my attention. In Fukushima 2003, some examples in which an adverb like *kinoo* 'yesterday' occurs in an unusual constituent are judged to be acceptable. As Fukushima himself acknowledges, native speakers do not necessarily agree with his judgments, however.

16. In the right-node-raising construction, a slight pause is placed at the right boundary of each constituent out of which the verb is extracted. No such pause is necessary in the case of the unusual coordinate structure. Koizumi (2000) observes that the clausemate condition does not apply to the right-node-raising construction.

17. Fukui and Sakai (2003) suggest that Japanese does not have overt verb raising (in narrow syntax). Takano (2002) holds that verb raising does not take place in Japanese.

18. This analysis assumes that the object is moved without going through *v*P. Note, however, that if *v*P constitutes a phase that an argument needs to move through, the object can be moved across the subject even if the verb does not raise to T (see Chomsky 2000, 2001).

19. Ishihara (2001) argues that Miyagawa's analysis can capture the facts of nuclear stress in Japanese—the central prosodic stress assigned to sentences in neutral contexts—given Cinque's (1993) theory of nuclear stress, which says that nuclear stress falls on the mostly

embedded XP in a clause. To be more specific, Ishihara claims that the fact that nuclear stress falls on preverbal elements—but not the verb—follows from Miyagawa's analysis.

(vii) a. Taroo-ga **hon**-o kat-ta.
Taroo-NOM book-ACC buy-PAST
'Taroo bought a book.'
b. Hon-o$_i$ **Taroo**-ga t_i katta.
book-ACC Taroo-NOM buy-PAST
'A book, Taroo bought.'

In (viia), the object is the lowest XP (regardless of whether the verb moves up to a higher position), so the object is assigned nuclear stress. When the object is scrambled to the clause front, the subject receives nuclear stress. Ishihara suggests that this stress assignment can be accounted for on the assumption that the subject stays in Spec,vP, while the verb raises to T.

20. This does not mean that the addition of an adverbial particle to the negative head *nai* is always impossible. There are in fact cases in which *nai* can be followed by an adverbial particle, as illustrated in (viii).

(viii) Ano-ryoori-wa mibae-ga waru-i-dake-de-naku oisiku-naku-mo ar-u.
that-dish-TOP looking-NOM bad-PRES-only-NEG delicious-NEG-also be-PRES
'That dish not only looks bad, but also not delicious.'

In a case like (viii), however, the negative expression *nai* does not function as a sentential negator, as can be confirmed by the fact that it does not license any type of NPI.

(ix) *Ano-ryoori-wa mibae-ga waru-i-dake-de-naku sukosimo/tittomo
that-dish-TOP looking-NOM bad-PRES-only-NEG at.all/in.the.least
oisiku-naku-mo ar-u.
delicious-NEG-also be-PRES
'That dish not only looks bad, but also not delicious at all/in the least.'

The negative head's inability to license NPIs suggests that it counts as a negative affix akin to *un-* in *uninteresting* in English. This use of the negative element *nai* is not relevant to the present discussion.

21. The verbal predicate *warikira-nai* 'not decide', which takes a "nominative-accusative" case pattern, behaves like an ordinary negative expression. In the first place, *nai* in *warikira-nai* does not allow the addition of an adverbial particle on its right.

(x) *John-wa sono-koto-o konna-huu-ni warikira-naku-mo ar-u.
John-TOP that-matter-ACC this-way-in decide-NEG-also be-PRES
'John does not also decide on that matter in this way.'

In the second, the scope of negation spreads over the entire clause, as indicated in (xi).

(xi) Dare-mo sono-koto-o konna-huu-ni warikira-na-i.
anyone that-matter-ACC this-way-in decide-NEG-PRES
'No one decides on that matter in this way.'

These data show that the conditions restricting the idiomatic "adjectival" predicate *warikire-nai* do not apply to the "verbal" predicate *warikira-nai* (and its variants) taking an ordinary nominative-accusative case pattern.

REFERENCES

Aoyagi, Hiroshi. 1998. On the nature of particles in Japanese and its theoretical implications. Doctoral dissertation, University of Southern California, Los Angeles.

Carlson, Greg. 1987. Same and different: Some consequences of syntax and semantics. *Linguistics and Philosophy* 10:531–565.

Chomsky, Noam. 1991. Some notes on economy of derivation and representation. In *Principles and parameters in comparative grammar*, ed. Robert Freidin, 417–454. Cambridge, Mass.: MIT Press.

Chomsky, Noam. 1995. *The Minimalist Program*. Cambridge, Mass.: MIT Press.

Chomsky, Noam. 2000. Minimalist inquiries: The framework. In *Step by step: Essays on minimalist syntax in honor of Howard Lasnik*, ed. Roger Martin, David Michaels, and Juan Uriagereka, 89–155. Cambridge, Mass.: MIT Press.

Chomsky, Noam. 2001. Derivation by phase. In *Ken Hale: A life in language*, ed. Michael Kenstowicz, 1–52. Cambridge, Mass.: MIT Press.

Cinque, Guglielmo. 1993. A null theory of phrase and compound stress. *Linguistic Inquiry* 24:239–298.

Fukui, Naoki, and Hiromu Sakai. 2003. The visibility guideline for functional categories: Verb raising in Japanese and related issues. *Lingua* 113:321–375.

Fukui, Naoki, and Yuji Takano. 1998. Symmetry in syntax: Merge and Demerge. *Journal of East Asian Linguistics* 7:27–86.

Fukushima, Kazuhiko. 2003. Verb-raising and numeral classifiers in Japanese: Incompatible bedfellows. *Journal of East Asian Linguistics* 12:313–347.

Halle, Morris, and Alec Marantz. 1993. Distributed morphology and the pieces of inflection. In *The view from Building 20: Essays in linguistics in honor of Sylvain Bromberger*, ed. Kenneth Hale and Samuel Jay Keyser, 111–176. Cambridge, Mass.: MIT Press.

Hoji, Hajime. 1995. Demonstrative binding and principle B. In *Proceedings of NELS* 25, ed. Jill N. Beckman, 255–271. Amherst, Mass.: GLSA Publications.

Hoji, Hajime. 1998. Null objects and sloppy identity in Japanese. *Linguistic Inquiry* 29:127–152.

Holmberg, Anders. 1986. Word order and syntactic features in the Scandinavian languages and English. Doctoral dissertation, University of Stockholm.

Holmberg, Anders. 1999. Remarks on Holmberg's generalization. *Studia Linguistica* 53:1–39.

Ishihara, Shinichiro. 2001. Stress, focus, and scrambling in Japanese. In *MITWPL 39: A few from Building E39: Papers in syntax, semantics, and their interfaces*, ed. Elena Guerzoni and Ora Matushansky, 151–185. Cambridge, Mass.: MIT Working Papers in Linguistics.

Kageyama, Taro. 1999. Word formation. In *The handbook of Japanese linguistics*, ed. Natsuko Tsujimura, 297–325. Oxford: Blackwell.

Kayne, Richard. 1994. *The antisymmetry of syntax*. Cambridge, Mass.: MIT Press.

Kishimoto, Hideki. 2001. Binding of indeterminate pronouns and clause structure in Japanese. *Linguistic Inquiry* 32:597–633.
Kishimoto, Hideki. 2005. *Toogokoozoo-to bunpookankei* [Syntactic structure and grammatical relations]. Tokyo: Kurosio.
Kishimoto, Hideki. 2007. Negative scope and head raising in Japanese. *Lingua* 117: 247–288.
Koizumi, Masatoshi 1995. Phrase structure in minimalist syntax. Doctoral dissertation, MIT, Cambridge, Mass.
Koizumi, Masatoshi. 2000. String vacuous overt verb raising. *Journal of East Asian Linguistics* 9:227–285.
Kuno, Susumu. 1978. Japanese: A characteristic OV language. In *Syntactic typology*, ed. Winfred P. Lehmann, 57–138. Austin: University of Texas Press.
Marantz, Alec. 1989. Clitics and phrase structure. In *Alternative conceptions of phrase structure*, ed. Mark Baltin and Anthony Kroch, 99–116. Chicago: University of Chicago Press.
McCawley, James. 1982. Parentheticals and discontinuous constituent structures. *Linguistic Inquiry* 13:91–106.
McCawley, James. 1987. Some additional evidence for discontinuity. In *Discontinuous constituency* (Syntax and Semantics 20), ed. Geoffrey J. Huck and Almerindo E. Ojeda, 185–200. San Diego, Calif.: Academic Press.
Miyagawa, Shigeru. 2001. The EPP, scrambling, and *wh*-in-situ. In *Ken Hale: A life in language*, ed. Michael Kenstowicz, 293–338. Cambridge, Mass.: MIT Press.
Müller, Gereon. 1996. A constraint on remnant movement. *Natural Language & Linguistic Theory* 14:355–407.
Otani, Kazuyo, and John Whitman. 1991. V-raising and VP-ellipsis. *Linguistic Inquiry* 22:345–358.
Pollock, Jean-Yves. 1989. Verb movement, Universal Grammar, and the structure of IP. *Linguistic Inquiry* 20:365–424.
Reinhart, Tanya. 1983. *Anaphora and semantic interpretation*. Chicago: University of Chicago Press.
Sag, Ivan. 1976. Deletion and logical form. Doctoral dissertation, MIT, Cambridge, Mass.
Saito, Mamoru. 1989. Scrambling as semantically vacuous A'-movement. In *Alternative conceptions of phrase structure*, ed. Mark Baltin and Anthony Kroch, 182–200. Chicago: University of Chicago Press.
Saito, Mamoru. 1992. Long distance scrambling in Japanese. *Journal of East Asian Linguistics* 1:69–118.
Saito, Mamoru. 1994. Additional-*wh* effects and the adjunction site theory. *Journal of East Asian Linguistics* 3:195–240.
Saito, Mamoru, and Hiroto Hoshi. 2000. The Japanese light verb constructions and the Minimalist Program. In *Step by step: Essays on minimalist syntax in honor of Howard Lasnik*, ed. Roger Martin, David Michaels, and Juan Uriagereka, 261–295. Cambridge, Mass.: MIT Press.
Sakai, Hiromu. 1998. Feature checking and morphological merger. *Japanese/Korean Linguistics* 8, ed. David J. Silva, 189–201. Stanford, Calif.: CSLI Publications.
Sohn, Keun-Won. 1994. Adjunction to argument, free ride and a minimalist program. *MITWPL 24: Formal approaches to Japanese linguistics 1*, ed. Masatoshi Koizumi and Hiroyuki Ura, 315–334. Cambridge, Mass.: MIT Working Papers in Linguistics.
Takano, Yuji. 2002. Surprising constituents. *Journal of East Asian Linguistics* 11:243–301.

Ueyama, Ayumi. 2003. Two types of scrambling constructions in Japanese. In *Anaphora: A reference guide*, ed. Andrew Barss, 23–104. Oxford: Blackwell.

Watanabe, Akira. 1992. Subjacency and S-structure movement of *wh*-in-situ. *Journal of East Asian Linguistics* 1:255–291.

Williams, Edwin. 1977. Discourse and Logical Form. *Linguistic Inquiry* 8:101–139.

CHAPTER 6

NOMINATIVE OBJECT

MASATOSHI KOIZUMI

6.1 INTRODUCTION

Japanese is a nominative-accusative language. Subjects of both transitive and intransitive verbs are usually case-marked in nominative, in contrast to objects of transitive verbs, which are typically marked with accusative. This is exemplified in (1).

(1) a. Masami-ga   ano kabin-o   wat-ta.
       Masami-NOM   that vase-ACC break(transitive)-PAST
       'Masami broke the flower vase.'
    b. Ano kabin-ga   ware-ta.
       that vase-NOM break(intransitive)-PAST
       'The flower vase broke.'

There are Japanese sentences, however, that implement what appears to be an ergative case pattern (Kuno 1973, Kuroda 1978, among others). Consider the following examples:

(2) a. Hiromi-ga   syuwa-ga   deki-ru.
       Hiromi-NOM sign language-NOM   capable-PRES
       'Hiromi can use a sign language.'
    b. Hiromi-ni   syuwa-ga   deki-ru.
       Hiromi-DAT sign language-NOM   capable-PRES
       'Hiroko can use a sign language.'

The objects in (2) are marked by the nominative case-marker *-ga* rather than the accusative case-marker *-o*. Sentences like (2) are referred to as the nominative object construction. The subject of the nominative object construction may appear either with the nominative case-marker *-ga* as in (2a) or with the dative postposition *-ni* as in (2b). Similar constructions are found in many languages of the world such as Hindi, Icelandic, Kannada, Korean, Russian, and Tibetan, among others, and have raised a number of questions interesting both descriptively and theoretically. In this chapter, I summarize major grammatical properties of the nominative object construction in Japanese, present formal analyses to them, and consider their theoretical implications.

6.2 Core Data

Let us briefly overview, in this section, some of the fundamental properties of the nominative object construction in Japanese.

6.2.1 The Nominative Object Is Not Subject

In the nominative object construction, the logical subject (experiencer or agent), which is marked either dative or nominative, functions as the grammatical subject, and the nominative object, which is a logical object (typically theme or patient), has no subject properties other than the nominative case marking (Kuno 1973, Shibatani 1977, Takezawa 1987, among others). This can be shown by such standard operational tests as subject honorification, reflexive binding, arbitrary *pro*, and so forth.

One of the most frequently used operational tests for subjecthood in Japanese is subject honorification. Subject honorification is a phenomenon in which a certain marking on the predicate indicates the speaker's sense of respect toward the referent of the grammatical subject of that predicate. In a subject honorification sentence, the intended target of the speaker's respect must be the referent of the grammatical subject, as in (3a), and when it is not, the sentence is judged deviant, as in (3b).

(3) a. Tigusa-sensei-ga   gakuseitati-o o-yobi-ni natta.
       Chigusa-prof.-NOM students-ACC called (SUB-HON)
       'Prof. Chigusa called students.'
   b. #Gakuseitati-ga Tigusa-sensei-o   o-yobi-ni natta.
       students-NOM Chigusa-prof.-ACC called (SUB-HON)
       'Students called Prof. Chigusa.'

If the predicate of a nominative object construction assumes the subject honorific form, the target of honorification is the experiencer/agent argument rather than the nominative object, as shown in (4) (Shibatani 1977).[1]

(4) Subject honorification
   a. Tigusa-sensei-ga   gakuseitati-ga o-suki-da.
      Chigusa-prof.-NOM students-NOM like (SUB-HON)
      'Prof. Chigusa likes students.'
   b. #Gakuseitati-ga Tigusa-sensei-ga   o-suki-da.
      students-NOM Chigusa-prof.-NOM like (SUB-HON)
      'Students like Prof. Chigusa.'
      (Infelicitous under the intended interpretation)

This suggests that in the nominative object construction, the logical subject functions as grammatical subject but the logical object in the nominative case does not.

Another diagnostic for identifying grammatical subjects in Japanese involves the reflexive anaphor *zibun* 'self', which generally takes a subject as its antecedent, as shown in (5) (cf. Kuno 1973, Harada 1976).

(5) Masami$_1$-ga   Hiromi$_2$-o   zibun$_{1/*2}$-no heya-de hometa.
    Masami-NOM Hiromi-ACC self-GEN   room-in praised
    'Masami$_1$ praised Hiromi in self's$_{1/*2}$ own room.'

In the nominative object construction, it is the experiencer/agent argument rather than the nominative object that functions as the antecedent of *zibun* (Shibatani 1977):

(6) Reflexive binding
    Masami$_1$-ga   Hiromi$_2$-ga zibun$_{1/*2}$-no kurasu-de itiban suki-da.
    Masami-NOM Hiromi-NOM self-GEN   class-in   best   like-COP
    'Masami$_1$ likes Hiromi$_2$ the best in self's$_{1/*2}$ class.'

A third grammatical phenomenon sensitive to grammatical subjecthood is the interpretation of unpronounced arguments. A phonologically null subject of certain-type nonfinite clauses can have an "arbitrary interpretation," but it is not possible with a null object (Saito 1982, Kuroda 1983, Kageyama 1993). Thus the subject in (7a) can be interpreted as "people in general" (= arbitrary interpretation), whereas the same is not possible with the null object in (7b): (7b) only has an interpretation in which the null object refers to some specific entity.

(7) a. (subject) kodomo-o sodateru no-wa   muzukashii.
             child-ACC raise   that-TOP difficult
       'To raise a child is difficult.'
    b. Oya-ga   (object) sodateru no-wa   muzukashii.
       parent-NOM   raise   that-TOP difficult
       'For parents to raise (a child) is difficult.'

The examples in (8) demonstrate that it is the logical subject rather than the nominative object that counts as subject in the nominative object construction in this regard.

(8) a. (logical subject) sampo-ga suki-na no-wa ii-koto-da.
　　　　　　　　　　　　walk-NOM like-COP that-TOP good-thing-COP
　　　'To like taking a walk is a good thing.'
　　b. *Masami-ga (nominative object) suki-na no-wa ii-koto-da.
　　　Masami-NOM　　　　　　　　　　　like-COP that-TOP good-thing-COP
　　　Lit. 'For Masami to like is a good thing.'

The three tests above all suggest that in the nominative object construction, the logical subject functions as the grammatical subject, but the logical object in the nominative case has none of the subject properties except for the case marking. It is thus safe to conclude that the nominative object is not a grammatical subject.

6.2.2 The Nominative Object Is Grammatical Object

Let us now turn to some diagnostic tests of objecthood. One such test involves the formal noun *koto*. The formal noun *koto* is devoid of its historically original meaning 'fact' and can be inserted only in the surface direct-object position, as shown in (9) (Tsunoda 1991, Kishimoto 2004).

(9) a. John-ga　Mary(-no-koto)-o　damasi-ta.
　　　John-NOM Mary-GEN-fact-ACC deceive-past
　　　'John deceived Mary.'
　　b. John(*-no-koto)-ga Mary-o　damasi-ta.
　　　John-gen-fact-NOM Mary-ACC deceive-PAST
　　　'John deceived Mary.'
　　c. Mary(*-no-koto)-ga John-ni-yotte damas-are-ta.
　　　Mary-GEN-fact-NOM John-by　　　deceive-PASS-PAST
　　　'Mary was deceived by John.'

In the nominative object construction, the nominative object may be accompanied by the formal noun *koto*, but the logical subject cannot.

(10) a. John-ga　Mary(-no-koto)-ga　suki-da.
　　　John-NOM Mary-GEN-fact-NOM fond-PRES
　　　'John is fond of Mary.'
　　b. John(*-no-koto)-ga Mary-ga　suki-da.[2]
　　　John-gen-fact-NOM Mary-NOM deceive-PRES
　　　'John is fond of Mary.' (Kishimoto 2004)

This is a clear indication that the nominative object has an object property.
　　Another operational test for objecthood is concerned with so-called double *-o* constraint (Harada 1973, Inoue 1976). In Japanese, multiple occurrences of direct objects marked with accusative case are prohibited. As shown in (11), the verb

su(-ru) 'do' allows either *Mootuaruto* 'Mozart' or *ensoo* 'play' to be marked with accusative case, but not both.

(11) a. John-ga   Mootuaruto-no ensoo-o   si-ta.
        John-NOM Mozart-GEN   play-ACC do-PAST
        'John played Mozart.'
     b. John-ga   Mootuaruto-o ensoo-si-ta.
        John-NOM Mozart-ACC   play-do-PAST
        'John played Mozart.'
     c. *John-ga   Mootuaruto-o ensoo-o   si-ta.
        John-NOM Mozart-NOM   play-ACC do-PAST
        'John played Mozart.'

Although the constraint responsible for the ungrammaticality of (11c) is often assumed to derive from a ban on the duplication of accusative case marking, it is in fact a more general ban on the duplication of direct objects (Shibatani 1973, Kageyama 1999, Kishimoto 2004). Thus, the same constraint applies to the predicate *deki(-ru)* 'can-do', which is a suppletive form of *su(-ru)* 'do' and *rare* 'can', and takes a nominative object, as illustrated in (12).

(12) a. John-ga/-ni   Mootuaruto-no ensoo-ga deki-ru.
        John-NOM/-DAT Mozart-GEN   play-NOM can.do-PRES
        'John can play Mozart.'
     b. John-ga/-ni   Mootuaruto-ga ensoo-deki-ru.
        John-NOM/-DAT Mozart-NOM   play-can.do-PRES
        'John can play Mozart.'
     c. *John-ga/-ni   Mootuaruto-ga ensoo-ga deki-ru.
        John-NOM/-DAT Mozart-NOM   play-NOM can.do-PRES
        'John can play Mozart.'   (Kishimoto 2004)

Given that the unacceptability of (12c) is on a par with (11c), and because there is no general ban on double-*ga* or double nominative case marking in Japanese, the deviance of (12c) must stem from a violation of a grammatical constraint that restricts the number of direct objects to one per clause. If this reasoning is on the right track, (12c) is taken to be evidence that the nominative object is a direct object (Kishimoto 2004).

To sum up, the two tests for objecthood as well as the three diagnostics for subjecthood all point to the conclusion that the nominative object is undoubtedly a grammatical object.[3]

6.2.3 The Nominative Object Construction Is Neither the Passive nor Major Subject Construction

The nominative object construction is superficially similar to the passive construction in that they both exhibit the nominative-dative case pattern. The two constructions are distinct, however. One difference has to do with thematic relation. Unlike in the nominative object construction, where logical subject (experiencer/agent) is the grammatical subject, in the passive construction, it is the logical object (theme/patient) that functions as the grammatical subject. Thus, compare the nominative object construction in (6), repeated here, with the passive construction in (13), in which the theme argument (*Hiromi*) can be the antecedent of *zibun* 'self' but the agent (*Masami*) cannot (Kuroda 1965, Kuno 1973).

(6) Reflexive binding
Masami$_1$-ga   Hiromi$_2$-ga   zibun$_{1/*2}$-no kurasu-de itiban suki-da.
Masami-NOM Hiromi-NOM self-GEN   class-in   best   like-COP
'Masami$_1$ likes Hiromi$_2$ the best in self's$_{1/*2}$ class.'

(13) Passive construction
Hiromi$_1$-ga   Masami$_2$-ni   zibun$_{1/*2}$-no heya-de   os-are-ta.
Hiromi-NOM Masami-DAT self-GEN   room-in push-PASS-PAST
'Hiromi was pushed by Masami in self's$_{1/*2}$ own room.'

A second difference between the nominative-object and passive constructions concerns case marking. As mentioned in relation to the examples in (2), the dative marker in the nominative object construction may alternate with the nominative case particle. The same is not possible, however, with the passive construction, as shown in (14).

(14) Hiromi-ga   Masami-ni/*-ga   os-are-ta.
Hiromi-NOM Masami-DAT/-NOM push-PASS-PAST
Intended: 'Hiromi was pushed by Masami.'

Another type of sentence superficially similar to the nominative object construction is the so-called major subject construction. The major subject construction, like the nominative object construction, has two nominative nominals. A crucial difference is that in the major subject construction, the second nominative NP, rather than the first, is the logical as well as grammatical subject (Kuno 1973, Kuroda 1983). Thus, consider (15).

(15) Major subject construction
Sendai-ga   sakana-ga uma-i.
Sendai-NOM fish-NOM   taste.good
'It is in Sendai that fish taste good.'

Fish may or may not taste good, but it does not make sense to say that the city of Sendai tastes good. The first nominative NP in the major subject construction is neither the logical subject nor the logical object of the predicate; rather it has some "aboutness relation" with the rest of the sentence. Neither of the two nominative case particles in the major subject construction can be replaced with the dative -*ni*.

6.2.4 The Nominative Object Occurs with a Stative Predicate

Sentences with a nominative object all involve a subset of stative predicates (Kuno 1973, Shibatani 1999). Predicates that occur in the nominative object construction include (a) all transitive adjectives such as *suki* 'fond of', (b) a subset of stative transitive verbs such as *dekiru* 'can do', and (c) complex predicates consisting of an action verb and a stative auxiliary verb such as *-rare* 'can' or an auxiliary adjective *-tai* 'want' (e.g., *tabe-tai* 'eat-want').

(16)   Predicates that take a nominative object[4]
    a. Transitive adjectives
       kowa(-i) 'afraid of', *hosi(-i)* 'want', *suki(-da)* 'like', *kirai(-da)* 'hate', *hituyoo(-da)* 'need', *tokui(-da)* 'good at', *heta(-da)* 'bad at', etc.
    b. Stative transitive verbs
       deki(-ru) 'can do', *waka(-ru)* 'understand', *ar(-u)* 'have', etc.
    c. Complex stative predicates
       i. Potential verbs (V-*rare/e(-ru)* 'can V')
          tabe-rare(-ru) 'can eat', *nom-e(-ru)* 'can drink', *hanas-e(-ru)* 'can speak', *tumur-e(-ru)* 'can close', etc.
       ii. Desiderative adjectives (V-*ta(-i)* 'want to V')
          tabe-ta(-i) 'want to eat', *nomi-ta(-i)* 'want to drink', *hanasi-ta(-i)* 'want to speak', *tsumuri-ta(-i)* 'want to close', etc.

6.2.5 The Nominative Object Tends to Have Wide Scope

Among the three types of predicates given in (16), the first two (i.e., those in (a) and (b)) only take nominative object (except for a few exceptions, such as *waka(-ru)* 'understand', which take either a nominative or accusative object). With a predicate of the third type (i.e., those in (c)), the object may be case-marked either in the accusative or in the nominative, as shown in (17).

(17)   a. Kiyomi-wa   migime-dake-o   tumur-e-ru.
       Kiyomi-TOP right.eye-only-ACC close-can-PRES
       Lit: 'Kiyomi can close only his right eye.'
       [can>only] 'Kiyomi can wink his right eye.'
    b. Kiyomi-wa   migime-dake-ga   tumur-e-ru.
       Kiyomi-TOP right.eye-only-NON close-can-PRES
       [only > can] 'It is only the right eye that Kiyomi can close.'

The accusative object takes narrow scope with respect to the second element of the complex predicate (the potential verb *-rare* 'can' in (17), V2 hereafter). Thus the prominent reading of (17a) is 'Kiyomi can wink his right eye' (can > only).[5] In contrast, the nominative object has wide scope over V2 (Sano 1985, Tada 1992), so that (17b) is interpreted as 'It is only the right eye that Kiyomi can close' (only > can).

In negative sentences, the accusative object falls within the scope of the sentential negation and V2 (neg > can > only), whereas the nominative object takes wider scope than the negation and V2 (only > neg > can) (Koizumi 1994, 1995).

(18) a. Kiyomi-wa   migime-dake-o   tumur-e-na-i.
      Kiyomi-TOP right.eye-only-ACC close-can-NEG-PRES
      Lit: 'Kiyomi cannot close only his right eye.'
      [not > can > only] 'It is not the case that Kiyomi can wink his right eye.'
   b. Kiyomi-wa   migime-dake-ga   tumur-e-na-i.
      Kiyomi-TOP right.eye-only-NOM close-can-NEG-PRES
      [only > not > can] 'It is only the right eye that Kiyomi cannot close.'

The nominative object has wide scope not only in sentences with a complex stative predicate but also in simplex stative sentences. Example (19) can be read as 'The only subject Hiromi is not capable of is math' (only > not), and it cannot be interpreted as 'It is not the case that Hiromi is only capable of math' (not > only) (Koizumi 1994, 1995).

(19) Hiromi-wa   suugaku-dake-ga deki-na-i.
      Hiromi-TOP math-only-NOM   capable-NEG-PRES
      *[not > only] 'It is not the case that Hiromi is only capable of math'
      [only > not] 'It is only mathematics that Hiromi is not capable of.'

To summarize so far, we have seen in this section that the nominative object is a grammatical object rather than some sort of subject, that it occurs with certain types of stative predicates, and that it tends to have wide scope.

6.3 ANALYTICAL ISSUES

In this section, I consider how the case and scope properties of the nominative object can be explained within the broad framework of current generative grammar.

6.3.1 Why Is the Object Case-Marked in Nominative?

There are three classes of hypotheses regarding why the object is marked with -*ga* in the nominative object construction. They all agree in assuming that the stative predicates that occur in this construction lack the ability to license accusative Case. They differ as to the nature or origin of the particle -*ga* of the nominative object. The three hypotheses are: (a) The particle -*ga* of the nominative object is a postposition rather than an instantiation of abstract nominative Case; (b) -*ga* is the nominative case marker and is licensed by a stative predicate (Kuno 1973, Tada 1992, Yatsushiro 1999, Takano 2003, among others); and (c) -*ga* is the nominative case marker and is licensed by a functional category, Tense (T) (Koizumi 1994, Ura 1999, Kishimoto 2001; see also Takezawa 1987).

That the first hypothesis is inadequate can be shown by facts about numeral quantifier float and *ga-no* (or nominative-genitive) conversion. Generally, floated numeral quantifiers can be associated with an NP bearing nominative or accusative Case, but they cannot be construed with an NP within PP, as shown in (20) (Shibatani 1978, Miyagawa 1989, among others).

(20) a. Gakusei-ga 3-nin ringo-o katta.
      student-NOM 3-CL apple-ACC bought
      'Three students bought apples.'
   b. Gakusei-ga ringo-o 3-tu katta.
      student-NOM apple-ACC 3-CL bought
      'A student bought three apples.'
   c. *Hiromi-ga gakusei-kara 3-nin ringo-o katta.
      Hiromi-NOM student-from 3-CL apple-NOM bought
      Intended: 'Hiromi bought apples from three students.'

Examples (21a,b) demonstrate that the logical subject and the nominative object, respectively, can readily host a numeral quantifier, the latter of which should be impossible if the particle *-ga* of the nominative object were a postposition such as *-kara* 'from', as in (20c).

(21) a. Kono kurasu-no gakusei-ga 3-nin tyuugokugo-ga hanas-e-ru.
      this class-GEN student-NOM 3-CL Chinese-NOM speak-can-PRES
      'Three students in this class can speak Chinese.'
   b. Masami-ga gaikokugo-ga 3-tu hanas-e-ru.
      Masami-NOM foreign language-NOM 3-CL speak-can-PRES
      'Masami can speak three foreign languages.'

As for the *ga-no* (or nominative-genitive) conversion, in certain configurations such as a relative clause, an NP may be optionally marked with the genitive case-marker *-no* instead of the nominative *-ga*, as shown in (22a). (For details of the *ga-no* conversion, see Maki and Uchibori, this volume, and the references cited there.) Comparable alternation is not possible with any of the postpositions (see (22b)).

(22) a. ame-ga/-no huru hi
      rain-NOM/-GEN fall day
      'the day when it rains'
   b. sora-kara/*-no huru hi
      sky-from/-GEN fall day
      Intended: 'the day when something falls from the sky'[6]

The nominative object may undergo *ga-no* conversion, as shown in (23), which again supports the idea that the *-ga* marking of the nominative object is a realization of structural nominative Case rather than a postposition.

(23) a. tyuugokugo-ga   hanas-e-ru   gakusei
       Chinese-NOM   speak-can-NONPAST   student
    b. tyuugokugo-no   hanas-e-ru   gakusei
       Chinese-GEN   speak-can-NONPAST   student
    'a student who can speak Chinese'

The second analysis—that -ga is the nominative Case marker licensed by a stative predicate—also faces several problems. For example, under this analysis, nominative Case is licensed by two distinct categories. The nominative Case of the subject is licensed by Tense, and the nominative Case of the nominative object is licensed by stative predicates. Tense is a functional category, whereas stative predicates are lexical categories (verbs and adjectives). These two categories have nothing in common, except for the alleged nominative Case-licensing ability. It is not clear at all why nominative Case should be licensed by two distinct sets of categories as different as Tense and stative predicates. This fact alone, of course, does not render the analysis untenable, but it surely makes it dubious (Koizumi 1994).

There are empirical problems with the second analysis as well. Consider the following examples (Koizumi 1994).

(24) a. Mary-wa   suugaku-dake-o   wakari-tuzuke-ta.
       Mary-TOP   mathematics-ACC   understand-continue-PAST
       Lit. 'Mary kept understanding only math.'
    b. Mary-wa   suugaku-dake-ga   wakari-tuzuke-ta.
       Mary-TOP   mathematics-NOM   understand-continue-PAST

The lower verb (V1) of these sentences (i.e., *wakar* 'understand') is a stative verb, and the higher verb (V2) (i.e., *tuzuke* 'continue') is a nonstative verb.[7] The object may be marked either with the nominative -*ga* or with the accusative -*o*. If the nominative object is Case-licensed by a stative verb as postulated by the second analysis, the nominative object in (24b) should be licensed within the embedded VP (or some larger phrase sister to the higher verb), as schematically shown in (25).

(25) ...[VP [VP [nominative object] understand] continue]

Here the nominative object is asymmetrically c-commanded by the higher verb. We would therefore expect that (24b) may not have the reading in which the object takes scope over the higher verb. The prediction fails, however. Example (24b) is interpreted such that it is only math that Mary had understood all the time throughout the relevant time span, which clearly shows that the object takes the wide scope reading. This suggests that (unlike the accusative object in sentences like (17a)) the nominative object in (24b) is licensed in a position higher than the higher verb, contrary to what is expected from the hypothesis that the nominative object is licensed by a stative predicate. Yet another problem with this analysis has to do with the fact that it cannot account for the obligatory wide scope of the nominative object over sentential negation (Neg) (see (18) and (19) above). If the nominative object is licensed by the stative verb within the projection of that verb as schematically shown in (26), much like the accusative object is licensed by a verb within its VP, there is no reason for the nominative object to take scope over negation obligatorily.[8]

(26) [TP [NegP [VP [nominative object] close-can] Neg] T] (cf. (18))

The third analysis—that the nominative Case of the nominative object is licensed by Tense—faces none of the above problems. Under this hypothesis, nominative Case is uniformly licensed by Tense regardless of which NP it appears on. The nominative object undergoes movement to the domain of T for the purpose of Case-licensing, and the domain of T is higher than (and hence outside the scope of) Neg. The wide scope reading of the nominative object therefore is readily explained (Koizumi 1994, 1995).

(27) [TP [NegP [VP [VP [nominative object] close] can] Neg] T]

6.3.2 Why Is the Narrow Scope Reading Absent?

Given that the nominative object is licensed by T within TP, the wide scope reading of the nominative object over sentential negation and stative verbs is explained in the way just sketched. A remaining question is why the nominative object cannot have narrow scope with respect to Neg and V2 in the V1-V2 compound. There are two main approaches for this. One approach postulates a VP-complementation structure as in (27) and assumes that a trace left behind by (a subtype of) A-movement is invisible for the purpose of scope interpretation (e.g., Koizumi 1998, Nevins and Anand 2003, Bobaljik and Wurmbrand 2005). The other approach assumes that complex predicates are formed prior to merger of the nominative object either as in (28a) or as in (28b) (e.g., Saito 2000; Hoshi 2001, 2005; see also Takano 2003). In either structure, the object is never lower than the second verb, and hence there is no possibility of scope reconstruction.

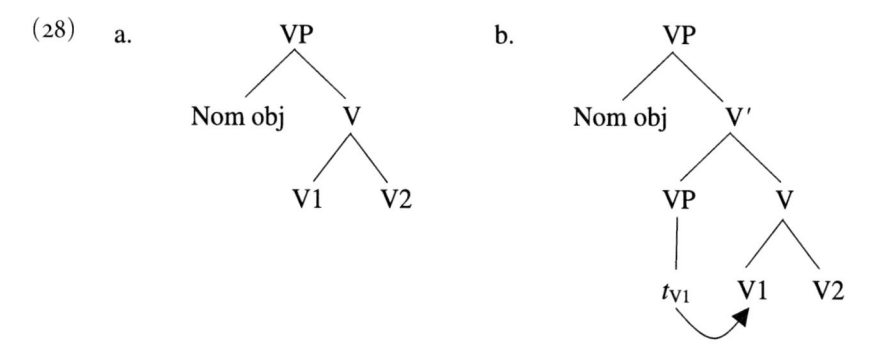

(28) a.   VP   b.   VP
           /   \   /   \
       Nom obj   V   Nom obj   V'
                 / \   / \
                V1 V2   VP   V
                                                  | / \
                                                 t_V1 V1 V2

Bobaljik and Wurmbrand (2007) note several potential problems with the analyses in (28). One of them is reproduced here, and the reader is referred to their original work for other problems. It is known that different time-span adverbials diagnose different aspectual classes of VPs. Bare time adverbials such as *iti-zikan* 'for one hour' modify the duration of an activity. Expressions like *iti-zikan-de* 'in one hour', however, serve to diagnose accomplishments (Vendler 1967). Aspectual distinctions hold at the VP-level rather than at the V-level, as shown by the English sentences in (29), where the transitive accomplishment-denoting VP *read the book* licenses *in an hour*, but the intransitive activity-denoting VP *read* cannot.

(29) a. John read the book in an hour.
b. John read *in an hour/for an hour.

Now consider the following example (Bobaljik and Wurmbrand 2007):

(30) Taroo-ga hon-ga iti-zikan-de yom-e-ru.
Taro-NOM book-NOM 1-hour-in read-can-PRES
'Taro can read the book in one hour.'

In (30), *iti-zikan-de* 'in one hour' is licensed, which shows that the nominative object construction contains an accomplishment-denoting VP. The problem with the structures in (28) is that there is no node corresponding to an accomplishment. The VP in (28a) and the higher VP in (28b) are states, whereas the lower VP (without an object) in (28b) would be an activity. Both states and activities are incompatible with *de*-marked adverbials. The structures in (28) therefore wrongly predict that (30) is ungrammatical. In contrast, the correct predictions are made by a VP-complementation structure in (27), because the lower VP contains an object trace and thus denotes an accomplishment, licensing the *-de* adverbial.

6.3.3 May the Narrow Scope Reading Be Marginally Available after All?

So far we have assumed that the nominative object takes scope over both sentential negation and stative verbs. Recently, however, Nomura (2005a,b) has challenged this generalization by pointing out that, with an appropriate context, the narrow scope reading of the nominative object is marginally possible for many speakers. Thus, consider the following example.

(31) Taroo-ga koyubi-dake-ga mage-rare-ru no-wa sit-te-ita-ga,
Taro-NOM pinkie-only-NOM crook-can-PRES that-TOP knew-but,
(kare-ga) kusuriyubi-dake-mo mage-rare-ru no-ni-wa odoro-ita.
(he-NOM) ring-finger-only-also crook-can-PRES that-at-TOP surprised
'I have known that Taro can crook only his pinkie, but I was surprised that he can also crook only his ring finger.'

If the example in (31) is interpreted in such a way that the nominative object takes scope over the potential verb, it would yield a contradictory reading—that is, 'I have known that Taro can bend none of his fingers except his pinkie, but I was surprised that he can bend none of his fingers except his ring finger.' Nomura (2005a, b) observed, however, that (31) is judged as noncontradictory, and this is only possible if the nominative object is interpreted within the scope of the potential verb (can > only). The noncontradictory reading available to (31) is 'I have known that Taro can bend only his pinkie, but I was surprised that he can also bend only his ring finger.'

As a further support for the claim that the nominative object can fall within the scope of the potential verb, consider example (33) in the context provided in (32).

(32) Context (Nomura's [2005a] context 4):
John has a white bookshelf, and he does not want it to be orange colored. He has two different color paints, red and yellow (mixing red and yellow will yield orange).

(33) John-wa subete-no iro-ga tuka-e-nai.
John-TOP all-GEN color-NOM use-POT-NEG
'John cannot use every color.'

There are three logically possible interpretations for the example in (33), with regard to whether the universally quantified object takes scope over negation and/or the potential verb, which are summarized in (34).

(34) a. all > not > can: For every color x, John cannot use x.
b. not > all > can: It is not the case that for every color x, John can use x.
c. not > can > all: It is not possible for John to use all the colors.

Let us consider the three interpretations in turn. Under the interpretation in (34a), there has to be no color that John can use. However, given that he can use a nonorange color, this is a false statement in the context of (32). Example (34b) denies that John can use any one of the colors. This denial is a false statement because he can use any single color. Example (34c) denies that using all the paints is a way of achieving the desired result. Given that mixture of red and yellow is orange, this is a true assertion in the given context. The fact that sentence (33) can be felicitously used (as a true statement) in the context given in (32) shows that given appropriate context the nominative object can take narrow scope with respect to both sentential negation and potential verb.

The correct generalization about the scope interpretation of the nominative object, therefore, seems to be that the wide scope reading is strongly preferred, but the narrow scope reading is marginally available given appropriate context.

6.3.4 Why Is the Narrow Scope Reading So Difficult to Obtain?

The new generalization calls for a new analysis. Why is the narrow scope reading so difficult to obtain? Although this is currently an open question, one promising way to pursue the issue has to do with pragmatics. According to this view, syntactically both the wide and narrow scope readings are available for the nominative object, and the extremely strong preference for the wide scope reading is due to pragmatic reasons along the lines of Grice's conversational principles, such as "avoid ambiguity as much as possible (manner)," which suppress (or disfavor) the narrow scope reading. As discussed in section 6.2, the nominative object construction with a complex stative predicate has a counterpart with an accusative object. A relevant set of examples are repeated here.

(35) a. Kiyomi-wa migime-dake-o   tumur-e-ru.
          Kiyomi-TOP right.eye-only-ACC close-can-PRES
          Lit: 'Kiyomi cannot close only his right eye.'
          [can > only] 'Kiyomi can wink his right eye.'
          *[only > can] 'It is only the right eye that Kiyomi cannot close.'
      b. Kiyomi-wa migime-dake-ga   tumur-e-ru.
          Kiyomi-TOP right.eye-only-NON close-can-PRES
          #[can > only] 'Kiyomi can wink his right eye.'
          [only > can] 'It is only the right eye that Kiyomi cannot close.'

In the pair of examples in (35), the accusative object is within the scope of the potential verb, giving rise to the interpretation [can > only] but not the interpretation [only > can]. In contrast, if Nomura's observation is correct, the nominative object is actually ambiguous in scope with respect to the potential verb. It can take either wide [only > can] or narrow [can > only] scope. Of the two interpretations available to the sentence with the nominative object, one is identical to the reading of the sentence with the accusative object (i.e., the object narrow scope reading [can > only]). Then, when a speaker intends to convey the meaning associated with the narrow scope of the object, there are two alternative expressions from which to choose: one with the accusative object, which is unambiguous; and the other with nominative object, which is ambiguous. In this situation, the speaker would choose the unambiguous sentence with the accusative object, given Gricean requirements on rational use of the language for communication ("avoid ambiguity," in particular): If a speaker has the means to express a certain idea clearly, he or she would not choose a less clear way to express it.

This is reminiscent of a case, discussed by Reinhart (1983) among others, of interpretation of pronouns. A pronoun in the object position usually cannot be coreferential with the subject, as shown in (36b), but there are various situations in which such coreferential reading is possible (e.g., (37)). Reinhart proposes that the coreferential reading of (36b) is usually unavailable not because it is ruled out by principles of sentence grammar (i.e., condition B) but because it is pragmatically unfavored given the Gricean principle "avoid ambiguity" (Reinhart's Rule I) (see also Dowty 1980). There is a clearer alternative to (36b) (i.e., (36a)), which is unambiguous, unlike (36b) in which *her* can be potentially coreferential with someone other than Zelda.

(36) a. Zelda saw herself.
b. Zelda saw her.

(37) I know what Bill and Mary have in common. Mary adores Bill, and Bill adores him too. (Reinhart 1983:169)

Since Reinhart 1983, several alternative analyses have been proposed to account for the (un)availability of the coreference reading in examples like (36b) (e.g., Grimshaw and Rosen 1990, Grodzinsky and Reinhart 1993, Wexler and Thornton 1999). Although it is beyond the scope of this chapter to compare and choose among them, whatever analysis turns out to be correct for (36b) may be readily extended to (35b), given the apparent parallelism between (35) and (36).

6.4 ACCUSATIVE OBJECT

We have considered how nominative objects are licensed. For the sake of completeness, let us now briefly turn to the question of how accusative objects are licensed. I lay out what may be considered "core data" in section 6.4.1, and in section 6.4.2, I discuss possible analyses.

6.4.1 Empirical Generalization

As discussed in the previous sections, the stative compounds shown in (16c)—that is, the complex potential verbs (V-*rare/e(-ru)* 'can V') and complex desiderative adjectives (V-*ta(-i)* 'want to V')—can take either a nominative or an accusative object. When the object is case-marked in nominative, it usually takes scope over the second element (i.e., *rare* 'can' or *tai* 'want') of the compound. When the object bears the accusative case, it has narrow scope with respect to 'can' or 'want'. In this section, I discuss nonstative compounds such as V-*hazime(-ru)* 'begin to V', in which the second element is a nonstative verb unlike the stative compounds, in which the second element is a stative predicate.

Nonstative compounds cannot take a nominative object. They take an accusative object if the first element (V1) is a transitive verb. Accusative objects of nonstative compounds exhibit different scope properties depending on the type of the second component verb (V2). When V2 is a control verb with an accusative Case feature (e.g., *wasure* 'forget'), the object obligatorily takes scope over V2. This is exemplified in (38).⁹

(38) V2 = Control verb with accusative feature
John-wa ringo-dake-o tabe-wasure-ta.
John-TOP apple-only-ACC eat-forget-PAST
'John forgot to eat only apples.'
   a. only > forget (Among many things John was supposed to eat, it was only apples that he forgot to eat.)
   b. *forget > only (It was eat only apples that John forgot to do.)

When V2 is a control verb without an accusative Case feature (39), a raising verb (40), or a verb ambiguous between raising and control (41), the accusative object may take either narrow or wide scope with respect to V2.

(39) V2 = Control verb without accusative feature
Yooko-wa furansu-ryuugaku-tyuu-ni pan-dake-o
Yoko-TOP France-study.abroad-during-at bread-only-ACC
tabe-nare-ta.
eat-get.used.to-PAST
'Yoko got used to eating only bread, while studying in France.'
   a. only > get.used.to (It is only bread that Yoko got used to eating while studying in France.)
   b. get.used.to > only (While studying in France, Yoko got used to eating bread without having anything else together.)

(40) V2 = Raising verb
John-wa niku-dake-o tabe-sugi-ta.
John-TOP meat-only-ACC eat-overdo-PAST
'John overdid eating only meat.'
   a. only > overdo (Among many things John ate, it was only meat that he overate.)
   b. overdo > only (For too long a time, John ate nothing but meat.)

(41) V2 = Ambiguous between raising and control
John-ga ringo-dake-o tabe-hazime-ta
John-NOM apple-only-ACC eat-start-PAST
'John started to eat only apples.'
   a. only > start (It was only apples that John started to eat.)
   b. start > only (It was eat only apples that John started to do.)

Representative verbs that can be used as V2 in stative and nonstative compounds are shown in (42), and the relationship between the type of V2 and the scope of the accusative object is summarized in (43).

(42) V2 in stative and nonstative compounds
   a. Control verb with accusative feature
      -*wasure* 'forget', -*oe* 'finish', -*age* 'complete', -*naos* 're-do'
      -*sokonaw* 'fail', etc.
   b. Control verb without accusative feature
      -*nare* 'get used to', -*tuke* 'be accustomed to', -*aki* 'get tired of',
      -*aw* 'do to each other', etc.
   c. Raising verb
      -*sugi* 'overdo', -*kake* 'be about to', -*owar* 'come to an end', etc.
   d. Ambiguous between raising and control
      -*hazime* 'begin', -*tuzuke* 'continue', -*das* 'start', etc.
   e. Stative (= stative control verb or adjective without accusative feature)
      -*rare* 'can', -*tai* 'want'

(43) Relationship between the type of V2 and the scope of the accusative object

	Scope	
V2	Object > V2	V2 > Object
Type 1 verbs (= Control w/ acc)	✓	*
Type 2 verbs (= Control w/o acc, raising, and raising/control)	✓	✓
Type 3 verbs (= Stative)	*	✓

Given the data above, the empirical generalization seems to be as follows (Koizumi 1995, 1998): When V2 has an accusative Case feature, it obligatorily takes narrow scope with respect to the accusative object. When V2 does not have an accusative Case feature, it may take either wide or narrow scope with respect to the accusative object if it is a nonstative verb, and it takes wider scope than the accusative object if it is a stative verb.

6.4.2 Analyses

Two families of analyses have been proposed to account for the generalization mentioned above: movement approaches (Kageyama 1993; Nishigauchi 1993; Koizumi 1995, 1998) and direct merge approaches (Kato 2003; Saito 2000; Hoshi 2001, 2005). Abstracting away from details, according to the movement approaches, the accusative object is first combined with V1 to form a verb phrase (V1P). When V1P is selected by v as in (44a), the object raises to the specifier of v and has its accusative Case licensed by v. Given that the object in this configuration is c-commanded by V2, it is within the scope of V2 (the subject positions are not represented in (44)).

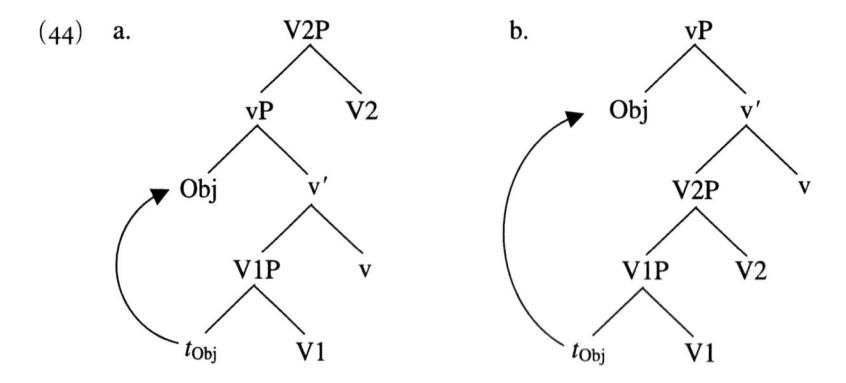

(44) a. [tree: V2P → vP, V2; vP → Obj, v'; v' → V1P, v; V1P → t_Obj, V1; with Obj moved from t_Obj]

b. [tree: vP → Obj, v'; v' → V2P, v; V2P → V1P, V2; V1P → t_Obj, V1; with Obj moved from t_Obj]

In contrast, when V1P is selected by V2 rather than v as in (44b), the object moves to the vP above V2P to have its accusative Case licensed. In this case, the object asymmetrically c-commands V2 and hence takes scope over V2. Both (44a,b) are available for type 2 verbs in (43) (such as raising verbs), whereas only (44b) is possible with type 1 verbs (control verbs such as *wasure* 'forget'). Within the movement camp, there are several competing ideas as to why there is such a selectional difference between the two types of verbs. See Kageyama 1993, Koizumi 1995, 1998, and Bobaljik and Wurmbrand 2005, among many others.

The direct merge approaches account for the scope ambiguity observed with type 2 verbs by positing that the object may be merged either before (as in (45)) or after (as in (46)) V2 (Kato 2003, Hoshi 2005).

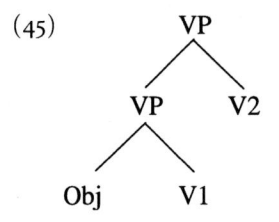

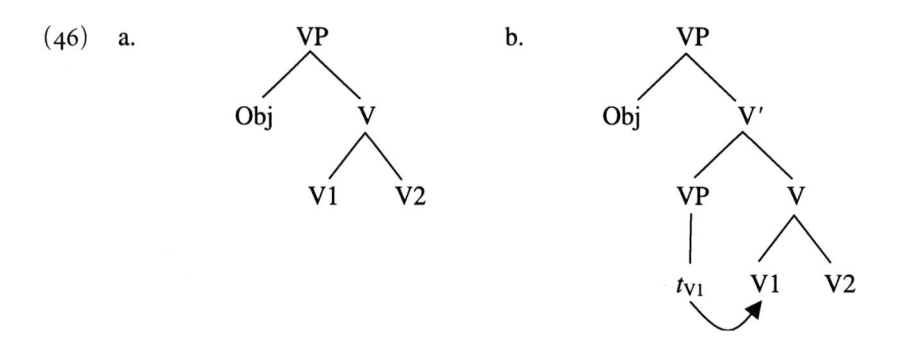

(45) [tree: VP → VP, V2; VP → Obj, V1]

(46) a. [tree: VP → Obj, V; V → V1, V2]

b. [tree: VP → Obj, V'; V' → VP, V; VP → t_V1; V → V1, V2; with V1 moved]

Under these approaches, type 1 verbs may occur in the structures in (46) but not in (45) for some reason. Because there is no movement of the object in (46), there is no possibility of reconstructing it below V2, and hence wide scope is guaranteed for the object of complex verbs with a type 1 V2.

The most crucial difference between the movement approaches and direct merger approaches is that the former posits an object trace in the embedded VP but the latter does not. An active debate is going on between the two camps. See Bobaljik and Wurmbrand 2005, 2007 for the most recent discussion.

6.5 Theoretical Implications

In this section, I consider two theoretical implications of the discussion in the previous sections.

6.5.1 Multiple Agree and EPP

It was discussed in section 6.3 that nominative object moves to TP. Koizumi (1994), adapting the insight of Tada (1992), suggests a Case-theoretic reason for this obligatory movement. However, given recent minimalist assumptions, in which a probe can enter into long-distance Agree (including case licensing) with a target in its c-commanding domain without ever invoking movement of the target, the nominative Case of the object should be able to be licensed by T through (long distance) Agree if the object does not move to TP. In fact, nominative objects in some languages clearly occur in a low position, as exemplified by the Icelandic sentence in (47).

(47) Barninu   viriðst [t hafa   batnað   veikin].
      child-DAT seems   to-have   recovered-from   disease-NOM
      'The child seems to have recovered from the disease.'   (Andrews 1982)

If the nominative Case of the object can be licensed by long-distance Agree, why is it the case that the object must move to TP? One conceivable reason has to do with EPP—that is, that the object movement is driven by the EPP feature of T. It has been argued that Japanese T has an EPP feature, and something must occupy Spec,TP (see, e.g., Miyagawa 2001). It is therefore tempting to say that the nominative object moves because of the EPP of T. There is, however, a potential problem with this idea. The EPP is satisfied by movement of the subject to Spec,TP. If so, there is no reason for the nominative object to move there as well.

This apparent paradox can be resolved if we adopt Hiraiwa's (2001) idea of Multiple Agree/Multiple Move, given in (48).

(48) Hiraiwa's (2001) Multiple Agree/Multiple Move
MULTIPLE AGREE (multiple feature checking) with a single probe is a single simultaneous syntactic operation; AGREE applies to all the matched goals at the same derivational point derivationally simultaneously. MULTIPLE MOVE (movement of multiple goals into multiple specifiers of the same probe H) is also a single simultaneous syntactic operation that applies to all the AGREEd goals.[10]

It has often been suggested that Japanese T can participate in Case-checking operations more than once (e.g., Ura 2000). According to Hiraiwa, however, it is not the case. What appears to be a series of Case-checking operations in fact is a single operation involving multiple NPs. T in Japanese enters into Agree/Move relation with more than one nominative NP simultaneously when there are such NPs in its c-command domain. Thus, in the nominative object construction, both the nominative subject and nominative object simultaneously enter into Multiple Agree/Multiple Move relation with T and move to the multiple specifiers of T to satisfy the EPP feature. This is schematically shown in (49).

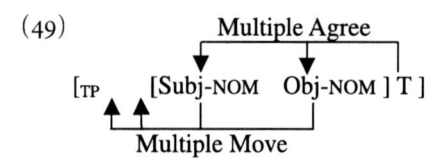

(49)   Multiple Agree
       [TP   [Subj-NOM   Obj-NOM] T]
                Multiple Move

If T enters into Agree/Move relation with the nominative subject alone first, its φ- and EPP features are all deleted, and hence it cannot participate in any further operation as a probe. Then the object remains with its Case feature unlicensed, leading to ungrammaticality.

What happens when the subject bears the dative postposition -*ni* (rather than a structural nominative Case), as shown in (50)?

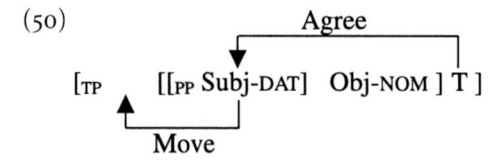

(50)   Agree
       [TP   [[PP Subj-DAT]   Obj-NOM] T]
                Move

In this case, T's EPP feature is satisfied by the movement of the subject, but its uninterpretative φ-features remain yet to be deleted because they cannot be deleted by a PP. Thus, T can still enter into Agree relation with the nominative object. Because the EPP feature of T is already satisfied by the subject, the nominative object in this case need not move to TP. Then, we would expect the nominative object to take narrow scope with respect to the matrix verb when the subject is in dative.[11] This expectation seems to be borne out. Consider (51).[12]

(51) Kiyomi-ni(-wa)   migime-dake-ga   tumur-e-na-i   (koto).
      Kiyomi-DAT(-TOP) right.eye-only-NOM close-can-NEG-PRES (fact)
      Lit. 'Kiyomi cannot close only the right eye.'
      Primary reading: [not > can > only]: 'Kiyomi cannot wink his right eye.'

This is in sharp contrast to the nominative object constructions with a nominative subject, in which, as we have observed, the nominative object takes widest scope.[13]

6.5.2 Nominative Object in Child Languages

As discussed in section 6.3.4, the object pronoun in (36b), repeated here as (52), usually cannot be coreferential with the subject in adult English. It has been observed, however, that children more readily accept such coreferential reading. More precisely, children's performance on sentences such as (52) is at chance level (Chien and Wexler 1990).

(52) Zelda saw her.

To decide if coreference is permitted in sentences such as (52), according to Reinhart (1983), one must evaluate two representations, (52) and a similar structure with a bound variable, and determine if the two are not equivalent in the given context. Grodzinsky and Reinhart (1993) argue that the computation required here exceeds the processing ability of children, so that children give up and make a guess, yielding the observed 50 percent error rate (i.e., chance-level performance). If this line of analysis is on the right track, and if the suggestion that the object narrow scope reading in the nominative object construction in Japanese is difficult to obtain for the same reason that the coreferential reading is difficult to obtain in sentences such as (52), we would then expect that Japanese learning children may go through stages in which they will accept the narrow scope reading for the nominative object more readily than adults. Future research should clarify whether this expectation is borne out.

6.6 CONCLUSION

In this chapter, we have first observed in section 6.2 that the nominative object is a grammatical object rather than some kind of subject; that the nominative object occurs with stative predicates, which lack the ability to license nominative Case; and that the nominative object tends to have wide scope with respect to sentential negation and V2. In section 6.3, I have reviewed several attempts to account for these facts and reached the conclusion that the nominative Case of the nominative object is uniformly licensed by T rather than by a set of heterogeneous categories. Then in section 6.4, I have briefly considered how accusative Case is licensed. Finally, in section 6.5, I have suggested that the nominative object, along with the nominative subject, moves to TP to satisfy the EPP requirement of T.

NOTES FOR CHAPTER 6

1. Matrix stative sentences, including the nominative object construction, sound most natural when the subject is topicalized and marked with the topic marker *wa*. The matrix subject of a stative sentence tends to be interpreted as focused if it is in the nominative case.
2. Example (10b) with the formal noun *koto* is grammatical under the interpretation that Mary is fond of John, in which case the nominative object is scrambled across the subject.
3. Additional evidence for this conclusion can be found in Takezawa 1987. For differing views, see Tonoike 1975/1976, Saito 1982, and Shibatani 1999, among others.
4. Adjectives here include *keiyoshi* (*i*-adjectives) and *keiyodoshi* (*na*-adjectives) in the terms of the traditional Japanese grammar. Some of the predicates that occur in the nominative object construction cannot take a dative subject. (e.g., *hosi(-i)* 'want', *suki(-da)* 'like').
5. The accusative object can take wide scope if it is stressed, which presumably is due to movement induced by the stress.
6. Example (22b) with the genitive case marker is acceptable if it is interpreted as 'the day when the sky falls,' which is irrelevant in the context of our discussion.
7. Predicates of this type are rare and hence not listed in (16).
8. See Koizumi 1994 for further problems with the second analysis.
9. All examples in section 6.4.1 are taken from Koizumi 1995 unless otherwise noted.
10. This is similar to what is proposed in Miyagawa 2001 for nominative objects as well but for an opposite reason. Miyagawa argues that it is possible to have multiple instances of "agreement" in languages such as Japanese that do not have formal ϕ-feature agreement (of Indo-European language type). This correctly differentiates Japanese, in which nominative object moves to TP, from Icelandic, in which nominative object stays in a lower position (see note 13).
11. See a similar point in Miyagawa 2001.
12. The object can take scope over the negation if it is stressed (Ura 1999).
13. As we have seen in (47), the subject of the nominative object construction in languages such as Icelandic is marked with a nonstructural case, such as an inherent case or a postposition, much like the Japanese example in (51). It cannot bear structural nominative Case unlike in Japanese. The nominative object remains in a low position. These languages differ from Japanese in that their T cannot enter into Multiple Agree/Multiple Move.

REFERENCES

Andrews, Avery. 1982. The representation of Case in Modern Icelandic. In *The mental representation of grammatical relations*, ed. Joan Bresnan, 427–503. Cambridge, Mass.: MIT Press.

Bobaljik, Jonathan David, and Susi Wurmbrand. 2005. The domain of agreement. *Natural Language & Linguistic Theory* 23:809–865.

Bobaljik, Jonathan David, and Susi Wurmbrand. 2007. Complex predicates, aspect, and anti-reconstruction. *Journal of East Asian Linguistics* 16:27–42.

Chien, Y.-C., and Ken Wexler. 1990. Children's knowledge of locality conditions in binding as evidence for the modularity of syntax and pragmatics. *Language Acquisition* 1:225–295.

Dowty, David. 1980. Comments on the paper by Bach and Partee. In *Papers from the Parasession on Pronouns and Anaphora*, ed. Jody Kreinman and Almerindo Ojeda, 29–40. Chicago: Chicago Linguistic Society.

Grimshaw, Jane, and Sara Thomas Rosen. 1990. Knowledge and obedience: The developmental status of the binding theory. *Linguistic Inquiry* 21:187–222.

Grodzinsky, Yosef, and Tanya Reinhart. 1993. The innateness of binding and the development of coreference: A reply to Grimshaw and Rosen. *Linguistic Inquiry* 24:69–103.

Harada, S.-I. 1973. Counter equi NP deletion. *Annual Bulletin* 7:113–147. Research Institute of Logopedics and Phoniatrics, Tokyo University.

Harada, S.-I. 1976. Honorifics. In *Japanese generative grammar* (Syntax and Semantics 5), ed. Masayoshi Shibatani, 499–561. San Diego, Calif.: Academic Press.

Hiraiwa, Ken. 2001. Multiple Agree and the Defective Intervention Constraint in Japanese. In *MITWPL 40*, ed. Ora Matushansky, Albert Costa, Javier Martin-Gonzalez, Lance Nathan, and Adam Szczgielniak, 67–80. Cambridge, Mass.: MIT Working Papers in Linguistics.

Hoshi, Hiroto. 2001 Relations between thematic structure and syntax: A study on the nature of predicates in Japanese. In *SOASWPL 11*, ed. Hyun-Joo Lee and Sam Hellmuth, 203–247. London: SOAS, University of London.

Hoshi, Hiroto. 2005. Functional categories and configurationality. Ms., Akita University, Akita, Japan.

Inoue, Kazuko. 1976. *Henkei-bunpoo-to nihongo* [Transformational grammar and Japanese]. Tokyo: Taishukan.

Kageyama, Taro. 1993. *Bunpoo to gokeisei* [Grammar and word formation]. Tokyo: Hituzi Syobo.

Kageyama, Taro. 1999. Word formation. In *The handbook of Japanese linguistics*, ed. Natsuko Tsujimura, 297–325. Oxford: Blackwell.

Kato, Sachiko. 2003. Derivational theta-marking: A minimalist approach to the complex predicate constructions in Japanese. *Gengo Kenkyu* 124:37–96.

Kishimoto, Hideki. 2001. Binding of indefinite pronouns and clause structure in Japanese. *Linguistic Inquiry* 32:597–633.

Kishimoto, Hideki. 2004. Transitivity of ergative-marking predicates in Japanese. *Studies in Language* 28(1):105–136.

Koizumi, Masatoshi. 1994. Nominative objects: The role of TP in Japanese. In *MITWPL 24*, ed. Masatoshi Koizumi and Hiroyuki Ura, 211–230. Cambridge, Mass.: MIT Working Papers in Linguistics.

Koizumi, Masatoshi. 1995. Phrase structure in minimalist syntax. Doctoral dissertation, MIT, Cambridge, Mass.

Koizumi, Masatoshi. 1998. Invisible Agr in Japanese. *The Linguistic Review* 15:1–39.

Kuno, Susumu. 1973. *The structure of the Japanese language*. Cambridge, Mass.: MIT Press.

Kuroda, S.-Y. 1965. Generative grammatical studies in the Japanese language. Doctoral dissertation, MIT, Cambridge, Mass.

Kuroda, S.-Y. 1978. Case marking, canonical sentence patterns, and counter Equi in Japanese. In *Problems in Japanese syntax and semantics*, ed. John Hinds and Irwin Howard, 30–51. Tokyo: Kaitakusha.

Kuroda, S.-Y. 1983. What can Japanese say about government and binding? In *Proceedings of the Western Conference on Formal Linguistics 2*, ed. Michael Barlow, Daniel P.

Flickinger, and Michael T. Wescoat, 153–164. Stanford, Calif.: Stanford Linguistics Association.

Miyagawa, Shigeru. 1989. *Structure and Case-marking in Japanese*. San Diego, Calif.: Academic Press.

Miyagawa, Shigeru. 2001. EPP, scrambling, and *wh*-in-situ. In *Ken Hale: A life in language*, ed. Michael Kenstowicz, 293–338. Cambridge, Mass.: MIT Press.

Nevins, Andrew, and Pranav Anand. 2003. Some AGREEment matters. In *Proceedings of WCCFL 22*, ed. Gina Garding and Mimu Tsujimura, 370–381. Somerville, Mass.: Cascadilla Press.

Nishigauchi, Taisuke. 1993. Long distance passives. In *Japanese syntax in Comparative Grammar*, ed. Nobuko Hasegawa, 74–114. Tokyo: Kurosio.

Nomura, Masashi. 2005a. Nominative Case and AGREE(ment). Doctoral dissertation, University of Connecticut, Storrs.

Nomura, Masashi. 2005b. Remarks on the scope of nominative objects in Japanese. Paper presented at TCP 2005, Tokyo.

Reinhart, Tanya. 1983. *Anaphora and semantic interpretation*. London: Croom Helm.

Saito, Mamoru. 1982. Case marking in Japanese: A preliminary study. Ms., MIT, Cambridge, Mass.

Saito, Mamoru. 2000. Predicate raising and theta relations. Ms., Nanzan University, Nagoya, Japan.

Sano, Masaki. 1985. LF movement in Japanese. *Descriptive and Applied Linguistics* 18:245–259.

Shibatani, Masayoshi. 1973. Semantics of Japanese causativization. *Foundations of Language* 9:327–373.

Shibatani, Masayoshi. 1977. Grammatical relations and surface case. *Language* 53:789–809.

Shibatani, Masayoshi. 1978. Mikami Akira and the notion of "subject" in Japanese grammar. In *Problems in Japanese syntax and semantics*, ed. John Hinds and Irwin Howard, 52–67. Tokyo: Kaitakusha.

Shibatani, Masayoshi. 1999. Dative subject constructions 22 years later. *Studies in the Linguistic Sciences* 29(2):45–76.

Tada, Hiroaki. 1992. Nominative objects in Japanese. *Journal of Japanese Linguistics* 14:91–108.

Takano, Yuji. 2003. Nominative objects in Japanese complex predicate constructions: A prolepsis analysis. *Natural Language & Linguistic Theory* 21:779–834.

Takezawa, Koichi. 1987. A configurational approach to Case-marking in Japanese. Doctoral dissertation, University of Washington, Seattle.

Tonoike, Shigeo. 1975/1976. The case ordering hypothesis. *Papers in Japanese Linguistics* 4:191–208.

Tsunoda, Tasaku. 1991. *Sekai-no gengo-to nihongo* [Languages of the world and Japanese language]. Tokyo: Kurosio.

Ura, Hiroyuki. 1999. Checking theory and dative subject constructions in Japanese and Korean. *Journal of East Asian Linguistics* 8:223–254.

Ura, Hiroyuki. 2000. *Checking theory and grammatical functions in Universal Grammar*. Oxford: Oxford University Press.

Vendler, Zeno. 1967. *Linguistics in philosophy*. Ithaca, N.Y.: Cornell University Press.

Wexler, Ken, and Rosalind Thornton. 1999. *Principle B, VP ellipsis, and interpretation in child grammar*. Cambridge, Mass.: MIT Press.

Yatsushiro, Kazuko. 1999. Case licensing and VP structure. Doctoral dissertation, University of Connecticut, Storrs.

CHAPTER 7

JAPANESE ACCENT

HARUO KUBOZONO

7.1 INTRODUCTION

Anyone who studies the word accent of Tokyo Japanese will be amazed at the complexity of its system. It appears complex in two ways. First, the system contains a large number of accent rules, including the loanword accent rule, a set of compound accent rules, and the accent rule for verbs and adjectives (Akinaga 1985, 2001). Second, the system is believed to involve a depth of accent specification in the lexicon. This latter point can be exemplified by the data in (1) (McCawley 1968). In (1) and throughout this chapter, words without an accent mark are *unaccented*, or words pronounced with a rather flat pitch even when they are followed by a particle like the nominative particle *ga*. This representation should not be taken as suggesting, however, that lack of an accent represents the unmarked or default accent pattern of the language.

(1) Lexical specification
 a. Initial accent, initial-accenting: néko 'cat', básu 'bus'
    e.g., perusya-néko 'Persian cat', koosoku-básu 'highway bus'
 b. Final accent, preaccenting: yukí 'snow', umá 'horse'
    e.g., niwaká-yuki 'sudden snow', abaré-uma 'unruly horse'
 c. No accent (unaccented), preaccenting: musi 'bug', tora 'tiger'
    e.g., kabutó-musi 'beetle', hitokúi-dora 'man-eating tiger'[1]
 d. Final accent, deaccenting: yamá 'mountain', simá 'island'
    e.g., asama-yama 'Mount Asama', takara-zima 'Treasure Island'

Two types of accent specification are given in (1). First, it is supposed that every lexical item is specified in the lexicon with respect to its own accent pattern. The words in (1a), for example, are listed as *initially accented*, whereas those in (1b) are represented as *finally accented* in the lexicon. Moreover, each monomoraic or bimoraic lexical item is believed to be specified in the lexicon as to its accent behavior in compound nouns of which they form the second member. The items in (1a), for example, are specified as *initial-accenting* morphemes because they attract a compound accent on their initial syllable in compound nouns. The items in (1b), on the other hand, are specified as *preaccenting* morphemes; they attract a compound accent on the syllable immediately before them. The morphemes in (1d) are registered as finally accented just like those in (1b), but they are also registered as *deaccenting* morphemes because they yield unaccented compound nouns (McCawley 1968).

Seen from the viewpoint of language acquisition, the analysis in (1) implies that children acquiring Tokyo Japanese must learn all of this lexical information to correctly produce the lexical and compound accent patterns for each morpheme. This would be a tough job to achieve because there are ten thousand or more morphemes in the language, including more than one thousand monomoraic or bimoraic ones. However, psycholinguistic work on phonological development reports very few accent errors, if any, although a number of segmental errors are reported (see, e.g., Ito 1990). This raises a fundamental question about the accent system of Tokyo Japanese: is the accent system really so complex as is generally believed in the literature?

This chapter answers this question negatively through a review of the recent studies of Japanese accent. Regarding lexical specification, I argue that word accent is only sparsely specified in the lexicon—that is, only certain classes of words in the whole vocabulary are lexically specified with their accent patterns, whereas the majority of words are literally unmarked in the lexicon. As for the number of accent rules, I claim that what have been characterized as major accent rules in Tokyo Japanese—such as the loanword accent rule, compound accent rules, and the accent rule for verbs and adjectives—can be generalized.

This new line of work on Japanese accent has significant implications for general phonological theories. In loanword phonology, for example, a heated debate has been going on regarding the very nature of the phonological patterns exhibited by loanwords: where do loanword patterns come from? For previous analyses, see Silverman 1992, Paradis and LaCharité 1997, Dupoux et al. 1999, Kenstowicz and Sohn 2001, and Kenstowicz and Uffmann 2006.

Japanese accent provides a very interesting case for this central question of loanword phonology because loanwords in this language appear to show radically different accent patterns from native words. This can be seen from the data in table 7.1, which shows the frequency of each of the two major accent patterns—accented and unaccented—for the three word types: native, Sino-Japanese (SJ), and foreign (loanwords) in trimoraic nouns (Kubozono 2006).[2]

Table 7.1 Word type and accent pattern in three-mora nouns

Word type	Accent pattern Accented [+ pitch fall]	Unaccented [−pitch fall]	Examples
Native (2,220 words)	29%	71%	ínoti 'life', sakana 'fish'
Sino-Japanese (4,939 words)	49%	51%	ténki 'weather', kiten 'tact, wit'
Loan (778 words)	93%	7%	púrasu 'plus', piano 'piano'

As mentioned earlier, accented words involve a sudden pitch drop at the phonetic output, whereas unaccented words are pronounced without such a pitch fall.

Table 7.1 reveals that a vast majority of native words are unaccented, whereas most loanwords are accented. In other words, the accent type that native words prefer is not favored by loanwords and vice versa. Sino-Japanese words, or old loanwords from Chinese, exhibit an intermediate pattern whereby they favor the accented and unaccented patterns equally well.

Where the prosodic pattern of loanword comes from has been a mystery in the study of Japanese phonology (e.g., Sibata 1994). This chapter shows that the prosodic pattern in question comes from native phonology—in particular, loanwords follow the accent rule for *accented* native nouns.

This chapter consists of six sections. Section 7.2 considers the accent rule of morphologically simplex nouns to argue for the following three points: (a) what has been proposed as the loanword accent rule is nothing but the native accent rule for accented nouns in this language (Haraguchi 1991, Kubozono 2006); (b) this rule crucially resembles the famous Latin-type accent rule (Kubozono 1996, 1999); and (c) native nouns do not constitute a multiple-pattern system, as is generally believed, but rather a two-pattern accent system with a certain number of lexical items that exhibit idiosyncratic accent patterns (Haraguchi 1991). In terms of accent specification, this last point implies that word accent is only sparsely specified in the lexicon. Section 7.3 proposes a further generalization of Japanese accent by showing that what appears to be complicated accent behavior of compound nouns can be attributed to a general rule that permits a certain class of lexical exceptions. Here, too, the idea of exhaustive lexical specification of accent is argued against, in favor of a sparse accent specification in the lexicon. Section 7.4 demonstrates that the generalized rule of compound accent can be further generalized with the accent rule of morphologically simplex nouns discussed in section 7.2 as well as with the accent rule of verbs and adjectives. I then discuss Japanese accent in view of loanword phonology in section 7.5, where I also consider implications of Japanese accent for the central issue of loanword phonology. Section 7.6 presents a summary of main points.

7.2 Antepenultimate Rule

7.2.1 Native Nouns and Loanwords

A standard view of noun accent in Tokyo Japanese characterizes its system as a multiple-pattern system—that is, a system that permits multiple accent patterns (Uwano 1999, 2007). More specifically, Tokyo Japanese permits N+1 accent patterns for nouns of N syllables, where N represents an integer starting from one (McCawley 1968, Poser 1984, Shibatani 1990). Thus, three-syllable nouns exhibit the four accent patterns shown in (2): initial accent, medial accent, final accent, and no accent (unaccented). Longer nouns are thought to permit a larger number of accent patterns.

(2) Four accent patterns for three-mora nouns in Tokyo Japanese
  a. Initial accent: í.no.ti 'life'
  b. Medial accent: ko.kó.ro 'heart'
  c. Final accent: o.to.kó 'man'
  d. No accent (unaccented): sa.ka.na 'fish'

This multiple-pattern system contrasts with the two-pattern system of verbs and adjectives. In Tokyo Japanese, verbs and adjectives exhibit only two accent patterns—accented versus unaccented—with the accented pattern almost always bearing an accent on the penultimate mora.

(3) Verbs and adjectives in Tokyo Japanese
  a. Penultimate accent: hasíru 'to run', sirabéru 'to examine', atúi 'hot', umái 'tasty', utukusíi 'beautiful'
  b. No accent (unaccented): ageru 'to raise', atui 'thick', amai 'sweet'

The accent system in (3) is quite similar to the accent system of Kagoshima Japanese, a regional dialect spoken in the south of Japan. This dialect permits only two accent patterns—accented versus unaccented—for every type of word regardless of its length. As shown in (4), the accented pattern always involves an accent on the penultimate syllable. In phonetic terms, the accented pattern has a high tone on the penultimate syllable, whereas the unaccented pattern shows a default high tone on the final syllable (Shibatani 1990; Kubozono 2007).[3]

(4) Kagoshima Japanese
  a. Penultimate accent: sakána 'fish', akáka 'red', agéru 'to raise'
  b. No accent (unaccented): inoti 'life', aoka 'blue', hasiru 'to run'

Although slightly different in phonetic details, the two-pattern accent system of verbs and adjectives in Tokyo Japanese illustrated in (3) is strikingly similar to this accent system of Kagoshima Japanese, yet it differs from the multiple-pattern system of nouns in the same dialect, given in (2). Still, the three accent systems are thought to have one thing in common: the relationship between lexical items and their accent patterns is arbitrary, so it is not possible to tell which accent pattern is taken by a given word. In (2), for example, it is not possible to explain, at least in the synchronic grammar of Tokyo Japanese, why /í.no.ti/ 'life' is initially accented, /ko.kó.ro/ 'heart' is medially accented, and /sa.ka.na/ 'fish' is unaccented. The assignment of a particular accent pattern to a particular lexical item thus seems arbitrary.

It must be noted, however, that this does not entail that the accent patterns must be learned word by word or specified for each and every item in the lexicon. Consider, for example, a hypothetical situation where the accent pattern in (3b) is quite uncommon—in other words, relatively few words take this accent pattern. It would then follow that this accent pattern is lexically marked, whereas the other pattern, in (3a), is unmarked or rule governed. In terms of language acquisition, children would only have to memorize the words that take the exceptional accent pattern, while mastering an accent rule that assigns the penultimate accent to the majority of words. In the case of noun accent in Tokyo Japanese, there are at least a few pieces of evidence to support this idea of accent underspecification in preference to the standard view that an accent pattern is specified for every item in the lexicon.

The first fact to consider is that the N+1 law does not hold in nouns with five or more morae/syllables. According to the standard view mentioned earlier, five-syllable nouns should exhibit six accent patterns, and six-syllable nouns seven patterns. This prediction cannot be empirically borne out. On the contrary, it is generally the case that fewer accent patterns emerge in longer words. Particularly, initial accent and final accent become very rare in long nouns: thus, very few six-mora nouns, if any at all, are accented on their initial or final syllable. It may be argued that relatively long nouns tend to show more or less uniform accent patterns because many of them are compound nouns whose accentuation is determined by the compound accent rule. This observation is partially correct, but it does not apply to loanwords in general, which are morphologically simplex and can be long but nevertheless display a strong bias as to their accentual preference. Loanwords are generally known to follow the famous antepenultimate rule in (5) regardless of their phonological length (McCawley 1968).

(5) Loanword accent rule
Put an accent on the syllable containing the antepenultimate mora.

This rule, as exemplified in (6), is responsible for the accent of loanwords in general. In particular, loanwords generally disfavor final accent regardless of their length, and, moreover, relatively long loanwords disfavor initial accent as well.

(6) bá.su 'bus'　　　　　　　á.zi.a 'Asia'
　　yoo.róp.pa 'Europe'　　　san.do.ít.ti 'sandwich'
　　ku.ri.sú.ma.su 'Christmas'　ma.sa.tyuu.sét.tu 'Massachusetts'
　　wa.sín.ton 'Washington'　　ba.do.mín.ton 'badminton'

Thus, it remains unclear why loanwords fail to obey the N+1 law and become subject to a certain accent rule. This has a close bearing on the long-standing question in the loanword phonology of Japanese—namely, where does the antepenultimate accent rule of loanwords come from?

This question can be answered at least in part by considering a second fact that the standard view of Tokyo Japanese accent has overlooked. Statistically, the antepenultimate accent pattern is the most productive pattern among accented native nouns. Recall from table 7.1 that native nouns favor the unaccented pattern, whereas loanwords show a marked bias toward the accented pattern. However, this difference disappears if we restrict the analysis to accented nouns. A comparison between trimoraic accented loanwords and their native counterparts is summarized in table 7.2 (Kubozono 2006).

Table 7.2 shows that most trimoraic loanword and SJ nouns take an accent on their antepenultimate mora, if they are accented. This is in full agreement with what the accent rule in (5) predicts. Interestingly enough, the same accent pattern is chosen by a majority of (accented) native nouns as well. This similarity between native and loanword nouns is suggestive of two things. First, the antepenultimate accent pattern in loanwords does not arise out of the blue, nor does it simply correspond to accent patterns "in marginal sectors of the native Japanese vocabulary, such as proper names and prosodically derived words" (Shinohara 2000:91). Rather, it is the most productive accent pattern of accented native words. In other words, the accent rule in (5) is nothing but a native accent rule that comes from the native phonology of the language. This shows how heavily loanword phonology is constrained by the native phonology of the recipient language.

Second, and seen conversely, the similarity between native and loanword nouns implies that the antepenultimate accent pattern in native nouns is also rule governed. It is certainly true that the native vocabulary permits the other accented patterns—penultimate or final accent—to a considerable extent, but these subdominant accent patterns can be regarded as lexical exceptions to the antepenultimate rule in (5).[4] In other words, native nouns and loanwords primarily differ in the extent to which they admit lexical exceptions.

Table 7.2 considers the accentuation of three-mora nouns for two reasons: there are not many bimoraic loanwords in the language, and, moreover, most four-mora or longer native nouns are morphologically complex, at least etymologically. However, native nouns display basically the same accent patterns and preference as loanwords regardless of their phonological length. Five-mora or longer

Table 7.2 Word type and accent pattern in accented three-mora nouns

Accent pattern	Initial accent (= antepenultimate)	Medial accent (= penultimate)	Final accent
Native (634 words)	59%	33%	9%
SJ (2,427 words)	95%	2%	3%
Loan (722 words)	96%	2%	2%
Total (3,783 words)	89%	7%	4%

native nouns, virtually all of which are compound nouns, exhibit basically the same accentual tendencies as their loanword counterparts. For one thing, unlike native nouns with up to four morae, they disfavor the unaccented pattern. Moreover, their accent location is strikingly similar to the location of accent in loanwords in that accent tends to go as close as possible to the end of the word while avoiding the final syllable. This second point is discussed in detail in section 7.4, where it is demonstrated that the loanword accent rule in (5) and the accent rule of compound nouns are, in fact, one and the same.

In sum, statistical data, including those in table 7.2, indicate that, as far as accented nouns are concerned, accent location is largely predictable and rule governed in Tokyo Japanese—accented nouns, whether native or foreign, follow the antepenultimate rule in (5). This has two significant implications. Regarding lexical specification of accent, it clearly speaks against the traditional view that accent pattern is specified for each and every word in the lexicon. Instead, it supports the idea that the antepenultimate pattern should be attributed to a rule, whereas the other accented patterns represent lexical exceptions to this rule. Thus, the three accented patterns in table 7.2 do not have the same status in the lexicon. Seen from the perspective of language acquisition, children acquiring the language need to distinguish between accented and unaccented words as a whole, but they do not have to memorize the accent pattern of every accented noun. All they have to do is memorize the words showing accented patterns other than the antepenultimate pattern and apply the rule in (5) to all other words marked as accented.

This sparse representation of accent in the lexicon is shown in (7), where * denotes a kind of floating accent that is to be assigned to a certain syllable by rule. This analysis, which was originally hinted at by Haraguchi (1991) for nouns with four or more morae, has been shown by Kubozono (2006) to apply to shorter nouns as well.

(7) Lexical specification: two-pattern system with lexically marked words
    a. Major distinction
       Accented: i.no.ti* (* = floating accent, assigned by rule)
       Unaccented: sa.ka.na
    b. Lexically marked patterns: ko.kó.ro, o.to.kó

It may be argued that this accent analysis does not differ radically from the traditional analysis illustrated in (2). Under the new analysis, people acquiring the language acquire the antepenultimate accent rule, the distinction as to whether a given word belongs to the accented or unaccented class, and the small group of idiosyncratic words that are accented on an idiosyncratic location of the word. This may look like a sufficiently complex analysis, maybe as complex as the standard analysis of exhaustive accent specification. However, this criticism is not appropriate. The two analyses differ crucially from each other in terms of lexical specification and language acquisition. This difference shows up very clearly if a new word enters the vocabulary of the language. The traditional analysis in (2) does not make any concrete prediction as to how this new word is to be pronounced. The underspecification analysis in (7), in contrast, predicts that the new word will be pronounced with the antepenultimate accent pattern or, otherwise, as an unaccented word. This prediction squares perfectly with the well-known fact that most words borrowed from other languages—Sino-Japanese words and loanwords—as well as nonsense words follow the antepenultimate accent rule in (5) if they are not processed as unaccented words (see section 7.5 for an analysis of unaccented nouns).

A second implication that comes from the new analysis in (7) concerns the accent system of the language per se. As mentioned before, Tokyo Japanese is believed to have a multiple-pattern system for nouns and a two-pattern system for verbs and adjectives. The data presented in this section require us to reconsider this interpretation. Specifically, they suggest that Tokyo Japanese has a two-pattern system for nouns just as it does for verbs and adjectives and that nouns differ from verbs and adjectives only in the extent to which they admit lexical exceptions. Tokyo Japanese also differs from Kagoshima Japanese in the same way: Tokyo admits more lexical exceptions than Kagoshima. All of these systems crucially involve a contrast between two major accent patterns, accented and unaccented, but permit lexical exceptions to differing degrees. This analysis is further reinforced by the discussion in section 7.4.2, where it is shown that the antepenultimate accent rule for nouns—the rule in (5)—can be generalized with the penultimate accent rule for verbs and adjectives.

7.2.2 Antepenultimate Rule versus Latin Rule

Having seen that the antepenultimate accent rule in (5) is a general accent rule for accented nouns in Tokyo Japanese, it is worth considering here the argument that this accent rule has strikingly similar effects as the Latin/English stress rule (Kubozono 1996, 1999, 2006; Shinohara 2000). Because the antepenultimate rule in (5) has been formulated with the mora as the basic unit of description, it has the effect of accenting either the second or third syllable from the end of the word if reinterpreted in terms of the syllable. Assuming that syllables fall into two kinds—heavy (or bimoraic) and light (or monomoraic) (Kubozono 1999)—the antepenultimate rule assigns an accent as in the following, where H and L stand for heavy and light syllables, respectively, and syllables in boldface represent those to which an accent has been assigned.

(8) a. ...HHH# b. ...HHL# c. ...LHH# d. ...LHL#
    e. ...HLH# f. ...HLL# g. ...LLH# h. ...LLL#

On the other hand, the famous Latin accent rule is formulated as in (9) and assigns an accent as shown in (10) (Hayes 1995).

(9) Latin Accent Rule

Accent the penultimate syllable if it is heavy (bimoraic); otherwise, accent the antepenultimate syllable.

(10)   a. ...HHH#   b. ...HHL#   c. ...LHH#   d. ...LHL#
       e. ...HLH#   f. ...HLL#   g. ...LLH#   h. ...LLL#

A comparison between (8) and (10) reveals a striking similarity between the antepenultimate rule of Japanese and the Latin accent rule, the latter being a very general accent rule observed in a variety of languages (Hayes 1995). Indeed, these two rules make one and the same prediction in six out of the eight phonological contexts. What is fundamentally shared by the two rules is the assignment of accent as close to the end of the word as possible, while avoiding the very final syllable. On the other hand, they assign an accent onto different syllables in (8/10e) and (8/10g). In these two environments, the Japanese rule assigns an accent onto the penultimate light syllable, whereas the Latin rule obviously avoids this light syllable to choose the antepenult instead as the docking site of the accent.

Interestingly enough, an accent change is taking place in exactly these two environments in Tokyo Japanese (Kubozono 1999). Thus, older generations tend to prefer the accent patterns in (8e,g), and younger generations favor the Latin-type accent patterns in (10e,g). This is exemplified in (11), where the accent pattern of the first member of each pair is the one preferred by the older generations.

(11)   ...LLH#   do.rá.gon vs. dó.ra.gon 'dragon', re.bá.non vs. ré.ba.non 'Lebanon', a.má.zon vs. á.ma.zon 'Amazon', e.ne.rú.gii vs. e.né.ru.gii 'energy'
       ...HLH#   myuu.zí.syan vs. myúu.zi.syan 'musician', han.gá.rii vs. hán.ga.rii 'Hungary', en.dé.baa vs. én.de.baa 'endeavor'

According to statistical studies that looked at the accentuation of loanwords in accent dictionaries as well as that of nonsense words (Kubozono 1996, 2002; Tanaka 1996), the preantepenultimate patterns as in /dó.ra.gon/ and /myúu.zi.syan/ outnumber the antepenultimate patterns of /do.rá.gon/ and /myuu.zí.syan/.[5]

7.3 COMPOUND ACCENT RULES

In the preceding section I showed that morphologically simplex nouns follow the antepenultimate rule whether they are native nouns or loanwords. In this section, I move on to analyze the accentuation of compound nouns. The accent patterns shown by compound nouns in Tokyo Japanese have been formulated quite differently from those shown by morphologically simplex nouns. A standard view classifies compound nouns into two major groups, those with a short second member (N2) and those with a long N2 (McCawley 1968, Akinaga 1985, Poser 1990). "Short" here means monomoraic or bimoraic, whereas "long" means trimoraic or longer words. These two groups of compound nouns are supposed to follow different accent rules, although they both obey the basic principle whereby their accentuation is determined by the phonological structure of their second (or final) member.

In this section, I show that these two types of compound nouns need not be distinguished from each other in accentual terms—that is, the accent patterns exhibited by the two groups of compound nouns can be generalized into one accent rule if a certain number of lexically marked items are removed from the scope of accent computation. In showing this point, I also demonstrate that only a certain type of monomoraic or bimoraic morpheme is specified in the lexicon with respect to its accentual behavior in compound nouns. This speaks against the traditional view that all monomoraic or bimoraic morphemes are lexically marked as to their compound accent behavior (see section 7.1).

7.3.1 Compound Nouns with a Short Second Member

Compound nouns with a short N2 may be classified into three categories, depending on the accent patterns they take: those with a compound noun accent (CA) on the initial syllable of their N2, those with a CA on the final syllable of their first member (N1), and those that are unaccented. Traditionally, these three CA patterns have been attributed to the morphological property of N2, as briefly mentioned in section 7.1. Thus, morphemes that yield the first two types of CA patterns are called initial-accenting and preaccenting morphemes, respectively, whereas those that produce unaccented compounds are referred to as deaccenting morphemes (McCawley 1968). These three types of morphemes and their CA behavior are illustrated in (12).

(12) Compound nouns with a short N2
　　　a. *Initial-accenting* morphemes
　　　　　néko 'cat': perusya-néko 'Persian cat', maneki-néko 'cat with a beckoning paw'
　　　　　básu 'bus': maikuro-básu 'mini-bus', koosoku-básu 'highway bus'
　　　b. *Pre-accenting* morphemes
　　　　　sí 'city': hirosimá-si 'Hiroshima City', nagasakí-si 'Nagasaki City'
　　　　　ko 'child': tinomí-go 'baby at the breast; infant', minasí-go 'orphaned child'
　　　　　inú 'dog': akitá-inu 'Akita dog', mayoí-inu 'lost dog'
　　　　　híme 'princess': kaguyá-hime 'Princess Kaguya', sirayukí-hime 'Snow White'
　　　　　musi 'bug': kabutó-musi 'beetle', tentóo-musi 'ladybug'
　　　c. *Deaccenting* morphemes
　　　　　iró 'color': orenzi-iro 'orange color', nezumi-iro 'gray'
　　　　　tóo 'party': minsyu-too 'Democratic Party', kyoowa-too 'Republican Party'
　　　　　gó 'word, language': nihon-go 'the Japanese language', ei-go 'English'

This traditional analysis fails to explain the following three facts. First, a statistical study shows that the three types of morphemes are not equally popular; rather, the preaccenting morpheme is by far the most common (Kubozono 1997). Second, there is a certain correlation between the accent pattern of the N2 morphemes and the CA pattern they exhibit. Specifically, deaccenting and initial-accenting patterns arise only from N2s that are accented on their final and initial syllables, respectively, although not vice versa (Kubozono 1997). This is shown in table 7.3, where ✓✓ and ✓ mean that the correlation in question is very strong and relatively strong, respectively.

Finally, there is psycholinguistic evidence that children learning to speak Tokyo Japanese tend to acquire the deaccenting pattern later than the other two patterns (Shirose, Kubozono, and Kiritani 1997). All these facts suggest that the three types of morphemes in (12) do not have an equal status in the phonology of Japanese or in the mental lexicon of its speakers.

These three facts have led to a new CA analysis that distinguishes lexically marked patterns from lexically unmarked ones. This analysis assumes that only deaccenting morphemes are lexically marked—that is, that they are specified in the lexicon with respect to their accent behavior in compounds (Kubozono 1997). In terms of language acquisition, children have only to memorize this set of morphemes and their compound accent behavior. However, the other two types of morphemes—initial-accenting and preaccenting morphemes—are not lexically marked, but their accent behavior in compounds is accounted for largely by rule on the basis of their own lexical accent patterns.

More specifically, the compound accent patterns in (12a,b) can be attributed to the two basic principles in (13a, b), one specifying the condition on the parsability of the input N2 accent in the output, and the other defining the location of a default CA (Kubozono 1997).

(13) Generalization of the preaccenting and initial-accenting patterns
   a. Keep the accent of N2 as compound accent (CA) *except when* it is on the very final syllable.
      néko 'cat': perusya-néko 'Persian cat'
      inú 'dog': akitá-inu 'Akita dog'
   b. Otherwise, put a CA on the final syllable of N1.
      inú 'dog': akitá-inu 'Akita dog'
      musi 'bug': kabutó-musi 'beetle'

Table 7.3 Relationship between lexical and compound accent patterns

	Accent of compound nouns		
N2 accent	(12a)	(12b)	(12c)
Initial (= nonfinal) accent	✓✓	✓	—
Final accent	—	✓✓	✓
No accent	—	✓✓	—

The generalization in (13a) is based on two facts: (i) that the CA pattern in (12a) comes only from N2s that are originally accented on their initial—or nonfinal—syllable; and (ii) that if N2 is accented on its final syllable in the lexicon, this lexical accent is almost never preserved in compound nouns. There are a certain number of bimoraic morphemes, such as /híme/ in (12b), that are originally accented on their nonfinal syllable but do not nevertheless preserve their accent in compound nouns. But this type of morpheme is outnumbered by the /néko/-type morpheme, which readily retains its nonfinal accent in compounds.

The generalization in (13b), on the other hand, is based on the fact that a CA is placed on the N1-final syllable if N2 is lexically accented on its final syllable or is unaccented. This location of accent can be identified as the default location of CA in compound nouns with a short N2. It must be noted in this connection that the deaccenting morphemes in (12c) do not follow this generalization. They do follow the generalization in (13a) in that their final accent is never preserved in compound nouns. However, they do not attract a default CA in compound nouns of which they form the second member. This is where their idiosyncratic nature is manifested. This idiosyncratic pattern contrasts with the one shown by a large number of morphemes, including /inú/ and /sí/ in (12b), which are accented on their final syllable when pronounced in isolation but attract a default CA in compound nouns.

In sum, it is reasonable to assume that not all short morphemes are specified in the lexicon with respect to their accent behavior in compound nouns. Rather, only two types of morphemes are subject to such lexical specification: the so-called deaccenting morphemes that follow the generalization in (13a) but not the one in (13b), and the /híme/-type morpheme that does not keep its nonfinal accent in compound nouns. All other types of morphemes need not be specified in the lexicon with respect to their compound accent behavior. In terms of language acquisition, children have to memorize the idiosyncratic accent behavior of the first two types of morphemes while acquiring the two generalizations in (13) to produce the compound patterns in (12a,b) correctly.

7.3.2 Compound Nouns with a Long Second Member

As mentioned before, in previous studies of Japanese accent, compound nouns with a three-mora or longer N2 have been treated separately from those with a shorter N2. The most traditional analysis of this type of compound nouns was that of McCawley (1968), who proposed the following generalization.

(14)   a. If N2 is unaccented or accented on the final syllable, then a CA emerges on the initial syllable of N2.
      b. Otherwise, the accent of N2 survives as the CA.

The two subparts of this CA rule are exemplified in (15a,b), respectively.

(15) a. otokó 'man': yuki-ótoko 'snow, man; yeti'
       amerika 'America': minami-ámerika 'South America'
    b. nadésiko 'lady': yamato-nadésiko 'Japanese lady'
       báree 'volleyball': biiti-báree 'beach volleyball'

Poser (1990) revised this generalization by introducing the notion "bimoraic foot" in the analysis of Japanese accent:

(16) a. Mark the final foot of N2 as invisible.
    b. If the visible portion of N2 is unaccented, assign an accent to its initial syllable.
    c. Otherwise, leave the existing accent in place.

According to Poser's analysis, the final two morae of N2 become invisible to the CA rule with the result that the accent existent in this invisible portion is never preserved in compound nouns. In contrast, any accent in the remaining portion is visible to the CA rule and is retained in compounds, as formulated in (16c). Compound nouns cannot be unaccented and, hence, attract a CA onto the N2-initial syllable if the visible portion of N2 contains no accent.

Poser's analysis is superior to his predecessors' in incorporating the notion of bimoraic foot in the analysis of Japanese accent. However, his analysis is oversimplified in that it fails to account for the fact that compound nouns can and often do preserve an accent on the penultimate mora of N2. Some examples are given in (17).

(17) derawéa 'Delaware': kita-derawéa 'north Delaware'
     ototói 'the day before yesterday': saki-ototói 'three days ago'

Moreover, many words show a fluctuation between two accent patterns, one in which N2 preserves its accent on its penultimate mora and the other in which this accent is not respected.

(18) tamágo 'egg':   nama-tamágo, nama-támago 'raw egg'
     itóko 'cousin': mata-itóko, mata-ítoko 'second cousin'
     omútu 'diaper': kami-omútu, kami-ómutu '(disposable) paper diaper'

All these examples suggest that an accent on the nonfinal syllable of N2 can be faithfully preserved in compound nouns. This leads to a new generalization, summarized in (19).

(19) Compound nouns with a long N2
    a. Keep the accent of N2 as CA *except when* it is on the very final syllable.
    b. Otherwise, put a CA on the initial syllable of N2.

Notice that this generalization is very similar to the one proposed for compound nouns with a short N2. In fact, the parsability conditions in (13a) and (19a) are identical. In both types of compound nouns, the input accent of N2 is preserved quite faithfully in the output compounds except when it is on the very final syllable. How then are the other subparts of the generalizations—(13b) and (19b)—related to each other?

In (13b), a default CA appears on the final syllable of N1, whereas it emerges on the initial syllable of N2 in (19b). These are compared in (20) and illustrated in (21) with unaccented N2s.

(20) a. If N2 is either monomoraic or bimoraic, a CA falls on the final syllable of N1.
      b. If N2 is three morae long or longer, a CA falls on the initial syllable of N2.

(21) a. ti.no.mi + ko   → ti.no.mí-go 'milk drinking, baby; breastfeeding baby'
         ku.wa.ga.ta + mu.si   → ku.wa.ga.tá-mu.si 'stag beetle'
         tu.ki + ki.zu   → tu.kí-ki.zu 'to push, bruise; prick or stab'
      b. nó + ne.zu.mi   → no-né.zu.mi 'field, mouse; field mouse'
         sín + yo.ko.ha.ma   → sin-yó.ko.ha.ma 'New Yokohama (Station)'
         mi.na.mi + a.me.ri.ka   → mi.na.mi-á.me.ri.ka 'South America'

At a glance, these appear to be entirely different effects of CA. If one looks at the location of the default accent from the end of the compound, however, one can see their identity. The two rules in (20) both avoid placing an accent on the final syllable (Nonfinality-syllable) and on the final two morae (Nonfinality-foot) unless the final mora itself constitutes an independent word in compounds. Moreover, both rules avoid placing an accent on a syllable too far from the right edge of the word (Edgemostness). The Nonfinality effect can be seen clearly from the fact that /no-né.zu.mi/, /sin-yó.ko.ha.ma/, and /mi.na.mi-á.me.ri.ka/ in (21b) cannot be accented on the penultimate syllable (i.e., */no-ne.zú.mi/, */sin-yo.ko.há.ma/, */mi.na.mi-a.me.rí.ka/), whereas /sin-yo.kó.ha.ma/ and /mi.na.mi-a.mé.ri.ka/ can be accepted as variant accent patterns of /sin-yó.ko.ha.ma/ and /mi.na.mi-á.me.ri.ka/, respectively.

Similarly, the tendency to put an accent toward the end of the word can be confirmed by the fact that the rule in (20b) does not apply to compound nouns with a five-mora or longer unaccented N2, a fact that has been overlooked by most previous studies. Compounds with this type of N2 generally become unaccented or otherwise bear a CA on the third or fourth mora from the end of the word (Kubozono and Mester 1995; Kubozono, Ito, and Mester 1997). This is illustrated in (22), where loanword N2 is used in the absence of an appropriate noncompound native noun. These exceptional compound patterns, which contrast with the one in (21b), suggest that assigning an accent on the fifth or six mora from the right edge of the word is banned or disfavored in Japanese compounds.

(22) minami + kariforunia → mi.na.mi-ka.ri.fo.ru.ni.a, mi.na.mi-ka.ri.fo.rú.ni.a
                              *mi.na.mi-ká.ri.fo.ru.ni.a 'Southern California'
      nyúu + karedonia   → nyuu-ka.re.do.ni.a, nyuu-ka.re.dó.ni.a
                              *nyuu-ká.re.do.ni.a 'New Caledonia'

In any case, the two CA rules in (20) have basic features in common. This observation prompted Kubozono and Mester (1995) to propose that the two rules represent the two sides of a single coin and can be unified. By using "bimoraic foot" as a key notion and assuming that foot formation is bound by morpheme boundaries, Kubozono (1995) proposed the following descriptive generalization for the two rules in (20).

(23) a. Accent the rightmost, nonfinal foot (Nonfinality-foot, Edgemostness).
      b. Within the rightmost, nonfinal foot, accent the syllable that is closer to the word-internal morpheme boundary (Align-CA).[6]

When combined with the parsability condition in (13a) and (19a), repeated in (24), (23) allows us to account for the accent pattern of compound nouns in general, irrespective of the accentuation and phonological length of N2. Some examples with an accented N2 are given in (25), where foot structure [ ] is shown only in relevant places (see Kubozono 1995, 1997 for a detailed analysis).

(24) Keep the accent of N2 as CA *except when* it is on the very final syllable (Max-accent).

(25) ten.zyoo + [ka.wá]   → ten.[zyóo]-ga.wa 'ceiling, river; raised bed river'
      á.ka + [kái]   → [a.ká]-gai 'red, shellfish; arch shell'
      ma.ne.ki + [né.ko]   → ma.ne.ki-[né.ko] 'inviting, cat; a cat with a beckoning paw'
      yá.ma.to + na.[dé.si].ko → ya.ma.to-na.[dé.si].ko 'Japan, lady; Japanese lady'
      na.tú + ya.su.mí   → na.tu-[yá.su].mi 'summer, holiday; summer holiday'

In sum, the compound accent patterns exhibited by compounds with a short N2 and those with a long N2 can be generalized. There are several keys to this generalization. One of them is to make a distinction between lexically marked and rule-governed patterns in compound nouns with a short N2. This allows us to exclude the unaccented pattern in (12c) from the scope of phonological computation, which is an accent pattern that is never produced by compound nouns with a three- or four-mora N2. Another key to the new generalization in question is to define precisely the extent to which the lexical accent of N2 can be preserved in compound nouns. The two types of compound nouns exhibit a crucial similarity in that they both tend to preserve an input accent of N2 unless it is on the very final syllable. Third, the default accent location in the two types of compound nouns can be identified by computing the CA from the end of the word and by using the notion of bimoraic foot. The two types of compound nouns both display a strong tendency to put a CA as close to the end of the word while avoiding the final two morae.

7.4 FURTHER GENERALIZATION

7.4.1 Compound Accent and Antepenultimate Accent

We have seen in the preceding section that compound nouns—whether with a short or long N2—tend to maximally preserve the input accent of N2 on the one hand, and on the other hand, put a default CA toward the end of the word while avoiding the last two morae. This second part of the CA rule, it must be noticed, looks very similar to the effect of the antepenultimate rule in (5), which, as pointed out in section 7.2, accounts for the accent location of accented nouns that are morphologically simplex. Indeed, both rules can be attributed to two factors, one that forces an accent away from the final syllable and another that prohibits the accent from docking too far from the right edge of the word. In theoretical terms, these two factors are equivalent to Nonfinality and Edgemostness, the two constraints that govern the accentuation of compound nouns in general (see (23a)).

The basic identity between the antepenultimate rule in (5) and the CA rule leads to the generalization that these two rules essentially represent one and the same process, which is a conclusion independently reached by Kubozono (2002) and Shinohara (2002). The only difference between the two rules is that the antepenultimate rule only consists of the default rule in (23a), whereas the CA rule involves the Align-CA principle in (23b) and the faithfulness principle in (24) in addition to the default rule in (23a). Note that the two principles in (23b) and (24) vacuously apply to morphologically simplex nouns. What this means is that all nouns, both morphologically simplex and complex, are subject to one and the same set of principles. On the one hand, morphologically complex words are subject to Align-CA and Max-accent, the two principles that apply to morphologically complex inputs, in addition to the default accent rule. On the other hand, morphologically simplex nouns are free from compound-related constraints because they lack internal structure and are hence subject only to the default rule in (23a). Obviously, this difference arises from the differences in input structure between simplex and compound nouns and not from any difference in the system in which their accentuation is computed.

That morphologically simplex accented nouns follow the default rule in (23a) can be shown in (26), where loanwords are used for illustration.

(26) su.[tó.re].su   'stréss'
      [sái].daa   'cíder'
      yoo.[róp].pa   'Européa'
      ku.ri.[sú.ma].su   'Chrístmas'
      wa.[sín].[ton]   'Wáshington'
      an.[dáa].[son]   'Ánderson'
      pai.[náp].[pu.ru]   'píneapple'
      ba.do.[mín].[ton]   'bádminton'

This leads me to conclude that the antepenultimate accent rule is fundamentally the same as the CA rule responsible for the accentuation of accented four-mora and longer nouns. This reinforces the argument developed in section 7.2 that the antepenultimate rule—or the principle behind it—accounts for the default accent pattern of accented native nouns: it reflects the default accent pattern in the core part of the accented native vocabulary. Moreover, the antepenultimacy effect is, after all, an epiphenomenon that results from the interaction between the Nonfinality and Edgemostness effects.

7.4.2 Noun Accent and Verb/Adjective Accent

Finally, let us consider the accent rule for verbs and adjectives, which represents another major accent rule in Japanese. As mentioned in section 7.2, verbs and adjectives are either accented or unaccented and, if accented, they are accented on their penultimate mora. Some examples from (3) are repeated here as (27).

(27) a. Penultimate accent: hasíru 'to run', sirabéru 'to examine', umái 'tasty', utukusíi 'beautiful'
      b. No accent (unaccented): ageru 'to raise', amai 'sweet'

Previous studies of Japanese accent pointed out three crucial differences between noun and verb/adjective accentuation. First, nouns supposedly constitute a multiple-pattern system, whereas verbs and adjectives form a two-pattern system. Second, the default accent location of accented nouns is the third mora from the end of the word, whereas that of accented verbs and adjectives is the second mora from the end of the word. Third, the majority of native nouns are unaccented, as illustrated in table 7.1, and the vast majority of (native) verbs and adjectives are accented (Tanaka and Kubozono 1999). I have already argued against the first characterization, by pointing out that nouns also have a two-pattern system—accented versus unaccented—with a certain number of lexical exceptions taking an idiosyncratic accent pattern. It is puzzling then why accent location differs between accented nouns and accented verbs and adjectives.

A fact that has a crucial bearing on this question is that the two groups of words differ in morphological complexity. Nouns can be either morphologically simplex or complex. Morphologically complex nouns are called compound nouns whose accentuation, as discussed in the preceding section, crucially resembles that of morphologically simplex nouns. However, verbs and adjectives are all morphologically complex, given that they consist of a stem (or root) and a suffix (or ending). Verbs fall into consonant-final and vowel-final verbs, but, in either case, they are morphologically complex with a monomoraic ending.[7]

(28) hasír-u, sirabé-ru, umá-i, utukusí-i

Given the morphological complexity of verbs and adjectives, it is easy to explain why they are accented on their penultimate mora if they are accented at all.

Verbs and adjectives are accented on the second mora from the end of the word because of the same compound accent rule that assigns an accent on the same position in compound nouns with a monomoraic second member, such as /minasí-go/ 'orphaned child' and /hirosimá-si/ 'Hiroshima City' in (12b). Penultimate accent in verbs and adjectives at a boundary presumably aids in parsing the words into their two constituents. This analysis also has the advantage of accounting for the fact, mentioned above, that unlike morphologically simplex nouns, verbs and adjectives tend to be accented rather than unaccented. Morphologically complex words, whether they are nouns or verbs and adjectives, are generally accented rather than unaccented as an effect of the compound accent rule.

In sum, verbs and adjectives, too, are governed by the same accent rule as accented nouns—namely, by the rule (23a) that assigns an accent to the rightmost, nonfinal foot. This explains why most verbs and adjectives are accented, although a majority of morphologically simplex (native) nouns are unaccented.

7.5 NATIVE VERSUS LOANWORD ACCENTUATION

Until now I have deferred the question regarding the crucial accentual difference between native words and loanwords. At the beginning of the chapter, I illustrated that most loanwords become accented, whereas their native counterparts tend to be unaccented (see table 7.1). It is clear from the discussion in section 7.2 that the accent pattern shown by accented loanwords is directly attributable to the accent rule responsible for accented native nouns. However, it remains unclear why loanwords do not tend to become unaccented. Kubozono (2006) proposes two factors to account for this apparent difference between the two groups of words: one concerns phonological structure, and the other has to do with input-output relationship.

Table 7.4 Word type and syllable structure in trimoraic words

		Syllable structure		
Word type	LLL	HL	LH	Total
Native	2,084 (94%)	112 (5%)	24 (1%)	2,220 (100%)
Sino-Japanese	1,110 (22%)	2,257 (46%)	1,572 (32%)	4,939 (100%)
Loan	296 (38%)	350 (45%)	132 (17%)	778 (100%)

$N = 7{,}937$ words.
Source: NHK 1998.

Table 7.5 Correlation between syllable structure and accent pattern in four-mora loanwords

Syllable structure	#LLLL#	#HLL#	#LHL#	#LLH#	#HH#	Average
Unaccentedness ratio	54%	45%	24%	19%	7%	29%

N = 963 words.
Source: NHK 1998.

Loanwords are crucially different from native words in containing an abundance of heavy syllables and epenthetic vowels. Compare the words for 'smoke', for example. The native noun is /ke.mu.ri/, which is an unaccented word consisting of three light syllables with no epenthetic vowel. In contrast, its loanword counterpart, /su.móo.ku/, has an accented heavy syllable with the other two syllables containing an epenthetic vowel. That loanwords differ from native words in syllable composition is illustrated in table 7.4, where three-mora native nouns are compared with their loanword counterparts.

It is well known that heavy syllables tend to attract an accent as compared with light syllables across languages (Prince and Smolensky 1993/2004). This is true in Japanese, too, where words with a heavy syllable tend to attract an accent. Stated conversely, words consisting solely of light syllables resist being accented in a language like Japanese, where unaccented words are tolerated as an independent accent category. This analysis can be supported by the fact that loanwords tend to become unaccented if they consist of light syllables. This is particularly so in four-mora loanwords, which, in fact, display a high degree of variability in the ratio of the unaccented pattern depending on the syllable structure of the word. As shown in table 7.5, although the unaccented pattern accounts for only about 30 percent of all four-mora loanwords, it accounts for 54 percent of four-mora loanwords with no heavy syllable. The same accent pattern accounts for only 7 percent of those with only heavy syllables (Kubozono and Fukui, 2006).

Furthermore, the ratio of the unaccented pattern also varies depending on the presence or absence of an epenthetic vowel, especially in word-final position. Thus, four-mora loanwords that end in a sequence of light syllables are mostly unaccented (90 percent) if their final vowel is underlying, whereas the ratio goes down to about 30 percent in words ending in an epenthetic vowel. This is shown in table 7.6 and exemplified in (29), where <>means that the syllable contains an epenthetic vowel (Kubozono and Fukui, 2006).

Table 7.6 Epenthetic vowel and the percentage of the unaccented pattern in LLLL and HLL loanwords

Epenthetic/nonepenthetic	..LL#	..L<L>#	Average
Unaccentedness ratio	90%	32%	50%

N = 355 words.

(29) Examples of unaccented loanwords
　　　s<u>.te.re.o 'stereo'
　　　si.na.ri.o 'scenario'
　　　in.h<u>.re 'inflation'
　　　a.ri.zo.na 'Arizona'
　　　i.ta.ri.a 'Italy'
　　　ho.no.ru.ru 'Honolulu'
　　　a.to.ri.e 'atelier'
　　　ma.ka.ro.ni 'macaroni, a kind of pasta'
　　　u.ku.re.re. 'ukulele'
　　　he.r<u>.ni.a 'hernia (Latin)'

　　According to Sibata (1994), 64 percent of four-mora nonloanwords—that is, native and SJ nouns combined—take the unaccented pattern. The data in table 7.6 indicate that loanwords can show a higher percentage of the unaccented pattern if they are given a nativelike phonological structure—that is, a sequence of light syllables and no epenthetic vowel. This reinforces the argument that loanwords do not crucially differ from native words in accent structure and preference. What appears to be an accentual difference between the two types of words—such as the one in table 7.1—stems largely from their differences in syllable structure and in the nature of vowels. If these factors are properly controlled, as shown in tables 7.5 and 7.6, then the two types of words display much the same accent structure and preference.

　　A second reason for the high percentage of the accented pattern in loanwords is that loanwords, but not native or SJ words, have correspondents in the source language. According to Sibata (1994), 84 percent of loanwords used in modern Japanese come from English, whose words are produced with a sudden pitch drop when pronounced in isolation. As is well known, almost every Japanese person receives English instruction at school and, moreover, pitch fall is a distinctive phonetic feature in the accent system of Tokyo Japanese. Given these facts, it will come as no surprise if native speakers of Japanese become sensitive to the pitch fall in the pronunciation of English words. It can be easily understood that this pitch feature is preserved in Japanese as a lexical accent although accent location is adjusted by the native accent rule (Kubozono 2006): for example, Wáshington → wa.[sín].ton, *wásinton, *wasinton (no accent). Unlike loanwords, native and SJ words do not have such an input prosodic feature to preserve in the output. This explains why many SJ words are unaccented although they involve many heavy syllables and epenthetic vowels.

　　That loanwords inherit a certain prosodic property of their source words is not a language-specific phenomenon. Kagoshima Japanese, a dialect described in section 7.2, distinguishes between two accent patterns—one with a pitch fall and the other without. In this dialect, the two accent patterns compete in nonloanwords in frequency, but the pattern with a pitch fall is by far the more common in loanwords, accounting for 95 percent of the loanword data (Kibe and Hashimoto 2003).[8] This is illustrated in (30), where high-toned syllables are capitalized: words with a high tone on their final syllable are pronounced without a pitch fall, whereas those with a high tone on their penultimate syllable involve a pitch fall at the phonetic output.

(30)   ya.KYUU vs. bee.su.BOO.ru   'baseball'
         dan.RO vs. su.TOO.bu   'heater'
         koo.kuu.BIN vs. e.a.MEE.ru   'airmail'
         hu.ku.SYUU vs. ri.BEN.zi   'revenge'
         a.O vs. BU.ruu   'blue'
         A.ka vs. RED.do   'red'
         si.roo.TO vs. a.ma.TYU.a   'amateur'

Kagoshima Japanese differs from Tokyo Japanese in permitting closed (and hence heavy) syllables quite freely in the native vocabulary as in the foreign vocabulary (Kubozono 2006). However, loanwords and native words nevertheless display an apparent difference in accentual preference in this dialect just as they do in Tokyo Japanese. This apparent difference can be attributed to the perceptual role in loanword adaptation, which is entirely absent in the accentuation of native and SJ words.

7.6 Conclusion and Implications for Phonological Theory

7.6.1 Conclusion

In this chapter I argue that the accent system of Tokyo Japanese is not as complex as is generally assumed. It is not so complex for two reasons: one regards the degree to which words are accentually specified in the lexicon, and the other concerns the number of accent rules in the system. As for accent specification, I claim that accent is only sparsely specified in the lexicon. This shows up in two independent ways. First, the antepenultimate pattern that accounts for the majority of accented words in Tokyo Japanese in all lexical strata—native, SJ, or foreign—is not lexically specified but is rule governed. This explains why new words—words borrowed from other languages as well as newly coined words—exhibit the antepenultimate pattern among the multiple accent patterns. Therefore, words showing the antepenultimate pattern need not be specified in the lexicon with respect to their accent location. Thus, /ínoti/ 'life' and /azárasi/ 'harbor seal' are free from the specification of accent location in the lexicon, whereas /kokóro/ 'heart' and /koohíi/ 'coffee' must be lexically specified as to the accent location.

Second, only a portion of monomoraic and bimoraic morphemes are lexically specified with respect to their accent behavior in compound nouns. Among the three types of short morphemes, only deaccenting morphemes such as /iró/ and /tóo/ and the /híme/-type morphemes must be marked in the lexicon: the former does not attract a default compound accent, and the latter does not keep a nonfinal accent when it forms the second member of compound nouns. In contrast, the other two general types of morphemes—so-called preaccenting and initial-accenting morphemes—need not be marked in the lexicon as their accent behavior in compound nouns can be readily computed by rule on the basis of their own accent structure.

In sum, I argue for two types of accent underspecification in the lexicon—one for lexical items themselves and the other for their accent behavior in compounds. These two types of sparse accent representation share the following basic property or tendency: the shorter the word becomes, the more likely it is to be lexically marked.[9] For example, a good portion of three- and four-mora nouns do not obey the antepenultimate rule, whereas longer words show a stronger tendency to follow the rule. Similarly, a portion of monomoraic and bimoraic morphemes must be marked in the lexicon as to their accent behavior in compounds, whereas three-mora and longer morphemes are not subject to such lexical markedness.

A second major claim of this chapter is that major accent rules in Tokyo Japanese can be unified into a single basic rule. First of all, the accent pattern shown by accented native nouns can be attributed to the famous antepenultimate accent rule that has been proposed specifically for loanwords (McCawley 1968). It is true that native nouns exhibit accent patterns other than the antepenultimate one, but a reinterpretation of the data in terms of phonological markedness leads to a different analysis whereby these other accented patterns are lexically marked. After all, native nouns share with loanwords the same accent rule but differ in the number of lexical exceptions they permit. This analysis also suggests that nouns in Tokyo form a two-pattern accent system just as verbs and adjectives do in the same dialect. Here again, nouns differ from verbs and adjectives in the degree to which they permit lexical exceptions.

The general accent rule for morphologically simplex nouns can be further generalized with the set of compound accent rules responsible for the accentuation of morphologically complex nouns. Although the accent patterns exhibited by compound nouns with a short second member and those with a long second member are formulated in entirely different ways in the literature, they can be generalized if a lexically marked pattern—the one yielded by deaccenting morphemes—is excluded from the scope of accent computation. Moreover, this generalized accent rule for compound nouns can be unified with the antepenultimate accent rule mentioned earlier. It follows from this that Tokyo Japanese has one general rule for nouns, regardless of whether they are morphologically complex or simplex or whether they are loanwords or native words. Additionally, I propose a further generalization of this accent rule by showing that it can also be unified with the accent pattern displayed by accented verbs and adjectives.

What underlies the accentuation of all these various kinds of words in Tokyo Japanese is the principle that puts an accent as close to the end of the word as possible while avoiding the very final syllable. To put it another way, the basic rule of accentuation in this language places an accent on the rightmost, nonfinal foot.

7.6.2 Implications

The new analysis of Japanese accent has certain implications beyond Japanese phonology. One implication concerns the fact that Japanese pitch accent is strikingly similar to the Latin accent rule, which is also employed in English. English and Japanese have been characterized as different kinds of accent languages—stress accent versus pitch accent (Beckman 1986). However, they share fundamental properties with respect to accent computation, as discussed in section 7.2.2. Specifically, both languages display a clear tendency to put an accent toward the end of the word while avoiding the very final syllable. This suggests that pitch accent languages can be analyzed on the same grounds as stress accent languages as far as the computation of accent location is concerned.

However, the pitch accent system of Tokyo Japanese exhibits one crucial difference from the stress accent system of English. That is, Tokyo Japanese has a number of unaccented words, or words that are pronounced with a rather flat pitch and, hence, lack a tonal prominence. This difference is reminiscent of and quite consistent with Hyman's (2005) claim that "a language with stress-accent is one in which... every word has AT LEAST one syllable marked for the highest degree of metrical prominence (primary stress)" [emphasis in original].

Another interesting implication of the Japanese data for general linguistic theory has to do with the central issue in loanword phonology: where do loanword patterns come from? Tokyo Japanese presents a challenging case for this question because loanwords and native words favor different accent patterns: most loanwords are accented as opposed to unaccented, which sharply contrasts with the dominance of the unaccented pattern in the native vocabulary. We have seen, first of all, that the loanword accent rule is the very rule that governs *accented* native words. This demonstrates that loanword prosody is heavily constrained by native prosody. On the other hand, the fact that loanwords favor the accented pattern over the unaccented one can be attributed to several general and independent factors, such as (i) differences in phonological structures—syllable structure and the nature of vowels—between the two types of words, and (ii) the fact that loanwords but not native words are subject to the influence of source word prosody. The latter factor speaks for the relevance of a perceptual effect of source words on adapted forms.

7.6.3 Future Agenda

Before concluding this chapter, I would like to sum up some remaining problems for future research. It is interesting, for example, to ask if the general accent rule proposed here—or the descriptive generalization summarized in (23) and (24)—can be extended to cover accent rules other than those discussed in this chapter, particularly the seemingly complex accent patterns exhibited by conjugated verb forms (Akinaga 2001) and the miscellaneous accent rules discussed in Kubozono 2001. This line of research may show that the general accent rule is indeed more general than has been claimed in this chapter.

Another interesting question for future research is how to formalize the general accent rule of Tokyo Japanese in the nonderivational framework of Optimality Theory. Optimality-theoretic analyses have thus far analyzed different aspects of Japanese accent: for example, Katayama (1998) and Shinohara (2000) examined loanword accent, Kubozono (1995, 1997) and Shinohara (2002) looked at compound noun accent, and so forth. It is necessary to incorporate all these studies into one picture and, by using only those constraints that are independently motivated, to propose a general and comprehensive constraint-based grammar of Japanese accent. This task may not be easy, given that Japanese accent appears quite complicated in some respects: for example, loanwords and native words assign different accent patterns for words with one and the same phonological (syllable) structure, epenthetic vowels often display somewhat ad hoc accent behavior (Kubozono 2001), and so on. Theoretical research along this line will illuminate both the universal and language-specific properties of Japanese accent, on the one hand, and the importance of Japanese accent for the general study of word accent on the other hand.

NOTES FOR CHAPTER 7

An earlier version of this article was presented at the Workshop on Linguistic Theory and the Japanese Language held at Harvard University in July 2005. I would like to thank the audience of that meeting, particularly Armin Mester, Junko Ito, Michael Kenstowicz, and Alan Prince, for various valuable comments. I am also grateful to Donna Erickson for checking and commenting on this manuscript. All errors that remain are, of course, my own. This work has been supported by Grant-in-Aid for Scientific Research (A) and (B) (Japan Society for the Promotion of Science, grant nos. 17202010 and 14310222) and Grant-in-Aid for Exploratory Research (Ministry of Education, Culture, Sports, Science and Technology, grant no. 15652027).

1. Voiceless obstruents such as /t/ and /s/ often undergo *rendaku*, or sequential voicing, when they stand in the initial position of a noninitial member of compounds.

2. The data in this table as well as those in table 7.2 come from *The NHK Pronunciation and Accent Dictionary* (1998).

3. Unlike Tokyo Japanese and many other Japanese dialects, Kagoshima Japanese is a syllable-based language in which the syllable is the relevant phonological unit: thus, phonological distance is measured in terms of the syllable and high tones are assigned to a

particular syllable, not to a particular mora. The loanword /wa.sin.ton/ 'Washington', for example, is pronounced with a high tone on /sin/, which is the second syllable from the end of the word.

4. The relatively high popularity of the penultimate accent pattern in native nouns in table 7.2 is attributable largely to the fact that most of the words showing this accent type are morphologically complex—that is, compound nouns, whose accentuation can be explained by the compound accent pattern discussed in section 7.3; for example, /ha.ná-ya/ 'flower, house; flower shop', /ha.tá-bi/ 'flag, day; holiday'.

5. Native and SJ nouns do not exhibit the preantepenultimate patterns in question, because those that have the syllable composition in (11) are compound nouns and, hence, attract a compound noun accent near the compound-internal morpheme boundary; for example, /gakú#mon/ 'learning'. See the next section for details.

6. This indicates that compound noun accent in Japanese basically has a boundary-marking effect. This is a feature that compound accent shares with other phonological processes observed in compounds such as *rendaku* (or sequential voicing) and vowel alternation (Ito and Mester 2003). Boundary marking presumably aids in parsing the compound into its two constituents.

7. Verbal and adjectival conjugations and their accent patterns are beyond the scope of this chapter.

8. Basque seems to display a similar situation with its loanwords, which show a stronger tendency to be accented than native words (Jose Hualde, pers. comm.).

9. Kenstowicz and Sohn (2001) also observe in Kyungsang Korean that accent is contrastive in shorter nouns but predictable in longer ones.

REFERENCES

Akinaga, Kazue. 1985. Kyootuugo no akusento [Accent of Standard Japanese]. In *NHK pronunciation and accent dictionary*, ed. NHK, 70–116. Tokyo: Nippon Hoso Shuppan Kyokai.

Akinaga, Kazue. 2001. Tookyoo akusento no syuutoku hoosoku [Rules for learning Tokyo accent]. In *Sin meikai nihongo akusento ziten*, ed. Haruhiko Kindaichi, 10–106. Tokyo: Sanseido.

Beckman, Mary. 1986. *Stress and non-stress accent*. Dordrecht: Foris.

Dupoux, E., K. Kakehi, Y. Hirose, C. Pallier, and J. Mehler. 1999. Epenthetic vowels in Japanese: A perceptual illusion? *Journal of Experimental Psychology: Human Perception and Performance* 25:1568–1578.

Haraguchi, Shosuke. 1991. *A theory of stress and accent*. Dordrecht: Foris.

Hayes, Bruce. 1995. *Metrical stress theory: Principles and case studies*. Chicago: University of Chicago Press.

Hyman, Larry M. 2005. Word-prosodic typology. Paper presented at the BeST (Between Stress and Tone) Conference, Leiden University, the Netherlands, June.

Ito, Junko, and Armin Mester. 2003. *Japanese morphophonemics: Markedness and word structure*. Cambridge, Mass.: MIT Press.

Ito, Katsuhiko. 1990. *Kodomo no kotoba* [Child language]. Tokyo: Keisoo Shoboo.

Katayama, Motoko. 1998. Optimality Theory and Japanese loanword phonology. Doctoral dissertation, University of California, Santa Cruz.

Kenstowicz, Michael, and Hyang-Sook Sohn. 2001. Accentual adaptation in North Kyungsang Korean. In *Ken Hale: A life in language*, ed. Michael Kenstowicz, 239–270. Cambridge, Mass.: MIT Press.

Kenstowicz, Michael, and Christian Uffmann, eds. 2006. *Lingua: A special issue on loanword phonology*.

Kibe, Nobuko, and Yumi Hashimoto. 2003. Kagoshimashi hoogen no gairaigono onchoo [Tone of loanwords in Kagoshima Japanese]. *The Journal of the Phonetic Society of Japan* 7(3): 92–100.

Kubozono, Haruo. 1995. Constraint interaction in Japanese phonology: Evidence from compound accent. *Phonology at Santa Cruz (PASC)* 4:21–38.

Kubozono, Haruo. 1996. Syllable and accent in Japanese: Evidence from loanword accentuation. *The Bulletin* (Phonetic Society of Japan) 211:71–82.

Kubozono, Haruo. 1997. Lexical markedness and variation: A non-derivational account. *WCCFL* 15:273–287.

Kubozono, Haruo. 1999. Mora and syllable. In *The handbook of Japanese linguistics*, ed. Natsuko Tsujimura, 31–61. Oxford: Blackwell.

Kubozono, Haruo. 2001. Epenthetic vowels and accent in Japanese: Facts and paradoxes. In *Issues in Japanese phonology and morphology*, ed. Jeroen van de Weijer and Tetsuo Nishihara, 113–142. Berlin: Mouton de Gruyter.

Kubozono, Haruo. 2002. Syllable weight and Japanese accent. Paper presented at LP 2004, Meikai University. (To appear in *Proceedings of LP 2002*. Prague: Charles University Press.)

Kubozono, Haruo. 2006. Where does loanword prosody come from? A case study of Japanese loanword accent. *Lingua* 116(7):1140–1170.

Kubozono, Haruo. 2007. Tonal change in language contact: Evidence from Kagoshima Japanese. In *Tones and tunes: Vol. 1: Typological studies in word and sentence prosody*, ed. Carlos Gussenhoven and Tomas Riad, 323–351. Berlin: Mouton de Gruyter.

Kubozono, Haruo, and Misa Fukui. 2006. Phonological structure and unaccented nouns in Tokyo and Osaka Japanese. *Japanese/Korean Linguistics* 14, ed. Timothy Vance and Kimberly Jones, 39–50. Stanford, Calif.: CSLI Publications and SLI.

Kubozono, Haruo, Junko Ito, and Armin Mester. 1997. On'in koozoo kara mita go to ku no kyookai [The phonological boundary between the word and the phrase]. In *Bunpoo to onsei [Speech and grammar]*, ed. Spoken Language Research Group, 147–166. Tokyo: Kurosio.

Kubozono, Haruo, and Armin Mester. 1995. Foot and accent: New evidence from Japanese compound accentuation. Paper presented at the annual LSA meeting, New Orleans, January.

McCawley, James D. 1968. *The phonological component of a grammar of Japanese*. The Hague: Mouton.

NHK, ed. 1985/98. *NHK pronunciation and accent dictionary*. Tokyo: Nippon Hoso Shuppan Kyokai.

Paradis, Carole, and Darlene LaCharité. 1997. Preservation and minimality in loanword adaptation. *Journal of Linguistics* 33:379–430.

Poser, William. 1984. The phonetics and phonology of tone and intonation in Japanese. Doctoral dissertation, MIT, Cambridge, Mass.

Poser, William. 1990. Evidence for foot structure in Japanese. *Language* 66:78–105.

Prince, Alan, and Paul Smolensky. 1993. *Optimality Theory: Constraint interaction in generative grammar*. Technical Report 2, Rutgers Center for Cognitive Science, Rutgers University. (Published 2004. Oxford: Blackwell.)

Shibatani, Masayoshi. 1990. *The languages of Japan*. Cambridge: Cambridge University Press.
Shinohara, Shigeko. 2000. Default accentuation and foot structure in Japanese: Evidence from Japanese adaptations of French words. *Journal of East Asian Linguistics* 9:55–96.
Shinohara, Shigeko. 2002. Metrical constraints and word identity in Japanese compound nouns. *MIT Working Papers in Linguistics* 42:311–328.
Shirose, Ayako, Haruo Kubozono, and Shigeru Kiritani. 1997. The acquisition of compound accent in Japanese. *Proceedings of the 16th International Congress of Linguists* (CD-ROM). Amsterdam: Elsevier.
Sibata, Takesi. 1994. Gairaigo ni okeru akusento kaku no ichi [On the location of accent in loanwords]. In *Gendaigo hoogen no kenkyuu* [*Studies on modern dialects*], ed. Kiyoji Sato, 338–418. Tokyo: Meiji Shoin.
Silverman, Daniel. 1992. Multiple scansion in loanword phonology: Evidence from Cantonese. *Phonology* 9:289–328.
Tanaka, Shin'ichi. 1996. Nihongo no onsetu koozoo to on'in gensyoo [Syllable structure and phonological phenomena in Japanese]. Master's thesis, Osaka University of Foreign Studies, Osaka, Japan.
Tanaka, Shin'ichi, and Haruo Kubozono. 1999. *Nihongo no hatuon kyoositu* [*Introduction to Japanese pronunciation*]. Tokyo: Kurosio.
Uwano, Zendo. 1999. Classification of Japanese accent systems. In *Proceedings of the symposium "Cross-Linguistic Studies on Tonal Phenomena, Tonogenesis, Typology, and Related Topics,"* ed. Shigeki Kaji, 151–186. Tokyo: ILCAA.
Uwano, Zendo. 2007. Two-pattern accent systems in three Japanese dialects. In *Tones and tunes: Vol. 1: typological studies in word and sentence prosody*, ed. Carlos Gussenhoven and Tomas Riad, 147–165. Berlin: Mouton de Gruyter.

CHAPTER 8

GA/NO CONVERSION

HIDEKI MAKI AND ASAKO UCHIBORI

8.1 INTRODUCTION

Japanese has a Case alternation phenomenon called the *ga/no* (nominative/genitive) conversion (hereafter, GNC). This conversion takes place in embedded contexts, such as sentential modifiers to nouns, but not in independent clauses. This phenomenon has led to a variety of approaches, all attempting to deal with the emergence of genitive Case *no* on the subject of the sentential modifier. The GNC was originally discussed by Harada (1971) and subsequently discussed by many linguists, such as Bedell (1972), Shibatani (1975, 1977, 1978), Inoue (1976), Nakai (1980), Saito (1983), Fukui (1986), Miyagawa (1993), Ura (1993), Sakai (1994), Watanabe (1996), Hiraiwa (2001a), and Ochi (2001), among others. Here we review two major approaches—Miyagawa (1993) and Ochi (2001) on the one hand, and Hiraiwa (2001a) on the other—and clarify the potential problems of each approach. We then suggest a refined approach, which crucially relies on core ideas from the two approaches. In the refined approach, D licenses genitive Case, as in the Miyagawa/Ochi-type approach, and movement into Spec,DP is not involved in genitive Case licensing, as in the Hiraiwa-type approach.

8.2 DESCRIPTION OF THE CORE DATA

The core data discussed in this chapter are shown in (1) and (2). Examples of type (2) are amply provided in Hiraiwa 2001a.

(1) Watasi-wa [[John-ga/no   kita] riyuu]-o   sitteiru.
    I-TOP   John-NOM/GEN came reason-ACC know
    'I know the reason why John came.'

(2) John-wa [ame-ga/no   yamu made] ofisu-ni ita.
    John-TOP rain-NOM/GEN stop until office-at was
    'John was at his office until the rain stopped.'

In (1) the DP marked genitive, *John-no* 'John-GEN', appears in the sentential modifier of a noun. In (2) the genitive DP *ame-no* 'rain-GEN' appears in a clause that does not directly modify a noun, unlike (1), because *made* 'until' is not a noun but a postposition. The examples in (1) and (2) raise central questions for this construction—namely, where is the genitive DP in the phrase structure, and what licenses its Case?

8.3 CONTROVERSIES REGARDING ANALYSIS

Two major approaches have been proposed in terms of what licenses genitive Case: (a) the DP approach by Miyagawa (1993) and Ochi (2001), among others, and (b) the non-DP approach by Hiraiwa (2001a), among others. Both approaches have their own strengths and weaknesses. The first approach is consistent with the fact that a DP is marked genitive whenever it is in a local relation to the outer N/D.[1] However, this approach cannot account for (2), in which there appears to be no nominal head to license genitive Case.

The second approach straightforwardly accounts for the GNC in examples such as (2). When the GNC is allowed, the predicate always takes its *rentai* (attributive) form. The *rentai* form of a predicate is, in most cases, identical to its *syuusi* (conclusive) form.

However, in a certain class of adjectives, the morphological distinction between the *rentai* and *syuusi* forms is retained.[2] Consider the examples in (3).

(3) a. Ano hito-wa sizuka-da/*na.
       that man-TOP quiet-DA(conclusive)/*NA(attributive)
       'That man is quiet.'
    b. sizuka-na/*da   hito
       quiet-NA(attributive)/*DA(conclusive)   man
       'a quiet man'

Example (3a) is an independent matrix clause. The sentence is grammatical when it ends with the conclusive form of the adjective, but it is ungrammatical when it ends with the attributive form of the adjective. However, (3b) contains a relative clause that has the same adjective. The sentence is grammatical when the adjective takes the attributive form, but it is ungrammatical when it takes the conclusive form.[3] Based on this fact and examples such as (2), Hiraiwa (2001a) claims that in a sentential modifier, it is the φ-feature of a special type of C that licenses the genitive DP via Agree in the sense of Chomsky (2000), but not the nominal head, thus arguing against the DP approach. Under this approach, the *rentai* morphology of the embedded predicate is a manifestation of the agreement relation among the special C, T, (*v*), and V. However, a potential problem with this approach is that it is possible to insert a nominal head to be modified by the sentential modifier, such as *toki* 'time', between *yamu* 'stop', and *made* 'until' in (2), as shown in (4).

(4) John-wa [ame-ga/no yamu toki made] ofisu-ni ita.
    John-TOP rain-NOM/GEN stop time until office-at was
    'John was at his office until the rain stopped.'

One may then argue that there is an invisible noun corresponding to *toki* 'time', which would lead us to conclude that examples such as (2) may not provide strong support for the non-DP approach. Also, this approach does not explain the fact that a genitive DP appears in simple possessive structures such as [DP's N], where no predicate in the *rentai* (attributive) form appears.

After reviewing the two approaches, we present an approach that draws from both of them. In particular, we suggest that D licenses genitive Case, as in the DP approach, and that movement into Spec,DP is not involved in genitive Case licensing, as in the non-DP approach. We also discuss the transitivity restriction on the GNC, which prohibits co-occurrence of an accusative DP with the genitive DP (Harada 1971, Miyagawa 1993, and Watanabe 1996, among others), and show how it is handled with Miyagawa's (2003) proposal that there are two types of Tense (T) in Japanese.

8.3.1 The DP Approach

8.3.1.1 *Miyagawa (1993)*

Miyagawa (1993) proposes the three hypotheses in (5).

(5) a. The genitive subject in a prenominal gapless clause raises into Spec,DP.
    b. This movement takes place in LF.
    c. Spec,DP may be A- or A'-position.

The first hypothesis (5a) is motivated by scope interactions between the nominative/genitive subject and the head noun. The example in (6a), which has a nominative subject, only has the reading in which the head noun *kanoosee* 'probability' takes scope over the nominative subject *rubii-ka sinzyu* 'ruby or pearl'. We call this reading the "in-situ" reading. The example in (6b), which has a genitive subject, allows an additional reading in which the subject takes scope over the head noun *kanoosee* 'probability'. We call this reading the "raising" reading.

(6) a. [[[Rubii-ka sinzyu]-ga yasuku-naru] kanoosee]-ga 50% izyoo da.
   ruby-or pearl-NOM cheap-become probability-NOM 50% over is
   i. 'The probability that rubies or pearls become cheap is over 50%.'
   ii. *'The probability that rubies become cheap or the probability that pearls become cheap is over 50%.'
   probability>[ruby or pearl]; *[ruby or pearl] > probability
 b. [[[Rubii-ka sinzyu]-no yasuku-naru] kanoosee]-ga 50% izyoo da.
   ruby-or pearl-GEN cheap-become probability-NOM 50% over is
   i. 'The probability that rubies or pearls become cheap is over 50%.'
   ii. 'The probability that rubies become cheap or the probability that pearls become cheap is over 50%.'
   probability > [ruby or pearl]; [ruby or pearl] > probability

Miyagawa (1993) points out that (6a) is unambiguous because the nominative subject does not raise out of the prenominal sentential modifier and is c-commanded by the head noun, as schematically shown in (7).

(7) [DP [NP [IP [ruby or pearl]-NOM predicate] N] D]

However, (6b) allows scope ambiguity because the genitive subject raises into Spec,DP at some point in the derivation and c-commands the head noun, as schematically shown in (8).

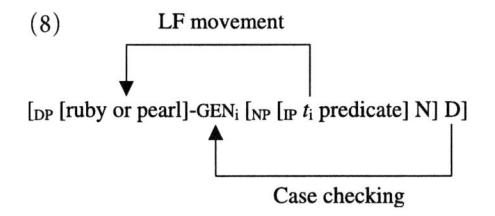

(8) LF movement

[DP [ruby or pearl]-GEN_i [NP [IP t_i predicate] N] D]

Case checking

The second hypothesis is motivated by Nakai's (1980) observation that the genitive subject may be preceded by other elements in the prenominal sentential modifier. Consider the example in (9).

(9) [kotosi sinzyu-no yasuku-naru] kanoosee
   this year pearl-GEN cheap-become probability
   'the probability that pearls become cheap this year'

In (9), the adverb *kotosi* 'this year' is at the left edge of the sentential modifier, preceding the genitive subject *sinzyu* 'pearl'. Therefore, the genitive subject cannot be in Spec,DP in overt syntax. This led Miyagawa to conclude that the genitive subject raises out of the sentential gapless clause into Spec,DP at LF.

Finally, the third hypothesis is motivated by the left-edge effect on scope exhibited by examples such as (10). According to Miyagawa (1993), whereas (10a), in which the genitive subject is at the left edge of the sentential modifier, allows scope ambiguity, (10b), in which it is preceded by an adverb in the sentential modifier, only allows the in-situ reading.

(10) a. [[[Rubii-ka sinzyu]-no kotosi-kara yasuku-natta] riyuu]-o osiete.
ruby-or pearl-GEN this year-from cheap-became reason-ACC tell-me
   i. 'Tell me the reason that rubies or pearls became cheap starting this year.'
   ii. 'Tell me the reason that rubies became cheap starting this year or the reason that pearls became cheap starting this year.'
   reason > [ruby or pearl]; [ruby or pearl] > reason
b. [[Kotosi-kara [rubii-ka sinzyu]-no yasuku-natta] riyuu]-o osiete.
this year-from ruby-or pearl-GEN cheap-became reason-ACC tell-me
   i. 'Tell me the reason that rubies or pearls became cheap starting this year.'
   ii. *'Tell me the reason that rubies became cheap starting this year or the reason that pearls became cheap starting this year.'
   reason > [ruby or pearl]; *[ruby or pearl] > reason

To explain this fact, Miyagawa proposes that Spec,DP may be either an A- or A'-position. When the genitive subject raises to Spec,DP as an A-position, (10a) only has a raising reading, under the assumption that there is no reconstruction with A-movement (Miyagawa 1993, Chomsky 1995, and Lasnik 1999, among others). However, when the genitive subject raises to Spec,DP as an A'-position, (10a) has an in-situ reading, if A'-movement allows reconstruction. As for (10b), Miyagawa argues that the PP *kotosi-kara* 'from this year' blocks A-movement of the genitive subject, and thus, (10b) only allows A'-movement of the genitive subject. Therefore, (10b) only has an in-situ reading on the assumption that A'-movement forces reconstruction.

So far, we have seen examples with prenominal gapless sentential modifiers. Before leaving this subsection, let us briefly summarize Miyagawa's analysis of relative clauses containing a disjunctive quantifier. Consider the example in (11).

(11) [[[John-ka Mary]-ga/no t_i katta] hon$_i$]-o misete.
John-or Mary-NOM/GEN bought book-ACC show-me
a. 'Show me the book that John or Mary bought.'
b. 'Show me the book that John bought or the book that Mary bought.'
book > [John or Mary]; [John or Mary] > book

Miyagawa observes that in (11), regardless of whether the subject is marked nominative or genitive, both the in-situ and raising readings are allowed. The in-situ reading is possible because the head noun *hon* 'book' c-commands the subject in the relative clause. That the raising reading is allowed, according to Miyagawa, is attributed to the fact that there is a relative gap within the relative clause coindexed with the head noun *hon* 'book', and this gap is c-commanded by the subject within the relative clause.

8.3.1.2 *Ochi (2001)*

Ochi (2001) inherits the core idea of Miyagawa's (1993) approach—namely, that the Case feature of a genitive subject is licensed by D. What is new in Ochi's approach is the claim that in certain cases, not the genitive subject as a whole but only the relevant feature of the genitive subject moves to D in covert syntax, based on Chomsky's (1995) Move-F hypothesis.[4] Specifically, Ochi (2001) proposes the three hypotheses in (12).

(12)   a. The genitive subject in a prenominal gapless clause is licensed by moving into Spec,DP in overt syntax or by moving the Case feature of the genitive subject to D in covert syntax.
       b. The genitive subject in a relative clause is licensed by moving the Case feature of the genitive subject to D in covert syntax.
       c. Spec,DP is consistently an A-position.

Let us start by examining how the first hypothesis (12a) captures the left-edge effect on scope illustrated by the examples in (10). Example (10b) only has an in-situ reading. This is expected because the genitive subject has not moved out of the sentential modifier in overt syntax due to the left-edge element. Ochi (2001) argues that in this case, the Case feature of the genitive subject moves out of the sentential modifier in covert syntax, and given the independent evidence that covert feature movement does not affect scope relations (Lasnik 1995, among others), the genitive subject cannot take scope over the head noun in (10b).

In contrast, in (10a), nothing prevents the genitive subject from moving to Spec,DP out of the sentential modifier in overt syntax, because there is no left-edge element in the clause. If the genitive subject moves to Spec,DP in overt syntax, it takes scope over the head noun, and if it does not, only the Case feature raises, at which point, the head noun takes scope over the genitive subject, just as in the case of (10b). Therefore, the hypothesis (12a) straightforwardly explains the scope facts in (10).

Next, let us turn to the second hypothesis in (12b). Consider (13), where the subject of the relative clause is preceded by an adverb.

(13)   [kinoo   John-ga/no   unten-site-ita]   kuruma
        yesterday John-NOM/GEN   drive-doing-was   car
        'the car John was driving yesterday'

In (13), the genitive subject is within the relative clause and, thus, is not in Spec,DP in overt syntax. If the genitive subject is forced to overtly move into Spec,DP, the example becomes ungrammatical, as shown in the contrast between (14a) and (14b).

(14)   a. [totemo atarasii] [kinoo   John-no   unten-site-ita]   kuruma
           very   new   yesterday John-GEN   drive-doing-was   car
           'the very new car that John was driving yesterday'
       b. *John-no [totemo atarasii] [kinoo   t unten-site-ita]   kuruma
           John-GEN very   new   yesterday   drive-doing-was   car

In (14a), the adjective phrase *totemo atarasii* 'very new', which modifies the head noun *kuruma* 'car', is placed in the position preceding the relative clause. In (14b), the genitive subject is moved to Spec,DP across the adjective phrase. Example (14b) is totally ungrammatical, in contrast to (14a), when the intended reading of (14b) is identical to that of (14a).[5] Therefore, the genitive subject in a relative clause cannot move into Spec,DP in overt syntax. Based on this fact, Ochi (2001) proposes that the genitive subject in a relative clause is licensed by moving the Case feature of the genitive subject to D in covert syntax.

Finally, let us turn to the third hypothesis in (12c). Consider the examples in (15). In (15a), the genitive subject of the sentential modifier is preceded by a relative clause, and in (15b), the genitive subject of the sentential modifier is moved to the sentence-initial position and precedes the relative clause.

(15) a. [kono   kompyuutaa-ga keesan-sita] [[rubii-ka sinzyu]-no
       this   conputer-NOM   calculated   ruby-or pearl-GEN
       kotosi   yasuku-naru]   kanoosee
       this year cheap-become   probability
    i. 'the probability [that rubies or pearls become cheap this year] [which this computer calculated]'
    ii. (?)'[[the probability that rubies become cheap this year] or [the probability that pearls become cheap this year]] [which this computer calculated]'
       probability > [ruby or pearl]; (?)[ruby or pearl] > probability
   b. [[rubii-ka sinzyu]-no, [kono kompyuutaa-ga keesan-sita],
      ruby-or pearl-GEN   this computer-NOM   calculated
      kotosi   yasuku-naru   kanoosee]
      this year cheap-become   probability
    i. *'the probability [that rubies or pearls become cheap this year] [which this computer calculated]'
    ii. '[[the probability that rubies become cheap this year] or [the probability that pearls become cheap this year]] [which this computer calculated]'
       *probability > [ruby or pearl]; [ruby or pearl] > probability

Ochi (2001) reports that, although (15a) has two readings—namely, the in-situ and raising readings—(15b) only has the raising reading. The fact that (15a) is ambiguous is readily explained under Ochi's approach, because in (15a), the genitive subject *rubii-ka sinzyu* 'ruby or pearl' is either in Spec,DP or within the sentential modifier in overt syntax, and the former case yields the raising reading, and the latter case the in-situ reading. The relevant structures for the in-situ and raising readings are shown in (16a,b), respectively.

(16) a. [DP [IP ...] [NP [IP [ruby or pearl]-GEN Adv predicate] N] D]
     b. [DP [IP ...] [DP [ruby or pearl]-GEN$_i$ [NP [IP t_i Adv predicate] N] D]]

The fact that (15b) has the raising reading is also expected under Ochi's approach, because in this case, the genitive subject *rubii-ka sinzyu* 'ruby or pearl' must be in Spec,DP in overt syntax, as shown in the structure in (17).

(17) [DP [ruby or pearl]-GEN_i [DP [IP ...] [NP [IP t_i Adv predicate] N] D]]

The remaining question is why (15b) does not have the in-situ reading. On the basis of the independent claims that A'-movement allows (scope) reconstruction (Miyagawa 1993, among many others), and that A-movement does not allow (scope) reconstruction (Miyagawa 1993, Chomsky 1995, and Lasnik 1999, among others), Ochi answers this question by claiming that in (15b), the movement of the genitive subject to Spec,DP is A-movement, which implies that Spec,DP is consistently an A-position. If this is true, there is no scope reconstruction in (15b), and the fact that the in-situ reading is absent in (15b) is expected.

8.3.1.3 *A problem*

We have seen that the DP/movement approach by Ochi (2001) is attractive and accounts for important data. However, it contains one theoretical problem: it is not clear why overt raising of the genitive subject is optional—that is, in some cases, it may move to Spec,DP in overt syntax, and in other cases, only the Case feature of the genitive subject moves to D in covert syntax. Ochi (2001:sect. 4.3.) attempts to answer this question. He states that what actually checks genitive Case is N, not D, and D, when it is present, triggers the overt raising of the genitive subject. If this is correct, though, a problem emerges in terms of the categorical status of a given nominal expression, because a complex NP with a prenominal gapless clause is an NP in cases such as (15a) with the in-situ reading, and the same complex NP is a DP in cases such as (15a) with the raising reading. It is theoretically desirable if nominal expressions are consistently NPs or DPs.

8.3.2 The Non-DP Approach

8.3.2.1 *Hiraiwa (2001a)*

Hiraiwa's (2001a) approach to the GNC essentially follows another important previous study by Watanabe (1996), which provides an insight that cross-linguistic observation is useful in elucidating the nature of the GNC.[6] In fact, Hiraiwa observes that GNC phenomena are broadly found in relative clauses in many other languages, such as Cuzco Quechua, Chamorro, Turkish, and so on, and argues that a certain typological difference in C is crucially related to the possibility of the GNC, which we briefly discuss later. Furthermore, Hiraiwa argues that the Japanese GNC depends on the existence of the *rentai* form, but not any overt D, showing that there is a set of clauses allowing the GNC that do not involve a noun. Hiraiwa's data are listed in (18) (with the exception of (18a), which is from Watanabe 1996).

(18) a. John-wa [Mary-ga/no yonda yori] takusan-no hon-o yonda.
John-TOP Mary-NOM/GEN read than many-GEN book-ACC read
'John read more books than Mary did.'
b. John-wa [ame-ga/no yamu made] ofisu-ni ita.
John-TOP rain-NOM/GEN stop until office-at was
'John was at his office until the rain stopped.'
c. [Boku-ga/no omoo-ni], John-wa Mary-ga sukini tigainai.
I-NOM/GEN think-DAT John-TOP Mary-NOM like must
'I think that John likes Mary.'
d. Kono atari-wa [hi-ga/no kureru ni-ture] hiekonde-kuru.
this around-TOP sun-NOM/GEN go-down as colder-get
'It gets chillier around here as the sun goes down.'
e. John-wa [toki-ga/no tatu to tomoni] Mary-no koto-o
John-TOP time-NOM/GEN pass with as Mary-GEN thing-ACC
wasurete-itta.
forget-went
'Mary slipped out of John's memory as time went by.'
f. [John-ga/no kuru to konai to]-dewa, ootigai da.
John-NOM/GEN come and come-not and-TOP great-difference be
'It makes a great difference whether John comes or not.'
g. [John-ga/no sikar-are-ta-no]-wa, Mary-ni da.
John-NOM/GEN scold-PASS-PAST-COMP-TOP Mary-by be
'It is by Mary that John was scolded.'
h. John-ga [sara-no ue-ni ringo-ga/no oiteatta-no]-o
John-NOM plate-GEN on-DAT apple-NOM/GEN put-COMP-ACC
katteni tabeta.
without-permission ate
'Without permission, John ate an apple, which was on the plate.'
i. [Sengetu ikkai John-ga/no soko-ni it-ta (k)kiri] daremo
last month once John-NOM/GEN there-to go-PAST since anybody
itte inai.
go not-PRES
'Nobody went there since John went once last month.'

All of the examples in (18) do not involve an overt nominal head inside the brackets, yet each example allows the subject to be marked genitive. This fact led Hiraiwa to claim that what licenses a genitive DP in a clause is not a noun (or an outer D) but a special inflection—that is, the *rentai* (attributive) form of the predicate.

Based on Chomsky's (2000) theory of agreement in terms of the operation called Agree, Hiraiwa (2001a) proposes that in Japanese, the inflectional morphology in the normal declarative sentence is a result of an Agree relation of T, (*v*), and V. For example, the normal inflection (the *syuusi*, or conclusive, form) corresponds to the T-(*v*)-V amalgamate created via Agree in syntax. However, the special inflection (the *rentai*, or attributive, form) results from an Agree relation of T, (*v*), V, and a special type of C. Hiwaira hypothesizes that C in Japanese relative clauses is null and affixal and that the affixal C requires an Agree relation with the T-(*v*)-V to circumvent the situation where the affixal C is left stranded. Through this type of Agree relation, T's ϕ-feature is copied or transferred onto the special C (i.e., C$_{affix}$ in Hiraiwa's terms), creating the C-T-(*v*)-V amalgamate, which obtains a single set of ϕ-features. In Hiraiwa's approach, the crucial difference between the *syuusi* (conclusive) and *rentai* (attributive) forms is, thus, whether the Agree relation involves the special type of C. Furthermore, adopting Chomsky's framework for Case in terms of the operation Agree between the probe and its matching goal, Hiraiwa assumes that the categorical property of the probe determines Case values on the goal. That is, when the probe is the ϕ-feature of C, the Case of the goal is valued genitive. However, when it is the ϕ-feature of T, the Case of the goal is valued nominative.

Given this, the examples in (18) are analyzed in the following way. In each, the clause in the brackets is assumed to be dominated by C$_{affix}$, and this C$_{affix}$ licenses genitive Case of the subject of the clause via Agree. This is schematically shown in (19).

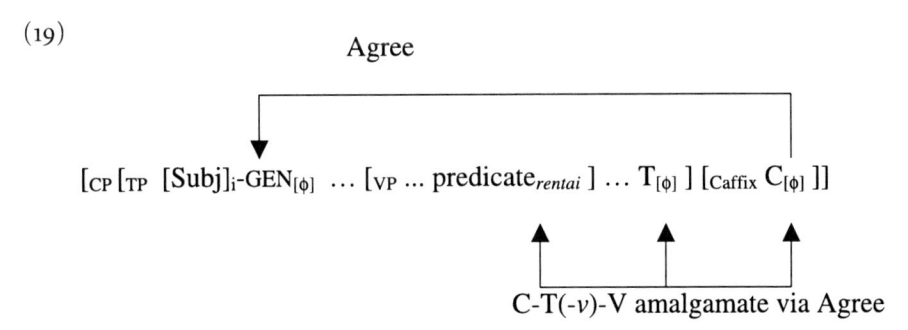

(19)

Agree

[$_{CP}$ [$_{TP}$ [Subj]$_i$-GEN$_{[ϕ]}$ ... [$_{VP}$ ... predicate$_{rentai}$] ... T$_{[ϕ]}$] [C$_{affix}$ C$_{[ϕ]}$]]

C-T(-*v*)-V amalgamate via Agree

The *rentai* form thus indicates an occurrence of the Agree relation among C$_{affix}$, T, (*v*), and the predicate, which enables licensing of genitive Case for the subject.

Two examples in (18) pose an apparent problem. The cleft sentence in (18g) and the head-internal relative clause in (18h) seem to have an overt complementizer *no* rather than a C$_{affix}$ in the brackets. Under Hiraiwa's hypothesis, such an overt Comp does not license genitive Case in Japanese. However, he argues that under these constructions, the morpheme *no* itself is not a complementizer but a manifestation of the Agree relation between C$_{affix}$ and the genitive subject, and as such, it appears on C$_{affix}$ as *no*, the same morphology of the genitive Case marker. In relation to this, Hiraiwa points out that clauses headed by genuine overt complementizers—such as *ka* 'Q', *to* 'that', *to-no* 'that-GEN', and *to-iu* 'that-say'— do not allow the GNC. This is because these overt complementizers are not affixal and do not trigger the Agree relation necessary for licensing genitive Case of the subject.

Moreover, Hiraiwa (2001a) claims that the distribution of the GNC follows from the locality condition on Agree. Specifically, Hiraiwa adopts his theory of multiple applications of the operation, which he calls Multiple Agree (Hiraiwa 2001b). That is, Agree is applicable to more than one matching goal derivationally simultaneously. Let us briefly review how it works. According to Hiraiwa, in the multiple feature-checking configuration, the probe has a [+multiple] feature and continues its search, even after it matches with the closest matching goal. Suppose that the search reaches the second-closest matching goal and stops there (because there is no other matching element in the search domain). Multiple Agree takes place in this configuration, and the probe agrees with the two matching goals simultaneously, violating no locality condition on Agree (hence, triggering no defective intervention effect; Chomsky 2000). Hiraiwa claims that the mechanism of Multiple Agree accounts for the GNC in a clause with a nominative object and the GNC in the possessor raising construction. The relevant examples are shown in (20).

(20) a. Totemo yoku John-ga/*no   nihongo-ga/*no   dekiru.
         very   well John-NOM/*GEN Japanese-NOM/*GEN do-can
         'John can speak Japanese very well.'
     b. [totemo yoku John-ga/no   nihongo-ga/no   dekiru] riyuu
         very   well John-NOM/GEN Japanese-NOM/GEN do-can reason
         'the reason why John can speak Japanese very well'
     c. John-ga/no   se-ga/*no   takai.
         John-NOM/GEN height-NOM/*GEN high
         'John is tall.'
     d. [John-ga/no   se-ga/no   takai] riyuu
         John-NOM/GEN height-NOM/GEN high   reason
         'the reason why John is tall.'

The agentive subject and the thematic object in (20a) and the possessor subject and the thematic subject in (20c), when they appear in a clause modifying a noun, can be marked either nominative or genitive in any combination, as shown in (20b) and (20d). Let us, for instance, consider the case of the *ga-no* combination in the possessor raising construction in (20d), in which the higher and lower subjects are marked nominative and genitive, respectively. What is peculiar about this example is that the genitive subject is not closest to its licensor (whether it is C or the outer N/D), because the higher nominative subject intervenes between them. In terms of Hiraiwa's Multiple Agree, the nominative subject and the genitive subject are simultaneously licensed by the same probe—that is, the φ-feature that is copied/transferred onto C_{affix} from T. Here, no Minimality violation or defective intervention effect is induced, even though there is more than one matching goal. Furthermore, according to Hiraiwa's assumption on valuing Case via φ-feature agreement, which was briefly mentioned before, the Case for the subjects in (20d) can be freely valued either genitive or nominative on the grounds that the probe φ-feature on C_{affix} has a twofold character—that is, the property of both C and T (given that the φ-feature originates from T).[7] As for the case of the nominative object construction in (20b), the same analysis applies, if we assume that there is no probe for the nominative object other than the ϕ-feature on C$_{affix}$.

Hiraiwa's (2001a) approach is briefly summarized in (21).[8]

(21) a. The special inflection of a predicate, such as the *rentai* (attributive) form in Japanese, results from an Agree relation among V, *v*, T, and C$_{affix}$.
b. T's ϕ-feature is transferred onto C$_{affix}$ through the Agree relation in (21a).
c. C$_{affix}$ with the ϕ-feature transferred from T can license genitive Case of the subject in Spec,TP via Agree.

8.3.2.2 *A problem*

The non-DP approach proposed by Hiraiwa (2001a) is highly attractive, because it deals with a broader range of facts, such as the GNC in clauses without an overt head noun. There are some empirical problems, however, including one that we believe to be particularly serious. Let us again look at the examples in (18), which do not contain a head noun, at least overtly. What we have noticed is that examples (18a–f) have counterparts that do contain a noun, as shown in (22a–f). A question that naturally arises is whether Hiraiwa's "head noun-less" examples are simply instances of GNCs with head nouns where the head noun is somehow implicit. (For the remaining two examples, (18g,h), we also show that they contain a head noun.)

(22) a. John-wa [Mary-ga/no yonda-*teedo/no* yori] takusan-no
John-TOP Mary-NOM/GEN read-degree/NO than many-GEN
hon-o yonda.
book-ACC read
'John read more books than Mary did.'
b. John-wa [ame-ga/no yamu *toki/zikan* made] ofisu-ni ita.
John-TOP rain-NOM/GEN stop time/time until office-at was
'John was at his office until the rain stopped.'
c. [Boku-ga/no omoo-*no*-ni], John-wa Mary-ga sukini tigainai.
I-NOM/GEN think-NO-DAT John-TOP Mary-NOM like must
'I think that John likes Mary.'
d. Kono atari-wa [hi-ga/no kureru-*no*
this around-TOP sun-NOM/GEN go-down-NO
ni-ture] hiekonde-kuru.
DAT-go-together colder-get
'It gets chillier around here as the sun goes down.'
e. John-wa [toki-ga/no tatu-*no* to-tomo-ni] Mary-no
John-TOP time-NOM/GEN pass-NO and-together-DAT Mary-GEN
koto-o wasurete-itta.
thing-ACC forget-went
'Mary slipped out of John's memory as the time went by.'

f. [John-ga/no   kuru-*no* to konai-*no*   to]-dewa,
   John-NOM/GEN   come-NO   and come not-NO   and-TOP
   ootigai   da.
   great-difference be
   'It makes a great difference whether John comes or not.'

In (22a) -*teedo/no* 'degree/NO' are inserted between the *rentai* form of the verb and *yori* 'than', and in (22b) *toki/zikan* 'time/time' are inserted between the *rentai* form of the verb and *made* 'until'. In (22c–f), -*no* 'NO' is inserted after the *rentai* form of the verb. It is natural to consider *teedo/toki/zikan* 'degree/time/time' as nouns. In the case of (22a), given that *no* 'NO' and the noun *teedo* 'degree' appear in the same position, it is natural to claim that *no* 'NO' in (22a) is either a noun or a nominalizer, which makes the entire clause function as a noun.

Could we analyze *no* 'NO' in (22c–f) as the same noun/nominalizer as in (22a)? One might argue, following Hiraiwa (2001a), that *no* 'NO' in (22c–f) is a complementizer (to be precise, a morphological realization of the Agree relation among V, (*v*), T, and C_{affix} on C_{affix}). The strength of Hiraiwa's analysis rests on the parallelism between the morphologically realized C and the *no* that appears in the cleft sentence in (18g) and the head-internal relative clause in (18h). It is normally assumed that the instance of *no* in (18g,h) is a complementizer. We question this assumption about (18g,h) and, in turn, question the status of *no* as a complementizer for (22c–f).

Let us consider the cleft sentence in (18g), reproduced as (23).

(23) [John-ga/no   sikar-are-ta-no]-wa,   Mary-ni da.
      John-NOM/GEN   scold-PASS-PAST-COMP-TOP   Mary-by be
      'It is by Mary that John was scolded.'

Hiraiwa (2001a) assumes that (23) is a perfectly grammatical sentence. However, Murasugi (1991) states that a genitive subject makes the cleft sentence in which it appears less acceptable and provides examples such as those in (24).[9]

(24) a. [[Mary-ga   nigedasita]-no]-wa gakkoo kara da.
          Mary-NOM ran-away-NO-TOP   school from is
          'It is from school that Mary ran away.'
      b. ??[[Mary-no   nigedasita]-no]-wa gakkoo kara da.
          Mary-GEN   ran-away-NO-TOP   school from is
          'It is from school that Mary ran away.'

Murasugi, pursuing Hoji's (1990) work on cleft sentences in Japanese, claims that *no* 'NO' in cleft sentences is not a pronoun but a complementizer, based on data from the Toyama dialect of Japanese. In Murasugi's analysis, Comp does not license genitive Case, so that (24b) should be predicted to be ungrammatical. However, she suggests that a genitive subject is allowed in cleft sentences such as (24b), when *no* 'NO' is interpreted as a pronoun corresponding to something such as 'action' or 'event'. If Murasugi's suggestion is correct, the *no* 'NO' in (23) is considered a pronoun or nominal, not a complementizer, which constitutes an argument for the approach that genitive Case is licensed by N/D.[10]

Next, let us consider the head-internal relative example in (18h), reproduced as (25).

(25) John-ga [sara-no ue-ni ringo-ga/no
     John-NOM plate-GEN on-DAT apple-NOM/GEN
     oiteatta-no]-o katteni tabeta.
     put-COMP-ACC without-permission ate
     'Without permission, John ate an apple, which was on the plate.'

In (25), the elements in the brackets are replaced by the pronoun *sore* 'it', as shown in (26).

(26) John-ga [sore]-o katteni tabeta.
     John-NOM it-ACC without-permission ate
     'Without permission, John ate it.'

This indicates that the head of the head-internal relative clause *no* 'NO' in (25) should be a nominal, just like the pronoun *sore* 'it'. Therefore, the claim that *no* 'NO' in the clause-final position is uniformly C is contradicted by the above data. Hence, we conclude that *no* 'NO' in the examples (18g,h) and (22c–f) is either a noun or a nominalizer. This, again, questions the non-DP analysis of GNC.

Turning to the final example from Hiraiwa, (18i), we question the status of the morpheme *kiri* 'since' that "heads" the clause with the GNC. Hiraiwa's assumption is that it is not a noun, so that the entire clause is a CP, but, in fact, we can show that it is a noun. The morpheme *kiri* 'since' has the basic meaning of "endpoint," such as the endpoint of a temporal duration. This *kiri* is the *renyoo* (continuous) form of the verb *kiru* 'cut/break'. The *renyoo* form of a verb can be used as a noun in Japanese, as seen in examples such as *kikoe* 'hearing' (continuous) < *kikoeru* 'hear' (conclusive) and *oyogi* 'swimming' (continuous) < *oyogu* 'swim' (conclusive). The use of -*kiri* as a noun is found in examples such as *hutari-(k)kiri* [two-only] 'only two' and *pin-kara kiri-made* [the first-from-the last-to] 'from the best to the worst'. In the latter case, *kiri* is a complement of the postposition *made* 'to', and it is obvious that it functions as a noun.

To summarize the problem for the non-DP approach, the examples that Hiraiwa (2001a) provides to support the non-DP approach all turn out to have counterparts that contain a noun or a clause nominalizer. This suggests that the "head-noun-less" examples that Hiraiwa offers are instances in which a nominal element such as a head noun or a nominalizer is simply unpronounced in the overt form but present in the structure.

8.3.3 A Refinement of the Two Approaches

Thus far, we have reviewed the strengths and limitations of the two types of approaches: the DP-approach (Miyagawa 1993, Ochi 2001) and the non-DP approach (Hiraiwa 2001a). In this section, we suggest a refinement of the two approaches by integrating the core ideas of the approaches. We show (a) that the proposed analysis allows unified treatment of the regular genitive and the genitive in GNC and (b) that it captures scope facts. We then demonstrate how the proposed approach can deal with two other distinctive properties of the GNC, the transitivity restriction and optionality, which have not been discussed thus far.

In section 8.3.1.3, we pointed out a potential problem in Ochi's DP approach concerning movement of the genitive DP to Spec,DP. In section 8.3.2.2, we also pointed out a problem in Hiraiwa's non-DP approach, which is that the occurrence of a nominal element such as a head noun, overt or covert, in the GNC construction suggests the existence of D. We therefore suggest a refinement of the two approaches. Specifically, we suggest that D licenses genitive Case in the GNC construction and that the DP marked genitive does not move to Spec,DP, as shown in (27).[11]

(27) [[[... DP-GEN ... predicate] N (overt/covert)] D]

An Altaic language called Dagur provides cross-linguistic evidence for the refined DP approach. Hale (2002) reports that in the Dagur object relative construction, the subject of the relative clause is marked genitive, and the head noun, but not the verb in the relative clause, is obligatorily accompanied by a postpounded reduced copy of the genitive subject pronoun. This is shown in (28).

(28) [mini   au-sen]   mer^y-min^y]   sain.
      1SG.GEN buy-PERF   horse-1SG.GEN   good
      'The horse I bought is good.'

In (28), the subject of the relative clause is *mini* '1SG.GEN', and the head noun *mer^y* 'horse' is accompanied by the copy of the genitive subject pronoun *min^y* '1SG.GEN'. Hale states that this agreement pattern is also seen in simple possessive constructions, as shown in (29).

(29) [mini   mer^y-min^y]   sain.
      1SG.GEN horse-1SG.GEN   good
      'My horse is good.'

In (29), the head noun is accompanied by the copy of the possessor pronoun. However, in simple verbal clauses, agreement holds between the subject and verb, and the subject is in the nominative, as shown in (30).

(30) bi   nek mer^y au-sem.   (au-sema < au-sen-bi)
      1SG.NOM one horse   buy-PERF:1SG.NOM
      'I bought a horse.'

These facts clearly suggest that in the Dagur object relative construction, the genitive subject of the relative clause is in agreement with the head noun (D) and provides cross-linguistic support for the refined DP approach.

The refined DP approach explains the facts in Japanese thus far observed, as we show. First, the proposed analysis allows unified treatment of the regular genitive and the genitive in GNC. A simple possessor construction, such as (31), and the

GNC construction, such as (32), share a common property—that is, a DP-GEN appears within a phrase headed by a nominal element.

(31) [John-no [neko] D]
 John-GEN cat
 'John's cat'

(32) [[[John-no kita] hi] D]
 John-GEN came day
 'the day John came'

This fact is correctly accounted for by the analysis suggested here, because genitive Case is licensed by D in either case.

Note that although the DP approach also correctly captures this parallelism, the non-DP approach cannot, because under this approach, the element that licenses genitive Case in the GNC construction is not identical to the element that licenses genitive Case in the possessor construction. Also, the fact that genitive Case appears in the former construction and the fact that the same Case appears in the latter construction are coincidental.

Furthermore, under the refined approach, Hiraiwa's problem does not arise. This is because under the refined approach, the parallelism with respect to the GNC between the seemingly "head-noun-less" examples and their counterparts with head nouns is naturally captured. They are all instances of DPs, with the structure shown in (27).

Second, the proposed analysis correctly captures scope facts, without invoking Ochi's (2001) problem. Because genitive Case licensing does not require movement into D/Spec,DP, no question arises as to why overt movement of the genitive subject takes place, when the raising reading is allowed, whereas covert movement of the genitive Case feature occurs when the in-situ reading is allowed. Furthermore, under our analysis, the category of the genitive subject is consistently DP, regardless of the scope of the genitive subject. This is theoretically desirable, whereas under Ochi's approach, the distinction between overt and covert movement is linked to the difference in the categorical status of the genitive subject (i.e., NP vs. DP).

The proposed analysis provides an account of the left-edge effect on scope, different from Ochi's (2001) approach. Consider again the examples in (10a,b), reproduced here as (33a,b), respectively.

(33) a. [[[Rubii-ka sinzyu]-no kotosi-kara yasuku-natta] riyuu]-o
 ruby-or pearl-GEN this year-from cheap-became reason-ACC
 osiete.
 tell-me
 i. 'Tell me the reason that rubies or pearls became cheap starting this year.'
 ii. 'Tell me the reason that rubies became cheap starting this year or the reason that pearls became cheap starting this year.'
 reason > [ruby or pearl]; [ruby or pearl] > reason

b. [[Kotosi-kara [rubii-ka sinzyu]-no yasuku-natta] riyuu]-o
　　this year-from ruby-or pearl-GEN cheap-became reason-ACC
　　osiete.
　　tell-me
　　i. 'Tell me the reason that rubies or pearls became cheap starting this year.'
　　ii. *'Tell me the reason that rubies became cheap starting this year or the reason that pearls became cheap starting this year.'
　　reason > [ruby or pearl]; *[ruby or pearl] > reason

Although (33a), in which the genitive subject is at the left edge of the sentential modifier, allows scope ambiguity, (33b), in which it is preceded by an adverb in the sentential modifier, only allows the in-situ reading. We suggest that under the approach proposed here, the left-edge effect actually indicates that the genitive subject at issue is base-generated in Spec,DP and functions as a modifier of the noun rather than as a subject of the sentential modifier, based on the fact that (34), with a structure slightly different from (33a), has the raising reading.

(34) [[Rubii-ka sinzyu]-nituite-no [(sore-ga) kotosi-kara yasuku-natta]
　　 ruby-or pearl-about-GEN it-NOM this year-from cheap-became
　　 riyuu]-o osiete.
　　 reason-ACC tell-me
　　 i. *'Tell me the reason, about rubies or pearls, that rubies or pearls became cheap starting this year.'
　　 ii. 'Tell me, about rubies or pearls, the reason that rubies became cheap starting this year or the reason that pearls became cheap starting this year.'
　　 *reason > [ruby or pearl]; [ruby or pearl] > reason

In (34), the genitive subject in (33a) has been changed to the form [DP-about-GEN], and (34) has the raising reading. Let us consider why this is so. Suppose that *rubii-ka sinzyu-nituite-no* '[ruby or pearl]-about-GEN' is base-generated in Spec,DP. Under the assumption that the PP headed by *nituite* 'about' is transparent, and thus, the complement DP can c-command the elements c-commanded by the PP, *rubii-ka sinzyu* 'ruby or pearl' c-commands the head noun *riyuu* 'reason'. Therefore, the former may take scope over the latter, which yields the raising reading.

The fact that (34) cannot have the in-situ reading, in spite of the fact that the pronoun in the parentheses *sore* 'it' referring to *rubii-ka sinzyu* 'ruby or pearl' is c-commanded by the head noun *riyuu* 'reason', is treated in the same way as the English example in (35), where the quantifier *at least three students* cannot take scope over the pronoun *it* referring to the quantifier *every book* base-generated in the clause-initial position, although the former c-commands the latter (Mamoru Saito, pers. comm.).

(35) For every book, there were at least three students who read it.
　　 every book > at least three students; *at least three students > every book

Thus, the left-edge effect is correctly predicted if we assume that the genitive subject in (33a) is actually base-generated in Spec,DP, just like the [DP-about-GEN] in (34). In this case, the nonovert nominative subject is base-generated within the sentential modifier. Also, the fact that (33b) only has the in-situ reading follows from the fact that the genitive subject is simply within the sentential modifier due to the adverb in the clause-initial position, and the genitive subject is unable to be at the position as high as Spec,DP.

Furthermore, the base-generation hypothesis under the refined approach in turn accounts for the scope facts of Ochi's (2001) examples in (15a,b), reproduced here as (36a,b).

(36) a. [kono   kompyuutaa-ga   keesan-sita]   [[rubii-ka   sinzyu]-no
          this   conputer-NOM   calculated   ruby-or   pearl-GEN
          kotosi   yasuku-naru]   kanoosee
          this year cheap-become   probability
       'the probability [that rubies or pearls become cheap this year]
       [which this computer calculated]'
       (?)'[[the probability that rubies become cheap this year] or [the
           probability that pearls become cheap this year]] [which this
           computer calculated]'
       probability > [ruby or pearl]; (?)[ruby or pearl] > probability
    b. [[rubii-ka sinzyu]-no, [kono kompyuutaa-ga   keesan-sita],
        ruby-or   pearl-GEN   this computer-NOM   calculated
        kotosi   yasuku-naru   kanoosee]
        this year cheap-become   probability
       *'the probability [that rubies or pearls become cheap this year] [which
         this computer calculated]'
       '[[the probability that rubies become cheap this year] or [the proba-
         bility that pearls become cheap this year]] [which this computer
         calculated]'
       *probability > [ruby or pearl]; [ruby or pearl] > probability

Example (36a) has both the in-situ and raising readings, whereas (36b) has only the raising reading. The fact that (36a) is ambiguous is expected under the refined approach, because in (36a), the genitive subject *rubii-ka sinzyu* 'ruby or pearl' may be base-generated in Spec,DP or within the sentential modifier. The former case yields the raising reading, because the genitive subject c-commands the head noun, and the latter case yields the in-situ reading, because the head noun c-commands the genitive subject.

The fact that (36b) has the raising reading is also expected under the refined approach, because in this case, the genitive subject *rubii-ka sinzyu* 'ruby or pearl' is base-generated in Spec,DP and c-commands the head noun. The fact that (36b) cannot have the in-situ reading is given the same account as example (34).

Having examined the coverage of the proposed analysis, let us see how it can deal with the transitivity restriction on the GNC and the optionality of the GNC.

First, let us consider the transitivity restriction (hereafter, TR) on the GNC. The TR prohibits co-occurrence of an accusative DP with the genitive DP (Harada 1971, Miyagawa 1993, Watanabe 1996, among others), as shown in (37).

(37) [Taroo-ga/*no hon-o   kasita] hito
     Taroo-NOM/GEN book-ACC lent   man
     'the man Taroo lent the book to'

In (37), the predicate in the relative clause is a transitive verb *kas* 'lend', and the subject and object are marked nominative *ga* and accusative *o*, respectively. However, in this configuration, a genitive subject is not allowed. The effect of the TR is, therefore, that the subject cannot be marked genitive as long as the object is marked accusative. Next, we show Miyagawa's (2003) treatment of the TR based on his hypothesis about the nature of Tense (T) in Japanese and suggest that the proposed analysis is not inconsistent with Miyagawa's hypothesis on T, so that it can potentially deal with the TR.[12]

Miyagawa (2003) first argues that in Japanese, morphological case marking must be licensed by T; he bases this analysis on scrambling data, where the object undergoes A-movement scrambling (by the EPP feature on T). Then, Miyagawa suggests that there are two types of T in Japanese—one that licenses the morphological case markers *ga* 'NOM', *o* 'ACC', and *ni* 'DAT' (call this type T1), and another that does not (call it T2).[13] Miyagawa's idea is that T1 appears in a normal sentence, where the predicate takes the *syuusi* form, and licenses *ga* 'NOM', *o* 'ACC', and *ni* 'DAT', whereas T2 appears in the GNC contexts, where the predicate takes the *rentai* form, and licenses the genitive Case *no* 'GEN' but not any of the morphological case markers. Given this, (37) with the nominative subject, which has *ga* 'NOM' and *o* 'ACC' simultaneously, is predicted to be grammatical, because these morphological cases are licensed by T1. However, (37) with the genitive subject, which has *no* 'GEN' and *o* 'ACC' at the same time, is predicted to be ungrammatical, because the accusative case, one of the morphological cases, is not licensed by T2.

Note here that, at first sight, Miyagawa's (2003) claim that T2 licenses genitive Case and our claim that N/D licenses genitive Case seem to be inconsistent. However, these two claims are not inconsistent, because in Miyagawa's approach, genitive Case and T2 co-occur, and in our approach, genitive Case and N/D co-occur, so that whenever T2 appears, N/D appears at the same time. Therefore, the claim that T2 licenses genitive Case and the claim that N/D licenses genitive Case are not incompatible.

Miyagawa (2003) presents another piece of evidence supporting the hypothesis that only the morphological case marking is licensed by T1. Harada (1971) points out that unlike the accusative object, a dative goal phrase can occur in the GNC with the genitive subject, as shown in (38).

(38) [Mary-ni$_i$ John-no t_i kasita] hon
     Mary-DAT John-GEN   lent   book
     'the book that John lent to Mary'

If Miyagawa's hypothesis is correct that only morphological case marking is licensed by T1, the grammaticality of (38) suggests that the tense of the prenominal clause should be T2, because it co-occurs with a genitive subject, and the dative marker of the dative goal phrase should not be a Case marker but a postposition. Miyagawa (1989) points out that there are two types of "dative"—that is, Case marker and postposition—and the latter, but not the former, cannot co-occur with a floated numeral quantifier. Miyagawa (2003) shows that this suggestion is correct based on an example with a floated numeral quantifier:

(39) [gakusei-ni   san-nin$_i$ John-ga/*no   t$_i$ kasita] hon
     student-DAT   3-CL   John-NOM/GEN lent   book
     'the book that John lent to three students'

In (39), when the subject is genitive, the example is ungrammatical. This is because either (a) the occurrence of the genitive subject forces the tense of the prenominal clause to be T2, which does not license the morphological dative case, or (b) the occurrence of the floated numeral quantifier forces the dative to be a morphological case, which in turn forces the tense of the prenominal clause to be T1, which cannot license the genitive subject. However, when the subject is nominative, (39) is perfect, because the tense of the prenominal clause is T1, which licenses the nominative subject and the dative goal phrase at the same time. Therefore, the data with the dative goal subject provides support to Miyagawa's (2003) hypothesis that only morphological case marking is licensed by T1.

The hypothesis that only morphological case marking is licensed by T1, along with a certain assumption on abstract Case, explains the grammaticality of examples with an overt genitive subject and a covert accusative object originally noted by Harada (1971), as shown in (40).

(40) [Taroo-ga/no   e$_i$ kaita] hon$_i$
     Taroo-NOM/GEN   wrote book
     'the book Taroo wrote'

Miyagawa (2003) states that in (40), the covert object presumably has Case, but it is only abstract Case. If this is true, the covert object in (40) does not need morphological case marking by T1, and the example is correctly predicted to be grammatical, given a proper licensing mechanism for abstract Case on the covert object. If, as Miyagawa suggests, abstract Case on the covert object is licensed by v (Chomsky 1995), the grammaticality of (40) is expected under the assumption that only morphological case marking is licensed by T1. Therefore, as long as Miyagawa (2003) is correct, the proposed analysis, which is not inconsistent with Miyagawa's hypothesis on T, can potentially capture (the lifting of) the TR.

Second, let us address the issue of the optionality of the GNC from the viewpoint of the hypothesis on the Japanese T proposed by Miyagawa (2003). Although the GNC has been extensively studied since Harada 1971, it seems that none of the previous analyses has come up with an ultimate solution to the optional nature of the GNC as well as the TR in Japanese. According to Miyagawa, T1 licenses morphological case marking. Therefore, it can appear with a nominative subject. On the other hand, T2 does not retain the ability to license morphological case marking or accusative Case on a covert object. Therefore, it may only appear with a genitive subject (along with elements that are not Case related, such as adverbs). Notice that if there are two types of T in Japanese, then the optionality issue of the GNC does not actually arise because a genitive subject may only appear with T2, and a nominative subject may appear only with T1. These combinations are completely fixed. Therefore, the optionality of the appearance of genitive and nominative subjects in the GNC is only apparent under the following circumstances: (a) whenever T1 is selected out of the lexicon, only the nominative subject is allowed; and (b) whenever T2 is selected from the lexicon, only the genitive subject is permitted. The other two combinations (the nominative subject and T2, and the genitive subject and T1) are excluded due to an unlicensed Case.[14] This argument, if correct, indicates that there is no optionality with the GNC in Japanese, and the apparent optionality is not an issue in light of the (strong) minimalist thesis that does not allow any optional operation.

8.4 Implications for the General Theory of Syntax

Investigation into the GNC in Japanese provides us with interesting implications for the general theory of syntax, especially with respect to the nature of operation Agree and the nature of Case systems.

First, as seen in the approaches reviewed in sections 8.3.1 and 8.3.2, any account of the GNC crucially concerns the mechanism of Case licensing, which has been an important issue concerning theory in generative grammar. Based on the empirical generalization shown here, we have suggested a refinement of some previous approaches, essentially following the findings and core ideas by the three researchers whose ideas we presented. That is, genitive Case in the GNC is licensed via Agree with D. Thus, the GNC in Japanese indicates a pure instance of Case licensing by Agree, in contrast to licensing by raising, in which agreement is followed by movement of a genitive DP to the specifier of the agreeing head. Therefore, the GNC in Japanese provides support to the hypothesis that Agree is an operation independent of movement.

Second, as discussed in section 8.3.3, the transitivity restriction (TR) on the GNC suggests that there are two types of T in Japanese, and the ways they license Case are different. If this is correct, Japanese has two completely different types of Case-licensing systems. This implies that Universal Grammar (UG) allows these two types of Case-licensing systems and, at the same time, raises interesting questions concerning in what languages the two types of Case-licensing systems may appear and what factors correlate with the appearance of the two types of Case-licensing systems.

NOTES FOR CHAPTER 8

An earlier version of this chapter was presented at the Workshop on Linguistic Theory and the Japanese Language of the 2005 MIT–Harvard LSA Summer Institute held at Harvard University on July 29, 2005. We would like to thank the audience at the meeting, as well as the following people: Fiona Clark, Ronald Craig, Jessica Dunton, Michiyo Hamasaki, Hironobu Kasai, Jaklin Kornfilt, Elizabeth Laurençot, Michael LoPresti, Keiko Miyagawa, Shigeru Miyagawa, Yoichi Miyamoto, Takashi Munakata, Fumikazu Niinuma, Kunio Nishiyama, Masao Ochi, Naoko Okura, Paul Rankin, Mamoru Saito, Shigeki Taguchi, Yukiko Ueda, Akira Watanabe, and an anonymous reviewer for their helpful comments. We are especially indebted to Shigeru Miyagawa and Mamoru Saito for their suggestions at various stages of this work. All errors are our own. Research by the first author was supported in part by Center for Linguistics, Nanzan University, of which he was an adjunct researcher (from June 1, 2004 to March 31, 2006).

1. In what follows, we refer to the category D, omitting N, just for simplicity of discussion.

2. The class of adjectives is called *keeyoo doosi* (adjectival verb) in terms of traditional Japanese linguistics. The morphological distinction between the *rentai* and *syuusi* forms was once clear in many predicates in Old Japanese, as shown by the contrast of *ari* 'have/be' (the conclusive form) versus *aru* (the attributive form). It is said that the distinction had been gradually lost somewhere between the twelfth and sixteenth centuries (the Kamakura era through the Muromati era). Accordingly, in Modern Japanese, the predicate form in a prenominal position is morphologically ambiguous between the two forms. The class of adjectives discussed in the text (i.e., *keeyoo doosi*) is the only case in which the contrast is retained.

3. The adjective appears in the prenominal position. This is the reason why the *rentai* form is alternatively dubbed the "prenominal form" in English.

4. Chomsky (1995) argues that any movement operation simply affects features rather than categories, because feature checking only requires a relevant feature. He attributes the impossibility of moving a feature alone in overt syntax to a PF requirement that only a category can be phonetically interpreted. This hypothesis about movement is called the Move-F hypothesis.

5. Note that (14b) is grammatical if it has the different reading shown in (i), in which *John* functions as a possessor of the car.

(i) John's very new car that he was driving yesterday

6. Watanabe (1996) points out that the GNC is allowed, even when there seems no outer N/D, based on comparative clauses in Japanese, such as (18a). Given that comparative clauses as well as relative clauses both involve *wh*-movement of some kind, Watanabe claims that the GNC results from *wh*-agreement. Watanabe observes that Japanese GNC and French stylistic inversion show a striking similarity in distribution, and he argues that both phenomena are explained under his framework of *wh*-agreement. Furthermore, under Watanabe's analysis, the presence of a predicate in *rentai* form means that the

inflectional system of the clause is changed from the normal inflection to a special inflection due to some factor such as *wh*-agreement.

7. It is not clear, however, how and why the categorical property of the head (e.g., T or C) that has the probe feature (e.g., φ-feature) is connected to the process of Agree operation between the probe and the goal in terms of the matching feature (e.g., φ-feature); in particular, the determination of Case value of the goal.

8. Based on Turkish Case alteration, Kornfilt (2003) independently proposes an approach along almost the same line as Hiraiwa's, which holds that there is a mechanism that crucially relies on Agree in C (between nominalized Agr that is raised up to C and the genitive subject).

9. We thank Mamoru Saito (pers. comm.) for bringing this set of data to our attention.

10. As Murasugi (1991) notes, however, the question remains as to what noun the *no* 'NO' in (24b) is the pro-form of. We leave this issue open here.

11. See Lees 1965 for the same type of analysis of genitive Case marking in Turkish subordinate clauses. Lees (1965) proposes that nominalized argument clauses are actually complements of phonologically unrealized nominal heads. See Kornfilt 2003, however, for a more promising approach to genitive Case marking in Turkish syntax.

12. Watanabe (1996) regards the TR as one of the core properties of Japanese GNC, as well as French stylistic inversion, arguing that the TR follows from his analysis of *wh*-agreement. However, Hiraiwa's (2001a) treatment of the TR is entirely different. Hiraiwa points out that the TR on the GNC is found in languages such as Japanese and Chamorro but not languages such as Turkish. Under Hiraiwa's approach, the TR follows independently of the mechanisms of the GNC. See also Saito 2004 and Ochi 2005, among others, for other promising approaches to (the lifting of) the TR.

13. See also Miyagawa and Ekida 2003 for an analysis of morphological case marking in Old Japanese and its relationship with the historical change in the verbal inflection system (briefly mentioned in note 2).

14. There is a fact that might be a potential problem for Miyagawa's (2003) two-T hypothesis, on which our refined approach relies. Under Miyagawa's hypothesis, T1, the licensor of the morphological case such as -*ga*, co-occurs only with a predicate in its *syuusi* (conclusive) inflection. It is thus predicted that the GNC is never allowed in a clause without a *syuusi* (conclusive) predicate. In the case of a clause in which the predicate is a verb, this prediction cannot be checked, because, as we briefly discussed in section 8.2, verbs in modern Japanese do not show morphologically visible distinction between the *syuusi* (conclusive) and *rentai* (attributive) forms. The only class of predicate maintaining this morphological distinction is the so-called *keeyoo doosi* (adjectival verb). In a clause with the *rentai* form of this type of predicate (i.e., an adjectival verb), the GNC is actually possible, as shown in (ii).

(ii) Watasi-wa [[John-ga/no   kenkoo-na]   riyuu]-o   sitteiru.
      I-TOP   John-NOM/GEN   healthy-NA(attributive) reason-ACC know
      'I know the reason why John is healthy.'

Unless we take the inflectional morphology of the adjectival verb to be just an exception (assuming, e.g., that its *rentai* form is an allomorph of the *syuusi* form and can appear under limited conditions such as this case), this fact suggests, contrary to the two-T hypothesis, that the *rentai* predicate has a feature compatible both with the licensor of nominative Case and with the licensor of genitive Case. Examples such as (ii) then suggest that the predicates appearing in GNC contexts all take the *rentai* inflections, whether the subjects are marked nominative or genitive.

There is evidence that the *rentai* inflection does not signify the mechanism of the Case conversion. Rather, a certain structural condition causes the special inflection on a predicate apart from the condition on the GNC. This is shown by the fact that the GNC is impossible, even if there is a *rentai* predicate in the sentence, as shown in (iii).

(iii) a. [Hanako-ga/*no   yuushuu-na-noni]   hoka-wa
       Hanako-NOM/GEN excellent-NA(attributive)-but the-others-TOP
       dameda.
       not-good
       'Hanako is excellent, but the others are not good.'
       (Shigeki Taguchi, pers. comm.)
    b. Taroo-wa [Hanako-ga/*no   itsumo yuushuu-na-noka]
       Taroo-TOP Hanako-NOM/GEN always excellent-NA(attributive)-Q
       sira-nakat-ta.
       know-not-PAST
       'Taroo did not know whether Hanako was always excellent.'

In these examples, the predicates in the bracketed clauses are *rentai* forms, yet the genitive subject is disallowed. These examples clearly indicate that the presence of a *rentai* form is certainly a necessary, but not sufficient, condition for licensing of genitive Case. Therefore, it is necessary to separate the source of the GNC from that of the *rentai* inflection. We suggest that the unavailability of genitive Case in (iii) indicates that the elements right after the *rentai* predicates (*noni* 'but' in (iia) and *noka* 'Q' in (iiib)) do not have the same feature as the one in N/D that can license genitive Case.

REFERENCES

Bedell, George. 1972. On *no*. In *UCLA papers in syntax 3: Studies in East Asian syntax*, ed. George Bedell, 1–20. Los Angeles: University of California.

Chomsky, Noam. 1995. Categories and transformations. In *The Minimalist Program*, 219–394. Cambridge, Mass.: MIT Press.

Chomsky, Noam. 2000. Minimalist inquiries: The framework. In *Step by step*, ed. Roger Martin, David Michaels, and Juan Uriagereka, 89–155. Cambridge, Mass.: MIT Press.

Fukui, Naoki. 1986. A theory of category projection and its applications. Doctoral dissertation, MIT, Cambridge, Mass.

Hale, Ken. 2002. On the Dagur object relative: Some comparative notes. *Journal of East Asian Linguistics* 11:109–122.

Harada, Shin-Ichi. 1971. *Ga-no* conversion and ideolectal variations in Japanese. *Gengo Kenkyu* 60:25–38.

Hiraiwa, Ken. 2001a. On nominative-genitive conversion. In *MITWPL 39: A few from Building E39*, ed. Elena Guerzoni and Ora Matushansky, 66–125. Cambridge, Mass.: MIT Working Papers in Linguistics.

Hiraiwa, Ken. 2001b. Multiple Agree and Defective Intervention Constraint. In *MITWPL 40: HUMIT 2000*, ed. Ora Matushansky, Albert Costa, Javier Martin-Gonzalez, Lance Nathan, and Adam Szczegielniak, 67–80. Cambridge, Mass.: MIT Working Papers in Linguistics.

Hoji, Hajime. 1990. Sloppy identity in Japanese. Ms., University of Southern California, Los Angeles.

Inoue, Kazuko. 1976. *Henkee bunpoo to nihongo* [Transformational grammar and Japanese]. Tokyo: Taishukan.
Kornfilt, Jaklin. 2003. Subject Case in Turkish nominalized clauses. In *Syntactic structures and morphological information*, ed. U. Junghanns and L. Szucsich, 129–215. Berlin: Mouton de Gruyter.
Lasnik, Howard. 1995. Last Resort and Attract F. In *Proceedings of the 6th annual meeting of the Formal Linguistics Society of Mid-America* 1, ed. Leslie Gabriele, Debra Hardison, and Robert Westmoreland, 62–81. Bloomington: Indiana University Linguistics Club.
Lasnik, Howard. 1999. Chains of arguments. In *Working minimalism*, ed. Samuel D. Epstein and Norbert Hornstein, 189–216. Cambridge, Mass.: MIT Press.
Lees, Robert B. 1965. Turkish nominalizations and a problem of ellipsis. *Foundations of Language* 1–2:112–121.
Miyagawa, Shigeru. 1989. *Structure and Case marking in Japanese*. San Diego, Calif.: Academic Press.
Miyagawa, Shigeru. 1993. Case-checking and Minimal Link Condition. In *MITWPL 19: Papers on Case and agreement II*, ed. Colin Phillips, 213–254. Cambridge, Mass.: MIT Working Papers in Linguistics.
Miyagawa, Shigeru. 2003. A-movement scrambling and options without optionality. In *Word order and scrambling*, ed. Simin Karimi, 177–200. Oxford: Blackwell.
Miyagawa, Shigeru, and Fusae Ekida. 2003. Historical development of the accusative Case marking in Japanese as seen in classical literary texts. *Journal of Japanese Linguistics* 19:1–109.
Murasugi, Keiko. 1991. Noun phrases in Japanese and English: A study in syntax, learnability, and acquisition. Doctoral dissertation, University of Connecticut, Storrs.
Nakai, Satoru. 1980. A reconsideration of *ga-no* conversion in Japanese. *Papers in Linguistics* 13:279–320.
Ochi, Masao. 2001. Move F and *ga/no* conversion in Japanese. *Journal of East Asian Linguistics* 10:247–286.
Ochi, Masao. 2005. *Ga/no* conversion and overt object shift in Japanese. *Nanzan Linguistics* 2:61–80.
Saito, Mamoru. 1983. Case and government in Japanese. In *Proceedings of the 2nd West Coast Conference on Formal Linguistics*, ed. Michael Barlow, David P. Flickinger, and Michael T. Westcoat, 247–259. Stanford, Calif.: CSLI Publications.
Saito, Mamoru. 2004. Genitive subjects in Japanese: Implications for the theory of null objects. In *Non-nominative subjects* 2, ed. Peri Bhaskararao and Karumuri Venkata Subbarao, 103–118. Amsterdam: John Benjamins.
Sakai, Hiromu. 1994. Complex NP Constraint and case-conversions in Japanese. In *Current topics in English and Japanese*, ed. Masaru Nakamura, 179–203. Tokyo: Hituzi Syoboo.
Shibatani, Masayoshi. 1975. Perceptual strategies and the phenomena of particle conversion in Japanese. In *Papers from the Parasession on Functionalism*, ed. Robin E. Grossman, L. James San, and Timothy J. Vance, 469–480. Chicago: Chicago Linguistic Society.
Shibatani, Masayoshi. 1977. Grammatical relations and surface Case. *Language* 53:789–809.
Shibatani, Masayoshi. 1978. *Nihongo no bunseki* [Analyses of Japanese]. Tokyo: Taishukan.
Ura, Hiroyuki. 1993. L-relatedness and its parametric variation. In *MITWPL 19: Papers on Case and agreement II*, ed. Colin Phillips, 377–399. Cambridge, Mass.: MIT Working Papers in Linguistics.
Watanabe, Akira. 1996. Nominative-genitive conversion and agreement in Japanese: A cross-linguistic perspective. *Journal of East Asian Linguistics* 5:373–410.

CHAPTER 9

PROCESSING SENTENCES IN JAPANESE

EDSON T. MIYAMOTO

9.1 Introduction

This chapter summarizes research investigating how sentences are processed in Japanese (see Nakayama, Mazuka, and Shirai 2006, for a recent collection of papers on Japanese psycholinguistics; see also Kess and Miyamoto 1994 for an extensive survey of early work). The goal in this field is to examine how people uncover the meaning intended when they read (or hear) a sentence. Ambiguity plays a central role. At each point in the sentence, how do readers choose among alternative interpretations often available? What do those preferences tell us about the way grammatical knowledge (as well as world knowledge and social conventions) is put to use? What are the cognitive resources (e.g., working memory, attention) used, and how do they shape this process?

Sections 9.2 and 9.3 provide basic background. Section 9.4 introduces a controversy involving head-final languages and summarizes related experimental results in Japanese. Sections 9.5–9.7 discuss how clause boundaries are determined in Japanese and how readers recover from initial misanalyses. Section 9.8 describes the processing of long-distance dependencies for fronted *wh*-phrases. The remaining sections summarize work related to such dependencies in relative clauses, scrambling, and in-situ *wh*-phrases.

9.2 Description of the Core Data

The simplest way to collect data on sentence comprehension is to ask readers to rate sentences (according to their naturalness, acceptability, and so on). This type of questionnaire data is *off-line* as it only provides a measurement after reading of the entire sentence has finished.

Although off-line results provide critical information, they often have to be complemented with *on-line* studies in which measurements are taken as the sentence is being read. The time scale of interest is usually in the order of a few hundred milliseconds (ms).

9.2.1 Reading Time Measurements

This discussion draws primarily from reports of reading experiments, in which similar sentences are compared and relatively longer reading times are taken as a sign of difficulty. In *eye-tracking*, eye movements are recorded every few milliseconds and measures of difficulty include *fixations* (how long the eyes fixate on a word or sequence of words) and *regressions* (how often the eyes return to a prior region; see Rayner 1998 for a summary).

Because eye-tracking requires special equipment and can be taxing on participants (accurate data collection may require participants' heads to be kept immobile through the use of chin rests and bite-bars), computer-based methods are often used. In *self-paced reading*, participants press a button to see the next region of the sentence, and the elapsed time between button presses is assumed to correspond to the reading time for that region. A region can include one or more words (usually one or more *bunsetsus* in Japanese) depending on the hypothesis being tested, but it is crucial that the segmentation be chosen carefully so that it does not lead to artificial breaks or groupings (words in a region tend to be grouped together during reading). Presentation can be *center-screen*, so that a new region replaces the previous region in the center of the screen at each button press. Or it can be of the *noncumulative moving-window* type, in which case the whole sentence is presented masked, with each character replaced with dashes or dots (in Japanese, spaces are used to indicate the regions of presentation), and for each button press a new region is revealed while all other regions remain masked. Although readers cannot return to previous regions, self-paced results (of the noncumulative moving-window type in particular) are well correlated with eye-tracking data (Just, Carpenter, and Woolley 1982).

To determine whether a word is read slowly in a given sentence, its reading times are compared to those of a word in a similar baseline sentence. The choice of an adequate baseline is crucial. Such comparisons are only meaningful if the words are similar in terms of length, part of speech, frequency, and familiarity. Moreover, because readers may speed up as they read more words in the sentence, comparisons are preferentially made between words that occupy similar linear positions in the sentences.

In *rapid serial visual presentation* (RSVP), words are flashed on a computer monitor for short periods of time—around 350 ms per word in English, and 700 ms per bunsetsu in Japanese. The difference in presentation rates in the two languages is largely explained by the fact that bunsetsus usually include both a content word and a functional word; therefore, they contain twice as much information. RSVP is particularly useful in brain imaging studies, in which participants are required to read sentences without moving their bodies (including hands and eyes).

9.2.2 Brain Responses

The brain responses discussed are similar to those observed for other languages. For *event-related potentials* (ERP), difficulty in integrating a word into the syntactic representation of the sentence (in syntactic violations in particular) leads to a *P600* response (i.e., a positive deflection peaking 600 ms after the onset of the ungrammatical word; e.g., after the declarative particle *yo* following a *wh*-phrase, Nakagome et al. 2001). Semantically unexpected words (e.g., *dekaketa* 'went out' in *zisyo-ni dekaketa* 'went out to a dictionary') elicit an *N400* (a negative response that peaks 400 ms after the offending word; Nakagome et al. 2001; see also Kiguchi and Miyamoto 2004, for its localization using *magnetoencephalography*, MEG).

In *functional magnetic resonance imaging* (fMRI), Broca's area, a brain region usually associated with grammatical functions (see, e.g., Sakai et al. 2002 and references therein for more specific localizations), is more active during the processing of scrambling (Koizumi 2005) and center-embedding constructions (Inui et al. 1998).

9.3 WORKING MEMORY

Working memory (see Baddeley 1992 for a summary; Baddeley 2000 for recent developments; and Just and Carpenter 1992, Caplan and Waters 1999 for models specific to language processing) plays a role in much of the following discussions. Working memory is where information is held for short periods of time (roughly up to two seconds) in order for various types of cognitive tasks to be performed, and it is severely constrained in the amount of information it can hold (consider how hard it is *not* to forget a phone number while dialing it). Item length is also important as the number of words that can be recalled decreases if the words are long. This *word length effect* indicates that one of the components of working memory is phonologically based (the other component handles visual information). The phonological nature of the encoding is further supported by the *phonological similarity effect*—the difficulty in recalling items that sound similar.

The small capacity in working memory is compensated by *chunking* (Miller 1963), an operation that associates items together so that they occupy fewer slots in working memory. Consider how much harder it is to recall the sequence of ten digits 6-5-1-9-4-5-2-0-1-0 than the three numbers 65-1945-2010, or that in 2010 it will have been sixty-five years since the end of World War II. A rough parallel can be drawn with sentence processing as we associate words together (e.g., a subject with a verb) creating links with our long-term memory (e.g., that a war ended in 1945) to create a more abstract representation that occupies fewer slots so that we have more capacity to process upcoming words in the sentence.

9.3.1 Individual Differences and Reading Ability

Individual differences in working memory capacity for reading can be measured with *reading span* (Daneman and Carpenter 1980), which is defined as the largest number of sentences a person is able to read aloud and later recall the last word for each one of them. Readers with different reading spans have been argued to display divergent reading patterns to long-distance dependencies (King and Just 1991; but see Caplan and Waters 1999 for criticisms).

Using the Japanese version of the reading span task (Osaka 1998), in which the word to be recalled is not necessarily the last one in the sentence so that its part of speech can be varied, reading span has been shown to improve if the word to be recalled is the one regarded independently as being the most important in the sentence (Osaka et al. 2002).

Whereas reading span reflects readers' abilities in handling transient information in working memory, reading also requires retrieving information from long-term storage. In one such a measure, participants are shown words (written in kanji) that are commonly used in Japanese but rarely written in kanji and asked to write down their pronunciation (the *Hyakurakan test*; Amano and Kondo 1999). Reading span correlates poorly with vocabulary tests but correlates well with general reading abilities (as measured by multiple-choice university entrance examinations). In contrast, the Hyakurakan test has not only a high correlation with vocabulary but also a higher correlation with reading abilities than reading span does (Jincho, Mazuka, and Namiki 2004). One way of understanding this contrast is that reading span is a better predictor of local processing (e.g., how fast a sentence segment will be read), whereas long-term memory measures may correlate better with how well a text is understood overall.

9.4 CONTROVERSIES

One basic question is how similar the processing of sentences is across different languages. One extreme view is that each language requires a specific processing algorithm apart from its own distinct grammar. In other words, not only is the grammar parameterized, but also the way people use the grammar to process sentences differs for each language. This approach raises issues in learnability (children have to set grammatical and processing parameters simultaneously, but see Mazuka 1998 for a constrained parameterization and its possible trigger and Hasegawa 1990 and Inoue and Fodor 1995 for criticisms of earlier versions of Mazuka's proposal), and it is also conceptually more complex than its alternative, which is the null hypothesis often assumed in the field. In this other type of proposal, the assumption is that all that children need to set are the parameters in the grammar, as the processing algorithm is universal to all languages (Fodor 1998).

9.4.1 Incremental Processing

One central topic within the parameterization debate is whether sentences in head-final languages like Japanese are processed *incrementally*, so that each word read is interpreted immediately in relation to the previous words in the sentence. The alternative is for comprehension to lag behind the actual reading of the words in the sentence (see Inoue and Fodor 1995 for discussion). For head-initial languages, there is a consensus that there is no delay. The problem is clearest at the clausal level. For example, in the fragment *Mary brought*, it is unnecessary to wait for the next words in order to interpret *Mary* as the agent of *brought*. Because verbs come at the end in head-final languages, incremental processing is more contentious. In the following example, each individual NP can be created and interpreted immediately (i.e., there are 'a student from Fukuoka', 'a teacher', and 'a letter').

(1) Fukuoka syussin-no gakusei-ga sensei-ni tegami-o
    Fukuoka native-GEN student-NOM teacher-DAT letter-ACC

The question is to what extent the NPs are associated together as part of a single representation before the verb is seen. An incremental solution is to assume that case markers provide enough information for readers to understand that the student did something to the letter for the benefit of the teacher, although the exact action is not known. But that is enough to bind the NPs together in one single chunk based on the prediction of an underspecified predicate (i.e., partial information about the predicate is used to project the necessary structure, e.g., a VP node, to associate the NPs; see Den and Inoue 1997, Miyamoto 2002, Yamashita 2000, for related discussions).

In contrast, in *head-driven* models the lexical head has to be present for a node to be projected (e.g., Pritchett 1991). As a by-product, processing must be non-incremental in Japanese, as all arguments (and adjuncts) cannot be associated together until the verb is read because only then is the VP node created. Few experimental studies claim to support this type of model (e.g., O'Grady, Nakamura and Lee 2002, but the result is compatible with incremental models that adopt a proposal such as Gibson 1998), and most arguments have been conceptual (head-driven processing is obligatory if one adopts Chomsky's [1981] Projection Principle in a strict fashion in performance; Pritchett 1991), computationally based (to circumvent limitations in top-down and bottom-up parsers, Abney 1989; but see Abney and Johnson 1991 for an alternative algorithm), or based on problems with incremental parsing in Japanese. One such problem is that case markers cannot aid in interpretation because they do not have a one-to-one correspondence with thematic roles (Pritchett 1991). However, it is known nowadays that lexical ambiguity does not prevent incremental interpretation. For example, when reading an ambiguous verb that allows more than one argument structure, English speakers interpret an NP using the argument structure most frequently used with that verb (Garnsey et al. 1997). Similarly, Japanese speakers may interpret a case-marked NP based on the most common use of that case marker with such a noun.

Head-driven models have serious problems of their own (see Miyamoto 2002 for discussion). For example, they predict a considerable memory load, as arguments have to be memorized individually until the predicate is read, whereas in incremental models constituents are associated together and can occupy fewer slots in working memory. The burden implied by head-driven models should be particularly problematic for the acquisition of head-final languages (e.g., leading to shorter utterances), but such typological discrepancies have not been reported.

Apart from detailed discussions based on intuitive judgments (A. Inoue 1991), current evidence supporting incremental models include studies examining reading times (Kamide and Mitchell 1999) and ERPs (Oishi and Sakamoto 2004) to clause-final predicates. More critical to the resolution of the controversy, various studies have examined reactions prior to the predicate. These include eye movements while listening to sequences of NPs (Kamide, Altmann, and Haywood 2003); ERPs for sequences of NPs (Garnsey et al. 2001) and for scrambled NPs (Ueno and Kluender 2003); and reading times for scrambled NPs (Mazuka, Itoh and Kondo 2002; Miyamoto and Takahashi 2002a, 2004), for scrambled *wh*-phrases (Aoshima, Phillips, and Weinberg 2004), for pronouns (Aoshima, Phillips, and Weinberg 2003), and for sequences of case-marked NPs (Miyamoto 2002). Although each result considered individually is unlikely to settle the issue, taken together the results make a strong case against a large class of nonincremental models. The following sections elaborate on two lines of evidence.

9.4.2 Anticipatory Eye Movements

While listening to instructions (e.g., *pick up the candy*), English speakers' eyes move to the relevant object about 145 ms after the end of its name. Because more than 150 ms are necessary to execute eye movements, the result suggests that the decision to move the eyes can occur even before the end of the word is heard (Tanenhaus et al. 1995; see Mazuka et al. 2005 for data on Japanese). Such rapid reactions allow this type of methodology to be used to investigate how listeners comprehend utterances in detail. In a study investigating incremental processing, Japanese speakers heard sentences as in (2) while looking at a picture of a waitress, a client, a hamburger, and other objects (Kamide, Altmann, and Haywood 2003).

(2) a. Dative object condition
Ueitoresu-ga   kyaku-ni   tanosigeni hanbaagaa-o   hakobu.
waitress-NOM   customer-DAT   merrily   hamburger-ACC   carry
'The waitress merrily carries the hamburger to the customer.'
b. Accusative object condition
Ueitoresu-ga   kyaku-o   tanosigeni karakau.
waitress-NOM   customer-ACC   merrily   tease
'The waitress merrily teases the customer.'

By the time the word 'merrily' is heard, the sentences in (2) differ only in the case marker of 'customer'. However, already by then, participants had made more anticipatory eye movements toward the hamburger while listening to the dative-object sentence in (2a) compared with when they heard the accusative condition in (2b) (Kamide, Altmann, and Haywood 2003). This result suggests that the participants considered the hamburger to be a more natural continuation for the dative object. The result is unexpected if NPs were processed independently as argued by nonincremental models.

9.4.3 Case Markers as Indicators of Clause Boundaries

If processing is incremental in Japanese, the question arises as to how readers interpret a sequence of NPs (and PPs) in relation to each other before the predicate is read. Because embedded clauses in Japanese do not have any markers to indicate their beginning (see A. Inoue 1991 for a discussion), readers may not even know how many clauses there are in a sequence of NPs unless they read the sentence until the end. But under some circumstances, case markers can indicate where clause boundaries lie. For example, in a sequence containing two accusative NPs, readers can assume that at least two clauses are necessary based on the *double-o constraint*, according to which two accusative NPs cannot be in the same clause in Japanese (Harada 1973 and references therein). In fact, long reading times can be observed at the second NP-*o* in such cases. That the long reading times are not simply a sign of surprise to an unusual sequence of NPs is suggested by faster reading times to the head of a relative clause later in the sentence (Miyamoto 2002). The result is compatible with the claim that the long reading times at the second accusative NP are used to create the initial boundary for an embedded clause, which facilitates processing at the head noun of the relative clause.

Furthermore, given the special properties of nominative NPs in Japanese (they cannot be scrambled, Saito 1985; they have to be associated with an inflected predicate, Takezawa 1987), it is possible that readers use such NPs as anchors around which other NPs in the same clause are interpreted (Miyamoto 2002; see also Uehara and Bradley 2002, experiment 3, on the preference to have each animate nominative NP in a separate clause, and Mazuka, Itoh and Kondo 2001, for a P600 to nominative NPs).

The use of case markers to determine clause boundaries is illustrated in the following example (from Kamide and Mitchell 1999).

(3) Kyoozyu-ga   gakusei-ni   tosyokansisyo-ga kasita
    professor-NOM student-DAT   librarian-NOM   lent
    komonzyo-o   miseta.
    manuscript-ACC showed
    'The professor showed the manuscript that the librarian had lent to the student.'

As in its English translation, 'student-DAT' in (3) is ambiguous and can be the recipient of 'showed' or 'lent'. In a self-paced reading experiment, the 'showed' interpretation was found to be preferred, even though 'student-DAT' is closer to 'lent' (Kamide and Mitchell 1999). Noting that no verb in Japanese can take the first three NPs as arguments, already at the third NP it is clear that at least two clauses are needed in this case. The result then can be explained if one assumes that there is a preference to insert a clause boundary where it is first clear to be necessary (at 'librarian-NOM') leaving 'student-DAT' in the matrix clause where it attaches to the matrix verb (see Miyamoto 2003 for discussion).

Another way of indicating the beginning of an embedded clause is to use numeral classifier mismatch as in the following example (from Yoshida, Aoshima, and Phillips 2004).

(4) San-satu-no   sensei-ga   yonda hon...
    three-CL-GEN   teacher-NOM   read   book
    'Three books that the teacher read...'

Because the numeral classifier *satu* cannot be used to count people, it creates the prediction for an upcoming noun such as 'book', and the noun 'teacher' is taken to be the beginning of a relative clause (Yoshida, Aoshima, and Phillips 2004).

Although particles are unlikely to be the only source of information (see Iguchi and Miyamoto 2006 and Muraoka and Sakamoto 2004 on the role of animacy), the research above suggests how sequences of NPs can be interpreted in complex multiple clauses before the predicate is seen.

9.4.4 A Single Processing Mechanism

The rest of this chapter assumes that processing is strictly incremental in Japanese and that there is a single processing mechanism that subserves the processing of all human languages. The goal then is to characterize this single processing mechanism and consider how its general properties are instantiated in Japanese. One line of research that can be pursued is to show that a strategy attested in various languages (e.g., for *wh*-phrases) is also adopted in Japanese. Another possibility is to investigate apparent differences in the way Japanese is processed (e.g., in relation to relative clauses) and the issues they raise for models that assume a single processing mechanism.

9.5 Reanalyses of Clause Boundaries

In section 9.4.3, some clause boundaries were claimed to be inferred from case markers. But in the absence of clause-initial markers, it is often the case that relative clauses are only detected when material after the verb is read (but see Misono et al. 1997; Venditti 2006; Venditti and Yamashita 1994, for prosodic cues in speech).

9.5.1 Subject Reanalyses

Up to 'delivered' in (5a) (from Inoue 1990a), the single-clause interpretation 'Taro delivered flowers to Masako' is favored.

(5) a. Subject reanalysis
      Taro-ga   Masako-ni   hana-o   todoketa   otoko-o   tasikameta.
      Taro-NOM   Masako-DAT   flower-ACC delivered man-ACC   scrutinized
      'Taro scrutinized the man who delivered flowers to Masako.'
   b. Taro-ga   Masako-ni   hana-o   todoketa   koto-ga   wakatta.
      Taro-NOM   Masako-DAT   flower-ACC delivered fact-NOM found out
      'It was found out that Taro delivered flowers to Masako.'
   c. Masako-ni   hana-o   todoketa   otoko-o   Taro-ga   tasikameta.
      Masako-DAT flower-ACC   delivered   man-ACC   Taro-NOM scrutinized
      'Taro scrutinized the man who delivered flowers to Masako.'

When the noun 'man' is read in (5a), it is clear that it is the head of a relative clause, and the subject 'Taro-NOM' must be reanalyzed out of the clause so that a gap can be created. A series of experiments by Masakatsu Inoue provide evidence for difficulty at the head noun. In an eye-tracking experiment, first-pass fixations were longer and more regressive eye movements were observed at 'man' in (5a) compared with 'fact' in (5b) and 'man' in (5c) (Inoue 1990a). The cost to reanalyze 'Taro' out of the simple clause initially built for (5a) has also been reported for transitive and intransitive clauses replacing the embedded ditransitive clause headed by 'delivered' (Inoue 1990b). Furthermore, the finding that reading times to 'man' are shorter if *Taro* is marked with the topic *wa* (M. Inoue 1991) is compatible with the claim that displacing topicalized NPs is relatively easy because they are in the periphery of the clause and only hold an aboutness relation with it.

An fMRI study detected more activity in Broca's area for subject reanalysis sentences such as (5a) compared with the left-branching (5c) with a transitive clause replacing the ditransitive embedded clause (Inui et al. 1998). The result was claimed to be due to the center-embedding configuration of (5a), but it is also possible that reanalysis contributed to the result.

9.5.2 Subject-Object Reanalyses

The sentences in (6) have been extensively compared (Mazuka and Itoh 1995; see also Kondo and Mazuka 1996 regarding eye movements while reading such constructions aloud).

(6) a. Subject reanalysis
Yoko-ga kodomo-o koosaten-de mikaketa onnanoko-ni
Yoko-NOM child-ACC intersection-LOC saw girl-DAT
koe-o-kaketa.
called
'Yoko called the girl who saw the child at the intersection.'
b. Subject-object reanalysis
Yoko-ga kodomo-o koosaten-de mikaketa takusii-ni noseta.
Yoko-NOM child-ACC intersection-LOC saw taxi-DAT put
'Yoko$_i$ made the child get on the taxi she$_i$ saw at the intersection.'

Up to the verb 'saw' in (6a,b), the single-clause interpretation 'Yoko saw the child at the intersection' is favored. When a head noun is detected next, the simple clause must be reanalyzed to insert a gap for the relative clause. Mazuka and Itoh (1995), based on intuitive judgments, observed that reanalysis is harder in (6b) than in (6a) because of the number of arguments that have to be displaced in each case. In (6a), only the subject 'Yoko' is displaced to the newly built matrix clause, whereas in (6b) both 'Yoko' and the object 'child' have to be displaced. This observation has been discussed within various reanalysis frameworks (e.g., Gorrell 1995, Sturt and Crocker 1996).

Experimental work suggests that the difficulty in (6b) comes from the ambiguity of 'taxi' (it can be the object or the subject of 'saw'), which hinders the reanalysis process (Hirose and Inoue 1998). However, another self-paced reading study indicates that even with unambiguous head nouns, (6b) is still difficult to process (Miyamoto 2002).

Displacing more NPs is not always dispreferred. The two objects in ditransitive constructions can be displaced together in situations where displacing the accusative NP alone would be sufficient, which thus argues against proposals in which the amount of revisions is always minimized during reanalysis (Miyamoto 2003).

9.6 Implicit Prosody in Silent Reading

The influence of prosody on the comprehension of utterances (see Venditti 2006 for a summary; see also Richards, this volume, on *wh*-phrases) has been recently expanded by claims that underlying prosodic contours influence processing decisions during silent reading as well (Fodor 2002). For example, a short modifier ('kind') is preferentially attached to the closer noun ('student'), but a long modifier ('extremely kind') is preferentially attached to the farther noun ('student's sister') so that the lengths of modifier and modifiee are similar (Hirose et al. 1998, Inoue and Fodor 1995).

(7) (kyokutanni) sinsetsuna gakusei-no imooto
 extremely kind student-GEN sister
 '(extremely) kind student's sister'

Implicit-prosody effects have also been observed in the resolution of clause-boundary ambiguities. Until 'trusted' in (8a,b), a single-clause interpretation is preferred.

(8) a. Single-name subject
 Morisita-ga sinyaku-o kokorokara sinyoosita yuuzintati-ni...
 Morisita-NOM medicine-ACC truly trusted friends-DAT
 b. Conjoined-name subject
 Hosokawa-to Morisita-ga sinyaku-o kokorokara sinyoosita
 Hosokawa-and Morisita-NOM medicine-ACC truly trusted
 yuuzintati-ni...
 friends-DAT
 c. ...syohoosen-o okutta.
 prescription-ACC sent
 Single name: 'Morisita sent the prescription to the friends who really trusted the medicine.'
 Conjoined names: 'Hosokawa and Morisita sent the prescription to the friends who really trusted the medicine.'

Reanalysis at 'friends' can build two types of relative clauses (see section 9.5.2). The object 'medicine-ACC' can remain as part of the relative clause (subject reanalysis) or be displaced to the matrix clause together with the subject (subject-object reanalysis).

The nominative subjects in the fragments in (8a,b) differ in their lengths (as measured by the number of *minor phrases* or *accentual phrases*), which lead to different prosodic contours when read aloud. A *major phrase* boundary (also known as *intermediate phrase*) tends to be produced immediately after the conjoined names, whereas with the single-name subject it is produced after 'medicine-ACC'

(Hirose 2003, experiment 2). Those two positions for the major phrase boundary correspond to the beginning of the embedded clause in the subject-reanalysis interpretation and the subject-object reanalysis, respectively.

When asked to write sentences starting with the fragments in (8a,b), Japanese speakers are more likely to produce completions with the subject-reanalysis interpretation after reading the conjoined names in (18b) (Hirose 2003, experiment 1; see Sato, Kobayashi, and Miyamoto 2007 for related data from deaf readers of Japanese). This is compatible with the claim that speakers assign implicit prosodic contours while reading in silence and that the position of the major phrase boundary influences the interpretation of the fragments.

Furthermore, when (8a,b) are continued as in (8c), the matrix clause contains 'prescription-ACC', thus only the subject-reanalysis interpretation is possible (two accusative NPs cannot be part of the same clause, hence 'medicine' has to be part of the embedded clause). For such sentences, readers take longer at 'prescription-ACC' in the single-name subject condition than in the conjoined-names condition. This suggests that 'medicine' is more likely to be interpreted as part of the matrix clause in the single-name condition, where it clashes with 'prescription' (Hirose 2003, experiments 4 and 5).

9.7 Verb Morphology

Apart from auxiliaries expressing animacy (e.g., production mistakes in animacy agreement with *iru* and *aru*; Nicol 1998), experimental studies have been reported on empathy markers (e.g., *kureru*) and on the internal structure of verbal compounds.

9.7.1 Subject Reanalysis with *Kureru*

The auxiliary *kureru* at the end of (9) expresses *empathy* (i.e., who benefits from the action) and has been used to force subject reanalysis (Mazuka et al. 1989).

(9) Yuuzin-ga mootyoo-de nyuin-siteita toki mimai-ni kite-kureta.
friend-NOM appendicitis-for hospitalized-was when visit-DAT came
'When I was hospitalized with appendicitis, my friend came to visit.'

The NP 'friend' is interpreted as the subject of 'hospitalized' until *kureta* signals that the speaker was the beneficiary of the visit. This forces a subject reanalysis to displace 'friend' to the matrix clause and insert a phonologically null subject (identified with the speaker) in the embedded clause. Mazuka and colleagues did not detect difficulty for (9) (78 percent correct in truth-false judgments and whole-sentence reading times comparable to other sentences). However, in other studies, in which participants were given the embedded verb and asked to produce its subject, performance was at chance at the end of the sentence and only improved gradually thereafter (Nagata 1993).

9.7.2 V-*te*-V Compounds

A self-paced reading study investigated sentences as in (10) (Nakatani 2006).

(10) a. Shuzii-ga   byoositu-ni   tyuusyaki-o   mot-te-kita.
       doctor-NOM   ward-DAT   syringe-ACC   brought in
       'The doctor brought a syringe into the hospital ward.'
    b. Shuzii-ga   byoositu-ni   tyuusyaki-o   mot-te   tootyakusita.
       doctor-NOM   ward-DAT   syringe-ACC   holding   arrived
       'The doctor arrived at the hospital ward holding a syringe.'

The critical words (from the dative NP until the last word shown in (10a,b)) were presented in one single region, and their reading times were longer in (10b) than in (10a) and in other baseline conditions. The longer reading times for (10b) are expected because the NP-*ni* is far from 'arrived', given the intervening embedded clause. Thus, the result suggests that there is no embedded clause in (10a) and *motte-kita* is processed as a unit.

9.8 FILLER-GAP DEPENDENCIES

The processing of *filler-gap dependencies* has been shown to underline a variety of phenomena across a number of different languages. The typical example is fronted *wh*-phrases in English as illustrated in the following sentence (adapted from Crain and Fodor 1985).

(11) Filled-gap effect (FGE)
     Who$_i$ did the children force [X] us to sing the songs for *gap*$_i$ last week?

As soon as the filler *who* in (11) is read, it triggers the search for a gap (the thematic position of the *wh*-phrase). As each ensuing word is processed, readers look for a position where the gap can be inserted. When *force* is read, the gap can be inserted (as indicated by [X]) and *who* can be interpreted as the direct object of this verb. A slow down occurs when the word *us* is read next as it becomes clear that the position of the gap is incorrect (Crain and Fodor 1985). This type of filled-gap effect is evidence for strict incremental processing as the required gap is inserted without look-ahead to check the next word in the sentence.

The preference to insert the gap as soon as possible is consistent with the claim that long dependencies consume cognitive resources such as working memory necessary to keep the filler and its gap requirement active until the gap position is found. In some models, this is a special case of a general phenomenon as readers are assumed to keep track of the syntactic heads necessary to complete the sentence. The memory cost at each point in the sentence depends on the number of predicted heads and the amount of material processed since each head was first predicted. The idea is that the maintenance of each prediction consumes cognitive resources, thus the more predictions and the longer they are kept active in working memory, the more costly their processing (Gibson 1998, and references therein, also Babyonyshev and Gibson 1999, for a discussion on Japanese).

Many of the discussions in the following sections revolve around filler-gap dependencies or generalizations of them. It is important to emphasize that the claims made here are related to the parsing process and not to syntax. For example, by handling scrambling in Japanese and fronted *wh*-phrases in English as a single phenomenon subsumed under filler-gap dependencies, the intention is not to claim that those constructions are syntactically identical. Rather, the point is that scrambling and fronted *wh*-phrases share similar types of configurations from the point of view of parsing in the sense that both constructions involve a dislocated filler that has to be held in working memory until its corresponding gap is found in the sentence.

9.9 RELATIVE CLAUSES

Cross-linguistic work on relative clauses has been particularly active in the investigation of gap position (the position that is relativized in the clause) and attachment ambiguities. Of particular interest is the fact that relative clauses across different languages can come after the head noun they modify (*postnominal* relative clauses) or precede the head noun (*prenominal* relative clauses). Such a difference in relative position is crucial because it changes the types of information available at each point.

9.9.1 Relative Clauses and Gap Position

Given that relative clauses involve a dependency between a filler (the modified noun) and a gap, a preference to minimize such dependencies has been claimed to explain why postnominal relative clauses with the gap in subject position are easier to understand than those with the gap in object position in a number of European languages (English: King and Just 1991; French: Holmes and O'Regan 1981; inter alia).

(12) a. Subject-gap relative clause
    the senator$_i$ that *gap*$_i$ accused the reporter
 b. Object-gap relative clause
    the senator$_i$ that the reporter accused *gap*$_i$

For prenominal relative clauses, the filler-gap distance predicts that object gaps should be easier to understand than subject gaps, contrary to results in Japanese using questionnaires (Sheldon 1976) and self-paced reading (Ishizuka, Nakatani and Gibson 2003, Miyamoto and Nakamura 2003).

Interestingly, self-paced reading results for prenominal relative clauses in Mandarin Chinese have been claimed to favor gaps in object position (Hsiao and Gibson 2003; see Hsu 2003 for criticisms; also Lin, Fong, and Bever 2005 for a subject preference with possessor relative clauses), and data from aphasic patients indicate that object gaps are also easier in Cantonese (Law and Leung 2000). Thus, Japanese may be exceptional, and its preference for subject gaps may be caused by the syntactic properties of its relative clauses (see Miyamoto and Nakamura 2003 for discussion), which may also explain the availability of constructions usually not seen in other languages (for the processing of some of such constructions, see Nakamura and Miyamoto 2006 on double-gap relative clauses, Yamashita 1995 on gapless relative clauses, Yoshida and Sano 2001 on head-internal relative clauses).

9.9.2 Relative Clause Attachment

Another line of research started with the finding that when reading *the daughter of the colonel who suffered the accident* in their native language, speakers of English prefer the interpretation in which the relative clause attaches to the low noun in the tree structure (*colonel*), whereas Spanish speakers prefer the high noun (*daughter*) interpretation (Cuetos and Mitchell 1988; for a list of results for various languages, see http://etm4rc.googlepages.com/table.html). Questionnaires indicate that there is an overall preference for the high noun in Japanese (Kamide and Mitchell 1997, experiment 1; also Hirose 2001; Sturt, Branigan, and Matsumoto-Sturt 1999). Reading times have also been measured for unambiguous sentences (disambiguated through plausibility manipulations) as in (13).

(13) a. High attachment
[RC Hoosekibako-no sumi-ni nokotteita] hannin no
      jewelry-box-GEN corner-LOC remained criminal GEN
simon o keisatu-ga nantoka mitukedasita.
fingerprint ACC police-NOM somehow found
'The police somehow found the fingerprint of the criminal that remained in the corner of the jewelry box.'
b. Low attachment
[RC Gozyuudai dansei-to suiteisareru] hannin no simon o
      50s male-as supposed criminal GEN fingerprint ACC
keisatu-ga nantoka mitukedasita.
police-NOM somehow found
'The police somehow found the fingerprint of the criminal who is supposed to be a male in his 50s.'

The high attachment sentence in (13a) was read more slowly at the low noun 'criminal', the genitive marker, and the high noun 'fingerprint', but it was faster at the end of the sentence (Kamide and Mitchell 1997, experiment 2). Three types of explanations have been suggested for this reversal in reading times. First, the genitive marker *no* was shown separate from the noun 'criminal' in the self-paced reading presentation, delaying the realization that another noun was upcoming, thus possibly giving an artificial advantage to the low noun interpretation (Kamide et al. 1998).

However, even when the two nouns and markers are shown in one single region (*hannin-no simon-o*), there is still an initial preference for the low noun interpretation (Miyamoto, Nakamura, and Takahashi 2004).

A second possibility is that readers are nondeterministically considering different interpretations at different points in the sentence (Kamide and Mitchell 1997), but recent evidence suggests otherwise as the same interpretation is maintained throughout (Aoyama and Inoue 2005).

A third explanation is that the relative clauses are initially interpreted as matrix clauses, and the reanalysis process to turn them into relative clauses favors the low noun as the attachment site. When canonical versions of (13a,b) are used, making the embedded clause reading available before the head nouns, the initial advantage for low attachment disappears (Miyamoto, Nakamura, and Takahashi 2004).

Other factors have also been investigated by varying the types (e.g., inalienables; Uetsuki and Tokimoto 2004) and number of head nouns (Miyamoto et al. 1999) involved.

9.10 SCRAMBLING

Some initial studies did not detect behavioral differences to scrambled orders and their canonical versions and have been used to support nonconfigurational models of Japanese syntax or gap-less representations for scrambled orders (Yamashita 1997; see also section 9.12 for discussions of Nakayama 1995, Sakamoto 2002). However, mounting evidence suggests that scrambled orders are harder to understand (apart from the studies discussed in the following sections, see Hagiwara and Caplan 1990 for data from aphasic patients, and Koizumi 2005 for an fMRI study).

9.10.1 Reading Times to Scrambled Orders

Self-paced reading studies did not find statistically reliable differences between scrambled and canonical orders when using ditransitive verbs (Yamashita 1997) or transitive verbs (Miyamoto and Takahashi 2002b, Nakayama 1995; see also section 9.12 for the probe recognition results of these experiments). Similarly, a center-screen self-paced reading experiment did not detect differences between the transitive sentences below (Mazuka, Itoh, and Kondo 2002; the coindexed gap indicates the canonical position of the scrambled constituent).

(14) a. Canonical order
Mariko-ga otooto-o yonda.
Mariko-NOM brother-ACC called
b. Scrambled order
Otooto-o$_i$ Mariko-ga gap$_i$ yonda.
brother-ACC Mariko-NOM called
'Mariko called her brother.'

However, in an eye-tracking experiment, 'Mariko-NOM' in the scrambled (14b) was read more slowly than 'brother-ACC' in the canonical (14a), according to total reading times and regressive eye movements, but not in more immediate measures such as first-pass fixations (Mazuka, Itoh, and Kondo 2002; see Kondo, Mazuka, and Kakehi 2002 for similar eye-tracking results and an interaction between lexical familiarity and word order; also Mazuka, Itoh, and Kondo 2001 for ERP data).

In the same studies, Mazuka and colleagues also included sentences like the following in which the second argument is modified by a prenominal relative clause.

(15) a. Canonical order
Mariko-ga [$_{RC}$ soto-de buranko-ni notte-ita] otooto-o yonda.
Mariko-NOM outside swing-DAT riding brother-ACC called
'Mariko called her brother who was riding on a swing outside.'
b. Scrambled order
Mariko-o$_i$ [$_{RC}$ soto-de buranko-ni notte-ita] otooto-ga
Mariko-ACC outside swing-DAT riding brother-NOM
gap$_i$ yonda.
called
'The brother who was riding on a swing outside called Mariko.'

The canonical sentence is initially misanalyzed as 'Mariko was riding the swing outside' and a subject reanalysis is necessary at the head noun (section 9.5); nevertheless, 'brother' is read more quickly in the canonical sentence than in the scrambled sentence. The difficulty at 'brother-NOM' in (15b) was detected in self-paced reading as well as in first-pass gaze time, total gaze time, and number of regressive eye movements (Mazuka, Itoh, and Kondo 2002).

Longer reading times were also detected in self-paced reading with ditransitive clauses followed by two other clauses in a left-branching configuration (Miyamoto and Takahashi 2002a, experiment 1). The extra clauses and the inclusion of a comprehension question after each sentence may have forced participants to read more carefully than usual, thus depleting cognitive resources and making the difficulty with scrambling more evident.

The results indicate that the difficulty in processing simple sentences with scrambled order is relatively small and may not be detected in self-paced reading. Slow reading times are more readily detected in complex sentences.

9.10.2 Plausibility Judgments and Word Order

A *plausibility task* has also been used to investigate scrambled word orders by measuring the time necessary to decide if a sentence makes sense. For transitive constructions (such as (14)), it took longer to decide that the sentence made sense when the order was scrambled (Chujo 1983). Recently, various constructions have been investigated (see Koizumi 2005 for a summary). For example, reaction times are faster for the *ga-ni-o* order than the *ga-o-ni* order for ditransitive verbs (Koizumi and Tamaoka 2004). The *ga-ni* order elicits faster reaction times for passives, but the *ni-ga* order is faster for potentials (Tamaoka et al. 2005, who also investigated causatives).

The results from the plausibility task confirm that there is a processing cost associated with scrambled orders, even in simple sentences without artifically long phrases. But because the whole sentence is shown at once, this task is not very informative and it cannot indicate where exactly in the sentence the reader is having difficulty. Therefore, it is unclear whether this type of task can be used to disentangle the various sources of difficulty in scrambling (for discussion, see Miyamoto and Nakamura 2005) or to make claims about nonincrementality (as in Tamaoka et al. 2005).

9.10.3 Sources of Difficulty in Scrambling

A number of factors may be involved in the longer reading times for scrambled sentences compared with their canonical versions as the ones in (14) (see Miyamoto and Takahashi 2002a for discussion). When the sentence-initial direct object is read, the subject may be assumed to have been dropped, thus some time may be necessary to create a null subject. Then, when the nominative subject is detected, reanalysis is necessary to remove the null subject.

A second factor is frequency. For example, an accusative object is rarely followed by a nominative NP (see section 9.10.5). Thus, there is the possibility that long reading times occur at the nominative NP because it is rarely expected in such a configuration.

Another factor is the *adjacency constraint*—the preference for direct objects to be next to the verb. After a scrambled accusative NP, a constituent other than the expected verb is likely to be disruptive. ERP data indicate that immediately after a scrambled NP-*o*, a demonstrative (the first word of a NP-*ga*) elicits a P600 (Ueno and Kluender 2003), which suggests difficulty in integrating this word into the syntactic representation.

Those factors are not necessarily independent of each other, and to some extent they may all be related to the filler-gap dependency needed for the interpretation of scrambled constituents. Whenever possible, readers may prefer to avoid the cost of such dependencies by assuming that a constituent is in its canonical position.

9.10.4 Filler-Gap Dependencies in Scrambling

In an ERP study, a long subject following a scrambled direct object elicited a sustained anterior negativity before the verb was seen (Ueno and Kluender 2003), a response usually associated with extra memory load. This may have been caused by the processing of a filler-gap dependency between the scrambled constituent (the filler) and its thematic position in a manner similar to the processing of fronted *wh*-phrases (section 9.8). The results of a self-paced reading experiment using sentences such as the following (from Miyamoto and Takahashi 2004) support this interpretation.

(16) a. Ueitoresu-wa doogu-ga okareteiru sooko-de kokku-o$_i$
 waitress-TOP tools-NOM stored room-LOC cook-ACC
 rezigakari-ni *gap*$_i$ syookaisita sooda.
 cashier-DAT introduced seems
 b. Ueitoresu-wa kokku-o$_i$ doogu-ga okareteiru sooko-de
 waitress-TOP cook-ACC tools-NOM stored room-LOC
 rezigakari-ni *gap*$_i$ syookaisita sooda.
 cashier-DAT introduced seems
 'The waitress seems to have introduced the cook to the cashier in the room where the tools are stored.'

In (16a,b), 'cook-ACC' was scrambled and a gap is necessary after the dative NP. The assumption is that the gap is created as soon as it is clear that the NP-*o* was scrambled, in other words at the dative NP, before the verb is seen (see Aoshima, Phillips, and Weinberg 2004 for related evidence). Because the distance between filler and gap is greater in (16b), it should be harder to create the gap in this sentence (see Gibson 1998 on the effects of dependency length). This was in fact the case, as the reading times for 'cashier-DAT' were longer in (16b) than in (16a), whereas no differences were found between similar sentences with the direct object in canonical position (Miyamoto and Takahashi 2004). Furthermore, corpus counts suggest that these reading time patterns cannot be explained by the frequency of these constructions in newspapers (Miyamoto and Takahashi 2002a).

It is possible that for simple sentences (as in (14)), the cost of the filler-gap dependency is too small to be detected in self-paced reading, and it is picked up only in more sensitive measurements such as eye-tracking. With long dependencies, the cost may be large enough to be revealed in self-paced reading as well. In

ERP, length seems to matter as well given that long NPs preceding transitive verbs lead to differences at the NPs themselves (Ueno and Kluender 2003), whereas short NPs in ditransitive constructions only lead to reliable differences at the predicate (Koso, Hagiwara, and Soshi 2005).

The filler-gap model is also supported by a self-paced reading result with scrambled *wh*-phrases in which a filled-gap effect (see section 9.8) was detected (Aoshima, Phillips, and Weinberg 2004; see also section 9.12 for reactivation effects).

9.10.5 Frequency of Scrambled Orders

Scrambled orders are commonly claimed to be infrequent, but there are few reports with exact figures. The subject-object-verb (SOV) order has been claimed to be seventeen times as frequent as the OSV order (Kuno 1973:353–354). In a survey of 2,635 sentences from various sources, fewer than 1 percent included scrambled constituents (Yamashita 2002).

Moreover, corpus counts and completion data indicate that a sentence-initial object NP is rarely in a scrambling configuration preceding an overt subject. Out of 4,621 sentence-initial accusative NPs in the Kyoto University Corpus (Kurohashi and Nagao 1997), fewer than 2 percent were followed by an overt subject; in the remaining 98 percent of the cases, the subject was left implicit (Miyamoto and Nakamura 2005). Similarly, when asked to write a sentence starting with a NP-*o*, native speakers of Japanese dropped the subject in 210 instances (84.3 percent) and included a subject in 39 instances (15.7 percent). For NP-*ni*, 47 completions (19.8 percent) were followed by an overt subject (Miyamoto and Nakamura 2005).

In the same completion study, NP-*o* was likely to be immediately followed by a predicate (64.7 percent) but rarely by NP-*ni* (2 percent). In contrast, NP-ni was equally likely to be followed by a predicate (36.7 percent) or NP-*o* (33.3 percent; Miyamoto and Nakamura 2005). In other words, the canonical *ni-o* order is frequent, but the scrambled *o-ni* is rare.

9.11 PRODUCTION

A survey of sentence production is beyond the scope of this chapter; however, two studies are discussed as examples of how production may affect the frequency with which people are exposed to different constructions.

Whether frequency-based accounts can explain comprehension difficulty remains an open question, and they may seem unsatisfactory conceptually. If a construction is easy to understand because it is frequently used, that begs the question as to why the construction is frequently used in the first place. One possibility is that production factors determine the frequency with which syntactic constructions are used. Two factors often claimed to affect the production of scrambled constituents are NP length and information status in discourse.

With short NPs, fewer than 5 percent of utterances produced are scrambled (OSV). However, when the object is long, that number rises to 20 percent (Yamashita and Chang 2001). One possible explanation is that speakers prefer to front the long object to keep the argument heads close to the predicate, thus shortening the dependencies.

However, another study did not find effects of information status on scrambling. After hearing ditransitive constructions, speakers were more likely to reverse the order of the two objects when the original order was scrambled (thus, recalling *ni-o* after hearing *o-ni* 67.2 percent of the time) than when the original order was canonical (29.2 percent). There was also a preference to recall given information before new information, but information status did not interact with word order, as the advantage for the given-new order was virtually the same for both orders (20.2 percent for *ni-o* and 20.3 percent for *o-ni*; Ferreira and Yoshita 2003, figure 3); this suggests that scrambling in Japanese is not used to indicate information status in discourse.

9.12 ANTECEDENT RESOLUTION FOR PRONOUNS AND GAPS

Work in English indicates that the antecedent of pronouns and gaps is reactivated when those elements are processed during sentence comprehension (Bever and McElree 1988). Immediately after reading sentences such as the following, participants are shown a probe word and have to decide whether it appeared in the sentence.

(17) a. [The astute lawyer who faced the female judge]$_i$ was suspected *gap*$_i$ constantly.
b. The astute lawyer who faced the female judge was suspicious constantly.

Participants are faster to recognize the probe *astute* in the passive condition (17a) than in the adjective condition (17b). The assumption is that the gap in the passive condition has to access its antecedent, refreshing its representation and facilitating recognition.

9.12.1 Antecedent Reactivation in Scrambling

Reactivation observed in unaccusative constructions (compared with unergatives) indicates that reactivation at gaps occurs in Japanese as well (Nakayama 1991, also briefly reported in Nakayama 1995). Hence, if scrambled constituents involve filler-gap dependencies, facilitation should be observed for (18a) compared with (18b) (Nakayama 1995).

(18) a. Scrambling condition
[Syukudai-o   wasureta seito-o]$_i$ mondai-o   dasita
homework-ACC forgot   student-ACC question-ACC posed
sensei-ga   gap$_i$ sikatta.
teacher-NOM   scolded
'The teacher who posed the question scolded the student who forgot the homework.'

b. Canonical condition
Mondai-o   dasita sensei-ga   syukudai-o   wasureta
question-ACC posed teacher-NOM homework-ACC forgot
seito-o   sikatta.
student-ACC scolded
'The teacher who posed the question scolded the student who forgot the homework.'

Contrary to the filler-gap predictions, 'homework' was recognized faster after the canonical (18b). But note that 'homework' is closer to the sentence end in (18b), thus potentially facilitating recognition (also (18b) requires a subject reanalysis, as discussed in section 9.5.1; see Miyamoto and Takahashi 2002b for discussion). When the probe is in the same linear position, either no difference is detected (Nakayama 1995, experiment 2) or the probe in the scrambled NP is recognized faster as predicted by the filler-gap model (Miyamoto and Takahashi 2002b; see Nakano, Felser, and Clahsen 2002 for cross-modal priming with long-distance scrambling).

9.12.2 Antecedent Reactivation with *Zibun*

In (19), the antecedent for the reflexive pronoun *zibun* can be either the subject 'Taro-TOP' or the agent of the passive 'Hanako-DAT'.

(19) Taro-wa   Hanako-ni zibun-no kazoku-no hanasi bakari sareta.
Taro-TOP   Hanako-DAT self-GEN   family-GEN talk   only   was
'Taro$_i$ was told by Hanako$_j$ nothing but stories about his$_i$/her$_j$ own family.'

At various points during the 1-second per bunsetsu RSVP, a probe was shown surrounded by angle brackets and participants had to decide whether it had appeared previously in the sentence. Reaction times were faster for subject probes than passive-agent probes immediately after *zibun* as well as at sentence end (Nagata 1991, experiment 1; see also experiment 2 for similar results when the order of the first two NPs is swapped, although the difference was not reliable immediately after *zibun*; see Nagata 1992 for evidence that there is no subject advantage in sentences without *zibun*). With contexts favoring the passive-agent reading, no difference was detected at the sentence end, although the subject advantage remained immediately after *zibun* (Nagata 1991, experiment 3). When causatives are used as in (20), only the dative NP can be the antecedent; nevertheless, subject probes were recognized faster immediately after *zibun* as well as at the sentence end.

(20) Simizusan-wa Katosan-ni zibun-no sigoto-o tanosimaseta.
   Simizu-TOP Kato-DAT$_i$ self$_i$-GEN work-ACC enjoy-made
   'Simizu made Kato$_i$ enjoy self$_i$'s work.'

One possibility is that the verb morphology has a late effect. Alternatively, it is conceivable that the causative did not have the effect intended, and participants maintained the subject interpretation throughout.

9.12.3 Antecedent Resolution in Control Constructions

Studies with control constructions (*Kooiti-ga Tamae-ni Tokyo iki-o* V, where V was a subject-control verb such as *moosideru* 'offered' or an object-control verb such as *saisokusuru* 'urge', as in 'Kooiti offered/urged Tamae PRO going to Tokyo') have yielded inconclusive results. After hearing a sentence with a subject and an object in the matrix clause, Japanese speakers were faster to recognize the antecedent for PRO in the embedded clause if the matrix predicate was a subject-control verb rather than an object-control verb (Sakamoto 2002, experiment 1; see also experiment 2 for the same outcome when the object is scrambled prior to the subject). Because the stimuli were created by splicing words pronounced individually, the experiment was replicated using sentences spoken with normal prosody. The task was also modified so that participants had to say aloud the antecedent for PRO. With this setup, reaction times for object-control verbs were faster (Sakamoto 2002, experiment 3; see also experiment 4 for the same result when the object was scrambled). A methodological problem in those experiments is that, for all sentences, participants were instructed to determine which person in the sentence had gone to Tokyo, which potentially allowed for the use of task-specific strategies (see Sakamoto 2002 and references therein for other factors that may explain the diverging results).

9.13 Center-Embedding and Multiple Nominative NPs

Center-embedding constructions, in which clauses are nested within one another, are known to be difficult to understand compared with sentences with the same clauses arranged in right- or left-branching structures (Miller and Chomsky 1963). Sentence (21) is probably unprocessable for most speakers (from Uehara and Bradley 2002; see also Mazuka et al. 1989 for whole-sentence reading times to center-embedding and left-branching sentences; see section 9.5 for a discussion of

Inui et al. 1998, who reported an fMRI study comparing center-embedding and left-branching sentences).

(21) Sensei-ga   gakusei-ga   onnanoko-ga syoonen-o mikaketa-to
     teacher-NOM student-NOM   girl-NOM   boy-ACC   saw-that
     hanasita-to itta.
     told-that   said
     'The teacher said that the student told that the girl saw the boy.'

Ambiguity in nominative NPs (they usually mark subjects but can mark the object of stative predicates) is unlikely to be the source of the difficulty. When asked to write sentences starting with an animate nominative NP, Japanese speakers virtually always (98 percent of the time) use the nominative NP as the subject of the sentence (Nakamura and Miyamoto 2007). Moreover, because the topic marker *wa* is even more ambiguous (it is preferentially interpreted as a subject in 78 percent of sentence completions; Nakamura and Miyamoto 2007), it should make the sentence harder to understand if the issue is ambiguity. However, the sentence becomes easier when the first nominative marker is replaced by the topic marker (Babyonyshev and Gibson 1999, experiment 1; Uehara and Bradley 2002, experiment 1, for questionnaire studies; Miyamoto 2002, for self-paced reading data).

Moreover, according to completion data (Uehara and Bradley 2002, experiment 3), each nominative NP tends to be interpreted as part of a separate clause. Speakers do not interpret an NP-*ga* as the object of a stative verb, even though that would decrease the number of predicates (and of embedding levels) necessary to complete the sentence.

The difficulty in processing multiple nominative NPs can be explained in terms of the load that such sequences impose, because they require the prediction of several syntactic heads to complete the sentence (see section 9.8; see also Babyonyshev and Gibson 1999 and Nakatani and Gibson 2003 for comparisons of different types of embeddings and the predictions of various versions of memory-load models of processing). However, this still fails to explain why topicalization facilitates comprehension. The proposal that the same case marker used in succession leads to phonological interference (Lewis and Nakayama 2002) is supported by Korean data, according to which a sequence of nominative NPs is easier to process when they are phonologically distinct (Lee and Nakayama 2003, but see Uehara and Bradley 2002, experiment 2).

9.14 IN-SITU *WH*-PHRASES

In-situ *wh*-phrases do not require a gap, thus they lack the feature that has attracted the most attention in fronted *wh*-phrases. However, they require a question particle (see Nakagome et al. 2001 for a P600 response to the declarative particle *yo*, instead of a question particle, following a *wh*-phrase). In (22), 'what kind of computer-ACC' is in situ and is licensed by the question particle *no*.

(22) Senmu-ga   donna-pasokon-o   tukatteiru-to kakarityoo-ga
     director-NOM what-kind-computer-ACC using-is-that supervisor-NOM
     itta-no?
     said-Q
     'What kind of computer did the supervisor say the director is using?'

Self-paced reading experiments indicate that in-situ *wh*-phrases trigger the search for a question particle in a manner similar to gap searching for *wh*-phrases in English. Readers slow down at the embedded verb with the declarative complementizer *to* 'that' in (22) in comparison with a similar sentence containing the question particle *ka* after the embedded verb. In this *typing mismatch effect*, the expectation for a question particle at the earliest point allowed by the grammar is violated by a constituent with declarative typing (Miyamoto and Takahashi 2002c). This effect has been claimed to be the in-situ equivalent of the filled-gap effect (see section 9.8) and has been shown to obey grammatical constraints and to be observable even when the initial segment of the sentence indicates that another possible position for the question particle is upcoming in the sentence (Miyamoto and Takahashi 2002d, experiments 2 and 3). The typing mismatch effect has also been detected for scrambled dative *wh*-phrases (Aoshima, Phillips, and Weinberg 2004), negative polarity items (Yoshida 2004), and exclamatives (Ono et al. 2006).

Wh-phrases exemplify how the same processing strategy can surface in different guises in different languages. To be interpreted, *wh*-phrases require their scope and thematic role to be determined. English indicates the scope position by pronouncing the *wh*-phrase at the relevant clausal level, and the thematic-role requirement is satisfied by searching for a gap. In Japanese, by contrast, *wh*-phrases are pronounced at the thematic position, and scope requires searching for a question particle. In short, the constituent sought (a gap or question particle) is determined by the grammar of each language, but the search process is similar, as would be expected if a single processing algorithm is used for all human languages.

9.15 IMPLICATIONS FOR THE GENERAL THEORY

An implicit assumption throughout this chapter is that grammatical knowledge guides processing by providing alternative interpretations, from which factors such as cognitive resources and plausibility choose (e.g., when a *wh*-phrase is read, the grammar of Japanese indicates the possible positions where a question particle can occur, but it is memory cost that eventually favors the earliest one among them).

However, alternative views for the role of the grammar have been proposed. In the *competition model*, the grammar is not as crucial and can be overridden if enough cues supporting an ungrammatical interpretation are available (see Sasaki and MacWhinney 2006 for results on Japanese within this framework). It remains to be seen whether the competition model is able to cover constructions more complex than the single-clause structures usually examined.

There are also approaches in which the grammar takes an even more critical role than assumed here, as syntactic complexity is claimed to be the primary determinant of processing difficulty. Those include recent proposals linking the difficulty in scrambled orders with the complexity of their syntactic representation (Koizumi 2005, Koizumi and Tamaoka 2004) and proposals based on the height of the syntactic structure (see Hagiwara 2006 for a summary of how the number of Merge operations counted from the bottom up in the structure explains data from aphasic patients and ERP studies). Since the 1970s it has been known that a large portion of processing difficulty lies in extracting the meaning intended from superficial cues in the sentence (Fodor, Bever, and Garrett 1974). Hence, the challenge for competence-based models of performance is to describe how their metrics affect processing on-line, as each word is read, and then support their predictions with evidence that cannot be explained by independent factors (e.g., plausibility, frequency, ambiguity).

Clearly, whichever the approach adopted, many issues still need to be addressed in the mapping between grammar and its use in parsing, and their resolutions are likely to affect our understanding of performance as well as competence-related issues in language.

REFERENCES

Abney, Steven P. 1989. A computational model of human parsing. *Journal of Psycholinguistic Research* 18:129–144.

Abney, Steven P., and Mark Johnson. 1991. Memory requirements and local ambiguities of parsing strategies. *Journal of Psycholinguistic Research* 20:233–250.

Amano, Shigeaki, and Tadahisa Kondo. 1999. *Nihongo-no goitokusei* [Lexical properties of Japanese]. Tokyo: Sanseido.

Aoshima, Sachiko, Colin Phillips, and Amy Weinberg. 2003. On-line computation of two types of structural relations in Japanese. Paper presented at the 16th annual CUNY Conference on Human Sentence Processing, Cambridge, Mass., March.

Aoshima, Sachiko, Colin Phillips, and Amy Weinberg. 2004. Processing filler-gap dependencies in a head-final language. *Journal of Memory and Language* 51:23–54.

Aoyama, Ikuko, and Masakatsu Inoue. 2005. Kouzou aimaisei-no kaisyou katei-ni okeru tougo/goyouronteki zyouhou-ni motoduku syorino senkousei [Syntactic/plausibility information precedence in structural ambiguity resolution]. In *Proceedings of the 22nd annual meeting of the Japanese Cognitive Science Society*, 372–373.

Babyonyshev, Maria, and Edward Gibson. 1999. Japanese nesting complexity. *Language* 75:423–450.

Baddeley, Alan. 1992. Working memory. *Science* 255:556–559.

Baddeley, Alan. 2000. The episodic buffer: A new component of working memory? *Trends in Cognitive Science* 4:417–423.

Bever, Thomas G., and Brian McElree. 1988. Empty categories access their antecedents during comprehension. *Linguistic Inquiry* 19:35–43.

Caplan, David, and Gloria S. Waters. 1999. Verbal working memory and sentence comprehension. *Brain and Behavioral Sciences* 22:77–94.

Chomsky, Noam. 1981. *Lectures on government and binding*. Dordrecht: Foris.

Chujo, Kazumitsu. 1983. Nihongo tanbun-no rikai katei: Bunrikai sutoratezi-no sougo kankei. *Japanese Journal of Psychology* 54:250–256.

Crain, Stephen, and Janet D. Fodor. 1985. How can grammars help parsers? In *Natural language parsing*, ed. David R. Dowty, Lauri Karttunen, and Arnold M. Zwicky, 94–128. Cambridge: Cambridge University Press.

Cuetos, Fernando, and Don C. Mitchell. 1988. Cross-linguistic differences in parsing: restrictions on the use of the Late Closure strategy in Spanish. *Cognition* 30:73–103.

Daneman, Meredyth, and Patricia A. Carpenter. 1980. Individual differences in working memory and reading. *Journal of Verbal Learning and Verbal Behavior* 19:450–466.

Den, Yasuharu, and Masakatsu Inoue. 1997. Disambiguation with verb-predictability: Evidence from Japanese garden-path phenomena. In *Proceedings of the 19th annual conference of the Cognitive Science Society*, ed. Michael G. Shafto and Pat Langley, 179–184. Mahwah, N.J.: Lawrence Erlbaum.

Ferreira, Victor S., and Hiromi Yoshita. 2003. Given-new ordering effects on the production of scrambled sentences in Japanese. *Journal of Psycholinguistic Research* 32:669–692.

Fodor, Janet D. 1998. Learning to parse? *Journal of Psycholinguistic Research* 27:285–319.

Fodor, Janet D. 2002. Prosodic disambiguation in silent reading. In *Proceedings of NELS 32*, ed. Masako Hirotani, 113–132. Amherst, Mass.: GLSA Publications.

Fodor, Jerry A., Thomas G. Bever, and Merrill F. Garrett. 1974. *The psychology of language*. New York: McGraw-Hill.

Garnsey, Susan, Neal J. Pearlmutter, Elizabeth Myers, and Melanie Lotocky. 1997. The contributions of verb bias and plausibility to the comprehension of temporarily ambiguous sentences. *Journal of Memory and Language* 37:58–93.

Garnsey, Susan M., Hiroko Yamashita, Kiwako Itoh, and Madelena McClure. 2001. What when the verb at the end is happens? An ERP study of Japanese sentence comprehension. Paper presented at the 14th annual CUNY Conference on Human Sentence Processing, Philadelpha, March.

Gibson, Edward. 1998. Linguistic complexity: Locality of syntactic dependencies. *Cognition* 68:1–76.

Gorrell, Paul. 1995. *Syntax and parsing*. Cambridge: Cambridge University Press.

Hagiwara, Hiroko. 2006. Neural basis of syntactic processing in Japanese. In *Handbook of Japanese psycholinguistics*, ed. Mineharu Nakayama, Reiko Mazuka, and Yasuhiro Shirai, 298–306. Cambridge: Cambridge University Press.

Hagiwara, Hiroko, and David Caplan. 1990. Syntactic comprehension in Japanese aphasics: effects of category and thematic order. *Brain and Language* 38:159–170.

Harada, S.-I. 1973. Counter equi NP deletion. *Annual Bulletin of the Research Institute of Logopedics and Phoniatrics* 7:113–147. Research Institute of Logopedics and Phoniatrics, University of Tokyo.

Hasegawa, Nobuko. 1990. Comments on Mazuka and Lust's paper. In *Language processing and language acquisition*, ed. Lyn Frazier and Jill de Villiers, 207–223. Dordrecht: Kluwer.

Hirose, Yuki. 2001. L1 and L2 processing of RC attachment ambiguity. Paper presented at the Japanese Language Processing Workshop, Nara Institute of Science and Technology, Ikoma, Japan, July.

Hirose, Yuki. 2003. Recycling prosodic boundaries. *Journal of Psycholinguistic Research* 32:167–195.

Hirose, Yuki, and Atsu Inoue. 1998. Ambiguity of reanalysis in parsing complex sentences in Japanese. In *Sentence processing: A crosslinguistic perspective*, ed. Dieter Hillert, 71–93. San Diego, Calif.: Academic Press.

Hirose, Yuki, Atsu Inoue, Janet D. Fodor, and Dianne Bradley. 1998. Adjunct attachment ambiguity in Japanese: The role of constituent weight. Paper presented at the 11th annual CUNY Conference on Human Sentence Processing, Rutgers University, New Brunswick, N.J., March.

Holmes, V. M., and J. K. O'Regan. 1981. Eye fixation patterns during the reading of relative clause sentences. *Journal of Verbal Learning and Verbal Behavior* 20:417–430.

Hsiao, Franny, and Edward Gibson. 2003. Processing relative clauses in Chinese. *Cognition* 90:3–27.

Hsu, Chun-Chieh. 2003. Revisiting the processing of prenominal relative clauses in Chinese. Paper presented at the University of Delaware Linguistics and Cognitive Science Graduate Student Conference, University of Delaware, April.

Iguchi, Yoko, and Edson T. Miyamoto. 2006. The interpretation of nominative NPs is modulated by possessor relations. In *Proceedings of the 23rd annual meeting of the Japanese Cognitive Science Society*, 118–119.

Inoue, Atsu. 1991. A comparative study of parsing in English and Japanese. Doctoral dissertation, University of Connecticut, Storrs.

Inoue, Atsu, and Janet Fodor. 1995. Information-paced parsing of Japanese. In *Japanese sentence processing*, ed. Reiko Mazuka and Noriko Nagai, 9–63. Mahwah, N.J.: Lawrence Erlbaum.

Inoue, Masakatsu. 1990a. Kouzou-teki aimai bun-no rikai-ni okeru gaaden pasu-ka [Garden paths in the comprehension of structurally ambiguous sentences]. In *Proceedings of the 32nd Japanese Association of Educational Psychology*, 378.

Inoue, Masakatsu. 1990b. Kouzou-teki aimai bun-no rikai-ni okeru goku-no nagasa-no kouka [Phrasal length effects in the comprehension of structurally ambiguous sentences]. In *Proceedings of the 54th Japanese Psychological Association*, 678.

Inoue, Masakatsu. 1991. Bun-no tougo syori-ni okeru zyosi-*wa*-no kinou [The function of the particle *wa* in sentence parsing]. In *Proceedings of the 33rd Japanese Association of Educational Psychology*, 55–56.

Inui, Toshio, Yukio Otsu, Shigeki Tanaka, Tomohisa Okada, Sadahiko Nishizawa, and Jyunji Konishi. 1998. A functional MRI analysis of comprehension processes of Japanese sentences. *Neuroreport* 9:3325–3328.

Ishizuka, Tomoko, Kentaro Nakatani, and Edward Gibson. 2003. Relative clause extraction complexity in Japanese. Paper presented at the 16th annual CUNY Conference on Human Sentence Processing, Cambridge, Mass., March.

Jincho, Nobuyuki, Reiko Mazuka, and Hiroshi Namiki. 2004. Bunsyo rikai-ni okeru wakingu memori youryou-to gengo chisiki-no eikyo [The influence of knowledge and working memory span in sentence comprehension]. In *Proceedings of the 68th annual conference of the Japanese Psychological Association*, 897.

Just, Marcel A., and Patricia A. Carpenter. 1992. A capacity theory of comprehension: individual differences in working memory. *Psychological Review* 99:122–149.
Just, Marcel A., Patricia A. Carpenter, and Jacqueline D. Woolley. 1982. Paradigms and processes in reading comprehension. *Journal of Experimental Psychology: General* 3:228–238.
Kamide, Yuki, Gerry T. M. Altmann, and Sarah L. Haywood. 2003. The time-course of prediction in incremental sentence processing: Evidence from anticipatory eye movements. *Journal of Memory and Language* 49:133–156.
Kamide, Yuki, and Don C. Mitchell. 1997. Relative clause attachment: Nondeterminism in Japanese parsing. *Journal of Psycholinguistic Research* 26:247–254.
Kamide, Yuki, and Don C. Mitchell. 1999. Incremental pre-head attachment in Japanese parsing. *Language and Cognitive Processes* 14:631–662.
Kamide, Yuki, Don C. Mitchell, Janet D. Fodor and Atsu Inoue. 1998. Relative clause attachment ambiguity: Further evidence from Japanese. Paper presented at the 11th annual CUNY Conference on Human Sentence Processing, Rutgers University, New Brunswick, N.J., March.
Kess, Joseph F., and Tadao Miyamoto. 1994. *Japanese psycholinguistics: a classified and annotated research bibliography*. Amsterdam: John Benjamins.
Kiguchi, Hirohisa, and Edson T. Miyamoto. 2004. MEG responses in the comprehension of Japanese sentences. In *Proceedings of the 5th Tokyo Conference on Psycholinguistics*, ed. Yukio Otsu, 207–228. Tokyo: Hitsuji Syobo.
King, Jonathan, and Marcel A. Just. 1991. Individual differences in syntactic processing: The role of working memory. *Journal of Memory and Language* 30:580–602.
Koizumi, Masatoshi. 2005. Syntactic structure of ditransitive constructions in Japanese: Behavioral and imaging studies. Paper presented at the Tokyo Conference on Psycholinguistics, Tokyo, March.
Koizumi, Masatoshi, and Katsuo Tamaoka. 2004. Cognitive processing of Japanese sentences with ditransitive verbs. *Gengo Kenkyu* 125:173–190.
Kondo, Tadahisa, and Reiko Mazuka. 1996. Prosodic planning while reading aloud: On-line examination of Japanese sentences. *Journal of Psycholinguistic Research* 25:357–381.
Kondo, Tadahisa, Reiko Mazuka, and Kazuhiko Kakehi. 2002. Nihon-go bun no dokkai-katei-ni okeru gotokusei oyobi gozyun no eikyo [The influence of word order and lexical properties in sentence reading in Japanese]. *Cognitive Studies: Bulletin of the Japanese Cognitive Science Society* 9:543–563.
Koso, Ayumi, Hiroko Hagiwara, and Takahiro Soshi. 2005. Cognitive processes involved in parsing Japanese ditransitives: An event-related potential study. Paper presented at the Tokyo Conference on Psycholinguistics, Tokyo, March.
Kuno, Susumu. 1973. *The structure of the Japanese language*. Cambridge, Mass: MIT Press.
Kurohashi, Sadao, and Makoto Nagao. 1997. Kyoto University text corpus project (in Japanese). In *Proceedings of the 3rd annual meeting of the Association for Natural Language Processing*, 115–118.
Law, Sam-Po, and Man-Tak Leung. 2000. Sentence processing deficits in two Cantonese aphasic patients. *Brain and Language* 72:310–342.
Lee, Sun-Hee, and Mineharu Nakayama. 2003. Effects of syntactic and phonological similarity in Korean center-embedding constructions. Paper presented at the 16th annual CUNY Conference on Human Sentence Processing, Cambridge, Mass., March.
Lewis, Richard, and Mineharu Nakayama. 2002. Syntactic and positional similarity effects in the processing of Japanese Embeddings. In *Sentence processing in East Asian languages*, ed. Mineharu Nakayama, 85–110. Stanford, Calif.: CSLI Publications.

Lin, Chien-Jer, Sandiway Fong, and Thomas G. Bever. 2005. Local dependencies aren't necessarily easier: Processing possessor relative clauses in Mandarin Chinese. Paper presented at the 11th International Conference on Processing Chinese and Other East Asian Languages (PCOEAL), Hong Kong, December.

Mazuka, Reiko. 1998. *The development of language processing strategies*. Mahwah, N.J.: Lawrence Erlbaum.

Mazuka, Reiko, Gary Feng, Youngon Choi, and Li Yi. 2005. Japanese and Korean speakers' errors and corrections during sentence comprehension: Evidence from eye-movement monitoring in a picture selection task. Paper presented at the 18th annual CUNY Conference on Human Sentence Processing, Tucson, Ariz., March.

Mazuka, Reiko, and Kenji Itoh. 1995. Can Japanese speakers be led down the garden path? In *Japanese sentence processing*, ed. Reiko Mazuka and Noriko Nagai, 295–329. Mahwah, N.J.: Lawrence Erlbaum.

Mazuka, Reiko, Kenji Itoh, Shigeru Kiritani, Shinich Niwa, Kayo Ikejiri, and Kazuo Naitoh. 1989. Processing of Japanese garden path, center-embedded, and multiply-left-embedded sentences: Reading time data from an eye movement study. *Annual Bulletin of the Research Institute of Logopedics and Phoniatrics* 23:187–212. Research Institute of Logopedics and Phoniatrics, University of Tokyo.

Mazuka, Reiko, Kenji Itoh, and Tadahisa Kondo. 2001. Event-related potential for scrambled word order in Japanese. Paper presented at the 14th annual CUNY Conference on Human Sentence Processing, Philadelphia, March.

Mazuka, Reiko, Kenji Itoh, and Tadahisa Kondo. 2002. Cost of scrambling in Japanese sentence processing. In *Sentence processing in East Asian languages*, ed. Mineharu Nakayama, 131–166. Stanford, Calif.: CSLI Publications.

Miller, George A. 1963. The magical number seven, plus or minus two: Some limits on our capacity for processing information. In *Readings in mathematical psychology* 1, ed. R. Duncan Luce, Robert R. Bush, and Eugene Galanter, 135–151. New York: John Wiley and Sons.

Miller, George A., and Noam Chomsky. 1963. Finitary models of language users. In *Handbook of mathematical psychology* 2, ed. R. Duncan Luce, Robert R. Bush, and Eugene Galanter, 419–491. New York: John Wiley and Sons.

Misono, Yasuko, Reiko Mazuka, Tadahisa Kondo, and Shigeru Kiritani. 1997. Effects and limitations of prosodic and semantic biases on syntactic disambiguation. *Journal of Psycholinguistic Research* 26:229–245.

Miyamoto, Edson T. 2002. Case markers as clause boundary inducers in Japanese. *Journal of Psycholinguistic Research* 31:307–347.

Miyamoto, Edson T. 2003. Reanalysis of clause boundaries in Japanese as a constraint-driven process. *Language and Speech* 46:23–52.

Miyamoto, Edson T., Edward Gibson, Neal J. Pearlmutter, Takako Aikawa, and Shigeru Miyagawa. 1999. A U-shaped relative clause attachment preference in Japanese. *Language and Cognitive Processes* 14:663–686.

Miyamoto, Edson T., and Michiko Nakamura. 2003. Subject/object asymmetries in the processing of relative clauses in Japanese. In *Proceedings of the 22nd West Coast Conference on Formal Linguistics*, ed. Gina Garing and Mimu Tsujimura, 342–355. Somerville, Mass.: Cascadilla Press.

Miyamoto, Edson T., and Michiko Nakamura. 2005. Unscrambling some misconceptions: A comment on Koizumi and Tamaoka 2004. *Gengo Kenkyu* 128:113–129.

Miyamoto, Edson T., Michiko Nakamura, and Shoichi Takahashi. 2004. Processing relative clauses in Japanese with two attachment sites. In *Proceedings of NELS 34*, ed. Keir Moulton and Matthew Wolf, 441–452. Amherst, Mass.: GLSA Publications.

Miyamoto, Edson T., and Shoichi Takahashi. 2002a. Sources of difficulty in the processing of scrambling in Japanese. In *Sentence processing in East Asian languages*, ed. Mineharu Nakayama, 167–188. Stanford, Calif.: CSLI Publications.

Miyamoto, Edson T., and Shoichi Takahashi. 2002b. Antecedent reactivation in the processing of scrambling in Japanese. In *MITWPL 43: Proceedings of HUMIT 2001*, ed. Tania Ionin, Heejeong Ko, and Andrew Nevins, 123–138. Cambridge, Mass.: MIT Working Papers in Linguistics.

Miyamoto, Edson T., and Shoichi Takahashi. 2002c. The processing of *wh*-phrases and interrogative complementizers in Japanese. In *Japanese/Korean linguistics 10*, ed. Noriko M. Akatsuka and Susan Strauss, 62–75. Stanford, Calif.: CSLI Publications.

Miyamoto, Edson T., and Shoichi Takahashi. 2002d. The processing of *wh*-phrases in Japanese. *Scientific Approaches to Language* 1:133–172.

Miyamoto, Edson T., and Shoichi Takahashi. 2004. Filler-gap dependencies in the processing of scrambling in Japanese. *Language and Linguistics* 5:153–166.

Muraoka, Satoru, and Tsutomu Sakamoto. 2004. Tougokaiseki-ni-okeru setsukyoukai-no goijouhou-no eikyou [The influence of lexical information during the parsing of clause boundaries]. In *Proceedings of the 21st annual meeting of the Japanese Cognitive Science Society*, 206–207.

Nagata, Hiroshi. 1991. Temporal course of activation of the antecedent by the reflexive in syntactically ambiguous sentences in Japanese. *Journal of Psycholinguistic Research* 20:501–520.

Nagata, Hiroshi. 1992. Activation of the antecedent by the reflexive in Japanese: A supplementary control experiment. *Perceptual and Motor Skill* 74:99–106.

Nagata, Hiroshi. 1993. Unimmediate construction of syntactic structure for garden path sentences in Japanese. *Journal of Psycholinguistic Research* 22:365–381.

Nakagome, Kazuyuki, Satoru Takazawa, Osamu Kanno, Hiroko Hagiwara, Heizo Nakajima, Kenji Itoh, and Ichiro Koshida. 2001. A topographical study of ERP correlates of semantic and syntactic violations in the Japanese language using the multichannel EEG system. *Psychophysiology* 38:304–315.

Nakamura, Michiko, and Edson T. Miyamoto. 2006. Crossed dependencies and plausibility factors in the interpretation of double-gap relative clauses in Japanese. *Cognitive Studies: Bulletin of the Japanese Cognitive Science Society* 13:369–391.

Nakamura, Michiko, and Edson T. Miyamoto. 2007. Relative preferences in the processing of relative clauses in Japanese. Ms., University of Tsukuba, Japan.

Nakano, Yoko, Claudia Felser, and Harald Clahsen. 2002. Antecedent priming at trace positions in Japanese long-distance scrambling. *Journal of Psycholinguistic Research* 31:531–571.

Nakatani, Kentaro. 2006. Processing complexity of complex predicates: A case study in Japanese. *Linguistic Inquiry* 37:625–647.

Nakatani, Kentaro, and Edward Gibson. 2003. An on-line study of Japanese nesting complexity. Paper presented at the 16th annual CUNY Conference on Human Sentence Processing, Cambridge, Mass., March.

Nakayama, Mineharu. 1991. *Japanese motion verbs and probe recognition*. Ms., Ohio State University, Columbus.

Nakayama, Mineharu. 1995. Scrambling and probe recognition. In *Japanese sentence processing*, ed. Reiko Mazuka and Noriko Nagai, 257–273. Mahwah, N.J.: Lawrence Erlbaum.

Nakayama, Mineharu, Reiko Mazuka, and Yasuhiro Shirai, eds. 2006. *Handbook of Japanese psycholinguistics*. Cambridge: Cambridge University Press.

Nicol, Janet L. 1998. The production of agreement in English and Japanese: Animacy effects (or lack thereof). In *Sentence processing: A crosslinguistic perspective*, ed. Dieter Hillert, 113–128. San Diego, Calif.: Academic Press.

O'Grady, William, Michiko Nakamura, and Miseon Lee. 2002. Processing Japanese and Korean: Full attachment versus efficiency. In *Japanese/Korean linguistics 10*, ed. Noriko M. Akatsuka and Susan Strauss, 18–49. Stanford, Calif.: CSLI Publications.

Oishi, Hiroaki, and Tsutomu Sakamoto. 2004. Tougo kaiseki-no sokuzi/chiensei-no kensyo: P600-wo sihyo-to site [Incrementality versus delay during parsing: Using the P600 as an index]. *Cognitive Studies: Bulletin of the Japanese Cognitive Science Society* 11:311–318.

Ono, Hajime, Masaya Yoshida, Sachiko Aoshima, and Colin Phillips. 2006. Real-time computation of Japanese exclamatives and the strength of locality biases in sentence comprehension. *Cognitive Studies: Bulletin of the Japanese Cognitive Science Society* 13:261–287.

Osaka, Mariko. 1998. Yomi to wakingu memori [Reading and working memory]. In *Yomi: No to kokoro-no zyohou syori* [Reading: Information processing in the brain and mind], ed. Naoyuki Osaka, 239–262. Tokyo: Asakura.

Osaka, Mariko, Yukiko Nishizaki, Mie Komori, and Naoyuki Osaka. 2002. Effect of focus on verbal working memory: Critical role of the focus word in reading. *Memory and Cognition* 30:562–571.

Pritchett, Bradley L. 1991. Head position and parsing ambiguity. *Journal of Psycholinguistic Research* 20:251–270.

Rayner, Keith. 1998. Eye movements in reading and information processing: 20 years of research. *Psychological Review* 124:372–422.

Saito, Mamoru. 1985. Some asymmetries in Japanese and their theoretical implications. Doctoral dissertation, MIT, Cambridge, Mass.

Sakai, Kuniyoshi L., Yasuki Noguchi, Tatsuya Takeuchi, and Eiju Watanabe. 2002. Selective priming of syntactic processing by event-related transcranial magnetic stimulation of Broca's area. *Neuron* 35:1177–1182.

Sakamoto, Tsutomu. 2002. Processing filler-gap constructions in Japanese. In *Sentence processing in East Asian languages*, ed. Mineharu Nakayama,189–221. Stanford, Calif.: CSLI Publications.

Sasaki, Yoshinori, and Brian MacWhinney. 2006. The competition model. In *Handbook of Japanese psycholinguistics*, ed. Mineharu Nakayama, Reiko Mazuka and Yasuhiro Shirai, 207–314. Cambridge: Cambridge University Press.

Sato, Kaori, Mari Kobayashi, and Edson T. Miyamoto. 2007. Lack of implicit prosody effects in deaf readers of Japanese. *Journal of Japanese Linguistics* 23:35–46.

Sheldon, Amy. 1976. Speaker's intuition about the complexity of relative clauses in Japanese and English. In *Papers from the 12th regional meeting of the Chicago Linguistic Society*, ed. Salikoko S. Mufwene, Carol A. Walker, and Steever B. Sanford, 558–567. Chicago: Chicago Linguistic Society.

Sturt, Patrick, Holly P. Branigan, and Yoko Matsumoto-Sturt. 1999. The effect of clausal and thematic domains on left branching attachment ambiguities. In *Proceedings of the 21st annual conference of the Cognitive Science Society*, ed. Martin Hahn and Scott C. Stoness, 718–723. Mahwah, N.J.: Lawrence Erlbaum

Sturt, Patrick, and Matthew Crocker. 1996. Monotonic syntactic processing: A cross-linguistic study of attachments and reanalysis. *Language and Cognitive Processes* 11: 449–494.
Takezawa, Koichi. 1987. A configurational approach to case-marking in Japanese. Doctoral dissertation, University of Washington, Seattle.
Tamaoka, Katsuo, Hiromu Sakai, Jun-Ichiro Kawahara, Yayoi Miyaoka, Hyungjung Lim, and Masatoshi Koizumi. 2005. Priority information used for the processing of Japanese sentences: Thematic roles, case particles or grammatical functions? *Journal of Psycholinguistic Research* 34:281–332.
Tanenhaus, Michael K., Michael J. Spivey-Knowlton, Kathleen M. Eberhard, and Julie C. Sedivy. 1995. Integration of visual and linguistic information in spoken language comprehension. *Science* 268:1632–1634.
Uehara, Keiko, and Dianne Bradley. 2002. Center-embedding problem and the contribution of nominative case repetition. In *Sentence processing in East Asian languages*, ed. Mineharu Nakayama, 257–287. Stanford, Calif.: CSLI.
Ueno, Mieko, and Robert Kluender. 2003. Event-related brain indices of scrambling in Japanese. *Brain and Language* 86:243–271.
Uetsuki, Miki, and Shingo Tokimoto. 2004. Kouzouteki aimai bun syori-ni okeru meisi houwasei-no eikyo [The influence of noun saturation in the processing of structurally ambiguous sentences]. In *Proceedings of the 21st annual meeting of the Japanese Cognitive Science Society*, 74–75.
Venditti, Jennifer J. 2006. Prosody in sentence processing. In *Handbook of Japanese psycholinguistics*, ed. Mineharu Nakayama, Reiko Mazuka, and Yasuhiro Shirai, 208–217. Cambridge: Cambridge University Press.
Venditti, Jennifer J., and Hiroko Yamashita. 1994. Prosodic information and processing of complex NPs in Japanese. In *MITWPL 24: Proceedings of Formal Approaches to Japanese Linguistics 1*, ed. Hiroyuki Ura and Masatoshi Koizumi, 375–391. Cambridge, Mass.: MIT Working Papers in Linguistics.
Yamashita, Hiroko. 1995. Verb argument information used in a pro-drop language: An experimental study in Japanese. *Journal of Psycholinguistic Research* 24:333–347.
Yamashita, Hiroko. 1997. The effects of word-order and case marking information on the processing of Japanese. *Journal of Psycholinguistic Research* 26:163–188.
Yamashita, Hiroko. 2000. Structural computation and the role of morphological markings in the processing of Japanese. *Language and Speech* 43:429–459.
Yamashita, Hiroko. 2002. Scrambled sentences in Japanese: Linguistic properties and motivations for production. *Text* 22:597–633.
Yamashita, Hiroko, and Franklin Chang. 2001. "Long before short" preference in the production of a head-final language. *Cognition* 81:B45–B55.
Yoshida, Masaya. 2004. When negative statements are easier: Processing polarity items in Japanese. Paper presented at the 17th annual CUNY Conference on Human Sentence Processing, College Park, Md., March.
Yoshida, Masaya, Sachiko Aoshima, and Colin Phillips. 2004. Relative clause prediction in Japanese. Paper presented at the 17th annual CUNY Conference on Human Sentence Processing, College Park, Md., March.
Yoshida, Masaya, and Tetsuya Sano. 2001. Psycholinguistic studies on Japanese head internal relative clauses. In *MITWPL 41: Proceedings of Formal Approaches to Japanese Linguistics 3*, ed. M. Cristina Cuervo, Daniel Harbour, Ken Hiraiwa, and Shinichiro Ishihara, 33–46. Cambridge, Mass.: MIT Working Papers in Linguistics.

CHAPTER 10

THE ACQUISITION OF JAPANESE SYNTAX

KEIKO MURASUGI AND KOJI SUGISAKI

10.1 Principal Questions

The knowledge of language comprises many complex and abstract properties that are not shared by other modules of the human mind. Knowledge of Japanese is no exception, as discussed in detail in other chapters of this book. As a simple illustration, consider the sentences in (1), discussed by Harada (1972) and Saito (1989).

(1) a. Ken-ga   [dare-ga   sono hon-o   katta   ka] siritagatteiru (koto).
       Ken-NOM   who-NOM   that book-ACC bought   Q   want-to-know (fact)
       'Ken wants to know who bought that book.'
    b. *Dare-ga   [Ken-ga   sono hon-o   katta   ka] siritagatteiru (koto).
       who-NOM   Ken-NOM   that book-ACC bought   Q   want-to-know (fact)

Adult native speakers of Japanese can tell that the sentence in (1a) is acceptable and the one in (1b) is not. The characterization of the knowledge responsible for this contrast is argued to involve the structural notion of c-command: Whereas the *wh*-phrase *dare-ga* is c-commanded by the question-particle *ka* in (1a), it is not in the case of (1b). This notion is abstract in that it depends on the phrase structure of sentences, which we cannot directly perceive from the given string of words. Additionally, no property that makes crucial use of this notion has been observed in other modules of human cognition.

In contrast, the linguistic experience available to children to acquire such properties is severely limited in that it is structurally simple for the most part and provides no systematic information as to which sentences are ungrammatical in the target language. The absence of systematic "negative evidence" can be illustrated by the following dialogue between a two-year-old girl (2;11) and her mother.[1,2]

(2) Mother: Ashita   minna-de   pikunikku ikou   ka?
            tomorrow everyone-with   picnic   go   Q
            'Shall we go on a picnic tomorrow?'
    Child: Osoto   tabe-i (=tabe-ni) iku,   mama.
            outside   eat-to   go   mom
            'Mom, I want to go outside to eat.'
    Mother: Doko-ni ikou ka?
            where-to go   Q
            'Where shall we go?'
    Child: Ike   kara iku?
            pond from go
            (Intended meaning) 'Shall we go to a pond?'
    Mother: Soudane. Ike, iine. Ike-ni   siyou.
            right   pond good pond-to let's
            'Right. A pond sounds good. Let's go to a pond.'

Notice that in her second turn, the child incorrectly said *ike kara iku?* ('Shall we go from a pond?'), when she intended to say *ike ni iku?* ('Shall we go *to* a pond?'). Despite this error, her mother did not point it out but, rather, agreed with what the child said.

Given the qualitative gap between linguistic experience and the acquired knowledge of language, a question arises as to why children are able to acquire the knowledge of their native languages under this "poverty of the stimulus" situation, also known as "Plato's problem" (Chomsky 1986) or "the logical problem of language acquisition" (Baker and McCarthy 1981, Hornstein and Lightfoot 1981).

The task for modern linguistic theory is to provide an answer to this problem. The proposed solution postulates that a human child is genetically equipped with Universal Grammar (UG), which narrowly constrains the space of hypotheses to entertain. Under the principles-and-parameters approach to UG (Chomsky 1981), UG consists of (a) a number of principles that specify the properties to be satisfied by any language, and (b) a small number of parameters that sharply restrict the range of possible cross-linguistic variation. The major task for modern linguistic theory, then, is to reveal the exact nature of such principles and parameters.

The theory of language acquisition aims to answer a broader question of how language is acquired in real time. The theory has to address (at least) the following two principal questions, in addition to specifying the exact nature of the initial state (UG).

(3) Principal questions
    a. When and how do principles of UG emerge in the child grammar?
    b. What factors explain the gradual, noninstantaneous nature of actual language development?

In this chapter, we review some representative studies on the acquisition of Japanese that attempt to answer the questions in (3) and hence have a direct bearing on the construction of the theory of language acquisition. Our summary is highly selective in that it is mainly limited to studies on the acquisition of syntax that provide intriguing empirical findings.[3] Given that Japanese has various syntactic characteristics that are not observed in Germanic or Romance languages, the investigation of its acquisition process can be especially valuable for acquisition theory. We hope that this chapter demonstrates this point in a convincing way.

10.2 Addressing the Principal Question 1: Early Emergence of UG Principles

Principles of UG are, by definition, innately given and are reflected in any adult grammar. Because no learning from experience is involved to acquire these principles, the simplest possibility for their emergence is that they constrain language acquisition from virtually the very beginning of life. In other words, their effects should be observed as soon as the child becomes able to use relevant lexical items and structures. A large number of experimental investigations of the acquisition of English indicate that this simplest possibility is, in fact, correct for various UG principles.[4] For example, Crain and McKee (1986) and Murasugi (1988) examined children's knowledge of condition C of the binding theory, which informally says that a referential NP cannot be coreferential with a pronoun that c-commands it (Reinhart 1976; Lasnik 1976, 1991, among others). This principle dictates that a coreferential interpretation between the pronoun and the referential NP is possible in (4a), but not in (4b).

(4) a. While he$_1$ was dancing, the Ninja Turtle$_1$ ate pizza.
    b. *He$_1$ ate the hamburger when the Smurf$_1$ was inside the fence.

Using the truth-value judgment task, Crain and McKee found that English-speaking three- and four-year-olds accepted the coreferential reading of (4a) 73 percent of the time and rejected it in (4b) 84 percent of the time. These findings suggest that the UG principle of condition C is operative in children's grammar before the age of three years. Along the same lines, Murasugi (1988) provided further supporting evidence for young children's knowledge of condition C by proposing that the pragmatic felicity condition termed "plausible denial" (adopted in Crain and Thornton 1998, among others) is required in order to avoid accidental coreference in the experimental situation.

Studies on the acquisition of Japanese have provided novel pieces of evidence for such early emergence of UG principles. As a first illustration, consider the configurationality of human languages, discussed in the introduction of this handbook.

In the early 1980s, Hale (1980) proposed that Japanese is a typical example of a non-configurational language and has a flat structure as in (5a), which is responsible for its flexible word order. Yet, Saito and Hoji (1983), Hoji (1985), and Saito (1985) argued against this proposal and presented strong evidence that Japanese is configurational (like English) and is hierarchically organized as in (5b). These studies revealed that there is a principle of UG, which in effect makes every human language fall into the class of configurational languages.[5]

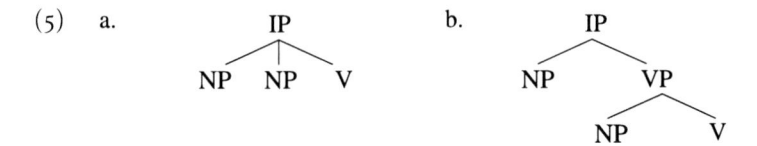

(5) a.
```
        IP
      / | \
    NP  NP  V
```
b.
```
        IP
       /  \
     NP   VP
          / \
         NP  V
```

In light of this finding, Otsu (1994a) investigated whether the principle relevant to configurationality is operative in early child Japanese, by making use of the Case Marker Drop (CMD) phenomenon. In colloquial speech, Case markers can sometimes drop. Yet, there seems to be a contrast between the nominative marker *ga* and the accusative marker *o*: Although the latter can easily be dropped, the former resists this process.

(6) a. Eri-ga   nani-o   tabeta no?
         Eri-NOM what-ACC ate   Q
         'What did Eri eat?'
     b. Eri-ga   nani-Ø   tabeta no?

(7) a. Dare-ga   kono ringo-o   tabeta no?
         who-NOM this apple-ACC ate   Q
         'Who ate this apple?'
     b. *Dare-Ø   kono ringo-o   tabeta no?

The contrast between (6b) and (7b) can be accounted for if we assume that Japanese sentences have hierarchically organized structures like (5b) and that CMD applies only to those Case markers that are structurally close enough to verbs (Saito 1985, Takezawa 1987).

In one of the two experiments reported in Otsu 1994a, twenty three- and four-year-olds were asked to answer questions such as (8).

(8) Dare-Ø taosita   no?
     who   knocked-down Q

In the adult grammar, this sentence is only interpreted as meaning 'Who did (someone) knock down?' because of a hierarchical structure like (5b) and the condition on CMD. The results succinctly showed that children are completely adultlike and never interpret (8) as meaning 'Who knocked down (someone)?' This finding suggests that child Japanese is just as configurational as adult Japanese, which in turn demonstrates that the UG principle relevant to configurationality is operative from the early stages of Japanese acquisition.[6,7]

Murasugi (1991) demonstrated the early emergence of UG principles in a complementary way, by analyzing children's apparent "errors" concerning genitive Case marking. In adult English, whereas NP complements to nouns require *of*-insertion, PP complements never trigger this operation.

(9) a. John's destruction *(of) [NP the building]
    b. John's claim (*of) [PP about his marriage]

Stowell (1981) attributed this difference to a principle of UG called the Case Resistance Principle, which states that projections of Case-assigning categories (such as P) cannot be assigned Case.

Murasugi (1991) reported that there are cases where Japanese-speaking children successfully insert the genitive Case marker *no* after NPs but still undergenerate it after PPs.

(10) a. Emi-no   zyuusu
        Emi-GEN   juice
        'Emi's juice'   (Emi, 2;9)
     b. murasaki-no ribon
        purple-GEN   ribbon
        'the purple ribbon'   (Emi, 2;9)
     c. Santa san kara   purezento
        Santa   from   present
        'a present from Santa'   (Emi, 3;0)

In adult Japanese, *no* is required after the PP, *Santa san-kara*, in (10c). Murasugi attributed this requirement to a language-particular operation of genitive Case-marker insertion that inserts *no* after NPs and PPs within noun phrases. Then, she suggested that because children have to learn this specific operation and, in particular, that it overrides the Case Resistance Principle, there can be a stage in which children strictly conform to the UG principle and do not insert *no* after PPs. Then, what appear to be "errors" made by Japanese-speaking children in fact provide another piece of evidence that principles of UG constrain language acquisition from the earliest observable stages.[8]

Sugisaki (2000) examined Japanese-speaking children's knowledge of a universal constraint on *wh*-movement. The sentence in (11a) is structurally ambiguous with respect to the position of the adjunct *wh*-phrase *naze* 'why': It can be contained in the adjunct clause, or it can be located outside the adjunct clause and hence can be an element of the matrix clause. Yet, the former possibility is excluded by the conflict between the LF *wh*-movement of *naze* to the matrix CP specifier and the principle of UG that bans extraction out of an adjunct clause (Huang 1982). This is why the example in (11a) is interpreted as a question asking the reason for John's anger but not asking why John read that book.

(11) a. Naze sono hon-o yomu maeni John-wa okotta no?
why that book-ACC read before John-TOP got angry Q
'Why did John get angry before reading that book?'
b. Dooiu riyuu de sono hon-o yomu maeni John-wa okotta no?
for-what-reason that book-ACC read before John-TOP got angry Q
'For what reason did John get angry before reading that book?'

Sugisaki conducted an experiment to determine how three- and four-year-old children respond to structurally ambiguous questions like (11a). The subjects were seventeen children, ages 3;4 to 4;8 (mean age 4;2). The task was comprehension. Each subject was told a story, which was accompanied by an animation presented on a laptop computer, and at several points during the story, the experimenter asked a question about the story. The child's task was to answer these questions. The results showed that children never interpret *naze* as an element of the adjunct clause, which in turn suggests that the relevant UG principle on the locality of *wh*-movement is already in the grammar of Japanese-speaking children. Kabuto (2007), furthermore, examined the acquisition of *wh*-questions such as (11a,b) and reported that three-year-old Japanese-speaking children can interpret these types of sentences like adults and know that *dooiu-riyuu* 'what reason' can be unselectively bound in situ, whereas *naze* 'why' cannot be unselectively bound and has to be moved out into the specifier position of the matrix CP.

In sum, the studies of Japanese acquisition reviewed in this section confirm the early emergence of UG principles, but the syntactic phenomena that are taken up to demonstrate this point are quite different from those in the acquisition of English, which makes these studies quite intriguing from the viewpoint of acquisition theory.

10.3 Addressing the Principal Question 2: Identifying Developmental Factors

The finding that many UG principles are functioning from the outset of development provides strong support for the innateness of these properties. Yet, at the same time, it raises the following important question, whose answer definitely constitutes a crucial part of acquisition theory: Why does grammar acquisition take time and proceed gradually?

As a first step to answering this question, we note that several factors are proposed as potentially relevant to the gradual, noninstantaneous nature of language development:

(12) a. Parameter setting
b. Maturation of UG properties
c. Acquisition of lexical items

In the following subsections, we review representative studies on the acquisition of Japanese that attempt to evaluate these developmental factors.[9]

10.3.1 Parameter Setting

Within the principles-and-parameters (P&P) framework, one major task for children is to identify the correct parameter settings for the community's language from among the possibilities permitted by the parameters of UG, as we can see in the following statement by Chomsky (1995:6).

(13) [Within the P&P approach] language acquisition is interpreted as the process of fixing the parameters of the initial state in one of the permissible ways.

Given that children determine correct parametric values by analyzing and accommodating the input data around them, there can in principle be a situation in which this process of data analysis and accommodation takes a certain amount of time, and hence the shift from the nontarget value to the target value gives rise to observable developmental effects. Hyams 1986 is the first study that attempted to show that this possibility is in fact realized in the course of child language acquisition. It is widely known that in the acquisition of obligatory subject languages such as English, children before or around the age of two years optionally omit subject pronouns, as illustrated in (14).

(14) a. See window.
b. Want more apple. (Hyams 1986:63)

Based on the observation that the availability of null-subject sentences is a distinctive property of adult Italian and Spanish, Hyams proposed that subject omission in the child's speech follows from an early nonadultlike setting of the null-subject parameter.

Even though Hyams's (1986) parametric account of null subjects ran up against a number of empirical challenges (e.g., Bloom 1990, Lillo-Martin 1991, Valian 1991, Hyams and Wexler 1993, among others), the important question of whether parameter setting contributes to the noninstantaneous and gradual nature of language development continues to be explored in acquisitional studies of many languages, including Japanese.

Murasugi (1991) provided evidence for such "delayed parameter setting" through investigating the syntax and acquisition of Japanese relative clauses. Japanese children, at one point in language acquisition, overgenerate *no* immediately after prenominal sentential modifiers, as observed by Nagano (1960) and Yokoyama (1990), among others.[10]

(15) a. kiiroi   no   ohana   (2;1)
     yellow-is   flower
     'the yellow flower'
   b. tigau   no   outi   (Emi, 3;0)
     differ   house
     'the different house'
   c. Emi-tyan-ga kaita no sinderera (Emi, 2;11)
     Emi-NOM   drew   Cinderella
     'the Cinderella that Emi drew'

This overgeneration of *no* has attracted much attention in the acquisition literature on Japanese. Regarding the syntactic status of the overgenerated *no*, three hypotheses have been proposed: (a) *no* as a noun (Nagano 1960, Murasugi and Hashimoto 2004a), (b) *no* as the genitive Case marker (Iwabuchi and Muraishi 1968, Clancy 1985, Yokoyama 1990, among many others), and (c) *no* as a complementizer (Murasugi 1991, Murasugi and Hashimoto 2004a).

One piece of evidence that the *no* in question is not the genitive Case marker can be found in the utterances of children speaking the Toyama dialect (a dialect spoken in the mid-north region of Japan). In the Tokyo dialect, *no* could be the genitive Case marker, a pronoun (corresponding to *one* in English), or a complementizer, as they are all homophonous as shown in (16).

(16) a. John-no   hon
       John-GEN book
       'John's book'
    b. akai   no
       red-is   one
       'the red one'
    c. Robusutaa-o tabeta no-wa Bosuton-de da.
       lobster-ACC ate   C-TOP Boston-in is
       'It is in Boston that (I) ate lobster.'

In the Toyama dialect, the genitive Case is realized as *no*, as in the Tokyo dialect, but the other two *no*'s (N and C) are realized as *ga*. Examples from this dialect are shown in (17)–(19).

(17) Genitive Case marker
    a. Emi-no   hon
       Emi   book
       'Emi's book'
    b. heya-no okatazuke
       room   cleaning-up
       'cleaning up of the room'

(18) Pronoun
   a. akai   ga
      red-is   one
      'the red one'
   b. hasittoru   ga
      running-is   one
      'the one that is running'

(19) Complementizer

   [John-ga   kane-o   nusunda ga]-wa [_PP_ koko-kara] da-t-tya
   John-NOM   money-ACC   stole   C-TOP   here-from   is
   'It is from here that John stole money.'

The overgeneration in (15) is observed also with children speaking the Toyama dialect. Interestingly, they overgenerate *ga* and not the genitive Case marker *no*. The following instances are reported in Murasugi 1991.[11]

(20) a. akai   ga   boosi
        red   cap
        'a red cap'   (Ken, 2;11)
     b. Anpanman   tuitoru   ga   koppu
        (a character) attaching   cup
        'a cup bearing the image of Anpanman'   (Ken, 2;11)

The data in (20) constitute evidence that the overgenerated element is not a pronoun, either. Those children who showed the overgeneration illustrated in (20) had already acquired the rule of genitive *no*-insertion in noun phrases, applying it properly in the position after prenominal NPs. Therefore, if they assumed that the *ga* in question was a pronoun, then they should have inserted the genitive *no* after the NP headed by this pronoun. This is illustrated in (21).

(21)   [_NP_ [_NP_ [Modifier ...] *ga*]-*no* head noun]

However, this prediction was not borne out. The subjects never inserted *no* in this context. That is, they did not produce ill-formed strings such as those in (22).

(22) a. akai   ga-no   boosi
        red-is   N-GEN   cap
        'the red cap'
     b. Anpanman   tuitoru   ga-no   koppu
        (a character) attaching-is N-GEN   cup
        'the cup bearing the image of Anpanman'

Hence, Murasugi (1991) concluded that the overgenerated *no* and *ga* in (15) and (20) are not pronouns but complementizers.

Building on this finding and independent syntactic analysis, Murasugi (1991) proposed that relative clauses in Japanese are TPs (IPs) whereas those in English are CPs.[12] Under this hypothesis, the overgeneration of *no/ga* can be construed as follows. Children initially take the CP value of the relative-clause parameter and realize the C head of the relative clause by inserting an overt morpheme. Positive evidence that C can be lexically realized as *no/ga* is provided, for example, by cleft sentences such as (16c). This implies that the unmarked setting for the CP/TP parameter for relative clauses is CP. Japanese-speaking children later reset the value to TP, based on the positive evidence available, and consequently retreat from the overgeneration of *no/ga* in the position of C.[13]

The above account raises the question of why the TP value of the relative-clause parameter is set at a later stage of acquisition. One possibility, suggested in Murasugi 1991, is that it takes time because the required positive evidence is not readily available in the input. The complementizer *that* is optional in English relative clauses. Hence, the mere absence of *no/ga* in adult Japanese relatives cannot serve as evidence that they are TPs. However, the complementizer is obligatory in English pure complex NPs, as shown in (23a).

(23) a. the fact *(that) John was fired
 b. John-ga kubi-ni natta (*no) zizitu
    John-NOM fired was   C   fact

If this property of (23a) follows from a principle dictating the distribution of empty C heads, as argued by Stowell (1981), then the absence of *no* in its Japanese counterpart in (23b) can serve as positive evidence that prenominal sentential modifiers lack the C-projection in Japanese. But then, Japanese-speaking children must be exposed to pure complex NPs and must analyze them to reset the value of the relative-clause parameter (or more generally, the parameter that dictates the categorial status of prenominal sentential modifiers) to TP. The acquisition of Japanese relative clauses, then, is plausibly a case of delayed parameter setting. If so, the process of parameter setting constitutes one important developmental factor.

Sugisaki and Isobe (2000) presented another piece of evidence from child Japanese for delayed parameter setting, by making use of the Compounding Parameter proposed by Snyder (1995, 2001, 2002). Through his cross-linguistic investigation of typologically diverse languages, Snyder found a generalization that any language that allows transitive resultatives as in (24a) necessarily allows novel endocentric compounds as in (24b). The results of his comparative survey are summarized in (25).

(24) a. John painted the house red.
 b. banana box 'box in which bananas are stored'

(25) Cross-linguistic survey (modified from Snyder 2002:34):

	Novel N-N compounds?	Transitive resultatives?
Khmer:	Yes	Yes
Estonian:	Yes	Yes
Dutch:	Yes	Yes
Mandarin:	Yes	Yes
Thai:	Yes	Yes
Japanese:	Yes	Yes
American Sign Language:	Yes	Yes
Basque:	Yes	No
Egyptian Arabic:	No	No
Javanese:	No	No
Spanish:	No	No
Serbo-Croatian:	No	No

Snyder formulated this cross-linguistic correlation in terms of the syntactic parameter given in (26).

(26) The Compounding Parameter (Snyder 2002:33)
The language {allows, disallows} formation of endocentric compounds during the syntactic derivation.

The fundamental idea behind this parameter is that in complex-predicate constructions like resultatives, the main verb and the secondary predicate constitute a single word (namely, an endocentric compound) at the point of semantic interpretation, and the operation necessary to form this is the same as the one required to create nominal compounds.

Building on this proposal, Sugisaki and Isobe performed a cross-sectional study on twenty three- and four-year-old Japanese children (mean age 4;2), to test the prediction that transitive resultatives would be available to a given child only if the child's grammar allowed novel, endocentric compounds. In their experiment, each child received a test of novel compounds (as in (27)) in the form of elicited production, and a test of transitive resultatives (as in (28b)) in the form of a truth-value judgment task. The story for (28b) is presented in (29).

(27) kame pan 'turtle bread' (i.e., bread in the shape of a turtle)

(28) a. Pikachu-wa aka-i isu-o nutte-imasu.
Pikachu-TOP red chair-ACC painting-is
'Pikachu is painting the red chair.'
b. Pikachu-wa aka-ku isu-o nutte-imasu.
Pikachu-TOP red chair-ACC painting-is
'Pikachu is painting the chair red.'

(29)   Sample story (translated from Japanese to English)

Today, Pikachu is playing in Ash's room. In the room, there are two chairs. One chair, which is blue, belongs to his good friend Ash, and the other chair, which is red and small, belongs to Pikachu. Pikachu wants these chairs to be the same color. He walks to Ash's chair and starts thinking about painting that chair with red paint. However, Pikachu realizes that he will be scolded very much if he paints that chair without Ash's permission. Then, what can he do? He gets a good idea. He can paint his own chair. Now, he gets blue paint and starts painting his chair with that paint.

If the child has the knowledge to interpret resultatives correctly, then s/he will judge that the sentence in (28b) is false in this situation, because even though Pikachu once thought about painting a chair red, he gave up that idea and started painting his own chair with blue paint. However, if the child does not have knowledge of the resultative and has wrongly assigned the interpretation that corresponds to (28a), then s/he will accept the test sentence in (28b) even in this situation.

The results showed a significant contingency between passing the compounding test and passing the resultative test ($p=.0194$ by two-tailed Fisher Exact Test). The children who failed both of these tests can be interpreted as having the negative value of the Compounding Parameter, and those who passed both tests can be viewed as having the positive value. Because the shift from the negative setting to the positive one is observable in the course of acquisition, this finding suggests that the Compounding Parameter undergoes delayed setting in the acquisition of Japanese, and again that parameter setting contributes to the non-instantaneous nature of actual language development.

In addition to such "global" parameters, a recent study by Goro and Akiba (2004) suggested that UG contains a lexical parameter governing the semantics of negation-disjunction expressions and that this parameter is initially misset by Japanese-speaking children. They observed that negated disjunctions in English and Japanese behave differently, as illustrated in (30). Whereas the English disjunction *or* is interpreted within the scope of local negation and yields the conjunctive interpretation, this interpretation is unavailable in the Japanese counterpart containing *ka*: The Japanese disjunction must take scope above local negation.

(30) a. John cannot speak English *or* Japanese.
         = John cannot speak English AND he cannot speak Japanese.
      b. John-wa   eigo   ka   nihongo-o   hanas-e-nai.
          John-TOP   English   or   Japanese-ACC   speak-able-NEG
          = John cannot speak English OR he cannot speak Japanese./*Neg>OR

Goro and Akiba argued that this contrast should be captured by assuming that Japanese disjunction is a positive polarity item (PPI), like English *some*, and went on to propose that the PPI-hood of disjunction is governed by a lexical parameter with values {±PPI}. Selecting the +PPI value yields Japanese-type PPI disjunction, and selecting the −PPI value yields English-type non-PPI disjunction.

To determine how Japanese-speaking children interpret negated disjunctions, Goro and Akiba (2004) conducted an experiment with thirty children, using a truth-value judgment task. The results revealed that children accepted adultlike "disjunctive" interpretation of *ka* only 25 percent of the time, which suggests that Japanese-speaking children interpret *ka* conjunctively, as in adult English. Goro and Akiba interpreted this finding as an indication that the −PPI value is the default setting of the relevant semantic parameter, and that the shift to the correct setting requires a certain amount of time, presumably due to the low frequency of the relevant input data.

So far, we have seen evidence from child Japanese that the setting of various parameters takes time and hence contributes to the noninstantaneous nature of language acquisition. Yet, it is not necessarily the case that *every* parameter undergoes such delayed setting. In fact, based on findings from the acquisition of Germanic and Romance languages, Wexler (1998) proposed the hypothesis in (31), which says that "basic" parameters such as those listed in (32) are already fixed to the target value when syntactically relevant production begins.

(31) Very Early Parameter-Setting (VEPS; Wexler 1998:25)
Basic parameters are set correctly at the earliest observable stages, that is, at least from the time that the child enters the two-word stage, around eighteen months of age.

(32) Basic parameters are (at least) the parameters relevant to:
a. Word order, such as VO versus OV (e.g., Swedish vs. German)
b. V-to-I or not (e.g., French vs. English)
c. V2 or not (e.g., German vs. English or French)
d. Null subject or not (e.g., Italian vs. English or French)

Sugisaki (2005) confirmed the early setting of the word-order parameter in Japanese, a free word-order language. In addition to its basic SOV order, Japanese permits English-like SVO order, at least in matrix contexts, as shown in (33). Yet, this SVO order exhibits various restrictions that do not apply to the SOV order, which indicates that the former is a marked order, derived in some way from the latter (see, e.g., Tanaka 2001). For example, the SVO order is incompatible with direct-object *wh*-questions, as illustrated in (34).

(33) a. SOV: Eri-ga   ringo-o   tabeta (yo).
            Eri-NOM apple-ACC ate   (PART)
            'Eri ate an apple.'
     b. SVO: Eri-ga   tabeta(yo), ringo-o.
            Eri-NOM ate (PART) apple-ACC

(34) a. SOV: Eri-ga   nani-o   tabeta no?
             Eri-NOM what-ACC ate   Q
             'What did Eri eat?'
     b. SVO: *Eri-ga   tabeta   no,   nani-o?
             Eri-NOM   ate   Q   what-ACC

Japanese-learning children around the age of 2;5 sometimes produce utterances that contain VO order. To determine whether such VO sentences in the child's speech have the same marked status as in adult language, Sugisaki (2005) analyzed two longitudinal corpora for Japanese (Aki and Ryo; Miyata 2004a, 2004b) from the CHILDES database (MacWhinney 2000), which provide a total sample of more than thirty-three thousand lines of child speech. The results showed that both VO sentences and direct-object *wh*-questions occurred reasonably often, but there was never an example of an object *wh*-question with VO order. This finding indicates that OV is the only basic word order even in early child Japanese and that the early setting of the word-order parameter holds even for the acquisition of Japanese, a free word-order language.

According to syntactic studies such as Fukui 1993 and Saito and Fukui 1998, the availability of scrambling in Japanese is tightly connected to its head-final setting. If so, the findings of Otsu (1994b) and Murasugi and Kawamura (2005) that scrambling in Japanese is acquired very early conform to the early setting of the word-order parameter. Yet, the view that scrambling is acquired early is a relatively new development.

In the late 1970s, Hayashibe (1975) and Sano (1977) examined how Japanese-speaking children interpret sentences with the canonical SOV order and those with the scrambled OSV order, illustrated in (35). In this task, children were asked to act out the meaning of the sentence by manipulating toy animals placed in front of them.

(35) a. SOV: Kamesan-ga   ahirusan-o   osimasita.
             turtle-NOM   duck-ACC   pushed
             'A turtle pushed a duck.'
     b. OSV: Kamesan-o   ahirusan-ga osimasita.
             turtle-ACC   duck-NOM   pushed
             'A duck pushed a turtle.'

The results indicated that there seems to be a period in development, sometimes up to five years old, where children tend to interpret scrambled sentences such as (35b) as if they were nonscrambled sentences such as (35a). This finding raised the possibility that the grammar of Japanese-speaking children lacks scrambling and that this operation is acquired fairly late.

Otsu (1994b) pointed out the possibility that even though the child grammar is equipped with the scrambling operation, children may have trouble creating the discourse context by themselves that makes the scrambled sentence sound natural. Specifically, he suggested that the scrambled NP usually needs to have been established as a discourse topic and, hence, that children cannot comprehend scrambled sentences in the absence of any discourse context. To evaluate this possibility, Otsu conducted an experiment in which each test sentence was preceded by another sentence that established the scrambled NP as the discourse topic. An example is given in (36).

(36) Kooen-ni   ahirusan-ga   imasita.
　　 park-in   duck-NOM   is-POL-PAST
　　 Sono   ahirusan-o   kamesan-ga   osimasita.
　　 the   duck-ACC   turtle-NOM   push-POL-PAST
　　 'There was a duck in the park. A turtle pushed the duck.'

The results showed that three- and four-year-old children had virtually no difficulty in understanding OSV sentences, once the discourse context was provided. This finding indicates that knowledge of scrambling is acquired early, even though the knowledge relevant to creating the discourse context for scrambled sentences may take more time to develop. Early acquisition of scrambling in Japanese is further supported by Murasugi and Kawamura 2005. In addition to children's comprehension of scrambled sentences, Murasugi and Kawamura tested the acquisition of the reconstruction property of scrambling, one of the syntactic properties associated with A'-movement. The sentences they used are exemplified in (37).

(37) a. SOV: Ahiru-ga$_1$ usi-o   [zibun-no$_1$ niwa-de]   oikaketa.
　　　　　　 duck-NOM   cow-ACC   self-GEN   garden-at   chased
　　　　　　 'The duck chased the cow at the garden of himself.'
　　 b. OSV: Usi-o$_1$ [zibun-no$_2$ niwa-de]$_3$ ahiru-ga$_2$ t_1 t_3 oikaketa.
　　　　　　 cow-ACC   self-GEN   garden-at   duck-NOM   chased
　　　　　　 'The cow, at the garden of himself, the duck chased.'

In (37a), the subject-oriented anaphor *zibun* is c-commanded and hence is bound by the subject NP *ahiru-ga*. In (37b), this c-command requirement is satisfied through reconstruction: The anaphor is properly licensed in its initial position. Using an act-out task, Murasugi and Kawamura showed that even three-year-olds have knowledge of the reconstruction property of scrambling. This finding is significant in that it suggests that the children had indeed acquired scrambling as a movement operation.

Going back to the issue of the early setting of parameters, Nakayama (1996) investigated whether the null-argument parameter is fixed correctly from the very beginning. Nakayama analyzed the use of empty arguments in the spontaneous speech of three Japanese-speaking children and compared the obtained frequencies with those of adults. The results revealed that the rate of empty arguments in the children's speech is not very different from that in the adults' speech, which led Nakayama to claim that Japanese-speaking children as young as one year old have the same knowledge about empty arguments as adults. This finding suggests that the null-argument parameter is also set correctly from the earliest stages of Japanese acquisition.

The findings from the various studies reviewed so far lead to the conclusion that there are two types of parameters—those that undergo early fixation (e.g., the word-order parameter) and those that undergo delayed fixation (e.g., the relative-clause parameter). Then, an important question arises as to what explains this dichotomy. Some recent acquisition studies offer interesting proposals. For example, Guasti (2003) suggested that early-set parameters are those that can be set on the basis of prosodic information. Rizzi (2004) speculated that some parameters, specifically those that are relevant to the dropping of materials, undergo delayed fixation due to a grammatically driven strategy to reduce the workload of the immature production system. Alternatively, the dichotomy might reflect the fact that UG parameters are structured hierarchically (Baker 2001) and hence that the settings of certain parameters depend on the settings of others. More evidence concerning each parameter is called for in order to obtain a more definite answer.

To summarize this subsection, we have reviewed evidence from the acquisition of Japanese that certain parameters take time to reach the target value and that this helps explain why actual language development is noninstantaneous. These studies in turn indicate that the time course of child language acquisition is a potentially rich source of evidence concerning the parameters of variation permitted by human language.[14]

10.3.2 Maturation of UG Properties

As we discussed in section 10.2, many principles of UG have been demonstrated to emerge early. However, this is not the only logical possibility. In principle, there could be properties of UG that emerge later in the course of acquisition due to maturation: Their emergence is biologically controlled and hence they are not available until the child reaches a certain stage of development.[15]

One area that several studies argued to involve maturation of UG properties is the development of functional categories (e.g., Radford 1990) and the later acquisition of IP and CP (e.g., Vainikka 1993/1994). It is widely observed that English-speaking children before or around the age of two years frequently omit functional elements such as determiners and auxiliaries.

(38) Bee going window. Wayne sitting gate. (Radford 1990:159)

Additionally, no productive use of modals, tense and agreement markers, complementizers, or *wh*-movement are observed in this stage of language acquisition.

To account for the lack of functional elements in the child's speech, Radford (1990) proposed that the early grammar is a lexical-thematic system that includes no functional categories (no D, I, or C) and that the availability of these categories is subject to maturation: Although functional categories are part of UG, they are programmed to emerge and become operative around the age of two years.[16]

Yet, later studies provided compelling evidence against the complete lack of functional categories in early grammars. Pierce (1992) examined natural production data from four French-speaking two-year-olds and made two striking findings. First, children incorrectly use nonfinite verbs as the matrix verb.[17] Second, they make virtually no errors with respect to the syntactic position of the verbs: Verbs precede the negation *pas* when they are finite but follow *pas* when they are nonfinite. The following table summarizes the data from one of the four children, Nathalie:

(39) Verb placement in negatives as a function of tense (Pierce 1992:66)

	+Finite	−Finite
Verb-Neg	68	0
Neg-Verb	3	82

This finding demonstrates that French children know that finite verbs must overtly move to I across negation, which in turn suggests that the functional category of I already exists in the children's grammar. This observation from child French and a similar observation from child German led Poeppel and Wexler (1993) to argue against Radford's (1990) claim and to propose instead that phrase structure in the grammar of two-year-olds is equipped with a full array of functional categories and is organized in exactly the same way that it is for adults (the Full Competence Hypothesis).

Murasugi and Hashimoto (2004b) presented evidence from Japanese that the child grammar projects the functional category of small *v*, which is responsible for the assignment of an external θ-role (Chomsky 1995:315). Their longitudinal study of the child called Akkun revealed that at around age 2;5, Akkun quite productively ended utterances with the words *tiyu/tita/tite*, which correspond in meaning to 'do/did/doing' in English.

(40) a. Mama   Akkun hai   doozyo   tiyu   (2;5)
     Mommy Akkun yes   please   do
     'Akkun(/ I) will give it to Mommy.'
   b. Akkun   nezi   kuyukuyu   tite,   konoko   syaberu (2;9)
     Akkun   screw   turn-around doing   this-one talk
     'When Akkun(/ I) will wind this one around, it will talk.'

Murasugi and Hashimoto further observed that Akkun used *tiyu/tita/tite* to describe an activity that caused a certain event or change of state, and they proposed the following structure for (40b).

(41)
```
          vP
         /  \
      Akkun  v'
            /  \
           /    v [+cause]
          /     |
       nezi  kiyukiyu
              tite
```

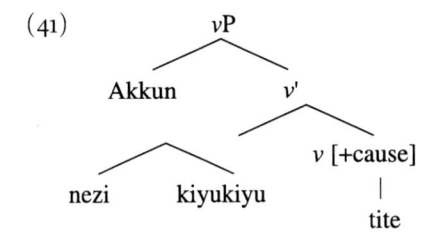

If this analysis of (40b) is correct, then the child's utterances involving *tiyu/tita/tite* provide evidence for the *v*-VP frame for agentive verbs in the child grammar and hence undermine Radford's (1990) proposal that the emergence of all functional categories is maturationally delayed.

Another UG property that has been argued to involve maturation is the ability to form A-chains, as proposed initially by Borer and Wexler (1987).[18] Their A-chain maturation hypothesis was based on the following two observations concerning the acquisition of passives in English. First, English-speaking children have difficulty in comprehending and producing passives of nonactional verbs as in (42) but not passives of actional verbs as in (43) (Maratsos et al. 1985).

(42) The doll was seen (by Mary).

(43) The doll was combed (by Mary).

The second observation is that passives without a *by*-phrase (short passives) are comprehended and produced earlier than passives with a *by*-phrase (long passives).

Borer and Wexler (1987) argued that these observations can be accounted for by assuming that children are unable to form A-chains: In passives, the underlying object moves to the subject position and forms an A-chain, but the child lacks the ability to handle this property. This hypothesis directly accounts for children's difficulty with sentences such as (42), which can only be analyzed as verbal passives. In contrast, the participle in (43) is potentially ambiguous between a passive and an adjectival interpretation. Thus, although the participle in (42) cannot appear prenominally, this is possible with the participle in (43):

(44) a. *the seen doll
      b. the combed doll

Given this distinction, Borer and Wexler claimed that children analyze examples such as (43) as adjectival passives and hence are able to provide an interpretation. They also suggested that the lack of long passives in the child's speech follows from the fact that adjectival passives are in many cases incompatible with *by*-phrases, as shown in (45).[19]

(45) The fact was unknown (*by Peter).

Sugisaki (1999) and Minai (2000), among others, argued that the acquisition of passives in Japanese is consistent with the prediction of the A-chain maturation hypothesis. Japanese has two major types of passives.[20] The *direct passive* corresponds to the English *be*-passive both structurally and functionally. In this construction, the passive morpheme -*rare* is attached to the verb stem, and the object NP of the active sentence appears in the subject position bearing nominative Case. The subject NP of the active optionally appears as a PP with *ni* 'by'.[21]

(46) a. Active transitive
Eri-ga   Ken-o   osita.
Eri-NOM   Ken-ACC pushed
'Eri pushed Ken.'
b. Direct passive
Ken-ga   (Eri-ni) os-are-ta.
Ken-NOM   Eri-by   push-PASS-PAST
'Ken was pushed by Eri.'

The other major type of passive—the *indirect passive*—can be created not only from a transitive verb but also from an intransitive verb. As in direct passives, the passive morpheme -*rare* is attached to the verb stem, and the subject of the active appears in a PP headed by *ni* 'by'. However, in indirect passives, an additional argument appears as the surface subject, and this NP is interpreted as being adversely affected by the state of affairs expressed in the rest of the clause. For this reason, the indirect passive is often called the *adversity passive*.

(47) a. Active intransitive
Ame-ga   hutta.
rain-NOM fell/rained
'It rained.'
b. Indirect passive
Ken-ga   ame-ni   hur-are-ta.
Ken-NOM   rain-by   fall-PASS-PAST
'Ken was adversely affected by rain.'
(48) a. Active transitive
Ken-ga   kuruma-o ketta.
Ken-NOM   car-ACC   kicked
'Ken kicked a car.'
b. Indirect passive
Eri-ga   Ken-ni   kuruma-o   ker-are-ta.
Eri-NOM   Ken-by   car-ACC   kick-PASS-PAST
'Eri was adversely affected by Ken's kicking a/her car.'

There are important structural differences between direct and indirect passives. First, Kuno (1973) pointed out that the subject-oriented anaphor *zibun* 'self' takes the surface subject as its antecedent in direct passives, but it can refer to the surface subject or the *ni*-phrase object in indirect passives. This contrast is illustrated in (49).

(49) a. Taroo-wa   Hanako-ni   zibun-no heya-de nagur-are-ta.
        Taroo-TOP   Hanako-by   self-GEN room-in hit-PASS-PAST
        'Taroo was hit by Hanako in his room.'
    b. Taroo-wa   Hanako-ni   zibun-no heya-de sawag-are-ta.
        Taroo-TOP   Hanako-by   self-GEN room-in make noise-PASS-PAST
        'Taroo was adversely affected by Hanako's making noise in his/her room.'

Based on this observation, Kuno proposed that the direct passive has a simple structure similar to the English passive, whereas -*rare* is an independent verb in the indirect passive. The passive morpheme takes a sentential complement in (49b), and *Hanako* qualifies as a potential antecedent of *zibun* because it is the subject of the embedded clause.

Second, Miyagawa (1989) observed that quantifier float is possible from the surface subject of a direct passive but not from that of an indirect passive:

(50) Direct passive
    Yuube,   kuruma-ga [VP doroboo-ni ni-dai nusum-are-ta].
    last-night car-NOM   thief-by   2-CL   steal-PASS-PAST
    'Last night, two cars were stolen by the thief.'

(51) Indirect passive
    *Kodomo-ga   [VP ame-ni futari fur-are-ta].
    children-NOM   rain-by 2-CL   fall-PASS-PAST
    'Two children were rained on.'

Miyagawa argued that this contrast can be captured by assuming that direct passives involve A-movement of the NP from object to subject position and that the locality requirement on quantifiers is satisfied between the numeral quantifier and the trace of that movement. If so, the contrast between (50) and (51) suggests that the formation of an A-chain between subject and object positions is involved in direct passives but not indirect passives.

Sugisaki (1999) and Minai (2000) reasoned that if direct passives contain A-chains but indirect passives do not, then the A-chain maturation hypothesis predicts that indirect passives are acquired earlier than direct passives. Using a picture-selection task, these studies showed that Japanese-speaking four- and five-year-olds have much difficulty in interpreting direct passives and that indirect passives are easier to comprehend for these children than direct passives.[22]

Other findings from child Japanese are consistent with the A-chain maturation hypothesis. Miyamoto et al. (1999) examined in detail the Case-Marker Drop phenomenon in the spontaneous speech data of one Japanese-speaking child (Aki; Miyata 2004a) and made the following observation: Even though Aki generally omitted Case markers only in environments that an adult would find acceptable, one possible exception occurred with arguments of unaccusative verbs. Aki dropped Case markers even in environments such as (52).

(52) a. Dare-ga kita no?
    who-NOM came Q
    'Who came?'
  b. ??Dare-ɸ kita no?

Miyamoto et al. speculated that the lack of A-chains at this stage forced Aki to leave the argument of unaccuatives within VP and thus the Case particle was close enough to the verb to undergo Case omission.

Sugisaki and Isobe (2001) investigated experimentally whether Japanese-speaking children around four years old can correctly interpret the ditransitive constructions given in (53).

(53) a. S-IO-DO-V
    Eri-ga   Ken-ni   sono hon-o   ageta.
    Eri-NOM   Ken-DAT   that book-ACC   gave.
    'Eri gave that book to Ken.'
  b. S-DO-IO-V
    Eri-ga   sono hon-o   Ken-ni   ageta.
    Eri-NOM   that book-ACC   Ken-DAT   gave.

The results from twenty children suggested that, although children showed no difficulty interpreting IO-DO order as in (53a), they had trouble interpreting DO-IO order as in (53b). If syntactic analyses such as Nemoto 1993 and Tada 1993 are correct in claiming that S-DO-IO-V order is derived from S-IO-DO-V order via A-movement of DO, then these results are consistent with the A-chain maturation hypothesis.[23]

In contrast, Sano (2000) and Sano, Endo, and Yamakoshi (2001) argued against the maturation of A-chains, based on their experiment on Japanese-speaking children's interpretation of full unaccusatives. They observed that quantifier float is possible not only with the subject of direct passives but also with the subject of "full unaccusatives" (unaccusaitves with -*ni* phrase), and they claimed that full unaccusatives also involve the formation of A-chains in their derivation.

(54) a. Direct passive
    Zousan-ga   butasan-ni   2-hiki   tukamae-rare-ta.
    elephant-NOM   pig-by   2-CL   catch-PASS-PAST
  b. Full unaccusative
    Zousan-ga   butasan-ni   2-hiki   tukamat-ta.
    elephant-NOM   pig-by   2-CL   catch(UNACC)-PAST
    'Two elephants were caught by a pig.'

Yet, contrary to the prediction of the A-chain maturation hypothesis, the three- to five-year-old children they tested did not have much difficulty in comprehending full unaccusatives, even though they made many errors in interpreting direct passives. In light of this finding, Sano (2000) and Sano, Endo, and Yamakoshi

(2001) argued that children's difficulty lies not in the formation of A-chains but rather in the transmission of an external θ-role from the passive affix to the *by*-phrase.

Murasugi and Kawamura (2005) compared the acquisition of scrambling and the direct passive and found not only that scrambling is acquired earlier than the direct passive but also that the discrepancy is surprisingly large. As noted in section 10.3.1, their (act-out) experiments indicated that even three-year-olds know the reconstruction property of scrambling. However, children start assigning correct interpretations to passive sentences around the age of four. Moreover, a further experiment with test sentences that contained the subject-oriented anaphor *zibun* 'self' suggested that the acquisition of direct passive is actually further delayed. In the direct passive, the surface subject is the unique possible antecedent of *zibun*, whereas in the indirect passive, both the surface subject and the semantic subject in the *ni*-phrase (*by*-phrase) qualify as possible antecedents. In their experiment, none of the six four-year-old subjects showed the ability to assign the correct antecedent to *zibun* in direct passive sentences, and even three of the eight older subjects (ages five and six years) were unsuccessful in this respect.

According to Murasugi and Kawamura (2005), these results suggest that the four-year-olds (and some older children) who successfully acted out direct passive sentences actually interpreted them as indirect passives. This is in line with the conclusion of Sugisaki (1999) and Minai (2000) that the indirect passive is acquired prior to the direct passive, which involves an A-chain, and hence the acquisition of Japanese passives is consistent with the A-chain maturation hypothesis. However, Murasugi and Kawamura pointed out that the delay in the acquisition of the direct passive is too extensive if A-chain maturation is its sole cause: It is dubious that A-chains take more than five years to mature. They speculated, then, that morphological complexity plays at least some role in the delayed acquisition of the direct passive. In the indirect passive, the passive morpheme -*rare* is a verb that assigns the affectee role to the subject and takes a sentential complement. In the direct passive, though, the morpheme's properties are more complex. Hoshi (1994), for example, argued that it not only absorbs the external θ-role and the objective Case of the root verb but also assigns the affectee role to the surface subject when a *ni*-phrase appears.[24] It seems quite possible, then, that these complex properties of -*rare* in the direct passive contribute to its delayed acquisition.

As we can see from this discussion, the maturation of A-chains is still not a settled issue (even) in the acquisition of Japanese, despite the fact that this issue is one of the better studied areas in Japanese acquisition.

Before closing this review of studies on the maturation of UG properties, let us look at another area in child Japanese that has been given a maturational account. It has long been observed in the acquisition of Japanese that young children occasionally produce errors with negation, as illustrated in (55a) (see, e.g., Clancy 1985). In this example, a finite verbal form is placed in front of the negation, even though the correct adult counterpart requires a nonfinite irrealis verbal form, as shown in (55b).

(55) a. *hairu   nai
        enter(NONPAST) NEG
        '(It) does not enter.'
     b. haira   nai
        enter(IRREALIS) NEG

To account for such errors, Sano (2002) proposed that the morphological operation of irrealis formation undergoes maturation and does not become operative until children reach a certain point in development.

To summarize this subsection, evidence from child Japanese argues against the maturation of functional categories, in line with evidence from the acquisition of other languages. In the case of the maturation of A-chains, however, there are still competing views in the literature, and further investigation is necessary to determine the validity of this hypothesis. Thus, we can reasonably say that the acquisition of Japanese leaves the maturation of UG properties as a potential contributor to the noninstantaneous nature of actual language development.

10.3.3 Acquisition of Lexical Items: On the Lexical Realization of Syntactic Categories

So far, we have seen two factors that may contribute to the noninstantaneous nature of language acquisition: parameter setting and the maturation of UG properties. Finally, we discuss the acquisition of lexical items and their syntactic properties. We take up as a case study Murasugi and Hashimoto's (2004b) longitudinal study on the acquisition of verbs—in particular, transitive-unaccusative pairs and causatives.

As noted earlier, Murasugi and Hashimoto (2004b) reported a longitudinal study of a Japanese-speaking child, Akkun, and observed that he initially seemed to realize *v* as *tiyu/tita/tite* 'do/did/doing'. A relevant example, (40b), is repeated here as (56).

(56) Akkun nezi   kuyukuyu   tite, konoko   syaberu (2;9)
     Akkun screw turn-around doing this-one talk
     'When Akkun (/I) will wind this one around, it will talk.'

At this point, he typically used onomatopoeic or mimetic expressions in place of the actual verb. Thus, *kuyukuyu* in (56), which corresponds to *kurukuru* in adult speech, is a mimetic word that describes things turning around. His acquisition of actual verbs, however, started early and proceeded step by step. Utterances such as (57) and (58) were observed before he turned three years old.

(57) Dango-ga   uta pakan   tite,   dango-ga   atta   (2;9)
     dumpling-NOM lid ONOMATOPOEIA doing dumpling-NOM there-be
     'There was a dumpling (when I) opened the lid of the dumpling (box).'

(58) Kinnou   Akkun akatyan toki, papa-ni   koe *ageta*   (2;10)
     yesterday Akkun baby   when   Daddy-to   this gave
     'Akkun gave this to Daddy when he was a baby yesterday (= in the past).'

The italicized verb in (57) is an unaccusative, and that in (58) is a ditransitive.

At the same time, Akkun showed interesting and consistent "errors" as he acquired the actual verbs. Note first that, in adult English, a transitive verb and an unaccusative verb often take the same phonetic form. Thus, we have alternations as in (59).

(59) a. John passed the ring to Mary.
     b. The ring passed to Mary.

If the argument structures of these sentences are realized as in (60), then *v* is a "zero morpheme" without phonetic content whether it is [+cause] as in the case of (59a) or [−cause] as in the case of (59b).

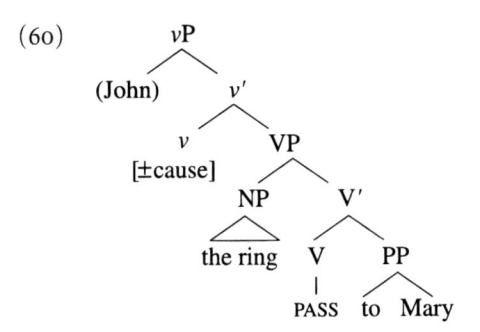

(60)   vP
           / \
      (John)   v'
              / \
             v   VP
         [±cause] / \
                NP   V'
              / \   / \
         the ring V   PP
                 | / \
               PASS to Mary

Consequently, '*v* [+cause] + PASS' and '*v* [−cause] + PASS' are both realized as 'PASS'.

In adult Japanese, in contrast, transitivity and unaccusativity are often marked by distinct suffixes, as illustrated in (61).

(61)   Transitive   Unaccusative
     a. mi-se-ru (= show-PRES)   / mi-e-ru (= see-PRES)
     b. utu-s-(r)u (= copy-PRES)   / utu-r-(r)u (= be copied-PRES)
     c. todok-e-ru (= deliver-PRES) / todok-(r)u (= be delivered-PRES)
     d. os-ie-ru (= teach-PRES)   / os-owar-(r)u (= be taught)

These examples show that the forms of the suffixes are idiosyncratic and probably have to be learned individually. These suffixes plausibly occupy the *v* position. For example, [+cause] *v* is realized as -*s* and [−cause] *v* as -*r*, in the case of (61b).

In the process of acquiring these lexical items that stand for V-*v* combinations, Akkun often produced transitive sentences with unaccusative verbs:

(62) Nee, ati-o   hirogat-te   (3;7)
     INT legs-ACC spread(UNACC)-REQUEST
     'Please spread your legs.'

(63) Kore, ai-toku   kara saa   (4;5)
     this   open(UNACC)-keep   as   INT
     '(I will) open this and keep it open.'

(64) Todok-ok-ka,   ano hito-ni   todok-oo   todok-oo   (4;8)
     arrive-shall we that person-to arrive-let's arrive-let's
     'Shall we send (it)? Let's send (it) to that person.'

In each of these examples, Akkun used the unaccusative form of the verb in place of the transitive. What he intended in (62), for example, was *hirog-e-te* 'spread-REQUEST' (transitive) and not *hirog-at-te* 'spread-REQUEST' (unaccusative). In adult Japanese, (63) and (64) mean 'I will remain open' and 'Let's be delivered to that person', respectively.

Fuji (2006) and Murasugi, Hashimoto, and Fuji (2007) examined a longitudinal corpus (Noji 1973–1977) from the CHILDES database (MacWhinney 2000) and observed that the subject, Sumihare, went through exactly the same stages as Akkun in the acquisition process of Japanese verbs. And interestingly, whereas Akkun consistently used unaccusatives for transitives, Sumihare sometimes used transitives for unaccusatives as well.[25] One of the examples is shown in (65).

(65) Koko-kara hi-ga   das-u   nze   (2;6)
     here-from sun-NOM take out PART
     'The sun comes out from here.'

These studies suggest that children initially assume that the pronounced verbs are Vs and that [±cause] *v* is phonetically empty. Accordingly, to them, unaccusatives and their transitive counterparts should be homophonous, as in English. They only later realize that the surface forms of the verbs are derived by suffixing *v* to the verbal root. As the actual realization of [±cause] *v* is idiosyncratic and sometimes even null, the acquisition of verbs requires complex morphological analysis. It is, then, not surprising at all that it requires some time.

Japanese has a well-known causative verbal suffix, *-sase*, and syntactically it takes a sentential (*v*P) complement. Thus, the subject-oriented reflexive pronoun, *zibun*, can take the causer as well as the causee as its antecedent in a causative sentence.

(66) Hanako-ga   Taroo-ni   zibun-no heya-o   katazuke-sase-ta.
     Hanako-NOM   Taroo-DAT   self-GEN room-ACC   clean-CAUSE-PAST
     'Hanako made Taroo clean up her/his room.'

This shows that causative sentences contain two subjects and, hence, an embedded clause. The causative *-sase*, then, is not a realization of [+cause] *v* but is itself a V (or a V-*v* combination).

Akkun started uttering causative sentences quite productively around the age of five years.[26] But sporadic uses of *-sase* were observed much earlier, at age three. A typical example is shown in (67).

(67) Akkun-ni   tabe-sase-tee   (3;6)
      Akkun-DAT   eat-CAUSE-REQUEST
      'Please feed Akkun.'

Interestingly, in all of those examples, the causee is not agentive. Thus, (67) was intended to mean 'Please feed me' rather than 'Please let me eat'. As this coincided with the period when Akkun was struggling with the idiosyncratic realization of [±cause] *v*, one can conjecture that he was using *-sase* as one possible form of [+cause] *v*. The acquisition of the causative construction with the full verb *-sase* took place more than a year later, as witnessed by the following example, where the causee is clearly agentive:[27]

(68) Name-tee, name-tee, name-sase-te.   (4;9)
      lick-want lick-want lick-CAUSE-REQUEST
      'I want to lick (the candy). Let me lick it.'

The discussion in Murasugi and Hashimoto 2004b indicates that children are equipped with the *v*-VP frame from the early stage of acquisition, but they require some time to discover the morphological makeup of the actual verbs, which are formed by combining V and *v*. The causative suffixal verb *-sase* is initially assumed to be a realization of [+cause] *v* and is only later acquired as a full verb that takes a sentential (*v*P) complement. Lexical items typically correspond to syntactic heads, but they are sometimes formed by combining two or more distinct morphemes that project phrases of their own. Children must perform morphological analysis to acquire those complex lexical items. We would then expect this analysis to take time in some cases, and this is exactly what we have seen in the acquisition of verbs in Japanese. (See Murasugi, Hashimoto, and Fuji 2007 for a detailed study.)

10.4 Concluding Remarks

In this chapter, we have reviewed studies on the acquisition of Japanese that directly bear on the construction of a theory of language acquisition. Specifically, we have summarized studies that attempt to answer the two principal questions listed in (3), repeated here in (69).

(69) Principal questions
      a. When and how do principles of UG emerge in the child grammar?
      b. What factors explain the gradual, noninstantaneous nature of actual language development?

As for the first question, we have presented evidence from child Japanese that various principles of UG constrain the course of acquisition from the very beginning. These findings in turn argue for the innateness of these principles. With respect to the second question, we have seen evidence from child Japanese that parameter setting, maturation of UG properties, and lexical acquisition play important roles in explaining why language acquisition is not instantaneous but proceeds gradually. As mentioned at the outset, Japanese has various syntactic characteristics that are not observed in Germanic or Romance languages, and hence the investigation of its acquisition process can be especially valuable for acquisition theory. We hope that this chapter has succeeded in demonstrating this point in a convincing way.

Descriptive and explanatory adequacies have to be met in acquisition research. Acquisition studies that explicitly make a contribution from child Japanese to the analysis of adult Japanese syntax are very much needed, as are acquisition studies that draw directly on proposed syntactic analyses of adult Japanese. Theory-based and theory-inspiring hypotheses that make use of solid data and theoretical analysis are much sought after in Japanese acquisition research.

To achieve these objectives, however, acquisition researchers need a keen eye for theoretically significant data. Empirical research is guided by theoretical ideas. For this reason exactly, a simple empirical discovery can have a profound effect on the foundations of linguistic theory. Recall the findings of Jane Goodall, who discovered that chimpanzees make and use tools. This finding revolutionized the understanding not only of chimps but also of human behavior itself. In *Jane Goodall's Wild Chimpanzees*, the discovery is recorded as follows:

> I [Jane Goodall] was walking through the forest, when I spotted a hunched figure through the vegetation. He [a chimpanzee] had his back to me, but I could see him stripping the leaves off a small twig.
> Then busying himself around the top of a termite mound, I could see him pushing the twig into a hole in the mound. I had no idea what he was up to.
> But then he pulled out the twig and expertly picked a few termites off it with his lips. I was mesmerized. I knew that what he had just done was considered to be outright impossible. A mere nonhuman had just fabricated a clever and effective tool right before my very eyes. [28]

When Jane first described termite-fishing, the ability to make and use tools was considered one of the defining features that set humans apart from the rest of the animal kingdom. We were known as "Man the Tool Maker."

In what has become a famous quote, Dr. Louis Leakey wrote to Jane, "Now we have to redefine tool, redefine man, or accept chimpanzees as humans." Jane replied, "I [Jane Goodall] have since discovered that all Gombe chimpanzees know how to termite-fish."

In the course of long and constant longitudinal study, a piece of important empirical data happened to appear in front of the researcher, and a fundamental assumption regarding human versus nonhuman behavior had to be reconsidered because of the observation. This discovery was made during Jane Goodall's forty years of research at Gombe.

We conclude this chapter by expressing our hope that the connection between acquisitional investigations and theoretical studies of the Japanese language will be further tightened in the future. This will undoubtedly inspire the discovery of more acquisition data of theoretical significance and the pursuit of a more accurate description of child Japanese. And more important, it will make the theoretical significance of empirical acquisition research more apparent. Child language offers a wealth of information for the construction of the theory of UG, and it is one of the important tasks of acquisitionists to make use of this information to contribute to linguistic theorizing.

NOTES FOR CHAPTER 10

We would like to thank Shigeru Miyagawa, Mamoru Saito, William Snyder, and the audience of the Workshop on Linguistic Theory and the Japanese Language for valuable comments and suggestions. Any remaining errors are, of course, our own. This research was supported in part by the Nanzan University Pache Research Grant I-A, JSPS Grant-in-Aid (C) (#17520282) to Nanzan University (Murasugi), and JSPS Grant-in-Aid (B) (#17320062; Project Leader: Seiki Ayano) to Mie University (Sugisaki).

1. This dialogue was collected by Keiko Murasugi.

2. There are also cases where adults attempt to correct children's "errors." In spite of these efforts, children typically ignore these corrections. The following dialogue with a child age 2;2 illustrates such a case (Suzuki 1987:172, trans. KM and KS).

(i) Child: Papa   fuusen   *fukurande*
          daddy   balloon   blow
          (Intended meaning) 'Daddy, please blow up the balloon.'
    Father: Fukurande   zyanai   desyo,   fukuramasite   desyo
            blow   not   isn't it blow up   isn't it
            'You should not say "fukurande" (blow). It should be "fukuramasite" (blow up).'
    Child: *Fukurande.*
           blow
           (Intended meaning) 'Blow up (the balloon).'
    Father: Fukuramasite.
            blow up
            '(You should say) blow up (the balloon).'
    Child: *Fukurande.*   *Fukurande.*
           blow   blow
           (Intended meaning) 'Blow up (the balloon)! Blow up (the balloon)!'

In his utterances, the father gives the child direct negative evidence by prompting for the correct lexical causative form *fukuramasite* 'blow up', but it never works. The child keeps producing the erroneous intransitive imperative form *fukurande* 'blow', instead.

3. For a survey of Japanese acquisition from a (slightly) different perspective, see Clancy 1985 and Otsu 1999. For a detailed description of Japanese acquisition based on naturalistic observation, see, for example, Okubo 1967 and Murata 1984.

4. See Otsu 1981 and Crain and Thornton 1998, among many others.

5. See Legate 2003 for evidence that Warlpiri is also a configurational language.

6. Yet, because judgments on the CMD phenomenon show significant individual and dialectal variation, different types of evidence are needed to further confirm the configurationality of early child Japanese.

7. See Morikawa 1997 and Matsuoka 1998 for detailed discussion of the acquisition of Case particles in Japanese.

8. Murasugi and Hashimoto (2004a) also reported that the possessive NP Case-marked by *no*, as in (ii), is acquired earlier than the modifier NP associated by *no*, as in (iii). Even at the age of 2;6, the Japanese-speaking child Akkun did not mark the modifier NP with *no* as in (iii), yet he never dropped the genitive Case marker for the possessive NP at that age. See Murasugi and Hashimoto 2004a for the detailed analysis.

(ii) a. Akkun-*no*   otya   (2;6)
       Akkun-GEN   tea
       'Akkun's tea'
    b. ziityan-*no*   mikan   (2;6)
       grandfather-GEN orange
       'Grandfather's orange (= the orange that Grandfather gave me)'

(iii) Mama, dobotto (=robotto) [Ø] outa. (2;6)
      mommy robot   song
      'Mommy, (please sing) the robot's song.'

9. Another developmental factor (not discussed in detail here) is the delayed development of "pragmatic" knowledge. One fundamental assumption in generative grammar is that linguistic knowledge (or more broadly, human knowledge in general) has a modular nature. For example, sentence grammar and pragmatic knowledge are assumed to constitute independent knowledge modules. This assumption allows the possibility that those modules of linguistic knowledge develop independently, taking different periods of time to reach their steady states. Studies on the acquisition of English suggest that this developmental difference among modules is the source of children's difficulty in understanding sentences involving condition B of the binding theory. See Chien and Wexler 1990, Grodzinsky and Reinhart 1993, and Thornton and Wexler 1999, among many others. However, see Elbourne 2005 for an alternative interpretation of the evidence.

10. Example (15a) is from Nagano 1960 and (15b,c) are from Murasugi 1991. The examples are all ungrammatical with *no* in adult Japanese.

11. Similar patterns are found in the Kumamoto dialect (Murasugi 1998) and in Korean (Kim 1987, Lee 1991) as well.

12. See Murasugi 2000a,b for further discussion on the syntax of Japanese relative clauses.

13. This account may not cover all cases of overgeneration of *no/ga* by Japanese-speaking children. Nagano (1960) and Yokoyama (1990) reported the overgeneration with much younger children (around age two years). Nagano observed that those children had not fully acquired tense and Case marking (including genitive Case), and Yokoyama noted that the overgeneration occurred only with a limited number of adjectives (those indicating color or size).

Murasugi and Hashimoto (2004a), on the other hand, conducted a six-year longitudinal study with a subject, Akkun, and reported that he overgenerated *no* in two distinct periods. In the first period, starting at age 2;4, he showed exactly those patterns noted by

Nagano and Yokoyama. Then, after the overgeneration ceased at 2;6, it "reemerged" at age 2;7. This coincides with the period when degree-1 embedding, tense, and nominative Case-marking started to show up in his spontaneous production (see also note 16). The overgeneration of *no/ga* that is analyzed in the text is from this second stage. See Murasugi and Hashimoto 2004a for details.

14. See Snyder 2001, 2002 and Sugisaki 2003 for a detailed discussion of how evidence from child language acquisition can help in evaluating the UG parameters proposed in the syntactic literature.

15. See Gleitman 1981 for a related discussion.

16. Murasugi and Hashimoto (2004a) reported that the overt marking of tense alternations/inflectional systems on verbal categories, the production of the nominative Case marker, and production of relative clauses with the overgenerated complementizer appeared in Akkun's corpus simultaneously. Such facts indicate that the child achieved command of the sentential functional categories that are necessary to project an IP and CP around the same time. At around 2;7, Akkun started to produce adjectives and verbs in the past tense as in (iv) and (v), respectively.

(iv) Mama, koe   atyukatta yo   (2;7)
      mommy this hot-was
      'Mommy, this was hot.'

(v) a. Akkun, ima, zingo tyukuyu (tyukuyu = tukuru) (2;6)
       Akkun   now   signal make
       'Akkun(/ I) will make the signal now.'
    b. Mama, okkii no, tyukutta (tyukutta = tukutta) (2;7)
       mommy big-is one made
       'Mommy made a big one.'

The employment of tense in (iv) and (v) coincided with the consistent use of the nominative Case marker, as illustrated in (vi).

(vi) a. Akkun-*ga*   tyatyatyatya   tiyu (tiyu = suru)   (2;7)
        Akkun-NOM   ONOMATOPOEIA   do
        'Akkun(/ I) will sprinkle (the salt).'
     b. mama-*ga*   oyoui   tiyu   (oyoui = ryouri) (2;7)
        mommy-NOM   cooking   do
        'Mommy is cooking.'
     c. anyo-*ga*   itai   (anyo = asi)   (2;7)
        legs-NOM   hurt
        '(My) legs hurt.'

This provides further confirmation for the development of the functional system in sentences.

17. For discussion of why the child grammar permits nonfinite verbs in matrix contexts, see Hoekstra and Hyams 1998; Phillips 1996; Rizzi 1993/1994; Sano 2002; and Wexler 1994, 1996, 1998, among many others.

18. See Babyonyshev et al. 2001 for further evidence and discussion of A-movement of the subject NP from a VP-internal position to Spec,IP. Wexler (2004) proposed a reformulation of the A-chain maturation hypothesis within the current minimalist framework. For counterarguments to Borer and Wexler 1987, see Demuth 1989; Fox and Grodzinsky 1998; Snyder, Hyams, and Crisma 1995; and Thornton 2001, among others.

19. As the qualification "in many cases" suggests, there are adjectival passives that are compatible with a *by*-phrase. The following example was suggested to Koji Sugisaki by Howard Lasnik (pers. comm.):

(vii) Antarctica is uninhabited by humans.

20. See Kuroda 1979, Washio 1989/1990, Kubo 1990, Hoshi 1994, and references cited therein for detailed discussion of Japanese passives.

21. Kuroda (1979) and Hoshi (1994) observed that the surface subject is interpreted as an affectee when the "semantic subject" shows up with the postposition *-ni*. Thus, an inanimate subject is incompatible with the *ni*-phrase.

(viii) Sono tou-wa   kigenzen   3000-nen-goro-ni   (*kodai eziputozin-ni)
       that tower-TOP   B.C.   3000-year-about-in   ancient Egyptians-by
       tate-rare-ta.
       build-PASS-PAST
       'That tower was built by the ancient Egyptians around 3000 B.C.'

The use of *-ni-yotte* 'by' instead of *-ni* would create a more neutral direct passive sentence, but we do not discuss it here because it is not colloquial and hence not part of a child's lexicon.

22. See Otsu 2000 for different experimental results.

23. See Miyagawa 1997 and Miyagawa and Tsujioka 2004 for different approaches to ditransitives in Japanese.

24. Kuroda (1979) was the first to point out the θ-role-assigning property of *-rare* in direct passives.

25. Morikawa (1997) analyzed the data of Sumihare in CHILDES, and she reported some examples where intransitive forms were erroneously used instead of transitive forms. For example, Sumihare, asking his parents to open the door, used the intransitive verb *aku* 'be open' instead of the transitive verb *akeru* 'open'. Morikawa also reported that Sumihare sometimes overextended transitive verbs and used them as intransitives as well, although the latter type of error was less frequent than the former.

26. Lexical causatives are acquired earlier than syntactic causatives. The order of the acquisition of the two kinds of causatives is reported in Murasugi, Hashimoto, and Kato 2004 based on Akkun's data, and in Fuji 2006 based on an experimental study.

27. Matsumoto (2000) argued that *-sase* need not be a full verb but can be a lexical suffix in adult Japanese when the causee is not agentive. Our conjecture supports this hypothesis. Once a child assumes that the morpheme is a possible realization of [+cause] *v*, negative evidence would be required to deny this, even after the usage of the same morpheme as a full verb is acquired. Given this learnability consideration, one would expect the assumption to be retained in adult Japanese.

28. From the DVD *Jane Goodall's Wild Chimpanzees* (2003, Sling Shot Studios).

REFERENCES

Babyonyshev, Maria, Jennifer Ganger, David Pesetsky, and Kenneth Wexler. 2001. The maturation of grammatical principles: Evidence from Russian unaccusatives. *Linguistic Inquiry* 32:1–44.

Baker, Carl L., and John McCarthy, eds. 1981. *The logical problem of language acquisition.* Cambridge, Mass.: MIT Press.
Baker, Mark. 2001. *The atoms of language.* New York: Basic Books.
Bloom, Paul. 1990. Subjectless sentences in child language. *Linguistic Inquiry* 21:491–504.
Borer, Hagit, and Kenneth Wexler. 1987. The maturation of syntax. In *Parameter setting,* ed. Tom Roeper and Edwin Williams, 123–172. Dordrecht: Reidel.
Chien, Yu-Chin, and Kenneth Wexler. 1990. Children's knowledge of locality conditions in binding as evidence for the modularity of syntax and pragmatics. *Language Acquisition* 1:225–295.
Chomsky, Noam. 1981. *Lectures on government and binding.* Dordrecht: Foris.
Chomsky, Noam. 1986. *Knowledge of language: Its nature, origin, and use.* New York: Praeger.
Chomsky, Noam. 1995. *The Minimalist Program.* Cambridge, Mass.: MIT Press.
Clancy, Patricia M. 1985. The acquisition of Japanese. In *The crosslinguistic study of language acquisition: Vol. 1,* ed. Dan I. Slobin, 373–524. Hillsdale, N.J.: Lawrence Erlbaum.
Crain, Stephen, and Cecile McKee. 1986. The acquisition of structural restrictions on anaphora. In *Proceedings of NELS 16,* ed. Stephen Berman, Jae-Woong Choe, and Joyce McDonough, 94–110. Amherst, Mass.: GLSA Publications.
Crain, Stephen, and Rosalind Thornton. 1998. *Investigations in Universal Grammar: A guide to experiments on the acquisition of syntax and semantics.* Cambridge, Mass.: MIT Press.
Demuth, Katherine. 1989. Maturation and acquisition of Sesotho passive. *Lingua* 65:56–81.
Elbourne, Paul. 2005. On the acquisition of principle B. *Linguistic Inquiry* 36:333–365.
Fox, Danny, and Yosef Grodzinsky. 1998. Children's passives: A view from the *by*-phrase. *Linguistic Inquiry* 29:311–332.
Fuji, Chisato. 2006. Two types of causatives in Japanese and Japanese Sign Language: A study in syntax and acquisition. Master's thesis, Nanzan University, Nagoya, Japan.
Fukui, Naoki. 1993. Parameters and optionality. *Linguistic Inquiry* 24:399–420.
Gleitman, Lila R. 1981. Maturational determinants of language growth. *Cognition* 10:103–114.
Goro, Takuya, and Sachie Akiba. 2004. Japanese disjunction and the acquisition of positive polarity. In *Proceedings of the 5th Tokyo Conference on Psycholinguistics,* ed. Yukio Otsu, 137–161. Tokyo: Hituzi Syobo.
Grodzinsky, Yosef, and Tanya Reinhart. 1993. The innateness of binding and coreference. *Linguistic Inquiry* 24:69–101.
Guasti, Maria Teresa. 2003. How parameters are set and the order of setting. In *Proceedings of the 4th Conference on Psycholinguistics,* ed. Yukio Otsu, 23–58. Tokyo: Hituzi Syobo.
Hale, Kenneth. 1980. Remarks on Japanese phrase structure: Comments on the papers on Japanese syntax. In *MITWPL 2: Theoretical issues in Japanese linguistics,* ed. Yukio Otsu and Ann Farmer, 185–203. Cambridge, Mass.: MIT Working Papers in Linguistics.
Harada, Kazuko I. 1972. Constraints on WH-Q binding. *Studies in Descriptive and Applied Linguistics* 5:180–206.
Hayashibe, Hideo. 1975. Word order and particles: A developmental study in Japanese. *Descriptive and Applied Linguistics* 8:1–18.
Hoekstra, Teun, and Nina Hyams. 1998. Aspects of root infinitives. *Lingua* 106:81–112.
Hoji, Hajime. 1985. Logical Form constraints and configurational structures in Japanese. Doctoral dissertation, University of Washington, Seattle.

Hornstein, Norbert, and David Lightfoot, eds. 1981. *Explanations in linguistics: The logical problem of language acquisition*. London: Longman.
Hoshi, Hiroto. 1994. Passive, causative, and light verbs: A study on theta role assignment. Doctoral dissertation, University of Connecticut, Storrs.
Huang, C.-T. James. 1982. Logical relations in Chinese and the theory of grammar. Doctoral dissertation, MIT, Cambridge, Mass.
Hyams, Nina. 1986. *Language acquisition and the theory of parameters*. Dordrecht: Reidel.
Hyams, Nina, and Ken Wexler. 1993. On the grammatical basis of null subjects in child language. *Linguistic Inquiry* 24:421–459.
Iwabuchi, Etsutaro, and Shozo Muraishi. 1968. Kotoba no syuutoku [Acquisition of language]. In *Kotoba no tanjoo: Ubugoe kara go sai made* [The birth of speech: From newborn babies to five-year-olds], ed. E. Iwabuchi, K. Hatano, J. Naito, I. Kirikae, T. Tokizane, M. Sawashima, S. Muraishi, and T. Takizawa, 109–177. Tokyo: Nihon Hoosoo Syuppan Kyookai.
Kabuto, Yoshie. 2007. The acquisition of the mechanism of unselective binding, LF-movement, and constraints on movement. Paper presented at the Connecticut–Siena–Nanzan Joint Workshop on Linguistic Theory and Language Acquisition, Nanzan University, Nagoya, Japan, February.
Kim, Young-Joo. 1987. The acquisition of relative clauses in English and Korean: Development in spontaneous production. Doctoral dissertation, Harvard University, Cambridge, Mass.
Kubo, Miori. 1990. Japanese passives. Ms., MIT, Cambridge, Mass..
Kuno, Susumu. 1973. *The structure of the Japanese language*. Cambridge, Mass.: MIT Press.
Kuroda, Shige-Yuki. 1979. On Japanese passives. In *Explorations in linguistics: Papers in honor of Kazuko Inoue*, ed. George Bedell, Eichi Kobayashi, and Masatake Muraki, 305–347. Tokyo: Kaitakusha.
Lasnik, Howard. 1976. Remarks on coreference. *Linguistic Analysis* 2:1–22.
Lasnik, Howard. 1991. On the necessity of binding conditions. In *Principles and parameters in comparative grammar*, ed. Robert Freidin, 7–28. Cambridge, Mass.: MIT Press.
Lee, Kwee-Ock. 1991. On the first language acquisition of relative clauses in Korean: The universal structure of Comp. Doctoral dissertation, Cornell University, Ithaca, N.Y.
Legate, Julie Anne. 2003. Warlpiri: Theoretical implications. Doctoral dissertation, MIT, Cambridge, Mass.
Lillo-Martin, Diane. 1991. *Universal Grammar and American Sign Language: Setting the null argument parameters*. Dordrecht: Kluwer.
MacWhinney, Brian. 2000. *The CHILDES Project: Tools for analyzing talk*. Mahwah, N.J.: Lawrence Erlbaum.
Maratsos, Michael, Dana Fox, Judith Becker, and Mary Anne Charlkley. 1985. Semantic restrictions on children's passives. *Cognition* 19:167–191.
Matsumoto, Yo. 2000. On the crosslinguistic parameterization of causative predicates: Implications from Japanese and other languages. In *Argument realization*, ed. Miriam Butt and Tracy Holloway King, 135–169. Stanford, Calif.: CSLI Publications.
Matsuoka, Kazumi. 1998. The acquisition of Japanese Case particles and the theory of Case checking. Doctoral dissertation, University of Connecticut, Storrs.
Minai, Utako. 2000. The acquisition of Japanese passives. In *Japanese/Korean Linguistics 9*, ed. Mineharu Nakayama and Charles J. Quinn, Jr., 339–350. Stanford, Calif.: CSLI Publications.

Miyagawa, Shigeru. 1989. *Structure and Case marking in Japanese*. San Diego, Calif.: Academic Press.

Miyagawa, Shigeru. 1997. Against optional scrambling. *Linguistic Inquiry* 28:1–25.

Miyagawa, Shigeru, and Takae Tsujioka. 2004. Argument structure and ditransitive verbs in Japanese. *Journal of East Asian Linguistics* 13:1–38.

Miyamoto, Edson T., Kenneth Wexler, Takako Aikawa, and Shigeru Miyagawa. 1999. Case-dropping and unaccusatives in Japanese acquisition. In *Proceedings of the 23rd annual Boston University Conference on Language Development*, ed. Annabel Greenhill, Heather Littlefield, and Cheryl Tano, 443–452. Somerville, Mass.: Cascadilla Press.

Miyata, Susanne. 2004a. *Japanese: Aki corpus*. Pittsburgh, Penn.: TalkBank. 1-59642-055-3.

Miyata, Susanne. 2004b. *Japanese: Ryo corpus*. Pittsburgh, Penn.: TalkBank. 1-59642-056-1.

Morikawa, Hiromi. 1997. *Acquisition of Case marking and argument structure in Japanese*. Tokyo: Kurosio.

Murasugi, Keiko. 1988. The acquisition of structural and pragmatic constraints on pronominal references. In *UConn Working Papers in Linguistics* 2, ed. Javier Ormazabal and Jaya Sarma, 40–68. Cambridge, Mass.: MIT Working Papers in Linguistics.

Murasugi, Keiko. 1991. Noun phrases in Japanese and English: A study in syntax, learnability, and acquisition. Doctoral dissertation, University of Connecticut, Storrs.

Murasugi, Keiko. 1998. Gengo (kakutoku) riron to hougen kenkyu [Theory of language (acquisition) and the dialectal studies]. *Academia* 65:227–259.

Murasugi, Keiko. 2000a. An antisymmetry analysis of Japanese relative clauses. In *The syntax of relative clauses*, ed. Artemis Alexiadou, Paul Law, André Meinunger, and Chris Wilder, 231–263. Amsterdam: John Benjamins.

Murasugi, Keiko. 2000b. Japanese complex noun phrases and the antisymmetry theory. In *Step by step: Essays on minimalist syntax in honor of Howard Lasnik*, ed. Roger Martin, David Michaels, and Juan Uriagereka, 211–234. Cambridge, Mass.: MIT Press.

Murasugi, Keiko, and Tomoko Hashimoto. 2004a. Two different types of overgeneration of "no" in Japanese noun phrases. In *Proceedings of the 4th Asian GLOW in Seoul*, ed. Hang-jin Yoon, 327–349. Seoul: Hankook.

Murasugi, Keiko, and Tomoko Hashimoto. 2004b. Three pieces of acquisition evidence for the *v*-VP frame. *Nanzan Linguistics* 1:1–19.

Murasugi, Keiko, Tomoko Hashimoto, and Chisato Fuji. 2007. VP-shell analysis for the acquisition of Japanese intransitive verbs, transitive verbs, and causatives. *Linguistics* 43:615–651.

Murasugi, Keiko, Tomoko Hashimoto, and Sachiko Kato. 2004. On the acquisition of causatives in Japanese. In *BUCLD 28 Proceedings Online Supplement*, ed. Alejna Brugos, Linnea Micciulla, and Christine E. Smith. http://www.bu.edu/linguistics/APPLIED/BUCLD/supp.html.

Murasugi, Keiko, and Tomoko Kawamura. 2005. On the acquisition of scrambling in Japanese. In *The free word order phenomenon: Its syntactic sources and diversity*, ed. Joachim Sabel and Mamoru Saito, 221–242. Berlin: Mouton de Gruyter.

Murata, Koji. 1984. *Youji no gengo hattatsu* [Language development of children]. Tokyo: Baifukan.

Nagano, Satoshi. 1960. Youji no gengo hattatu: Tokuni josi "no" no syuutokukatei nituite [Language development: A case study of Japanese "no"]. In *Kansai daigaku kokubun gakkai: Shimada kyooju koki kinen kokubungaku ronsyuu* [Papers on Japanese literature in honor of Professor Shimada on the occasion of his 70th birthday], ed. Kansai Daigaku Kokubun Gakkai, 405–418. Osaka: Kansai University.

Nakayama, Mineharu. 1996. *Acquisition of Japanese empty categories.* Tokyo: Kurosio.

Nemoto, Naoko. 1993. Chains and case positions: A study from scrambling in Japanese. Doctoral dissertation, University of Connecticut, Storrs.

Noji. Junya. 1973–1977. *Youji no gengoseikatu no jittai* I–IV [A longitudinal study of Japanese language acquisition]. Tokyo: Bunka Hyoron Shuppan.

Okubo, Ai. 1967. *Youji gengo no hattatsu* [The development of child Language]. Tokyo: Tokyodo Shuppan.

Otsu, Yukio. 1981. Universal Grammar and syntactic development in children: Toward a theory of syntactic development. Doctoral dissertation, MIT, Cambridge, Mass.

Otsu, Yukio. 1994a. Case-marking particles and phrase structure in early Japanese. In *Syntactic theory and first language acquisition: Cross-linguistic perspectives: Vol. 1*, ed. Barbara Lust, Margarita Suñer, and John Whitman, 159–169. Hillsdale, N.J.: Lawrence Erlbaum.

Otsu, Yukio. 1994b. Early acquisition of scrambling in Japanese. In *Language acquisition studies in generative grammar*, ed. Teun Hoekstra and Bonnie D. Schwartz, 253–264. Amsterdam: John Benjamins.

Otsu, Yukio. 1999. First language acquisition. In *The handbook of Japanese linguistics*, ed. Natsuko Tsujimura, 378–397. Oxford: Blackwell.

Otsu, Yukio. 2000. A preliminary report on the independence of sentence grammar and pragmatic knowledge: The case of the Japanese passive: A developmental perspective. *Keio Studies in Theoretical Linguistics* 2:161–170.

Phillips, Colin. 1996. Root infinitives are finite. In *Proceedings of the 20th annual Boston University Conference on Language Development*, ed. Andy Stringfellow, Dalia Cahana-Amitay, Elizabeth Hughes, and Andrea Zukowski, 588–599. Somerville, Mass.: Cascadilla Press.

Pierce, Amy E. 1992. *Language acquisition and syntactic theory: A comparative analysis of French and English grammars.* Dordrecht: Kluwer.

Poeppel, David, and Ken Wexler. 1993. The full competence hypothesis of clause structure in early German. *Language* 69:1–33.

Radford, Andrew. 1990. *Syntactic theory and the acquisition of English syntax.* Oxford: Blackwell.

Reinhart, Tanya. 1976. The syntactic domain of anaphora. Doctoral dissertation, MIT, Cambridge, Mass.

Rizzi, Luigi. 1993/1994. Some notes on linguistic theory and language development: The case of root infinitives. *Language Acquisition* 3:371–394.

Rizzi, Luigi. 2004. On the grammatical basis of language development: A case study. In *The handbook of comparative syntax*, ed. Guglielmo Cinque and Richard Kayne, 70–109. Oxford: Oxford University Press.

Saito, Mamoru. 1985. Some asymmetries in Japanese and their theoretical implications. Doctoral dissertation, MIT, Cambridge, Mass.

Saito, Mamoru. 1989. Scrambling as semantically vacuous A'-movement. In *Alternative conceptions of phrase structure*, ed. Mark R. Baltin and Anthony S. Kroch, 182–200. Chicago: University of Chicago Press.

Saito, Mamoru, and Naoki Fukui. 1998. Order in phrase structure and movement. *Linguistic Inquiry* 29:439–474.

Saito, Mamoru, and Hajime Hoji. 1983. Weak crossover and move α in Japanese. *Natural Language & Linguistic Theory* 1:245–259.

Sano, Keiko. 1977. An experimental study on the acquisition of Japanese simple sentences and cleft sentences. *Descriptive and Applied Linguistics* 10:213–233.

Sano, Tetsuya. 2000. Issues on unaccusatives and passives in the acquisition of Japanese. In *Proceedings of the 1st Tokyo Conference on Psycholinguistics*, ed. Yukio Otsu, 1–22. Tokyo: Hituzi Syobo.

Sano, Tetsuya. 2002. *Roots in language acquisition: A comparative study of Japanese and European languages.* Tokyo: Hituzi Syobo.

Sano, Tetsuya, Mika Endo, and Kyoko Yamakoshi. 2001. Developmental issues in the acquisition of Japanese unaccusatives and passives. In *Proceedings of the 25th annual Boston University Conference on Language Development*, ed. Anna H.-J. Do, Laura Dominguez, and Aimee Johansen, 668–683. Somerville, Mass.: Cascadilla Press.

Snyder, William. 1995. Language acquisition and language variation: The role of morphology. Doctoral dissertation, MIT, Cambridge, Mass.

Snyder, William. 2001. On the nature of syntactic variation: Evidence from complex predicates and complex word-formation. *Language* 77:324–342.

Snyder, William. 2002. Parameters: The view from child language. In *Proceedings of the 3rd Tokyo Conference on Psycholinguistics*, ed. Yukio Otsu, 27–44. Tokyo: Hituzi Syobo.

Snyder, William, Nina Hyams, and Paola Crisma. 1995. Romance auxiliary selection with reflexive clitics: Evidence for early knowledge of unaccusativity. In *Proceedings of the 26th annual Child Language Research Forum*, ed. Eve Clark, 127–136. Stanford, Calif.: CSLI Publications.

Stowell, Timothy. 1981. Origins of phrase structure. Doctoral dissertation, MIT, Cambridge, Mass.

Sugisaki, Koji. 1999. Japanese passives in acquisition. In *Cranberry Linguistics: UConnWPL 10*, ed. Dave Braze, Kazuko Hiramatsu, and Yutaka Kudo, 145–156. Cambridge, Mass.: MIT Working Papers in Linguistics.

Sugisaki, Koji. 2000. LF *wh*-movement in child Japanese: A preliminary study. In *UConnWPL 11: The syntax-semantics interface*, ed. Cedric Boeckx, Luisa Marti, and Douglas Wharram. Cambridge, Mass.: MIT Working Papers in Linguistics.

Sugisaki, Koji. 2003. Innate constraints on language variation: Evidence from child language. Doctoral dissertation, University of Connecticut, Storrs.

Sugisaki, Koji. 2005. Early acquisition of basic word order: New evidence from Japanese. In *Proceedings of the 29th annual Boston University Conference on Language Development*, ed. Alejna Brugos, Manuella R. Clark-Cotton, and Seungwan Ha, 582–591. Somerville, Mass.: Cascadilla Press.

Sugisaki, Koji, and Miwa Isobe. 2000. Resultatives result from the compounding parameter: On the acquisitional correlation between resultatives and N-N compounds in Japanese. In *Proceedings of the 19th West Coast Conference on Formal Linguistics*, ed. Roger Billerey and Brook Danielle Lillehaugen, 493–506. Somerville, Mass.: Cascadilla Press.

Sugisaki, Koji, and Miwa Isobe. 2001. What can child Japanese tell us about the syntax of scrambling? In *Proceedings of the 20th West Coast Conference on Formal Linguistics*, ed. Karine Megerdoomian and Leora A. Bar-el, 538–551. Somerville, Mass.: Cascadilla Press.

Suzuki, Seiichi 1987. Youji no bunpo nouryoku [Childen's grammatical competence]. In *Kodomo no gengo shinri* [Language and psychology in children], ed. S. Fukuzawa, 141–180. Tokyo: Dainihon Tosho.

Tada, Hiroaki. 1993. A/A' partition in derivation. Doctoral dissertation, MIT, Cambridge, Mass.

Takezawa, Koichi. 1987. A configurational approach to Case marking in Japanese. Doctoral dissertation, University of Washington, Seattle.

Tanaka, Hidekazu. 2001. Right-dislocation as scrambling. *Journal of Linguistics* 37:551–579.
Thornton, Rosalind. 2001. A-movement in early English. In *Proceedings of the 2nd Tokyo Conference on Psycholinguistics*, ed. Yukio Otsu, 227–250. Tokyo: Hituzi Syobo.
Thornton, Rosalind, and Kenneth Wexler. 1999. *Principle B, VP ellipsis, and interpretation in child grammar*. Cambridge, Mass.: MIT Press.
Vainikka, Anne.1993/1994. Case in the development of English syntax, *Language Acquisition* 3:257–325.
Valian, Virginia. 1991. Syntactic subjects in the early speech of American and Italian children. *Cognition* 40:21–81.
Washio, Ryuichi. 1989/1990. The Japanese passive. *Linguistic Review* 6:227–263.
Wexler, Kenneth. 1994. Optional infinitives, head movement, and the economy of derivations. In *Verb movement*, ed. David Lightfoot and Norbert Hornstein, 305–350. Cambridge: Cambridge University Press.
Wexler, Kenneth. 1996. The development of inflection in a biologically based theory of language acquisition. In *Toward a genetics of language*, ed. Mabel. L. Rice, 113–144. Mahwah, N.J.: Lawrence Erlbaum.
Wexler, Kenneth. 1998. Very early parameter setting and the unique checking constraint: A new explanation of the optional infinitive stage. *Lingua* 106:23–79.
Wexler, Kenneth. 2004. Theory of phasal development: Perfection in child grammar. In *MITWPL 48: Papers on language acquisition*, ed. Aniko Csirmaz, Andrea Gualmini, and Andrew Nevins, 159–209. Cambridge, Mass.: MIT Working Papers in Linguistics.
Yokoyama, Masayuki. 1990. Youji no rentai syuusyoku hatuwa ni okeru josi "no" no goyoo [Errors of particle "no" of young Japanese children in adjective-noun constructions]. *Hattatu Sinrigaku Kenkyuu* 1:2–9.

CHAPTER 11

THE SYNTAX AND SEMANTICS OF FLOATING NUMERAL QUANTIFIERS

KIMIKO NAKANISHI

11.1 INTRODUCTION

It is well known that a numeral quantifier in Japanese can appear in various locations, as illustrated in (1).[1,2]

(1) a. Kinoo   [**san-nin**-no   *kasyu*]-ga   utat-ta.
       yesterday   [three-CL-GEN singer]-NOM   sing-PAST
       'Three singers sang yesterday.'
    b. Kinoo   [*kasyu*   **san-nin**]-ga   utat-ta.
       yesterday   [singer   three-CL]-NOM   sing-PAST
    c. *Kasyu*-ga   kinoo   **san-nin**   utat-ta.
       singer-NOM yesterday   three-CL   sing-PAST

Over the past few decades, this paradigm has attracted a great deal of attention. Especially important among various issues discussed in the literature, and at the same time controversial, is the following question: how is the configuration in (1c) syntactically derived?[3] Although researchers agree that the numeral and the host NP *kasyu* 'singer' are in the same nominal projection in (1a) and (1b), opinions vary as to the status of (1c), where the numeral appears away from its host NP.[4]

There are at least two competing views addressing this question. One view holds that the numeral and host NP in (1c) are adjacent in the underlying structure and that the host NP moves somewhere higher in the structure, stranding the numeral. Under this view, the numeral in (1c) is "floated" in that it is left behind after the movement of the host NP, hence it has traditionally been called a floating numeral quantifier (FNQ). Another view holds that the numeral in (1c) is base generated as an adjunct to a verbal projection, just like an adverb. Under the second view, the numeral in (1c) is not floated, but rather it is base generated in situ. I refer to the family of proposals related to the first view as the "stranding view" and ones related to the second view as the "adverb view." Furthermore, I use the term "FNQ" simply to refer to the numeral in (1c) without implicating the stranding view. One of the main goals of this chapter is to shed light on some theoretical implications that emerge from the studies on FNQs by examining how the two competing theories fare with some characteristic syntactic and semantic properties of FNQs.

One core set of data comes from the well-known word-order restriction on FNQs: the subject and its FNQ need to be adjacent, as in (2a,a′), whereas the object and its FNQ need not, as in (2b) (Haig 1980, Kuroda 1980).

(2) a. *Gakusei-ga hon-o **san-nin** kat-ta.
    student-NOM book-ACC three-CL buy-PAST
    'Three students bought a book/books.'
  a′. Gakusei-ga **san-nin** hon-o kat-ta.
    student-NOM three-CL book-ACC buy-PAST
  b. Hon-o gakusei-ga **san-satu** kat-ta.
    book-ACC student-NOM three-CL buy-PAST
    'A student/Students bought three books.'

Ever since it was first noted in the literature, many researchers have attempted to account for the nature of this restriction. One of the most influential attempts can be found in Miyagawa's (1989) stranding analysis, which has been successful in accounting for various distributional restrictions on FNQs, including (2). However, this view has been challenged by alternative theories—most notably, the adverb view. The adverb view is supported by the existence of numerous counterexamples to distributional restrictions on FNQs, including counterexamples to (2). Another piece of evidence for the adverb view comes from the observation that FNQs are subject to some semantic restrictions that can be straightforwardly explained if the FNQs are VP- (or V′-) adjoined adverbs. In the following, I discuss these issues in more detail and examine the two views in light of various empirical data.

11.2 THE STRANDING VIEW AND ITS SYNTACTIC IMPLICATIONS

We have seen that, although Japanese FNQs need not be adjacent to their host NP in the surface, as in (1c) and (2b), it is not the case that FNQs can appear anywhere in a sentence, as in (2a). Indeed, it has been argued that, besides (2a), there are more distributional restrictions on FNQs, which are discussed shortly. The question then is what the source of such distributional restrictions is. Miyagawa (1989) answers this question by claiming that the distribution of FNQs is principled by some structural conditions—namely, c-command requirements. He first observes that the FNQ is unacceptable when it does not c-command its host NP. This observation is based on data such as in (3), where the difference in grammaticality is accounted for by the difference in structures.

(3) a. Tomodati-ga **huta-ri** Sinzyuku-de at-ta.
 friend-NOM two-CL Sinzyuku-in meet-PAST
 'Two friends met in Sinzyuku.'
 b. *Tomodati-ga Sinzyuku-de **huta-ri** at-ta.
 friend-NOM Sinzyuku-in two-CL meet-PAST (Miyagawa 1989:28)

Miyagawa suggests that the FNQ is a secondary predicate that does not form a constituent with the host NP (see also Ueda 1986, Miyamoto 1994), admitting ternary-branching structures (but see shortly below for a modification). Then, assuming that subjects are generated outside of the VP and that *Sinzyuku-de* is VP-internal, Miyagawa obtains (4a) as the structure for (3a), where the host NP, the FNQ, and the VP are sisters. In this structure, the FNQ c-commands its host NP (and vice versa). In contrast, in (3b), if *Sinzyuku-de* is VP-internal, the FNQ must also be VP-internal, yielding the structure in (4b). Because the FNQ in this structure does not c-command the host NP, (3b) is ungrammatical.

(4) a. [s Tomodati-ga **huta-ri** [VP Sinzyuku-de at-ta]]
 b. [s Tomodati-ga [VP Sinzyuku-de **huta-ri** at-ta]]

Note that, unlike (3b), examples such as (1c) are grammatical. The contrast naturally follows from the assumption that temporal adverbs such as *kinoo* 'yesterday' are VP-external. Then, in (1c), the host NP, the temporal adverb, the FNQ, and the VP are considered to be sisters. In this structure, the FNQ c-commands its host NP (and vice versa), just as in (4a).

Miyagawa further observes that the c-commanding in the other direction must hold—that is, the host NP must c-command the FNQ, based on data such as in (5) (and (8) below). In (5), the classifier *-nin* in the FNQ semantically agrees with *tomodati* 'friend' but not with *kuruma* 'car'. Under the intended interpretation, the host NP *tomodati* 'friend', being embedded, cannot c-command the FNQ, although the FNQ c-commands the host NP.

(5) *[Tomodati-no kuruma]-ga **san-nin** kosyoosi-ta.
    [friend-GEN car]-NOM three-CL break down-PAST
    'Three friends' car(s) broke down.' (Miyagawa 1989:29)

Based on these observations, Miyagawa argues that, for FNQs to be well formed, they must satisfy the mutual c-command requirement in (6).[5]

(6) Mutual c-command requirement: The NP or its trace and the numeral or its trace must c-command each other. (Miyagawa 1989:30)

Miyagawa further shows that the mutual c-command requirement is capable of accounting for the well-known observation that an FNQ can be associated with an argument but not an adjunct (Okutsu 1969, Harada 1976, Shibatani 1977, Inoue 1978, Kuno 1978b). More specifically, whereas subjects, objects, and what Inoue (1978) calls "quasi-objects" (such as the dative object in (7c)) are possible antecedents of the FNQ, as in (7), PPs cannot host the FNQ, as in (8).

(7) a. *Gakusei*-ga **san-nin** hon-o kat-ta.
       student-NOM three-CL book-ACC buy-PAST
       'Three students bought the book.' (Miyagawa 1989:24)
    b. Hanako-ga *pen*-o **san-bon** kat-ta.
       Hanako-NOM pen-ACC three-CL buy-PAST
       'Hanako bought three pens.' (Miyagawa 1989:24)
    c. Boku-wa *yuumeina gakusya*-ni **san-nin** at-ta.
       I-TOP famous scholar-DAT three-CL meet-PAST
       'I met three famous scholars.' (Miyagawa 1989:35)

(8) a. *Gakuseitati-wa *kuruma*-de **ni-dai** ki-ta.
       students-TOP car-in two-CL come-PAST
       'Students came in two cars.' (Miyagawa 1989:31)
    b. *Kyonen, Hanako-wa *paatii*-ni **mit-tu** ki-ta.
       last year Hanako-TOP party-to three-CL come-PAST
       'Last year, Hanako came to three parties.' (Miyagawa 1989:36)

Miyagawa claims that there is a structural difference between arguments and adjuncts; the particles in (7) are cliticized onto the NP, whereas the particles in (8) have their own projection. With these structures, the difference in grammaticality between (7) and (8) naturally follows from the mutual c-command requirement. In (7), the NP, FNQ, and VP are sisters, and so the mutual c-command requirement is met. In (8), however, assuming that the host NP is embedded in the PP whose head is -*de* 'in' or -*ni* 'to', the host NP cannot c-command the FNQ.

Most significantly, by applying the mutual c-command requirement to subsequent empirical data on FNQs, Miyagawa argues that the FNQs give evidence for NP trace (see Sportiche 1988 for the same line of argument based on English and French data; see also McCloskey 2000). The crucial examples are presented in (9), where an FNQ can be associated with the subject of a passive verb (in (9a)) or an unaccusative verb (in (9b)) but not with the subject of an unergative verb (in (9c)).

(9) a. *Kuruma*-ga   doroboo-ni   **ni-dai**   nusum-are-ta.
       car-NOM   thief-by   two-CL   steal-PASS-PAST
       'Two cars were stolen by a thief.'   (Miyagawa 1989:38)
   b. *Gakusei*-ga   ofisu-ni   **huta-ri**   ki-ta.
       student-NOM   office-to   two-CL   come-PAST
       'Two students came to the office.'   (Miyagawa 1989:43)
   c. **Kodomo*-ga   geragerato   **huta-ri**   warat-ta.
       children-NOM loudly   two-CL   laugh-PAST
       'Two children laughed loudly.'   (Miyagawa 1989:44)

The key to Miyagawa's analysis comes from the well-known hypothesis that the subject of a passive verb and that of an unaccusative verb differ from the subject of an unergative verb in that they are base generated as the object of the verb (Perlmutter 1978, among others). Miyagawa points out that, if we adopt this hypothesis, the contrast in (9) naturally follows. In (9), the PPs and the adverb (i.e., *doroboo-ni*, *ofisu-ni*, and *geragerato*) are assumed to be in the VP, which indicates that the FNQs are also in the VP. Suppose that the subjects in (9a,b) are base generated in the object position—that is, the position adjacent to the FNQ in the VP—and that they move out of the VP, stranding the FNQ, as schematized in (10a). In this case, positing the existence of the NP trace on the left of the FNQ, the mutual c-command requirement is met; the trace of the host NP and the FNQ c-command each other. In contrast, the subject of the unergative verb in (9c) originates at a VP-external position, as in (10b). In this structure, the FNQ cannot c-command its host NP, hence the mutual c-command requirement is violated.

(10) a. NP_1 [$_{VP}$ PP/Adv t_1 **FNQ** V]
     b. NP [$_{VP}$ PP/Adv   **FNQ** V]

Miyagawa's analysis is further supported by the fact that the subject of a transitive verb cannot be associated with an FNQ when a VP-internal PP or adverb intervenes, as in (11). Just like in the case of unergative verbs, there is no trace of the subject adjacent to the FNQ, hence the mutual c-command requirement cannot be satisfied.

(11) ?**Kodomo*-ga   kono   kagi-de   **huta-ri**   doa-o   ake-ta.
      child-NOM   this   key-with   two-CL   door-ACC   open-PAST
      'Two children opened a door with this key.'   (Miyagawa 1989:44)

In sum, by positing an NP trace, Miyagawa's analysis of FNQs explains why the subjects of unaccusative or passive verbs, but not the subjects of unergative or transitive verbs, can be associated with a VP-internal FNQ.[6] The subjects in the first group, being VP-internal arguments, originate in the object position, and so the trace of the subject and the FNQ can c-command each other. In contrast, the subjects in the second group, being VP-external arguments, do not originate as objects, thus failing to satisfy the mutual c-command requirement.

Although ternary-branching structures were permitted at the time of Miyagawa's (1989) proposal, all structures are considered to be binary in recent syntactic theories, assuming that structures are built by an operation called Merge (Chomsky 1995). To accommodate this, Miyagawa and Arikawa (2007) modify Miyagawa's (1989) original proposal and assume that the FNQ and its host NP form a nominal constituent (such as a Num[ber] phrase), following some previous work (Kamio 1977, 1983; Terada 1990; Kawashima 1998; Watanabe 2006, among others). This modification makes it possible to maintain the mutual c-command analysis even without ternary-branching structures. In (12), which is a modification of (10a), the trace of the host NP and the FNQ c-command each other.[7] Furthermore, in (1c), assuming that temporal adverbs such as *kinoo* 'yesterday' are adjoined somewhere higher in the structure (say, to vP), we can posit a structure in (13). In this structure, the trace of the subject and the FNQ c-command each other. In the following, adopting this modification, I assume that the FNQ and its host NP are in the same nominal projection under Miyagawa's stranding analysis.

(12) NP_1 [$_{VP}$ PP/Adv [$_{VP}$ [$_{NumP}$ t_1 **FNQ**] V]]

(13) NP_1 [$_{vP}$ Adv [$_{vP}$ [$_{NumP}$ t_1 **FNQ**] [$_{VP}$ O V]]]

Let us now go back to the word-order restriction in (2), which is repeated in (14), and see whether the mutual c-command requirement is capable of explaining this restriction.

(14) a. **Gakusei*-ga hon-o **san-nin** kat-ta.
         student-NOM book-ACC three-CL buy-PAST
         'Three students bought a book/books.'
      b. *Hon*-o gakusei-ga **san-satu** kat-ta.
         book-ACC student-NOM three-CL buy-PAST
         'A student/Student(s) bought three books.'

We could argue that (14a) is ungrammatical because there is no subject trace to the right of the object, as in (15a). In contrast, in (14b), the object is base generated within the VP and has undergone scrambling, leaving the trace to the right of the subject, as in (15b).

(15) a. S [$_{VP}$ O **FNQ** V]
      b. O_1 S [$_{VP}$ [$_{NumP}$ t_1 **FNQ**] V]]

However, there is a potential problem for the analysis of (14a) given in (15a). Presumably, (14a) can be derived if both the subject and object scramble, as in (16). The mutual c-command requirement is met in (16), which predicts (14a) to be grammatical.

(16) S_1 O_2 [[$_{NumP}$ t_1 **FNQ**] [$_{VP}$ t_2 V]]

To exclude this unwanted derivation, Saito (1985) claims that subjects in Japanese cannot undergo scrambling.[8,9] As Miyagawa and Arikawa put it, this claim is an economy statement banning string-vacuous movement. Clause-internal subject scrambling is often string vacuous, and thus it is difficult to provide a solid argument for such scrambling.

Summing up the discussion so far, Miyagawa (1989) observes that there is a certain syntactic locality constraint on the dependency between an FNQ and its host NP and further claims that the locality constraint can be formulated as the structural requirement of mutual c-command in (6). His claim is based on two kinds of distributional restrictions—one that is considered as a purely structural restriction, and the other that serves as a piece of evidence for an NP trace, as summarized in (17).

(17) Distributional restrictions on FNQs
Structural restrictions
 a. *Embedded NP as the host NP; (5)
 b. *NP within PP as the host NP; (8)
Locality restrictions
 c. *External argument as the host NP with a VP-internal adverb/PP; (3), (9), (11)
 d. *S_i-O-FNQ_i; (2)

As for the first kind, we have seen that an NP embedded within another NP cannot be associated with an FNQ in the main clause (e.g., (5)), and that the host NP must be an argument but not an adjunct (e.g., (7), (8)). As for the second kind, we have seen that the distributional restrictions on FNQs in (2), (3), (9), and (11) can be explained by positing the existence of an NP trace within the VP. More precisely, Miyagawa's analysis accounts for why internal arguments, but not external ones, can host an FNQ when a VP-internal modifier intervenes between the host NP and its FNQ (e.g., (3), (9), (11)). The analysis is also capable of explaining why the object cannot intervene between the subject and its FNQ (henceforth *S_i-O-FNQ_i, where the index i indicates that S and FNQ are associated with each other), whereas the subject can intervene between the object and its FNQ (e.g., (2)).

If Miyagawa's analysis is on the right track, it makes a strong prediction about where FNQs appear in a sentence: FNQs should be observed only at positions from (or through) which the host NP has moved (see also Sportiche 1988, McCloskey 2000). This approach to Japanese FNQs has come to be widely accepted, and FNQs are considered as one of the most significant diagnostics to investigate phrase structure and syntactic movement in the Japanese language. For instance, in the literature on Japanese syntax, FNQs have been used to examine where a certain NP originates in the structure (see, e.g., Takano, this volume). Moreover, FNQs can play a role in determining whether a certain NP is an internal or an external argument, as shown in (9) and (11).

11.3 CONTROVERSIES

In the previous section, we have seen that under the stranding view, a number of distributional restrictions on FNQs fall under a syntactic locality constraint on the dependency between an FNQ and its host NP. Thus, FNQs serve as a powerful tool for investigating Japanese syntax. This section reveals that the stranding view, powerful as it may be, is not without problems. First, I show in section 11.3.1 that the distributional restrictions on FNQs presented in section 11.2 are challenged by numerous counterexamples. Section 11.3.2 summarizes some attempts to cope with the counterexamples under the stranding view. Section 11.3.3 presents some semantic restrictions on FNQs that may be problematic to the analyses presented in section 11.3.2. Then, in section 11.3.4, I explore an alternative analysis—namely, the adverb view. In section 11.3.5, I briefly discuss examples where FNQs have different properties depending on prosody.

11.3.1 Counterexamples to the Stranding View

As shown in section 11.2, the stranding view is supported by the observation that the distribution of FNQs is syntactically restricted. However, a number of linguists object to the empirical generalization in (17) (Fukushima 1991; Katagiri 1991; Kikuchi 1994; Hamano 1997; Mihara 1998; Takami 1998, 2001; Gunji and Hashida 1998; Ishii 1999; Nishigauchi and Ishii 2003). First, (18) and (19) are grammatical even though the mutual c-command requirement is violated. In particular, in (18), contra (5), the host NP is within another NP, and so it cannot c-command the FNQ.[10] In (19), contra (8), the host NP is within a PP, thus it cannot c-command the FNQ.

(18) a. Yamada Sensei-ga [*gakusei*-no kami]-o **san-nin** kit-ta.
Yamada Professor-NOM [student-GEN hair]-ACC three-CL cut-PAST
'Prof. Yamada cut three students' hair.' (Takami 2001:137)
b. Ano isya-wa [*zidoo*-no me]-o **sanzyuu-nin** sirabe-ta.
that doctor-TOP [pupil-GEN eye]-ACC thirty-CL examine-PAST
'That doctor examined thirty pupils' eyes.' (Kikuchi 1994:82)

(19) a. Gantan-ni *osiego*-kara **go-nin** nengazyoo-o morat-ta.
New Year's Day-on my student-from five-CL card-ACC receive-PAST
'(I) received a card from five students of mine on New Year's Day.'
b. *Gakusei*-kara **nizyuu-mei-izyoo** okane-o atume-nakerebanaranai.
student-from twenty-CL-or more money-ACC collect-must
'(We) must collect money from twenty students or more.'
(Takami 2001:128–129)

Second, there are examples where the FNQ is licensed even when there is no NP trace adjacent to the FNQ. In (20), unlike in (9c) and (11), the subject of an unergative verb or a transitive verb hosts the FNQ, even with a VP-internal modifier intervening between the subject and the FNQ. The structure of these sentences is given in (21). The stranding view would predict these examples to be ungrammatical because the FNQ does not c-command the host NP in (21).

(20) a. *Kodomo*-ga butai-de **zyuu-nin** odot-ta.
child-NOM stage-at ten-CL dance-PAST
'Ten children danced at the stage.' (Takami 2001:129)

b. *Gakusei*-ga tosyokan-de **go-nin** benkyoosi-tei-ta.
   student-NOM library-at five-CL study-PROG-PAST
   'Five students were studying at the library.' (Mihara 1998:89)
c. *Gakusei*-ga naihu-de koremadeni **huta-ri** te-o kegasi-ta.
   student-NOM knife-with so-far five-CL hand-ACC injure-PAST
   'So far two students injured their hands with the knife.'
   (Fukushima 1991:52)

(21) NP [$_{VP}$ PP/Adv [$_{VP}$ **FNQ** (O) V]]

The examples in (22) serve as counterexamples to the observation in (2) that the object cannot intervene between the subject and its FNQ.

(22) a. A: Kono sinkan zassi uretemasu-ka?
        this new magazine is selling-Q
        'Is this new magazine selling well?'
     B: Ee, kesa-mo gakuseisan-ga sore-o **go-nin**
        Yes this morning-also student-NOM it-ACC five-CL
        katteikimasitayo.
        bought
        'Yes, five students bought it this morning.'
   b. Boku-wa apaato zumai-dakedo,
      I-TOP apartment living-although
      saikin *dooryoo*-ga ie-o **si, go-nin**
      recently colleague-NOM house-ACC four, five-CL
      tugitugito tate-ta.
      one-after-another build-CL
      'Although I live in an apartment, four or five colleagues built a house one after another recently.'
   c. *Gakusei*-ga repooto-o **san-nin**-dake teisyutusi-ta.
      student-NOM report-ACC three-CL-only hand in-PAST
      'Only three students handed in a report.' (Takami 2001:125–126)

Crucially, the object appears between the subject and its FNQ in these examples. This order is predicted to be unacceptable under the stranding view because there is no trace of the subject adjacent to the FNQ (see (15a)), hence the violation of the mutual c-command requirement.

These counterexamples challenge the validity of the stranding view. Especially important are the examples in (20) and (22) that cast doubt on the locality restriction between the FNQ and its host NP, which further leads us to the question of whether FNQs provide a solid diagnostic to investigate phrase structures, as has been assumed under the stranding view. In the case of (20), we may be able to say that the adverbs in these examples are adjoined not to VP but somewhere higher in the structure in the same way as temporal adverbs, as in (13) (although this is inconsistent with (4b)). If we were to adopt the structure in (13) as a structure of the sentences in (20), then the mutual c-command requirement would be met in (20). However, in (22), there does not seem to be any obvious way of saving the stranding view without any major modification to the theory, and thus the fact that the S$_i$-O-FNQ$_i$ order is (at least sometimes) acceptable remains a problem for the stranding view. The researchers who present the counterexamples in (22) argue that an FNQ and its host NP need not observe strict locality, and they advocate alternative analyses to the stranding view. The most prominent would be the adverb view where the FNQ is considered as a VP- (or a V'-) adverb that does not necessarily have a locality dependency with its host NP.[11] Clearly, the stranding and adverb views make different predictions about locality: the stranding view predicts that the FNQ and its host NP show certain locality restrictions (hence *S$_i$-O-FNQ$_i$), whereas the adverb view predicts that they need not show any locality restrictions (hence S$_i$-O-FNQ$_i$ is acceptable). On empirical grounds, however, S$_i$-O-FNQ$_i$ is sometimes acceptable, as in (2), and sometimes not, as in (22). Then, whichever view we adopt, we are faced with the questions in (23).

(23) a. Under the stranding view: why is S$_i$-O-FNQ$_i$ sometimes acceptable?
b. Under the adverb view: why is S$_i$-O-FNQ$_i$ sometimes unacceptable?

Along the way, I examine a possibility of maintaining both views that may eliminate the questions in (23) all together. I also review how different approaches cope with the counterexamples to the stranding view other than (22) (namely, (18), (19), and (20)).

11.3.2 Reconsideration of Locality

As briefly sketched above, the researchers who offered the counterexamples in (22), where S$_i$-O-FNQ$_i$ is acceptable, conclude that no locality is required between the FNQ and its host NP and thus reject the stranding view on the basis of such examples. In contrast, some researchers argue that the examples in (22) need not be considered as counterexamples to the stranding view. In other words, it is possible to maintain the stranding view even with the existence of examples such as (22). In section 11.3.2.1, I first review Miyagawa and Arikawa's (2007) claim that locality is preserved even in (22). Then, in section 11.3.2.2, I turn to Ishii's (1999) claim that the FNQs in (22) are different in nature from FNQs that obey locality.

11.3.2.1 *The stranding view*

Miyagawa and Arikawa (2007) acknowledge the examples in (22), but they claim that these examples are not counterexamples to locality. More precisely, they argue that the sentences in (22) are associated with a different structure from the structure of the ungrammatical S$_i$-O-FNQ$_i$ sentence and that syntactic locality is preserved in (22), maintaining the stranding view advanced by Miyagawa (1989). Let us illustrate their point by examining the examples in (24).

(24) a. *Gakusei*-ga   sake-o   **san-nin** non-da.
student-NOM sake-ACC three-CL drink-PAST
'Three students drank sake.'   (Gunji and Hashida 1998:47)

b. ?*Gakusei*-ga   sake-o   imamadeni **san-nin** non-da.
   student-NOM sake-ACC so far   three-CL drink-PAST
   'Three students drank sake so far.'   (Gunji and Hashida 1998:57)

Example (24a) is a case of Haig/Kuroda's "standard" paradigm where the S$_i$-O-FNQ$_i$ order is ungrammatical, whereas (24b) is a case of the "nonstandard" paradigm. Miyagawa and Arikawa argue that the two are structurally different and that the difference is marked by prosody. In (24a), in the neutral intonational contour, the FNQ and the preceding object are pronounced in the same intonation phrase. This pattern would wrongly lead us to the interpretation where the FNQ is associated with the object rather than with the subject. In contrast, in (24b), the stress is on the adverb *imamadeni* 'so far', which marks the FNQ to be phrasally separate from the object, unlike in (24a).

Then the question is: what structure is (24b) associated with? Instead of arguing that (24b) is insensitive to locality, Miyagawa and Arikawa argue that the strict locality holds in this case. In particular, they claim that the subject in Japanese may scramble (following Ko 2005 but contra Saito 1985) and provide a derivation in (25) for (24b) (as well as for (22)). They present various arguments showing that, whenever the S$_i$-O-FNQ$_i$ order is acceptable, the object has moved outside of the *v*P and the subject has undergone A'-scrambling (but see Hoji and Ishii 2004 for arguments against this claim).[12] Crucially, the mutual c-command requirement is met in this derivation—that is, there is no locality violation in (24b) and (22). Thus, under this analysis, the examples in (24b) and (22) are not considered as counterexamples to the stranding view.

(25)   [$_{TP}$ S$_1$ [$_{TP}$ O$_2$ [$_{vP}$ t'$_2$ [$_{NumP}$ t$_1$ **FNQ**] [$_{VP}$ t$_2$ V]]]]

Miyagawa and Arikawa's analysis would then predict that the S$_i$-O-FNQ$_i$ order is grammatical whenever prosody signals the object and the FNQ to be in a separate intonation phrase, just as in (24b). This prediction does not seem to be borne out, as shown in (26). In (26), the stress seems to naturally fall on the adverb *huunnimo* 'unfortunately', yielding the same prosodic pattern as (24b).[13] However, (26) is much more degraded than (24b), according to my informants' and my own judgments. In this way, prosodic patterns with grammatical and ungrammatical S$_i$-O-FNQ$_i$ examples are not as clear-cut as Miyagawa and Arikawa describe.

(26)   ??*Gakusei*-ga   sake-o   huunnimo   **san-nin** non-da.
   student-NOM sake-ACC unfortunately three-CL drink-PAST
   'Unfortunately, three students drank sake.'

11.3.2.2 *The "hybrid" view*

A different approach has been proposed by Ishii (1999). Ishii argues that the mixed acceptability of S$_i$-O-FNQ$_i$ is due to the existence of two types of FNQs. When S$_i$-O-FNQ$_i$ is unacceptable, the sentence involves a stranding of the FNQ, which then predicts that the FNQ obeys a locality constraint (hence *S$_i$-O-FNQ$_i$). In contrast, when S$_i$-O-FNQ$_i$ is acceptable, the FNQ is an adverb, which predicts that we do not necessarily observe a locality constraint (hence S_i-O-FNQ_i is acceptable). In the following, I refer to Ishii's approach as the "hybrid" view. The hybrid view is motivated by semantic considerations of FNQs. What plays a crucial role here is a distinction between distributive and nondistributive interpretations proposed by Kitagawa and Kuroda (1992): "the distributive construal necessarily implies the occurrence of multiple events while the non-distributive construal implies the occurrence of only a single event" (pages 88–89). In (27), these two interpretations are forced by the temporal expressions *kono issyuukan-no aida-ni* 'during this week' ((27a); distributive only) and *sono toki totuzen* 'then suddenly' ((27b); nondistributive only).

(27) a. Kono issyuukan-no aida-ni *syuuzin*-ga **san-nin** nigedasi-ta.
　　　　this　week　　　　 during　prisoner-NOM three-CL escape-PAST
　　　　'There have been three jailbreaks during the past week.'
　　b. Sono toki totuzen　*syuuzin*-ga　　**san-nin**　abaredasi-ta.
　　　　then　suddenly　prisoner-NOM three-CL start-to-act-violently-PAST
　　　　'Then, a group of three prisoners suddenly started acting violently.'
　　　　　　　　　　　　　　　　　　　　　　(Kitagawa and Kuroda 1992:89)

Ishii claims that the counterexamples to the mutual c-command requirement permit a distributive reading but not a nondistributive reading. Let us go back to example (22a). According to Ishii, this sentence can mean that each of the five students bought a copy of the new magazine separately (distributive) but cannot mean that the five students together bought a single copy (nondistributive).[14] Similarly, in (22b), the distributive reading is enforced by *tugitugito* 'one after another'. Moreover, (22c) lacks the nondistributive reading where three students handed in a single paper. Ishii's claim is further supported by (28), where *ubaiau* 'to fight over' forces a nondistributive reading.

(28)　A:　Kono zassi　　ninki arimasu-ka?
　　　　　this　magazine is-popular-Q
　　　　　'Is this magazine popular?'
　　　B: *Ee,　　sakki-mo　　　　sokode *gakuseisan*-ga saisin-goo-o
　　　　　Yes　a-while-ago-also　there　 student-NOM　recent-issue-ACC
　　　　　go-nin ubaiatteimasitayo.
　　　　　five-CL were-fighting-over
　　　　　'Yes. In fact, five students were fighting over the most recent issue over there just a while ago.'
　　　B': Ee, sakki-mo sokode *gakuseisan*-ga **go-nin** saisin-goo-o ubaiatteimasitayo.
　　　　　　　　　　　　　　　　　　　　　　(Nishigauchi and Ishii 2003:78)

As in (28B), the sentence is unacceptable when the mutual c-command requirement is violated (due to the S_i-O-FNQ_i order), whereas it is acceptable, as in (28B'), when there is no locality violation. The observation here leads Ishii to claim that there are two types of FNQs—the stranding type and the adverb type. The stranding type is not sensitive to any semantic restriction, but it must obey the mutual c-command requirement. The adverb type is identified by the semantic restriction of having only a distributive interpretation. FNQs of this type, being adverbs, need not satisfy the mutual c-command requirement.

Ishii further argues that the other counterexamples to the stranding view presented above also involve the adverb-type FNQ. In (18), we have seen that sentences can be acceptable even when the host NP, being embedded in another NP, does not c-command the FNQ. The examples in (29) show that such examples only have a distributive interpretation.

(29) a. ?*Hora, ima soko-de isya-ga   [*zidoo*-no me]-o   **sanzyuu-nin**
         see   now there doctor-NOM [pupil-GEN eye]-ACC thirty-CL
         sirabete-imasuyo.
         examine-PROG
         'See, the doctor is examining thirty pupils' eyes over there now.'
    b. Ano isya-wa   kono ni-zikan-de [*zidoo*-no me]-o
         that doctor-TOP this two-hour-in [pupil-GEN eye]-ACC
         sanzyuu-ninsirabeta.
         thirty-CL   examined
         'That doctor examined thirty pupils' eyes during the last two hours.'
                                                              (Ishii 1999:247)

Example (18b) is unacceptable when a nondistributive reading is forced, as in (29a), although it is acceptable when a distributive reading is forced, as in (29b). In the same vein, examples such as (19)—namely, the examples where the host NP is within the PP—are unacceptable under a nondistributive interpretation, as in (30).

(30) *Itido-ni *gakusei*-kara   **nizyuu-mei-izyoo** okane-o
      at once   student-from twenty-CL-or   more money-ACC
      atumeru-no-wa muri-desu.
      collect-NL-TOP impossible-COP
      'It is impossible to collect money from twenty students or more at once.'
                                                              (Ishii 1999:245)

Let us summarize what we have seen so far in terms of locality. Recall that, under the stranding view, there needs to be a strict locality restriction on the dependency between an FNQ and its host NP, which predicts S_i-O-FNQ$_i$ to be unacceptable. Counterexamples such as (22) are problematic, as pointed out in (23a), and thus some modification needs to be made on the original stranding view (e.g., Miyagawa and Arikawa's [2007] proposal discussed above). In contrast, under the hybrid view, the questions in (23) do not arise in the first place. When S_i-O-FNQ$_i$ is disallowed, the FNQ is derived by stranding, hence there is a locality constraint. In contrast, when S_i-O-FNQ$_i$ is possible, the FNQ is an adverb, hence there is no locality constraint. In this sense, the examples in (22) are not really counterexamples to locality, but they simply involve a different type of FNQ, namely, the adverb type. The hybrid view keeps the stranding analysis intact in that FNQs of the stranding type are analyzed by the original stranding view.

11.3.3 Semantic Restrictions on FNQs

Recall that Ishii's (1999) motivation for advocating the two types of FNQs comes from the semantic restriction on FNQs that only a distributive reading is available when the mutual c-command requirement is violated. However, it has been observed in the literature that FNQs in general are subject to a semantic restriction of the kind discussed by Ishii (Terada 1990; Nakanishi 2004, 2007a, 2007b). For instance, the examples in (31) have a distributive but not a collective reading.[15,16]

(31) a. *Otokonoko*-ga kinoo **san-nin** omotya-no booto-o tukut-ta.
   boy-NOM yesterday three-CL toy-GEN boat-ACC make-PAST
   'Three boys made a toy boat/toy boats yesterday.'
b. *Tomodati*-ga kinoo **huta-ri** kekkonsi-ta.
   friend-NOM yesterday two-CL marry-PAST
   'Two friends got married yesterday.' (Nakanishi 2004:75)

Example (31a) means that each of the three boys made a toy boat (or toy boats), but it does not mean that the three boys together made a toy boat (or toy boats). In the same vein, (31b) can involve two friends, each of whom got married to someone (i.e., there are two couples), but it cannot mean that two friends married each other, which involves only one couple. Note that, under the stranding view, the mutual c-command requirement is satisfied in (31), unlike in (22) (see (1c) and its derivation in (13)). Then, the examples in (31) seem to indicate that there is no strict correlation between the locality requirement and the semantic restriction, contra Ishii (1999). It is true that, whenever S_i-O-FNQ$_i$ is acceptable, only the distributive reading is available. However, as shown in (31), this semantic restriction seems to be more widespread. The seeming generalization is that the semantic restriction is observed whenever FNQs appear away from their host NP on the surface, regardless of whether the mutual c-command requirement is satisfied.[17] Then it seems inappropriate to argue for the hybrid view simply on the basis of the semantic restriction on distributivity discussed in Ishii (1999).

Interestingly, unlike in (31a), both distributive and collective readings are available in (32).

(32) a. [**San-nin**-no *otokonoko*]-ga kinoo omotya-no booto-o tukut-ta.
   [three-CL-GEN boy]-NOM yesterday toy-GEN boat-ACC make-PAST
b. [*Otokonoko* **san-nin**]-ga kinoo omotya-no booto-o tukut-ta.
   [boy three-CL]-NOM yesterday toy-GEN boat-ACC make-PAST

As briefly mentioned in section 11.1, the researchers agree that the numerals in (32) (or the ones in (1a,b)) quantify over the nominal predicate. Then the fact that FNQs are semantically different from numerals that apparently quantify over nominal predicates may suggest that FNQs quantify over something else. More specifically, it has been argued that a range of semantic restrictions on FNQs indicates some semantic dependency between FNQs and verbal predicates (Fukushima 1991; Fujita 1994; Gunji and Hashida 1998; Nakanishi 2004, 2007a, 2007b, among others). Besides the data on distributivity discussed above, it has been observed that FNQs, but not numerals in a nominal projection, have a restriction on what kind of verbal predicates they can occur with. In particular, as shown in (33), FNQs are incompatible with verbal predicates denoting an event that can occur only once, although numerals in a nominal projection do not have such a restriction, as in (34) (Nakanishi 2004, 2007a, 2007b). This can be straightforwardly explained if FNQs involve quantification over events denoted by a verbal predicate. In (33b), the FNQ expresses that there are three events of killing Peter. However, such a situation is impossible in a natural context, hence (33b) is unacceptable. In contrast, the numerals in (34) quantify over individuals denoted by the host NP, thus they are insensitive to the properties of verbal predicates.

(33) a. *Gakusei*-ga kinoo **san-nin** Peter-o tatai-ta.
  student-NOM yesterday three-CL Peter-ACC hit-PAST
  'Three students hit Peter yesterday.'
 b. ??*Gakusei*-ga kinoo **san-nin** Peter-o korosi-ta.
  student-NOM yesterday three-CL Peter-ACC kill-PAST
  'Three students killed Peter yesterday.' (Nakanishi 2004:67)

(34) a. [**San-nin**-no *gakusei*]-ga kinoo Peter-o tatai-ta/korosi-ta.
  [three-CL-GEN student]-NOM yesterday Peter-ACC hit-PAST/kill-PAST
 b. [*Gakusei* **san-nin**]-ga kinoo Peter-o tatai-ta/korosi-ta.
  [student three-CL]-NOM yesterday Peter-ACC hit-PAST/kill-PAST

Another piece of evidence for event quantification comes from the observation that FNQs cannot occur with verbal predicates that express more or less permanent states (i.e., individual-level predicates) (Harada 1976, Ohki 1987, Fukushima 1991, Nishigauchi and Uchibori 1991, Mihara 1998). In (35), for instance, although the FNQ is compatible with the predicate *genki-da* 'be healthy' that expresses a temporal state, it is incompatible with *osu-da* 'be male' that expresses a permanent state. No such restriction can be found with numerals in a nominal projection, as in (36). It has been independently argued that, unlike predicates expressing temporal states, predicates expressing permanent states lack event arguments in their denotation (Kratzer 1995). If we take this view, the contrast in (35) naturally follows: (35b) is unacceptable because there is no event that the FNQ quantifies over. In contrast, the numerals in (36) have nothing to do with event quantification, thus any predicate can be used with them.[18]

(35) a. Uti-no doobutuen-de-wa *kaba*-ga mada **san-too** genki-da.
  my zoo-at-TOP hippo-NOM still three-CL healthy
  'In my zoo, three hippos are still healthy.'
 b. *Uti-no doobutuen-de-wa *kaba*-ga zannennakotoni **san-too** osu-da.
  my zoo-at-TOP hippo-NOM unfortunately three-CL male
  'In my zoo, unfortunately, three hippos are male.' (Mihara 1998:110–111)

(36) a. Uti-no doobutuen-de-wa [**san-too**-no *kaba*]-ga genki-da /osu-da.
my zoo-at-TOP [three-CL-GEN hippo]-NOM healthy /male
b. Uti-no doobutuen-de-wa [*kaba* **san-too**]-ga genki-da /osu-da.
my zoo-at-TOP [hippo three-CL]-NOM healthy /male

Note that FNQs quantify not just over verbal predicates but also somehow over nominal predicates as well. Recall that FNQs contain a classifier that semantically agrees with the host NP. For example, in (33a), -*nin* agrees with *gakusei* 'student', indicating that the cardinality of the students is three. Moreover, (33a) is semantically different from (37), where *three times* is simply counting a number of events without being associated with the number of students. In particular, whereas (33a) means that three students hit Peter for unknown number of times, (37) means that a student or students whose cardinality is unspecified hit Peter three times.

(37) Gakusei-ga kinoo **san-kai** Peter-o tatai-ta.
student-NOM yesterday three-time Peter-ACC hit-PAST
'A student/students hit Peter three times yesterday.' (Nakanishi 2004:85)

Thus, if we were to argue that an FNQ is an adverb, it cannot be an adverb that simply modifies a verbal predicate; rather, it must be a special kind of adverb that modifies a verbal predicate as well as a nominal predicate (which may be somewhat similar to so-called subject-oriented adverbs such as *reluctantly* in *John reluctantly hit Peter*). Indeed, Fujita (1994) argues that an FNQ modifies its host NP via modification of the verbal predicate. Similarly, Nakanishi (2004, 2007a, 2007b) presents a semantic mechanism where an FNQ quantifies over events denoted by the verbal predicate as well as over individuals denoted by the host NP.

Note that semantic properties of FNQs per se do not rule out the stranding view. Indeed, we might expect to observe some semantic differences as a result of transformations involved in the stranding view. For example, Watanabe (2006, this volume) discusses another semantic difference between the FNQ and the numerals in a nominal projection—namely, partitivity (the FNQ, but not the numerals in a nominal projection, evokes a partitive interpretation: see Inoue 1978, Fujita 1994, Hamano 1997; see also section 11.3.5)—and argues that this semantic difference can be captured under the stranding view. The task for the stranding view then is to explain why FNQs have different semantic properties from numerals that apparently quantify over nominal predicates, as discussed in this section. In other words, the stranding view needs to show that movement can be the source of the semantic differences discussed here.

11.3.4 The Adverb View

To sum up the discussion so far, the stranding view advocated by Miyagawa (1989) confines the distribution of FNQs to environments where locality constraint is met, and by doing so, it successfully accounts for some distributional restrictions on

FNQs presented in section 11.2. However, the counterexamples to locality challenge the validity of such a constrained analysis. Some attempts have been made to deal with the counterexamples under the stranding view, as we have seen in Miyagawa and Arikawa's (2007) recent work. An alternative analysis is presented by Ishii (1999), who argues that there are two types of FNQs—a stranding type and an adverb type. Under this analysis, the counterexamples to locality involve the adverb-type FNQs, which are distinct from the stranding-type FNQs in that they are not sensitive to locality. Thus, these examples do not pose a problem for the stranding view. Although Ishii's analysis offers an attractive possibility of eliminating the questions in (23), we saw in (31) that there does not seem to be a strict correlation between locality and the semantic restriction on distributivity. Moreover, further semantic restrictions on FNQs in (33)–(36) seem to indicate that FNQs quantify over events denoted by verbal predicates. Together with the counterexamples to locality (e.g., (22) where S_i-O-FNQ$_i$ is acceptable), the semantic data above led some researchers to advocate the adverb view.[19] The substance of this view is that FNQs can occur in positions that cannot be straightforwardly associated with an NP trace, which indicates that locality does not play a crucial role for the distribution of FNQs (for cross-linguistic data on this point, see Bobaljik 1995, Fitzpatrick 2006, among others). Then the question that we need to address is the following: why is S_i-O-FNQ$_i$ sometimes unacceptable (see (23b))? I review here two analyses that directly address this question—namely, Takami's (1998, 2001) pragmatic approach and Mihara's (1998) semantic approach. Along the way, I also discuss how these approaches account for the distributional restriction on FNQs other than S_i-O-FNQ$_i$, which is summarized in (17).

11.3.4.1 *Pragmatic consideration*

Takami (1998, 2001) rejects Miyagawa's (1989) stranding analysis on the basis of the counterexamples to locality presented in section 11.3.1. The upshot of his analysis is that the distribution of FNQs does not depend on syntactic factors, as claimed in the stranding view, but rather on pragmatic factors. It has been independently claimed that, in Japanese, the most important information (or new information) must appear in an immediately preverbal position (Kuno 1978a). Takami argues that FNQs must obey this information structure. Let us illustrate his point by examining the contrast in (38), where both sentences are in the S_i-O-FNQ$_i$ order.

(38) a. ?*Gakusei*-ga   hon-o   **yo-nin**   kat-ta.
       student-NOM book-ACC four-CL   buy-PAST
       'Four students bought a book/books.'
   b. *Gakusei*-ga   {sore   /sono hon}-o   **yo-nin**   kat-ta.
       student-NOM {it   /that book}-ACC   four-CL   buy-PAST
       'Four students bought it/that book.'   (Takami 2001:139)

In (38a,b), the FNQ is interpreted as the most important information, being in a preverbal position. The difference in acceptability between the two comes from the information status of the object. In (38a), the object is an indefinite NP, which is interpreted to convey new information. Thus, there is a conflict between the object and the FNQ as to which one should be the focus of the sentence. In contrast, in (38b) (also in (22a)), the object is a definite NP, which conveys less-important information, thus the ideal information structure is preserved.

Furthermore, Takami observes that the S_i-O-FNQ_i order is always acceptable when the FNQ is followed by an emphatic particle such as -*dake* 'only' and -*tomo* 'all', as shown in (22c) (repeated in (39)). This also follows from the pragmatic condition: emphatic particles signal that the FNQ conveys the most important information, thus the sentence realizes the ideal information structure.

(39) *Gakusei*-ga   repooto-o   **san-nin**-dake teisyutusi-ta.
     student-NOM report-ACC three-CL-only hand-in-PAST
     'Only three students handed in a report.' (= (22c))

In the case of (22b) (repeated in (40)), the context that 'I live in an apartment' evokes the contrast with 'my friends build a house', so the object *ie* 'house' merely conveys predictable information. Thus, it does not need to be placed in a preverbal position, just as in (38b).

(40) Boku-wa apaato   zumai-dakedo,
     I-TOP   apartment   living-although
     saikin   *dooryoo*-ga ie-o   **si, go-nin**   tugitugito
     recently colleague-NOM house-ACC   four, five-CL   one after another
     tate-ta.
     build-CL
     'Although I live in an apartment, four or five colleagues built a house one after another recently.' (= (22b))

Takami further argues that his analysis is able to account for the contrast in (41), where both verbs are unergative and a VP-internal adverb intervenes between the subject and its FNQ. In (41a), *geragerato* 'loudly' conveys important new information, hence it needs to be placed in a preverbal position. In contrast, a locative adverb such as *butai-de* 'at the stage' or a temporal adverb such as *kinoo* 'yesterday' serves as a "scene-setter," and so they do not convey important information, which allows the FNQ to sit in a preverbal position.[20]

(41) a. *Kodomo-ga   geragerato **huta-ri**   warat-ta.
        children-NOM loudly   two-CL   laugh-PAST
        'Two children laughed loudly.' (= (9c))
     b. Kodomo-ga   butai-de   **zyuu-nin** odot-ta.
        child-NOM   stage-at   ten-CL   dance-PAST
        'Ten children danced at the stage.' (= (20a))

In this way, Takami's analysis appeals to pragmatic considerations to account for the mixed judgments on the S_i-O-FNQ_i order and on the external argument hosting the FNQ. There seem to be some examples, however, where the pragmatic analysis does not go through. Consider (42), which is slightly modified from (20c). Under Takami's analysis, *naihu-de* 'with the knife' conveys important new information, just like *geragerato* 'loudly' in (41a). Nevertheless, (41a) and (42) differ in their acceptability. Moreover, determining "appropriate" information structure is not always straightforward. In all the examples discussed in this section, the FNQ conveys new information. At the same time, some examples involve other elements expressing new information. Then, the question is how to decide which one conveys more important information that has to be placed in a preverbal position.

(42) *Gakusei*-ga   *naihu-de*   *koremadeni*   **huta-ri**   *kegasi-ta*.
     student-NOM   knife-with   so-far   five-CL   injure-PAST
     'So far two students injured (themselves) with a knife.'   (cf. (20c))

11.3.4.2 Aspectual consideration

Like Takami (1998, 2001), Mihara (1998) considers Miyagawa's (1989) mutual c-command requirement inadequate based on numerous counterexamples. He also claims that Takami's pragmatic condition is not sufficient and argues that, besides the pragmatic condition, FNQs require an aspectual delimitedness. In particular, the sentence with an FNQ must express a completed situation and the FNQ must be tied to the enumeration resulting from the situation.[21] Let us illustrate his analysis by examining the data on the S_i-O-FNQ$_i$ order. Regarding (22a,b), he points out that the sentences sound worse without the temporal adverbs *kesa-mo* 'also this morning' and *saikin* 'recently', respectively. These adverbs signal that the relevant counting under a described situation has been completed.

The examples in (43) seem to further support the validity of Mihara's claim that the resultant state of counting (often signaled by temporal adverbs) contributes to a well-formedness of FNQs.

(43) a. *Gaikokuzin kankookyaku*-ga *kyonen*   *Tokushima*-o   **gosen-nin**
        foreign   tourist-NOM   last year   Tokushima-ACC   5,000-CL
        otozure-ta.
        visit-PAST
        'Five thousand foreign tourists visited Tokushima last year.'
     b. *Gaikokuzin kankookyaku*-ga *kyonen*   **gosen-nin**   *Tokushima*-o
        foreign   tourist-NOM   last year   5,000-CL   Tokushima-ACC
        otozure-ta.
        visit-PAST

Under Mihara's analysis, the sentence with an FNQ is grammatical as long as it is aspectually delimited, regardless of where the FNQ appears in the sentence. Example (43) provides us with a context where the enumeration is salient. In such a case, the S_i-O-FNQ$_i$ order in (43a) is as acceptable as the S_i-FNQ$_i$-O order in (43b).

Regarding (22c) (repeated in (39)), Mihara argues that emphatic particles such as *-dake* 'only' and *-tomo* 'all' signal that the counting of events described by the sentence is ended. In other words, in (22c), with the presence of the emphatic particle, the sentence is aspectually delimited, hence the S_i-O-FNQ_i order is acceptable. His analysis further accounts for why FNQs are incompatible with predicates that express a permanent state (*osu-da* 'be male'), as in (35b). These predicates are not aspectually delimited. Interestingly, FNQs are compatible with such predicates when they are followed by emphatic adverbs, as in (44). This is because emphatic adverbs indicate that the speaker finished counting, thus (44) does not describe permanent states, unlike (35b).

(44) Uti-no doobutuen-de-wa *kaba*-ga zannennakotoni
our zoo-at-TOP hippo-NOM unfortunately
san-too{-dake/-tomo} osu-da.
three-CL{-only/-all} male
'In our zoo, unfortunately, {only/all} three hippos are male.'

Mihara's analysis further extends to the contrast between unaccusatives and unergatives. Mihara argues that unaccusative verbs always express a completion—that is, they are inherently aspectually delimited. Thus, his analysis predicts FNQs to be always compatible with unaccusative verbs. As discussed in section 11.2, we know that this prediction is empirically correct (see (9b)). Unlike unaccusative verbs, unergative verbs are not semantically restricted. Thus, when they occur with FNQs, there needs to be an expression that aspectually delimits the relevant sentence. For instance, (45a) is unacceptable just as (9c) is, but it is acceptable in a context that provides an aspectual delimitation, as in (45b).[22]

(45) a. ??*Gakusei*-ga tosyokan-de **sanzyuu-nin** benkyoosi-ta.
student-NOM library-at thirty-CL study-PAST
'Thirty students studied at the library.' (Mihara 1998:106)
b. Heikan-magiwa-made *gakusei*-ga tosyokan-de **sanzyuu-nin**
closing-close to-until student-NOM library-at thirty-CL
benkyoosi-ta.
study-PAST
'Until the closing time, thirty students studied at the library.'
(Mihara 1998:106)

As shown in (20b), (45a) is acceptable when the verb is in a progressive form. Mihara argues that this is because progressives express limited duration—that is, progressives are inherently aspectually delimited.

Mihara's analysis is also able to account for the contrast in (46) regarding the S_i-O-FNQ_i order.

(46) a. **Gakusei*-ga sake-o **san-nin** non-da.
student-NOM sake-ACC three-CL drink-PAST
'Three students drank sake.' (= (24a))

b. *Gakusei*-ga   sono botoru-no sake-o   **san-nin** non-da.
   student-NOM that bottle-GEN sake-ACC three-CL drink-PAST
   'Three students drank the sake in that bottle.'

   (Gunji and Hashida 1998:50)

Gunji and Hashida (1998) observe that the NP intervening between the subject and its FNQ must express an entity whose quantity is determinate. It is independently known that aspectual properties of a verbal predicate can be influenced by internal arguments (Krifka 1992, among many others). For instance, *John drank wine* is atelic (or aspectually nondelimited), whereas *John drank a glass of wine* is telic (or aspectually delimited). The difference can be shown by adding temporal modifiers; the former is compatible with *for ten minutes* and not with *in ten minutes*, and the opposite holds for the latter (Dowty 1979). Then, in (46), we can argue that only (46b) is felicitous because (46b), but not (46a), is aspectually delimited.

Although Mihara's analysis opens a new venue of research on FNQs, there seem to be examples where their acceptability does not depend on an aspectual consideration. For instance, consider the examples of the S_i-O-FNQ$_i$ order in (41b) (= (20a)) and (45a), where only the former is reported to be acceptable. These examples do not seem to differ in terms of aspectuality; the VP *dance at the stage* and the VP *study at the library* are both atelic in that they are compatible with *for one hour* but not with *in one hour*. Thus, Mihara's analysis would predict (41b) to be infelicitous, just as (45a) is.

Summing up section 11.3.4, we have seen that a range of counterexamples to locality led some researchers to advocate an alternative view of the stranding analysis—namely, the adverb view. The adverb view is further supported by some data suggesting that FNQs quantify over something other than nominal predicates—in particular, verbal predicates. Under the adverb view, we do not expect to observe any locality constraints (but see note 11), hence the S_i-O-FNQ$_i$ order is predicted to be always acceptable. To account for why this order is sometimes unacceptable, we need to appeal to semantic/pragmatic considerations such as Takami's (1998, 2001) and Mihara's (1998). However, as we have seen above, these semantic/pragmatic analyses are not without problems.

11.3.5 Some Notes on Prosodic Effects

Before concluding the chapter, I would like to briefly discuss the status of an FNQ that is adjacent to its host NP in the surface. Kitagawa and Kuroda (1992), followed by Fujita (1994), claim that when a numeral quantifier immediately follows its host NP, it can be structurally ambiguous between [NP-CASE Q] and [NP-CASE][Q] (the brackets indicate constituency). Their claim is supported by the data on cardinal/partitive readings. Although only a cardinal reading holds when the numeral and its host NP form a constituent, as in (47a), only a partitive reading holds when they are apart, as in (47b). Kitagawa and Kuroda observe that, when the numeral and its host NP are adjacent to each other, as in (47c), the sentence has both cardinal and partitive readings. They further claim that the two readings in (47c) can be teased apart by different prosodic patterns. In particular, with a prosodic boundary or a pause between the host NP and the numeral (indicated by //), (47c) has a partitive reading only, which implies that the host NP and the numeral are not in the same nominal projection, just as in (47b). In contrast, without any pause between them, (47c) only allows a cardinal reading, which indicates that the host NP and the numeral form a nominal constituent, just as in (47a).

(47) a. [Sokoni   iawase-ta   **go-nin**-no   *otoko*]-ga   tero-ni
       [there   be-PAST   five-CL-GEN   man]-NOM   terrorism-by
       makikom-are-ta.
       involve-PASS-PAST
       'Five (and only five) men who were there got involved in terrorism.'
   b. Sokoni iawase-ta *otoko*-ga   tero-ni   **go-nin** makikom-are-ta.
      there be-PAST   man-NOM   terrorism-by five-CL   involve-PASS-PAST
      'Five of the men who were there got involved in terrorism.'
                                                          (Fujita 1994:35–36)
   c. Sokoni iawase-ta *otoko*-ga (//) **go-nin** tero-ni makikom-are-ta.

Similarly, in (48), the presence of a prosodic boundary seems to influence the interpretation of the sentence. The sentence is ambiguous between distributive and collective readings without a boundary, whereas it only allows a distributive reading with a boundary.

(48) *Gakusei*-ga (//) **go-nin** tukue-o   motiage-ta.
     student-NOM   five-CL   desk-ACC lift-PAST   (cf. (31))

Throughout the chapter, to avoid this complication, I have focused on cases where some element intervenes between an FNQ and its host NP. However, it is important to question what implication the prosodic pattern has to the theory of FNQs (see Miyagawa and Arikawa 2007).

11.4 IMPLICATIONS FOR THE GENERAL THEORY

In this short overview, I have examined previous studies on Japanese FNQs by dividing them into two groups—namely, the stranding view and the adverb view. Among the numerous important issues that arise from the investigation of the phenomenon, I have focused on issues of locality. The stranding view advanced by

Miyagawa (1989) observes that there are certain locality restrictions on the dependency between an FNQ and its host NP, as summarized in (49).

(49) Distributional restrictions on FNQs (also in (17))
Structural restrictions
a. *Embedded NP as the host NP; (5) (counterexamples in (18))
b. *NP within PP as the host NP; (8) (counterexamples in (19))
Locality restrictions
c. *External argument as the host NP with a VP-internal adverb/PP; (3), (9), (11) (counterexamples in (20))
d. *S_i-O-FNQ$_i$; (2) (counterexamples in (22))

Under this view, FNQs have served as a powerful tool for the investigation of Japanese syntax. However, close scrutiny reveals that there are a number of counterexamples to locality, as indicated in (49), which led some researchers to the adverb view. Further support for the adverb view comes from a range of semantic properties of FNQs, summarized in (50).

(50) Semantic restrictions on FNQs
a. *Collective readings; (31)
b. *Single-occurrence events; (33)
c. *Predicates describing a permanent state; (35)[23]

Table 11.1 summarizes how the two views fare with the properties of FNQs. I would like to emphasize that, whatever theory of FNQs we may choose (the stranding view, the adverb view, the hybrid view, or something else), we need to make sure that the theory is capable of accounting for the range of properties of FNQs discussed here and of making further predictions about other properties of FNQs, such as scrambled FNQs (cf. note 2) and the scope property (see below).

The syntactic and semantic considerations of FNQs lead us to the larger question of how the syntactic and semantic components of grammar interact: when accounting for FNQs, is it possible to maintain the compositionality of grammar? That is, do semantic rules apply in accord with syntactic rules? In (1a,b), when the numeral combines with the host NP in syntax, a corresponding semantic

Table 11.1 Comparison of the stranding and adverb views

Properties of FNQs	Stranding view	Adverb view
Distributional restrictions in (49)	✓ (Locality restriction)	Not necessarily expected (but see section 11.3.4)
Counterexamples to the restrictions	Not necessarily expected (but see section 11.3.2)	✓ (No locality restriction)
Semantic restrictions in (50)	Not necessarily expected (but see section 11.3.2)	✓ (Result of quantification over verbal predicates)

rule makes the numeral express the number of relevant students. Does the FNQ in (1c) quantify over the host NP just as the numerals in (1a,b) do? The answer is affirmative for the stranding view. The FNQ, being in the same nominal projection as its host NP, should quantify over the host NP in the same way as the numerals in (1a,b). However, examples such as (31), (33), and (35) suggest that the FNQ has something to do with quantification over a verbal predicate. Then the challenge for the stranding view is to provide a mechanism of the FNQ having an effect on a verbal predicate. In contrast, under the adverb view, the FNQ syntactically combines with, and correspondingly semantically quantifies over, a verbal predicate. Then the challenge would be to account for the apparent connection between the FNQ and its host NP. As pointed out in section 11.3.3, the FNQ includes a classifier that semantically agrees with the host NP, and thus the relation between the FNQ and its host NP cannot be ignored.

I conclude this chapter with a discussion of some cross-linguistic issues. It is well known that floating quantifiers (FQs) exist in many other languages and that, just as in the case of Japanese, there are competing theories in cross-linguistic studies—namely, the stranding view (Sportiche 1988, Shlonsky 1991, Merchant 1996, McCloskey 2000), the adverb view (Dowty and Brodie 1984, Bobaljik 1995, Junker 1995, Hoeksema 1996, Doetjes 1997), and the hybrid view (Fitzpatrick 2006). Furthermore, various arguments used to argue for or against the competing views in the cross-linguistic literature largely overlap with the arguments used in Japanese—that is, the arguments based on distributional and semantic restrictions on FQs. Regardless of this fact, Japanese FQs and cross-linguistic FQs are strikingly different in that, whereas any quantifier can float in Japanese, quantifiers are often restricted to universal ones in other languages (e.g., in English, only *all*, *each*, and *both* are able to float). Indeed, the focus of this chapter is on floating *numeral* quantifiers. Although it is not entirely clear what the source of this difference is, I would like to make two remarks regarding this question. First, it has been pointed out that Japanese FQs may be more closely related to so-called split quantifiers than to FQs in other languages (Bobaljik 2003). Some languages are known to have a construction called Split Topicalization, where some part of a noun phrase gets topicalized to the sentence-initial position and, as a result, the noun phrase gets "split up." For instance, in the German example in (51a), the NP *Bekannte* 'acquaintances' is separated from the numeral *zwei* 'two' by Topicalization.

(51) a. *Bekannte   haben gestern   **zwei** geheiratet.*
       acquaintances have yesterday two   married
       'Two acquaintances married yesterday.'
   b. *[**Zwei** Bekannte]   haben gestern   geheiratet.*
       [two   acquaintances] have yesterday married

(Nakanishi 2004:75)

It is independently argued that split quantifiers as well as Japanese FQs are confined to narrow scope interpretations (for instance, van Geenhoven 1998 for German;

Hasegawa 1993, Yamashita 2001 for Japanese). Moreover, it has been pointed out that Split Topicalization in German is subject to the same semantic restrictions as Japanese FQs summarized in (50) (Nakanishi 2004, 2007a). For instance, although (51b) permits both distributive and collective readings, (51a) has a distributive reading only, just like (31b). It is interesting to explore why the two seemingly unrelated constructions, Split Topicalization and FQ constructions, share various semantic properties.

Second, there is another instance that may have a close connection to Japanese FQs—namely, so-called adverbs of quantification in English, such as *mostly* or *for the most part*. It has been argued that these expressions can quantify over a nominal predicate (Berman 1991). For example, the sentence *For the most part, John likes his friends* has the possible interpretation 'John likes most of his friends'. Similarly, (52) has the reading 'most of the boys built a model boat'. It has been claimed that, under this reading, (52) can be understood distributively (most of the boys built a model boat separately) but not collectively (most of the boys together built a model boat) (Nakanishi and Romero 2004).

(52) **For the most part**, *the boys* built a model boat.

The same restriction seems to obtain with the Japanese example in (53). As one of the possible interpretations, (53) could mean that most of the boys built a model boat and, under this interpretation, (53) is distributive, not collective.[24] Crucially, this is exactly the restriction we have observed with Japanese FNQs (see (31)).

(53)   (?)*Otokonoko*-ga   kinoo   **hotondo**   omotya-no booto-o   tukut-ta.
     boy-NOM   yesterday   most/mostly   toy-GEN   boat-ACC   make-PAST
     'For the most part, boys made a toy boat yesterday.'

The cross-linguistic data discussed above seem to suggest that we should compare Japanese FNQs not just with FQs in other languages but also with extended cross-linguistic phenomena (e.g., Split Topicalization, adverbs of quantification).

The research on Japanese FNQs has been advanced a great deal over the past few decades, although many questions still remain unanswered. It is hoped that this chapter serves as a partial overview of what has been done and sheds light on some of the issues that require further investigations.

NOTES FOR CHAPTER 11

I would like to thank Jonathan Bobaljik, Heidi Harley, Nobuko Hasegawa, Heejeong Ko, Martha McGinnis, Shigeru Miyagawa, Norvin Richards, Mamoru Saito, Andrew Simpson, Koichi Takezawa, Satoshi Tomioka, and Akira Watanabe for discussions and valuable comments.

    1. Nouns in Japanese lack obligatory grammatical markings of definiteness and of plurality, and bare nouns can be used freely as arguments, as in (i).

(i) Kasyu-ga   sinkyoku-o   utat-ta.
    singer-NOM   new song-ACC   sing-PAST
    'A singer/Singers/The singer(s) sang a new song/new songs/the new song(s).'

When these bare nouns occur with a numeral, the numeral must be followed by a classifier—a morpheme that indicates the semantic class of the host noun in terms of shape, size, animacy, and so forth (see Downing 1996 for details). For instance, in (1), with *kasyu* 'singer', the classifier *-nin* needs to be used, which carries some semantic information about *kasyu*.

2. When a numeral and its host NP are apart, as in (1c), the numeral can precede its host NP, as in (ii) and (iii). Although I do not have space for discussion on this type, readers are directed to previous literature such as Takano 1984; Miyagawa 1989; Terada 1990; Yatabe 1990; Fukushima 1991; Gunji and Hashida 1998; Kawashima 1998; Takami 1998, 2001; Ishii 1999; and Watanabe 2006, among others.

(ii)   Kinoo   **san-nin**   kasyu-ga   utat-ta.
       yesterday   three-CL   singer-NOM   sing-PAST
(iii) **San-nin** kinoo   kasyu-ga   utat-ta.
       three-CL   yesterday   singer-NOM   sing-PAST

3. In this chapter, I do not discuss another important question regarding the paradigm in (1): is there any transformational relation among the forms in (1)? This question is dealt with by Watanabe (this volume).

4. In the following, I refer to the noun phrase that the numeral is associated with as the host NP (e.g., *kasyu* 'singer' in (1)). I put aside the question of whether the relevant noun phrase is an NP or a DP (see Watanabe, this volume, for this issue).

5. Miyagawa (1989) later makes a revision and argues that the requirement applies throughout the derivation of the sentence. This is to accommodate data involving a scrambled host NP, such as (ii) and (iii) in note 2. Because these cases are not discussed in this chapter, the definition in (6) may suffice here.

6. Another piece of evidence for Miyagawa's analysis comes from the fact that the subject of a so-called indirect passive cannot host an FNQ, as in (iv). Crucially, it has been argued that this type of passive, unlike (9a), does not involve movement of the subject, and thus there is no NP trace that satisfies the mutual c-command requirement.

(iv)   *Kodomo-ga   ame-ni   **huta-ri**   hur-are-ta.
       child-NOM   rain-DAT   two-CL   fall-PASS-PAST
       'Two children were rained on.'   (Miyagawa 1989:41)

7. Strictly speaking, an assumption that the FNQ and its host NP are within the same nominal projection does not guarantee that the mutual c-command requirement will be necessarily satisfied. For instance, if we were to adopt the structure in (v), based on Li's (1999) proposal for Chinese noun phrases, the host NP does not c-command the numeral. Thus, to maintain the mutual c-command requirement, we need to assume a structure such as (vi) (Kawashima 1998). Although I put aside this question here, readers are referred to Watanabe, this volume.

(v)   [$_{NumP}$ three [$_{ClP}$ -CL student]]
(vi) [$_{NumP}$ student [$_{Num'}$ three-CL]]

8. Saito's (1985) account here needs to be reconsidered if we adopt the VP- (or *v*P-) internal subject hypothesis (Kitagawa 1986, Kuroda 1988, among others). The derivations

in (vii) and (viii) are plausible under this hypothesis: the object first adjoins to VP or vP, and the subject undergoes Case-driven movement to Spec,TP.

(vii) [TP S₁ [VP O₂ [VP [NumP t₁ **FNQ**] t₂   V]]]
(viii) [TP S₁ [vP O₂ [vP [NumP t₁ **FNQ**] [VP t₂ V]]]]

Then (14b) is predicted to be grammatical. Indeed, I show in section 11.3.1 that the word order in (14a) is not always unacceptable. Presumably, we could appeal to the derivations in (vii) and (viii) to account for grammatical examples. However, Miyagawa and Arikawa (2007) reject the derivation in (viii) (hence (vii) as well) and argue for an alternative derivation. See section 11.3.2.1 for a brief discussion.

9. Although it is not impossible to argue that (13) is an instance of subject scrambling, a more straightforward account is to say that the subject undergoes Case-driven movement (hence not scrambling) to Spec,TP, as in (ix) (cf. note 8; see also Miyagawa and Arikawa 2007). Then we can maintain Saito's (1985) claim that subjects do not scramble.

(ix) [TP NP₁ [vP Adv [vP   [NumP t₁ **FNQ**] [VP O V]]]]

10. Regarding the examples of the kind presented in (18) (i.e., inalienable possessions), my informants' and my own judgments vary depending on which example we are looking at; while the judgments vary from "acceptable" to "a little awkward" for the examples in (18) and (x), the speakers agree that (xi) is much worse. It seems to be the case that the examples improve whenever a one-to-one correspondence between the possessor and his/her body part is clear from the context. For instance, in (x), each child has one stomach being stabbed, whereas, in (xi), it is not clear how many fingers were broken per child.

(x) John-ga   [kodomotati-no hara]-o   **zyuu-nin** sasi-ta.
    John-NOM   [children-GEN   stomach]-ACC   ten-CL   stab-PAST
    'John stabbed ten children's stomachs.'
(xi) John-ga   [kodomotati-no yubi]-o   **zyuu-nin** ot-ta.
    John-NOM   [children-GEN   finger]-ACC   ten-CL   break-PAST
    'John broke ten children's fingers.'   (Kikuchi 1994:82)

11. Some researchers implement a certain locality restriction under the adverb view. For example, Doetjes (1997) argues that FQs in Dutch and French are adverbs and that they must c-command a trace of the host NP (see also Fitzpatrick 2006). The adverbial analyses on Japanese FNQs summarized here do not take such a view (but see Nakanishi 2004, 2007a, 2007b), and so it suffices to say here that, under the adverb view, FNQs are insensitive to locality.

12. More precisely, Miyagawa and Arikawa argue that, when the S_i-O-FNQ_i order is acceptable, the object first moves to the edge of vP, then moves to Spec,TP to meet the EPP requirement of T. Then the subject undergoes A'-scrambling to a higher position (to a higher Spec,TP, as in (25), or to Spec,CP). They argue for this derivation rather than the alternative derivation in (xii). For various empirical examples supporting their analysis, see Miyagawa and Arikawa 2007:section 5.

(xii) [TP S₁ [vP O₂ [vP [NumP t₁ **FNQ**] [VP t₂ V]]]] (= (viii) in note 8)

13. It is not the case that any unacceptable example of the S_i-O-Adverb-FNQ_i order can serve as a counterexample to Miyagawa and Arikawa's analysis. In particular, it is crucial to use a "high" rather than "low" adverb. Recall that adverbs such as *kinoo*

'yesterday' are considered to be high in the structure (see (1c) and (13)), whereas adverbs such as *geragerato* 'loudly' (see (9c) and (10b)) are considered to be low. The high adverbs, but not the low ones, can intervene between the subject and its FNQ. The fact that (xiii) is acceptable indicates that *imamadeni* 'so far' (used in (24b)) and *huunnimo* 'unfortunately' (used in (26)) are high adverbs.

(xiii) *Gakusei*-ga {imamadeni /huunnimo} **san-nin** sake-o
 student-NOM {so far /unfortunately} three-CL sake-ACC
 non-da.
 drink-PAST

Consider now (xiv), which is unacceptable just like (26) is.

(xiv) ??*Gakusei*-ga sake-o ikkini **san-nin** non-da.
 student-NOM sake-ACC in-one-breath three-CL drink-PAST

However, unlike *huunnimo* 'unfortunately' in (26), *ikkini* 'in one breath' in (xiv) is a low adverb; as shown in (xv), *ikkini* cannot intervene between the subject and its FNQ. Thus, the unacceptability of (xiv) has nothing to do with the unacceptability of the S$_i$-O-FNQ$_i$ order. In other words, (xiv) is unacceptable not because of the intervening object but because of the intervening low adverb. I thank Shigeru Miyagawa for clarifying this point.

(xv) ??*Gakusei*-ga ikkini **san-nin** sake-o non-da.
 student-NOM in-one-breath three-CL sake-ACC drink-PAST

14. We can imagine another scenario where each of the five students bought a copy of the new magazine at the same time, which amounts to a nondistributive reading under Kitagawa and Kuroda's (1992) definition. This nondistributive reading seems to be available in (22a), contra Ishii's generalization that sentences such as (22a) only allow distributive readings. The semantic notion relevant here seems to be the distinction between distributive and collective readings (Dowty 1987, among others): a distributive reading holds when each member expressed as the subject serves as an agent, and a collective reading holds when the subject as a group serves as an agent. Example (22a) permits a distributive reading where each of the five students bought a copy, but it lacks a collective reading where the five students as a group bought a single copy. Crucially, under the distributive-collective distinction, the situation where each of the five students bought a copy at the same time falls under a distributive reading, correctly predicting that such a situation is compatible with (22a). See section 11.3.3 for more examples.

15. See note 14 on why the distributive/collective distinction matters, rather than Kitagawa and Kuroda's (1992) distributive/nondistributive distinction. See also Nakanishi 2007a for further discussions.

16. When so-called collectivizing adverbs such as *together* co-occur with FNQs, as in (xvi), only collective readings are available. Nakanishi (2004, 2007a, 2007b) proposes that these adverbs serve to form a group, yielding the interpretation 'one group consisting of three boys'. It follows that (xvi) has the same semantic status as (xvii), where there is no ambiguity between distributive and collective readings in the first place. This is because the distributive/collective distinction is defined in terms of plural individuals; *the boys made a toy boat* can be ambiguous, as opposed to *the boy made a toy boat*, which does not have any ambiguity.

(xvi) *Otokonoko*-ga kinoo **san-nin** {issyoni /(hito-kumi)-de}
 boy-NOM yesterday three-CL {together /(one-group)-COP}

omotya-no booto-o tukutta.
toy-GEN boat-ACC made
'Three boys made a toy boat {together / as a group} yesterday.'
(xvii) Otokonoko-ga kinoo **hito-ri** omotya-no booto-o tukutta.
boy-NOM yesterday one-CL toy-GEN boat-ACC made
'One boy made a toy boat yesterday.'

17. I do not examine here the cases where the FNQ and its host NP are adjacent, as in (xviii). This is because the interpretation of the sentence changes depending on the prosodic pattern (see section 11.3.5; see also Nakanishi 2007a).

(xviii) Otokonoko-ga san-nin omotya-no booto-o tukut-ta.
boy-NOM three-CL toy-GEN boat-ACC make-PAST

18. Fukushima (1991) presents another set of data to show a semantic difference between FNQs and numerals in a nominal projection. In (xix), we obtain two completely different interpretations depending on where the numeral is: whereas the numeral in (xixa) expresses the number of cells in the beaker, the FNQ in (xixb) expresses the number of cells obtained by a proliferation. However, the numeral in (xixb) is different in nature from FNQs discussed in this chapter. More specifically, the numeral in (xixb) should be treated as a differential in comparative constructions (e.g., *two* in *John read two more books than Mary*) (see Nakanishi 2004, 2007a for details).

(xix) a. [**Hito-tu**-no *saiboo*]-ga biikaa-nonakade hue-ta.
[one-CL-GEN cell]-NOM beaker-inside increase-PAST
'One cell proliferated/increased in the beaker.'
b. *Saiboo*-ga biikaa-nonakade **hito-tu** hue-ta.
cell-NOM beaker-inside one-CL increase-PAST
'The number of cells increased by one in the beaker.' (Fukushima 1991:77)

19. Note that, under this view, as long as a close connection between FNQs and verbal predicates is captured, it may not matter so much whether FNQs are categorized as "adverbs" (Nakanishi 2004). Indeed, the approaches that I discuss in detail later in the chapter—namely, Mihara (1998) and Takami (1998, 2001)—do not explicitly state that FNQs are adverbs. Nonetheless, I include their approaches in the adverb view in that, under their analyses, there are no locality restrictions on the dependency between an FNQ and its host NP. Furthermore, their analyses assume a close relation between an FNQ and a verbal predicate.

20. Takami (1998, 2001) proposes another pragmatic condition in (xx), which accounts for the data on structural restrictions in (17a,b)—namely, the data on an embedded NP as the host NP and on the NP within PP as the host NP. For instance, *gakusei* 'student' in (xxia) can be topicalized but not the one in (xxib). That is, *gakusei* serves as a Theme in (xxia) but not in (xxib). For lack of space, I do not discuss this pragmatic condition further here.

(xx) An NP can host an FNQ only when it can serve as a Theme of the sentence.

(xxi) a. Yamada Sensei-ga [*gakusei*-no kami]-o **san-nin** kit-ta.
Yamada Professor-NOM [student-GEN hair]-ACC three-CL clip-PAST
'Prof. Yamada cut three students' hair.' (= (18a))
b. *Yamada Sensei-ga [*gakusei*-no tukue]-o **san-nin** ket-ta.
Yamada Professor-NOM [student-GEN desk]-ACC three-CL kick-PAST
'Prof. Yamada kicked three students' desks.' (Takami 2001:137)

21. Mihara (1998) argues that FNQs are subject to different aspectual conditions depending on whether they are associated with an external or internal argument. In particular, the aspectual delimitedness of FNQs associated with an external argument must come from contexts, whereas that of FNQs associated with an internal argument must come from a lexical conceptual structure of verbs. For lack of space, I only discuss the former case here.

22. Mihara (1998) briefly notes that his analysis is able to account for why the NP within PP is generally not a suitable host NP, as in (8). He claims that the NPs *kuruma* 'car' and *paatii* 'party' in (8) do not come to exist as a result of a described situation, and so the FNQs in these examples do not express the result of counting.

23. This property may be considered as a syntactic restriction rather than a semantic one, if we adopt a view such as Diesing's (1992) that the syntax of predicates describing a permanent state differs from the syntax of predicates describing a temporal state.

24. *Hotondo* is lexically ambiguous between being a quantifier, as in (xxii), or an adverb, as in (xxiii). Crucially, unlike (53), (xxii) has both distributive and collective readings.

> (xxii) [**Hotondo**-no *otokonoko*]-ga kinoo omotya-no booto-o tukut-ta.
> [most-GEN boy]-NOM yesterday toy-GEN boat-ACC make-PAST
> 'Most of the boys made a toy boat yesterday.'
> (xxiii) John-ga **hotondo** ne-tei-ta.
> John-NOM mostly sleep-PROG-PART
> 'Most of the time, John was sleeping.'

REFERENCES

Berman, Stephen. 1991. On the semantics and Logical Form of *wh*-clauses. Doctoral dissertation, University of Massachusetts, Amherst.

Bobaljik, Jonathan D. 1995. Morphosyntax: The syntax of verbal inflection. Doctoral dissertation, MIT, Cambridge, Mass.

Bobaljik, Jonathan D. 2003. Floating quantifiers: Handle with care. In *The second Glot International state-of-the-article book: The latest in linguistics*, ed. Lisa L.-S. Cheng and Rint Sybesma, 107–148. Berlin: Mouton de Gruyter.

Chomsky, Noam. 1995. *The Minimalist Program*. Cambridge, Mass.: MIT Press.

Diesing, Molly. 1992. *Indefinites*. Cambridge, Mass.: MIT Press.

Doetjes, Jenny. 1997. *Quantifiers and selection: On the distribution of quantifying expressions in French, Dutch, and English*. The Hague: Holland Institute of Generative Linguistics.

Downing, Pamela. 1996. *Numeral classifier systems: The case of Japanese*. Amsterdam: John Benjamins.

Dowty, David. 1979. *Word meaning and Montague Grammar: The semantics of verbs and times in generative semantics and Montague's PTQ*. Dordrecht: Reidel.

Dowty, David. 1987. Collective predicates, distributive predicates, and *all*. In *Proceedings of ESCOL '86*, ed. Fred Marshall, Ann Miller, and Zheng-sheng Zhang, 97–115. Columbus: Ohio State University.

Dowty, David, and Belinda Brodie. 1984. The semantics of "floated" quantifiers in a transformationless grammar. In *Proceedings of WCCFL 3*, ed. Mark Cobler, Susannah MacKaye and Michael T. Wescoat, 75–90. Stanford, Calif.: Stanford Linguistics Association.

Fitzpatrick, Justin. 2006. The syntactic and semantic roots of floating quantification. Doctoral dissertation, MIT, Cambridge, Mass.

Fujita, Naoya. 1994. On the nature of modification: A study of floating quantifiers and related constructions. Doctoral dissertation, University of Rochester, Rochester, N.Y.

Fukushima, Kazuhiko. 1991. Generalized floating quantifiers. Doctoral dissertation, University of Arizona, Tucson.

Geenhoven, Veerle van. 1998. *Semantic incorporation and indefinite descriptions: Semantic and syntactic aspects of noun incorporation in West Greenlandic*. Stanford, Calif.: CSLI Publications.

Gunji, Takao, and Koichi Hashida. 1998. Measurement and quantification. In *Topics in constraint-based grammar of Japanese*, ed. Takao Gunji and Koichi Hashida, 39–79. Dordrecht: Kluwer.

Haig, John. 1980. Some observations on quantifier floating in Japanese. *Linguistics* 18:1065–1083.

Hamano, Shoko. 1997. On Japanese quantifier floating. In *Directions in Functional Linguistics*, ed. Akio Kamio, 173–197. Amsterdam: John Benjamins.

Harada, Shin-Ichi. 1976. Quantifier float as a relational rule. *Metropolitan Linguistics* 1:44–49.

Hasegawa, Nobuko. 1993. Floating quantifiers and bare NP expressions. In *Japanese syntax in comparative grammar*, ed. Nobuko Hasegawa, 115–145. Tokyo: Kuroshio.

Hoeksema, Jacob. 1996. Floating quantifiers, partitives, and distributivity. In *Partitives: Studies on the syntax and semantics of partitive and related constructions*, ed. Jacob Hoeksema, 57–106. Berlin: Mouton de Gruyter.

Hoji, Hajime, and Yasuo Ishii. 2004. What gets mapped to the tripartite structure of quantification in Japanese. In *Proceedings of WCCFL 23*, ed. Vineeta Chand, Ann Kelleher, Angelo J. Rodríguez, and Benjamin Schmeiser, 101–114. Somerville, Mass.: Cascadilla Press.

Inoue, Kazuko. 1978. *Nihongo-no bunpoo kisoku* [Grammar rules in Japanese]. Tokyo: Taisyukan.

Ishii, Yasuo. 1999. A note on floating quantifiers in Japanese. In *Linguistics: In search of the human mind, A festschrift for Kazuko Inoue*, ed. Masatake Muraki and Enoch Iwamoto, 236–267. Tokyo: Kaitakusha.

Junker, Marie-Odile. 1995. *Syntax et semantique des quantifieurs flottants* tous *et* chacun: *Distributivite en semantique conceptuelle*. Geneva: Librarie Droz.

Kamio, Akio. 1977. Syuuryousi-no sintakkusu: Nihongo-no henkei-o meguru giron-eno iti siryou [Syntax of numeral quantifiers: A piece of data for debates on transformation in Japanese]. *Gengo* [Language] 6(8):83–91.

Kamio, Akio. 1983. Meishiku-no koozoo [The structure of noun phrases]. In *Nihongo-no kihon koozoo* [The basic structure of Japanese], ed. Kazuko Inoue, 77–126. Tokyo: Sanseido.

Katagiri, Masumi. 1991. Review article of Miyagawa (1989). *Studies in Language* 15:399–414.

Kawashima, Ruriko. 1998. The structure of extended nominal phrases: The scrambling of numerals, approximate numerals, and quantifiers in Japanese. *Journal of East Asian Linguistics* 7:1–26.

Kikuchi, Akira. 1994. Extraction from NP in Japanese. In *Current topics in English and Japanese*, ed. Masaru Nakamura, 79–104. Tokyo: Hituzi Syobo.

Kitagawa, Yoshihisa. 1986. Subject in Japanese and English. Doctoral dissertation, University of Massachusetts, Amherst.
Kitagawa, Yoshihisa, and S.-Y. Kuroda. 1992. Passive in Japanese. Ms., University of Rochester and University of California, San Diego.
Ko, Heejeong. 2005. Syntax of *why*-in-situ: Merge into [Spec,CP] in the overt syntax. *Natural Language & Linguistic Theory* 23:867–916.
Kratzer, Angelika. 1995. Stage-level predicates and individual-level predicates. In *The generic book*, ed. Gregory N. Carlson and Francis Jeffry Pelletier, 125–175. Chicago: University of Chicago Press.
Krifka, Manfred. 1992. Thematic relations as links between nominal reference and temporal constitution. In *Lexical matters*, ed. Ivan A. Sag and Anna Szabolcsi, 29–53. Stanford, Calif.: CSLI Publications.
Kuno, Susumu. 1978a. *Danwa-no bunpoo* [Discourse grammar]. Tokyo: Taishukan.
Kuno, Susumu. 1978b. Theoretical perspectives on Japanese linguistics. In *Problems in Japanese syntax and semantics*, ed. John Hinds and Irwin Howard, 213–285. Tokyo: Kaitakusha.
Kuroda, S.-Y. 1980. Bunkoozoo-no hikaku [A comparative study of the structure of sentences]. In *Nitieigo hikaku kooza 2: Bunpoo* [Lectures on a comparative study of Japanese and English 2: Grammar], ed. Tetsuya Kunihiro, 23–61. Tokyo: Taishukan.
Kuroda, S.-Y. 1988. Whether we agree or not: A comparative syntax of English and Japanese. *Lingvisticae Investigationes* 12:1–47.
Li, Yen-Hui Audrey. 1999. Plurality in a classifier language. *Journal of East Asian Linguistics* 8:75–99.
McCloskey, James. 2000. Quantifier float and *wh*-movement in an Irish English. *Linguistic Inquiry* 31:57–84.
Merchant, Jason. 1996. Object scrambling and quantifier float in German. In *Proceedings of NELS 26*, ed. Kiyomi Kusumoto, 179–193. Amherst, Mass.: GLSA Publications.
Mihara, Ken-Ichi. 1998. Suuryoosi renketu koobun-to 'kekka'-no gan'i [Quantifier linking construction and the implication of 'resultative']. *Gengo* [Language] 6:86–95, 7:94–102, 8:104–113.
Miyagawa, Shigeru. 1989. *Structure and Case marking in Japanese*. San Diego, Calif.: Academic Press.
Miyagawa, Shigeru, and Koji Arikawa. 2007. Locality in syntax and floated numeral quantifiers. *Linguistic Inquiry* 38:645–670.
Miyamoto, Yoichi. 1994. Secondary predicates and tense. Doctoral dissertation, University of Connecticut, Storrs.
Nakanishi, Kimiko. 2004. Domains of measurement: Formal properties of non-split/split quantifier constructions. Doctoral dissertation, University of Pennsylvania, Philadelphia.
Nakanishi, Kimiko. 2007a. *Formal properties of measurement constructions*. Berlin: Mouton de Gruyter.
Nakanishi, Kimiko. 2007b. Measurement in the nominal and verbal domains. *Linguistics and Philosophy* 30:235–276.
Nakanishi, Kimiko, and Maribel Romero. 2004. Two constructions with *most* and their semantic properties. In *Proceedings of NELS 34*, ed. Keir Moulton and Matthew Wolf, 453–467. Amherst, Mass.: GLSA Publications.
Nishigauchi, Taisuke, and Yasuo Ishii. 2003. *Eigo-kara nihongo-o miru* [Looking at Japanese from English]. Tokyo: Kenkyusya.

Nishigauchi, Taisuke, and Asako Uchibori. 1991. Japanese bare NPs and syntax-semantics correspondences in quantification. Ms., Osaka University and University of Connecticut, Storrs.
Ohki, Mitsuru. 1987. Nihongo-no yuuri suuryoosi-no danwa kinoo-ni tuite [On discourse functions of floating quantifiers in Japanese]. *Sityookaku Gaikokugokyooiku Kenkyuu* [Research in audio-visual education of foreign languages] 10:37–68.
Okutsu, Keiichiro. 1969. Suuryooteki-hyoogen-no bumpoo [The grammar of quantificational expressions]. *Nihongo Kyooiku* [Japanese Language Education] 14:2–60.
Perlmutter, David. 1978. Impersonal passives and the unaccusative hypothesis. In *Proceedings of the Berkeley Linguistics Society 4*, ed. A. C. Woodbury, F. Ackerman, C. Chiarelo, O. D. Gensler, J. J. Jaeger, J. Kingston, E. E. Sweetser, H. T. Thompson, and W. Whistler, 157–189. Berkeley, Calif.: Berkeley Linguistics Society.
Saito, Mamoru. 1985. Some asymmetries in Japanese and their theoretical implications. Doctoral dissertation, MIT, Cambridge, Mass.
Shibatani, Masayoshi. 1977. Grammatical relations and surface cases. *Language* 53:789–809.
Shlonsky, Ur. 1991. Quantifiers as functional heads: A study of quantifier float in Hebrew. *Lingua* 84:159–180.
Sportiche, Dominique. 1988. A theory of floating quantifiers and its corollaries for constituent structure. *Linguistic Inquiry* 19(3):425–449.
Takami, Ken-Ichi. 1998. Nihongo-no suuryoosi yuuri-ni tuite [On quantifier float in Japanese]. *Gengo* [Language] 1(3):86–95, 98–107.
Takami, Ken-Ichi. 2001. *Nitieigo-no kinooteki koobun bunseki* [A functional analysis of English and Japanese constructions]. Tokyo: Hoo Syoboo.
Takano, Yasukuni. 1984. The lexical nature of quantifiers in Japanese. *Linguistic Analysis* 14:289–311.
Terada, Michiko. 1990. Incorporation and argument structure in Japanese. Doctoral dissertation, University of Massachusetts, Amherst.
Ueda, Masanobu. 1986. On quantifier float in Japanese. In *UMOP 11*, ed. Nobuko Hasegawa and Yoshihisa Kitagawa, 203–238. Amherst, Mass.: GLSA Publications.
Watanabe, Akira. 2006. Functional projections of nominals in Japanese: Syntax of classifiers. *Natural Language & Linguistics Theory* 24:241–306.
Yamashita, Hideaki. 2001. "FNQ-scrambling" in Japanese. In *Second report of minimalization of each module in generative grammar*, 221–252. Nagoya, Japan: Nagoya University.
Yatabe, Shuichi. 1990. Quantifier floating in Japanese and the θ-hierarchy. In *Papers from CLS 26*, ed. Michael Ziolkowski, Manuela Noske, and Karen Deaton, 437–451. Chicago: Chicago Linguistic Society.

CHAPTER 12

V-V COMPOUNDS

KUNIO NISHIYAMA

12.1 INTRODUCTION

Ever since Chomsky 1970, the place of morphology in linguistic theory has been a matter of debate. Before that, transformation in the syntax was the only mechanism for word formation, but Chomsky (1970) proposed the lexicalist hypothesis. Despite Chomsky's original intention to the contrary (see Marantz 1997), the article inspired "lexicalism," an approach for word formation in the lexicon, and lexicalism was the main trend until the mid-1980s, both within Chomskian frameworks and others (such as Lexical Functional Grammar [LFG]). Baker 1988 was a turning point in this history. It resurrected the syntactic approach to word formation in restricted and thus principled ways, and this move has been strengthened with the advent of Distributed Morphology (Halle and Marantz 1993). Lexicalism, however, is also still active, not only within LFG but also in works with assumptions more or less along the lines of the main Chomskian framework (e.g., Li 2005, Reinhart and Siloni 2005). Such coexistence of the two approaches has yielded vigorous discussions on many constructions in various languages, such as noun incorporation.

The agglutinating nature of Japanese complex predicates also has been given a variety of treatments in the history of generative grammar. In fact, the history of the treatment of Japanese predicates goes hand in hand with the development of linguistic theory outlined above. Therefore, analyses of Japanese predicates have provided key insights at each stage of the development of the theory. In the earliest research, Kuroda (1965) and Kuno (1973) analyzed Japanese predicates in syntactic (i.e., transformational) terms. This analysis was reformulated as Incorporation (i.e., head movement) by Baker (1988). In the interim, there appeared lexical accounts of Japanese predicates, initiated by Miyagawa (1980, 1989), Farmer

(1980, 1984), and Kitagawa (1986). Their assumptions regarding the clause structure of Japanese are by no means uniform, but what they have in common is that they form Japanese predicates in the lexicon (i.e., presyntactically). This lexicalist view of Japanese predicates is also put forward by Sells (1995). Kageyama (1989, 1993), however, proposes a modular view of morphology, where predicates are formed in both the lexicon and syntax. Applications of Distributed Morphology to Japanese predicates are found in Nishiyama 1998b, 1999 and Volpe 2005.

In terms of constructions, the center of the lexicon-versus-syntax debates has been the causative construction (see Harley, this volume). By contrast, this chapter discusses V-V compounds as yet another construction that has inspired the debate on the place of morphology in grammar.[1] As I present in this chapter, V-V compounds contain complexities (and thus challenges) not observed in other constructions. Mainly owing to such complexities, many works on V-V compounds characterize and analyze them in lexical (and also often semantic) terms, as in Kageyama 1989, 1993; Li 1993; Matsumoto 1996, 1998; Ito and Sugioka 2002; Gamerschlag 2002; Fukushima 2005; and Yumoto 2005. On the other hand, syntactic approaches to V-V compounds include Nishiyama 1998a, 1998b; Hasegawa 1998, 2000; Furukawa 1999; and Saito 2001. This chapter reviews three lexical analyses (Kageyama 1993, Li 1993, and Fukushima 2005) and one syntactic analysis (Nishiyama 1998a). I show that each analysis has its own mechanisms and constraints that are motivated by certain aspects of V-V compounds. However, when faced with other aspects, the analyses often have difficulties, which may, in the worst case, remain counterexamples or perhaps be solved by additional stipulations.

The first issue of V-V compounds is the scope of the analysis and, if one aspect is excluded, how that is justified. Next, we must consider what kinds of mechanisms are utilized for the analysis and, crucially, whether the mechanisms are independently motivated on principled grounds. The final issue is, when difficulties arise, how they are solved—that is, whether the stipulations are again independently motivated.

This chapter is organized as follows. Section 12.2 presents the core data. Section 12.3, the main section, first introduces preliminaries and then reviews the major lexical and syntactic analyses. I then discuss some complex cases as illustrations of the recalcitrant aspects of V-V compounds. Section 12.4 concludes the chapter by eliciting theoretical implications from the discussion on V-V compounds.

12.2 CORE DATA

The following sentences represent core patterns of V-V compounds that I focus on in this chapter:

(1) a. John-ga   kimono-o   ki-kuzusi-ta.
       John-NOM   kimono-ACC   wear-make.out.of.shape-PAST
       'John wore the kimono and made it out of shape.'
    b. *John-ga   kimono-o   ki-kuzure-ta.
       John-NOM   kimono-ACC   wear-get.out.of.shape-PAST
       'John wore the kimono and it got out of shape.'
    c. Kimono-ga   ki-kuzure-ta.
       kimono-NOM   wear-get.out.of.shape-PAST
       'The kimono was worn and got out of shape.'
    d. John-wa   itumo   kaban-o moti-aruk-u
       John-TOP always bag-ACC hold-walk-PRES
       'John always carries the bag around.'

Example (1a) is a combination of transitive-transitive, and this pattern is very common. When the second verb (henceforth V_2) is intransitive, as in (1b), the compound cannot take an object. But the combination in (1b) itself is not ruled out. As shown in (1c), when the whole compound functions as an intransitive, the sentence is grammatical. What is striking about (1c) is that the agent of the first verb (henceforth V_1), which is transitive, is not realized in the sentence. Example (1d) is another kind of transitive-intransitive combination with a different pattern, where both arguments of V_1 are realized.

Additionally, there are more complicated patterns in V-V compounds, as described in detail by Tagashira (1978), Tagashira and Hoff (1986), Kageyama (1993), Matsumoto (1996), Himeno (1999), and Yumoto (2005), among others. I have chosen the patterns in (1) among diverse patterns because they are systematic, and the options in accounting for them reveal the strength and weakness of competing analyses, thus providing implications for linguistic theory. I briefly discuss other patterns (some systematic, some less systematic) in later sections.

12.3 Issues and Controversies

This section presents issues and controversies surrounding V-V compounds. After the preliminaries in section 12.3.1, sections 12.3.2 and 12.3.3 overview lexical and syntactic approaches to the issues. In those two subsections, the examples discussed are rather systematic. Some complex and unexpected cases are discussed in section 12.3.4.

12.3.1 Preliminaries

This subsection overviews issues that constitute the basis for considering several analyses of V-V compounds—aspectual and psychological compounds and headedness.

12.3.1.1 *Aspectual and psychological compounds*

Many researchers use the term "lexical" V-V compounds for the compounds in (1). The term implies that there are other types of compounds—namely, "syntactic" V-V compounds. Exact analyses aside, such a distinction is largely due to Kageyama's (1989, 1993) pioneering observation on the issue. Consider the following:

(2) a. John-ga   Bill-o   osi-taosi-ta.
       John-NOM Bill-ACC push-topple$_{TR}$-PAST
       'John pushed and toppled Bill.'
    b. John-ga   hasiri-hazime-ta.
       John-NOM run-begin-PAST
       'John began to run.'
    c. John-ga   hon-o   yomi-aki-ta.
       John-NOM book-ACC read-get.bored-PAST
       'John got bored of reading a book.'

Example (2a) is a "lexical" compound as in (1), and (2b,c) are what Kageyama claims to be "syntactic" compounds. Note that V$_2$ is either aspectual or psychological in (2b,c), and it is plausible that these examples involve a biclausal structure, just like the English counterparts *John began [PRO to run]* and *John got bored of [PRO reading a book]*. But the same structure does not seem to hold in (2a). Kageyama notes some differences between (2a) and (2b,c) to confirm such an intuition. For example, *soo su-* 'so do' can substitute V$_1$ in (2b) but not in (2a):

(3) a. John-ga   hasiri-hazime-te, Bill-mo [soo si]-hazime-ta.
       John-NOM run-begin-and   Bill-also so do-begin-PAST
       'John began to run and Bill began to do so, too.'
    b. *Mary-ga   Susan-o   osi-taosi-te,   John-mo Bill-o
        Mary-NOM Susan-ACC push-topple-and John–also Bill-ACC
        [soo si]-taosi-ta.
        so do-topple-PAST
        'Mary toppled Susan by pushing her, and John toppled Bill by doing so, too.'

Another difference comes from honorification:

(4) a. **o**-hasiri-**ni nari**-hazimeru   b. **o**-hasiri-hazime-**ni naru**
       run.HON-begin   [run-begin].HON
    c. ***o**-osi-**ni nari**-taosu   d. **o**-osi-taosi-**ni naru**
       push.HON-topple   [push-topple].HON

Honorification is a process of surrounding the verb with *o-* and *-ni naru*, deriving *o-V-ni naru*. Examples (4a,b) show that with aspectual compounds, it is possible to honorify only V$_1$ or the whole compound. In (4c,d), however, one cannot honorify only V$_1$ and the honorification must be on the whole compound.

Based on these and other differences, Kageyama (1989, 1993) proposes that, whereas the compounds in (2b,c) are formed in the syntax, that in (2a) is formed in the lexicon. Kageyama's analysis for "syntactic" V-V compounds seems to be widely accepted.[2] It is the analysis of "lexical" V-V compounds—that is, whether they are formed in the lexicon or in the syntax—that distinguishes between researchers. In the remainder of this chapter, I do not discuss aspectual and psychological compounds. See Nishiyama 1998a and Saito 2001 for ways to account for the contrast in (3) and (4) on the assumption that both types of compounds are formed in the syntax. I also refrain from using the terminology "lexical" compounds, for it presupposes the analysis.

12.3.1.2 Headedness

There is a general agreement among researchers that V_2 is the head in V-V compounds in Japanese, which is initially motivated by the universality of right-headedness in morphology (see Williams 1981a). Additional evidence comes from the case frame (see Kageyama 1993 and Nishiyama 1998a):

(5) John-ga   Mary-ni/*o   oi-tui-ta.
    John-NOM   Mary-DAT/ACC   chase-attach-PAST
    'John chased and attached to (i.e., caught up with) Mary.'

By itself, *oi-* 'chase' takes an accusative object, and *tui-* 'attach' a dative object. When they combine to form a compound, the object takes a dative marker, which shows the precedence of V_2 in the case frame. Which part is the head is an important issue in the analysis of V-V compounds. In addition to case, transitivity and argument realization of the compound are heavily influenced by those of the head. Although there are cases where the right-headedness of V-V compounds becomes obscure (e.g., dvandva (28) and noncompositional cases (30), discussed briefly later), this feature seems to be quite persistent in V-V compounds and is assumed by most researchers.

Li (1993) is exceptional among researchers regarding the position of the head. He assumes that in Japanese V-V compounds, both V_1 and V_2 are heads,[3] arguing that this assumption derives several differences between V-V compounds in Japanese and V-V compounds in Chinese. I return to Li's analysis shortly.

12.3.2 Lexical Approaches

This subsection reviews three lexical accounts: Kageyama 1993, Li 1993, and Fukushima 2005. Because the first two share common features, they are discussed together. Although Matsumoto 1996 is another comprehensive work on V-V compounds in lexical terms (i.e., within the LFG framework), it is not discussed here because, although rich in data, the analysis focuses on semantic characterizations of V-V compounds with constraints whose status is not clear in Universal

Grammar (UG). See Fukushima 2005 for a review of Matsumoto 1996 and its limitations.

12.3.2.1 *Kageyama 1993 and Li 1993*

Kageyama 1993 and Li 1993 propose "argument structure composition" as a lexical process[4] to produce the compound as follows:

(6) a. John-ga   Bill-o   osi-taosi-ta.   = (2a)
       John-NOM Bill-ACC push-topple$_{TR}$-PAST
       'John pushed and toppled Bill.'

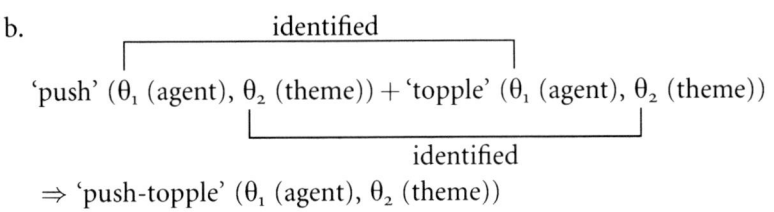

   b.   identified
       ┌───┐
       'push' (θ$_1$ (agent), θ$_2$ (theme)) + 'topple' (θ$_1$ (agent), θ$_2$ (theme))
                              └─────────────────────────────┘
                                     identified
       ⇒ 'push-topple' (θ$_1$ (agent), θ$_2$ (theme))

This is an extension of Grimshaw's (1990) theory of Argument Structure. In this process of composition, the more prominent θ-roles of the two verbs are identified, as well as the less prominent θ-roles. The result is one complex verb with two θ-roles. Thus, as far as the syntax is concerned, there is no difference between compounds and ordinary simplex verbs.

Let us next see the combination of transitive-intransitive ((1b,c) are repeated here).

(1) b. *John-ga   kimono-o   ki-kuzure-ta.
       John-NOM kimono-ACC wear-get.out.of.shape-PAST
       'John wore the kimono and it got out of shape.'
   c. Kimono-ga   ki-kuzure-ta.
       kimono-NOM wear-get.out.of.shape-PAST
       'The kimono was worn and got out of shape.'

Kageyama (1993) rules out (1b) by a constraint that prohibits a combination of a transitive and an unaccusative. To rule in (1c), Kageyama assumes that it is derived by back-formation from the transitive-transitive counterpart in (1a). That is, (1c) is not derived by compounding a transitive and an unaccusative directly but by detransitivizing the transitive-transitive counterpart.

However, there are problems with back-formation. Consider this example:

(7) Kouzyou-ga osui-o   tare-nagas-u.
    factory-NOM polluted.water-ACC drip$_{INTR}$-pour$_{TR}$-PRES
    'The factory drains polluted water.'   (Hasegawa 1998)

Example (7) involves a combination of unaccusative-transitive. Therefore, Kageyama (1993) would derive it by back-formation. However, as pointed out by

Hasegawa (1998), (7) cannot be derived by back-formation, for there is no "original" combination of transitive-transitive or unaccusative-unaccusative for the compound in (7); *tare-nagare(ru) 'drip$_{INTR}$-pour$_{INTR}$' and *tarasi-nagas(u) 'drip$_{TR}$-pour$_{TR}$' do not exist. The same problem is also pointed out by Matsumoto (1996:230).

Li (1993) rules out (1b) by a constraint that says that the most prominent argument of a head (both V$_1$ and V$_2$ for Japanese V-V compounds in his analysis) must remain the most prominent in the compound as well. Because the most prominent argument of the unaccusative V$_2$ (head) in (1b), which is the theme (trivially), is assigned to the object of the compound, (1b) violates this constraint. In the transitive-transitive pair as in (1a), in contrast, the most prominent argument of V$_2$, the agent, is assigned to the subject of the compound, thus obeying this constraint. However, Li does not discuss how (1c) can be ruled in. As for the headedness, the reason why Li assumes that V$_1$ is a head in Japanese V-V compounds is the following:

(8) *John-ga   Mary-o   odori-aki-ta.
      John-NOM Mary-ACC dance-bored-PAST
      'Mary danced and John got bored.'   (Li 1993:(12))

On the assumption that V$_1$ is a head in Japanese V-V compounds, Li rules out (8) by the prominence constraint, because the most prominent argument of V$_1$ is assigned to the object of the sentence.

We saw in section 12.2 that there is another pattern with the combination of transitive-intransitive. I repeat example (1d) as (9a) with an additional one:

(9) a. John-wa   itumo   kaban-o   moti-aruk-u.   = (1d)
        John-TOP always   bag-ACC   hold-walk-PRES
        'John always carries the bag around.'
     b. John-ga   kodomo-o   ture-sat-ta.
        John-NOM child-ACC   take-leave-PAST
        'John took the child away.'

One special character of (9) is that the object of the compound is originally the object of only V$_1$, given that V$_2$ is intransitive and does not take an object. In other words, there is no object sharing—a requirement often observed in serial verb constructions (see Baker 1989).

According to Kageyama (1993), the compounds in (9a) are formed as follows:

(10) V$_1$ <agent, theme> + V$_2$ <agent> ⇒ V-V <agent, theme>

Here, the agent roles of both V$_1$ and V$_2$ are identified, and are inherited by the entire compound. As for the theme, although argument inheritance usually takes place from the head V$_2$, V$_2$ in (10) contains no theme. Therefore, the theme argument of V$_1$ can be inherited by the compound. However, the compound in (9b) cannot be formed by argument structure composition. This is because, if, as assumed by Kageyama, V₂ sat- (⟨sar-¹⟩) 'leave' is an unaccusative and its sole argument is the theme, argument structure composition would wrongly compose it with the theme argument of V₁ (*kodomo* 'child'). Given that the themes of V₁ and V₂ are realized as distinct arguments, obviously no argument structure composition should be happening. Another problem is that, according to Kageyama's constraint that prohibits a combination of a transitive and an unaccusative, compounding in (9b) should not be possible. Kageyama stipulates that the compound in (9b) is formed not in Argument Structure but in Lexical Conceptual Structure. However, as pointed out by Nishiyama (1998a), there seems to be no principled way to predict whether a compound is formed in Argument Structure, by back-formation, or in Lexical Conceptual Structure.

12.3.2.2 *Fukushima 2005*

Fukushima (2005) offers yet another lexical account for V-V compounds. His analysis is like Kageyama's and Li's in that the locus of compounding is Argument Structure located in the lexicon. Unlike Kageyama and Li, however, Fukushima utilizes the notion "matching" for argument sharing, because he adopts Dowty's (1991) proposal to regard thematic roles as "prototypes."⁵ But the actual outputs of argument matching are not substantially different from those of θ-identification outlined in the last subsection, and I do not review how Fukushima forms transitive-transitive pairs. Let us see instead how Fukushima deals with transitive-intransitive pairs:

(11) a. *John-ga   kimono-o   ki-kuzure-ta.   = (1b)
        John-NOM   kimono-ACC   wear-get.out.of.shape-PAST
        'John wore the kimono and it got out of shape.'
     b. Kimono-ga   ki-kuzure-ta.   = (1c)
        kimono-NOM   wear-get.out.of.shape-PAST
        'The kimono was worn and got out of shape.'
     c. John-ga   kodomo-o   ture-sat-ta.   = (9b)
        John-NOM   take-leave-PAST
        child-ACC
        'John took the child away.'

The crucial operations and constraints that Fukushima postulates can be summarized as follows:

(12) a. Take the least oblique (i.e., most prominent) argument of each verb. If those arguments do not match, dismiss the argument of the nonhead and move to the next least oblique argument of the nonhead.
     b. If a match is found, move to the next arguments of the head and nonhead and find a match.
     c. After the first match is found, do not dismiss any more arguments from the nonhead.

The situation in (11b) is schematized as follows:

(13)

$$V_1 \langle x, y \rangle + V_2 \langle y \rangle \Rightarrow \text{V-V} \langle (\exists x), y \rangle$$

with "no matching" bracketing x of V$_1$ and the V$_2$ argument set, "dismissed" pointing to x of V$_1$, and "matching" on the y's.

Here, x represents the proto-agent, and y the proto-patient. The least oblique arguments—namely, x of V$_1$ and y of V$_2$—do not match. Thus, by (12a) the former is dismissed. The dismissed argument cannot be realized syntactically, and this rules out (11a). However, it is existentially quantified, as represented in the output in (13), and I will return to this shortly. Also by (12a), the next search should be in the nonhead (V$_1$), and we find a match between the two y's. The situation in (11c) is as follows:

(14)

$$V_1 \langle x, y \rangle + V_2 \langle x \rangle \Rightarrow \text{V-V} \langle x, y \rangle$$

with "matching" over the two x's, and "not dismissed" pointing to y of V$_1$.

Here, the two x's match,[6] and by (12c), y in V$_1$ is not dismissed and is realized syntactically, as *kodomo-o* in (11c).

The evaluation of Fukushima's analysis centers on the status, characterization, and predictions of (12). First, the status of (12) in UG is not clear and raises many questions. Why does dismissal happen in (13) but not (14)? Just like x in (13) fails to match with the argument in V$_2$, so does y in (14). Given that such a mechanism is not proposed in other languages or in other constructions in Japanese, it is desirable that (12) is derived from other independently motivated principles.

Second, the characterization of the dismissed argument needs more elaboration. Dismissal here is different from the "suppression" that happens to the agent in passivization, for (11b) does not license a *ni*-phrase ('*by*-phrase'). In this sense, dismissal of an argument is a novel operation in linguistic theory. This aspect aside, existential quantification of the dismissed argument seems empirically controversial. As discussed in the next subsection, Nishiyama (1998a) claims that the agent is completely missing in (11b). This is motivated by the following contrast:

(15) a. Wazato   kimono-ga   ki-kuzus-are-ta.
        deliberately kimono-NOM wear-make.out.of.shape-PASS-PAST
        'The kimono was deliberately worn and made out of shape.'
     b. *Wazato   kimono-ga   ki-kuzure-ta.
        deliberately kimono-NOM wear-get.out.of.shape-PAST

Example (15a) is a passive of the transitive-transitive pair, and it licenses the agent-oriented adverb *wazato* 'deliberately.'[7] Example (15b) uses the intransitive (unaccusative) counterpart of the transitive V₂ in (15a), and it cannot license *wazato*. According to Nishiyama, this is because the compound *ki-kuzure-* has no agent. Fukushima objects to this conclusion, citing the following examples:

(16) a. Dou site-mo kimono-ga ki-kuzure-ta.
        how do-even kimono-NOM wear-get.out.of.shape-PAST
        'The kimono lost its original shape due to (someone's) wearing it in whatever the manner the wearer tried wearing it.'
    b. Ukkari kimono-ga ki-kuzure-ta.
        unwittingly kimono-NOM wear-get.out.of.shape-PAST
        '(Due to someone's) unwittingly wearing (it), the kimono lost its original shape.' (adapted from Fukushima 2005)

In the sentences in (16), apparently an agent-oriented adverb is licensed by *ki-kuzure-*. Based on this, Fukushima claims that the agent is present semantically, if not syntactically, in the compound.

However, it is not straightforward what to do with (16). As pointed out by a referee for Fukushima 2005, *doo site-mo* can be analyzed as a full sentence involving a light verb *su-* 'do':

(17) [$_S$ *pro* [$_{VP}$ doo site]-mo]
                how do even
    'No matter how one does...'

Then (16a) is analogous to the following example and is irrelevant to the issue of whether the compound involves the agent:

(18) John-ga osi-tara door-ga ai-ta.
      John-NOM push-when door-NOM open-PAST
      'When John pushed (it), the door opened.'

In (18), there is no thematic relation between 'John' and 'open,' and the agentive reading in the second sentence, if it ever exists, is implied contextually from the first sentence. Example (16b) is cited by Fukushima to circumvent such a potential problem of (16a). But *ukkari* can also be analyzed in the same way as *doo site-mo*, for it can optionally take the light verb, as in *ukkari-site*. Apparently the existence and treatment of the alleged agent in combinations like (11b) needs further research.

As for the empirical side, there is at least one combination for which Fukushima's prediction is incorrect or unclear at best. Before discussing this example, let us first consider the following analysis by Fukushima:

(19) a. (Taroo-no) hoho-ga naki-nure-ta   (Fukushima 2005:(29b))
        Taroo-GEN cheek-NOM cry-get.wet-PAST
        '(Taroo's) cheeks got wet due to (his) crying.'

b.   no matching

$$V_1 \langle x \rangle + V_2 \langle y \rangle \Rightarrow \text{V-V} \langle (\exists x), y \rangle$$
   ↓
dismissed

Example (19a) is analyzed as in (19b). Given that x in V_1 and y in V_2 do not match, the former is dismissed.

Now consider the following example ((7) is repeated here), for which Fukushima does not give an analysis:

(7)   Kouzyou-ga   osui-o   tare-nagas-u.
      factory-NOM polluted.water-ACC drip$_{\text{INTR}}$-pour$_{\text{TR}}$-PRES
      'The factory drains polluted water.'

The problem here is that the prediction based on (12) is not borne out:

(20)   a.   *Prediction based on (12a)*

           no matching

$$V_1 \langle y \rangle + V_2 \langle x, y \rangle \Rightarrow \text{V-V} \langle x, (\exists ?y)? \rangle$$
↓
dismissed

    b.   *Actual situation*

           matching

$$V_1 \langle y \rangle + V_2 \langle x, y \rangle \Rightarrow \text{V-V} \langle x, y \rangle$$
↓
not dismissed

According to (12a), because y of V_1 and x of V_2 do not match, the former should be dismissed, as in (20a), contrary to fact. Note that in (7), y in V_1 is realized as *osui-o* 'polluted water'. Note also that it cannot be the case that at least one argument of a verb must survive, for the sole argument of V_1 is dismissed in (19b). The problem stems from the fact that (12a) stipulates that the next move should be in the *nonhead*, implying that when the nonhead is intransitive, the next move is impossible. For the matching between the two y's to happen as in (20b), the next move must be in the *head*. But if (12a) is modified to the effect that the next move can be in either the head or the nonhead, we would have a serious indeterminacy unless some principle is found that determines in which domain the next move should occur. Additionally, the fate of the nonmatching argument of the nonhead must be stipulated so that it is dismissed when the next move is in the nonhead (as in (11b) and (13)) or there is no second move (as in (19)) but survives when the next move is in the head (as in (7) and (20b)).

Other types of compounds discussed by Fukushima (2005) include mirror image compounds and compounds with flexible argument realization. I return to them in section 12.3.4.

12.3.3 Syntactic Account: Nishiyama 1998a

In contrast to the lexical approaches reviewed so far, Nishiyama (1998a) proposes a syntactic account of V-V compounds. The initial motivation for this is the parallelism between V-V compounds and serial verb constructions widely known cross-linguistically:[8]

(21) a. Femi ti Akin subu.
       push   Akin fall
       'Femi pushed Akin down.'   (Yoruba; Baker 1989)
    b. m-a   da   nu   du.
       I-FUT cook thing eat
       'I will cook something and eat it.'   (Ewe; Collins 1997)

Extending the analysis of serial verb constructions by Collins (1997) to V-V- compounds in Japanese, Nishiyama proposes that (22a) is analyzed as in (22b).

(22) a. John-ga   Bill-o   osi-taosi-ta   = (2a)/(6a)
       John-NOM   Bill-ACC   push-topple$_{TR}$-PAST
       'John pushed and toppled Bill.'

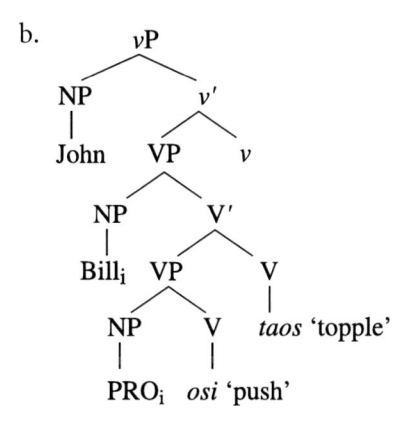

   b.   vP
                  /   \
               NP   v'
               | /   \
              John   VP   v
                     /   \
                   NP   V'
                   | /   \
                 Bill$_i$ VP   V
                        /   \ |
                      NP   V   taos 'topple'
                      | |
                    PRO$_i$ osi 'push'

Each verb assigns only the internal role (theme), and the external role (agent) is assigned by another head v. (Nishiyama 1998a uses the label TrP for vP.) Argument sharing of the internal role is implemented by control,[9] and compounding is due to head movement.

The combination of transitive-intransitive (unaccusative)[10] is analyzed as follows ((1b,c) are repeated here):

(1) b. *John-ga   kimono-o   ki-kuzure-ta.
       John-NOM kimono-ACC wear-get.out.of.shape-PAST
       'John wore the kimono and it got out of shape.'
    c. Kimono-ga   ki-kuzure-ta.
       kimono-NOM wear-get.out.of.shape-PAST
       'The kimono was worn and got out of shape.'

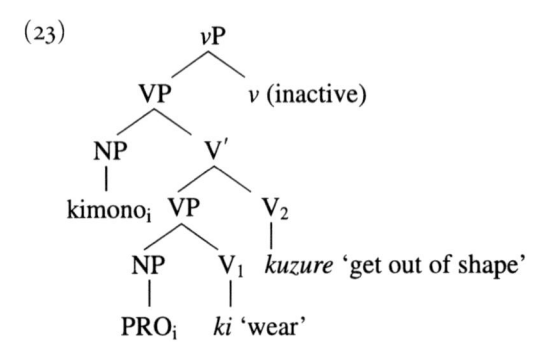

(23)
```
              vP
             /  \
           VP    v (inactive)
          /  \
        NP    V'
        |    /  \
    kimono_i VP   V_2
           /  \    |
         NP   V_1  kuzure 'get out of shape'
         |    |
        PRO_i ki 'wear'
```

Here, v is inactive and does not introduce the external argument. There is a selectional relation between v and VP: inactive v selects VP headed by an unaccusative. (In (22b), in contrast, active v selects transitive VP.) The surface subject is the underlying object of the unaccusative V_2 and is generated in the specifier of the matrix VP. Although V_1 is transitive, by hypothesis there is no external argument in the embedded VP. Nishiyama (1998a) takes (1c) as strong evidence that the external roles are not assigned by the verb but by v. Note that the selectional relation holds only one way. Thus, although active v requires a transitive verb, a transitive verb does not require active v. Given that (23) does not contain active v, there is no way to license an external argument, ruling out (1b).

The example in (19a), repeated here, would be given a similar account.

(19) a. (Taroo-no)   hoho-ga   naki-nure-ta.
        Taroo-GEN   cheek-NOM   cry-get.wet-PAST
        '(Taroo's) cheeks got wet due to (his) crying.'

The structure is like (23), except that embedded VP has no object. Because *naki-* 'cry' does not contain the agent as its argument, it can survive without the agent when it is selected by a verb, as in (23).

As a mirror image of the transitive-unaccusative combinations, there are also combinations of unaccusative-transitive. I provided one example in (7). The following is another example of such a combination:

(24) John-ga   soup-o   huki-kobosi-ta.   (Nishiyama 1998a:(43a))
     John-NOM soup-ACC boil.over$_{INTR}$-spill$_{TR}$-PAST
     'The soup boiled over and John spilled it.'

In the analysis of Nishiyama 1998a, (24) has a structure that is virtually identical to the transitive-transitive combination as in (22b). In this system, although active v selects transitive VP as V_2, there is no requirement that a transitive V_2 select transitive VP as V_1, and a transitive V_2 can freely select unaccusative VP as V_1.

Japanese V-V compounds can involve ditransitive verbs, exemplified as follows:

(25) a. John-ga   Mary-ni   hon-o   nage-watasi-ta.
       John-NOM Mary-DAT book-ACC throw-pass-PAST
       'John threw a book and passed it to Mary.'
   b. John-ga   hon-o   Mary-ni   yuzuri-watasi-ta.
       John-NOM book-ACC Mary-DAT yield-pass-PAST
       'John handed over the book to Mary by yielding it to her.'
$\hspace{5cm}$ ((25b) adapted from Fukushima 2005)

Example (25a) contains a transitive verb as V_1 and a ditransitive as V_2. In (25b), both verbs are ditransitives. Such combinations can be treated rather straightforwardly by lexical approaches. However, Nishiyama's control analysis of argument sharing requires a specific treatment of ditransitives among several choices. For this reason, I discuss ditransitive compounds in this subsection.

As pointed out by Fukushima (2005), if both the goal and theme are internal arguments of ditransitive verbs and two controls are involved, we cannot obtain a proper interpretation.

(26)   [goal theme [PRO PRO V] V]

Given that the closest c-commanding argument is the controller, the structure in (26) predicts that the theme is the controller for both PROs, which yields a wrong interpretation. One might circumvent the problem by adopting the movement analysis of control (see note 9). In this analysis, the PROs in (26) are traces, and our task is to guarantee the correct landing site for each argument. Another way out is as follows:

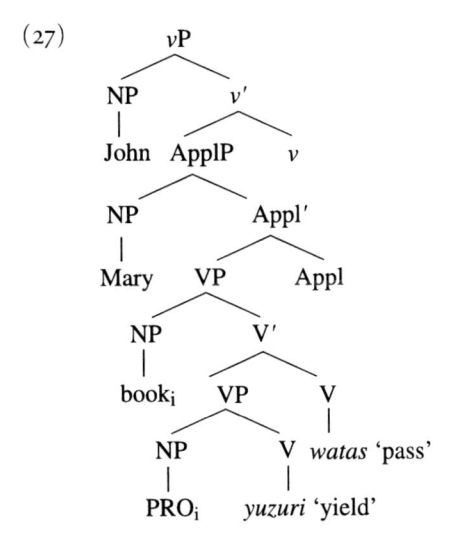

(27)
```
                vP
              /    \
            NP      v'
            |      /  \
           John ApplP   v
               /     \
              NP      Appl'
              |      /    \
            Mary    VP    Appl
                   /  \
                  NP   V'
                  |   /  \
               book_i VP   V
                     /  \   |
                    NP   V  watas 'pass'
                    |    |
                  PRO_i yuzuri 'yield'
```

Example (27) assumes that the goal is introduced by an independent head Appl (for applicative) (see Marantz 1993 and Pylkkänen 2002, among others). In this approach, there is a one-to-one relation between an argument and a head, and even the ditransitive verb has only the theme as its core (original) argument. Just like the agent is not included in the argument structure of the verb, the goal is not, either.[11]

Another potential challenge for Nishiyama's analysis is a dvandva:

(28) a. John-ga naki-saken-da.
   John-NOM cry-scream-PAST
   'John cried and screamed.'
   b. [agent [vp V₁] [vp V₂] v]

Dvandva V-V compounds typically consist of two unergatives. They can be analyzed as involving a coordinate VP structure as in (28b).[12]

Let us next consider (9a), repeated here.

(9) a. John-wa itumo kaban-o moti-aruk-u.   = (1d)
   John-TOP always bag-ACC hold-walk-PRES
   'John always carries the bag around.'

In this example, there is no object sharing, and the object of V₁ is overtly realized. Given that this overt object requires Case, by Burzio's Generalization there is an external argument in the embedded clause. Nishiyama (1998a) stipulates that motion verbs are specified to c-select vP as follows:

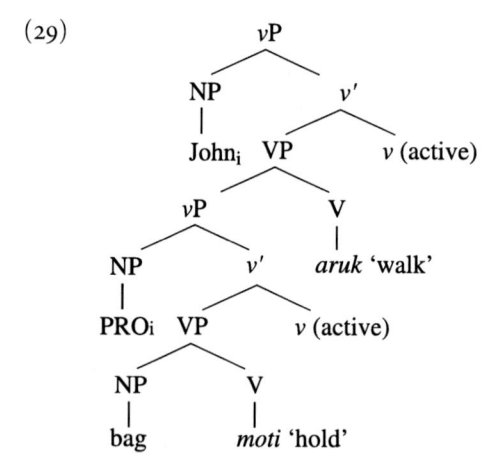

(29)
```
              vP
             /  \
           NP    v'
           |    /  \
         Johnᵢ VP   v (active)
              /  \
            vP    V
           /  \   |
         NP    v' aruk 'walk'
         |    /  \
       PROᵢ  VP   v (active)
            /  \
          NP    V
          |     |
         bag   moti 'hold'
```

Here, *John* is the agent introduced by active *v*. It controls PRO, which is the external argument of the embedded clause. This analysis can basically be extended to *ture-sar-* 'take-leave' in (9b). Given that 'leave' is a motion verb, it takes vP, as in (29). If *aruk-* 'walk' and *sar-* 'leave' belong to the same verb class, the same structure as in (29) holds for *ture-sar-* 'take-leave'. If, however, *sar-* is an unaccusative distinct from *aruk-* 'walk', there is a slight difference. Unlike the structure for (9a) in (29), where the subject is the agent introduced by active *v*, the subject is the underlying object of the unaccusative V₂.

As we have seen in (22b) and (23), VP-complementation is crucial for other types of combination for Nishiyama's analysis. Therefore, the selection of *v*P as in (29) should be restricted somehow. For Nishiyama, this is obtained by stipulating that only motion verbs c-select *v*P. Fukushima (2005:599) objects to this, claiming that *taore*- 'fall' is as good a "motion" verb as *sar*- 'leave' but still cannot serve as V$_2$ when V$_1$ is transitive. This is illustrated by the following:

(30) a. John-ga   Bill-o   osi-taosi-ta.   = (2a)/(6a)/(22a)
         John-NOM Bill-ACC   push-topple$_{TR}$-PAST
         'John pushed and toppled Bill.'
     b. *John-ga   Mary-o   osi-taore-ta.
         John-NOM Mary–ACC   push-fall-PAST
         'John pushed Mary and he fell.'

The compound in (30b) is transitive-unaccusative, and the sentence is ungrammatical. The translation is meant to parallel the situation in (29). (Example (30a) is cited for comparison.) Although one can say that including the notion "change of location" into the definition of motion verbs excludes *taore*- 'fall' as a motion verb, the proper treatment of the pattern in (9) awaits further research.

12.3.4 Complex and Unexpected Cases

So far, we have seen cases where the combination of verbs and argument realizations are more or less straightforward. Although each analysis reviewed here resorts to its own specific mechanisms and stipulations, the data discussed have been rather "systematic," and it seems somehow that the pattern should be generated by grammar (either the syntax or the lexicon). This section is concerned with more recalcitrant cases. In section 12.3.4.1, idiosyncratic characteristics in compounding (i.e., noncompositionality and restriction in nominalization) are discussed. It is generally believed that idiosyncrasies are the hallmarks of the lexicon, so this subsection focuses on how syntactic approaches to morphology can handle idiosyncrasies. In particular, I develop possible ways to treat the idiosyncrasies of V-V compounds syntactically within principles of Distributed Morphology (Halle and Marantz 1993), building on Volpe 2005 and Arad 2003. In sections 12.3.4.2 and 12.3.4.3, accidental gaps and some peculiar combinations are discussed.

12.3.4.1 *Idiosyncrasies and Distributed Morphology*

12.3.4.1.1 Noncompositionality

The following examples illustrate compounds whose meanings are not compositional:

(31) a. oti-tuk(u)   fall-attach$_{INTR}$ 'get calm'
     b. sikari-tuker(u) scold-attach$_{TR}$ 'scold harshly'
     c. tori-simar(u)   take-tighten$_{INTR}$ 'crack down on'

In (31a), the original meaning of each verb is bleached and the compound as a whole assumes a new meaning. In (31b), from Matsumoto 1996, although V$_1$ *sikar-* 'scold' retains its original meaning, the semantic contribution of V$_2$ seems to be limited to modification.[13] Such a drift proceeds further in (31c) (from Fukushima 2005), which has a peculiar thematic relation in addition to the new meaning. Thus, whereas V$_2$ is originally intransitive (unaccusative), the whole compound is transitive, in apparent violation of right-headedness in V-V compounds.

For Fukushima (2005), noncompositional compounds as in (31) are outside the scope of his analysis to generate systematic patterns in V-V compounds in the lexicon. But if one adopts the view that the syntax always predicts regularity and that the lexicon is a kind of "trash box" that deals with all kinds of idiosyncrasies, the only conclusion drawn from (31) is that V-V compounds are generated in the lexicon. But nowadays not every researcher takes such a view of the lexicon. In fact, Distributed Morphology abandons the lexicon altogether as a locus of word formation. Below I discuss how and to what extent the idiosyncrasies in (31) can be treated in Distributed Morphology.

Volpe (2005) proposes an analysis of Aronoff's (1976) pioneering generative insights into derivational morphology within the principles of Distributed Morphology outlined by Marantz (1997) (see also Arad 2003, Embick 2004, and in particular Embick and Marantz 2008). According to Marantz, roots are categorially neutral and obtain categorial status by being selected by a functional head such as *v*, *n*, or *a*. Volpe adopts this and proposes an account of the following adjectival doublets:

(32) a. compárable   b. cómparable
     c. separatable d. separable

As noted by Aronoff (1976), *compárable* and *separatable* are transparent to the meanings of the corresponding verbs *compare* and *separate*, but *cómparable* and *separable* bear some additional meanings. Thus, *compárable* is 'capable of being compared,' whereas *cómparable* is the same as 'equivalent.' Volpe proposes that this is accounted for as follows:[14]

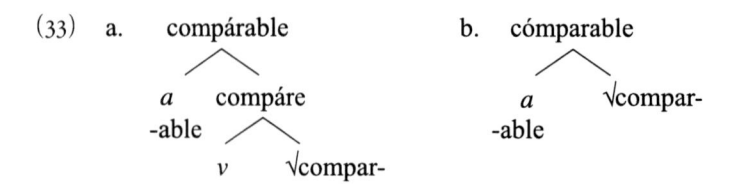

(33) a.   compárable   b.   cómparable
         /\   /\
        a   compáre   a   √compar-
       -able /\   -able
             v   √compar-

In (33a), *compárable* contains the functional head *v*, which explains why it is like the verb *compare* in terms of meaning and stress. In (33b), in contrast, there is no v node, which is why *cómparable* bears a particular meaning. According to Volpe, roots are uninterpretable by themselves, and their meanings are fixed when they are selected by a functional head. In the case of (33a), the meaning of √*compar-* is fixed when it is selected by *v*. Because this fixed meaning remains unchanged, *compárable* carries the meaning of the verb *compare* throughout the derivation. The same accounts hold for the doublets in (32c,d). Here, the root is √*separ-*, and *-at-* is an overt realization of *v*.

Now, let us apply this concept of the so-called derivation to the idiosyncrasies in V-V compounds in (30). Example (30a) is a straightforward case. With the structure [$_{vP}$ [$_{VP}$ V$_1$ V$_2$] *v*], the meaning is fixed only after the merge of *v*. Thus, regardless of the original meanings of the verbs, the new compound can bear a new meaning. However, nothing prevents the newly produced compounds from having compositional meanings, as we have been observing in regular cases.

Example (30b) is a little less straightforward, for the semantic drift is selective and only the meaning of V$_1$ is inherited by the compound. But the situation may well be the same as in (30a). The hard case is (30c). If we assume that, in addition to meanings, the transitivity of each verb is flexible until *v* merges, we would lose the account for compositional compounds. For example, (30c) is exactly parallel with the ungrammatical (1b) in terms of transitivity. Thus, even if the exact semantics is unspecified until *v* is merged, syntactic principles (transitivity selection, in this case) must be at work within *v*P. This means that in (30c), although V$_2$ looks like an unaccusative, it is actually behaving like a transitive, making the compound also a transitive. In this analysis, (30c) has no anomaly at least in transitivity.

In short, although semantic noncompositionality can be accommodated into the syntactic approaches to V-V compounds, noncompositionality of other kinds, such as transitivity, must be handled with some kind of stipulations.

12.3.4.1.2 Nominalization

Fukushima (2005) notes an interesting property of V-V compounds from the perspective of derivational morphology: there are combinations that can appear only as nominalized forms:

(34) a. tati-gui   b. osi-uri
         stand-eat   push-sell
         'eating while standing'   'selling things aggressively'

Although each morpheme can be a verb by itself, the above compounds lack verbal counterparts; **tati-gu(u)* and **osi-ur(u)* do not exist. Fukushima claims that this is a problem for a syntactic approach to V-V compounds, for there are no "original" verbal counterparts for (34). But the notion of categories outlined in section 12.3.4.1.1 provides a way to handle (34) in syntactic terms. In fact, according to the root-as-categorially-neutral view, there is no process of "nominalization" in the lexicon,[15] and there is no need for the so-called derived nominals to be verbs originally. Let me elaborate on this by considering zero-related noun-verb pairs in English. Kiparsky (1982) notes the following contrast:

(35) a. He hammered the nail with a rock.
  b. *She taped the picture to the wall with pushpins.

Whereas the verb *hammer* licenses an adjunct distinct from its nominal counterpart, the verb *tape* does not. Arad (2003) analyzes this contrast as follows:

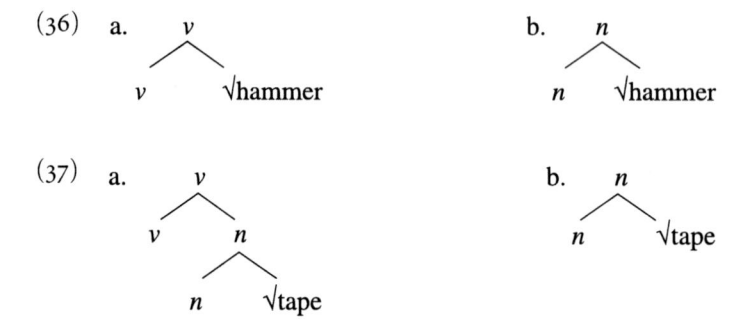

(36) a. v   b. n
      / \   / \
     v   √hammer   n   √hammer

(37) a. v   b. n
      / \   / \
     v   n   n   √tape
        / \
       n   √tape

In (36a), the verb *hammer* does not contain the noun *hammer*, and this licenses a distinct adjunct (35a). In contrast, the verb *tape* contains the noun *tape*, as in (37a). Because the functional head *n* fixes the meaning of the root, the verb *tape* entails the existence of the noun *tape*. Thus, it cannot have a distinct adjunct, as shown by (35b).

The situation of nominal-only compounds in (34) is treated in a similar way. According to the above analysis, √hammer can be selected either by *v* or *n*, but √tape is specified so that it is selected only by *n*. In the same way, *tati-gu(w)-* 'eat-stand' is selected only by *n*. Given that V₂ *ku(w)-* 'eat' by itself can be selected by *v* ([g] is due to *rendaku* [sequential voicing]), the analysis implies that the categorial selectional property is determined after compounding at the point of the merger of the functional head.[16] The verbal-only compounds noted by Fukushima (2005:574) can be given a similar account.

There are complications regarding nominal-only compounds, however. Note first that (34b) contains some idiomatic meaning; the first root *osi-* 'push' is used metaphorically, as in 'pushy.' Consider also the following:

(38) a. naguri-gaki   b. oki-biki
    beat-write   put-pull
    'disorderly writing' 'stealing (a bag)'

These examples are nominal-only. Example (38a) is related to a verbal compound *kaki-nagur(u)* 'write-beat' 'write in an disorderly manner.' This verbal counterpart is discussed by Fukushima (2005) as a case where one of the two verbs has lost its original meaning, but note that the order of the roots is reversed in the nominal counterpart in (38a). In (38b), *oki-biki* 'put-pull' refers to stealing a thing (typically a bag) that someone has put somewhere in a public place. Semantically, the alleged agents of the first root (the victim) and the second root (the thief) are different. Although this is a peculiar situation, it is compatible with the hypothesis of introducing the agent by *v*. If *oki-biki* cannot be selected by *v*, there is no agent, and there is no need for the alleged agents of the two roots to be identical. The alleged agents (the victim and thief) are only contextually implicated.

12.3.4.2 *Accidental gaps*

Note that there are accidental gaps in V-V compounds:[17]

(39) a. Ziroo-ga   Hanako-o   maneki-ire-ta.
        Ziroo-NOM   Hanako-ACC   beckon-put.in-PAST
        'Ziroo had Hanako come in by beckoning her.'
   b. *Ziroo-ga   Hanako-o   maneki-dasi-ta.
        Ziroo-NOM   Hanako-ACC   beckon-put.out-PAST
   c. *John-ga   sushi-o   tukuri-tabe-ta.
        John-NOM   sushi-ACC   make-eat-PAST
        'John cooked sushi and ate it.'
   d. *Taroo-ga   sirase-o   kiki-kaet-ta.
        Taroo-NOM   news-ACC   hear-return-PAST
        'Taroo returned due to hearing the news.'

Given that (39a) is possible, there seems to be no principled account for the absence of the compound in (39b). The absence of the compound in (39c) is also noteworthy, for 'cook' and 'eat' is a common combination in serial verb constructions (cf. (21b)). Regarding examples such as (39d), Matsumoto (1996, 1998) offers a semantic constraint on causal V-V compounds. Put simply, it says that the event denoted by V_2 cannot be intended when it is caused by the event denoted by V_1. This constraint might also rule out (39b,c), given that the event denoted by V_2 is intended. However, there is a caveat. Because (39a) is a minimal pair with (39b) but is still grammatical, the constraint should not apply to (39a,b). The difference is that, whereas (39a,b) involve a means/manner relation between the two events, (39d) involves a causal relation. The distinction is reflected in the translations by Fukushima, who endorses this constraint. If one adopts this constraint, the consequence is that although (39b) is really an accidental gap, at least the ungrammaticality of (39c,d) has semantic basis.

However, the distinction between means/manner and causal compounds, which is crucial for the constraint, is often obscure. Consider *osi-taos-* 'push-topple$_{TR}$' (see (2a), (6a), (22a)), for example. Because the event denoted by V_2 is intended but the compound is grammatical, it must be a means/manner compound such as 'to topple by pushing.' But it seems equally possible to interpret it as involving a causal relation, for pushing is obviously the cause of the patient being toppled. Unless there is a clear criterion to sort out between means/manner and cause, the constraint does not seem to have much substance and (39b–d) are all considered accidental gaps. See Fukushima 2005 for relevant discussion on productivity in V-V compounds, utilizing Bauer's (2001) definition of morphological productivity.

12.3.4.3 Peculiar combinations

This subsection discusses two types of compounds that are analyzed in detail by Fukushima (2005). Such compounds are peculiar in that, although they are compositional semantically, they show noncanonical ways of argument realization.

A first type is mirror-image compounds:

(40) Taroo-ga hon-o Hanako-kara yuzuri-uke-ta.
Taroo-NOM book-ACC Hanako-from yield-receive-PAST
'Taroo received a book from Hanako who yielded it to him.'

This type is strange because, using the conventional labels for θ-roles, the composition is: (agent, goal, theme) + (agent, source, theme) ⇒ (agent, source, theme). That is, despite semantic incompatibility, the source of V_1 and the goal of V_2 are matched, producing the source in the output. Fukushima's solution is that in this case, the argument structure of V_1 is modified as (agent, source, theme) so as to match that of V_2. Fukushima acknowledges that the solution overgenerates, but he justifies it by observing that the pattern is "more widespread than one might imagine" (Fukushima 2005:577).

Within the syntactic approach, we can postulate the same structure for canonical ditransitive compounds, as in (27), for the compound in (40). In this analysis, the applicative head introduces a location-related argument, but whether it is a goal or a source is unspecified. The exact interpretation is obtained based on the verb that Appl selects. In (40), Appl selects *uke-* 'receive,' which yields the source interpretation for the argument.

A second peculiar type is a compound with flexible argument realization:

(41) a. Karera-ga sono yoru-ni omoide-o katari-akasi-ta.
they-NOM that night-during memory-ACC talk-spend.the.night-PAST
'They talked about the memories that night until dawn.'
b. Karera-ga omoidebanasi-de itiya-o katari-akasi-ta.
they-NOM memory.story-with one.night-ACC talk-spend.the.night-PAST
'They spent one night telling reminiscent stories until dawn.'

According to Fukushima, the situation here is that there is no argument matching for the internal arguments, and both arguments can be realized in a peculiar way; either of the arguments can be selected as the direct object of the compound, but if one is selected, the other is relegated to an adjunct. Fukushima (2005:588f.) shows how the prototype approach to θ-roles guarantees that both arguments can be inherited to the whole compound, although only one of them can be the direct object.

It seems to me that this characterization of (41) is disputable. In particular, it is not clear whether V_1 and V_2 are transitive verbs in both (41a,b), although this is assumed by Kageyama (1993) and Matsumoto (1996), as well as Fukushima (2005). *Katar-* can be either intransitive (like *talk*) or transitive (like *tell*). Thus, when it has no overt object, it merely describes the act of talking, without implying any content established in discourse.[18] Thus, *katar-* in (41b) may well be intransitive. As for *akas-*, note that Fukushima's gloss is 'spend the night', hence having an object *itiya-o* 'one night' is almost redundant semantically.[19] By itself, the verb means 'make open' and is used as in (42a).

(42) a. Taroo-ga himitu-o akasi-ta.
Taroo-NOM secret-ACC make.open-PAST
'Taroo revealed the secret.'
b. Taroo-ga himitu-o katat-ta.
Taroo-NOM secret-ACC tell-PAST
'Taroo told the secret.'
c. *Taroo-ga himitu-o karari-akasi-ta.
Taroo-NOM secret-ACC tell-make.open-PAST
'Taroo revealed the secret by telling it.'

Example (42b) shows that the same object *himitu* 'secret' can be used with *katar-* 'tell.' Crucially, as in (42c), when the two verbs are compounded, the object can no longer be used. This is unexpected if the compound is really compositional. The contrast between (41a) and (42c) suggests that some kind of idiomaticity is involved in (41). That is, compounding renders *akas-* an intransitive and, as a consequence, renders the apparent object in (41b) an adjunct. If this is correct, (41a) is treated as transitive-intransitive on a par with (9), and (41b) as intransitive-intransitive on a par with (28).

For the analysis in Nishiyama 1998a, analogizing (41a) with (9) significantly weakens the stipulation to limit *v*P complementation to motion verbs. However, the pattern in (41) does not seem to be widespread or systematic enough to call for a novel mechanism in the grammar. I briefly return to the issue of how and to what extent we should accommodate peculiar patterns into the scope of the analysis in the next section on theoretical implications.

12.4 THEORETICAL IMPLICATIONS

I have reviewed several issues with V-V compounds and showed how competing analyses handle them. They all point to one question: where is morphology? If lexical analyses are correct, then we still need the "productive" lexicon equipped with Argument Structure in the sense of Williams (1981b) and Grimshaw (1990). If, however, the syntactic analysis is correct, the implication is that we can dispense with the lexicon as the place of word formation, in accord with the fundamental standpoint of Distributed Morphology. Although the purpose of this chapter has not been to choose one analysis as optimal, I would like present a guideline for future research.

Because of their many complexities and idiosyncrasies, V-V compounds offer a bona fide example of the tension between explanatory and descriptive adequacy, which has provided an important perspective throughout the history of generative grammar. On the explanatory side, the optimal analysis should be equipped with mechanisms that are independently motivated. In this sense, Nishiyama's transitivity selection seems to be more desirable than Kageyama's transitivity harmony or Fukushima's matching convention. But we have seen that Nishiyama's analysis must make stipulations on motion verbs and *v*P complementation.

As for the empirical side, the crucial questions are how and to what extent the analysis should accommodate exceptions, without rendering it a restatement of the fact and losing its explanatory strength. Because idiosyncrasies are generally believed to be aliens to the syntax, I investigated in section 12.3.4.1 the kinds of idiosyncrasies of V-V compounds that Distributed Morphology can account for. As it turns out, at least semantic idiomaticity and categorial idiosyncrasy can be accommodated, if not explained, but the status of transitivity idiosyncrasies must be stipulated. Although not covered in this chapter, V-V compounds involve many other examples with idiosyncrasies (whether of the same kind as reviewed or different). Further study of V-V compounds would shed light on the scope and limitations of the roots-as-categorially-neutral hypothesis and thus contribute to the development of the theory.

In conclusion, I hope to have provided a basis for further research on V-V compounds, which directly touch on the important issue of the place of morphology in linguistic theory.

NOTES FOR CHAPTER 12

I would like to thank the following people for comments and suggestions: the organizers of the Workshop on Linguistic Theory and the Japanese Language (Shigeru Miyagawa and Mamoru Saito), the participants of the workshop, Heidi Harley, and an anonymous referee for the handbook.

1. Another construction that has yielded controversies is adjectives. See Nishiyama 1999, 2005 and Namai 2002. Sells (1995) also treats various constructions, such as honorifics and polite forms, to argue for the lexical approach. See Nishiyama 1998b for a review of Sells 1995, and Koopman 2005 for a syntactic reinterpretation of the data and insights by Sells.

2. But see Matsumoto 1996 for some complications.

3. On completely different grounds, Carstens (2002) argues that serial verb constructions in Ijo, a head-final language related to Yoruba, are underlyingly head initial like those in Yoruba. She derives the word order by movement in the sense of Kayne (1994). This analysis implies that in serial verb constructions in Ijo, V_1 is the head, despite their apparent similarity to Japanese V-V compounds. Because Kayne's theory is supposed to apply universally, the issue of headedness in Japanese V-V compounds bears relevance to headedness and phrase structure in general.

4. Strictly speaking, Li's (1993) theta-identification is analogous to the process of modification in the sense of Higginbotham (1985). As noted by Nishiyama (1998a) and

Fukushima (2005), this is a *syntactic* process, despite the fact that it targets argument structure. Li 2005 can be regarded as a development of this hybrid standpoint.

5. See Newmeyer 2001 (p. 65ff.) for problems with proto-θ-roles.

6. Because Fukushima adopts the prototype approach and rejects the unaccusativity hypothesis, he has no problem matching the 'taker' and 'leaver' in (11c).

7. Fukushima (2005:598) argues that *wazato* is subject-oriented rather than agent-oriented, based on the following example:

(i) *Wazato   sebiro-ga   Taroo-ni(-yotte)   ki-rare-ta.
    deliberately suit.jacket-NOM   Taroo-DAT(-by)   wear-PASS-PAST
    'The suit jacket was deliberately worn by Taroo.'

Although the grammatical status of (i) itself requires an account, the contrast in (15) is real, and this seems to be sufficient to justify the agent-orientation of *wazato*.

8. Saito's (2001) analysis also features the parallelism between V-V compound and serial verb constructions. Haseagawa's (1998, 2000) analysis also shares the same spirit, for it features the parallelism between V-V compound and resultative constructions. Their analyses are, however, empirically more limited than Nishiyama's (1998a) in that they do not cover all the core data cited in section 12.2. For this reason and also due to space limitation, I focus on Nishiyama's (1998a) analysis as a representative of syntactic approaches to V-V compounds.

9. PRO in (22b) is licensed on the assumption that PRO appears in a non-Case position and accusative Case is assigned to the object position only if the verb is dominated by an active *v*P (i.e., *v*P introducing the external argument). Alternatively, the empty category in (22b) is a trace/copy of the matrix object and the chain receives two θ-roles, as in Hornstein's (1999) control-as-movement analysis. Furukawa 1999 is an implementation of this insight.

10. The exact definitions and characterization of unaccusatives are controversial (see Alexiadou, Anagnostopoulou, and Everaert 2004), and Matsumoto (1996) and Fukushima (2005) do not adopt the unaccusativity hypothesis in their analyses of V-V compounds. For the purposes of this subsection, unaccusatives are defined as intransitive verbs that have morphologically related transitive counterparts, and I believe that at least this definition is less controversial. See Harley, this volume, for examples and discussion.

11. The analysis in (27) implies that the case order of accusative-dative in (25b) is due to scrambling, contra Miyagawa (1997). See also Takano, this volume.

12. The structure is entertained by Nishiyama (1998a) for a certain type of V-V compound in Chinese. See Li 2005 for arguments against this structure for Chinese. The operation of head movement as a way of compounding in (28) seems hard to implement, due to the coordinate structure. This makes "morphological merger" in the sense of Marantz (1988) and Embick and Noyer (2001) more promising for the compound in (28) and, by extension, probably for other kinds of combinations.

13. In Matsumoto's (1996) terms, V2 is deverbalized semantically. There are also cases where V1 loses its original meaning:

(ii) sasi-ager(u)   thrust$_{TR}$-give   'give (honorific)'

Here, V$_1$ seems to be functioning to yield an honorific form of ordinary *ager*- 'give'. See Matsumoto 1996 for more examples of compounds where one of the two verbs has lost its original meaning.

14. The structures in (33) simplify Volpe's analysis based on Aronoff 1976, where there are two types of -*able*, depending on whether -*able* selects a root or a verb.

15. See Ogawa 2001 for another view on nominalization in syntactic terms.

16. Ito and Sugioka (2002:140) note that there are few V-V compounds involving *rendaku*, and they claim that such V-V compounds are derived by "back-formation":

(iii)   ki-bukure-ru   ← ki-bukure
        wear-swell-PRES   wear-swell
        'to wear too much'   'wearing too much'

('Swell' is originally *hukure-*, and *bukure-* is due to *rendaku*.) According to Ito and Sugioka, *ki-bukure-ru* (the verb) is derived from a noun, *ki-bukure*. In the present terms, *ki-bukure-ru* has the structure of (37a), and *rendaku* applies in a domain selected by *n*.

17. Examples (39a,b) are from Fukushima 2005, and (39c) is from Nishiyama 1998a. Example (39d) is originally attributed to Matsumoto 1998 and is taken from Fukushima 2005.

18. Fukushima (2005:601) cites the following as ungrammatical:

(iv)   *Taroo-ga   (omoide banasi-de)   katat-ta.
        Taroo-NOM   memory.story-with   talk-PAST

I agree that the sentence is ungrammatical with the bracketed part, but for me it is grammatical without the bracketed part.

19. Even the 'one' part is redundant, for *katari-akas-* cannot be used when one spends more than one night.

REFERENCES

Alexiadou, Artemis, Elena Anagnostopoulou, and Martin Everaert, eds. 2004. *The unaccusativity puzzle*. Oxford: Oxford University Press.

Arad, Maya. 2003. Locality constraints on the interpretation of roots: The case of Hebrew denominal verbs. *Natural Language & Linguistic Theory* 21:737–778.

Aronoff, Mark. 1976. *Word formation in generative grammar*. Cambridge, Mass.: MIT Press.

Baker, Mark C. 1988. *Incorporation: A theory of grammatical function changing*. Chicago: University of Chicago Press.

Baker, Mark C. 1989. Object sharing and projection in serial verb constructions. *Linguistic Inquiry* 20:513–553.

Bauer, Laurie. 2001. *Morphological productivity*. Cambridge: Cambridge University Press.

Carstens, Vicki. 2002. Antisymmetry and word order in serial constructions. *Language* 78:3–50.

Chomsky, Noam. 1970. Remarks on nominalization. In *Readings in English transformational grammar*, ed. Roderick A. Jacobs and Peter S. Rosenbaum, 184–221. Waltham, Mass.: Ginn & Co. (Reprinted in Noam Chomsky, 1972, *Studies on semantics in generative grammar*, 11–61. The Hague: Mouton.)

Collins, Chris. 1997. Argument sharing in serial verb constructions. *Linguistic Inquiry* 28:461–497.

Dowty, David. 1991. Thematic proto-roles and argument selection. *Language* 67:547–619.

Embick, David. 2004. On the structure of resultative participles in English. *Linguistic Inquiry* 35:335–392.

Embick, David, and Alec Marantz. 2008. Architecture and blocking. *Linguistic Inquiry* 39:1–53.

Embick, David, and Rolf Noyer. 2001. Moving operations after syntax. *Linguistic Inquiry* 32:555–595.
Farmer, Ann K. 1980. On the interaction of morphology and syntax. Doctoral dissertation, MIT, Cambridge, Mass.
Farmer, Ann K. 1984. *Modularity in syntax.* Cambridge, Mass.: MIT Press.
Fukushima. Kazuhiko. 2005. Lexical V-V compounds in Japanese: Lexicon vs. syntax. *Language* 81:568–612.
Furukawa, Yukio. 1999. Argument sharing in JVVCs' constructions and relativized minimality. In *Proceedings of TACL Summer Institute of Linguistics*, 13–24. Department of English language and literature, Tokyo Metropolitan University, Tokyo.
Gamerschlag, Thomas. 2002. Complex predicate formation and argument structure of Japanese V-V compounds. *Japanese/Korean linguistics 10*, ed. Noriko Akatsuka and Susan Strauss, 532–544. Stanford, Calif.: CSLI Publications.
Grimshaw, Jane. 1990. *Argument structure.* Cambridge, Mass.: MIT Press.
Halle, Morris, and Alec Marantz. 1993. Distributed morphology and the pieces of inflection. *The view from Building 20*, ed. Kenneth Hale and Samuel Jay Keyser, 111–176. Cambridge, Mass: MIT Press.
Hasegawa, Nobuko. 1998. Syntax of resultatives. In *Researching and verifying an advanced theory of human languages* (2-A), 31–57. Graduate School of Language Sciences, Kanda University of International Studies, Chiba, Japan.
Hasegawa, Nobuko. 2000. Resultatives and language variations: Result phrase and VV compounds. *Japanese/Korean linguistics 9*, ed. Mineharu Nakayama and Charles J. Quinn, Jr., 269–282. Stanford, Calif.: CSLI Publications.
Higginbotham, James. 1985. On semantics. *Linguistic Inquiry* 16:547–593.
Himeno, Masako. 1999. *Hukugoodoosi-no koozoo-to imiyoohoo* [Structure and semantic usage of compound verbs]. Tokyo: Hituzi Shobo.
Hornstein, Norbert. 1999. Movement and control. *Linguistic Inquiry* 30:69–96.
Ito, Takane, and Yoko Sugioka. 2002. *Go-no sikumi-to gokeisei* [Mechanism of words and word formation]. Tokyo: Hituzi Shobo.
Kageyama, Taro. 1989. The place of morphology in grammar: Verb-verb compounds in Japanese. *Yearbook of Morphology* 2:73–94.
Kageyama, Taro. 1993. *Bumpoo-to gokeisei* [Grammar and word formation]. Tokyo: Hituzi Syobo.
Kayne, Richard. 1994. *The antisymmetry of syntax.* Cambridge, Mass.: MIT Press.
Kiparsky, Paul. 1982. Word formation and the lexicon. In *Proceedings of the Mid-America Linguistics Conference*, ed. Fred Ingeman, 3–29. Lawrence: University of Kansas.
Kitagawa, Yoshihisa. 1986. Subjects in Japanese and English. Doctoral dissertation, University of Massachusetts, Amherst. (Published 1994, New York: Garland.)
Koopman, Hilda. 2005. Korean (and Japanese) morphology from a syntactic perspective. *Linguistic Inquiry* 36:601–633.
Kuno, Susumu. 1973. *The structure of the Japanese language.* Cambridge, Mass.: MIT Press.
Kuroda, S.-Y. 1965. Generative grammatical studies in the Japanese language. Doctoral dissertation, MIT, Cambridge, Mass.
Li, Yafei. 1993. Structural head and aspectuality. *Language* 69:480–504.
Li, Yafei. 2005. X^0. Cambridge, Mass: MIT Press.
Marantz, Alec. 1988. Clitics, morphological merger, and the mapping to phonological structure. In *Theoretical morphology*, ed. Michael Hammond and Michael Noonan, 253–270. San Diego, Calif.: Academic Press.

Marantz, Alec. 1993. Implications of asymmetries in double object constructions. In *Theoretical aspects of Bantu grammar 1*, ed. Sam I. Mchombo, 113–151. Stanford, Calif.: CSLI Publications.

Marantz, Alec. 1997. No Escape from syntax: Don't try morphological analysis in the privacy of your lexicon. In *Proceedings of the 21st annual Penn Linguistic Colloquium: University of Pennsylvania working papers in linguistics 4.2*, ed. Alexis Dimitriadis, Laura Siegel, Clarissa Surek-Clark, and Alexander Williams, 201–225. Philadelphia: University of Pennsylvania.

Matsumoto, Yo. 1996. *Complex predicates in Japanese*. Stanford, Calif.: CSLI Publications.

Matsumoto, Yo. 1998. Nihongo-no hukugoodoosi-ni okeru doosi-no kumiawase [Combination of verbs in Japanese lexical compound verbs]. *Gengo Kenkyuu* 114:37–83.

Miyagawa, Shigeru. 1980. Complex verbs and the lexicon. Doctoral dissertation, University of Arizona, Tucson.

Miyagawa, Shigeru. 1989. *Structure and case marking in Japanese* (Syntax and Semantics 22). San Diego, Calif.: Academic Press.

Miyagawa, Shigeru. 1997. Against optional scrambling. *Linguistic Inquiry* 28:1–25.

Namai, Kenichi. 2002. The word status of Japanese adjectives. *Linguistic Inquiry* 33:340–349.

Newmeyer, Frederick J. 2001. Grammatical functions, thematic roles, and phrase structure: Their underlying disunity. In *Objects and other subjects: Grammatical functions, functional categories, and configurationality*, ed. William D. Davies and Stanley Dubinsky, 53–75. Dordrecht: Kluwer.

Nishiyama, Kunio. 1998a. V-V compounds as serialization. *Journal of East Asian Linguistics* 7:175–217.

Nishiyama, Kunio. 1998b. The morphosyntax and morphophonology of Japanese predicates. Doctoral dissertation, Cornell University, Ithaca, N.Y.

Nishiyama, Kunio. 1999. Adjectives and the copulas in Japanese. *Journal of East Asian Linguistics* 8:183–222.

Nishiyama, Kunio. 2005. Morphological boundary of Japanese adjectives: Reply to Namai. *Linguistic Inquiry* 35:134–143.

Ogawa, Yoshiki. 2001. *A unified theory of verbal and nominal projections*. Oxford: Oxford University Press.

Pylkkänen, Liina. 2002. Introducing arguments. Doctoral dissertation, MIT, Cambridge, Mass.

Reinhart, Tanya, and Tal Siloni. 2005. The lexicon-syntax parameter: Reflexivization and other arity operations. *Linguistic Inquiry* 36:389–436.

Saito, Mamoru. 2001. Movement and θ-roles: A case study with resultatives. In *Proceedings of the 2nd Tokyo Conference on Psycholinguistics*, ed. Yukio Otsu, 35–60. Tokyo: Hituzi Syobo.

Sells, Peter. 1995. Korean and Japanese morphology from a lexical perspective. *Linguistic Inquiry* 26:277–235.

Tagashira, Yoshiko. 1978. Characterization of Japanese compound verbs. Doctoral dissertation, University of Chicago.

Tagashira, Yoshiko, and Jean Hoff. 1986. *Handbook of Japanese compound verbs*. Tokyo: Hokuseido.

Volpe, Mark Joseph. 2005. Japanese morphology and its theoretical consequences: Derivational morphology in Distributed Morphology. Doctoral dissertation, Stony Brook University, New York.

Williams, Edwin. 1981a. On the notions lexically related and head of a word. *Linguistic Inquiry* 12:245–274.
Williams, Edwin. 1981b. Argument structure and morphology. *The Linguistic Review* 1:81–114.
Yumoto, Yoko. 2005. *Hukugoo-doosi, hasei-doosi-no imi-to toogo* [The semantics and syntax of compound verbs and derived verbs]. Tokyo: Hituzi Shobo.

CHAPTER 13

WH-QUESTIONS

NORVIN RICHARDS

13.1 INTRODUCTION

Among the properties of Japanese that have been of theoretical interest is the behavior of its *wh*-phrases, which may be left in situ:[1]

(1) Taroo-wa [Hanako-ga **nani**-o katta to] omoimasita ka?
    Taro-TOP Hanako-NOM what-ACC bought that thought Q

(2) **What** did Taro think [that Hanako bought __]?

Approaches to this difference between English and Japanese may be classified into two camps. One type of approach makes use of cross-linguistic differences in the mapping of the syntax to the phonological representation. The other posits differences in the mapping of the syntax onto the semantic representation.

For the first type of approach, the syntax of *wh*-questions is always essentially the same, but the *wh*-movement that such questions universally involve is difficult to detect in some languages, having little or no effect on the phonology. This difference in phonology might itself be the result of some syntactic difference; this is the claim of theories that follow the lead of Huang (1982) in suggesting that Japanese *wh*-movement takes place during a part of the syntactic derivation that never feeds the phonology ("covert movement").[2]

In the second type of approach, the relation between the syntax and the phonology is comparatively simple, at least in this domain; *wh*-movement occurs only where it has an effect on the phonology. The point of variation between languages, on this approach, has to do with the mapping between the syntax and the semantics; a *wh*-question may have a semantic representation with the *wh*-phrase in situ or in a moved position, and languages vary in which of these types of semantic representations they allow. Shimoyama (2001, 2006, this volume) offers arguments for an approach of this kind.

In section 13.2, I outline the distribution of island effects in Japanese and consider what each of these types of theories might have to say about them. Section 13.3 considers other kinds of phenomena that might bear on the choice between the theories. Section 13.4 touches on a series of interesting recent papers on the phonology of *wh*-in-situ in Japanese, and section 13.5 summarizes this chapter.

13.2 CORE DATA: JAPANESE ISLANDS

Watanabe (1992a, 1992b) claims that Japanese *wh*-in-situ exhibits *wh*-island effects. A *wh*-phrase in an interrogative complement clause, as in (3a), is prevented from taking wide scope; by contrast, a *wh*-phrase in a declarative complement clause, as in (3b), can freely take wide scope.

(3) a. *John-wa   [Mary -ga   **nani**-o   katta   ka dooka]   siritagatteiru no?
       John-TOP   Mary-NOM what-ACC bought   whether   know-want   Q
       'What does John want to know whether Mary bought?'
    b. John-wa   [Mary-ga   **nani**-o   katta   to]   omotteiru no?
       John-TOP   Mary-NOM what-ACC bought   that   thinks   Q
       'What does John think that Mary bought?'

Other types of islands, however, seem to be absent for Japanese *wh*-in-situ; the examples in (4) involve a complex NP island and an adjunct island.

(4) a. Mary-wa   [John-ga   **nani**-o   nusunda koto]-o
       Mary-TOP John-NOM what-ACC stole   fact-ACC
       mondai-ni   siteiru no?
       problem-DAT make   Q
       'What is Mary making an issue out of [the fact that John stole __]?'
    b. John-wa   [**dono hon**-o   yonde   kara]   dekaketa no?
       John-TOP   which book-ACC   read   after   went.out Q
       'Which book did John go out [after he read __]?'

Unlike their English translations, the examples in (4) are well formed in Japanese. This type of island effect does reappear, however, for certain *wh*-phrases, notably *naze* 'why' and *wh*-phrases modified by *ittai* '... in the world':

(5) *Mary-wa   [John-ga   **naze**   sore-o   nusunda   koto]-o
     Mary-TOP   John-NOM why   that-ACC stole   fact-ACC
     mondai-ni   siteiru no?
     problem DAT make   Q
     'Why is Mary making an issue out of [the fact that John stole it __]?'

(6) a. Mary-wa [John-ga   **nani**-o   ageta   hito]-ni   atta no?
       Mary-TOP John-NOM what-ACC gave person-DAT met Q
       'What did Mary meet [the person that John gave __ to]?'
    b. *Mary-wa [John-ga   **ittai   nani**-o   ageta hito]-ni atta no?
       Mary-TOP John NOM ITTAI what-ACC gave person-DAT   met Q
       'What in the world did Mary meet [the person that John gave __ to]?'

This, then, is the array of facts about islands that theories about Japanese *wh*-questions are attempting to capture. If these islands reflect conditions on syntactic operations, then the distribution of island effects for *wh*-in-situ represents a challenge for both of the above types of theories about *wh*-in-situ.

On one kind of theory, *wh*-in-situ is syntactically like *wh*-movement; on this approach, the main difference between overt movement and *wh*-in-situ is a phonological one. The difficulty for a theory of this kind is how to account for the gaps in the distribution of islands outlined above; if *wh*-in-situ is simply a phonologically masked version of *wh*-movement, then why are some of the familiar islands for *wh*-movement absent for *wh*-in-situ?

The second type of theory is one in which *wh*-in-situ and *wh*-movement differ syntactically; both *wh*-movement and *wh*-in-situ can yield syntactic structures with the semantics of *wh*-questions. The challenge for this kind of theory is to explain why *wh*-in-situ exhibits any island effects at all, if it is syntactically completely unlike *wh*-movement.

Let us consider how these types of theories might account for the distribution of island effects. In what follows I concentrate on the difference between *wh*-islands and other types of islands. I also reexamine the facts about *ittai* '...in the world' in section 13.3.1.1, but I do not discuss the facts about *naze* 'why', mainly for reasons of space; see Tsai 1994 for one approach.

13.2.1 Covert Movement Theories: Why Are Some Islands Missing?

A theory that posits covert movement for Japanese *wh*-phrases must offer some explanation for why some island effects are missing; why, for example, are sentences such as (4), repeated here as (7), acceptable in Japanese?

(7) a. John-wa [**nani**-o   katta   hito]-o   sagasiteiru no?
       John-TOP what-ACC bought person-ACC looking.for Q
       'What is John looking for [the person who bought __]?'
    b. John-wa [**dono hon**-o   yonde kara] dekaketa no?
       John-TOP which book-ACC read   after went.out Q
       'Which book did John go out [after he read __]?

Much work on covert *wh*-movement follows the influential proposal of Nishigauchi (1986, 1990) and Choe (1987), who argued that although there is indeed covert movement in examples such as (7), the moving phrases are not simply the boldfaced *wh*-phrases but in fact the entire islands containing these phrases. In (7a), for instance, the moving phrase is *nani-o katta hito-o* 'the person who bought what', and in (7b) the moving phrase is *dono hon-o yonde kara* 'after he read which book'. Given that these phrases do not in fact exit any islands when they undergo movement, the absence of island effects is expected.

On this account, covert movement in Japanese is much like overt *wh*-movement in certain languages, which sometimes appears to avoid island effects by pied-piping the island. In Imbabura Quechua, for instance, Cole (1982) notes that *wh*-movement may pied-pipe clauses:

(8) a. **Ima** -ta -taj ya -ngui [Juan randi -shka] -ta?
      what ACC INT think 2 Juan buy NLZ ACC
      'What do you think that Juan bought?'
   b. [**Ima** -ta Juan randi -shka] -ta -taj ya -ngui?
      what ACC Juan buy NLZ ACC INT think 2
      'What do you think that Juan bought?'

For ease of processing, I have underlined the *wh*-fronted phrases. Example (8a) shows *wh*-movement without clausal pied-piping; the *wh*-word *ima* has moved to its scope position at the beginning of the matrix clause. In (8b), *wh*-movement has pied-piped the entire complement clause. In either case, the fronted phrase is followed by the suffix *-taj*, glossed here as INT(errogative).[3] As Cole points out, wide-scale pied-piping may be used as a means for avoiding island effects:

(9) a. *****Ima** -ta -taj riku -rka -ngui [randi -shka runa-ta]?
      what ACC INT see past 2 buy NLZ man ACC
      'What did you see the man who bought?'
   b. [**Ima** -ta randi -shka runa -ta -taj] riku -rka -ngui?
      what ACC buy NLZ man ACC INT see PAST 2
      Lit. '[The man that bought what] did you see?'

As we can see in (9a), Imbabura Quechua exhibits complex NP island effects; (9b) shows that these effects may be circumvented by moving the whole island.

Cable (2007) discusses similar facts for Tlingit. Like Imbabura Quechua, Tlingit can pied-pipe islands to circumvent them. A *wh*-phrase embedded in a relative clause, for example, cannot simply be extracted, as in (10a), but it may pied-pipe the relative clause together with the head noun, as in (10b).

(10) a. *****Waa** sá [kligéiyi xáat] i tuwáa sigóo?
       how INT it.is.big fish your spirit be.happy
    b. [**Waa** kligéiyi xáat sá] i tuwáa sigóo?
       how it.is.big fish INT your spirit be.happy
       '[A fish that is how big] do you want?'

Ortiz de Urbina (1989) also analyzes Basque as a language with overt *wh*-movement and with pied-piping as a way of avoiding island violations (here, adjunct island and complex NP island violations):[4]

(11) a. [**Zer** ikusi ondoren] joan ziren hemen-dik?
what see after go AUX here from
'What did they leave [after seeing __]?'
b. ***Zer** joan ziren hemen-dik [__ ikusi ondoren]?
what go AUX here from see after

(12) a. [**Nork** idatzi zuen liburua] irakurri du Peruk?
who-ERG write AUX book read AUX Peter-ERG
'Who did Peter read [the book that __ wrote]?'
b. ***Nork** irakurri du Peruk [__ idatzi zuen liburua]?
who-ERG read AUX Peter-ERG write AUX book

Interestingly, Ortiz de Urbina also notes that this strategy does not work for *wh*-islands, which cannot be pied-piped:

(13) a. *[**Nor** etorriko d-en] galdetu duzu?
who came AUX-Q asked AUX
'Who have you asked [whether __ has come]?'
b. ***Nor** galdetu duzu [__ etorriko d-en]?
who asked AUX come AUX Q

Thus, we need a theory of movement that allows languages to circumvent islands by means of pied-piping the entire island; this strategy is straightforwardly present for several languages with overt movement of *wh*-phrases. At least for Basque, we can also see that this strategy does not work for *wh*-islands, which cannot be pied-piped.[5] The only question, then, once we have developed such a theory, is whether to apply it to Japanese. We have seen that *wh*-in-situ in Japanese is subject just to *wh*-islands—that is, just to the type of island that cannot be avoided by pied-piping. The possibility arises, then, that Japanese is simply a covert version of Tlingit, Quechua, or Basque.

Of course, we would like to have a theory of pied-piping that gets these results; what makes *wh*-islands special in this way, so that they are impervious to pied-piping? We might start by exploiting another special property of *wh*-islands; they are the one type of island that is fairly straightforwardly captured via approaches involving the Minimal Link Condition.[6] Movement out of a *wh*-island involves movement past a position where the moving phrase could in principle land, and it often moves it past another *wh*-phrase that could in principle be undergoing a (shorter) movement into the higher clause. Other islands (e.g., CED islands) are less susceptible to explanations of this kind.

In Richards 2000, I try to make use of this distinction between these types of islands to develop an account of why *wh*-islands were not susceptible to pied-piping. The account makes use of van Riemsdijk's (1984) observation that pied-piping typically requires the operator to be in a high position within the pied-piped phrase (see also Heck 2004) and that in cases of clausal pied-piping, the operator in question often moves to the periphery of the clause, a type of movement van Riemsdijk dubs "internal movement" (the example in (14) is Imbabura Quechua, from Hermon 1984:152).

(14) [**Ima**-ta   wawa __   miku-chun-taj]   Maria   muna-n?
     what ACC child   eat   FIN   INT   Maria   want 3.PRES
     'What does Maria want (that) the child eat __?'

Just in the case of a *wh*-island, pied-piping of the island would require internal movement of the pied-piping *wh*-phrase to the specifier of the interrogative CP, which is a possible scope position. Consequently, I have suggested, the *wh*-phrase doing the pied-piping must take scope in the interrogative CP rather than in the matrix one. Wide scope would be ruled out by whatever conditions rule out (15), in which a *wh*-phrase moves from one scope position to another.

(15) *Who does John wonder __ Mary saw __ ?

Of course, if we do decide to invoke internal movement, a new question arises: does Subjacency constrain internal movement? I return to this question in section 13.3.4. But it seems clear that whatever mechanism we use for excluding *wh*-islands from the rescuing effects of island pied-piping, the special status of *wh*-islands is not unexpected, from a syntactic point of view.

13.2.2 Interpretation-in-situ Theories: Why Are Some Islands Present?

In a theory in which Japanese *wh*-phrases never move, the task is to understand why some island effects nevertheless appear. Why should nonmoving phrases be subject to *wh*-islands, for example?

Shimoyama (2001, 2006, this volume) offers an account in which the "*wh*-island" effects are only apparent; in fact, the effect follows from the way the relevant structures are interpreted. Shimoyama, following Hamblin (1973), has *wh*-words such as *dare* 'who' denote sets of individuals. When such an expression combines with, for example, a predicate, the function denoted by the predicate applies pointwise to the members of the set, giving a set of propositions. Shimoyama gives the example in (16); the words *dare* 'who' and *odorimasu* 'dance' have the denotations in (17).

(16) Dare-ga   odorimasu ka?
     who NOM   dance   Q
     'Who dances?'

(17) For all possible worlds w and variable assignments g,
     a. $[\![\mathbf{dare}]\!]^{w,g} = \{x \in D_e : \text{person}(x)(w)\}$
     b. $[\![\mathbf{odorimasu}]\!]^{w,g} = \{\lambda x \lambda w'[\text{dance}(x)(w')]\}$

To derive the meaning of (16), we apply the function in (17b) pointwise to the set in (17a), giving the set of propositions in (18).

(18) ⟦**dare-ga odorimasu**⟧^{w,g}={f(x):f ∈ ⟦**odorimasu**⟧^{w,g}, x ∈ ⟦**dare**⟧^{w,g}}
={λw′[dance (x)(w′)]: person (x)(w)}

The question in (16) thus has a denotation that is a set of propositions, essentially the propositions of the form 'x danced', where x is a member of the (contextually restricted) set of people. This is a reasonable denotation for a question, following Hamblin (1973) and Karttunen (1977).

Following a suggestion that she credits to Angelika Kratzer, Shimoyama then suggests that the question particle *ka* takes a set of propositions and returns a singleton set whose sole member is a question denotation. The apparent *wh*-island effect in (19) follows.

(19) Mary-wa [John-ga **nani**-o tabeta **ka**] siritagatteimasu **ka**?
Mary-TOP John-NOM what-ACC ate Q wonders Q
a. 'Does Mary wonder what John ate __?'
b. ?*'What does Mary wonder if John ate __ ?'

The preference for the reading in (19a) over the reading in (19b) looks like a *wh*-island violation, but in this kind of account, it is not. Once the lower instance of *ka* (the one after *tabeta* 'ate') is added to the structure, the result is no longer a set of propositions—that is, it is no longer the kind of thing with which *ka* combines to form a *wh*-question. As a result, the higher *ka* cannot create a *wh*-question.

In this type of account, Japanese *wh*-questions are not in fact subject to any island effects at all. They appear to be subject to *wh*-islands, but this is an illusion created by the conditions on interpretation of *ka*. Because no movement is involved, other islands are not expected to appear.

13.3 Controversies: Distinguishing the Theories

In both types of theories that we just considered, the distribution of island effects can be captured using independently needed assumptions. In the movement approach, Japanese exhibits a type of pied-piping that we already know exists and must be accounted for. Even if the existing theories of pied-piping are not the correct ones, we know that some theory of pied-piping must be constructed to account for the data from Basque, Quechua, and Tlingit, and once we have that theory we can apply it to covert movement in Japanese. In the nonmovement approach, the apparent *wh*-island effects are a result of general principles of semantic composition.

If this is a fair summary of the situation, then we cannot make this choice on the basis of theoretical simplicity; the complications that the two approaches make use of are unavoidable ones. Choosing between the approaches has to involve finding more data bearing on the relevant questions.

13.3.1 Non-*wh*-islands and *Wh*-in-situ

One piece of evidence that all islands are relevant, even for *wh*-in-situ languages such as Japanese, involves the distribution of a morpheme appearing in *wh*-questions in some languages. In section 13.2.1, I have shown that for some languages that do wide-scale pied-piping, such as Imbabura Quechua and Tlingit, the moved phrase is followed by a particle I glossed INT(-*taj* in Quechua and -*sá* in Tlingit):

(20) a. **Ima -ta -taj** ya -ngui [Juan randi -shka] -ta
what ACC INT think 2 Juan buy NLZ ACC
'What do you think that Juan bought?'
b. **Goodéi sá** uwajée [wugóot] i shagóonich?
where.to INT they.think he.went your parents
'Where do your parents think he went?'

We also have seen that in sentences involving islands, INT is attached not to the *wh*-word itself but to the island containing the *wh*-word. In other words, INT never appears separated from the *wh*-scope position by an island:

(21) a. [**Ima -ta randi -shka runa -ta -taj**] riku -rka -ngui
what ACC buy NLZ man ACC INT see PAST 2
Lit. '[The man that bought what] did you see?'
b. [**Waa kligéiyi xáat sá**] i tuwáa sigóo?
how it.is.big fish INT your spirit be.happy
'[A fish that is how big] do you want?'

Kishimoto (1992, 2005) and Hagstrom (1998) discuss data from Sinhala that show that for that language, although islands do not constrain the distribution of *wh*-in-situ, they do constrain the distribution of the Sinhala version of INT, -*də*. Sinhala *wh*-in-situ is exemplified in (22).

(22) Siri **mokak də** keruwe?
Siri what INT did-E
'What did Siri do?'

As (22) exemplifies, the *wh*-word *mokak* 'what' is left in situ in Sinhala, followed by the INT particle *də*; the verb in *wh*-questions also bears a special suffix -*e*. When *wh*-in-situ is in an island, the INT particle *də* appears outside the island:

(23) a. Oyaa [**kauru** liyəpu potə] **də** kieuwe?
you who wrote book INT read-E
'Who did you read [a book that __ wrote]?'

b. *Oyaa [**kauru də** liyəpu potə] kieuwe?
   you   who   INT wrote book read-E

Similar facts are discussed in the literature on Shuri Okinawan (Sugahara 1996, Hagstrom 1998) and premodern Japanese (Whitman 1997, Hagstrom 1998, Watanabe 2002); the data are omitted here for reasons of space.

In Sinhala, Shuri Okinawan, and premodern Japanese, then, *wh*-phrases co-occur with a particle that cannot be separated from the scope position of the *wh*-phrase by islands—not just *wh*-islands, but all the familiar types of islands. If these are *wh*-in-situ languages,[7] and if these islands are reliable diagnostics of a movement operation, then apparently some kind of movement operation takes place in some *wh*-in-situ languages.[8]

Of course, modern Japanese has no INT attaching to the *wh*-phrase in *wh*-questions.[9] We might conclude that, although there are indeed *wh*-in-situ languages in which movement operations relate the *wh*-phrase to its scope position, Japanese is not one of them. The next three sections discuss phenomena in Japanese *wh*-questions that militate against this approach.

13.3.1.1 *Ittai*

Hoji (1985), Pesetsky (1987), and Hagstrom (1998), among others, note that islands appear to constrain the distribution of *ittai* '... in the world'. Example (24) is a straightforward case containing *ittai*.

(24) John-wa *ittai* **nani**-o   kaimasita ka?
     John-TOP *ittai* what-ACC   bought   Q
     'What in the world did John buy?'

In (24), *ittai* immediately precedes the *wh*-word that it modifies. This is not necessary, however. In fact, when a *wh*-word is inside an island, *ittai* must be outside the island (Pesetsky 1987:112, 126):

(25) a. Mary-wa   *ittai* [John-ni   **nani**-o   ageta hito-ni]   atta no?
        Mary-TOP *ittai* John-DAT what-ACC   gave   person-DAT met Q
        'What in the world did Mary meet [the person that gave __ to John]?'
     b. *Mary-wa [John-ni *ittai* **nani**-o ageta hito-ni] atta no?

The facts about *ittai* are quite similar to the facts discussed earlier about the distribution of INT particles. In both cases, although *wh*-words themselves may freely occur inside islands, certain other morphemes associated with the *wh*-question must be outside the island. Again, the facts seem to urge against theories in which non-*wh*-islands such as the one in (25) are simply irrelevant for *wh*-questions in Japanese. If *wh*-questions are interpreted via unselective binding, then why is the distribution of *ittai* constrained by movement islands? Of course, in principle, one could posit a hybrid theory, in which *ittai*-questions involve covert movement but questions without *ittai* involve no movement.

13.3.1.2 Intervention effects

In Japanese, when certain types of quantifiers c-command *wh*-in-situ, intervening between *wh*-in-situ and its scope position, the result is ill formed (for much discussion of the relevant phenomena in Japanese and other languages, see Hoji 1985; Beck 1996; Beck and Kim 1997; Tanaka 1997, 1999a, 2002; Hagstrom 1998, and references cited there). One example is given in (26).

(26) *John-ka Bill-ga **nani-o** katta no?
John or Bill-NOM what-ACC bought Q
'What did John or Bill buy?'

In (26) the subject *John-ka Bill* 'John or Bill' intervenes between the *wh*-word *nani* and its scope position, causing ungrammaticality.

Nishigauchi (1986, 1990) notes that intervention effects do not always constrain the relation between a *wh*-word and its scope position, per se. In particular, when *wh*-words are inside islands, intervention effects hold for the relation between the island containing the *wh*-word and the scope position. The result is that embedding an example like (26) in an island actually improves its grammaticality, as long as the potentially offending intervener is inside the island with the *wh*-word (Hagstrom 1998:54–55):

(27) a. Mary-wa [John-ka Bill-ga **nani-o** katta ato de] dekaketa no?
Mary-TOP John or Bill-NOM what-ACC bought after left Q
'What did Mary leave [after John or Bill bought __]?'
b. *John-ka Bill-wa [Mary-ga **nani-o** katta ato de] dekaketa no?
John or Bill-TOP Mary-NOM what-ACC bought after left Q
'What did John or Bill leave [after Mary bought __]?'

The ill-formedness of (27b) shows that we do not want to simply claim that *wh*-words in islands are somehow not sensitive to intervention effects. Rather, the intervention effect constrains the relation between the island and the scope position; the intervener therefore intervenes in (27b), where the intervener c-commands the island, but not in (27a), where it is contained in the island.

Here we see, again, that the formation of Japanese *wh*-questions is crucially influenced by islands—not just *wh*-islands, but islands of all types. If we take the relevance of non-*wh*-islands to be a reliable sign of movement, then there must be movement going on here. In an approach assuming pied-piping, the data in (27) show that covert movement involves pied-piping of the entire island and that intervention effects constrain the operation of (covert) movement.

13.3.1.3 Multiple-wh "trapping"

Watanabe (1992a) and Richards (2000) offer another argument for covert pied-piping of islands, which Watanabe attributes to a personal communication from Mamoru Saito. The argument concerns multiple *wh*-phrases inside islands.

Consider a Japanese sentence with two *wh*-phrases and two potential scope positions:

(28) Keesatu-wa [**dare**-ga **dare**-o korosita ka] sirabeteiru no?
police-TOP who-NOM who-ACC killed Q are.investigating Q

Speakers of Japanese vary in how they can interpret (28) (cf. Nishigauchi 1986, 1990; Saito 1994; Richards 1997; Shimoyama 2001, 2006). The easiest reading for (28) is one in which both *wh*-phrases take scope in the embedded clause (informally represented in (29a)). Some speakers also allow readings such as (29b), in which both *wh*-phrases take scope in the matrix clause.

(29) a. Are the police investigating for which x and which y, x killed y?
b. ?For which x and which y are the police investigating whether x killed y?

Some speakers also allow a reading in which the two *wh*-phrases take distinct scopes. For speakers who allow this, the reading with hierarchically crossed paths (30a) is preferred to the one with hierarchically nested paths (30b).

(30) a. ?For which x are the police investigating for which y, x killed y?
b. *For which y are the police investigating for which x, x killed y?

The facts change when we add an island containing both *wh*-phrases:

(31) Keesatu-wa [Nakamura-san-ga [**dare**-ga **dare**-o
police-TOP Nakamura-HON-NOM who-NOM who ACC
korosita tatemono-o] katta ka] sirabeteiru no?
killed building-ACC bought Q are.investigating Q
Lit. 'Q the police are investigating Q Nakamura-san bought [a building where who killed who]?'

In examples such as (31), in which both *wh*-phrases are contained in an island, the two *wh*-phrases must both have the same scope, even for speakers who can give sentences such as (28) readings where the *wh*-phrases have distinct scopes (that is, speakers for whom (28) can have the reading in (30a)). In other words, (31) can have a reading such as (32a) but not a reading such as (32b).

(32) a. Are the police investigating for which x and which y, Nakamura-san bought a house where x killed y?
b. *For which x are the police investigating for which y, Nakamura-san bought a house where x killed y?

This state of affairs is expected under a theory in which *wh*-phrases in Japanese get their scope by covert *wh*-movement, sometimes pied-piping the islands that contain them. In an example such as (31), the two *wh*-phrases have to pied-pipe their island to a single scope position, and this is the scope position for both phrases; neither then is able to move to a different scope position, because this crucially involves exiting the island.

In a theory in which Japanese *wh*-phrases get their scope by unselective binding, on the other hand, these facts are unexpected; the whole point of this kind of theory is that islands (perhaps with the exception of *wh*-islands) are irrelevant for *wh*-in-situ. These facts suggest that that conclusion is too hasty. Although *wh*-in-situ may freely appear inside an island, islands do constrain the behavior of *wh*-in-situ in ways which the pied-piping approach predicts.

13.3.1.4 *Summary*

In section 13.2, I described Japanese as a language whose *wh*-words obey only *wh*-islands. Sections 13.3.1.1–13.3.1.3 have shown that this is not quite true. We have now seen three kinds of arguments that in Japanese *wh*-questions, some domain that contains the *wh*-word is related to the scope position of the *wh*-phrase, in a way that respects islands—not just *wh*-islands, but islands of all kinds. This domain is the one that *ittai* precedes; it is the domain whose relation with the scope position may be interrupted by intervention effects; and it appears to be the domain whose position determines *wh*-scope, given that multiple *wh*-phrases in a single domain must have the same scope. Viewed in this way, Japanese appears to have all the familiar island effects (though these effects are sometimes masked, because the domain in question can be larger than the *wh*-word itself; in other words, Japanese *wh*-movement allows pied-piping).

13.3.2 Additional-*wh* effects

Watanabe (1992a, 1992b) discusses the data in (33).

(33) a. *John-wa [Mary-ga **nani**-o katta ka dooka] siritagatteiru no?
 John-TOP Mary-NOM what-ACC bought whether wants.to.know Q
 'What does John want to know whether Mary bought __?'
 b. John-wa [Mary-ga **nani**-o katta ka dooka] **dare**-ni tazuneta no?
 John-TOP Mary-NOM what-ACC bought whether who-DAT asked Q
 'Who did John ask __ whether Mary bought what?'

Example (33a) is a familiar ill-formed example; on one approach, it is a *wh*-island violation. Example (33b) demonstrates that adding another *wh*-phrase outside the island (in this case *dare-ni* 'who-DAT') improves the example.

Richards (1997, 2001) notes that similar additional-*wh* effects can be found in languages with overt *wh*-movement. The examples in (34) are from Bulgarian (Roumyana Pancheva, Ani Petkova, Roumyana Slabakova, pers. comm.).

(34) a. ***Koja kniga** otreče senatorăt [mălvata če iska
 which book denied the.senator the.rumor that wanted
 da zabrani __]?
 to ban
 'Which book did the senator deny [the rumor that he wanted to ban __]?'

b. ?**Koj senator koja kniga** __ otreče [mălvata če iska da zabrani __]?
which senator which book denied the.rumor that wanted to ban
'Which senator denied [the rumor that he wanted to ban which book]?'

Example (34a) involves extraction from a complex NP and is ill formed. In (34b), an additional *wh*-phrase (*koj senator* 'which senator') has been added outside the island, and the result is better than the straightforward island violation in (34a). For Richards, the Japanese and Bulgarian facts are both instances of the Principle of Minimal Compliance; a Probe that has Agreed with one Goal in a way that creates a well-formed dependency is free to violate island conditions in later Agree operations. In this case, the Agree operation with the additional *wh*-phrase is the one that amnesties the later, island-violating *wh*-movement.

The Bulgarian case is clearly an instance of movement. The additional-*wh* effect that the Bulgarian and Japanese cases share, then, is one that demonstrably occurs when movement is involved, and in a theory in which Japanese *wh*-questions are created via movement, the commonality between Bulgarian and Japanese is expected. However, if the Japanese effect in (33a) follows from the nature of semantic composition, then it is unclear why Japanese should be mimicking Bulgarian in this way.

13.3.3 Also, *Mo*

Japanese *wh*-phrases may be combined with the particle *mo* to give universal expressions. The *wh*-phrase may be adjacent to *mo*, but need not be:

(35) a. **Dono** gakusei-mo odotta.
    which student-MO danced
    'Every student danced.'
  b. [**Dono** gakusei-no okaasan]-mo odotta.
    which student-GEN mother-MO danced
    'Every student's mother danced.'

The particle *mo* can also be associated with multiple *wh*-phrases:

(36) [**Dono** gakusei-ga dono ie-ni syootaisita sensei]-mo
    which student-NOM which house-to invited teacher-MO
    odotta.
    danced
    'For every student x and every house y, the teacher(s) x had invited to y danced.'

The particle *mo* may also appear without a *wh*-phrase, in which case it means 'also' or 'even':

(37) Ano gakusei-mo odotta.
　　　that student-MO danced
　　　'That student also danced.'

Shimoyama (2001, 2006, this volume) offers compelling arguments that the relation between Japanese *wh*-phrases and *mo* in examples such as (35)–(37) parallels the relation between *wh*-phrases and the question particle *ka* (see also Nishigauchi 1990, Ohno 1991, Watanabe 1992a, von Stechow 1996, and Takahashi 2002 for important discussion). In particular, she shows that just as *wh*-phrases prefer to be associated with the closest instance of *ka* (that is, they exhibit apparent *wh*-island effects), they prefer to be associated with the closest instance of *mo*. The easiest reading for (38) is the one given below.[10]

(38) [[Taroo-ga **nan**-nen-ni **nani**-ni-tuite kaita ronbun]- mo
　　　Taro-NOM what-year-in what-about wrote paper MO
　　　yonda sensei]-mo totemo tukareta.
　　　read teacher MO very got.tired
　　　'The teacher who read, for every topic x, every year y, the paper that Taro wrote on x in y also got very tired.'

In (38), the preference is to translate the higher *mo*, the one attached to *sensei* 'teacher', with 'also', rather than interpreting it in tandem with one of the *wh*-phrases. In other words, given the two instances of *mo* in (38), the *wh*-phrases prefer to associate with the lower *mo* rather than the higher *mo*.

In fact, the generalization appears to be that *mo* and *ka* are equivalent as far as this type of intervention is concerned; *mo* intervenes for association with *ka*, and *ka* intervenes for association with *mo*. Thus, the *wh*-phrases in (39) prefer to associate with the closer *ka*, not with the higher *mo*, and are interpreted as *wh*-phrases with scope in the lowest clause, rather than as universal expressions:

(39) [Yamada-ga **dare**-ni **nani**-o okutta ka] sitteiru syoonin]-mo
　　　Yamada-NOM who-DAT what-ACC sent Q know witness MO
　　　damatteita.
　　　was.silent
　　a. 'The witness who knew what Yamada sent to whom was also silent.'
　　b. *'For every person x, for every thing y, the witness who knew whether Yamada sent y to x was silent.'

However, association with *mo* disregards other familiar types of islands:

(40) [**Dono** TA-ga osieta gakusei-ga syootaisita sensei]-mo kita.
　　　which TA-NOM taught student-NOM invited teacher MO came
　　　'For every TA x, [the teacher(s) [that the student(s) that x had taught] invited] came.'

As Shimoyama (2001, 2006, this volume) points out, this is a powerful prima facie argument for giving the same type of explanation both for the relation between *wh*-phrases and *ka* and for the relation between *wh*-phrases and *mo*.[11] Any arguments that bear on the nature of one of these relations, then, ought to be tried on the other. I leave investigation of the properties of *mo* to other work (see Shimoyama 2001, 2006, this volume, for much careful discussion).

13.3.4 Pied-piping and the Semantics of *Wh*-Questions

Ohno (1989) and von Stechow (1996) point out a very serious problem with Nishigauchi's (1986, 1990) LF pied-piping analysis: it predicts the wrong readings. Their point holds, as far as I can see, for any type of pied-piping:

(41) Whose book did you buy?

The problem with an example such as (41) is that the *wh*-moved object is not just *whose* but *whose book*. Given the type of semantics for *wh*-questions that Nishigauchi assumes, the syntactic structure in (41) would be mapped onto the semantic representation informally represented in (42).

(42) For which x, y, x a book, y the book's owner, you read x?

The problem with the representation in (42) is that the nucleus of the question ('you read x') contains only one variable, x, which corresponds to a book. But the question should not be answered with the name of a book; it is a question about a person. The real semantic representation should be one in which the variable in the nucleus corresponds to a person:

(43) For which y, you read y's book?

In other words, although the entire phrase *whose book* has moved overtly, interpretation of (41) must involve reconstruction of everything but *who* to create the representation in (43).

Ohno's and von Stechow's point is that Nishigauchi's examples have the same problem; Nishigauchi gives the Japanese sentence in (44a) the semantics in (44b), which makes the question one about books. In fact, it must have the semantic structure in (44c), that of a question about people.

(44) a. John-wa   [**dare**-ga   kaita   hon-o]   yomimasita ka?
         John-TOP who-NOM wrote   book-ACC read   Q
         'Who did John read [a book that ___ wrote]?'
      b. For which x, y, x a book, y a person that wrote x, John read x?
      c. For which y, y a person, John read a book that y wrote?

If we posit covert pied-piping in examples such as (44), then, the process of interpretation must apparently involve operations that give a representation such as the one in (44c). In other words, even if the covert derivation begins by pied-piping the entire island *dare-ga kaita hon-o* 'a book that who wrote' into a scope position, we must then go on to extract the *wh*-word *dare* 'who' out of the island

and then reconstruct the island back into the base position. This is in fact the type of derivation von Stechow (1996) outlines. In (45b), the *wh*-phrase pied-pipes the entire island, so that *dare-ga kaita hon-o* 'a book that who wrote' moves to the specifier of CP. In (45c), the *wh*-phrase *dare-ga* 'who' moves out of the pied-piped island, and finally, in (45d), the remnant of the island reconstructs.[12]

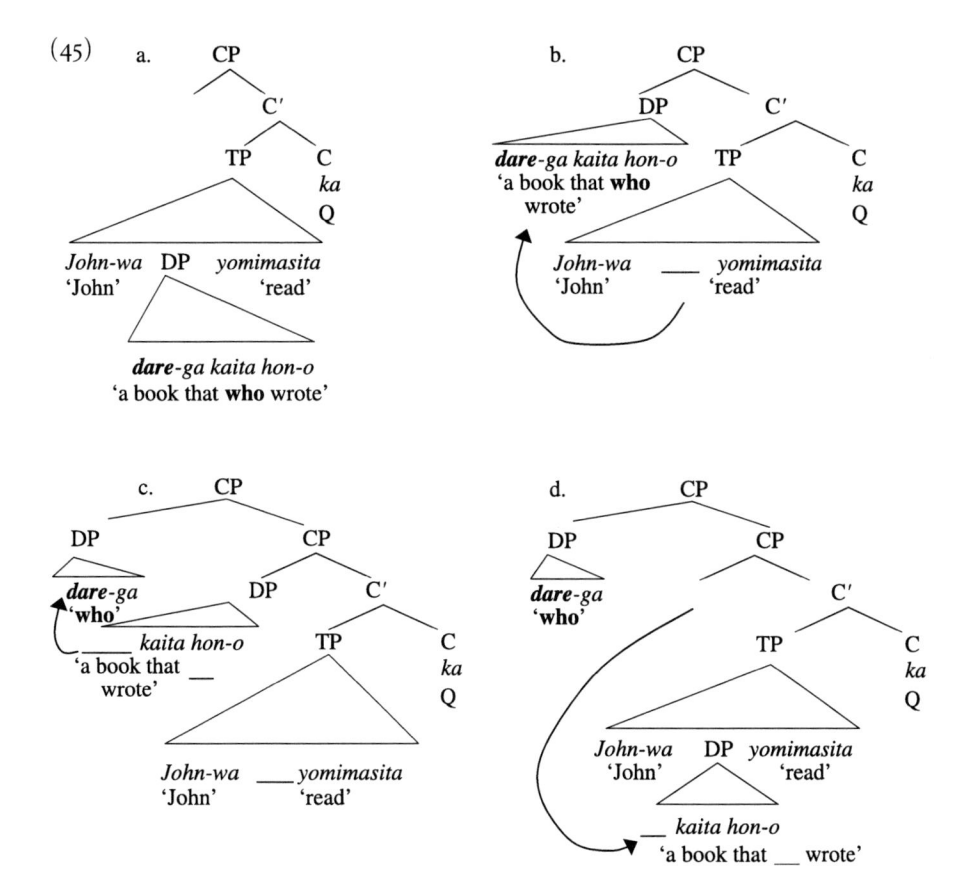

(45) [Tree diagrams a, b, c, d illustrating the derivation described in the text.]

Although it gets us the right semantic representation, the derivation in (45) has some unsettling properties. For one thing, it is fairly baroque. Do we really need a derivation with all these steps?[13] One way of avoiding this derivation would be to revise the assumptions Ohno and von Stechow make about the semantics of questions. This is the tack taken by Hagstrom (1998) and Cable (2007), who propose a semantics for questions that can interpret pied-piped structures.

One can imagine several possible solutions, then, to the problems raised by Ohno and von Stechow; we might avail ourselves of the derivation in (45), or adopt different assumptions about the semantics or questions, for example. But it seems clear that we cannot simply deny the existence of large-scale pied-piping as a way of circumventing island effects. In section 13.2.1 we saw that in some languages (e.g.,

Quechua, Tlingit, and Basque), pied-piping to avoid islands is a property of overt movement:

(46) a. ***Ima** -ta -taj   riku -rka -ngui [randi -shka runa -ta]?
       what ACC INT   see PAST 2   buy   NLZ   man ACC
       'What did you see the man who bought?'
   b. [**Ima** -ta   randi -shka   runa -ta   -taj] riku -rka -ngui?
       what ACC buy   NLZ   man ACC INT   see PAST 2
       Lit. '[The man that bought what] did you see?'

If this is the correct analysis for languages such as Quechua, and if Ohno's and von Stechow's claims about the interpretation of *wh*-questions are correct, then we cannot have a simpler theory in which this kind of derivation is impossible; some version of this derivation must be possible to deal with the interpretation of languages like Quechua. The only question is whether we want to use covert versions of these operations in Japanese.

The derivation in (45) has another, more serious problem, however. Recall that the whole point of positing covert pied-piping was to deal with islands. Nishigauchi's proposal was that Japanese lacks certain types of island effects, because covert *wh*-movement pied-pipes the entire island, so that the *wh*-word itself never actually exits the island, and thus no island violation is incurred. But the derivation in (45) does appear to have an island violation; the pied-piping step in (45b) may not violate any islands, but subextraction of the *wh*-word itself in (45c) certainly does. Von Stechow acknowledges this and suggests that, if we are to employ derivations such as (45), we need to posit a derivation with multiple levels on which covert movements can take place. The first, which he calls WH-structure, is the one constrained by Subjacency; this is the level on which pied-piping of islands takes place. WH-structure is followed by LF, which is not constrained by Subjacency and in which the *wh*-word itself is moved out of the island, which creates a structure that can be correctly interpreted semantically.

This proposal is disturbing in several ways. For one thing, the introduction of a new level is always cause for suspicion (as Heck 2004 points out). Perhaps more important, the original goal of the pied-piping proposal seems to have been lost. Nishigauchi first proposed covert pied-piping to explain why island effects seem not to appear. Rather than simply stipulating that island effects do not apply to covert operations, he allowed island effects to remain constant and gave covert movement another way of circumventing them. Now, it seems, we are back to stipulating that island effects do not appear for certain types of movement.

As it happens, a related proposal has been made on independent grounds. Richards (1997, 2001) and Hiraiwa (2001) claim that the conditions on a Probe are not uniform through the derivation; in particular, they claim that once a Probe has undergone its first Agree operation, it becomes subject to looser locality conditions. They explicitly avoid making any reference to differences in levels of representation. The relevant distinction is simply between the first

Agree operation by a given Probe and subsequent Agree operations, regardless of the levels on which these take place. Richards's (1997, 2001) Principle of Minimal Compliance allows a Probe that has participated in one well-formed Agree relation to subsequently ignore the locality conditions that normally constrain Probes. Hiraiwa's (2001) notion of Multiple Agree allows Probes to ignore Goals with which they have previously Agreed, when locality conditions are computed.

From this perspective, von Stechow's version of Nishigauchi's proposal no longer looks so peculiar. Richards and Hiraiwa have already proposed that when a Probe performs multiple Agree operations, instances of Agree after the first one are subject to looser locality conditions. This is precisely what von Stechow proposes; Japanese interrogative C first Agrees with the island, triggering pied-piping, and may then pull the *wh*-word out of the island with impunity. The stipulation that the second of these Agree operations is less subject to islands than the first turns out to be a special instance of a more generally observable phenomenon.

Shimoyama (2006) suggests that this version of a pied-piping analysis, in which *wh*-phrases eventually do exit the pied-piped island, loses the result described in section 13.3.1.3, in which multiple *wh*-phrases inside an island must all take the same scope. She offers the derivation in (48), which begins with two interrogative CPs, with an island containing two *wh*-phrases embedded inside the lower CP:

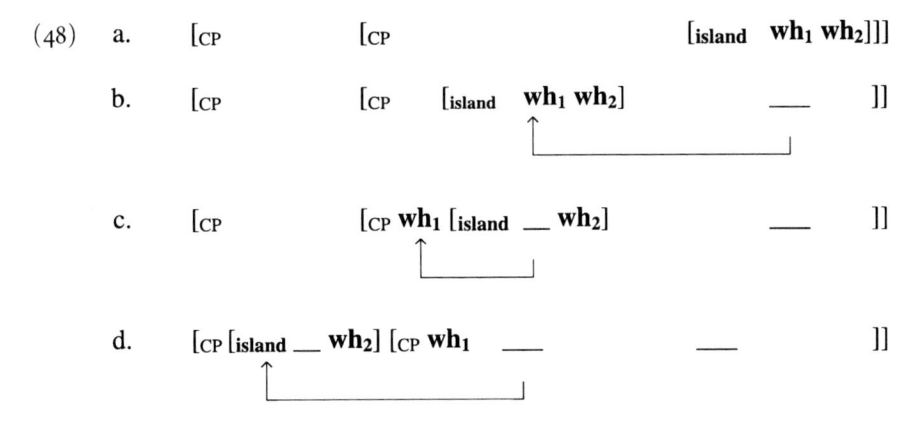

(48) a.   [CP   [CP   [island **wh₁ wh₂**]]]

      b.   [CP   [CP   [island **wh₁ wh₂**]   __   ]]

      c.   [CP   [CP **wh₁** [island __ **wh₂**]   __   ]]

      d.   [CP [island __ **wh₂**] [CP **wh₁**   __   ]]

In the derivation in (48), the island first moves to Spec,CP in the embedded clause, and one of the *wh*-phrases moves out of it. The island then moves up to the higher clause, where the second *wh*-phrase ought to be able to move out of it, thereby taking scope in a different clause.

Shimoyama's point is well taken. The Minimal Link Condition might be enough to rule out this derivation, however. At the point in the derivation in (48c), the first *wh*-phrase moves out of the island to a higher specifier of the embedded CP. As a result, the move of the island in (48d) violates the Minimal Link Condition; *wh*₁ is a closer possible Goal for the matrix C than the island is. The prediction that multiple *wh*-phrases that share an island must have the same scope thus appears to be safe, at least from this particular derivation.[14]

None of this, of course, is a positive argument that Japanese *wh*-movement ought to be done in this way. All we have seen here is that we need the type of derivation under consideration, in any event, to deal with the facts from Basque, Quechua, and Tlingit, and that the tools we need to do *wh*-movement in this way are already present in the syntactic literature, having been proposed on independent grounds.

13.4 INTERLUDE: *WH*-INTONATION

The intonation associated with Japanese *wh*-questions has been the subject of a number of recent papers (including Deguchi and Kitagawa 2002; Ishihara 2002, 2003; Sugahara 2003; Kitagawa, Roehrs, and Tomioka 2004; Hirotani 2005; Smith 2005). In Tokyo Japanese, the special *wh*-intonation involves an area of pitch compression, beginning with the *wh*-phrase and ending at the C marking the scope position for that *wh*-phrase.

Some of the work on Japanese *wh*-intonation (see, in particular, Ishihara 2002, Deguchi and Kitagawa 2002, Kitagawa, Roehrs, and Tomioka 2004) argues for the conclusion that some of the data under discussion here are in fact illusory. For instance, they reanalyze examples like (33a), repeated here as (49).

(49) *John-wa [Mary-ga **nani**-o katta ka dooka] siritagatteiru no?
John-TOP Mary-NOM what-ACC bought whether wants.to.know Q
'What does John want to know whether Mary bought __?'

The proposal, as I understand it, is that (49) is not in fact ill formed but is simply frequently given an improper intonation, in which the intonational domain following the *wh*-phrase ends in the embedded clause rather than in the matrix clause. Because this intonational domain must end at the scope position of the *wh*-phrase, and the embedded clause in this case is headed by *ka dooka* 'whether' and is therefore not a scope position for a *wh*-phrase, the result is a semantic anomaly.

This is an extremely interesting proposal. My understanding is that there is some debate among native speakers about whether intonation can make (49) completely well formed or simply easier to interpret. It is very difficult to know how to adjudicate this type of debate. Similarly, it is difficult to see how to find out whether Japanese *wh*-island effects are like *wh*-island effects in other languages (for instance, in English) or qualitatively different in some way that we want the theory to capture. In both Japanese and English, speakers vary in how robust they find the *wh*-island effect. It may be that we need to consider more semantically sophisticated kinds of effects on interpretation; rather than simply asking whether the sentences are ill formed, we may wish to concentrate on the distribution of pair-list readings, interactions between *wh*-phrases and quantifiers, and so forth.[15]

13.5 IMPLICATIONS AND CONCLUSIONS

Our access to the syntactic and semantic properties of *wh*-in-situ is necessarily somewhat indirect, and it is probably no surprise that no complete consensus on these topics has been reached. I have reviewed here two types of proposals from the literature. In one of these, *wh*-in-situ remains in situ throughout the derivation and is given a semantic type that allows it to be interpreted without movement. In the other, *wh*-in-situ is moved via a syntactic operation not unlike overt *wh*-movement; the particular derivation that we considered was first proposed by Nishigauchi and refined by von Stechow.

The proponents of these theories often offer simplicity arguments in favor of their approaches. Researchers championing the first type of approach point to the complex array of steps that the Nishigauchi derivation requires, once it is modified as von Stechow has argued it must be. Researchers arguing for the second type of approach tend to push for the desirability of a single type of syntax for *wh*-questions, with variation appearing only in the phonology.

Although I have certainly been guilty of this type of argumentation in my own work, I think that it is misplaced. Theories such as Shimoyama's (2001, 2006, this volume) cover a wide range of data elegantly and simply and without recourse to semantic trickery that is unneeded in other domains. No simplicity arguments should be leveled against such an approach.

The pied-piping proposal does force us to either alter our assumptions about the semantics of questions or posit a derivation with more steps than we are typically familiar with. I have argued here, however, that we cannot avoid positing some type of pied-piping derivation in certain languages (namely, languages such as Quechua, which use overt pied-piping as a way of avoiding islands). It seems to me, then, that a simplicity argument is out of place here as well, given that our theory of Universal Grammar (UG) must allow for derivations of this kind. Of course, we could simplify our theory of Japanese by pretending that these derivations do not exist, but this does nothing to simplify our overall theory.

In my opinion, then, the relevant evidence bearing on the choice between these theories must come not from considerations of simplicity but from the kind of evidence reviewed in section 13.3—that is, evidence gathered by investigating the properties of the syntax-semantics interface.

Several recent theories have focused on the properties of the particles I glossed with INT (Hagstrom 1998; Kishimoto 1992, 2005; Cable 2007). The discussion here has centered on the relation between *wh*-phrases and interrogative C, but once the behavior of INT is taken seriously, we have a third morpheme to investigate. It may well be that the correct theory is a hybrid of the two extremes I have been considering, with different types of relations holding between the different syntactic objects participating in a *wh*-question.

NOTES FOR CHAPTER 13

Many thanks to Danny Fox, Takako Iseda, Shigeru Miyagawa, and Mamoru Saito for useful discussion of these topics. Any mistakes are my own responsibility.

1. Abbreviations used in this chapter are: ACC = accusative, PRES = present tense, INT = interrogative, Q = question particle. NLZ = nominalizer, TOP = topic, NOM = nominative.

2. The literature offers us a number of models for covert movement, including post-Spell-Out movement of the type first suggested by Huang (1982), pronunciation of a lower copy (e.g., Bobaljik 2002), and movement of some object other than the *wh*-phrase itself (a null operator, as in Watanabe 1992a, 1992b, or the *wh*-particle *ka*, as in Hagstrom 1998).

3. I discuss these particles in more depth in section 13.3.1. They do not appear to be instances of C, given that multiple questions contain multiple instances of INT:

(i) **Pi** -taj, **ima** -ta -taj, riku-rka Utavalu-pi -ka?
 who INT what ACC INT see PAST. 3 Otavalo in TOP
 'Who saw what in Otavalo?' (Imbabura Quechua; Cole 1982:27)

(ii) **Aa** sá **daa** sá aawax̱aa?
 who INT what INT they.ate.it
 'Who ate what?' (Tlingit; Cable 2007)

4. Though see Arregi 2002 for another analysis of Basque *wh*-questions.

5. As of this writing, I have not been able to find the relevant data for Tlingit or Quechua.

6. See Ochi 1999, Tanaka 1999b, and references cited there for discussion.

7. These languages have all typically been analyzed as having *wh*-in-situ. However, Watanabe (2002) claims that older Japanese had overt *wh*-movement.

8. On the basis of these data, because it is the particle whose position is partly determined by islands, we might conclude that it is the particle, or the projection headed by the particle, that undergoes covert movement in these cases. See Hagstrom 1998; Kishimoto 2005; Cable 2007.

9. See Hagstrom 1998, however, for arguments that the Japanese interrogative particle *ka* is identical to the INT particle *ka* in premodern Japanese but undergoes overt movement in modern Japanese to its scope position.

10. For more discussion of the possible readings, see Shimoyama's (2001, 2006, this volume) discussion.

11. We might instead try to relate the facts about *mo* to the intervention effects in section 13.3.1.2.

12. I represent reconstruction as a lowering operation, but this is just for graphic convenience; any approach to reconstruction would work equally well.

13. Some readers may particularly object to the step in (45c), in which C apparently Probes into its own specifier, pulling the *wh*-word *dare* out and moving it to another specifier. See Richards 2004 for arguments that operations like this are in principle possible. Briefly, what I claim there is that we should not impose a c-command requirement (or "search domain") on Probes. Approaches to Cyclicity in which Probes must perform Agree operations early in the derivation will handle many of the cases that a c-command requirement on Agree would rule out; the potentially offending Goals will simply not be present in the structure at the point in the derivation at which the Goal is active. The only purpose of a c-command requirement on Agree, I claim, would be to rule out derivations like the one in (45); I offer evidence from Bulgarian that such derivations are in fact licit. See also Rezac 2003 for related discussion and Ko 2005 for counterarguments.

14. Another derivation, in which wh_1 does indeed move into the matrix clause and wh_2 later moves to a scope position in the embedded clause, could be ruled out by Cyclicity.

15. Kitagawa, Roehrs, and Tomioka (2004), for example, note that Japanese *wh*-phrases separated by a *wh*-island cannot have a pair-list reading, even on the correct intonation. They propose that covert movement is required just for pair-list readings and that single-pair readings may be generated without such movement (and hence without *wh*-island effects).

REFERENCES

Arregi, Karlos. 2002. Focus on Basque movements. Doctoral dissertation, MIT, Cambridge, Mass.

Beck, Sigrid. 1996. Quantified structures as barriers for LF movement. *Natural Language Semantics* 4:1–56.

Beck, Sigrid, and Shin-Sook Kim. 1997. On *wh*- and operator scope in Korean. *Journal of East Asian Linguistics* 6:339–384.

Bobaljik, Jonathan. 2002. A-chains at the PF interface: Copies and "covert" movement. *Natural Language & Linguistic Theory* 20:197–267.

Cable, Seth. 2007. The grammar of Q: Q-particles and the nature of *wh*-fronting, as revealed by the *wh*-questions of Tlingit. Doctoral dissertation, MIT, Cambridge, Mass.

Choe, Jae W. 1987. LF movement and pied-piping. *Linguistic Inquiry* 18:348–353.

Cole, Peter. 1982. *Imbabura Quechua* (Lingua Descriptive Studies vol. 5). Amsterdam: North Holland.

Deguchi, Masanori, and Yoshihisa Kitagawa. 2002. Prosody and *wh*-questions. In *Proceedings of NELS 32*, ed. Masako Hirotani, 73–92. Amherst, Mass.: GLSA Publications.

Hagstrom, Paul. 1998. Decomposing questions. Doctoral dissertation, MIT, Cambridge, Mass.

Hamblin, Charles. 1973. Questions in Montague English. *Foundations of Language* 10:41–53.

Heck, Fabian. 2004. A theory of pied piping. Doctoral dissertation, University of Tübingen, Germany.

Hermon, Gabriella. 1984. *Syntactic modularity*. Dordrecht: Foris.

Hiraiwa, Ken. 2001. Multiple Agree and the Defective Intervention Constraint in Japanese. In *MITWPL 40: The proceedings of HUMIT 2000*, ed. Ora Matushansky, Albert Costa, Javier Martín-González, Lance Nathan, and Adam Szczegielniak, 67–80. Cambridge, Mass.: MIT Working Papers in Linguistics.

Hirotani, Masako. 2005. Prosody and LF interpretation: Processing Japanese *wh*-questions. Doctoral dissertation, University of Massachusetts, Amherst.

Hoji, Hajime. 1985. Logical Form constraints and configurational structures in Japanese. Doctoral dissertation, University of Washington, Seattle.

Huang, C.-T. James. 1982. Logical relations in Chinese and the theory of grammar. Doctoral dissertation, MIT, Cambridge, Mass.

Ishihara, Shinichiro. 2002. Invisible but audible *wh*-scope marking: *Wh*-questions and deaccenting in Japanese. In *Proceedings of WCCFL 21*, ed. Line Mikkelsen and Christopher Potts, 180–193. Somerville, Mass.: Cascadilla Press.

Ishihara, Shinichiro. 2003. Intonation and interface conditions. Doctoral dissertation, MIT, Cambridge, Mass.

Karttunen, Lauri. 1977. Syntax and semantics of questions. *Linguistics and Philosophy* 1:3–44.

Kishimoto, Hideki. 1992. LF pied piping: Evidence from Sinhala. *Gengo Kenkyu* 102:46–87.

Kishimoto, Hideki. 2005. *Wh*-in-situ and movement in Sinhala questions. *Natural Language & Linguistic Theory* 23:1–51.

Kitagawa, Yoshihisa, Dorian Roehrs, and Satoshi Tomioka. 2004. Multiple *wh*-interpretations. In *Generative grammar in a broader perspective: Proceedings of the 4th GLOW in Asia 2003*, ed. Hang-Jin Yoon, 209–233. Seoul: Hangkook.

Ko, Heejeong. 2005. Syntactic edges and linearization. Doctoral dissertation, MIT, Cambridge, Mass.

Nishigauchi, Taisuke. 1986. Quantification in syntax. Doctoral dissertation, University of Massachusetts, Amherst.

Nishigauchi, Taisuke. 1990. *Quantification in the theory of grammar*. Dordrecht: Kluwer.

Ochi, Masao. 1999. Constraints on feature checking. Doctoral dissertation, University of Connecticut, Storrs.

Ohno, Yutaka. 1989. Mo. In *Papers on quantification*, ed. Emmon Bach, Angelika Kratzer, and Barbara Partee, 223–250. Amherst: University of Massachusetts, Department of Linguistics.

Ohno, Yutaka. 1991. Arguments against unselective binding in Korean. In *Harvard studies in Korean linguistics IV*, ed. Susumu Kuno, John Whitman, Young-Se Kang, Ik-Hwan Lee, Joan Maling, and Young-Joo Kim, 553–562. Seoul: Hanshin.

Ortiz de Urbina, Jon. 1989. *Parameters in the grammar of Basque*. Dordrecht: Foris.

Pesetsky, David. 1987. *Wh*-in-situ: Movement and unselective binding. In *The representation of (in)definiteness*, ed. Eric Reuland and Alice ter Meulen, 98–129. Cambridge, Mass.: MIT Press.

Rezac, Milan. 2003. The fine structure of cyclic Agree. *Syntax* 6:156–182.

Richards, Norvin. 1997. What moves where when in which language? Doctoral dissertation, MIT, Cambridge, Mass.

Richards, Norvin. 2000. An island effect in Japanese. *Journal of East Asian Linguistics* 9:187–205.

Richards, Norvin. 2001. *Movement in language: Interactions and architectures*. Oxford: Oxford University Press.

Richards, Norvin. 2004. Against bans on lowering. *Linguistic Inquiry* 35:453–463.

Riemsdijk, Henk van. 1984. On pied-piped infinitives in German relative clauses. In *Studies in German grammar*, ed. Jindrich Toman, 165–192. Dordrecht: Foris.

Saito, Mamoru. 1994. Additional-*wh* effects and the adjunction site theory. *Journal of East Asian Linguistics* 3:195–240.

Shimoyama, Junko. 2001. *Wh*-constructions in Japanese. Doctoral dissertation, University of Massachusetts, Amherst.

Shimoyama, Junko. 2006. Indeterminate phrase quantification in Japanese. *Natural Language Semantics* 14:139–173.

Smith, Jennifer. 2005. On the *wh*-question intonational domain in Fukuoka Japanese: Some implications for the syntax-prosody interface. In *UMOP 30: Papers on prosody*, ed. Shigeto Kawahara, 219–237. Amherst, Mass.: GLSA Publications.

Stechow, Arnim von. 1996. Against LF pied-piping. *Natural language Semantics* 4:57–110.

Sugahara, Mariko. 1996. Shuri Okinawan *kakari-musubi* and movement. In *MITWPL 29: Formal approaches to Japanese linguistics 2*, ed. Masatoshi Koizumi, Masayuki Oishi, and Uli Sauerland, 235–254. Cambridge, Mass.: MIT Working Papers in Linguistics.

Sugahara, Mariko. 2003. Downtrends and post-FOCUS intonation in Tokyo Japanese. Doctoral dissertation, University of Massachusetts, Amherst.

Takahashi, Daiko. 2002. Determiner raising and scope shift. *Linguistic Inquiry* 33:575–615.

Tanaka, Hidekazu. 1997. Invisible movement in *sika-nai* and the linear crossing constraint. *Journal of East Asian Linguistics* 6:143–188.

Tanaka, Hidekazu. 1999a. Conditions on logical form derivations and representations. Doctoral dissertation, McGill University, Montreal.

Tanaka, Hidekazu. 1999b. LF *wh*-islands and the Minimal Scope Principle. *Natural Language & Linguistic Theory* 17:371–402.

Tanaka, Hidekazu. 2002. Remarks on Beck's effects. *Linguistic Inquiry* 34:314–323.

Tsai, Wei-tien Dylan. 1994. On economizing the theory of A-bar dependencies. Doctoral dissertation, MIT, Cambridge, Mass.

Watanabe, Akira. 1992a. Wh-in-situ, Subjacency, and chain formation. *MIT occasional papers in linguistics 2*. Cambridge, Mass.: MIT Working Papers in Linguistics.

Watanabe, Akira. 1992b. Subjacency and S-structure movement of *wh*-in-situ. *Journal of East Asian Linguistics* 1:255–291.

Watanabe, Akira. 2002. The loss of overt *wh*-movement in Old Japanese. In *Syntactic effects of morphological change*, ed. David Lightfoot, 179–195. Oxford: Oxford University Press.

Whitman, John. 1997. *Kakarimusubi* from a comparative perspective. In *Japanese/Korean linguistics 6*, ed. Ho-min Sohn and John Haig, 161–178. Stanford, Calif.: CSLI Publications.

CHAPTER 14

INDETERMINATE PRONOUNS

JUNKO SHIMOYAMA

14.1 Introduction

This chapter surveys some of the major issues surrounding so-called indeterminate pronouns in Japanese such as *dare* 'who' and *nani* 'what'. One of the questions that has attracted the most attention in this domain concerns how indeterminate pronouns associate with quantificational particles that occur higher in the structure. Two major approaches to this question—namely, the movement and nonmovement analyses—are reviewed from the perspective of the syntax-semantics interface, and the challenges that these analyses face are presented. Closely related to this issue is the question of what the semantics of indeterminate pronouns is. I survey two views on this and point out the advantages and disadvantages.

14.2 Brief Introduction of the Problem: Indeterminate Pronouns

Japanese expressions such as *dare* 'who', *nani* 'what', *doko* 'where', and so forth—although typically given English translations using *wh*-words—do not have interrogative meanings inherently. The quantificational force of these expressions depends on the particles that they co-occur with, as table 14.1 shows (the table is

Table 14.1 Japanese indeterminate pronouns and their quantificational meanings

a. Interrogative		b. Existential	c. Universal	d. NPI any	e. FC any
da're...ka	'who'	da're-ka	da're-mo	dare-mo	dare-de-mo
na'ni...ka	'what'	na'ni-ka	(na'ni-mo)	nani-mo	nan-de-mo
do're...ka	'which (one)'	do're-ka	do're-mo	dore-mo	dore-de-mo
do'no N...ka	'which$_{Det}$'	do'no N-ka	do'no N-mo	dono N-mo	dono N-de-mo
do'tira...ka	'which of the two'	do'tira-ka	do'tira-mo	dotira-mo	dotira-de-mo
do'ko...ka	'where'	do'ko-ka	do'ko-mo	doko-mo	doko-de-mo
i'tu...ka	'when'	i'tu-ka	i'tu-mo	—	itu-de-mo
na'ze...ka	'why'	na'ze-ka	—	—	—
do'o...ka	'how'	(do'o-ka)	(do'o-mo)	(doo-mo)	doo-de-mo

not intended to be an exhaustive list of indeterminate pronouns). The apostrophes in the table indicate the location of accent in the standard dialect.

Because of their varying semantics, the expressions in question are referred to as *huteigo* 'indeterminate words' in traditional Japanese grammar and as indeterminate pronouns by Kuroda (1965:91). Indeterminate pronouns are interpreted as interrogative when they associate with the question particle *ka* that occurs at the right periphery of a clause as in column (a) of the table. When the indeterminates are immediately followed by *ka* as in column (b), they take on existential meaning. Columns (c) and (d) show that accented indeterminates and the particle *mo* give rise to universal meaning, whereas nonaccented indeterminates and *mo* give rise to meaning similar to the negative polarity item (NPI) *any*. Finally, column (e) shows that nonaccented indeterminates and *-de-mo* are interpreted as free choice *any*.

What we have just seen is by no means a phenomenon peculiar to Japanese, as can be seen in cross-linguistic studies such as Haspelmath 1997. To provide just one sample, table 14.2 shows a list of what we might call indeterminate pronouns in Basque and how they take on various quantificational meanings depending on the co-occurring particles (Haspelmath 1997:315).

When the common cores of all the series (*nor, zer, non,* etc.) occur on their own as in column (a), interrogative meaning arises. The *-bait*-series in column (b) are nonemphatic indefinites used in nonnegative polarity contexts, and the *i*-series in column (c) are negative polarity items. The *edo*-series and *-nahi*-series in columns (d) and (e) are found in free choice contexts.

Among the various uses of indeterminate pronouns in Japanese, the interrogative use, or more precisely its syntax, has received the most attention in the literature. As overviewed by Richards in this volume, Japanese indeterminates in the context of *wh*-questions have figured more prominently in the development of syntactic theory in the last few decades than those in any other contexts. However, given the way quantification is expressed in general in Japanese as observed in table 14.1 and the fact

Table 14.2 Basque indeterminate pronouns and their quantificational meanings

a. Interrogative	b. -bait-series	c. i-series	d. edo-series	e. -nahi-series
nor 'who'	nor-bait	i-nor	edo-nor	nor-nahi
zer 'what'	zer-bait	i-zer	edo-zer	zer-nahi
non 'where'	non-bait	i-non	edo-non	non-nahi
noiz 'when'	noiz-bait	i-noiz	edo-noiz	noiz-nahi
nola 'how'	nola-bait	i-nola	edo-nola	nola-nahi
zein 'which$_{Det}$'	—	—	edo-zein	zein-nahi

that the Japanese-type indeterminate pronouns are found cross-linguistically, we can say that looking at *wh*-questions in isolation may not necessarily give us an insight into learning how quantification in general works in Japanese. For any of the contexts where indeterminates show up, its analysis should be couched within a general theory of indeterminate pronoun quantification in Japanese. Of course, we would ultimately want to see a theory of quantification involving indeterminate pronouns across languages. First steps toward that direction have been taken by Kratzer and Shimoyama 2002 and Kratzer 2005, to which the reader is referred.

14.3 Description of the Core Data: Association of Indeterminate Pronouns and Particles

One of the central questions that has been addressed in the literature concerns how indeterminate pronouns associate with particles that do not occur locally. This section introduces the core data in this domain.

14.3.1 Nonlocal Association

Looking at table 14.1, one might get the impression that except for the interrogative case, Japanese is not that different from Basque, or English for that matter, because the particles from which indeterminates derive their quantificational force occur right next to them. This, however, is not always the case. The examples in (1) illustrate that the particle *mo* or *ka* can occur at either side of the postposition *ni* 'to' or *kara* 'from'.

(1) a. Dare-mo-ni/-ni-mo denwa-o kaketa.
     who-MO-to/-to-MO phone-ACC rang
     '(I) called everyone.'

b. Dare-ka-kara/-kara-ka denwa-ga atta.
   who-KA-from/from-KA phone-NOM existed
   'There was a call from someone.'

These are cases of universal and existential quantification, but a similar observation can be made for the NPI and free choice contexts. In these contexts, however, the particles *mo* and *de-mo* must occur to the right of postpositions.

In the universal construction, the distance between indeterminates and associating particles can even be farther than just across postpositions. The example in (2a) illustrates that the universal particle *mo* can associate with *dare* 'who' across a noun phrase boundary. The example in (2b) is even more striking—the association takes place across a complex NP, which contains a relative clause.

(2) a. [Dare-no hahaoya]-mo naita.
       who-GEN mother-MO cried
       'For everyone x, the mother of x cried.'
    b. [Dare-ga katta ie]-mo takakatta.
       who-NOM bought house-MO was.expensive
       'For everyone x, a/the house(s) that x bought was/were expensive.'

Such data have attracted the attention of Kuroda (1965), Hoji (1985), Nishigauchi (1986, 1990), Ohno (1989), von Stechow (1996), Shimoyama (1999, 2001, 2006a), and Takahashi (2002), among many others. Korean has a very similar construction, as shown in (3), taken from Ohno 1991.

(3) [Enu sonye-ka pon koyangi] -na kwiyewessta.
    which girl-NOM saw cat -NA were.cute
    'The cats that each girl saw were cute.'

The universal *mo* (and perhaps the free choice *de-mo*) most freely allows the long-distance association of the kind we just observed. The existential particle *ka*, for instance, does not seem to allow nonlocal association as freely, as shown in (4) and (5), though Takahashi (2002) and Yatsushiro (2004) report on data from more permissive dialects.[1]

(4) a. Taroo-wa dare-ka-no hon-o nakusita.
        Taroo-TOP who-KA-GEN book-ACC lost
        'Taroo lost someone's book.'
    b. ?/??Taroo-wa dare-no hon-ka-o nakusita.
        Taroo-TOP who-GEN book-KA-ACC lost

(5) a. Taroo-wa [dare-ka-kara karita hon]-o nakusita.
        Taroo-TOP who-KA-from borrowed book-ACC lost
        'Taroo lost a/the book that he had borrowed from someone.'
    b. ??/*Taroo-wa [dare-kara karita hon]-ka-o nakusita.
        Taroo-TOP who-from borrowed book-KA-ACC lost

14.3.2 Locality

Data such as (2b), where an indeterminate depends on the particle *mo* outside the complex NP it is embedded in, are familiar from indeterminates in the interrogative context. In (6), association of *doko* 'where' and the question particle *ka* is established across complex NP (see Richards, this volume).[2]

(6) Hanako-wa [doko-kara kita hito]-ni aimasita ka?
    Hanako-TOP where-from came person-DAT met Q
    'Where_x did Hanako meet a/the person/people who came from x?'

This seemingly long-distance association in the interrogative context as well as in the universal context is in fact constrained by a certain locality condition. An important observation made by Nishigauchi (1986, 1990) is that the association does not result in full grammaticality in the presence of a *wh*-island. Starting from a *wh*-question example in (7), we can see that the sentence is most readily interpreted as a matrix *yes/no*-question and an embedded multiple question.[3]

(7) Sabu-wa [Masako-ga dare-ni nani-o ageta ka] oboeteimasu ka?
    Sabu-TOP Masako-NOM who-DAT what-ACC gave Q remember Q
    a. 'Does Sabu remember what Masako gave to whom?'
    b. ?*'Who_x does Sabu remember what Masako gave to x?'
    c. *'What_x does Sabu remember to whom Masako gave x?'
    d. ?*'Who_x does Sabu remember whether Masako gave what to x?'

In a similar manner, the association between indeterminates and *mo* is blocked by a *wh*-island. Note first that the particle *mo* has a use in which it means 'also' or 'even'. So, when there is no indeterminate pronoun in the scope of *mo* as in (8), 'also' or 'even' is the only possible interpretation.

(8) Sono hito-mo Sabu-ni denwasita.
    that hito-MO Sabu-DAT called
    'That person also called Sabu./Even that person called Sabu.'

In (9), we see that an attempt to interpret *dare* 'who' and/or *nani* 'what' as having a universal force fails.

(9) [[[Masako-ga dare-ni nani-o ageta ka] siritagatteiru]
        Masako-NOM who-DAT what-ACC gave Q want.to.know
    hito]-mo Sabu-ni denwasita.
    person-MO Sabu-DAT called
    a. 'The person who wanted to know what Masako gave to whom also called Sabu.'
       'Even the person who wanted to know what Masako gave to whom called Sabu.'
    b. *'For every person x, the person who wanted to know what Masako gave to x called Sabu.'

c. **'For every thing x, the person who wanted to know to whom Masako gave x called Sabu.'
d. *'For every person x, for every thing y, the person who wanted to know whether Masako gave y to x called Sabu.'

Based on observations of this kind, Nishigauchi (1986, 1990) has established that a uniform analysis should be sought for the two types of indeterminate-particle association.

To reinforce the need for such a uniform analysis, we can add here that a *mo*-marked phrase functions similarly to a *wh*-island in that it blocks indeterminate-particle association. Examples (10) and (11) from Shimoyama 2006a illustrate this point. Both show that an indeterminate cannot be construed with a higher particle (either *ka* or *mo*) when the lower particle, *mo*, is interpreted as universal.[4]

(10) Yoko-wa [[[Taroo-ga nan-nen-ni nani-nituite kaita]
 Yoko-TOP Taroo-NOM what-year-in what-about wrote
 ronbun] -mo yuu-datta ka] siritagatteiru.
 paper -MO A-was Q want.to.know
 a. 'Yoko wonders whether for every topic x, every year y, the paper that Taroo wrote on x in y got an A.'
 b. ?*'Yoko wonders for which year y, for every topic x, the paper that Taroo wrote on x in y got an A.'
 c. *'Yoko wonders for which topic x, for every year y, the paper that Taroo wrote on x in y got an A.'
 d. (?)'Yoko wonders for which topic x and for which year y, the paper that Taroo wrote on x in y also got an A.'

(11) [[[[Taroo-ga nan-nen-ni nani-nituite kaita] ronbun] -mo yonda]
 Taroo-NOM what-year-in what-about wrote paper -MO read
 sensei]-mo totemo tukareta.
 teacher-MO very.much got.tired
 a. 'The teacher who read, for every topic x, every year y, the paper that Taroo wrote on x in y also got very tired.'
 b. *'For every year y, the teacher who read, for every topic x, the paper that Taroo wrote on x in y got very tired.'
 c. **'For every topic x, the teacher who read, for every year y, the paper that Taroo wrote on x in y got very tired.'
 d. (?)'For every topic x, every year y, the teacher who also read the paper that Taroo wrote on x in y got very tired.'

In summary, indeterminate pronouns can associate with higher particles *ka* and *mo* in a long-distance manner, except when these particles occur in the association path as shown in (12).

(12) *[...[...indeterminate...]-ka/mo...]-ka/mo
 |_____|

This locality pattern observed in Japanese has created an intriguing challenge to the theory of *wh*-dependencies. The pattern is different in interesting ways from the well-studied dependency between a *wh*-phrase and its trace in English, created by overt or covert movement. Overt *wh*-movement in English is subject to island constraints including not just *wh*-islands but also complex NP, adjunct, and subject islands, whereas covert *wh*-movement is not. Providing explanation to this cross-linguistic variation has been a central concern in syntactic research (see Richards, this volume). In the next two sections, I provide an overview of two major types of analyses—namely, the movement and nonmovement analyses—mainly from the perspective of the syntax-semantics interface. I mainly focus on how they fare in providing a uniform analysis of the interrogative and universal constructions.

14.4 Issues and Controversies Regarding Analysis: The Movement Analysis, Covert Pied-Piping, and the Syntax-Semantics Interface

The fact that the indeterminate-particle dependency is sensitive to *wh*-islands has been taken by many researchers to indicate that this dependency is mediated through movement (see, e.g., Nishigauchi 1986, 1990; Watanabe 1992a, 1992b; Maki 1995; von Stechow 1996; Richards 1997, 2000, 2001; Hagstrom 1998; Ochi 1999; Tanaka 1999). A challenge for the movement analysis, then, is to explain the lack of all other island constraints. An influential syntactic proposal in this area was made by Nishigauchi (1986, 1990) and Choe (1987), to which we now turn.

14.4.1 Covert Pied-Piping

A special mechanism that allows covert pied-piping of a whole island was proposed to account for the lack of island effects other than the *wh*-island effect (Nishigauchi 1986, 1990; Choe 1987). According to the pied-piping analysis, a whole island embedding an indeterminate pronoun counts as a *wh*-phrase due to feature percolation, and it is this big constituent that undergoes covert movement. The key in this proposal is that indeterminate pronouns within islands are never extracted out of them throughout the derivation, thus circumventing island violation. Though the authors cited in the previous paragraph do not necessarily agree on what moves at what level, most of them rely on some form of pied-piping analysis. For precise syntactic mechanisms of pied-piping, see Nishigauchi 1986, 1990 and Richards 2000.[5]

14.4.2 Pied-Piping and Semantic Interpretation

From the perspective of syntax-semantics mapping, however, the pied-piping analysis comes with an undesirable consequence and therefore needs to be augmented with reconstruction of the pied-piped material, as discussed in detail in von Stechow 1996 (see also Chomsky 1977; Heim 1987; and Fiengo, Huang, Lasnik, and Reinhart 1988). Below I summarize von Stechow's main point—namely, that the LF structure with pied-piping is not suitable for deriving appropriate semantic interpretation for *wh*-questions, and I show how the revised pied-piping analysis solves the problem.[6]

According to the movement analysis, a *wh*-question such as (13a) has a Logical Form such as (13b).

(13) a. Yoko-ga   dono hon-o   yomimasita ka?
     Yoko-NOM which book-ACC read   Q
     'Which book did Yoko read?'
   b. [$_{CP}$ [dono hon-o]$_1$ [$_{TP}$ Yoko-ga t_1 yomimasita] ka]

This LF has basically the same structure as the LF of the English *wh*-question *Which book did Yoko read?* and thus a standard interrogative semantics can be derived compositionally following a standard procedure proposed for its English counterpart. That is, we can assume, for example, that indeterminates introduce existential quantifiers that bind variables created by their movement, and that there is an interrogative operator, say in C^0, that forms a set of propositions that are possible answers to the question, along the lines of Hamblin (1973) and Karttunen (1977).[7] The formula in (14), a suitable semantics for the question in (13a), can then be read off from the LF in (13b).

(14) $\lambda p \exists x [\text{book}(x)(w) \ \& \ p = \lambda w'. \text{read}(x)(\text{Yoko})(w')]$

The question denotes a set of propositions of the form Yoko read x, where x is a book in the actual world.

When an indeterminate pronoun is embedded in an island other than a *wh*-island, the whole island undergoes covert movement, according to the pied-piping analysis.[8] In (15a), for example, where *dare* 'who' occurs inside the complex NP *dare-ga kaita hon* 'book that who wrote', the LF structure is derived by moving this entire object, as shown in (15b). The LF in (15b) also shows the movement of *dare* 'who' within the complex NP. It moves within the relative clause according to Nishigauchi (1986, 1990, 1999) and outside the relative clause according to Richards (2000). For Nishigauchi, the purpose of this type of internal movement is to make the *wh*-feature percolation from *dare* 'who' possible (see also van Riemsdijk 1984).

(15) a. Kimi-wa [[dare-ga   kaita] hon]-o   yomimasita ka?
       you-TOP who-NOM wrote book-ACC read   Q
       'Who$_x$ did you read a book that x wrote?'
   b. [[[dare-ga]$_1$ t_1 kaita] hon-o]$_2$ kimi-wa t_2 yomimasita ka
        who-NOM   wrote book-ACC you-TOP read   Q

It is proposed by Nishigauchi (1986, 1990) that variables introduced by both *dare* 'who' and *hon* 'book' are bound unselectively by *ka* and the question is claimed to receive the paraphrase in (16a), which can be translated into (16b).

(16) a. For which x, y, x a book, y a person that wrote x, did you read x?
b. $\lambda p \exists x \exists y [\text{book}(x)(w) \ \& \ \text{person}(y)(w) \ \& \ \text{wrote}(x)(y)(w) \ \& \ p = \lambda w'.\text{read}(x)(\text{you})(w')]$

As von Stechow (1996) points out, this semantic interpretation derived from the pied-piped LF structure incorrectly predicts that the sentence in (17a) is a possible answer to the question.

(17) a. *Umibe-no   Kafuka-o   yomimasita.*
       shore-GEN   Kafka-ACC   read
       '(I) read *Kafka on the Shore*.'
    b. *Murakami-ga   kaita   hon-o   yomimasita.*
       Murakami-NOM   wrote   book-ACC   read
       '(I) read a book that Murakami wrote.'

A possible answer to this question should in fact have the form represented in (17b). Given this fact, the denotation of the question should be (18), which can be derived from the LF in (19).

(18) $\lambda p.\exists x [\text{person}(x)(w) \ \& \ p = \lambda w'.\exists y [\text{book}(y)(w') \ \& \ \text{wrote}(y)(x)(w') \ \& \ \text{read}(y)(\text{you})(w')]]$

(19) [*dare-ga*]$_1$ [[[t_1 *kaita*] *hon-o*]$_2$ *kimi-wa* t_2 *yomimasita ka*]
     who-NOM   wrote book-ACC   you-TOP   read   Q

According to von Stechow, a series of three covert movements are involved in the derivation of this LF structure. First, the entire island *dare-ga kaita hon-o* 'book that who wrote' undergoes covert pied-piping. At the second step, where no island constraints are operative, *dare-ga* 'who' is extracted out of the island and adjoined to it.[9] Finally the pied-piped material [t *kaita hon-o*] is reconstructed to an interpretable position in the nucleus (this step does not leave a trace).

One might wonder why we even bother to covertly move the entire island to begin with, if most of it should be reconstructed for interpretational purposes. This is necessitated by the fundamental idea in the movement analysis that the locality effect we observed in section 14.3.2 is an indication of a movement relation between indeterminates and the particle *ka* or *mo*. One is then forced to assume that *wh*-movement takes place in Japanese at a level where island constraints do apply.[10]

14.4.3 A Consequence for the Universal Construction

So far in this section we have focused on indeterminate pronouns in the interrogative context. In particular, we have seen how the movement analysis, coupled with the amended pied-piping analysis, accounts for the puzzling pattern of island effects and derives appropriate interpretations. If we are to seek a general theory of indeterminate pronouns, and in particular, a uniform analysis of the interrogative and universal constructions, we want this analysis to extend to the universal construction. As becomes clear shortly, this turns out to be a difficult task. Therefore, if one insists on the movement analysis sketched for the interrogative construction, a uniform analysis of the interrogative and universal constructions has to be given up, which goes against Nishigauchi's (1986, 1990) original insight.

The main problem lies in the fact that the LF structure derived for the nonlocal universal construction following the successive steps assumed in the amended pied-piping analysis is not suitable for appropriate semantic interpretation. An example of the nonlocal universal construction is repeated here:

(20) a. [Dare-ga   katta   ie]-mo   takakatta.
        who-NOM bought house-MO was.expensive
      'For everyone x, the house that x bought was expensive.'
    b. [[dare-ga]$_1$ [[t_1 katta ie]-mo]] takakatta.
       who-NOM   bought house-MO was.expensive

Following the steps described above, [*dare-ga katta ie*] 'house that who bought' first undergoes covert pied-piping to the specifier position of the phrase headed by *mo*. Then the indeterminate *dare-ga* 'who' is extracted out of the island and adjoined to it, and finally the pied-piped part undergoes reconstruction, which results in the LF in (20b).

The semantic interpretation we want for the quantified sentence in (20a) is (21), disregarding tense and possible worlds (Ohno 1989, von Stechow 1996).[11]

(21) $\forall x[\text{person}(x) \rightarrow \text{expensive}(\iota y[\text{house}(y) \ \& \ \text{person}(x) \ \& \ \text{buy}(y)(x)])]$

The LF structure in (20b), however, cannot be transparently mapped to the semantic representation (21) given that it does not have the typical tripartite structure that corresponds to the semantic interpretation. A technical device for the purpose of deriving (21) from the LF in (20b) is indeed proposed by von Stechow (1996), which I cannot go into here for reasons of space (see Shimoyama 2006a for a brief review). The proposed device, however, is not an attractive solution, relying on ad hoc assumptions made only for this type of sentence and hence not well motivated in the grammar of Japanese.

14.4.4 More Questions Surrounding Covert Pied-piping

There are many other issues surrounding the pied-piping analysis that cannot be fully discussed in this survey. For example, for the amended pied-piping analysis to be complete, pied-piped *wh*-islands should be blocked in a principled manner. Richards (2000, this volume) addresses this important question and tries to derive why pied-piping of *wh*-islands does not give rise to grammatical sentences. Readers are referred to his work, where a connection is made between the non-pied-pipability of *wh*-islands in overt *wh*-movement in Basque and the putative non-pied-pipability of *wh*-islands in covert *wh*-movement in Japanese (see also Ortiz de Urbina 1990 and Arregi 2003).

Richards (2000) also presents examples similar to (22) as an argument for covert pied-piping in Japanese. The example in (22) is taken from Watanabe (1992a:fn. 9), where the observation is attributed to Mamoru Saito (pers. comm.).

(22) John-wa [Mary-ga [[nani-o doko-de katta] hito]-o
John-TOP Mary-NOM what-ACC where-LOC bought person-ACC
sagasiteiru ka] siritagatteiru no?
looking.for Q want.to.know Q
a. [_{CP}...[_{CP}...[_{CNP}...indeterminate₁...indeterminate₂...]...Q₂]...Q₁]
*'For which x, x a thing, John wants to know for which y, y a place, Mary is looking for the person who bought x at y?'
b. [_{CP}...[_{CP}...[_{CNP}...indeterminate₁...indeterminate₂...]...Q]...Q_{1,2}]
??/?*'For which x, x a thing, for which y, y a place, John wants to know whether Mary is looking for the person who bought x at y?'[12]
c. [_{CP}...[_{CP}...[_{CNP}...indeterminate₁...indeterminate₂...]...Q_{1,2}]...Q]
'Does John want to know for which x, x a thing, for which y, y a place, Mary is looking for the person who bought x at y?'

Readings (a) and (b) both involve *wh*-island violations. The observation is that reading (a), where the two indeterminates in the same complex NP are assigned distinct scopes, is worse than typical *wh*-island violations.

It is claimed in Watanabe 1992a and Richards 2000 that the contrast in grammaticality between (22a) and (22b) is accounted for straightforwardly by assuming that covert pied-piping takes place in Japanese. One crucial assumption there is that the reading in (22a) cannot be derived without extracting one indeterminate, in this case, *nani* 'what', out of the complex NP, whereas the reading in (22b) can be derived without extracting any indeterminate from the complex NP. Hence, an additional island effect is detected for (22a) but not for (22b), where only the *wh*-island effect is detected.

However, given that the original pied-piping analysis needs to be augmented with subsequent *wh*-extraction out of islands and reconstruction for the semantic reasons discussed above, extraction out of complex NPs always takes place, even in the same scope readings. That is, extraction out of the complex NP occurs not just in (22a) but in (22b) as well. Thus, the degradedness of the distinct scope reading does not follow simply from the assumption that covert pied-piping takes place in Japanese.

Consider, for instance, the derivation of the reading in (22a) in which the complex NP first moves to the lower scope position, and then indeterminate₂ is extracted out of the complex NP. From this second step on, no island constraints are operative in the amended pied-piping analysis. Then, indeterminate₁ can move out of the complex NP to the matrix scope position without any island violation (see also Richards, this volume). Thus, covert pied-piping and the distinct scope reading do not necessarily exclude each other in the amended pied-piping analysis.[13]

The contrast between (22a) and (22b) does not seem to follow, either, if we further augment the amended pied-piping analysis so that Subjacency needs to be satisfied only once per C^0, as briefly touched on in note 9. Starting from a derivation of (22b), the movement of the complex NP to the matrix scope position incurs a *wh*-island violation. Because Subjacency has not yet been obeyed at the matrix Q level, the subsequent extraction of the two indeterminates incurs two complex NP island violations. In a derivation of (22a), it is possible to first move the complex NP to the lower scope position and extract indeterminate$_2$ without incurring any violation. Then, we either further move the complex NP to the higher scope position, extract indeterminate$_1$, and reconstruct the island, or move only indeterminate$_1$ to the higher scope position out of the complex NP. Either way, we have at most one *wh*-island violation and one complex NP violation.[14]

The upshot is that in the amended pied-piping analysis, a possible source of the contrast between (22a) and (22b) cannot be as simple as the former having one extra island violation. That a possible source of the contrast is, in fact, of a more general nature than having to do with a complex NP island violation is suggested by the following example. Example (23) is a slight variation of example (22): The complex NP in the original example has now been replaced by a simple NP, *dare-no nan-nen-no syasin* 'a photo of whom from what year'. The pattern of grammaticality stays more or less the same in this example.

(23) John-wa   [Mary-ga   [dare-no   nan-nen-no   syasin]-o
      John-TOP Mary-NOM   who-GEN   what-year-GEN   photo-ACC
      sagasiteiru   ka]   siritagatteiru   no?
      looking.for   Q   want.to.know   Q
   a.   *'For which x, x a person, John wants to know for which y, y a year, Mary is looking for a photo of x from y?'
   b.   ??/?*'For which x, x a person, for which y, y a year, John wants to know whether Mary is looking for a photo of x from y?'
   c.   'Does John want to know for which x, x a person, for which y, y a year, Mary is looking for a photo of x from y?'

More research is needed to provide a satisfactory answer to the question as to where the contrast in the (a) and (b) examples stems from in (22) and (23).

14.5 More Issues and Controversies Regarding Analysis: The Nonmovement Analysis and *Wh*-Island

As I have discussed, the movement analysis takes the presence of the *wh*-island effect to be indicative of a movement relation between indeterminates and higher particles and attempts to provide an account for the lack of other island effects. Alternatively, one could consider the lack of most island effects to be evidence that there is no such movement relation, as proposed in Toyoshima 1996 and Shimoyama 1999, 2001, for example. The challenge now is turned around: the presence of the *wh*-island effect requires an explanation.

14.5.1 The Hamblin Analysis and Locality

To see how the apparent *wh*-island effect can be accounted for without appealing to a movement relation between indeterminates and particles, we should first address what the semantic denotations of indeterminate pronouns are. Two proposals are found in this domain—one says that indeterminate pronouns denote sets of alternatives, and the other says that they denote open propositions. In what follows I first summarize the former proposal and present how it accounts for the apparent *wh*-island effect without *wh*-movement. I then summarize the latter proposal and evaluate its way of handling the apparent *wh*-island effect.

The idea that indeterminate pronouns denote sets of alternatives is based on a proposal in Hamblin 1973 that English *wh*-pronouns denote sets of alternatives. For example, *who* denotes the set of all persons. The application of Hamblin's semantics to indeterminate pronouns is found in Ramchand 1997 for Bengali, as well as in Lin 1996 for the Chinese *wulun* 'no matter'-construction. For Japanese, a Hamblin semantics is adopted by Hagstrom (1998) for indeterminate pronouns that occur in the interrogative and existential contexts. Its extension to the universal context is suggested in Shimoyama 2001 and more fully explored in Kratzer and Shimoyama 2002. Starting from the interrogative context, *dare* 'who' in (24) denotes the set of all people (with appropriate contextual restriction) as in (25a). The VP *utaimasu* 'sing', in contrast, denotes a singleton set whose sole member is its ordinary denotation, as shown in (25b).

(24) [Dare-ga   utaimasu] ka?
     who-NOM sing   Q
     'Who sings?'

(25) For all possible worlds w and variable assignments g,
   a. $[\![dare]\!]^{w,g} = \{x \in D_e : person(x)(w)\}$
   b. $[\![utaimasu]\!]^{w,g} = \{\lambda x \lambda w'[sing(x)(w')]\}$

In composing these two pieces, we apply the function $\lambda x \lambda w'[\text{sing}(x)(w')]$ to each of the members in the set denoted by *dare* 'who' and create a bigger set—namely, the set of propositions in (26).

(26) $[\![\text{dare-ga utaimasu}]\!]^{w,g} = \{f(x): f \in [\![\text{utaimasu}]\!]^{w,g}, x \in [\![\text{dare}]\!]^{w,g}\}$
$= \{\lambda w'[\text{sing}(x)(w')]: \text{person}(x)(w)\}$

Thus we arrive at an appropriate basic form of interrogative semantics.

The question now is whether this view of *wh*-questions due to Hamblin can make a uniform analysis possible with the universal construction. A uniform analysis in fact becomes possible if we leave our standard conception of the nonlocal universal construction. The nonlocal universal construction is standardly assumed to involve quantification at a distance or some kind of inverse linking as represented in (28) (see, for example, Ohno 1989, von Stechow 1996, and Takahashi 2002).

(27) [Dare-ga   katta   ie]-mo   takakatta.
     who-NOM bought   house-MO was.expensive
     'For everyone x, the house that x bought was expensive.'

(28) $\forall x[\text{person}(x) \to \text{expensive}(\iota y[\text{house}(y) \,\&\, \text{person}(x) \,\&\, \text{buy}(y)(x)])]$

Alternatively, one could conceive the nonlocal universal construction as involving a rather direct quantification, as proposed in Shimoyama 1999, 2001. More specifically, we could assume that the restriction of the universal quantification is not provided by the embedded indeterminate pronoun but is provided directly by the sister constituent as a whole as in (29).[15]

(29) $\forall x[x \in \{\iota y[\text{house}(y) \,\&\, \text{buy}(y)(z)]: \text{person}(z)\} \to \text{expensive}(x)]$

The domain of quantification in (29), the set of unique individuals that are houses each person bought, is exactly what is obtained through successive pointwise functional application. We thus obtain a uniform analysis of the interrogative and universal constructions based on a Hamblin semantics of indeterminate pronouns.

In the Hamblin analysis of indeterminate pronouns, the relation between indeterminates and particles is not mediated through movement. Rather, the relation is established by the fact that indeterminate pronouns introduce Hamblin alternatives, which expand as they compose with the denotations of other constituents, and the particles *ka* and *mo* select such denotations. In this mode of association, the lack of island effects is expected.

Crucially, the expansion of the Hamblin alternatives introduced by indeterminates is stopped when the first operator that selects Hamblin alternatives is encountered. The particles *ka* and *mo* take the Hamblin alternatives and return singleton sets, thereby making the alternatives created by indeterminates inaccessible to even higher particles.[16] This is how the locality constraint illustrated in (12) follows, whether there is a single indeterminate or multiple indeterminates in the scope of the lower particle. Other long-distance associations across, for example, complex NP islands, are allowed as desired. Thus the puzzling locality pattern simply comes out as a consequence of the interpretation system.[17]

14.5.2 Indeterminate Pronouns as Open Propositions

A more widely held view on the semantics of *wh*-pronouns or indeterminate pronouns (other than the one in which they introduce existential quantifiers) is that they introduce free variables and denote open propositions. This type of proposal for English *wh*-phrases is explored by Baker (1970), Pesetsky (1987), Berman (1991), and Reinhart (1998) among many others. The idea builds on influential work by Kamp (1981) and Heim (1982) on indefinites in English. As for Japanese indeterminate pronouns, Kuroda (1965:101) was the first to observe that "the role of the indeterminate pronouns [is] very much like that of yet unbounded logical variables," and his insight was pursued further by Nishigauchi (1986, 1990). The idea has been adopted for other languages, such as Chinese (Aoun and Li 1993, Tsai 1994, and Lin 1996, among others) and Malayalam (Jayaseelan 2001).

Although the Hamblin analysis of indeterminates introduced above made in-situ interpretation of indeterminates possible, the idea that indeterminates denote open propositions makes semantic interpretation possible with short movement of indeterminates and without movement to the specifier of CP or of the phrase headed by *mo*. As is discussed shortly, a uniform analysis of the interrogative and universal construction is achieved under the assumption that the semantics of the nonlocal universal construction is perceived as proposed in Shimoyama 1999, 2001, introduced in section 14.5.1. Thus similar results are achieved in the Hamblin analysis, on the one hand, and in the open proposition analysis, on the other hand. When we consider how the locality puzzle is dealt with within the latter analysis, a difference emerges. Let us first see the basic syntax-semantics mapping in the open proposition analysis and then consider how the locality puzzle is accounted for.

Following Heim (1982), we can assume that *dare* 'who' in (30a) and (31a), for example, receives index 1 and is interpreted as: the individual assigned to variable 1 is a person. Because this is not of the suitable semantic type to be combined with *utaimasu* 'sing' or *katta* 'bought', *dare* 'who' has to move to an interpretable position. For example, moving out of VP (normal subject movement) or adjoining to TP would do (see Heim 1982).

(30) a. [Dare-ga utaimasu] ka?
     who-NOM sing Q
     'Who sings?'
   b. [[dare$_1$-ga [$_{TP/VP}$ t$_1$ utaimasu]] Op$_1$] ka

(31) a. [Dare-ga katta ie]-mo takakatta.
     who-NOM bought house-MO was.expensive
     'For everyone x, the house that x bought was expensive.'
   b. [[[dare$_1$-ga [$_{TP/VP}$ t$_1$ katta]] ie] Op$_1$]-mo takakatta.

It is proposed in Shimoyama 2001 that interpretability forces an introduction of a set creating operator (*Op*) at LF, which gets copies of indices and is interpreted as in (32) along the lines of Heim 1982 and Berman 1991. The part $g' \approx^{1,\ldots,n} g$ in (32b) says that assignment g' is just like assignment g, except possibly for values assigned to the variables $1, \ldots, n$.

(32) a. *Op*-indexing: Copy the index of each indeterminate pronoun onto the c-commanding *Op*.
 b. $[\![\text{XP } Op_{1,\ldots,n}]\!]^g = \{[\![\text{XP}]\!]^{g'}: g' \approx^{1,\ldots,n} g\}$
  $= \{z: \exists g'[g' \approx^{1,\ldots,n} g \ \& \ z = [\![\text{XP}]\!]^{g'}]\}$

In the LFs in (30b) and (31b), for instance, *Op* combines with its sister constituent and forms the set of propositions {that x is a person and x sings: $x \in D$} and the set of individuals {$\iota y[\text{house}(y) \ \& \ \text{person}(x) \ \& \ \text{buy}(y)(x)]: x \in D$}, respectively, by abstracting over the free variable that it is coindexed with. The steps are shown in (33) and (34).[18]

(33) $[\![[\text{dare}_1\text{-ga } [t_1 \text{ utaimasu}]] \ Op_1]\!]^g$
 $= \{[\![[\text{dare}_1\text{-ga } [t_1 \text{ utaimasu}]] \ Op_1]\!]^{g'}: g \approx^1 g'\}$
 $= \{p: \exists x[p = \lambda w'[\text{person}(x)(w') \ \& \ \text{sing}(x)(w')]\}$
 $= \{\lambda w'[\text{person}(x)(w') \ \& \ \text{sing}(x)(w')]: x \in D\}$

(34) $[\![[[\text{dare}_1\text{-ga } [t_1 \text{ katta}]] \text{ ie}] \ Op_1]\!]^g$
 $= \{ [\![[\text{dare}_1\text{-ga } [t_1 \text{ katta}]] \text{ ie}]\!]^{g'}: g \approx^1 g'\}$
 $= \{z: \exists x[z = \iota y[\text{house}(y) \ \& \ \text{person}(x) \ \& \ \text{buy}(y)(x)]]\}$
 $= \{\iota y[\text{house}(y) \ \& \ \text{person}(x) \ \& \ \text{buy}(y)(x)]: x \in D\}$

Once the denotation in (34) is available, the universal quantifier *mo* can directly quantify over it, giving us the appropriate semantics.

So far, the open-proposition analysis does not seem to differ significantly from the Hamblin analysis—both derive appropriate semantics from LF structures. Now, though, I show a difference. Recall that in the Hamblin analysis, the puzzling locality pattern simply falls out from the interpretation mechanism. In the open-proposition analysis, however, a Relativized Minimality–type locality principle (Rizzi 1990) needs to be stated independently. That is, the *Op*-indexing rule in (32a) should be modified to: "Copy the index of each indeterminate pronoun onto the *lowest* c-commanding *Op*." Note that Heim's (1982) rule of Quantifier Indexing, which the *Op*-indexing rule builds on, also has the locality clause built in. The purpose there is to block a certain LF representation that corresponds to an unavailable reading in sentences with indefinites and adverbs of quantification. This way of looking at the *wh*-island effect is specifically proposed in Toyoshima 1996 and Shimoyama 1999, 2001 and in a more general form in works such as Ochi 1999, Tanaka 1999, and Yoshida 1999. The Hamblin analysis fares better in this respect, because any independent statement of such locality principles is made unnecessary.[19] For further exploration and consequences of the Hamblin analysis, see Kratzer and Shimoyama 2002 and Kratzer 2005.[20]

14.6 Implications and Open Questions

I have reviewed two major approaches (i.e., movement vs. nonmovement) to the nonlocal association of indeterminates and particles. The focus of the discussion on association in the literature has been on the interrogative and universal contexts—two contexts where nonlocal association is most naturally allowed. The nature of limitations in nonlocal association in other series (existential, NPI, free choice) is yet to be investigated carefully, and the question whether the reviewed proposals can be extended to handle the syntax and semantics of the Japanese indeterminate pronoun system in general, as well as the indeterminate pronoun system in natural language, remains to be examined.

Another important question that has been addressed in the literature but needs more work is whether various uses of *ka* and *mo* should or can be related to one another. As is well known, *ka* is not just a question particle but also marks existential quantification (e.g., *nani-ka* 'something') as well as disjunction (e.g., *Hanako-ka Taro[-ka]* 'Hanako or Taro'). *Mo* is used to mark universal quantification but can also be used to mean *even* or *also* when there is no indeterminate in its scope.[21] Although works such as Hagstrom 1998 and Suzuki 2003 take up this question, we are still far from a good understanding of it.

NOTES FOR CHAPTER 14

I would like to thank Shigeru Miyagawa and Mamoru Saito, the editors of this volume and organizers of the Workshop on Linguistic Theory and the Japanese Language held at Harvard University in July 2005. I also wish to thank the participants at the workshop, in particular, Norvin Richards, Akira Watanabe, and Jim Huang, as well as an anonymous reviewer and Bernhard Schwarz for useful comments and discussions. All remaining errors are my own.

1. Interestingly, somewhat similar speaker variations in Malayalam are reported by Jayaseelan (2001:72) with respect to the distance between a *wh*-word and a disjunction marker, which form an existential quantificational phrase.

2. *Naze* 'why' cannot be associated with *ka* across complex NP or adjunct island for some reason, as shown in (i) and (ii). See Huang 1982, Saito 1994, Tsai 1994, Ochi 1999, and Ko 2005, for example.

   (i) *Hanako-wa [Kyoto-ni naze kita hito]-o yobimasita ka?
       Hanako-TOP Kyoto-to why came person-ACC invited Q
       'Why$_x$ did Hanako invite a person who came to Kyoto for reason x?'

   (ii) *Yumi-wa [Mika-ga naze kaetta-ra] okorimasu ka?
        Yumi-TOP Mika-NOM why left-if get.angry Q
        'Why$_x$ would Yumi get angry if Mika left for reason x?'

3. Certain cases of *whether*-island violations are known to improve with particular prosodic renditions (see, e.g., Deguchi and Kitagawa 2002, Ishihara 2003, and Hirotani 2004). However, prosody does not rescue all cases of *wh*-island violations, as can be seen from the examples to follow in the text. See Kratzer 2005 for speculation on how certain prosodic conditions might affect the scope of indeterminates.

4. It is tempting to try to work out a unification of *mo* as universal and *mo* as 'also' (see Suzuki 2003). The (d)-readings in (10) and (11), however, are in principle available as long as the presupposition that comes with the lower *mo* as 'also' is satisfied. This suggests that the two instances of *mo* should be treated as distinct lexical items.

5. It is proposed by Nishigauchi (1986, 1990) that examples such as (i) in note 2 are ruled out because of the category mismatch between *naze* 'why' and the head noun of the relative clause. It is not obvious how an analysis along those lines would extend to explaining why (ii) in note 2 is not possible, or why nominals such as *dare* 'who' and *nani* 'what' occur freely in adjunct clauses such as the *if*-clause in (ii).

6. Sharvit (1998) and Watanabe (2001:222–223) attempt to assign semantic interpretation to the pied-piped structure. See Shimoyama 2006a (pp. 160–161) for comments on the latter attempt. See also Sauerland and Heck 2003.

7. Alternatively, indeterminates may introduce free variables, which are bound by existential closure, as proposed for D-linked *wh*-in-situ in English and Japanese by Pesetsky (1987). Nishigauchi (1986, 1990) assumes that this interpretational device applies to covertly moved indeterminates. See von Stechow 1996 for the spelling out of this idea.

8. This is not the case in Hagstrom's (1998) movement analysis of *wh*-questions in Japanese. There, it is the question particle *ka* that undergoes overt movement from the position next to a *wh*-phrase.

9. The stipulation that island constraints do not apply at this second step—namely, in the derivation from what von Stechow refers to as WH-structure to LF—may not be necessary if we assume with Brody (1995) and Richards (1997, 2001) that Subjacency needs to be satisfied only once per C^0 (as an effect of the Principle of Minimal Compliance in Richards's terms).

10. In Watanabe's (1992a, 1992b) analysis, the movement relevant here is not the *wh*-movement at LF but the invisible operator movement at S-structure, whereas in Hagstrom's (1998) analysis, it is the overt movement of the particle *ka/no*. In the former analysis, subsequent LF *wh*-movement of the standard kind is assumed, including large-scale pied-piping, which raises the same problem as it does for Nishigauchi's (1986, 1990) LF.

11. The domain of quantification is, in the end, narrower presumably due to accommodation of the existence presupposition of the definite description (see Shimoyama 2006a).

12. This reading is marked "ok" in Watanabe (1992a:fn. 9), but it is at least as difficult to get as cases where there is no complex NP island in addition to a *wh*-island (see (7)). See also Richards 2000 (fn. 6) for a clarifying note on degrees of ungrammaticality.

13. The following examples also show that pied-piping and distinct scope readings are, in principle, not incompatible with each other ((iii) is from van Riemsdijk and Williams 1981:196 and (iv) is from Fiengo, Huang, Lasnik, and Reinhart 1988:88). According to van Riemsdijk and Williams, *whom* in (iii) can take either matrix scope or embedded scope. (I thank Jon Nissenbaum for confirming this judgment.)

(iii) Who$_i$ t_i knows [[which picture of whom]$_j$ Bill bought t_j]?

(iv) ?Who$_i$ do you wonder [[which pictures of t_i]$_j$ t_j are on sale]?

Fiengo and his colleagues also discuss Spanish examples similar to (iv) from Chomsky 1986 (pp. 25–26), originally observed by Torrego (1985).

14. The first of the two subderivations is possibly blocked by an independent principle, given that there is a stage, before reconstruction, at which the trace of indeterminate$_2$ is not bound by its antecedent (see, e.g., Saito 1992).

15. An extensional system is used here for simplicity. It remains to be seen whether truly parallel analyses can be given to the local and nonlocal cases of association with *mo* when the denotation is relativized to possible worlds.

16. *Ka* presumably returns a singleton set whose sole member is a question denotation as proposed by Groenendijk and Stokhof (1982).

17. For Hagstrom (1998), who adopts Hamblin denotations for indeterminates in the interrogative context, the source of the apparent *wh*-island effect is still movement.

18. Note that, unlike in (26), the system derives the nontransparent interpretation of *dare* in (33). See Beck and Rullmann 1999 for discussion.

19. See Wold 1996 for related discussion in the domain of association with focus. See also Beck 2007 for more recent discussion in a broader context.

20. It does not necessarily follow that all indeterminate pronouns across languages should have a Hamblin semantics. For example, it is reported in Jayaseelan 2001 that Malayalam indeterminates can associate with a conjunction or disjunction particle across a closer particle. This suggests that this language presumably employs a selective version of the *Op*-indexing without the locality clause added.

21. Nishigauchi (1990) and, more recently, Yamashina and Tancredi (2005) assume that *mo* lacks quantificational force on its own (see also Shimoyama 2006b).

REFERENCES

Aoun, Joseph, and Yen-hui Audrey Li. 1993. Wh-elements in situ: Syntax or LF? *Linguistic Inquiry* 24:199–238.

Arregi, Karlos. 2003. Clausal pied-piping. *Natural Language Semantics* 11:115–143.

Baker, C. L. 1970. Notes on the description of English questions: The role of an abstract question morpheme. *Foundations of Language* 6:197–219.

Beck, Sigrid. 2007. The grammar of focus interpretation. In *Recursion + Interfaces = Language? Chomsky's minimalism and the view from syntax and semantics*, ed. Uli Sauerland and Hans-Martin Gärtner, 255–280. Berlin: Mouton de Gruyter.

Beck, Sigrid, and Hotze Rullmann. 1999. A flexible approach to exhaustivity in questions. *Natural Language Semantics* 7:249–298.

Berman, Stephen. 1991. On the semantics and Logical Form of *wh*-clauses. Doctoral dissertation, University of Massachusetts, Amherst.

Brody, Michael. 1995. *Lexico-logical form: A radically minimalist theory*. Cambridge, Mass.: MIT Press.

Choe, Jae W. 1987. LF movement and pied-piping. *Linguistic Inquiry* 18:348–353.

Chomsky, Noam. 1977. On *wh*-movement. In *Formal syntax*, ed. Peter Culicover, Thomas Wasow, and Adrian Akmajian, 71–132. New York: Academic Press.

Chomsky, Noam. 1986. *Barriers*. Cambridge, Mass.: MIT Press.

Deguchi, Masanori, and Yoshihisa Kitagawa. 2002. Prosody and *wh*-questions. In *Proceedings of NELS 32*, ed. Masako Hirotani, 73–92. Amherst, Mass.: GLSA Publications.

Fiengo, Robert, C.-T. James Huang, Howard Lasnik, and Tanya Reinhart. 1988. The syntax of *wh*-in-situ. In *Proceedings of WCCFL 7*, ed. Hagit Borer, 81–98. Stanford, Calif.: CSLI Publications.

Groenendijk, Jeroen, and Martin Stokhof. 1982. Semantic analysis of *wh*-complements. *Linguistics and Philosophy* 5:175–233.

Hagstrom, Paul. 1998. Decomposing questions. Doctoral dissertation, MIT, Cambridge, Mass.

Hamblin, C. L. 1973. Questions in Montague English. *Foundations of Language* 10: 41–53.

Haspelmath, Martin. 1997. *Indefinite pronouns*. Oxford: Oxford University Press.

Heim, Irene. 1982. The semantics of definite and indefinite noun phrases. Doctoral dissertation, University of Massachusetts, Amherst.

Heim, Irene. 1987. Where does the definiteness restriction apply? Evidence from the definiteness of variables. In *The representation of (in)definiteness*, ed. Alice ter Meulen and Eric Reuland, 21–42. Cambridge, Mass.: MIT Press.

Hirotani, Masako. 2004. Prosody and LF: Processing Japanese *wh*-questions. Doctoral dissertation, University of Massachusetts, Amherst.

Hoji, Hajime. 1985. Logical Form constraints and configurational structures in Japanese. Doctoral dissertation, University of Washington, Seattle.

Huang, C.-T. James. 1982. Logical relations in Chinese and the theory of grammar. Doctoral dissertation, MIT, Cambridge, Mass.

Ishihara, Shinichiro. 2003. Intonation and interface conditions. Doctoral dissertation, MIT, Cambridge, Mass.

Jayaseelan, K. A. 2001. Questions and question-word incorporating quantifiers in Malayalam. *Syntax* 4:63–93.

Kamp, Hans. 1981. A theory of truth and semantic representation. In *Formal methods in the study of language* (Mathematical Centre Tracts 135), ed. J. Groenendijk, T. Janssen, and M. Stokhof. 277–322. Amsterdam: Mathematisch Centrum. (Reprinted in *Truth, interpretation, and information*, ed. J. Groenendijk, T. Janssen, and M. Stokhof, 1–41. Dordrecht: Foris, 1984.)

Karttunen, Lauri. 1977. Syntax and semantics of questions. *Linguistics and Philosophy* 1:3–44.

Ko, Heejeong. 2005. Syntax of *wh*-in-situ: Merge into [Spec, CP] in the overt syntax. *Natural Language & Linguistic Theory* 23:867–916.

Kratzer, Angelika. 2005. Indefinites and the operators they depend on: From Japanese to Salish. In *Reference and quantification: The Partee effect*, ed. Gregory N. Carlson and F. Jeffry Pelletier, 113–142. Stanford, Calif.: CSLI Publications.

Kratzer, Angelika and Junko Shimoyama. 2002. Indeterminate pronouns: The view from Japanese. In *The Proceedings of the 3rd Tokyo Conference on Psycholinguistics*, ed. Yukio Otsu, 1–25. Tokyo: Hituzi Syobo.

Kuroda, S.-Y. 1965. Generative grammatical studies in the Japanese language. Doctoral dissertation, MIT, Cambridge, Mass.

Lin, Jo-wang. 1996. Polarity licensing and *wh*-phrase quantification in Chinese. Doctoral dissertation, University of Massachusetts, Amherst.

Maki, Hideki. 1995. The syntax of particles. Doctoral dissertation, University of Connecticut, Storrs.

Nishigauchi, Taisuke. 1986. Quantification in syntax. Doctoral dissertation, University of Massachusetts, Amherst.
Nishigauchi, Taisuke. 1990. *Quantification in the theory of grammar.* Dordrecht: Kluwer.
Nishigauchi, Taisuke. 1999. Quantification and *wh*-constructions. In *The handbook of Japanese linguistics*, ed. Natsuko Tsujimura, 269–296. Oxford: Blackwell.
Ochi, Masao. 1999. Constraints on feature checking. Doctoral dissertation, University of Connecticut, Storrs.
Ohno, Yutaka. 1989. *Mo.* In *Papers on quantification*, NSF Grant Report, Department of Linguistics, University of Massachusetts, Amherst, ed. Emmon Bach, Angelika Kratzer, and Barbara H. Partee, 224–250. Amherst, Mass.: GLSA Publications.
Ohno, Yutaka. 1991. Arguments against unselective binding in Korean. In *Harvard Studies in Korean Linguistics* 4, ed. Susumu Kuno et al. 553–562. Seoul: Hanshin.
Ortiz de Urbina, Jon. 1990. Operator feature percolation and clausal pied-piping. In *MITWPL 13: Papers on* wh-*movement*, ed. Lisa Cheng and Hamida Demirdache, 193–208. Cambridge, Mass.: MIT Working Papers in Linguistics.
Pesetsky, David. 1987. *Wh*-in-situ: Movement and unselective binding. In *The representation of (in)definiteness*, ed. Eric Reuland and Alice ter Meulen, 98–129. Cambridge, Mass.: MIT Press.
Ramchand, Gillian C. 1997. Questions, polarity, and alternative semantics. In *Proceedings of NELS 27*, ed. Kiyomi Kusumoto, 383–396. Amherst, Mass.: GLSA Publications.
Reinhart, Tanya. 1998. *Wh*-in-situ in the framework of the Minimalist Program. *Natural Language Semantics* 6:29–56.
Richards, Norvin. 1997. What moves where when in which language? Doctoral dissertation, MIT, Cambridge, Mass.
Richards, Norvin. 2000. An island effect in Japanese. *Journal of East Asian Linguistics* 9:187–205.
Richards, Norvin. 2001. *Movement in language: Interactions and architectures.* Oxford: Oxford University Press.
Riemsdijk, Henk van. 1984. On pied-piped infinitives in German relative clauses. In *Studies in German grammar*, ed. Jindrich Toman, 165–192. Dordrecht: Foris.
Riemsdijk, Henk van, and Edwin Williams. 1981. NP-structure. *The Linguistic Review* 1:171–217.
Rizzi, Luigi. 1990. *Relativized minimality.* Cambridge, Mass.: MIT Press.
Saito, Mamoru. 1992. Long distance scrambling in Japanese. *Journal of East Asian Linguistics* 1:69–118.
Saito, Mamoru. 1994. Additional-*wh* effects and the adjunction site theory. *Journal of East Asian Linguistics* 3:195–240.
Sauerland, Uli, and Fabian Heck. 2003. LF-intervention effects in pied-piping. In *Proceedings of NELS 23*, ed. Makoto Kadowaki and Shigeto Kawahara, 347–366. Amherst, Mass.: GLSA Publications.
Sharvit, Yael. 1998. Possessive *wh*-expressions and reconstruction. In *Proceedings of NELS 28*, ed. Pius N. Tamanji and Kiyomi Kusumoto, 409–423. Amherst, Mass.: GLSA Publications.
Shimoyama, Junko. 1999. Complex NPs and *wh*-quantification in Japanese. In *Proceedings of NELS 29*, ed. Pius N. Tamanji, Masako Hirotani, and Nancy Hall, 355–365. Amherst, Mass.: GLSA Publications.
Shimoyama, Junko. 2001. *Wh*-constructions in Japanese. Doctoral dissertation, University of Massachusetts, Amherst.

Shimoyama, Junko. 2006a. Indeterminate phrase quantification in Japanese. *Natural Language Semantics* 14:139–173.

Shimoyama, Junko. 2006b. A QVE-like phenomenon in the Japanese universal construction and its implications. In *In search of the essence of language science: Festschrift for Professor Heizo Nakajima on the occasion of his 60th birthday*, ed. Yubun Suzuki, Keizo Mizuno, and Ken-Ichi Takami, 297–309. Tokyo: Hituzi Syobo.

Stechow, Arnim von. 1996. Against LF pied-piping. *Natural Language Semantics* 4:57–110.

Suzuki, Shogo. 2003. Additive *mo*. Ms., MIT, Cambridge, Mass.

Takahashi, Daiko. 2002. Determiner raising and scope shift. *Linguistic Inquiry* 33:575–615.

Tanaka, Hidekazu. 1999. LF *wh*-islands and the minimal scope principle. *Natural Language & Linguistic Theory* 17:371–402.

Torrego, Esther. 1985. On empty categories in nominals. Ms., University of Massachusetts, Boston.

Toyoshima, Takashi. 1996. LF Subjacency and stationary *wh*-in-situ. Ms., Cornell University, Ithaca, N.Y.

Tsai, Wei-tien Dylan. 1994. On economizing the theory of A-bar dependencies. Doctoral dissertation, MIT, Cambridge, Mass.

Watanabe, Akira. 1992a. *Wh*-in-situ, Subjacency, and chain formation. *MIT occasional papers in linguistics* 2. Cambridge, Mass.: MIT Working Papers in Linguistics.

Watanabe, Akira. 1992b. Subjacency and s-structure movement of *wh*-in-situ. *Journal of East Asian Linguistics* 1:255–291.

Watanabe, Akira. 2001. *Wh*-in-situ languages. In *The handbook of contemporary syntactic theory*, ed. Mark Baltin and Chris Collins, 203–225. Oxford: Blackwell.

Wold, Dag E. 1996. Long distance selective binding: The case of focus. In *Proceedings from SALT 6*, ed. Teresa Galloway and Justin Spence, 311–328. Ithaca, N.Y.: CLC Publications.

Yamashina, Miyuki and Christopher Tancredi. 2005. Degenerate plurals. In *Proceedings of SuB 9*, ed. Emar Maier, Corien Bary, and Janneke Huitink, 522–537. Nijmegen, the Netherlands: NCS.

Yatsushiro, Kazuko. 2004. *Mo* and *ka*. Ms., University of Connecticut, Storrs.

Yoshida, Tomoyuki. 1999. LF Subjacency effects revisited. In *MITWPL 34: Papers on morphology and syntax: Cycle two*, ed. Vivian Lin, Cornelia Krause, Benjamin Bruening, and Karlos Arregi, 1–34. Cambridge, Mass.: MIT Working Papers in Linguistics.

CHAPTER 15

NOUN PHRASE ELLIPSIS

DAIKO TAKAHASHI

15.1 INTRODUCTION

A well-known feature that distinguishes Japanese from languages such as English is the availability of null subjects and objects in finite clauses, which can be illustrated in the following examples:

(1) A: Taroo-wa doo simasita ka?
Taroo-TOP how did Q
'What happened to Taroo?'
B: *e* ie-ni kaerimasita.
he home-to returned
'He returned home.'
C: Sensei-ga *e* sikarimasita.
teacher-NOM him scolded
'The teacher scolded him.'

(2) Taroo-ga Hanako-ni [*e e* kekkonsuru to] yakusokusita.
Taroo-NOM Hanako-DAT he her marry that promised
'Taroo promised Hanako that he would marry her.'

In (1), speakers B's and C's utterances are intended as replies to speaker A's question. In speaker B's utterance, the subject is not overtly expressed but is most naturally interpreted as referring to Taroo. In speaker C's utterance, on the other hand, the object is empty and yet it is taken as referring to Taroo. Also, null subjects and null objects can occur simultaneously. In the embedded clause in (2), both the subject and object are covert and interpreted most naturally as referring to Taroo and Hanako, respectively.

Since Kuroda 1965 it has been more or less standard to analyze null arguments as empty pronouns (see Ohso 1976, Hoji 1985, and Saito 1985, among many others). One indication comes from the fact that they can serve as variables bound by quantifiers, as discussed in detail by Hoji (1985). Consider the following examples:

(3) Daremo-ga [e susi-o taberu to] itta.
everyone-NOM he sushi-ACC eat that said
'Everyone said that he would eat sushi.'

(4) Daremo-ga [Hanako-ga e butta to] itta.
everyone-NOM Hanako-NOM him hit that said
'Everyone said that Hanako hit him.'

The null subject in (3) and the null object in (4) can be interpreted as bound by the quantificational matrix subjects. This is straightforward if those null arguments are pronominal, because, in general, pronouns can serve interpretively as variables associated with quantifiers (see the English translations of (3) and (4)).

Another argument can be constructed on the basis of condition B of the binding theory, which particularly prohibits pronouns in object positions from taking the subjects in the same clauses as their antecedents (see Chomsky 1981 and Chomsky and Lasnik 1993, among others). Thus, we have ungrammatical sentences in English such as the following, where the intended interpretation is indicated by placing the same subscript on the subjects and the objects:

(5) *John$_1$ criticized him$_1$.
(6) *Everyone$_1$ loves him$_1$.

Bearing this in mind, let us consider the following Japanese examples:

(7) *Taroo$_1$-ga e$_1$ semeta.
Taroo-NOM him criticized
'Taroo criticized him.'

(8) *Daremo$_1$-ga e$_1$ aisiteiru.
everyone-NOM him love
'Everyone loves him.'

These examples do not permit the reading in which the null object takes the subject as its antecedent. If the null object is a pronoun, (7) and (8) can be treated on a par with (5) and (6) as violations of condition B.

This pronoun theory has not necessarily been unchallenged, however (see especially Huang 1984 and Hasegawa 1984/1985). Since the late 1980s, researchers have pointed out a number of examples that pose problems for the pronoun theory. I consider some of them in the next section. The existence of such data has led linguists to seek an alternative analysis of null arguments. In section 15.3, I illustrate two analyses of null arguments in terms of ellipsis, which might look similar on the surface but should be distinguished in details. In section 15.4, I point out some implications of the ellipsis theory on the typology of languages with null arguments. In section 15.5, I summarize the entire discussion.

15.2 CORE DATA

Among the important observations that show the limitation of the pronoun theory is the one illustrated by the following examples, which are constructed on the basis of similar examples from Chinese in Xu 1986:[1]

(9) A: Dare-ga zibun-o sememasita ka?
who-NOM self-ACC criticized Q
'Who criticized himself?'
B: Taroo$_1$-ga/Daremo$_1$-ga e_1 sememasita.
Taroo-NOM/Everyone-NOM criticized
'Taroo/Everyone criticized himself.'

(10) Ken-ga zibunzisin-o semeta atode, Taroo$_1$-wa e_1 tataeta.
Ken-NOM himself-ACC criticized after Taroo-TOP praised
'After Ken criticized himself, Taroo praised himself.'

As a reply to the question in (9A), the utterance in (9B) can mean that Taroo or everyone criticized himself. In (10), the main clause follows the adverbial clause, which contains an anaphoric object, and can have the interpretation that Taroo praised himself. That is, the null object can take the subject of the same clause as its antecedent in (9B) and (10). If null objects (or arguments) were always pronominal, these cases would be ruled out by condition B on a par with (7) and (8).

Similar but slightly different examples are provided by Huang (1991) and Otani and Whitman (1991). They consider cases such as the following, paying attention to the interpretation of the null object in the main clause:

(11) Ken-ga zibun-no sensei-o semeta atode,
Ken-NOM self-GEN teacher-ACC criticized after
Taroo mo e semeta.
Taroo also criticized
Lit. 'After Ken criticized his teacher, Taroo criticized, too.'

With the subordinate clause as the antecedent, the main clause is ambiguous: it means either that Taroo criticized Ken's teacher or that Taroo criticized his own teacher. Under the empty pronoun analysis, although the availability of the first reading is straightforward, the second, sloppy interpretation appears to be unexpected. This can be shown by considering English examples such as the following:

(12) After John criticized his teacher, Bill criticized him, too.

Here the pronominal object in the main clause can refer to John's teacher but significantly cannot mean Bill's teacher. This difference between the null object in (11) and the pronominal object in (12) seems to cast doubt on the approach that analyzes the empty object as a pronoun.

Concerning cases such as (11), Hoji (1998) makes an important remark about how the null object is interpreted. He considers examples such as the following:

(13) a. Taroo-ga   zibun-no kuruma-o aratta.
        Taroo-NOM self-GEN car-ACC   washed
        'Taroo washed his car.'
     b. Taroo igai-no   subete-no hito   mo e aratta.
        Taroo except-GEN all-GEN   person also   washed
        Lit. 'Everyone other than Taroo washed e, too.'

Observing that (13b) does not allow the "distributed reading" of the sort found in (14a), Hoji (1998) points out that (13b) is rather similar to (14b), where an indefinite nominal phrase appears in place of the null object in (13b).

(14) a. Taroo igai-no   subete-no hito   mo zibun-no kuruma-o
        Taroo except-GEN all-GEN   person also self-GEN car-ACC
        aratta.
        washed
        'Everyone other than Taroo washed his car, too.'
     b. Taroo igai-no   subete-no hito   mo kuruma-o aratta.
        Taroo except-GEN all-GEN   person also car-ACC   washed
        'Everyone other than Taroo washed a car, too.'

Based on the similarity between (13b) and (14b), Hoji claims that the null object in the former is better analyzed as a null indefinite nominal phrase.[2]

If some null objects such as the ones in (11) and (13) are indefinite expressions, one might think that the pronoun theory could accommodate the relevant data, by analyzing them in the same way as the following cases (see Tomioka 2003 for related discussion):

(15) a. John wants to marry a Martian if he can find one.
     b. John bought his favorite car, but Bill hasn't yet found one.

In addition to definite pronouns like *him*, *her*, *it*, and so on, English has the indefinite pronoun *one*. Proponents of the pronoun theory might say that indefinite pronouns as well as definite counterparts can be empty in Japanese, so that (11) and (13b) can be analyzed in the same way as *After Ken criticized his teacher, Taroo criticized one, too* and *Hanako washed one, too*, respectively.

When null objects are interpreted indefinitely, there seems to be a way to maintain the pronoun theory, as noted just above. As Saito (2003) and Shinohara

(2004) point out, however, the range of interpretation actually available for null objects is much wider.[3] Saito (2003) considers cases such as the following:

(16) a. Taroo-ga   zibun-no kuruma-o aratta.
        Taroo-NOM self-GEN car-ACC   washed
        'Taroo washed his car.'
    b. (Demo) Hanako-wa   e arawanakatta.
        (but)   Hanako-TOP   not-washed
        Lit. '(But) Hanako did not wash e.'

Although (16a) is the same as (13a), (16b) differs from (13b) in that it is a negative sentence. Crucially, Saito observes that (16b) can be true if Hanako did not wash her own car but washed other cars. This interpretation is undoubtedly different from what the following sentence means:

(17) Hanako-wa   kuruma-o arawanakatta.
     Hanako-TOP car-ACC   not-washed
     'Hanako did not wash a car.'

The object here is an indefinite, and the whole sentence is true if and only if Hanako did not wash any car, including hers.

Shinohara (2004) provides sentences such as the following:[4]

(18) Sono ryokan-wa itiniti-ni   okyaku-o sankumi
     the hotel-TOP one-day-per guest-ACC three-group
     izyoo   tomeru   ga,   ano ryokan-wa e
     more-than   accommodate though that hotel-TOP
     tomenai.
     not-accommodate
     Lit. 'Though the hotel accommodates more than three groups of guests per day, that hotel does not accommodate.'

The null object here can specifically mean more than three groups of guests. It is not obvious how this interpretation is derived from the indefinite pronoun analysis.

Further data similar to (18) is given here:

(19) Hanako-ga   taitei-no   sensei-o   sonkeisiteiru.
     Hanako-NOM most-GEN   teacher-ACC   respect
     Sosite Taroo mo   e sonkeisiteiru.
     and   Taroo also   respect
     Lit. 'Hanako respects most teachers. And Taroo respects, too.'

In the preceding clause, the object is a quantified phrase (QP). Taking it as the antecedent sentence, the second clause contains a null object and means that Taroo respects most teachers. That is, the null object seems to behave as a QP meaning *most teachers*.

One might think that the interpretation of the second clause is derivable even from the analysis of the null object as an empty pronoun taking as its antecedent the QP *taitei-no sensei* 'most teachers' in the preceding clause. In that case, (19) might be analyzed in a way analogous to the following example:

(20) Hanako-ga   taitei-no   sensei-o   sonkeisiteiru.
      Hanako-NOM   most-GEN   teacher-ACC   respect
      Sosite Taroo mo   karera-o   sonkeisiteiru.
      and   Taroo also them-ACC   respect
      'Hanako respects most teachers. And Taroo respects them, too.'

Note that the lexical pronoun *karera* 'them' occurs in the second clause, somehow taking *most teachers* in the first clause as the antecedent. Although the first clause is the same as (19a), the interpretation of the second clause is slightly different from that of (19b): it means that Taroo also respects those teachers mentioned in the preceding clause (namely, those teachers that Hanako respects). That is, the pronoun in (20) seems to serve as what is called an E-type pronoun (Evans 1980) rather than as a genuine quantificational expression. Given that the null object in (19) is interpreted differently, it is questionable to treat it as a pronoun.

Any theory of null arguments must be able to account for the facts described above, but the pronoun theory would have difficulty accommodating them. Note that these considerations do not lead to complete abandonment of empty pronouns: they are still needed to account for cases such as (3), (7), and (8). What this section has shown is that there are cases for which something other than empty pronouns must be postulated.

15.3 ANALYSES

15.3.1 The VP-Ellipsis Analysis

To account for cases such as (9)–(11), Huang (1991) and Otani and Whitman (1991) put forth the idea that the sentences in questions involve VP-ellipsis. Whereas Huang mainly deals with Chinese null-object constructions and offers a very sketchy discussion of VP-ellipsis, Otani and Whitman elaborate on his proposal, extending it to Japanese. In what follows, therefore, let us consider Otani and Whitman's analysis of sentences with null objects in terms of VP-ellipsis.

Otani and Whitman's (1991) analysis is based on two assumptions. The first is Williams's (1977a) so-called copying theory of ellipsis, according to which ellipsis involves base-generation of empty constituents and subsequent copying of antecedent material onto the empty slots at LF. This is illustrated by (21), an example of VP-ellipsis in English.

(21) John will see Mary, and Bill will, too.

(22) a. [TP John will [VP see Mary]], and [TP Bill will [VP e]], too.
b. [TP John will [VP see Mary]], and [TP Bill will [VP **see Mary**]], too.

Example (21) is supposed to be derived as indicated in (22). Example (22a) is the overt-syntactic representation, where the VP in the second clause is empty. After the derivation enters into LF, the VP in the first clause is copied onto the empty VP, which is now fully materialized (the reconstructed VP is shown in boldface). Otani and Whitman's second assumption is that those languages that have null objects with the relevant properties, such as Chinese and Japanese, have overt V-to-T raising just like French, Italian, and so on (see Emonds 1978; Huang 1991; Kishimoto, this volume; Koizumi 1995; Miyagawa 2001; and Pollock 1989). Thus, the sentence in (23a) is represented as in (23b) in overt syntax.

(23) a. Taroo-ga   Hanako-o   semeta.
Taroo-NOM Hanako-ACC criticized
'Taroo criticized Hanako.'
b. [TP Taroo-ga [T' [VP Hanako-o t_V] [T seme$_V$-ta$_T$]]]

In (23b) the verb *seme* moves out of VP and adjoins to T.

Bearing these points in mind, let us illustrate Otani and Whitman's (1991) analysis of null-object sentences in terms of VP-ellipsis. Let us start with (11), the derivation of which is given in (24).

(24) a. [TP Ken-ga   [T' [VP zibun-no sensei-o t_V] [T seme$_V$-ta$_T$]]]
Ken-NOM   self-GEN teacher-ACC   criticize-T
atode, [TP   Taroo mo   [T' [VP e] [T seme$_V$-ta$_T$]]]
after   Taroo also   criticize-T
Lit. 'After Ken criticized his teacher, Taroo criticized, too.'
b. [TP Ken-ga [T' [VP zibun-no sensei-o t_V] [T seme$_V$-ta$_T$]]] atode,
[TP Taroo mo [T' [VP **zibun-no sensei-o t_V**] [T seme$_V$-ta$_T$]]]

Example (24a) is the overt representation, where the main verbs appear in T and the VP in the second clause is empty. In LF, the antecedent VP is copied onto the empty VP, yielding (24b), where the second clause contains the anaphor as well. Example (24b) represents the right interpretation of the sentence, especially accounting for its sloppy interpretation.[5]

The VP-ellipsis analysis also accommodates the examples in (9) and (10), which are assigned the derivations in (25) and (26), respectively.

(25) a. [TP Dare-ga   [VP zibun-o t_V] [T sememasi$_V$-ta$_T$]] ka?
who-NOM   self-ACC   criticize-T   Q
'Who criticized himself?'
[TP Taroo-ga/Daremo-ga [VP e] [T sememasi$_V$-ta$_T$]].
Taroo-NOM/everyone-NOM   criticize-T
Lit. 'Taroo/Everyone criticized.'

b. [TP Dare-ga [VP zibun-o t_V] [T sememasi_V-ta_T]] ka?
[TP Taroo-ga/Daremo-ga [VP **zibun-o t_V**] [T sememasi_V-ta_T]].

(26) a. [TP Ken-ga [VP zibunzisin-o t_V] [T seme_V-ta_T]] atode,
　　　　Ken-NOM　himself-ACC　　　　criticize-T　after
[TP Taroo-wa　[VP e] [T　tatae_V-ta_T]].
　Taroo-TOP　　　　　　praise-T
Lit. 'After Ken criticized himself, Taroo praised.'

b. [TP Ken-ga [VP zibunzisin-o t_V] [T seme_V-ta_T]] atode,
[TP Taroo-wa [VP **zibunzisin-o t_V**] [T tatae_V-ta_T]].

Examples (25a) and (26a) are overt syntactic representations, where the clauses with null objects actually involve elliptic VPs. These empty VPs are reconstructed at LF by copying the VPs in the antecedent clauses. This yields (25b) and (26b), where the second clauses contain anaphors and are correctly predicted to have sloppy interpretations.[6]

Cases such as (18) and (19) where null objects are understood as quantificational fall into place as well. Examples (18) and (19) are analyzed as in (27) and (28), respectively.

(27) a. [TP Sono　　ryokan-wa　　[VP itiniti-ni　　okyaku-o sankumi
　　　　the　　　hotel-TOP　　　　one-day-per　guest-ACC three-group
izyoo t_V]　[T tome_V-ru_T]]　　ga,　　[TP ano　　　ryokan-wa
more-than　　accommodate-T　though　　　　that　　hotel-TOP
[VP e] [T tome_V-na_Neg-i_T]]
　　　　　accommodate-not-T
Lit. 'Though the hotel accommodates more than three groups of guests per day, that hotel does not accommodate.'

b. [TP Sono ryokan-wa [VP itiniti-ni okyaku-o sankumi izyoo t_V]
[T tome_V-ru_T]] ga, [TP ano ryokan-wa [VP **itiniti-ni okyaku-o sankumi izyoo t_V**] [T tome_V-na_Neg-i_T]]

(28) a. [TP Hanako-ga　　[VP taitei-no　sensei-o t_V]
　　　　Hanako-NOM　　most-GEN　teacher-ACC
[T sonkeisi_V-teiru_T]]. Sosite [TP Taroo mo　[VP e] [T sonkeisi_V-teiru_T]].
respect-T　　　　　　　　And　　　Taroo also　　　　　　　　　respect-T
Lit. 'Hanako respects most teachers. And Taroo respects, too.'

b. [TP Hanako-ga [VP taitei-no sensei-o t_V] [T sonkeisi_V-teiru_T]].
Sosite [TP Taroo mo [VP **taitei-no sensei-o t_V**] [T sonkeisi_V-teiru_T]].

Examples (27a) and (28a) are overt representations, where the second clause contains an empty VP. Examples (27b) and (28b) are obtained by copying the VP in the preceding clause onto the empty VP. The quantifiers are reconstructed in the elliptic VPs, as desired.

The VP-ellipsis analysis is successful in explaining the data considered above as well as others (see Otani and Whitman 1991). It is not free from problems, however.

First of all, let us reconsider (10). It is repeated as (29) and its derivation in (26) is given as (30).

(29) Ken-ga   zibunzisin-o semeta   atode, Taroo-wa   e tataeta.
     Ken-NOM himself-ACC criticized after Taroo-NOM   praised
     'After Ken criticized himself, Taroo praised himself.'

(30) a. [TP Ken-ga [VP zibunzisin-o t_V] [T seme_V-ta_T]] atode,
        [TP Taroo-wa [VP e] [T tatae_V-ta_T]].
     b. [TP Ken-ga [VP zibunzisin-o t_V] [T seme_V-ta_T]] atode,
        [TP Taroo-wa [VP **zibunzisin-o t_V**] [T tatae_V-ta_T]].

Notice that the two verbs are different in (29): the verb in the antecedent clause is *seme* 'criticize' whereas the verb in the second clause is *tatae* 'praise'. In (30), this difference does not pose a problem. At the point where copying takes place, namely at LF, the antecedent VP contains the trace of *seme* and the entire VP is copied onto the empty VP. The trace of the verb inside the reconstructed (or copied) VP is now associated with the verb *tatae*, and the resulting verbal chain seems to be licit.

Note, however, that this explanation only works with the trace theory of movement, which assumes that movement leaves behind nondistinct traces in the original positions. This view of movement has changed with the advent of the Minimalist Program. Chomsky (1995) claims that syntactic derivations are constrained by what he calls the Inclusiveness Condition, which prohibits introduction of new material during the course of derivation except already-selected lexical items. The trace theory is a clear deviation from the Inclusiveness Condition because it introduces a new entity, namely traces, during the derivation of sentences. The trace theory, therefore, is now replaced with the copy theory, which posits that movement leaves copies of moved items behind. Under the copy theory, (29) should be reanalyzed as follows (copies created by movement are italicized):

(31) a. [TP Ken-ga [VP zibunzisin-o *seme*] [T seme_V-ta_T]] atode,
        [TP Taroo-wa [VP e] [T tatae_V-ta_T]].
     b. [TP Ken-ga [VP zibunzisin-o *seme*] [T seme_V-ta_T]] atode,
        [TP Taroo-wa [VP **zibunzisin-o *seme***] [T tatae_V-ta_T]].

The antecedent VP in the overt form in (31a) contains the copy of *seme*. After this VP is reconstructed onto the empty VP, (31b) is derived. Notice that the representation of the second clause in (31b) should be illicit, given that the verb in T and the verbal copy inside VP do not match. This consideration poses a conceptual, albeit somewhat theory-internal, problem to the VP-ellipsis analysis (see Kim 1999, Moriyama and Whitman 2004, and Otani and Whitman 1991 for related discussion).[7]

In addition to the problem just noted, several empirical counterarguments are pointed out in the literature. Let us consider three of them here. The first argument, due to Kim (1999), has to do with the so-called whole-part construction in Korean. I repeat it here by using the corresponding Japanese data:[8]

(32) a. ??Taroo-wa zibun-no kodomo-o ude-o tataita.
     Taroo-TOP self-GEN child-ACC arm-ACC hit
     'Taroo hit his child on the arm.'
   b. Hanako-wa e asi-o tataita.
     Hanako-TOP leg-ACC hit
     Lit. 'Hanako hit on the leg.'

In (32a), the first accusative phrase *zibun-no kodomo-o* 'self's child-ACC' serves as the "whole" expression, whereas the second accusative object *ude-o* 'arm-ACC' is the "part" phrase. The latter is understood as part of the former. Example (32a) is intended as the antecedent of (32b), where although the "whole" phrase is missing, the sloppy interpretation is available that Hanako hit her child on the leg. To apply the VP-ellipsis analysis here, we need an elliptic or empty VP. But the VP in (32b) does not appear to be empty, because it contains the overt "part" phrase *asi-o* 'leg-ACC', clearly a VP-internal object.

Advocates of the VP-ellipsis analysis might say that the part phrase is somehow dislocated from VP in (32b), creating an empty VP:

(33) [TP Hanako-wa asi-o [VP e] [T tatai_V-ta_T]]
     Hanako-TOP leg-ACC   hit-T

However, this does not seem to be possible. The following examples show that part phrases are inert for dislocation:

(34) a. ??Taroo-wa Ken-o ude-o tataita.
     Taroo-TOP Ken-ACC arm-ACC hit
     'Taroo hit Ken on the arm.'
   b. *Ude-o Taroo-wa Ken-o tataita.
     arm-ACC Taroo-TOP Ken-ACC hit
   c. *Taroo-wa ude-o Ken-o tataita.
     Taroo-TOP arm-ACC Ken-ACC hit

In (34b,c) the part phrases are dislocated from their normal positions (namely, the positions between the whole phrases and the verbs), and the examples are completely degraded in clear contrast with (34a), where the canonical word order for the construction is reserved. Thus, the VP-ellipsis analysis has difficulty accommodating cases such as (32b), where some missing VP-internal material can be understood sloppily despite the fact that entire VPs are not empty.

The second counterargument to the VP-ellipsis analysis, due to Oku (1998), pertains to sentences containing adjuncts, such as the following:

(35) a. Taroo-wa kono hoohoo de katta.
     Taroo-TOP this way in won
     'Taroo won (in) this way.'
   b. Hanako mo e katta.
     Hanako also won
     'Hanako also won.'

(36) a. Taroo-wa kono riyuu de sinda.
       Taroo-TOP this reason for died
       'Taroo died for this reason.'
    b. Hanako mo e sinda.'
       Hanako also   died
       'Hanako also died.'

Examples (35a) and (36a) are intended to serve as the antecedent sentences for (35b) and (36b), respectively. Example (35a) contains the adjunct *kono hoohoo de* 'in this way' and (36a) *kono riyuu de* 'for this reason'. As Oku (1998) correctly points out, if VP-ellipsis were available in Japanese, the (b)-sentences above would have the readings comparable to those of their antecedent sentences. Consider the following cases of VP-ellipsis in English:

(37) a. John won this way, and Mary did, too.
    b. John died for this reason, and Mary did, too.

The elliptic clauses in (37a,b) can mean that Mary also won this way and that Mary also died for this reason, respectively. This is because the adjuncts in the antecedent clauses are internal to the VP, so that they can be reconstructed in the VP in the elliptic clauses when the entire VP is copied. That (35b) and (36b) behave differently from (37) casts doubts on the availability of VP-ellipsis in Japanese.

The third problem with the VP-ellipsis analysis comes from null subjects. As Oku (1998) points out, the VP-ellipsis analysis predicts that the kind of interpretation exhibited by the null-object construction should not be available for null subjects because they are arguably outside of VP.[9] This is not borne out, however. Oku provides cases such as the following, showing that null subjects exhibit sloppy interpretation as well:[10]

(38) a. Taroo-wa [zibun-no teian-ga   Hanako-o
       Taroo-TOP self-GEN proposal-NOM Hanako-ACC
       odorokasu to] omotteiru.
       surprise   that think
       'Taroo thinks that his proposal will surprise Hanako.'
    b. Ken-wa [e Yumiko-o   odorokasu to] omotteiru.
       Ken-TOP   Yumiko-ACC surprise   that think
       Lit. 'Ken thinks that *e* will surprise Yumiko.'
(39) a. Taroo-wa [zibun-no kodomo-ga Hanako-o   tataita
       Taroo-TOP self-GEN child-NOM Hanako-ACC hit
       toyuu uwasa]-o   kiita.
       that rumor-ACC heard
       'Taroo heard the rumor that his child hit Hanako.'
    b. Ken-wa [e Yumiko-o   tataita toyuu uwasa]-o kiita.
       Ken-TOP   Yumiko-ACC hit   that rumor-ACC heard
       Lit. 'Ken heard the rumor that *e* hit Yumiko.'

Examples (38a) and (39a) serve as the antecedents for (38b) and (39b), respectively, where the subjects of the embedded clauses are empty. The (b)-examples can be understood sloppily: (38b) can mean that Ken thinks that Ken's proposal will surprise Yumiko, and (39b) can mean that Ken heard the rumor that Ken's child hit Yumiko. The VP-ellipsis analysis would be silent about this fact, since what is missing is VP-external material.[11]

15.3.2 The NP-Ellipsis Analysis

Given those difficulties faced by the VP-ellipsis analysis, Kim (1999), Moriyama and Whitman (2004), Oku (1998), and Tomioka (2003) put forth an alternative account of the data in question in terms of NP-ellipsis.[12] I use Oku's (1998) analysis in terms of LF copying to illustrate the NP-ellipsis analysis.[13] Let us consider the example in (10), repeated as (40):

(40) Ken-ga   zibunzisin-o semeta   atode, Taroo-wa   e tataeta.
      Ken-NOM   himself-ACC criticized   after   Taroo-NOM   praised
      'After Ken criticized himself, Taroo praised himself.'

(41) a. [TP Ken-ga   [NP zibunzisin-o] semeta]   atode,
           Ken-NOM   himself-ACC   criticized after
         [TP Taroo-wa   [NP e]   tataeta].
            Taroo-NOM   praised
     b. [TP Ken-ga [NP zibunzisin-o] semeta] atode,
        [TP Taroo-wa [NP **zibunzisin-o**] tataeta].

Example (41a) is the overt-syntactic representation of (40) according to the NP-ellipsis analysis. In (41a) the object position in the second clause is elliptic, indicated as [NP e]. After the derivation enters into LF, the antecedent NP—namely, the anaphoric object in the first clause—is copied onto the empty slot, resulting in (41b), which represents the correct interpretation for the sentence. Note in particular that because NP-ellipsis base-generates empty NP positions and just copies the content of other NPs onto them, it is no longer problematic that the two verbs are different in (40). Note also that once NP-ellipsis is adopted, V-raising is no longer necessary so far as the null-object construction in question is concerned, though it might be needed in other aspects of Japanese syntax (see Koizumi 1995 and Miyagawa 2001).

The examples in (9), (11), and (19) are dealt with easily as well. Their derivations under the NP-ellipsis analysis are given in (42)–(44), respectively.

(42) a. A: [TP Dare-ga   [NP zibun-o] sememasita] ka?
            who-NOM   self-ACC   criticized   Q
         'Who criticized himself?'
      B: [TP Taroo-ga/Daremo-ga [NP e] sememasita].
         Taroo-NOM/everyone-NOM   criticized
         Lit. 'Taroo/Everyone criticized.'

b. A: [TP Dare-ga [NP zibun-o] sememasita] ka?
B: [TP Taroo-ga/Daremo-ga [NP **zibun-o**] sememasita].

(43) a. [TP Ken-ga   [NP zibun-no sensei-o]   semeta] atode,
         Ken-NOM   self-GEN teacher-ACC criticized after
      [TP Taroo mo [NP e] semeta].
         Taroo also   criticized
      Lit. 'After Ken criticized his teacher, Taroo criticized, too.'
   b. [TP Ken-ga [NP zibun-no sensei-o] semeta] atode,
      [TP Taroo mo [NP **zibun-no sensei-o**] semeta].

(44) a. [TP Hanako-ga   [NP taitei-no   sensei-o]   sonkeisiteiru].
         Hanako-NOM   most-GEN teacher-ACC respect
      Sosite [TP Taroo mo   [NP e] sonkeisiteiru].
      and   Taroo also   respect
      Lit. 'Hanako respects most teachers. And Taroo respects, too.'
   b. [TP Hanako-ga [NP taitei-no sensei-o] sonkeisiteiru].
      Sosite [TP Taroo mo [NP **taitei-no sensei-o**] sonkeisiteiru].

In (42) and (43) the reconstructed parts contain the anaphors, which correctly accounts for the presence of sloppy interpretation, whereas in (44) the quantified phrase is reconstructed in the second clause, as desired.[14]

Let us turn to the whole-part construction in (32). Its derivation under the NP-ellipsis analysis is given here:

(45) a. [TP Taroo-wa   [VP [NP zibun-no kodomo-o] ude-o
         Taroo-TOP   self-GEN   child-ACC   arm-ACC
      tataita]]. [TP Hanako-wa [VP [NP e] asi-o   tataita]].
      hit   Hanako-TOP   leg-ACC   hit
      Lit. 'Taroo hit his child on the arm. Hanako hit on the leg.'
   b. [TP Taroo-wa [VP [NP zibun-no kodomo-o] ude-o tataita]].
      [TP Hanako-wa [VP [NP **zibun-no kodomo-o**] asi-o tataita]].

In the second clause in (45a), the NP position for the whole object is empty. It is lexicalized at LF by copying the corresponding NP in the antecedent clause, deriving (45b). Note that this analysis works just fine even if the part phrase remains in VP in the second clause.

Further, note that in principle NP-ellipsis should be able to create empty positions as long as they are designated for NP. Thus, we expect that null subjects as well as null objects can be elliptic. We saw that this expectation is borne out by the cases in (38) and (39) earlier, where the null subjects exhibit sloppy interpretation.

At this point, let us consider how the proponents of the NP-ellipsis analysis approach the question of why Japanese, unlike English, allows elliptic null arguments. Tomioka (2003) follows Chierchia (1998) in assuming that languages differ in the way nominal arguments are represented: In one type of language, nominal expressions are headed by determiners taking NPs as their complements; in another type, they are bare NPs lacking determiners. Tomioka assumes that English belongs to the first type but Japanese is an instance of the second type (see also Fukui 1986):

(46) a. John read a/the/this/that/these/those/some/many book(s).
  b. Taroo-ga   hon-o   yonda.
     Taroo-NOM   book-ACC   read
     'Taroo read a/the book.'

(47) a. John read [DP [D a/the/this/that/these/those/some/many] [NP book(s)]]
  b. Taroo-ga [NP hon]-o yonda

The object in the English sentence in (46a) is represented as in (47a), where it is headed by the determiners. In contrast, the object in the Japanese example in (46b) is analyzed as in (47b), where it is a bare NP. When NP-ellipsis takes place in these languages, it should leave determiners stranded in English but delete entire arguments in Japanese, as shown here (the struck-through material represents elliptic constituents):[15]

(48) a. John read [DP [D this/that/these/those/some/many] [NP book(s)]].
  b. Taroo-ga [NP hon]-o yonda.

Tomioka's (2003) idea is quite appealing because it just posits a single general operation (that is, NP-ellipsis) for the two languages, attributing their difference in the presence or absence of null arguments to another independently attested difference between them in the way nominal expressions are projected. At the same time, however, it gives rise to at least two questions. The first has to do with bare NP arguments in English:

(49) a. Mary loves novels.
  b. *But John hates [NP e].

Here the bare plural NP *novels* is supposed to undergo ellipsis in the second clause. As Tomioka (2003) notes, his analysis should expect it to be possible, contrary to fact.

The second question pertains to the existence of those cases of NP-ellipsis in Japanese where quantifiers are stranded (see Moriyama and Whitman 2004).[16] Consider the following examples:

(50) a. Hanako-wa   [DP [NP hon] [D nisatu]]-o yonda.
     Hanako-TOP   book   two-ACC   read
     'Hanako read two books.'
  b. Taroo-wa   [DP [NP hon] [D sansatu/motto ooku/subete]]-o yonda.
     Taroo-TOP   book   three/more many/all-ACC   read
     'Taroo read three/more/all.'

With (50a) as the antecedent sentence, (50b) has the NP part of the object elided. Although I label the quantifiers above as D, it is just for expository purposes and their categorial identity is immaterial; what is important is the fact that nominal arguments in Japanese can sometimes be headed by what seem to be functional categories, which allow their complement NPs to be elliptic. Even more important is that entire objects including quantifiers can be elliptic as well. Consider the following examples:

(51) a. Hanako-wa [DP [NP zibun-ni kansuru hon] [D subete]]-o yonda.
Hanako-TOP   self-to   related   book   all-ACC   read
'Hanako read all the books about herself.'
b. Taroo mo e yonda.
Taroo also read
Lit. 'Taroo read, too.'

Example (51b) can mean that Taroo read all the books about himself, which indicates that what is elliptic is the projection headed by *subete* 'all'.

Further, Saito and Murasugi (1990) argue that cases such as the following involve NP-ellipsis with a stranded genitive phrase (see also Jackendoff 1971 and Lobeck 1995):

(52) a. [DP Gakubusei-no   [NP sensei-e-no   izon] [D e]] -wa
undergraduates-GEN   teacher-on-GEN reliance   -TOP
yuruseru.
is-permissible
'Undergraduates' reliance on teachers is permissible.'
b. [DP Insei-no   [NP e] [D e]]-wa yurusenai.
graduate student-GEN   -TOP is-impermissible
'Graduate students' is impermissible.'

Preceded by (52a), (52b) can mean that graduate students' reliance on teachers is impermissible. Saito and Murasugi (1990) argue that (52b) has the NP part of the subject DP elided, with the genitive phrase and the empty D head stranded. Bearing this in mind, let us consider the following examples:

(53) a. Hanako-wa   [DP zibun-no[NP kusuri-e-no izon] [D e]] -o
Hanako-TOP   self-GEN   drug-on-GEN reliance   -ACC
haziteiru.
is-ashamed
'Hanako is ashamed of her reliance on drugs.'
b. Taroo mo [DP e] haziteiru.
Taroo also   is-ashamed
'Taroo is ashamed, too.'

Taking (53a) as its antecedent, (53b) means that Taroo is ashamed of his reliance on drugs. Thus, what is elliptic in (53b) is the entire object, which, according to Saito and Murasugi, is bigger than NP and arguably a DP.

In short, although NP-ellipsis no doubt is operative in the grammar of Japanese, it cannot be responsible for all the cases of elliptic null arguments, given that there are elliptic nominal arguments that are bigger than NP.

Unlike Tomioka (2003), Oku (1998) avoids the problems noted above. Although he assumes that elliptic null arguments involve NP-ellipsis, the categorial status of elliptic elements is not crucial. What is crucial for him is not the NPhood but the argumenthood of elliptic constituents. Let us illustrate Oku's analysis with the example in (41), repeated as (54):

(54) a. [TP Ken-ga   [NP zibunzisin-o] semeta]   atode,
        Ken-NOM   himself-ACC   criticized after
        [TP Taroo-wa [NP e]   tataeta].
        Taroo-TOP   praised
     Lit. 'After Ken criticized himself, Taroo praised.'
   b. [TP Ken-ga [NP zibunzisin-o] semeta] atode,
      [TP Taroo-wa [NP **zibunzisin-o**] tataeta].

The overt form of the second clause in (54a) is shown as if the vacant NP position were existent. For Oku, however, that position is literally absent, so that (54a) should be represented more precisely as:

(55) [TP Ken-ga   [VP[NP zibunzisin-o] semeta]]   atode,
     Ken-NOM   himself-ACC   criticized after
     [TP Taroo-wa   [VP tataeta]].
     Taroo-TOP   praised
   Lit. 'After Ken criticized himself, Taroo praised.'

Whereas the first clause has a usual transitive configuration, the second clause has a simplex VP. The LF representation in (54b) is derived from (55) by merging the copy of the object in the first clause with the verb in the second clause. That is, the second clause has a licit transitive configuration only at LF. Of course, a question immediately arises as to how the selectional property of the verb in the second clause does not have to be satisfied in overt syntax in (55).

To answer this question, Oku (1998) adopts Bošković and Takahashi's (1998) proposal that selectional features can be weak (namely, they do not have to be satisfied in overt syntax) in Japanese. Bošković and Takahashi are concerned with the question of how scrambling—an apparently optional, non-feature-driven movement operation—is ever possible in languages such as Japanese. For instance, cases such as (56a), where the embedded object undergoes scrambling and is placed in front of the matrix subject, have been analyzed as in (56b) in the literature (Saito 1985).

(56) a. Ken-o   Taroo-ga   Hanako-ga   sikatta to   itta.
        Ken-ACC   Taroo-NOM   Hanako-NOM   scolded that said
      Lit. 'Ken, Taroo said that Hanako scolded.'
   b. [TP Ken-o   [TP Taroo-ga   [CP Hanako-ga   [VP t
        Ken-ACC   Taroo-NOM   Hanako-NOM
        sikatta] to]   itta]]
        scolded that   said

The traditional view assumes that the object is base-generated in the canonical object position in the embedded VP and is moved by scrambling to the matrix TP-adjoined position. Given that this movement lacks any semantic effect or morphological reflex (see Saito 1989), it has been regarded as an exception to the so-called Last Resort principle, which demands that movement be driven for the purpose of feature checking (Chomsky 1995). In an effort to solve this problem, Bošković and Takahashi propose an alternative way to analyze cases such as (56a). According to them, the example is derived as follows:

(57) a. [TP Ken-o   [TP Taroo-ga   [CP Hanako-ga   [VP sikatta]
         Ken-ACC   Taroo-NOM   Hanako-NOM   scolded
         to] itta]]
         that said
         Lit. 'Ken, Taroo said that Hanako scolded.'
    b. [TP Taroo-ga   [CP Hanako-ga   [VP Ken-o   sikatta]
         Taroo-NOM   Hanako-NOM   Ken-ACC   scolded
         to] itta]]
         that said

In overt syntax, the sentence is represented as in (57a), where the "scrambled" object is actually base-generated in its surface position and the embedded VP consists of the transitive verb alone. The verb's selectional requirement does not need to be met in overt syntax because it is "weak." At LF, the object merges with the verb, to satisfy the verb's selectional property (or to check its selectional feature), and (57b) is obtained. Considered this way, scrambling is recast as a covert movement operation motivated by checking of selectional features (see Bošković and Takahashi 1998 for details).

Given that selectional features are weak in Japanese, overt-syntactic representations such as (55) should be permissible. In fact, Oku (1998) goes further, claiming that LF copying of antecedent NPs onto elliptic sites is triggered by satisfaction of selectional requirements: the derivation from (55) to (54b) is caused by the need to satisfy the selectional property of the verb in the elliptic clause. The presence of elliptic null arguments is now linked with the possibility of scrambling, both arising from the weakness of selectional features. Turning our attention to English, we are led to assume that selectional features are strong (that is, must be checked in overt syntax soon after verbs are introduced into the derivation) in English, given that scrambling is absent in the language. This in turn implies that elliptic arguments, too, are absent in English.

Notice that Oku's (1998) analysis entails that any category—whether an NP, a DP, or any other phrase—should be able to be elliptic to the extent that it is an argument (hereafter I call Oku's analysis the argument ellipsis analysis, following Saito 2003). Thus, Oku does not suffer from the problem faced by Tomioka (2003). Further, the two analyses can be distinguished by considering the possibility of PP-ellipsis. First, Oku would predict that if they are arguments, PPs should be able to be elliptic. This is actually borne out. Takahashi (2006) provides cases such as the following, observing that argument PPs can undergo ellipsis:

(58) a. Taroo to Hanako-ga otagai kara meeru-o
        Taroo and Hanako-NOM each other from e-mail-ACC
        uketotta.
        received
        'Taroo and Hanako received e-mail from each other.'
   b. Ken to Yumiko-wa tegami-o uketotta.
        Ken and Yumiko-TOP letter-ACC received
        Lit. 'Ken and Yumiko received letters.'

The verb *uketotta* 'received' selects a source PP argument as well as a theme nominal argument, as shown in (58a). In (58b), which takes (58a) as the antecedent, the source PP is missing but the sentence can have the interpretation that Ken and Yumiko received letters from each other. That is, the source PP is elliptic in (58b). Under the argument ellipsis analysis, (58) is derived as follows:

(59) a. [TP Taroo to Hanako-ga [VP [PP otagai kara] meeru-o uketotta]].
     [TP Ken to Yumiko-wa [VP tegami-o uketotta]].
   b. [TP Taroo to Hanako-ga [VP [PP otagai kara] meeru-o uketotta]].
     [TP Ken to Yumiko-wa [VP [PP **otagai kara**] tegami-o uketotta]].

In the overt form in (59a), the VP in the second clause consists of the theme object and the verb. After copying the source PP in the first clause into the defective VP, the complete form in (59b) is derived. In the second clause in (59b), the verb takes two internal arguments as desired and the source argument contains the reciprocal anaphor, which accounts for the interpretation of the sentence. Further, the copying in this case is licit with respect to Last Resort: it is caused by the need to satisfy one of the selectional properties of the verb in the second clause.

Let us consider how the NP-ellipsis analysis treats (58). It has to assign the following representation to the example:

(60) a. Taroo to Hanako-ga [PP [NP otagai] [P kara]] meeru-o
        Taroo and Hanako-NOM   each other from e-mail-ACC
        uketotta.
        received
        'Taroo and Hanako received e-mail from each other.'
   b. Ken to Yumiko-wa [PP [NP ~~otagai~~] [P e]] tegami-o uketotta.
        Ken and Yumiko-TOP   each other letter-ACC received
        Lit. 'Ken and Yumiko received letters.'

Only NPs can be elliptic under the NP-ellipsis analysis, so what is elided in (60b) is the NP complement of the source PP. Note that because the entire PP is empty in (58b), it is necessary to postulate an empty postposition as indicated in (60b). In general, however, empty postpositions do not seem to be possible in Japanese. Thus, the following example is ill formed:

(61) a. Taroo-ga   [PP Hanako kara] meeru-o   uketotta.
       Taroo-NOM   Hanako from   e-mail-ACC received
       'Taroo received e-mail from Hanako.'
    b. *Ken-wa   [PP Yumiko eP] tegami-o   uketotta.
       Ken-TOP   Yumiko   letter-ACC received
       Lit. 'Ken received letters Yumiko.'

The NP-ellipsis analysis has difficulty accommodating, or is silent about, those cases where categories other than NP undergo ellipsis. The argument ellipsis analysis, in contrast, can deal with cases such as (58) in the same way as those cases where nominals are elided.

Let us now turn to the examples in (35) and (36), which show the impossibility of adjunct ellipsis. Example (35) is repeated as (62).

(62) a. Taroo-wa   kono hoohoo de katta.
       Taroo-TOP this way   in won
       'Taroo won (in) this way.'
    b. Hanako mo   e katta.
       Hanako also   won
       'Hanako also won.'

The point here is that (62b) cannot have the intended reading that Hanako also won this way. According to what we have said about the argument ellipsis analysis, the example is explained as follows:

(63) a. [TP Taroo-wa [VP kono hoohoo de katta]].
         [TP Hanako mo [VP katta]].
    b. *[TP Taroo-wa [VP kono hoohoo de katta]].
         [TP Hanako mo [VP **kono hoohoo de** katta]].

Example (63a) is the overt form, where there is no adjunct position in the second clause. To derive the relevant reading, the adjunct in the antecedent clause might be copied and merged with the verb in the second clause, yielding the LF representation in (63b). This copying of the adjunct, however, is not selectionally motivated and hence should be ruled out by Last Resort. This is why adjunct ellipsis is impermissible.[17]

Although argument ellipsis works well for the cases considered so far, there is a complication with regard to null subjects. The relevant case in (38) is repeated as (64).

(64) a. Taroo-wa   [zibun-no teian-ga   Hanako-o
       Taroo-TOP self-GEN proposal-NOM Hanako-ACC
       odorokasu to] omotteiru.
       surprise that think
       'Taroo thinks that his proposal will surprise Hanako.'
    b. Ken-wa   [e Yumiko-o   odorokasu to] omotteiru.
       Ken-TOP   Yumiko-ACC surprise   that think
       Lit. 'Ken thinks that e will surprise Yumiko.'

The fact here is that the null subject in (64b) can exhibit sloppy interpretation. The argument ellipsis analysis accounts for this case in the following way: In overt syntax, (64b) lacks an argument that serves as the embedded subject, and in LF the copy of the embedded subject in (64a) is merged into the embedded clause in (64b).[18] Given that the embedded verb in (64b) requires a subject argument in addition to an object argument, the copying operation conforms to Last Resort: it operates to satisfy one of the selectional properties of the verb. Because Oku (1998) assumes that argument ellipsis correlates with scrambling, it is expected that subjects can undergo scrambling.

Saito (1985) makes an observation to the contrary, however, based on the relative unacceptability of cases such as the following:

(65) *?Taroo₁-ga Ken-ga   [t₁ Hanako-o   aisiteiru to] itta.
       Taroo-NOM Ken-NOM   Hanako-ACC love   that said
       Lit. 'Taroo, Ken said loved Mary.'

This sentence is fairly degraded with the intended reading where Taroo serves as the embedded subject. This fact seems to indicate that subjects cannot undergo scrambling. In Bošković and Takahashi's (1998) terms, the feature of a head that licenses subject positions, whatever it is, is strong and has to be checked in overt syntax. This in turn implies that subject ellipsis is impossible. Therefore, Oku argues contra Saito (1985) that scrambling of subjects is actually possible, and suggests that the awkwardness of (65) is due to some parsing difficulty. I refer the interested readers to Oku 1998 and the references therein for somewhat detailed discussion of this issue (see also Ko 2007 for an argument that subjects can scramble, as well as Kikuchi 1987, which examines the properties of operator movement in comparative constructions in Japanese and argues that subjects can undergo A′-movement in Japanese).

15.4 IMPLICATIONS

The ellipsis analysis of null arguments explicated in the last section should make a number of predictions. I consider here one of its implications on the typology of languages with null arguments. Recall that for Oku (1998), the presence of argument ellipsis is closely linked to the existence of scrambling, both of which share the weakness of selectional features as one of their necessary conditions. We would expect, then, that languages that permit null arguments like Japanese but disallow scrambling (or free word order) unlike Japanese should exhibit yet a different behavior. Below I examine two such languages, Spanish and Chinese.

Let us first consider Spanish, which permits null subjects as in (66) but does not have scrambling as shown in (67) and (68) (examples (66) and (68) are cited from Jaeggli 1982 and (67) from Green 1987).

(66) Baila bien.
 dances well
 'He/She dances well.'
(67) a. Elena compró un coche.
  Elena bought a car
  'Elena bought a car.'
 b. *Elena un coche compró.
(68) a. Me parece que Juan no tiene el libro.
  I think that Juan not have the book
  'I think that Juan does not have the book.'
 b. *El libro me parece que Juan no tiene.

Given that Spanish does not allow scrambling, it should not permit argument ellipsis, either. This is in fact borne out, as Oku (1998) points out on the basis of the following data:

(69) a. María cree que su propuesta será aceptada.
  Maria believes that her proposal will-be accepted
  'Maria believes that her proposal will be accepted.
 b. Juan también cree que e será aceptada.
  Juan also believes that it will-be accepted
  'Juan also believes that it will be accepted.'

Preceded by (69a), (69b) contains a null subject in the embedded clause. Although the null subject can mean Maria's proposal, it cannot mean Juan's proposal. The absence of the sloppy interpretation shows that the null subject cannot be elliptic.

Let us turn our attention to Chinese, which provides a more interesting test because although it allows null arguments exactly like Japanese (see Huang 1984), researchers do not classify it as a free-word-order language. First of all, let us note that null objects in Chinese exhibit the sloppy interpretation, as Huang (1991) and Otani and Whitman (1991) observe. The examples here are from Otani and Whitman 1991:

(70) a. Zhangsan bu xihuan guany ziji de yaoyan.
  Zhangsan not like about self GEN rumor
  'Zhangsan does not like rumors about himself.'
 b. Mali ye bu xihuan e.
  Mali also not like
  Lit. 'Mali does not like either.'

The null object in (70b) can mean either rumors about Zhangsan or rumors about Mali. The possibility of the second reading shows that the sentence involves ellipsis, as argued by Huang (1991) and Otani and Whitman (1991). Notice, however, that (70b) should not be analyzed as an instance of argument ellipsis, because Chinese does not allow scrambling and hence selectional features there must be strong. Then, it may well be that (70b) involves VP-ellipsis accompanied by V-raising, as proposed by the authors mentioned above.

That Chinese does not allow argument ellipsis is supported by the fact that in contrast with null objects, null subjects do not permit sloppy interpretation, which was pointed out to me by Shigeru Miyagawa (pers. comm.) and Jonah Lin (pers. comm.). The data here are supplied by Jonah Lin:

(71) a. Zhangsan shuo ziji de haizi mei na qian.
　　　 Zhangsan say self GEN child take not money
　　　 'Zhangsan said that his child did not take money.'
　　 b. Lisi ye shuo e mei na qian.
　　　 Lisi too say take not money
　　　 Lit. 'Lisi also said that *e* did not take money.'

The null subject in (71b) may refer to Zhangsan's child but cannot mean Lisi's child. If argument ellipsis is impossible and only VP-ellipsis is available in Chinese, it is expected that null subjects cannot be elliptic: they themselves cannot be elliptic because argument ellipsis is not allowed, nor can they be contained in elliptic VP because subjects are outside VP. The fact is in accordance with this expectation. Thus, although we have considered in section 15.3 several arguments that VP-ellipsis is not available in Japanese, it does seem to take place in Chinese, as originally proposed by Huang (1991) and Whitman (1988).[19]

15.5 SUMMARY

To summarize, I have explicated the ellipsis theory of null arguments in Japanese, focusing on those data that are difficult to account for under the pronoun theory but can be easily explained by the ellipsis theory. Two varieties of the ellipsis theory have been considered: the VP-ellipsis analysis and the NP-ellipsis analysis. The latter has two subtypes: one is due to Tomioka (2003) and the other is put forth by Oku (1998). We have considered several arguments that Oku's argument ellipsis analysis is empirically preferred. The hypothesis that argument ellipsis is closely tied to scrambling makes a number of Japanese-particular and cross-linguistic predictions. For example, it has been shown that adjuncts are inert for ellipsis and scrambling, and that in Spanish and Chinese (null argument languages without scrambling) null arguments behave differently from their Japanese counterparts.

I wish to close this article with the following question: Is it possible to analyze all instances of null arguments in Japanese uniformly as elliptic? The answer seems to be negative. According to Hankamer and Sag's (1976) taxonomy of anaphoric expressions, ellipsis (or surface anaphora in their terms) requires the presence of linguistically expressed antecedents whereas pronouns (or deep anaphora) can do without them and be "pragmatically controlled." The following examples are cited from Hankamer and Sag 1976:

(72) [Hankamer attempts to stuff a 9-inch ball through a 6-inch hoop]
 a. Sag: #It's not clear that you'll be able to.
 b. Sag: It's not clear that you'll be able to do it.

(73) Hankamer: I'm going to stuff this ball through this hoop.
 Sag: It's not clear that you'll be able to.

The bracketed part in (72) is intended to show the situation, not verbally expressed, where the utterances in (72a,b) are produced. In this context, (72a), which involves VP-ellipsis, is unnatural (as indicated by the # prefixed to the sentence), whereas (72b), which is constructed by using the pronoun *it*, is fully acceptable. Example (73) indicates that once provided with a linguistic antecedent, the sentence in (72a) becomes acceptable.

Bearing this in mind, let us consider the following examples:

(74) [Observing a student smoking in the classroom]
 a. Taroo: e hai gan-de sinu kamosirenai.
  lung cancer-of die may
  'He may die of lung cancer.'
 b. Taroo: Sensei-ga e sikaru daroo.
  teacher-NOM scold will
  'The teacher will scold him.'

The subject in (74a) and the object in (74b) are empty, and they can refer to the student that appears in the nonverbal situation. Given that they are pragmatically controlled, the null arguments here are arguably pronouns.[20] Then we must allow for two options in analyzing null arguments in Japanese: they may be elliptic or pronominal.

NOTES FOR CHAPTER 15

Some portions of this chapter were presented at Workshop on Linguistic Theory and the Japanese Language, held at Harvard University in July 2005. I am grateful to the participants for useful comments and questions. For helpful discussion and comments I thank Jim Huang, Jonah Lin, Shigeru Miyagawa, Mamoru Saito, and an anonymous reviewer.

 1. Xu (1986) actually discusses a Japanese example (his (51)) very similar to (9), attributing it to Kuno (1980, 1982).
 2. I do not agree with Hoji (1998) on the interpretation of (13b), which seems to me to have the interpretation of (14a). Also, a reviewer pointed out the following data in English, where each of (ib,c) is intended as a continuation of (ia).

 (i) a. Taroo washed his car.
  b. Hanako washed a car, too.
  c. Hanako washed one, too.

According to the reviewer, (ib,c) are pragmatically odd in the context where Hanako washed her own car. Given that (13b) does not seem (at least to me) to have the oddness of (ib,c) on the reading that everyone except Taroo washed his own car too, it casts doubts on analyzing the null object in (13b) as a sort of indefinite expression.

3. I have not had the chance to read Shinohara 2004. The information below is obtained from Arimoto and Murasugi 2005.

4. Precisely speaking, the Japanese expression *izyoo* means 'more than or equal to'. Thus, *sankumi izyoo* should be translated as 'three groups or more'. Just for convenience, I gloss it as 'more than' here.

5. The strict reading can be obtained when the second clause contains an empty pronoun in the object position, rather than involving VP-ellipsis.

6. The second clause in (10) (or (26b)) can have the strict reading that Taroo praised Ken. In that case, it may involve an empty pronominal object referring to Ken, instead of VP-ellipsis (see also note 5).

7. As a reviewer pointed out, the problem is more general. Consider the example in (iia).

(ii) a. John was criticized, and Bill was, too.
 b. [TP John was-T [VP *was* criticized *John*]],
  and [TP Bill was-T [VP *was* criticized *John*]]

Assuming that passives involve NP-movement and that *be* verbs undergo overt raising, one might analyze (iia) as in (iib), where the antecedent VP with the copy of *John* is reconstructed in the elliptic clause.

8. The example in (32a) is a little degraded due to the violation of the so-called Double-*o* Constraint (Harada 1973, Shibatani 1973), which disallows the occurrence of more than one accusative phrase in a clause in Japanese. I abstract away from this mild deviance.

9. That subjects are outside VP in Japanese is indicated by the following examples, due to Miyagawa (2001):

(iii) a. Zen'in-ga sono tesuto-o uke-nakat-ta.
  all-NOM that test-ACC take-NEG-PAST
  'All did not take that test.'
 b. Taroo-ga zen'in-o home-nakat-ta.
  Taroo-NOM all-ACC praise-NEG-PAST
  'Taroo did not praise all.'

In (iiia) the subject quantifier is interpreted outside the scope of negation, whereas in (iiib) the object quantifier is interpreted inside the scope of negation. The reading of (iiib) is explained by saying that because the object is inside VP, it is c-commanded by negation (on the assumption that the negation head appears between Tense and V). Then, the interpretation of (iiia) indicates that the subject is beyond the c-command domain of negation (arguably in the specifier position of TP).

10. Whitman (1988) proposes an analysis of the null-object construction in terms of VP-ellipsis and considers cases similar to (38), pointing out that they do not exhibit the sloppy interpretation. I concur with Oku (1998) in regard to the judgment of the relevant examples.

11. A confirmation that null subjects can be elliptic comes from the fact that given quantificational antecedents, null subjects can be quantificational as well, as illustrated here (see also Oku 1998, where an argument based on indefinite subjects is provided):

(iv) a. Taitei-no gakusei-ga Taroo-o sonkeisiteiru.
most-GEN student-NOM Taroo-ACC respect
'Most students respect Taroo.'
b. e Hanako-o sonkeisiteiru koto mo akiraka da.
Hanako-ACC respect that also obvious is
Lit. 'That e respect Hanako is obvious too.'

(v) a. Hanbun izyoo-no gakusei-ga ronbun ippon-o
Half more than-GEN student-NOM paper one-ACC
kaita sooda.
wrote I-heard
'I heard that more than half the students wrote one paper.'
b. Boku-wa e hon issatu-o kaita to mo kiita.
I-TOP book one-ACC wrote that also heard
Lit. 'I heard that e wrote one book too.'

Examples (ivb) and (vb) are intended to be continuations of (iva) and (va), respectively. The null subjects in (ivb) and (vb) can be understood as *taitei-no gakusei* 'most students' and *hanbun izyoo-no gakusei* 'more than half the students', respectively.

Incidentally, a reviewer noted that this argument may not be convincing because the English counterparts of (iv) and (v) with pronominal subjects have the same interpretation.

(vi) a. Most students respect Taroo and it is obvious that they respect Hanako, too.
b. I heard that more than half the students wrote one paper and I heard that they wrote one book, too.

According to the reviewer, the pronominal subjects in (via,b) do not have to denote exactly the same sets as their antecedents in the preceding clauses—namely, they do not have to be E-type pronouns. If this is the case, the null subjects in (ivb) and (vb) can be analyzed as pronouns.

12. By this I do not mean that VP-ellipsis of the form assumed by Huang (1991) and Otani and Whitman (1991) is ruled out universally. VP-ellipsis with concomitant V-raising is argued to be existent in Irish by McCloskey (1991) and in Hebrew by Doron (2000).

13. The analyses proposed by Kim (1999), Moriyama and Whitman (2004), Oku (1998), and Tomioka (2003) differ from one another in some details. Due to space limitations I cannot replicate all of them here, and hence I refer readers to those references.

14. Moriyama and Whitman (2004) propose to treat cases such as (44) in the following way:

(vi) Ken-ga [DP zibun-no [NP sensei-o]] semeta atode,
Ken-NOM self-GEN teacher-ACC criticized after
Taroo mo [DP pro [NP e]] semeta.
Taroo also criticized
Lit. 'After Ken criticized his teacher, Taroo criticized, too.'

When the example has the sloppy interpretation, the null object in the elliptic clause has a complex DP structure, where the NP part is elided with the stranded empty pronominal possessor. This kind of NP-ellipsis has been independently shown to be available in Japanese by Saito and Murasugi (1990) (see (52)). However, as Moriyama and Whitman assume that nominal arguments are DPs and that only NP complements can be elliptic, they have difficulty accounting for cases where entire DPs are elliptic, such as (44) and (51).

15. For some unclear reason, English disallows NP-ellipsis with some determiners such as *the*, *a*, and *every*. We do not concern ourselves with these exceptions here. See Elbourne 2001 and Lobeck 1995 for related discussion.

16. See Watanabe, this volume, for extensive discussion of quantifiers such as the ones in (50) and their relation to the structure of DP in Japanese.

17. The impossibility of adjunct ellipsis correlates with the absence of adjunct scrambling, which is noted by Saito (1985) on the basis of cases such as the following:

(vii) *Riyuu mo naku Mary-ga [John-ga *t* sono
 reason even without Mary-NOM John-NOM that
 setu-o sinziteiru to] omotteiru.
 theory-ACC believe that think
 Lit. 'For no reason, Mary thinks that John believed in that theory.'

This sentence disallows the reading where the sentence-initial adjunct modifies the embedded clause. Under the traditional view that scrambling is optional and not feature driven, this fact is hard to explain. In Bošković and Takahashi's (1998) analysis, in contrast, it is accounted for readily. According to them, the adjunct should be base-generated in its surface position and be moved into the embedded clause. Notice, however, that because adjuncts are not selected, there is no selectional motivation for the adjunct to undergo covert movement in (vii). The impossibility of adjunct scrambling, therefore, is regarded as a consequence of Last Resort.

18. A reviewer pointed out the following data (the original is slightly modified here to avoid an irrelevant complication):

(viii) a. Taroo-wa zibun-no sensei-o semeta.
 Taroo-TOP self-GEN teacher-ACC criticized
 'Taroo criticized his teacher.'
 b. Hanako-wa [*e* kakkoii to] itta.
 Hanako-TOP cool-is that said
 Lit. 'Hanako said that *e* was cool.'

The null subject in (viiib) is intended to take the object in (viiia) as its antecedent. Under the argument ellipsis analysis, nothing prevents the object in (viiia) from being copied onto the empty subject position in (viiib), so that (viiib) can mean that Hanako said that her own teacher was cool. The reviewer noted, however, that the reading is difficult to obtain, suggesting instead that argument ellipsis be subject to some sort of parallelism constraint such as the one discussed in Fox 2000. Exactly to what extent and how argument ellipsis obeys parallelism is left to future research.

19. If VP-ellipsis is indeed available in Chinese, the example in (ix), supplied by Luming Wang (pers. comm.), is predicted to be possible on a par with the English example in (x).

(ix) Zhangsan yong zhege fangfa yíng-le. Lisi ye *e* yíng-le.
 Zhangsan in this way win-ASP Lisi also win-ASP
 'Zhangsan won this way. Lisi also won.'
(x) John won this way, and Mary did, too.

The second sentence in (ix) is intended to mean that Lisi also won this way, just as the second clause in (x) means that Mary won this way, too. Native speakers of Chinese seem to vary about the judgment of (ix). I leave it for future research to examine cases such as (ix).

20. Following Williams (1977b), a reviewer pointed out that Hankamer and Sag's (1976) dichotomy between pronouns and ellipsis is problematic, and the reviewer provided the following examples to show that NP-ellipsis can be pragmatically controlled:

(xi) a. [In a car lot] I like the white [$_{NP}$ e].
b. [In a coatroom] You took his [$_{NP}$ e].

However, Lasnik and Saito (1992) present evidence to the contrary:

(xii) [Lasnik and Saito are in a yard with several barking dogs belonging to various people.]
Lasnik: #Harry's is particularly noisy.

(xiii) Lasnik: These dogs keep me awake with all their barking.
Saito: Harry's is particularly noisy.

Further, argument ellipsis seems to resist pragmatic control:

(xiv) [Watching a boy hitting himself]
Taroo: Hanako mo e tataku daroo.
       Hanako also hit   will
Lit. 'Hanako will hit, too.'

Although the null object can refer to the boy in the nonlinguistic situation, it cannot have the anaphoric reading: that is, Taroo's utterance cannot mean that Hanako will hit herself. Because the anaphoric interpretation is a sign of ellipsis, its absence in (xiv) indicates that argument ellipsis cannot be licensed pragmatically. Then, it may be that the examples in (xi) do not involve ellipsis, though I have no answer to offer to the question of exactly how they are analyzed.

REFERENCES

Arimoto, Masatake, and Keiko Murasugi. 2005. *Sokubaku to sakuzyo* [Binding and deletion]. Tokyo: Kenkyusha.
Bošković, Željko, and Daiko Takahashi. 1998. Scrambling and Last Resort. *Linguistic Inquiry* 29:347–366.
Chierchia, Gennaro. 1998. Reference to kinds across languages. *Natural Language Semantics* 6:339–405.
Chomsky, Noam. 1981. *Lectures on government and binding*. Dordrecht: Foris.
Chomsky, Noam. 1995. Categories and transformations. In *The Minimalist Program*, 219–394. Cambridge, Mass.: MIT Press.
Chomsky, Noam, and Howard Lasnik. 1993. The theory of principles and parameters. In *Syntax: An international handbook of contemporary research*, ed. Joachim Jacobs, Arnim von Stechow, Wolfgang Sternefeld, and Theo Vennemann, 506–569. Berlin: Walter de Gruyter.

Doron, Edit. 2000. VSO and left-conjunct agreement: Biblical Hebrew vs. Modern Hebrew. In *The syntax of verb-initial languages*, ed. Andrew Carnie and Eithne Guilfoyle, 75–95. Oxford: Oxford University Press.

Elbourne, Paul. 2001. E-type anaphora as NP-deletion. *Natural Language Semantics* 9:241–288.

Emonds, Joseph. 1978. The verbal complex V'-V in French. *Linguistic Inquiry* 9:151–175.

Evans, Gareth. 1980. Pronouns. *Linguistic Inquiry* 11:337–362.

Fox, Danny. 2000. *Economy and semantic interpretation*. Cambridge, Mass.: MIT Press.

Fukui, Naoki. 1986. A theory of category projection and its applications. Doctoral dissertation, MIT, Cambridge, Mass.

Green, John N. 1987. Spanish. In *The world's major languages*, ed. Bernard Comrie, 236–259. Oxford: Oxford University Press.

Hankamer, Jorge, and Ivan Sag. 1976. Deep and surface anaphora. *Linguistic Inquiry* 7:391–428.

Harada, S.-I. 1973. Counter equi NP deletion. *Annual Bulletin* 7:113–147. Research Institute of Logopedics and Phoniatrics, Tokyo University.

Hasegawa, Nobuko. 1984/1985. On the so-called "zero pronouns" in Japanese. *The Linguistic Review* 4:289–342.

Hoji, Hajime. 1985. Logical Form constraints and configurational structures in Japanese. Doctoral dissertation, University of Washington, Seattle.

Hoji, Hajime. 1998. Null object and sloppy identity in Japanese. *Linguistic Inquiry* 29:127–152.

Huang, C.-T. James. 1984. On the distribution and reference of empty pronouns. *Linguistic Inquiry* 15:531–574.

Huang, C.-T. James. 1991. Remarks on the status of the null object. In *Principles and parameters in comparative grammar*, ed. Robert Freidin, 56–76. Cambridge, Mass.: MIT Press.

Jackendoff, Ray S. 1971. Gapping and related rules. *Linguistic Inquiry* 2:21–35.

Jaeggli, Osvaldo. 1982. *Topics in Romance syntax*. Dordrecht: Foris.

Kikuchi, Akira. 1987. Comparative deletion in Japanese. Ms., Yamagata University, Yamagata, Japan.

Kim, Soowon. 1999. Sloppy/strict identity, empty objects, and NP ellipsis. *Journal of East Asian Linguistics* 8:255–284.

Ko, Heejeong. 2007. Asymmetries in scrambling and cyclic linearization. *Linguistic Inquiry* 38:49–84.

Koizumi, Masatoshi. 1995. Phrase structure in minimalist syntax. Doctoral dissertation, MIT, Cambridge, Mass.

Kuno, Susumu. 1980. Discourse deletion. In *Harvard studies in syntax and semantics 3*, ed. Susumu Kuno, 1–144. Cambridge, Mass.: Harvard University, Department of Linguistics.

Kuno, Susumu. 1982. Principles of discourse deletion: Case studies from English, Russian, and Japanese. *Journal of Semantics* 1:61–93.

Kuroda, S.-Y. 1965. Generative grammatical studies in the Japanese language. Doctoral dissertation, MIT, Cambridge, Mass.

Lasnik, Howard, and Mamoru Saito. 1992. *Move α*. Cambridge, Mass.: MIT Press.

Lobeck, Anne. 1995. *Ellipsis: Functional heads, licensing, and identification*. Oxford: Oxford University Press.

McCloskey, James. 1991. Clause structure, ellipsis, and proper government in Irish. *Lingua* 85:259–302.

Miyagawa, Shigeru. 2001. The EPP, scrambling, and *wh*-in-situ. In *Ken Hale: A life in language*, ed. Michael Kenstowicz, 294–338. Cambridge, Mass.: MIT Press.
Moriyama, Yoshiyuki, and John Whitman. 2004. Null objects in Japanese revisited. Paper read at a linguistics colloquium at Nanzan University, Nagoya, Japan, September.
Ohso, Mieko. 1976. A study of zero pronominalization in Japanese. Doctoral dissertation, Ohio State University, Columbus.
Oku, Satoshi. 1998. A theory of selection and reconstruction in the minimalist perspective. Doctoral dissertation, University of Connecticut, Storrs.
Otani, Kazuyo, and John Whitman. 1991. V-raising and VP-ellipsis. *Linguistic Inquiry* 22:345–358.
Pollock, Jean-Yves. 1989. Verb movement, Universal Grammar, and the structure of IP. *Linguistic Inquiry* 20:365–424.
Saito, Mamoru. 1985. Some asymmetries in Japanese and their theoretical implications. Doctoral dissertation, MIT, Cambridge, Mass.
Saito, Mamoru. 1989. Scrambling as semantically vacuous A'-movement. In *Alternative conceptions of phrase structure*, ed. Mark R. Baltin and Anthony S. Kroch, 182–200. Chicago: University of Chicago Press.
Saito, Mamoru. 2003. Notes on discourse-based null arguments. Paper presented at the 13th Japanese/Korean Linguistic Conference, Michigan State University, East Lansing, August.
Saito, Mamoru, and Keiko Murasugi. 1990. N'-deletion in Japanese: A preliminary study. *Japanese/Korean Linguistics* 1:285–301.
Shibatani, Masayoshi. 1973. Semantics of Japanese causativization. *Foundations of Language* 9:327–373.
Shinohara, Michie. 2004. Nihongo-no sakuzyo gensyoo-nituite [On the deletion phenomena in Japanese]. B.A. thesis, Nanzan University, Nagoya, Japan.
Takahashi, Daiko. 2006. Apparent parasitic gaps and null arguments in Japanese. *Journal of East Asian Linguistics* 15:1–35.
Tomioka, Satoshi. 2003. The semantics of Japanese null pronouns and its cross-linguistic implications. In *The interfaces: Deriving and interpreting omitted structures*, ed. Kerstin Schwabe and Susanne Winkler, 321–339. Amsterdam: John Benjamins.
Whitman, John. 1988. Discourse ellipsis and the identity of zero pronouns. *Linguistics in the morning calm* 2:149–175. Seoul: The Linguistic Society of Korea.
Williams, Edwin. 1977a. Discourse and Logical Form. *Linguistic Inquiry* 8:101–139.
Williams, Edwin. 1977b. On "deep and surface anaphora." *Linguistic Inquiry* 8:692–696.
Xu, Liejiong. 1986. Free empty category. *Linguistic Inquiry* 17:75–93.

CHAPTER 16

DITRANSITIVE CONSTRUCTIONS

YUJI TAKANO

16.1 INTRODUCTION

This chapter is concerned with the structure and derivation of ditransitive constructions (DCs) in Japanese. Focusing particularly on the structural relation between two objects, this work closely examines syntactic properties of Japanese DCs and discusses how competing theories account for them. I also consider consequences and implications following from the study of Japanese DCs, discussing in particular how the study of Japanese DCs contributes to the development of linguistic theory.

16.2 MAJOR QUESTIONS ABOUT JAPANESE DCs

One noticeable property of Japanese DCs is that they allow the order between the theme/accusative phrase and the goal/dative phrase to be free, as shown in (1), in contrast to English equivalents such as those in (2) and (3).

(1) a. Masao-ga   Yumi-ni   syasin-o   ageta.
Masao-NOM   Yumi-DAT   picture-ACC   gave
'Masao gave Yumi a picture/gave a picture to Yumi.'
b. Masao-ga   syasin-o   Yumi-ni   ageta.
Masao-NOM   picture-ACC   Yumi-DAT   gave

(2) a. John gave Mary a picture.
    b. *John gave a picture Mary.

(3) a. John gave a picture to Mary.
    b. *John gave to Mary a picture.

Another important property to note is that, disregarding surface order, Japanese apparently has only one morphosyntactic pattern for double complements, unlike English, which has the double-object construction in (2) and the dative construction in (3).

These facts about Japanese DCs immediately raise the following questions:

- What are the structures of the two variants in (1)? How are they derived?
- How does free order of the two objects arise?

It is difficult to answer these questions by just looking at the superficial patterns of Japanese DCs. To answer them, it is necessary to closely examine their syntactic properties.

In fact, a lot of work has been done to provide answers to these questions, yielding interesting empirical discoveries and theoretical consequences. Two major approaches to these questions have been proposed in the literature, which I review in section 16.3. I discuss various arguments for and against those approaches in sections 16.4 and 16.5. It becomes clear that some of the previous proposals are incompatible with each other. Given this state of affairs, we might ask if it is possible to unify the results of the previous studies. This is the topic of section 16.6.

The rich results of the previous studies of Japanese DCs have various important consequences and implications in a broader context. Given this, it is also a goal of this chapter to make clear the contribution that the study of Japanese DCs makes to linguistic theory in general. Specifically, I raise the following question: How does the study of Japanese DCs contribute to the development of linguistic theory? I address this question in section 16.7, which concludes the chapter.

16.3 Two Major Approaches to Japanese DCs

16.3.1 The Scrambling Approach: Hoji (1985)

The alternation in (1) shows a free-word-order phenomenon with two internal arguments of Japanese DCs. Two major approaches have been proposed to account for this phenomenon—Hoji (1985) and Miyagawa (1996, 1997). In this subsection, I review Hoji's approach. Miyagawa's approach is discussed in section 16.3.2.

On the basis of an extensive investigation of Japanese DCs, Hoji (1985) observes that despite the free word order between the two objects, Japanese DCs show asymmetries between goal-theme and theme-goal orders with respect to (backward) pronominal variable binding. The following are Hoji's original examples (Hoji 1985:122–125):

(4) a. *Kimi-wa [$_{NP}$ [$_S$ e_i e_j okuttekita] hito$_i$]-ni nani$_j$-o okurikaesita no.
 you-TOP   sent.over person-DAT what-ACC sent.back Q
 'What did you send back to the person that had sent it to you?'
 a'. Kimi-wa nani$_j$-o [$_{NP}$ [$_S$ e_i e_j okuttekita] hito$_i$]-ni okurikaesita no.
 you-TOP what-ACC   sent.over person-DAT sent.back Q
 b. Kimi-wa [$_{NP}$ [$_S$ e_i e_j okuttekita] hon$_j$]-o dare$_i$-ni okurikaesita no.
 you-TOP   sent.over book-ACC who-DAT sent.back Q
 'Who did you send back the book that he had sent to you?'
 b'. Kimi-wa dare$_i$-ni [$_{NP}$ [$_S$ e_i e_j okuttekita] hon$_j$]-o okurikaesita no.
 you-TOP who-DAT   sent.over book-ACC sent.back Q

The empty elements e_j in (4a) and e_i in (4b) are regarded as empty pronouns (i.e., *pro*). Hoji points out that there is a contrast between (4a) and (4b) with respect to the possibility of a bound-variable interpretation: e_i in (4b) can be interpreted as bound by the goal *wh*-phrase *dare* 'who', but e_j in (4a) cannot be interpreted as bound by the theme *wh*-phrase *nani* 'what'.[1] The contrast cannot be accounted for in linear terms, given that the *pro* precedes the *wh*-phrase in both cases. Hoji proposes an account of the contrast based on the following claims:

(5) a. Whereas the theme argument is base-generated in the complement of V, the goal argument is base-generated in the specifier of V.
 b. The theme-goal order results from scrambling of the theme over the goal.

Hoji in effect claims that the VP-internal structure of Japanese is configurational rather than flat. On the assumption that Japanese is head-final and that both complements and specifiers appear to the left of their sisters, (5a) ensures that the goal precedes the theme on the surface if no movement takes place. The claim in (5b) explains the other order. Let us refer to the type of scrambling invoked in (5b) as short scrambling, to distinguish it from longer scrambling—that is, short scrambling is scrambling to a postsubject position inside a clause, and longer scrambling is scrambling to a presubject position inside a clause or scrambling out of a clause. Hoji claims that short scrambling involves adjunction to VP. On Hoji's analysis, the lack of the bound-variable interpretation in (4a) follows from the fact that the *pro* is not c-commanded by the *wh*-phrase at any point in the overt derivation.[2] The status of (4b), Hoji argues, is a consequence of short scrambling of the theme shown in (6).

(6) Kimi-wa [$_{NP}$ ... pro_i ...]-o$_j$ dare$_i$-ni t_j okurikaesita no.

The theme phrase has moved from a position c-commanded by the goal phrase, so that the *pro* contained in the former can be bound by the latter through reconstruction. Hoji's analysis thus captures the contrast between (4a) and (4b).[3]

Hoji argues that his proposal in (5) accounts for facts related to quantifier scope as well. He discusses the examples in (7) (Hoji 1985:257–258).

(7) a. John-ga   daremo-ni   Bill-ka Mary-o   syookaisita.
       John-NOM everyone-DAT   Bill-or Mary-ACC introduced
       'John introduced Bill or Mary to everyone.'
   b. John-ga   Bill-ka Mary-o   daremo-ni   syookaisita.
       John-NOM Bill-or Mary-ACC everyone-DAT   introduced

Hoji observes that whereas (7a) is unambiguous, having only a reading on which *daremo* has wider scope than *Bill-ka Mary*, (7b) is ambiguous, permitting the opposite scope reading in addition to the one available in (7a). The contrast follows under the proposal in (5), with the assumption about scope relations in Japanese that if no movement is involved, scope relations between two quantifiers correspond to their surface order, whereas if one quantifier moves over the other, scope ambiguity results (Kuroda 1970). On Hoji's view, (7a) involves no movement and hence only *daremo* has wide scope, but in (7b) *Bill-ka Mary-o* has scrambled over *daremo-ni* and this makes the inverse scope reading, as well as the surface scope reading, possible.

Thus, Hoji's (1985) approach rests crucially on the idea that short scrambling is responsible for the free-word-order phenomenon seen in Japanese DCs. Let us call Hoji's approach the scrambling approach.

16.3.2 The Base-Generation Approach: Miyagawa (1996, 1997)

Whereas Hoji (1985) claims that the goal is always higher than the theme in the base structure, Miyagawa (1996, 1997) challenges this claim.[4] Among the arguments Miyagawa provides for his approach, I take up one here that is based on an observation about forward binding of the Japanese reciprocal *otagai* 'each other.'

Recall that the examples in (4) show an asymmetry between the goal-theme order and the theme-goal order with respect to backward binding. Miyagawa (1996, 1997) points out that such an asymmetry is not found with forward binding. Let us first look at the examples in (8) (from Miyagawa 1997:4–5).

(8) a. ???[John-to   Mary]-o$_i$ otagai-ga   t$_i$ mita.
           John-and Mary-ACC   each.other-NOM   saw
           'John and Mary, each other saw.'
    b. [John-to   Mary]-o$_i$ otagai-no   sensei-ga   t$_i$ mita.
        John-and Mary-ACC   each.other-GEN   teacher-NOM   saw
        'John and Mary, each other's teachers saw.'

Both examples have the object in front of the subject. It is standardly assumed that these cases involve scrambling of the object from the position of the trace. Although forward binding is perfect in (8b), it is degraded in (8a). Miyagawa attributes the latter fact to the effects of Rizzi's (1986) Chain Condition, which is defined in (9).[5]

(9) $C = (\alpha_1, \ldots, \alpha_n)$ is a chain iff, for $1 < i < n$, α_i is the local binder of α_{i+1}.

(10) α is a binder of β iff, for α, β = any category, α and β are coindexed, and α c-commands β; α is the local binder of β iff α is a binder of β and there is no γ such that γ is a binder of β, and γ is not a binder of α.

In (8a) the object has moved over the subject. Given that the subject c-commands the trace of the object and is coindexed with it, the subject is the local binder of the trace, according to (10). The Chain Condition in (9) then requires that the subject, not the moved object, form a chain with the trace of the object. Because the moved object cannot form a chain with its trace, it cannot be interpreted properly and hence the sentence is excluded.

Let us now consider (11) ((11b), together with the judgment, is from Miyagawa 1997:5).

(11) a. John-ga   [Hanako-to   Mary]$_i$-ni (paatii-de) otagai$_i$-o
        John-NOM   Hanako-and   Mary-DAT   party-at   each.other-ACC
        syookaisita.
        introduced
        'John introduced each other to Hanako and Mary (at the party).'
    b. (?)John-ga   [Hanako-to   Mary]$_i$-o   (paatii-de) otagai$_i$-ni
        John-NOM   Hanako-and   Mary-ACC   party-at   each.other-DAT
        syookaisita.
        introduced
        'John introduced Hanako and Mary to each other (at the party).'

Snyder (1992) and Miyagawa (1996, 1997) observe that the example in (11b) is acceptable, in contrast to the example in (8a).[6] The fact that (11b) is better than (8a) is puzzling if the theme phrase has undergone movement, as in Hoji's (1985) analysis. Given the Chain Condition, the grammatical status of (11b) implies that no movement is involved in this example. These considerations led Miyagawa to the following claims:

(12) a. The goal and theme arguments are freely base-generated in VP in either order.
    b. VP-internal scrambling does not exist.

Like Hoji (1985), Miyagawa takes a configurational approach to the structure of Japanese VP. Under this approach, (12) means that the theme and the goal can freely appear in the complement or specifier of V. Therefore, on Miyagawa's view, word-order permutations between the two arguments cannot result from short scrambling but must rather result from base-generation. Let us call Miyagawa's approach the base-generation approach.

Recall that Hoji (1985) points out that there is an asymmetry in scope interpretation between (7a) and (7b). Miyagawa (1997) takes up the same issue but claims that there is no such asymmetry. He judges both (13a,b) to be ambiguous.[7]

(13) a. Hanako-ga   dareka-ni   daremo-o   syookaisita.
        Hanako-NOM   someone-DAT   everyone-ACC introduced
        'Hanako introduced everyone to someone.'
    b. Hanako-ga   dareka-o   daremo-ni   syookaisita.
        Hanako-NOM   someone-ACC   everyone-DAT introduced

Miyagawa argues that the ambiguity in both examples in (13) follows from his proposals in (12), coupled with another proposal he makes—namely, that focus movement can move the lower object overtly over the higher object. Thus, on his analysis, the order in (13a) can be associated with a derivation in which *dareka-ni* has moved (by focus movement) from a position lower than *daremo-o*, and the order in (13b) with a derivation in which *dareka-o* has moved from a position lower than *daremo-ni*. The availability of focus movement in the two cases makes it possible for each of the two quantifiers to take wide scope (recall that in Japanese, scope ambiguity arises only when one quantifier overtly moves over the other).

There is an important issue arising here. As pointed out by Takano (1998: 850–852), the postulation of focus movement causes a problem for Miyagawa's approach. As in the case of quantifier scope, it predicts no asymmetry between the goal-theme and theme-goal orders. This cannot be correct, given Hoji's (1985) observation that there is indeed an asymmetry between the two orders with respect to (backward) pronominal variable binding, as illustrated in (4a,b) (and (ia,b) in note 1).

So far, I have reviewed two major approaches to Japanese DCs—Hoji's (1985) scrambling approach and Miyagawa's (1996, 1997) base-generation approach. There is in fact a third approach proposed in the literature, one that has the properties of both the base-generation and scrambling approaches. This account has been developed by Kitagawa (1994).[8] Details aside, Kitagawa proposes that Japanese has both the double-object and dative constructions, and that the two constructions differ in surface order. Thus, according to him, the goal-theme order corresponds to the double-object structure in (2a), whereas the theme-goal order corresponds to the dative structure in (3a). Kitagawa claims that the two constructions are derived without movement of either internal argument. In this sense, it is a variant of the base-generation approach.[9]

However, Kitagawa (1994) also allows scrambling to move the lower object over the higher one in both constructions. On this approach, then, there should be no asymmetries between the two orders—either one can be base-generated and can also involve scrambling of the lower object over the higher one. In fact, Kitagawa claims, like Miyagawa (1997), that there is no asymmetry with respect to quantifier scope, with both orders yielding ambiguity. Kitagawa addresses pronominal variable binding, too, observing that examples such as (4a) are not as bad as standard weak crossover effects induced by SOV sentences in which the object is a quantifier and the subject contains a pronoun bound by the object quantifier, and that examples such as (4b) are not as good as standard reconstruction effects induced by OSV sentences in which the subject is a quantifier and the moved object contains a pronoun bound by the subject quantifier. Hoji (1985:122, 125, 302–303) notes these points, too (in fact, Kitagawa cites Hoji's observations) but crucially claims that there is still a contrast between (4a) and (4b) (and between (7a) and (7b)) that supports his proposal in (5) (see also note 3). Kitagawa's approach thus has the same properties as Miyagawa's (1996, 1997) approach equipped with the focus-movement strategy (recall the discussion surrounding (13)).

As mentioned before, Kitagawa makes another important claim—namely, that Japanese has both double-object and dative structures. I return to this issue in section 16.5.2 when I discuss a proposal of Miyagawa and Tsujioka (2004).

To sum up so far, I have discussed the two major approaches to free word order in Japanese DCs—the scrambling approach and the base-generation approach. We have seen that the scrambling approach can explain the fact that backward binding is possible only in the theme-goal order, whereas the base-generation approach can explain the lack of Chain Condition effects in the theme-goal order. We have also seen that Hoji (1985) and Miyagawa (1997) report different judgments on quantifier-scope phenomena that are consistent with their respective proposals.[10]

The scrambling approach and the base-generation approach have been explored in subsequent work by various researchers. In the next two sections, I review developments of the two approaches advanced in the literature.

16.4 ARGUMENTS FOR THE SCRAMBLING APPROACH

The scrambling approach is advocated by Koizumi (1995), Takano (1998), and Yatsushiro (2003). Let us discuss their arguments in turn.

16.4.1 Koizumi (1995)

Koizumi (1995) argues for the scrambling approach on the basis of examples involving quantifier floating. Let us first consider the following examples (CL = classifier):

(14) a. Sannin-no gakusei-ga piza-o tabeta.
     three.CL-GEN student-NOM pizza-ACC ate
     'Three students ate pizza.'
   b. Gakusei-ga sannin piza-o tabeta.
     student-NOM three.CL pizza-ACC ate
   c. Gakusei-ga piza-o nikire tabeta.
     student-NOM pizza-ACC two.CL ate
     'A student ate two slices of pizza.'

In Japanese, if a numeral quantifier (NQ) occurs inside an NP, it necessarily has the genitive case particle -no, as in (14a). The NQ sannin in (14b) does not have a genitive case particle, which indicates that it is outside an NP. It is thus a floating NQ construed with the subject NP. The NQ in (14c) is also a floating NQ; it is construed with the object NP.

There is a locality restriction on the relation between a floating NQ and its host NP (i.e., the NP with which it is construed). Consider the following:

(15) a. *Gakusei-ga piza-o sannin tabeta.
      student-NOM pizza-ACC three.CL ate
      'Three students ate pizza.'
    b. Piza-o gakusei-ga nikire tabeta.
      pizza-ACC student-NOM two.CL ate
      'A student ate two slices of pizza.'

As (15a) shows, an NQ construed with the subject cannot appear between the object and the verb. This indicates that a floating NQ must be close enough to its host NP. Defining the notion of locality relevant here is a matter of debate and does not concern us here (see Koizumi 1995 for his own analysis of (15) and references cited therein for earlier analyses). What matters is the fact that an argument phrase cannot intervene between a floating NQ and its host NP. In this light, the grammaticality of (15b) is interesting, given that the subject intervenes between the NQ *nikire* and its host NP *piza-o*, which is the object. The standard analysis of this fact appeals to scrambling (see Haig 1980 and Kuroda 1980, 1983). Thus, (15b) is grammatical because the object NP has scrambled from its base-generated position and hence the NQ is close enough to the trace/copy of the object NP. Put differently, this analysis connects the grammaticality of (15b) with that of (14c) by way of scrambling.

Koizumi (1995:108) extends this analysis to DCs, claiming that the grammaticality of (16a) is accounted for in terms of short scrambling of the theme over the goal.

(16) a. John-ga piza-o Mary-ni nikire ageta.
      John-NOM pizza-ACC Mary-DAT two.CL gave
      'John gave two slices of pizza to Mary.'
    b. John-ga Mary-ni piza-o nikire ageta.
      John-NOM Mary-DAT pizza-ACC two.CL gave

In (16a) the goal argument intervenes between the NQ *nikire* and its host *piza-o*, which is the theme argument. Koizumi claims that the grammaticality of (16a) is to be assimilated to that of (15b)—that is, he claims that (16a) receives the same account as (16b) if the theme, generated lower than the goal, scrambles over the goal to yield the theme-goal order. Koizumi's analysis of (16a) thus constitutes an argument for the scrambling approach.

16.4.2 Takano (1998)

The next argument for the scrambling approach is provided by Takano (1998). Takano supports the scrambling approach from the point of view of the generality of Hoji's (1985) claim, arguing that short scrambling exists not only in Japanese but also in English.

Recall that Hoji (1985) claims that the goal argument is base-generated higher than the theme argument. In contrast, Larson (1988) advocates an opposite thematic hierarchy in which the theme is higher than the goal. Larson put forth this proposal to account for the properties of DCs in English.

Takano (1998) points out that it is highly unlikely that the properties of thematic prominence differ from language to language and argues that Hoji's thematic hierarchy in fact holds for English as well. English has a double-complement construction where the two complements are both PPs, as in (17a). Moreover, this construction allows the order of the two PPs to be free, as shown by the alternation between (17a) and (17b).

(17) a. I talked to John about Mary.
 b. I talked about Mary to John.

Takano claims that (17) is parallel to (1). Following Larson (1988), Takano assumes that the *to*-phrase is the goal and the *about*-phrase is the theme. If so, and if Hoji (1985) is correct, (17a) should be the base order and (17b) should involve scrambling of the *about*-phrase over the *to*-phrase, as shown in (18).

(18) I talked$_i$-v [$_{VP}$ [about Mary]$_j$ [$_{VP}$ to John t_i t_j]].

Takano argues that this is the correct analysis by pointing out the examples in (19) (Takano 1998:837–838).

(19) a. *I talked to each other's mothers about the boys.
 a'. ?I talked about the boys to each other's mothers.
 b. ?I talked about each other's mothers to the boys.
 b'. I talked to the boys about each other's mothers.

Particularly important here is the contrast between (19a) and (19b), which Takano argues is exactly parallel to the contrast between (4a) and (4b) in Japanese. Extending Hoji's (1985) proposal, Takano argues that the property in (5a) is universal, so that the order in (19a) reflects the base structure, whereas that in (19b) results from short scrambling of the theme (the *about*-phrase) over the goal (the *to*-phrase). On this view, (19a) violates condition A of the binding theory, but (19b) satisfies it due to reconstruction.

On the basis of this analysis of the cases in (19), Takano (1998) concludes that English, too, has scrambling of the theme over the goal, thus supporting the scrambling approach from a cross-linguistic point of view.

The hypothesis that (5a) is universal also led Takano (1998) to propose a new analysis of the English dative construction in (20).

(20) John gave a picture to Mary.

Specifically, Takano proposes that the theme necessarily moves over the goal in such cases, as shown in (21), contrary to Larson (1988), who argues that theme-goal reflects the base order.[11]

(21) John gave [a picture]$_i$ to Mary t_i.

One valuable consequence of this analysis is that it can treat the acceptable status of cases such as (22), originally noted by Burzio (1986), in exactly the same way as that of English (19b) and Japanese (4b).[12]

(22) ?I gave each other's babies to the mothers.

Takano (1998) claims that the unification of (4b), (19b), and (22) lends additional support to the scrambling approach, according to which the theme-goal order is derived by short scrambling of the theme from a position lower than the goal (thereby making backward binding possible through reconstruction).

A further consequence of Takano's (1998) proposal concerns the important difference between cases such as (17) and those such as (20): order between the goal and the theme is free in the former but not in the latter (see (3)). Takano provides a Case-theoretic account of this fact and also proposes to generalize the English-internal difference between (17) and (20) to the cross-linguistic difference between Japanese (1) and English (3) noted in section 16.2. His proposal has nontrivial implications for parametric variation between English and Japanese and for the nature of Universal Grammar (UG). I return to these issues in section 16.7.

16.4.3 Yatsushiro (2003)

As previously discussed, one of Takano's (1998) contributions is to show the generality of Hoji's (1985) claims in (5), by demonstrating that short scrambling exists in English as well, thereby lending further support to the scrambling approach. Recall, however, that the fact shown in (11) that forward binding is possible in either order supports the base-generation approach. Takano leaves this issue untouched, but it is squarely addressed by Yatsushiro (2003). Yatsushiro argues that a close examination of Chain Condition effects with Japanese DCs in fact leads us to conclude that the scrambling approach is correct.

Yatsushiro (2003) claims that the reciprocal anaphor, due to its semantics, cannot be subject to the Chain Condition and that both the deviance in (8a) and the lack of deviance in (11b) are due to special properties of the reciprocal anaphor instead of the Chain Condition. She provides an account of (8a) and (11b) compatible with the scrambling approach by appealing to covert movement of the 'each'-part of the reciprocal, in the spirit of the analysis of English *each other* proposed by Heim, Lasnik, and May (1991a,b) (see Yatsushiro 2003 for details).

Under the scrambling approach, Yatsushiro's claim about (11b) predicts that the example should become deviant if the reciprocal is replaced by a reflexive, which is clearly subject to the Chain Condition. Yatsushiro (2003:147, 149) gives the examples in (23) to show that the prediction is partially borne out.

(23) a. (?*)Uli-o karezisin-ga hometa.
Uli-ACC himself-NOM praised
'Himself praised Uli.'

b. (*)Uli-ga   Jonathan-o   karezisin-ni miseta.
      Uli-NOM   Jonathan-ACC   himself-DAT   showed
      'Uli showed Jonathan to himself.'
   c. ?Uli-ga   Jonathan-ni   karezisin-o   miseta.
      Uli-NOM   Jonathan-DAT   himself-ACC   showed
      'Uli showed himself to Jonathan.'

Example (23a) involves scrambling of the object over the subject, and (23b), given the scrambling approach, involves scrambling of the theme over the goal, in contrast to (23c), which is derived without scrambling. Yatsushiro reports that speakers' judgments vary on (23a,b) in such a way that whereas some speakers find them to be deviant, others find them to be acceptable.[13]

So, to the extent that there are speakers who find a significant contrast between (23b) and (23c), the fact shows that the theme-goal order of the Japanese DC exhibits Chain Condition effects, thereby supporting the scrambling approach.

Yatsushiro's (2003) view on Chain Condition effects in Japanese is challenged by Miyagawa and Tsujioka (2004). I return to this issue in section 16.6.

16.5 Arguments against Hoji's (1985) Analysis

Let us turn now to arguments against Hoji's (1985) analysis of Japanese DCs. I take up two proposals here—one by Matsuoka (2003) and the other by Miyagawa and Tsujioka (2004).

16.5.1 Matsuoka (2003)

Matsuoka (2003) proposes that Japanese ditransitive verbs do not constitute a uniform class but come in two types—the *pass*-type and the *show*-type—and that *pass*-type verbs take a theme and a goal, whereas *show*-type verbs take a theme and an experiencer. According to Matsuoka, the *pass*-type includes such verbs as *watasu* 'pass', *kakeru* 'put', and *todokeru* 'deliver', whereas the *show*-type includes *miseru* 'show', *abiseru* 'pour', *kasu* 'lend', and *kiseru* 'put (clothes)'. Matsuoka moreover claims that with the *pass*-type, the theme phrase is higher than the goal phrase in the base structure, which is exactly opposite to Hoji's (1985) view.[14] Among the arguments Matsuoka presents for this view, I discuss two here—one relating to variable binding and the other relating to a pattern of alternation seen between DCs and their inchoative counterparts.

Matsuoka (2003:183) observes that the following example allows bound-variable interpretation (the judgment is Matsuoka's):

(24) ?John-ga [[e$_i$ pro$_j$ tyuumonsita] seito$_i$]-ni [subete-no hon]$_j$-o watasita.
      John-NOM   ordered   student-DAT all-GEN book-ACC passed
      'John passed every book to the student who ordered it.'

The availability of the bound-variable interpretation is unexpected under Hoji's (1985) view, according to which goal-theme reflects the base order. Given that the sentence in (24) has the goal-theme order, no movement should be involved and the bound-variable reading should be disallowed. If this sentence allows the bound-variable reading, as Matsuoka claims, then it is a counterexample to Hoji's approach. On the basis of the judgment indicated in (24), Matsuoka proposes that the base position of the theme is higher than that of the goal and that the goal-theme order in (24) is derived by scrambling of the goal over the theme, which makes binding possible through reconstruction.

Matsuoka (2003) also argues for the theme being higher than the goal on the basis of the sentence pattern of inchoative variants of *pass*-type verbs. The basic pattern of interest is illustrated in (25) (Matsuoka 2003:173).

(25) a. John-ga   {Mary-ni   hanataba-o/ hanataba-o   Mary-ni}
          John-NOM Mary-DAT bouquet-ACC bouquet-ACC Mary-DAT
          watasita.
          passed
          'John passed a bouquet to Mary.'
      b. Hanataba-ga   Mary-ni   watatta.
          bouquet-NOM   Mary-DAT   passed
          'A bouquet passed to Mary.'
      c. *Mary-ga   hanataba-o   watatta.
          Mary-NOM   bouquet-ACC passed
          'Mary got a bouquet passed to her.'

The ditransitive verb *watas(u)* and its inchoative counterpart *watar(u)* are morphologically related. The interesting facts in (25) are that the (accusative) theme object of the ditransitive sentence in (25a) becomes the (nominative) subject of the inchoative sentence in (25b) and that the (dative) goal of the ditransitive can never become the subject of the inchoative, as shown in (25c). Following the spirit of Baker's (1993, 1995) original proposal for similar cases in English, Matsuoka argues that this alternation pattern is explained in syntactic terms. More specifically, he claims that the theme is higher than the goal in the base and hence that in the inchoative, the theme, which is closer to T than the goal, is attracted by T in accordance with the Minimal Link Condition.

Both of Matsuoka's (2003) arguments are intended to show that the theme is higher than the goal in the base structure, contrary to Hoji's (1985) proposal. However, there are problems with his arguments. I return to this point in section 16.6.

16.5.2 Miyagawa and Tsujioka (2004)

Miyagawa and Tsujioka (2004) argue against Hoji's (1985) view on Japanese DCs from a new perspective, making several new claims about Japanese DCs. First, they claim that Japanese, just like English, has both the double-object and the dative constructions.[15] It is well known that the double-object construction has properties that its dative counterpart does not have. Miyagawa and Tsujioka take up two such properties—the effects of causation and those of possession (see Oerhle 1976; Bresnan 1978, 1982; and references cited in Miyagawa and Tsujioka 2004). Consider (26) and (27).

(26) a. The article gave me a headache.
 b. *The article gave a headache to me.

(27) a. I sent the boarder/*the border a package.
 b. I sent a package to the boarder/the border.

The contrast in (26) shows that the verb of the double-object construction can carry a causative meaning, whereas that of the dative construction cannot. The examples in (27) show that whereas the first object of the double-object construction is necessarily construed as a possessor of the theme and hence must be animate, the same does not hold for the object of the preposition in the dative. Miyagawa and Tsujioka regard the object of the preposition in the dative construction as a location rather than a possessor.

This means that there are two kinds of goal. Miyagawa and Tsujioka (2004) call the goal interpreted as a possessor the "high goal" and the goal interpreted as a location the "low goal." As these names suggest, the high goal appears in a high position, and the low goal appears in a low position.

The fact that the double-object construction (with the high goal) and the dative construction (with the low goal) have different properties strongly suggests that they have different structures. To account for the properties of the double-object construction, Miyagawa and Tsujioka (2004) adopt the structure in (28) proposed by Marantz (1993).[16]

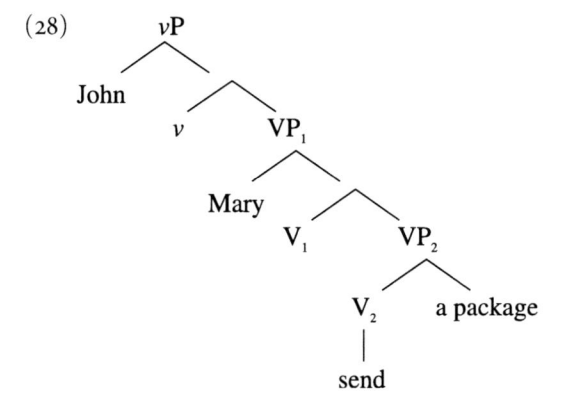

(28)
```
         vP
        /  \
    John    \
           v  VP₁
              /  \
          Mary    \
              V₁   VP₂
                   /  \
                 V₂   a package
                  |
                 send
```

In this structure, V_1 is regarded as an applicative head that relates the event in the VP_2 to the DP in its specifier, namely, the high goal. This applicative head is assumed to give rise to the causative interpretation in (26a). It is also considered to be the source of the animacy restriction on the goal argument seen in (27a): the applicative head, due to its semantics, forces the argument in its specifier to be interpreted as a possessor of the theme and so the inanimate goal is impossible in (27a).

The dative construction, in contrast, is claimed to lack the applicative head in its structure. Therefore, both the theme and the low goal appear in the same VP, as shown in (29).

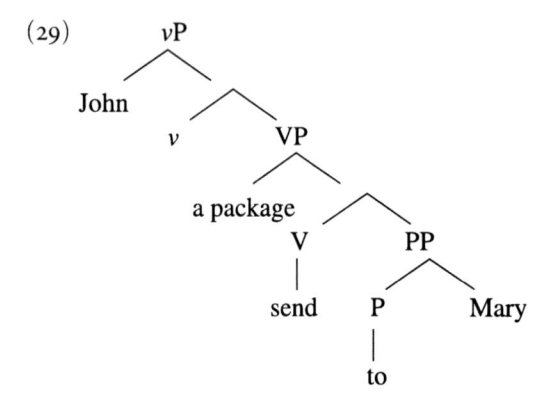

(29)
```
            vP
           /  \
       John    \
              / \
             v   VP
                / \
        a package \
                  / \
                 V   PP
                 |  / \
              send P   Mary
                   |
                   to
```

The absence of the applicative head is argued to derive the facts in (26b) and (27b). That is, (26b) is ungrammatical because the sentence cannot receive a causative interpretation due to the lack of the applicative head, and (27b) can have an inanimate goal because its structure does not have the applicative head, which forces a possessor interpretation on the argument in its specifier.

Miyagawa and Tsujioka (2004) extend this analysis to Japanese DCs. They propose that there are two kinds of goals in Japanese DCs as well and that the high goal is generated in the specifier of the applicative head in the same structure as that in (28) (modulo the complement-head order), whereas the low goal is generated in the (lower) VP, as in (29). They also propose that when both the low goal and the theme are present, they are generated freely within the same VP, in the spirit of the base-generation approach. On this view, then, the high goal is always generated in the specifier of the applicative head and so its position is fixed, whereas the low goal is subject to free generation inside VP. As is discussed later, scrambling of the theme over the high goal is blocked. As a result, in this new theory, word-order permutation occurs only between the theme and the low goal (through base generation).

Note that Japanese DCs, unlike the English equivalents, do not have two morphologically distinct ways of marking the goal argument. Thus, Japanese has only one morphosyntactic form, as in (31), for the two English sentences in (30).

(30) a. John sent Mary a package.
      b. John sent a package to Mary.

(31) John-ga   {Mary-ni   nimotu-o/   nimotu-o   Mary-ni} okutta.
     John-NOM Mary-DAT package-ACC package-ACC Mary-DAT sent

As a result, it is not clear which of the two variants in (30) the sentence in (31) corresponds to. Recall that whereas the high goal is interpreted as a possessor, the low goal is interpreted as a location. On Miyagawa and Tsujioka's (2004) analysis, *Mary-ni* in (31), being animate, can be a high goal as well as a low goal, and hence the sentence is structurally ambiguous: it can involve the double-object structure (with the applicative head) or the dative structure (without the applicative head). However, if the goal is inanimate, as in (32), the sentence is unambiguously of the dative variety.

(32) John-ga   {Tokyo-ni   nimotu-o/   nimotu-o   Tokyo-ni} okutta.
     John-NOM Tokyo-DAT package-ACC package-ACC Tokyo-DAT sent

In (32) *Tokyo-ni* is necessarily the low goal.

To support their two-goal analysis of Japanese DCs, Miyagawa and Tsujioka (2004:5–6) point out that there is a difference in scope interpretation between (33a), which has an animate goal, and (33b), which has an inanimate goal.

(33) a. Taroo-ga   dareka-ni   dono nimotumo okutta.
        Taro-NOM someone-DAT   every package   sent
        'Taro sent someone every package.'
     b. Taroo-ga   dokoka-ni   dono nimotumo okutta.
        Taro-NOM some.place-DAT   every package   sent
        'Taro sent every package to some place.'

They observe that whereas (33a) is unambiguous, permitting only a 'some'>'every' reading, (33b) is ambiguous, permitting both a 'some' > 'every' reading and an 'every' > 'some' reading.[17] They then assimilate the contrast to the well-known contrast in (34) (Aoun and Li 1989).

(34) a. John sent some student every article.   some > every, *every > some
     b. John sent some article to every student. some > every, every > some

Marantz (1993) attributes the lack of ambiguity in (34a) to the existence of the complex VP structure in the double-object construction (see (28)) and the presence of ambiguity in (34b) to the absence of the complex VP structure in the dative (see (29)). Miyagawa and Tsujioka adopt this analysis for the Japanese cases in (33), arguing that (33a,b) have different structures, as predicted by the two-goal analysis.[18]

Miyagawa and Tsujioka (2004) also claim that the high goal (in the double-object construction) and the low goal (in the dative construction) differ in categorial status, even though they look identical superficially, in such a way that the former is a DP, whereas the latter is a PP. They provide evidence for this claim from floating numeral quantifiers (NQs). Consider (35).

(35) a. Taroo-ga   mati-o   hutatu otozureta.
       Taro-NOM   town-ACC   two.CL visited
       'Taro visited two towns.'
    b. *Hito-ga   mati-kara   hutatu kita.
       people-NOM   town-from   two.CL came
       'People came from two towns.'

Both examples in (35) contain floating NQs (see section 16.4.1). The contrast in (35) illustrates that an NQ can float off its host if the host is a DP but not if the host is a PP (Shibatani 1978:59–60).

Now consider (36).

(36) a. Taroo-ga   gakusei-ni   hutari nimotu-o   okutta.
       Taro-NOM   student-DAT two.CL package-ACC sent
       'Taro sent two students a package.'
    b. *Daitooryoo-ga kokkyoo-ni hutatu heitai-o   okutta.
       president-NOM border-to   two.CL soldier-ACC sent
       'The President sent two borders soldiers.'

The goal is animate in (36a) but inanimate in (36b), which indicates, given Miyagawa and Tsujioka's theory, that (36a) can be a double-object construction, whereas (36b) must be a dative construction. On the basis of their observation that the NQ can float in (36a) but not in (36b), Miyagawa and Tsujioka conclude that the high goal is a DP, whereas the low goal is a PP. This is another argument for their two-goal analysis.

Furthermore, Miyagawa and Tsujioka (2004) present what they consider to be the clearest evidence for their claim that there are two goal positions—it is possible for both goals to appear in the same sentence (Miyagawa and Tsujioka 2004:9):[19]

(37) Taroo-ga Hanako-ni   Tokyo-ni nimotu-o   okutta.
     Taro-NOM Hanako-DAT Tokyo-to package-ACC sent
     'Taro sent Hanako a package to Tokyo.'

According to Miyagawa and Tsujioka, (37) means that Taro sent a package to Tokyo, which is a location, with the intention that Hanako, who may not be in Tokyo, will come to possess it. This sentence, with the interpretation just given, shows that we need to have two positions for the *ni*-marked objects, one for the possessor (high goal) and another for the location (low goal). Moreover, the position for the possessor must be higher than that for the location, given the ungrammaticality of (38), according to Miyagawa and Tsujioka (2004:9).

(38) *Taroo-ga Tokyo-ni Hanako-ni   nimotu-o   okutta.
      Taro-NOM Tokyo-to Hanako-DAT package-ACC sent

The ungrammaticality of (38) also indicates that the low goal cannot scramble over the high goal. Similarly, (39) shows that the theme cannot scramble over the high goal (Miyagawa and Tsujioka 2004:9).

(39) */?Taroo-ga nimotu-o Hanako-ni Tokyo-ni okutta.
    Taro-NOM package-ACC Hanako-DAT Tokyo-to sent

The ungrammaticality of (38) and (39) supports the hypothesis that scrambling is not a free operation (Miyagawa 1996, 1997). Miyagawa and Tsujioka suggest that the applicative head is not a phase and therefore never bears an EPP-feature, the assumption here being that movement is triggered by an EPP-feature (Chomsky 2000). This is why neither the low goal nor the theme can move to the domain of the applicative head. If scrambling were a free operation, taking place without any driving force, (38) and (39) would be possible.

Notice that (39) also shows that the theme cannot move across the high goal to vP. To account for this, Miyagawa and Tsujioka appeal to locality, claiming that if v has an EPP-feature, it should attract the closest phrase, which is not the theme but the high goal. Thus, the theme can never be attracted by *v*.

Unlike the order between the high goal and the theme/low goal, the order between the low goal and the theme is free, so that the acceptability of (37) does not change if the low goal and the theme are switched around, as in (40) (Miyagawa and Tsujioka 2004:10).

(40) Taroo-ga Hanako-ni nimotu-o Tokyo-ni okutta.
    Taro-NOM Hanako-DAT package-ACC Tokyo-to sent

Miyagawa and Tsujioka claim that this fact follows under their analysis, according to which the low goal and the theme are freely base-generated within VP. Thus, on their view, the word-order alternation between (37) and (40) arises from base generation.

Finally, Miyagawa and Tsujioka (2004) provide a new argument for the base-generation approach based on idioms. Larson (1988:340) claims that the existence of "discontinuous idioms" such as those in (41) supports the idea that a verb and its outer complements can form a single thematic complex.

(41) a. Lasorda *sent* his starting pitcher *to the showers*.

  b. Mary *took* Felix *to the cleaners/to task/into consideration*.

  c. Felix *threw* Oscar *to the wolves*.

Larson observes that in each case in (41), the verb and its PP complement form a single thematic complex that assigns a θ-role to the DP object. To account for these idioms, Larson argues that in the English V-DP-PP constructions, the PP is base-generated in the complement of V, so that the verb and the PP complement form an underlying constituent excluding the DP object, which he claims occupies Spec,V.

Miyagawa and Tsujioka (2004:20–21) observe that Japanese has idioms of both the dative-V type and the accusative-V type, as illustrated in (42) and (43).

(42) a. Taroo-wa omotta koto-o *kuti-ni* *dasu*.
       Taro-TOP thought thing-ACC mouth-DAT let.out
       'Taro says what's on his mind.'

b. Taroo-wa hito-no koto-ni *kuti-o dasu.*
   Taro-TOP person-GEN thing-DAT mouth-ACC let.out
   'Taro cuts in on others' business.'

(43) a. Taroo-wa kuruma-o *te-ni ireta.*
   Taro-TOP car-ACC hand-DAT put.in
   'Taro acquired a car.'
   b. Taroo-wa genkoo-ni *te-o ireta.*
   Taro-TOP draft-DAT hand-ACC put.in
   'Taro revised the draft.'

These examples show that the same verb can appear in both dative-V and accusative-V idioms. On Larson's (1988) reasoning, this fact indicates that Japanese allows both the dative phrase and the accusative phrase to form an underlying constituent with the verb. Miyagawa and Tsujioka take this to be independent evidence that both the goal and the theme can be base-generated in the complement of V.

16.6 Prospects for Unification

So far, I have discussed studies arguing for Hoji's (1985) original approach to Japanese DCs and those arguing against it. These previous studies have produced many interesting, and sometimes conflicting, empirical discoveries and theoretical proposals. Given this state of affairs, it is important to consider how things stand now regarding the study of Japanese DCs and to ask if we can imagine a way of unifying the results of these previous studies, despite the fact that some of the proposals are incompatible with each other. In this section, I attempt to do this and suggest a possible direction in which such unification might be achieved.

16.6.1 Reexamination of Yatsushiro's (2003) and Matsuoka's (2003) Proposals

To this end, we first need to resolve conflicts arising from some of the claims made in the previous studies. For this purpose, I reexamine the proposals of Yatsushiro (2003) and Matsuoka (2003) and show that their original claims cannot be upheld.

Let us consider Yatsushiro's (2003) proposal again. Recall that her proposal rests on the claim that the reciprocal anaphor cannot be subject to the Chain Condition. She bases this claim on the idea that the relation between the reciprocal and its antecedent is strictly speaking not one of coreference, so that the Chain Condition does not apply to the reciprocal if it is relevant only to coreferential phrases (see Yatsushiro 2003:sect. 3.2). She then argues that Japanese *karezisin* 'he.self', unlike *otagai* 'each.other', does obey the Chain Condition, as we have reviewed. This part of her claim has been challenged by Miyagawa and Tsujioka (2004), however. Miyagawa and Tsujioka (2004:24–27) point out that *karezisin* can never function as a bound variable and hence cannot enter into binding.[20] Given that the Chain Condition is couched in terms of binding, they argue that *karezisin* cannot be subject to the Chain Condition, contrary to Yatsushiro's proposal.

I add nothing to this debate here but instead focus on an empirical argument Yatsushiro (2003) provides against treating the lack of deviance in (11b) by recourse to base generation. Consider (44) (from Yatsushiro 2003:152).

(44) ?Uli-ga Jonathan-to Susi-o otagai-ni hihans-ase-ta.
Uli-NOM Jonathan-and Susi-ACC each.other-DAT criticize-make-PAST
'Uli made each other criticize Jonathan and Susi.'

The example in (44) is a causative construction where *otagai-ni* 'each.other-DAT' is a causee and *Jonathan-to Susi-o* 'Jonathan-and Susi-ACC' is an object of the embedded verb *hihans* 'criticize.' Assuming that the dative causee is the subject of the embedded clause and that the object cannot be base-generated higher than the subject, Yatsushiro points out that (44) cannot be derived by base generation but should involve scrambling of the embedded object over the embedded subject. Yatsushiro judges (44) to be better than (8a) even though (44), like (8a), involves movement of the kind prohibited by the Chain Condition. Yatsushiro argues that this constitutes a problem for the analysis that attributes the grammaticality of (11b) to base generation of the theme higher than the goal.

This argument based on (44) is not as convincing as it appears. First of all, I am not sure how much better (44) is than (8a). In fact, examination of similar cases involving a control complement clause seems to show that *otagai* does induce Chain Condition effects:

(45) Yumi-ga Masao-to Ken-o otagai-no tomodati-ni hihansuru
Yumi-NOM Masao-and Ken-ACC each.other-GEN friend-DAT criticize
yooni meezita.
that ordered
'Yumi ordered each other's friends to criticize Masao and Ken.'

In (45) *Masao-to Ken-o* is an object of the embedded verb *hihansuru* 'criticize' and *otagai-no tomodati-ni* 'each.other-GEN friend-DAT' is an object of the matrix verb *meezita* 'ordered.' Thus, the former has clearly been scrambled from within the embedded control clause. In this context, the scrambled object can license *otagai*, as evidenced by the grammaticality of (45) (see Nemoto 1993 for much relevant discussion). If the matrix object is replaced by *otagai-ni* 'each.other-DAT', however, the sentence becomes as deviant as (8a), in my judgment:

(46) ??Yumi-ga Masao-to Ken-o otagai-ni hihansuru yooni meezita.
Yumi-NOM Masao-and Ken-ACC each.other-DAT criticize that ordered
'Yumi ordered each other to criticize Masao and Ken.'

These observations strongly suggest that *otagai* is subject to the Chain Condition, contrary to Yatsushiro's (2003) claim.[21] If so, the acceptability of (11b), which is unexpected under the scrambling approach, does seem to require an analysis invoking base generation of the theme higher than the (low) goal, a conclusion backed up by the idiom facts discovered by Miyagawa and Tsujioka (2004).

Let us return next to Matsuoka's (2003) proposal that the theme is generated higher than the goal. He presents (24) as evidence in favor of this proposal. This argument, however, seems weak. First of all, it is not clear that (24) allows the intended bound-variable interpretation. Matsuoka (2003:fn. 11) even notes that half of the speakers he consulted rejected the bound-variable interpretation in (24). I find (24) quite unacceptable on the bound-variable reading and see a clear contrast between (24) and (47).

(47) John-ga [[*pro$_i$ e$_j$* rirekisyo-o okutta] kaisya$_j$]-ni
John-NOM   CV-ACC   sent   company-DAT
[subete-no   gakusei]$_i$-ni iku   yooni   meezita.
all-GEN   student-DAT go   that   ordered
'John ordered every student to go to the company to which he sent his CV.'

In (47) the dative phrase that belongs to a control complement clause is placed in front of the dative object of the matrix verb. Thus, the first dative phrase has clearly been scrambled from within the embedded clause. The intended bound-variable interpretation is much more readily available in (47) than in (24), in my judgment. This suggests that (24) does not involve scrambling of the dative phrase over the accusative phrase, contrary to Matsuoka's analysis.

One factor that makes judgment obscure in (24) is the use of *pro* as a bound element. Hoji (2003) claims that examples containing *pro* cannot be reliable data showing the presence of a bound-variable interpretation in Japanese because Japanese *pro* can be plural-denoting. Another potential factor that may affect judgment in (24) is the QP *subete-no hon* 'all-GEN book'. Hoji (2003) points out, citing Ueyama (1998), that QPs such as *subete-no hon* can be used to refer to a specific group of entities and that this obscures judgment on the bound-variable interpretation. Thus, in (24) *pro* can be understood to refer to the entire group of books under discussion, in which case *pro* is not interpreted as a variable bound by the QP (but instead as coreferential with the QP). To avoid these interfering factors, we should use an overt element, in place of *pro*, and a QP that is not (easily) interpretable as referring to a specific group of individuals. So let us change (24) to (48a).

(48) a. *John-ga [[e$_i$ sore$_j$-o   tyuumonsita]   seito$_i$]-ni
        John-NOM   it-ACC   ordered   student-DAT
        [sansatu-izyoo-no   hon]$_j$-o   watasita.
        three.CL-or.more-GEN   book-ACC   passed
        'John passed three or more books to the students who ordered them.'

b. John-ga   [sansatu-izyoo-no   hon]ⱼ-o
   John-NOM   three.CL-or.more-GEN book-ACC
   [[eᵢ soreⱼ-o tyuumonsita] seitoᵢ]-ni   watasita.
        it-ACC ordered   student-DAT passed

I believe that (48a) does not have a reading on which *sore* 'it' is bound by the QP *sansatu-izyoo-no hon* 'three.CL-or.more-GEN books', in contrast to its variant in (48b), which does have this reading. I also believe that the judgment is clearer here than in (24), consistent with Hoji's (2003) observations.

Incidentally, Hoji's (1985) contrast in (4) can be reproduced in the same way. Thus, (49) contrasts with (48a).[22]

(49) ?John-ga   [[soitui-ga   tyuumonsita] hon-o]
     John-NOM   that.person-NOM ordered   book-ACC
     [sannin-izyoo-no   seito]i-ni   watasita.
     three.CL-or.more-GEN student-DAT passed
     'John passed the books that they ordered to three or more students.'

These considerations undermine Matsuoka's (2003) argument based on pronominal variable binding in favor of theme being higher than goal. What about his other argument based on the behavior of the inchoative variants of *pass*-type verbs? Recall that his argument is built on the facts in (25): only the theme/accusative object of the ditransitive sentence becomes the nominative subject of the inchoative sentence. From this fact, Matsuoka concludes that the theme is necessarily higher (and hence closer to T) than the goal in the base structure.

This argument is also not conclusive. On Matsuoka's (2003) analysis, the goal phrase can never be higher than the theme phrase in the base structure of inchoative sentences. However, evidence suggests the contrary. Consider (50).

(50) Kenᵢ-ga   Yumiⱼ-ni   zibunᵢ/*ⱼ-no syasin-o   todoketa.
     Ken-NOM Yumi-DAT self-GEN   picture-ACC delivered
     'Ken delivered a picture of himself to Yumi.'

As is well known, Japanese *zibun* 'self' is subject-oriented. In (50) the agent argument is the subject, so only *Ken* can be the antecedent of *zibun*. Interestingly, in the inchoative counterpart of (50), *zibun* can be bound by the goal phrase:

(51) a. Zibunᵢ-no syasin-ga   Yumiᵢ-ni   todoita.
        self-GEN   picture-NOM Yumi-DAT reached
        'A picture of herself reached Yumi.'
     b. Yumiᵢ-ni   zibunᵢ-no syasin-ga   todoita.
        Yumi-DAT self-GEN   picture-NOM reached

On the basis of this fact, one might claim that the dative phrase is the subject of these sentences. But this does not seem correct, given that the dative phrase in this construction does not license subject honorification:

(52) a. #Nimotu-ga   Yamada-sensei-ni   o-todoki-ninzatta.
         package-NOM Yamada-teacher-DAT reach(honorific form)
         'A package reached Prof. Yamada.'
    b. #Yamada-sensei-ni   nimotu-ga   o-todoki-ninatta.
         Yamada-teacher-DAT package-NOM reach(honorific form)

We thus have apparently conflicting results: the facts in (51) and (52) show that in the inchoative construction in question, the dative phrase can antecede *zibun*, which is usually subject-oriented, but is not the subject of the sentence.[23] We might resolve this problem by interpreting subject-orientation in terms of thematic prominence, along the lines of Giorgi (1983).[24] On this view, the antecedent of *zibun* is an element bearing the most prominent θ-role in the same sentence. Then (50) shows that agent is more prominent than goal and theme, and (51) shows that goal is more prominent than theme.[25] If thematic prominence is reflected in structural prominence, as is standardly assumed in current literature, then the base position of the (high/low) goal argument can be higher than that of the theme argument. The conclusion is consistent with Hoji's (1985) view but not with Matsuoka's (2003).

This view leaves open the question of why the theme, not the goal, becomes the nominative phrase in the inchoative. Whatever the ultimate explanation, it is clear, if the above argument is correct, that it cannot be due to the theme being higher than the goal.

16.6.2 Toward a Unified Approach

Given these results, let us now explore a possible direction in which the discoveries of the previous studies on Japanese DCs could be unified. We have seen that free base generation of the theme and the low goal is necessary and that there is no strong syntactic evidence that the theme must be higher than the goal. We can then summarize the results obtained so far as follows:

(53) a. The high goal is generated in the specifier of the applicative head, whereas the low goal and the theme can be freely generated within VP.
    b. Scrambling cannot take place to the domain of the applicative head.
    c. The theme can scramble over the low goal.
    d. The low goal cannot scramble over the theme.

The proposals in (53a,b) are due to Miyagawa and Tsujioka (2004). The claim in (53c) is necessary to explain the binding facts (in (4), (19)/(22), (48)/(49), and (i) of note 1) and the quantifier floating facts (in (16)). Miyagawa and Tsujioka (2004:fn. 28) are also aware of the necessity of movement of the theme over the low goal, citing the following example, where the floating NQ is construed with the theme phrase:

(54) Taroo-ga   nimotu-o   Hanako-ni   futatu   okutta.
     Taro-NOM   package-ACC   Hanako-to   two.CL   sent
     'Taro sent two packages to Hanako.'

Recall that the theme cannot scramble over the high goal. Given this, (54) must involve movement over the low goal. We can make the point even clearer by using the two-goal sentence in (55).

(55) Taroo-ga Hanako-ni nimotu-o Tokyo-ni futatu okutta.
Taro-NOM Hanako-DAT package-ACC Tokyo-to two.CL sent
'Taro sent Hanako two packages to Tokyo.'

In (55) the NQ is construed with the theme phrase that occurs between the high goal and the low goal. This sentence seems to have the same grammatical status as its variant without the NQ. The position of the theme phrase unambiguously indicates that it can scramble over the low goal and land in a position below the high goal.

Note that although the theme can move over the low goal, the low goal cannot move over the theme, given the contrasts between (4a) and (4b), between (19a) and (19b), between (48a) and (49), and between (ia) and (ib) of note 1. Hence we need to ensure (53d) as well.

A unified approach thus needs to derive the properties in (53c,d) while maintaining (53a,b). To do this, I suggest the following:

(56) a. There is a functional head F between V and the applicative head.
b. There is no VP-internal scrambling; short scrambling is movement to Spec,F.
c. Although the theme is necessarily interpreted within VP, the low goal can be interpreted either within VP or in Spec,F.

The claim in (56a) is not new. F may be Agr$_O$, as proposed by Koizumi (1995), or Asp(ect), as proposed by Travis (1991).[26] The proposal in (56b) follows straightforwardly if scrambling is feature-driven, as argued for by Miyagawa (1996, 1997) and Miyagawa and Tsujioka (2004), on the standard assumption that only functional heads can bear formal features inducing movement. What is new is the second half of (56c), which in effect states that the low goal is an argument that has an adjunctlike property, in the sense that it can be interpreted in more than one position. That this is not totally inconceivable is shown by the fact that the low goal can sometimes be left out, whereas the theme can never be, as shown in (57) and (58) (cf. Kitagawa 1994).

(57) a. John sent *(a letter) to Mary.
b. John bought *(a dress) for Mary.

(58) a. John sent a letter (to Mary).
b. John bought a dress (for Mary).

On this view, scrambling of the theme over the low goal occurs as illustrated in (59).[27]

(59) [$_{FP}$ theme [$_{VP}$ low goal [t_{theme} V]] F]

In contrast, scrambling of the low goal over the theme, as shown in (60), cannot occur.

(60)　*[FP low goal [VP theme [$t_{\text{low goal}}$ V]] F]

This is because the low goal can be base-generated in Spec,F, so the movement option in (60) is excluded. The absence of scrambling of this kind is independently motivated by the following considerations. Consider first the example in (61).

(61)　*Ken-ga　　soko$_i$-no　　　　syatyoo-o
　　　Ken-NOM　that.place-GEN　president-ACC
　　　[mittu-izyoo-no　　　　　kaisya]$_i$-de　hihansita.
　　　three.CL-or.more-GEN　company-at　criticized
　　　'Ken criticized their presidents at three or more companies.'
　　　cf.　Ken-ga　　[mittu-izyoo-no　　　　　kaisya]$_i$-de
　　　　　Ken-NOM　three.CL-or.more-GEN　company-at
　　　　　soko$_i$-no　　　　syatyoo-o　　hihansita.
　　　　　that.place-GEN　president-ACC　criticized

Example (61) does not permit a bound-variable reading. This fact shows two things: first, the locative adjunct *mittu-izyoo-no kaisya-de* 'at three or more companies' can be base-generated lower than the theme, consistent with Larson's (1988) proposal; and second, (61) cannot have a derivation in which the theme is generated lower than the adjunct and moved past the adjunct to a higher position. Consider now (62).

(62)　*John-ga　　soko$_i$-no　　　　syatyoo-no　　　mae-de
　　　John-NOM　that.place-GEN　president-GEN　front-at
　　　[mittu-izyoo-no　　　　　kaisya]$_i$-o　　hihansita.
　　　three.CL-or.more-GEN　company-ACC　criticized
　　　'John criticized three or more companies in front of their presidents.'
　　　cf.　John-ga　　[mittu-izyoo-no　　　　　kaisya]$_i$-o
　　　　　John-NOM　three.CL-or.more-GEN　company-ACC
　　　　　soko$_i$-no　　　　syatyoo-no　　　mae-de　hihansita.
　　　　　that.place-GEN　president-GEN　front-at　criticized

The lack of the intended bound-variable reading in (62) shows that the locative adjunct *soko-no syatyoo-no mae-de* 'it-GEN president-GEN front-at' is interpreted in the position where it appears and cannot be interpreted as scrambled from a lower position (see Takano 1998:833 for original discussion of this effect). Given that the locative adjunct can be base-generated lower than the theme, as evidenced by (61), the absence of scrambling of the low goal in (60) can be attributed to the same property that prevents the adjunct from scrambling in (62).[28]

In this way, we might be able to achieve a unified theory of Japanese DCs, incorporating the insights of the scrambling approach into the theory of Japanese DCs proposed by Miyagawa and Tsujioka (2004).

16.7 IMPLICATIONS FOR LINGUISTIC THEORY

I began this chapter by questioning the possible structures and derivations of the two variants in (1) and wondering how to account for the free order of the two objects. I have investigated how these questions have been addressed and have just suggested one possible way of unifying the results of the previous studies. Let me address now the final, broader question: How does the study of Japanese DCs contribute to the development of linguistic theory?

In fact, the results of the previous studies (including the suggestions made in section 16.6) of Japanese DCs have many consequences and implications for linguistic theory in general. I briefly discuss the following areas:

- Scrambling
- θ-marking/argument licensing
- The nature of reconstruction
- Chain Condition
- Case-licensing mechanisms
- Psycholinguistic experimental research

First, an important implication follows regarding the nature of scrambling from the work by Miyagawa and Tsujioka (2004), who have shown that neither the low goal nor the theme can scramble over the high goal (recall (38) and (39)). This implies that scrambling is not an optional operation, which has a great impact on the general theory of movement. The same conclusion follows from the unified approach suggested in section 16.6, according to which short scrambling is necessarily movement to Spec,F rather than movement inside VP (see (56b)).

Another consequence derives from Takano's (1988) work on short scrambling in Japanese and English DCs. The traditional view on scrambling in Japanese and English—that Japanese has it but English lacks it—has been challenged by various researchers. For instance, Fukui (1993) and Saito and Fukui (1998) argue that English has scrambling though it is necessarily rightward (more specifically, they identify English heavy NP shift, analyzed as rightward movement, with scrambling). However, Takano claims, on the basis of close examination of Japanese and English DCs, that both Japanese and English have leftward short scrambling (recall the discussion in section 16.4.2), though only Japanese has longer scrambling. These results make clear the necessity of constructing a general theory of scrambling and parametric variation that accounts for the availability of scrambling both in terms of languages and in terms of structural domains. This is an important topic for future research.

Next, recall that the study of Japanese DCs has discovered that the theme can scramble over the low goal, but not vice versa (see (53c,d)). This is a striking property, given that the theme and the low goal can be base-generated in either hierarchical order (see (53a)). It implies a fundamental asymmetry between the theme and the low goal with respect to how they are θ-marked or licensed, thereby calling for a principled explanation in terms of UG mechanisms. The traditional intuition about this is Hoji's (1985) thematic hierarchy (goal higher than theme). A new way of looking at the issue in the context of a unified theory of Japanese DCs is suggested in section 16.6. However, there have also been proposals based on studies on languages other than Japanese that argue for a different structural relationship between the theme and the goal (see, e.g., Larson 1988 and Baker 1993 and references cited there). Given this state of affairs, an important issue for linguistic theory is whether there is parametric variation regarding this property, and if there is, how such variation arises.

The investigation of Japanese DCs has also discovered an important property of reconstruction. As is evident in Hoji's (1985) work, close examination of reconstruction effects plays an essential role in determining the structure and derivation of Japanese DCs; the theme-goal order is derived by movement of the theme because reconstruction effects are found with the theme in this order, but the goal-theme order involves no movement because no reconstruction effects are found with the goal in this order. In addition to this result, Hoji's work also reveals an interesting property of reconstruction. As mentioned in notes 1 and 3, the effects of reconstruction are weaker with short scrambling than with longer scrambling. The examples in (63) show the relevant contrast.

(63) a. Soko$_i$-no   syatyoo-no   syasin-o
       that.place-GEN   president-GEN   picture-ACC
       [mittu-izyoo-no   kaisya]$_i$-ga   Ken-ni   okutta.
       three.CL-or.more-GEN   company-NOM   Ken-DAT   sent
       'Three or more companies sent pictures of their presidents to Ken.'
    b. Ken-ga   soko$_i$-no   syatyoo-no   syasin-o
       Ken-NOM   that.place-GEN   president-GEN picture-ACC
       [mittu-izyoo-no   kaisya]$_i$-ni   okutta.
       three.CL-or.more-GEN   company-DAT   sent
       'Ken sent pictures of their presidents to three or more companies.'

Example (63a) involves scrambling of the theme/accusative phrase past the subject, whereas (63b) involves short scrambling of the theme/accusative phrase. In both cases the scrambled phrase contains *soko* 'that.place', which is to be bound by a QP through reconstruction. Although both examples allow *soko* to be bound by the QP, the intended bound-variable reading is less acceptable in (63b) than in (63a), as originally pointed out by Hoji (1985) (recall (4b) of section 16.3). Whereas it is significant both for Hoji and for the discussion of this chapter that cases such as (63b) do allow a bound-variable reading, it is also an important question why they allow that reading only weakly, as compared with cases such as (63a). This question is left open in Hoji 1985 and is briefly discussed in Takano 1998, with some suggestions about possible accounts. The issue is not settled, however. The situation reminds us of another issue related to reconstruction effects—namely, whether both A'- and A-movement induce reconstruction effects. Addressing these issues requires more careful and systematic investigation of the relationship between movement and reconstruction effects, as well as of the exact mechanisms of reconstruction.

The study of Japanese DCs also sheds new light on the nature of the Chain Condition. Recall that the Japanese data discussed by Miyagawa (1997) and in section 16.6 strongly suggest that the Chain Condition effects arise with *otagai* 'each other'. This means that the Chain Condition applies not only to reflexives but also to reciprocals, as Miyagawa and Tsujioka (2004) claim. The debate between Yatsushiro (2003) and Miyagawa and Tsujioka (briefly reviewed in section 16.6) also raises the important question of whether the Chain Condition is a condition on (variable) binding. These results thus have a direct bearing on the issue of exactly how the Chain Condition is to be formulated.[29]

The properties of Japanese DCs revealed through the previous studies have an implication for mechanisms of licensing Case as well. Recall from section 16.2 that Japanese DCs contrast sharply with English DCs in that they allow word order between the two objects to be free (see (1)–(3)). Given Miyagawa and Tsujioka's (2004) proposal, we can be more specific about this: the order between the high goal and the theme is fixed (high goal–theme, that is) in both English and Japanese; however, the flexibility of the order between the low goal and the theme differs in the two languages—fixed in English but free in Japanese. To account for this difference, Miyagawa and Tsujioka adopt an idea put forth in Takano 1998—namely, that the accusative DP is licensed in different ways in English and Japanese. More specifically, Takano argues that the necessity of Case checking requires the accusative DP to always be higher than the PP in English and that the lack of this effect is an indication that Japanese employs a mechanism of licensing accusative DPs that does not appeal to feature checking (see Kuroda 1978 for an earlier proposal of this nature).[30] If correct, this leads to the claim that UG has two mechanisms of licensing Case.

Finally, let us discuss the influence of the study of Japanese DCs on psycholinguistic research. The fact that competing hypotheses exist on the structure and derivation of Japanese DCs has prompted researchers to conduct psycholinguistic experiments to find new evidence in favor of one hypothesis over the others. As a result, a number of experimental studies have been reported. Sugisaki and Isobe (2001) report on language-acquisition experiments showing that children have more difficulty comprehending sentences with theme-goal order than those with goal-theme order. They interpret this result as indicating that the theme-goal order involves short scrambling (more specifically, A-movement) of the theme, whereas the other order results from base generation. Miyamoto and Takahashi (2002) report on sentence-processing experiments showing sentences with theme-goal order require longer reading time than those with goal-theme order. They propose that the difficulty of processing with theme-goal sentences is due to the necessity of associating a displaced element with its gap, thus supporting the hypothesis that theme-goal order results from movement of the theme, whereas the other order involves no movement. Koizumi (2005) also reports on experiments on sentence processing and brain imaging where all the results point to the conclusion that the goal-theme order is basic, with the theme-goal order derived by movement of the theme. The authors of these experimental studies thus all support Hoji's (1985) scrambling approach over the other alternatives proposed by Miyagawa (1996, 1997), Matsuoka (2003), and Miyagawa and Tsujioka (2004).[31]

Given that the unified approach suggested in section 16.6 adopts the idea of free base generation of the theme and the low goal, it is necessary to consider how the results of these experiments can be interpreted under this approach. Here I can only speculate. Under the approach presented here, the crucial difference between the goal-theme and theme-goal orders is that the former is associated only with derivational possibilities involving base generation, whereas the latter is associated with a derivation involving base generation and one involving short scrambling of the theme over the low goal. Should the existence of the movement option among derivational possibilities for sentences with the theme-goal order affect processing and comprehension of those sentences, the results of the experiments will be seen as compatible with the unified approach.

These comments are tentative and speculative. What is more important in this connection is the clear influence that the study of Japanese DCs has had on psycholinguistic research. The results of the study of Japanese DCs have driven interesting experimental studies that produced new evidence bearing on the issues in syntactic theory. These studies also show us how psycholinguistic evidence can relate to syntactic theory, which shows another way in which the study of Japanese DCs influences research in a broader context.

In this way, the study of Japanese DCs has contributed to revealing many interesting, and sometimes surprising, properties that lead us to a better understanding of language and linguistic theory. Although many issues still remain to be settled, it is hoped that future research will resolve the remaining questions and further deepen our understanding of the nature of Japanese syntax and UG.

NOTES FOR CHAPTER 16

Parts of this chapter were presented at the Workshop on Linguistic Theory and the Japanese Language, held at Harvard University on July 29–30, 2005. I am grateful to the audience there for comments and questions. I am also grateful to an anonymous reviewer for very helpful comments on a draft version of this chapter. Finally, I would like to thank Shigeru Miyagawa and Mamoru Saito for valuable suggestions and discussion at various stages of this work.

1. The same pattern as that shown in (4) can be reproduced by using a quantifier, instead of a *wh*-phrase, as a binder and an overt element, instead of *pro*, as a bindee:

(i) a. *Ken-wa [$_{NP}$ [$_S$ e_i sore$_j$-o okuttekita] hito$_i$]-ni
      Ken-TOP   it-ACC sent.over   person-DAT
      sansatu-izyoo-no   hon$_j$-o   okurikaesita.
      three.CL-or.more-GEN book-ACC sent.back
      'Ken sent back three or more books to the persons that had sent them to him.'

a'. Ken-wa   sansatu-izyoo-no   hon$_j$-o
Ken-TOP   three.CL-or. more-GEN   book-ACC
[$_{NP}$ [$_S$ e_i sore$_j$-o okuttekita] hito$_i$]-ni   okurikaesita.
                   it-ACC sent.over person-DAT sent.back
b. Ken-wa [$_{NP}$ [$_S$ soko$_i$-ga e_j okuttekita] hon$_j$]-o
   you-TOP   that.place-NOM sent.over book-ACC
   mittu-izyoo-no   syuppansya$_i$-ni okurikaesita.
   three.CL-or.more-GEN   publisher-DAT   sent.back
   'Ken sent back the books that they had sent to him to three or more publishers.'
b' Ken-wa   mittu-izyoo-no   syuppansyai-ni
   you-TOP   three.CL-or.more-GEN   publisher-DAT
   [$_{NP}$ [$_S$ sokoi-ga e_j okuttekita] hon$_j$]-o okurikaesita.
            that.place-NOM sent.over book-ACC   sent.back

In my judgment, (ib) is not fully acceptable but is much better than (ia). The contrast exists and it is important. The same holds for Hoji's examples in (4a,b). See also note 3. Perhaps the contrast between (ia) and (ib) is clearer than that between (4a) and (4b). See Hoji 2003 for an important discussion of factors that affect judgment on data involving variable binding in Japanese. See also section 16.6 on this.

2. Hoji (1985) assumes that the *wh*-phrase in situ moves covertly to its scope position. However, it is also assumed that covert movement does not affect possible binding relations.

3. Hoji (1985:125) notes that the bound-variable reading in (4b) is not perfect but, importantly, it is better than that in (4a). See Takano 1998 for a possible account of the slightly degraded status of binding in cases such as (4b) that is compatible with Hoji's analysis.

4. Miyagawa (1995) originally presented arguments for the base-generation approach.

5. That Chain Condition effects can be found with Japanese *otagai* was originally pointed out by Snyder (1992) and Koizumi (1995).

6. Koizumi (1995) judges an example such as (11b) to be deviant. I find (11a,b) to be equally acceptable.

7. Miyagawa (1997) puts "(?)" in front of the wide-scope reading of *daremo* in (13a) but considers it to be basically acceptable. Contrary to Miyagawa (1997), Miyagawa and Tsujioka (2004) report the same judgments as Hoji's (1985) but point out that animacy of the goal phrase affects scope interpretation. See the discussion of the examples in (33) in section 16.5.2. See also Kitagawa 1994 for possible factors that affect judgment on scope interpretation.

8. Ishii (1998) also argues for an analysis of Japanese DCs in which both base-generation and scrambling are possible.

9. It is important to note, however, that the base-generation analysis originally argued for in Miyagawa 1995 (see note 4) and developed in Miyagawa 1996, 1997 was proposed independently of Kitagawa's (1994) work.

10. It may be misleading, as a reviewer points out, to say that Hoji (1985) and Miyagawa (1997) report different judgments here, given that the examples they consider (i.e., Hoji's (7) and Miyagawa's (13)) contain different scope-taking elements. If the choice of scope-taking elements affects judgment on scope interpretation, their observations simply mean that different phenomena support different conclusions. See note 7 as well for a related issue.

11. On grounds independent of Takano's (1998) argument, several researchers have suggested the opposite derivation for DCs from Larson (1988). See works cited in Larson 1988 (note 18) for such proposals. See also Aoun and Li 1989 for another proposal of the same nature.

12. See Takano 1998 for other approaches to cases such as (22).

13. The examples in (23) are all fairly acceptable to me. The factor that affects judgment here is that *karezisin* can be used as an emphatic variant of *kare* 'he' rather than as a reflexive. Given that the emphatic reading of *karezisin* is always available, it is very hard (for me at least) to exclude this reading when judging sentences containing *karezisin*. See also note 7 in Yatsushiro 2003 for this and other possible factors that may affect judgment on (23).

14. For *show*-type verbs, Matsuoka claims that the experiencer is higher than the theme.

15. As mentioned in section 16.3.2, Kitagawa (1994) makes the same claim, though his theoretical implementation is different from Miyagawa and Tsujioka's. Kishimoto (2001) also argues for the existence of the two constructions in Japanese. However, he proposes that in Japanese, the semantics of verbs determines whether they can take the double-object construction or the dative construction, so that only verbs with certain semantic properties license double objects.

16. See Harley 1995, 2002 and Pesetsky 1995 for other proposals that assign different structures to the double-object and dative constructions.

17. Two remarks on the judgments reported here are in order. First, recall that Miyagawa (1997) judges (13a) to be ambiguous, contrary to Hoji's (1985) observation, and attributes the inverse scope reading to focus movement. However, Miyagawa and Tsujioka's (2004) judgment on (33a) is identical to Hoji's. Second, the reported contrast in (33) does not seem to exist for all speakers. Miyagawa and Tsujioka (2004:6) note that there are speakers who do not get ambiguity in (33b). I find it hard to see a contrast between (33a) and (33b).

18. There is a problem with Miyagawa and Tsujioka's analysis of the contrast in (33). In (33a) the goal is animate, so it can be a possessor in the double-object construction. But nothing excludes the possibility that it is a location in the dative construction. Then (33a) should be ambiguous, contrary to their judgment. Miyagawa and Tsujioka (2004:12) are aware of this problem and suggest that there is a preference to interpret an animate goal in the goal-theme order to be a possessor and not a location.

19. Miyagawa and Tsujioka (2004:fn. 8) observe that the two-goal sentences are acceptable only with verbs that are associated with some sort of a "path." They also report (Miyagawa and Tsujioka 2004:fn. 9) that there are speakers who reject two-goal sentences. I find them marginal at best.

20. The following example (from Miyagawa and Tsujioka 2004:26) shows that *karezisin* cannot be a bound variable:

(ii)   Taroo$_i$-ga/*Dareka$_i$-ga   kare$_i$-no kodomo-o sikatta.
       Taro-NOM/someone-NOM he-GEN   child-ACC scolded
       'Taro/Someone scolded his child.'

21. Note also that *otagai*, unlike *karezisin*, can be used as a bound variable:

(iii) Dono hitotati-ga   otagai-o   hihansita no?
       which people-NOM   each.other-ACC criticized Q
       'Which people criticized each other?'

22. The "?" in front of the sentence in (49) indicates that the bound-variable reading is less than perfect. The status of (49) is the same as that of (4b). See notes 1 and 3.

23. One might wonder if the theme argument in this construction can antecede *zibun* and also if it can trigger subject honorification. Unfortunately, we cannot test for these questions for an independent reason: although the antecedent of *zibun* and the target of subject honorification must be an animate DP, verbs of this construction, including the verbs in (51) and (52), cannot take an animate DP for the theme argument.

24. Thanks to Jun Abe for suggesting this possibility to me.

25. A question arises for cases such as (iv).

(iv) Yumi$_i$-ga   Ken$_j$-ni(yotte)   zibun$_i$/*$_j$-no heya-de   sikarareta.
Yumi-NOM   Ken-by   self-GEN   room-in   was.scolded
'Yumi was scolded by Ken in her room.'

In (iv) the antecedent of *zibun* is the theme argument of the passivized verb *sikarareta* 'was scolded' despite the presence of the agent argument of the verb. So this is a counterexample to the thematic prominence theory suggested in the text. There are at least two factors that may account for this case. For one thing, (iv) is a passive sentence and Japanese passives may involve biclausal structures (see Kitagawa and Kuroda 1992 and Huang 1999 for different proposals that assign biclausal structures to Japanese passives). If so, *Yumi* and *Ken* belong to different sentences (they are not arguments of the same verb). Another factor that may be relevant here is the fact that *Ken* in (iv) can never c-command outside the *ni(yotte)* phrase, as is evidenced by the quantifier floating fact in (v).

(v) *Yumi-ga   sensei-ni(yotte)   hutari   sikarareta.
Yumi-NOM   teacher-by   two.CL   was.scolded
'Yumi was scolded by two teachers.'
cf. Yumi-ga   hutari-no sensei-ni(yotte)   sikarareta.
Yumi-NOM   two-GEN teacher-by   was.scolded

Given that *Ken* is not a possible binder of *zibun* in (iv), it may be disregarded for the purpose of determining the antecedent of *zibun* in terms of thematic prominency. I thank Mamoru Saito for bringing cases such as (iv) to my attention.

26. In fact, Koizumi (1995) proposes that short scrambling is movement to Spec,Agr$_O$.

27. Given (56c), the low goal can also be a lower Spec,F, with the scrambled theme being a higher Spec,F.

28. The effect has a flavor of economy (derivations with fewer operations are preferred) and may be extended to the second conclusion drawn from (61) (that in (61) the theme cannot be generated lower than the adjunct and moved past the adjunct). But the exact nature of this property is left open here.

29. See McGinnis 2004 for a new approach to Chain Condition effects.

30. Recall from section 16.4.2 that Takano proposes to analyze Japanese DCs and English double PP constructions on a par.

31. One point worth mentioning here, brought to my attention by Shigeru Miyagawa, is that these experimental studies do not control for animacy of a goal argument (their examples involve animate goals). Given the results in Miyagawa and Tsujioka 2004, we might want to know if there are any differences between cases involving animate versus inanimate goals. This is yet another issue that needs to be addressed in future research.

REFERENCES

Aoun, Joseph, and Yen-hui Audrey Li. 1989. Constituency and scope. *Linguistic Inquiry* 20:141–172.

Baker, Mark. 1993. Why unaccusative verbs cannot dative-shift. In *Proceedings of NELS* 23, ed. Amy J. Schafer, 33–47. Amherst, Mass.: GLSA Publications.

Baker, Mark. 1995. On the structural positions of themes and goals. In *Phrase structure and the lexicon*, ed. Johan Rooryck and Laurie Zaring, 7–34. Dordrecht: Kluwer.

Bresnan, Joan. 1978. Computational psycholinguistics. Course taught at MIT, Fall semester. [Lecture notes dated October 12, 1978; initially cited in Gropen et al. 1989.]

Bresnan, Joan. 1982. *The mental representation of grammatical relations*. Cambridge, Mass.: MIT Press.

Burzio, Luigi. 1986. *Italian syntax*. Dordrecht: Reidel.

Chomsky, Noam. 2000. Minimalist inquiries: The framework. In *Step by step: Essays on minimalist syntax in honor of Howard Lasnik*, ed. Roger Martin, David Michaels, and Juan Uriagereka, 89–155. Cambridge, Mass: MIT Press.

Fukui, Naoki. 1993. Parameters and optionality. *Linguistic Inquiry* 24:399–420.

Giorgi, Alessandra. 1983. Toward a theory of long distance anaphors: A GB approach. *The Linguistic Review* 3:307–361.

Gropen, Jess, Steven Pinker, Michelle Hollander, Richard Goldberg, and Ronald Wilson. 1989. The learnability and acquisition of the dative alternation in English. *Language* 65:203–257.

Haig, John H. 1980. Some observations on quantifier floating in Japanese. *Linguistics* 18:1065–1083.

Harley, Heidi. 1995. Subjects, events, and licensing. Doctoral dissertation, MIT, Cambridge, Mass.

Harley, Heidi. 2002. Possession and the double-object construction. *Linguistic Variation Yearbook* 2:31–70.

Heim, Irene, Howard Lasnik, and Robert May. 1991a. On "reciprocal scope." *Linguistic Inquiry* 22:173–192.

Heim, Irene, Howard Lasnik, and Robert May. 1991b. Reciprocity and plurality. *Linguistic Inquiry* 22:63–101.

Hoji, Hajime. 1985. Logical Form constraints and configurational structures in Japanese. Doctoral dissertation, University of Washington, Seattle.

Hoji, Hajime. 2003. Falsifiability and repeatability in generative grammar: A case study of anaphora and scope dependency in Japanese. *Lingua* 113:377–446.

Huang, C.-T. James. 1999. Chinese passives in comparative perspective. *Tsing Hua Journal of Chinese Studies* 29:423–509.

Ishii, Yasuo. 1998. Scrambling of weak NPs in Japanese. In *Japanese/Korean linguistics 8*, 431–444. Stanford, Calif.: CSLI Publications.

Kishimoto, Hideki. 2001. The role of lexical meanings in argument encoding: Double object verbs in Japanese. *Gengo Kenkyu* 120:35–65.

Kitagawa, Yoshihisa. 1994. Shells, Yolks, and scrambled e.g.s. In *Proceedings of NELS 24*, ed. Merce Gonzàlez, 221–239. Amherst, Mass.: GLSA Publications.

Kitagawa, Yoshihisa, and S.-Y. Kuroda. 1992. Passive in Japanese. Ms., University of Rochester and University of California, San Diego.

Koizumi, Masatoshi. 1995. Phrase structure in minimalist syntax. Doctoral dissertation, MIT, Cambridge, Mass.

Koizumi, Masatoshi. 2005. Syntactic structure of ditransitive constructions in Japanese: Behavioral and imaging studies. In *The proceedings of the sixth Tokyo Conference on Psycholinguistics*, ed Yukio Otsu, 1–25. Tokyo: Hituzi Syobo.

Kuroda, S.-Y. 1970. Remarks on the notion of subject with reference to words like *also*, *even*, and *only*: Part I. In *Annual Bulletin* 3, 111–129. Tokyo: Research Institute of Logopedics and Phoniatrics, University of Tokyo.

Kuroda, S.-Y. 1978. Case-marking, canonical sentence patterns, and Counter Equi in Japanese (a preliminary survey). In *Problems in Japanese syntax and semantics*, ed. John Hinds and Irwin Howard, 30–51. Tokyo: Kaitakusha.

Kuroda, S.-Y. 1980. Bunkoozoo-no hikaku [Comparison of sentence structures]. In *Nitieigo hikakukooza 2: Bunpoo*, ed. Tetsuya Kunihiro, 23–61. Tokyo: Taishukan.

Kuroda, S.-Y. 1983. What can Japanese say about government and binding? In *Proceedings of the WCCFL 2*, ed. Michael Barlow, Daniel P. Flickinger, and Michael T. Wescoat, 153–164. Stanford, Calif.: Stanford Linguistics Association.

Larson, Richard. 1988. On the double object construction. *Linguistic Inquiry* 19:335–391.

Marantz, Alec. 1993. Implications of asymmetries in double object constructions. In *Theoretical aspects of Bantu grammar*, ed. Sam A. Mchombo, 113–150. Stanford, Calif.: CSLI Publications.

Matsuoka, Mikinari. 2003. Two types of ditransitive constructions in Japanese. *Journal of East Asian Linguistics* 12:171–203.

McGinnis, Martha. 2004. Lethal ambiguity. *Linguistic Inquiry* 35:47–95.

Miyagawa, Shigeru. 1995. Scrambling as an obligatory movement. In *Proceedings of the Nanzan University International Symposium on Japanese Language Education and Japanese Language Studies*, 81–92. Nagoya, Japan: Nanzan University.

Miyagawa, Shigeru. 1996. Word order restrictions and nonconfigurationality. In *MITWPL 29: Proceedings of FAJL 2*, 117–141. Cambridge, Mass.: MIT Working Papers in Linguistics.

Miyagawa, Shigeru. 1997. Against optional scrambling. *Linguistic Inquiry* 28:1–26.

Miyagawa, Shigeru, and Takae Tsujioka. 2004. Argument structure and ditransitive verbs in Japanese. *Journal of East Asian Linguistics* 13:1–38.

Miyamoto, Edson T., and Shoichi Takahashi. 2002. Sources of difficulty in processing scrambling in Japanese. In *Sentence processing in East Asian languages*, ed. Mineharu Nakayama, 167–188. Stanford, Calif.: CSLI Publications.

Nemoto, Naoko. 1993. Chains and Case positions: A study from scrambling in Japanese. Doctoral dissertation, University of Connecticut, Storrs.

Oerhle, Richard. 1976. The grammatical status of the English dative alternation. Doctoral dissertation, MIT, Cambridge, Mass.

Pesetsky, David. 1995. *Zero syntax*. Cambridge, Mass.: MIT Press.

Rizzi, Luigi. 1986. On chain formation. In *Syntax and semantics 19: The syntax of pronominal clitics*, ed. Hagit Borer, 65–95. New York: Academic Press.

Saito, Mamoru, and Naoki Fukui. 1998. Order in phrase structure and movement. *Linguistic Inquiry* 29:439–474.

Shibatani, Masayoshi. 1978. Mikami Akira and the notion of "subject" in Japanese grammar. In *Problems in Japanese syntax and semantics*, ed. John Hinds and Irwin Howard, 52–67. Tokyo: Kaitakusha.

Snyder, William. 1992. Chain-formation and crossover. Ms., MIT, Cambridge, Mass.

Sugisaki, Koji, and Miwa Isobe. 2001. What can child Japanese tell us about the syntax of scrambling? In *Proceedings of the West Coast Conference on Formal Linguistics 20*, 538–551. Somerville, Mass.: Cascadilla Press.

Takano, Yuji. 1998. Object shift and scrambling. *Natural Language & Linguistic Theory* 16:817–889.

Travis, Lisa deMena. 1991. Derived objects, inner aspect, and the structure of VP. Ms., McGill University, Montreal.

Ueyama, Ayumi. 1998. Two types of dependency. Doctoral dissertation, University of Southern California, Los Angeles.

Yatsushiro, Kazuko. 2003. VP internal scrambling. *Journal of East Asian Linguistics* 12:141–170.

CHAPTER 17

PROMINENCE MARKING IN THE JAPANESE INTONATION SYSTEM

JENNIFER J. VENDITTI, KIKUO MAEKAWA, AND MARY E. BECKMAN

17.1 INTRODUCTION

Beginning at least as early as Trubetskôi 1939, Arisaka 1941, and Hattori 1961, Japanese has played an important role in developing our understanding of prosodic structure and its function in the grammar of all human languages. In much of this literature, the primary consideration has been to account for apparent similarities between the culminative distribution of lexical stress in the lexicon of languages such as English and the distribution of pitch accents in simple and derived words of Japanese. For example, McCawley (1970) and Hyman (2001) both cite Japanese in rejecting an older typology of word-level prosodic systems in which languages are categorized by a simple dichotomy between stress languages (such as English or Catalan) and tone languages (such as Yoruba or Cantonese). More recently, the analysis of Japanese has played a critical role in the development of computationally explicit compositional theories of the elements of intonation contours and their relationship to the prosodic organization of utterances. For example, Fujisaki and Sudo (1971) and Pierrehumbert and Beckman (1988) provide two different accounts of Japanese intonation patterns in which phrase-level pitch range is specified by continuous phonological control parameters that are independent of the categorical specification of more local tone shapes in the lexicon. This incorporation of continuous (or "paralinguistic") specifications of phrasal pitch range directly into the phonological description was a critical element in the development of what

Ladd (1996) named the Autosegmental-Metrical (AM) framework. Beginning with Pierrehumbert's (1980) model of the grammar of English intonation contours, the AM framework has been widely adopted in descriptions of intonation systems and in comparisons of prosodic organization across languages. (See Jun 2005 for a recent collection of such descriptions and Gussenhoven 2004 for a review of work in this framework since Ladd 1996.)

Such cross-language comparisons, in turn, are critical for our understanding of *prominence marking* and of the ways in which prosody is used in the articulation of discourse-level categories such as *topic* and *focus*. Japanese is widely cited as a language that has a morphological marker for topic. Work on other languages, including English, Catalan, and Hungarian (e.g., Vallduví 1992, Roberts 1996), strongly suggests that the morphosyntactic articulation of topic and focus is related, at least in part, to phonological constraints on the prosodic marking of prominence contrasts. For Japanese, too, we see reference to contrasting degrees of prosodic prominence as a necessary condition on some interpretations of phrases marked for topic (see, e.g., Kuno 1973; Nakanishi 2007; Heycock, this volume). To fully understand how such categories as topic and focus are realized in Japanese, therefore, it is critical to understand how the prosodic marking of contrasts between prominent versus nonprominent elements works in the language.

In this chapter, we review the currently standard AM framework account of how the prosodic marking of prominence works in the Japanese system (section 17.3). We show that, just as in the English prosodic system, there are several different prosodic mechanisms in Japanese for marking some constituents as having focal prominence and others as being relatively reduced and out of focus. In section 17.4, we then describe four phenomena that are the locus of lively discussion and controversy in the further development of this AM framework account, before discussing the larger implications that these phenomena have for the development of a tenable general theory of the role of prosody in the marking of discourse prominence (section 17.5). Before we begin this description, however, we need to make explicit some assumptions about what prosody is and about the nature of phonetic representations that we use to study it. An understanding of these assumptions is essential background for understanding the AM framework description of Japanese. Section 17.2 lays out this background.

17.2 Elements of an AM Description of Japanese Intonation

In describing the prominence-marking mechanisms of Japanese, we use the account of the Japanese intonation system that is encoded in the X-JToBI labeling conventions (Maekawa et al. 2002). These conventions build on the earlier J_ToBI conventions described by Venditti (1997, 2005), adding tags for elements of intonation contours that have not been noted in the previous literature in English, although they are observed even in relatively formal spontaneous speech such as the conference presentations in the Corpus of Spontaneous Japanese (henceforth CSJ; Maekawa 2003, Kokuritsu Kokugo Kenkyuujo [National Institute for Japanese Language] 2006). Both the original and expanded tag sets are intended to describe intonation contours for standard (Tokyo) Japanese. The intonation systems of other dialects are known to differ, some rather dramatically. However, they either have not been studied at all (most regional dialects) or have been studied less extensively (e.g., the Osaka system, as described by Kori [1987] and others). Both tag sets also assume a description couched in the AM framework.

17.2.1 The AM framework

As already noted, the term *Autosegmental-Metrical* was coined by Ladd (1996) to refer to a class of models of phonological structure that emerged in work on intonation in the 1980s, beginning with Pierrehumbert's (1980) incorporation of Bruce's (1977) seminal insights about the composition of Swedish tone patterns into a grammar for English intonation contours. All AM models are deeply compositional, analyzing sound patterns into different types of elements at several different levels. The most fundamental level is the separation of autosegmental content features from the metrical positions that license them. This is roughly comparable to the separation of lexis from phrase structure in a description of the rest of the language's grammar.

More specifically, the "A" (Autosegmental) part of an AM description refers to the specification of content features that are autonomously segmented—that is, that project as strings of discrete categories specified on independent tiers rather than being bundled together at different positions in the word-forms that they contrast. For example, in Japanese, changing specifications of stricture degree for different articulators can define as many as six different manner autosegments within a disyllabic word-form, as in the word *sanpun* [sampuɴ] '3 minutes', where there is a sequence of stricture gestures for sibilant airflow, for vowel resonances, for nasal airflow, for a complete stopping of air, and then a vowel and a nasal again. However, there are constraints on which oral articulators can be involved in making these different airflow conditions, so that only one place feature can be specified for the middle two stricture specifications in a word of this shape. Therefore, in the grammar of Japanese (as in many other languages), place features should be projected onto a different autosegmental tier from the manner features. This projection allows for a maximally general description of the alternation among labial nasal [m] in *sanpun*, dental nasal [n] in *sandan* '3 steps', velar nasal [ŋ] in *sangai* '3rd floor', and uvular nasal [ɴ] in the citation form *san* '3'. That is, the projection of consonant place features onto a separate autosegmental tier from the manner features accounts for the derivational alternation in these Sino-Japanese forms in terms of the same general phonological constraints that govern how postvocalic nasals are adapted into the language in monomorphemic loanwords such as *konpyuuta* 'computer' or *hamu* 'ham' (where the [m] corresponds to a postvocalic [m] in the English source word), *handoru* 'steering wheel' (where the [n] corresponds to a postvocalic [n]), *hankachi* 'handkerchief' (where [ŋ] < [n]), and *koon* 'corn' (where [N] < [n]). A key insight of Firth (1957), which has been translated into Autosegmental Phonology by North American interpreters such as Langendoen (1968), Haraguchi (1977), and Goldsmith (1979), is that the traditional consonant and vowel "segments" that are named by symbols such the [s], [a], [m], [p], [u], and [N] in *sanpun* are not primitive elements in the phonological grammar. Rather, they are complex categories defined by the intersection of place and manner specifications for the word-form when the array of parallel streams of autosegments on different tiers is collapsed into a one-dimensional string.

These traditional "segments" are also the names for the C or V leaf nodes in the other part of an AM description of a spoken utterance. More generally, the "M" (Metrical) part specifies the hierarchy of prosodic constituents that defines the meter or rhythm of an utterance containing the word-form. For example, in Japanese, there is a low-level prosodic constituent *syllable* (typically abbreviated σ) that coordinates the place and manner features of words to alternate between more sonorant manners licensed to occur at the head and less sonorant manners licensed to occur only at the edges. In an utterance of *sanpun*, this syllable-level meter is CVC.CVC. In many other words, there is a more regular rhythmic alternation between C and V leaf-node types, as illustrated by the utterances in figure 17.1.

All but five of the thirty-three syllables in these utterances have a perfectly alternating CV structure. The exceptional cases are of two types. The first is the bare V at the beginning of the verbs *oyoideru* and *utatteru* in figures 17.1a and 17.1c. These two V-shape syllables, like the twenty-eight CV-shape syllables, are *short*. That is, each contains just one *mora* (abbreviated μ), a constituent between the syllable and the CV leaf nodes that licenses the specification of vowel place and height features as the head of the syllable.

The other three exceptional syllables are *long*. A long syllable contains at least one extra mora after the head V that is the sole obligatory leaf constituent. This following mora can be either a V or a C. If it is a V, it can be the second part of a geminate vowel or it can be a less sonorous vowel than the head vowel, as in figure 17.1a, where the [i] in the second syllable of *oyoideru* has lesser sonority than the preceding head vowel [o]. If the following mora is a C, it can be a moraic nasal, as in each of the two syllables of *sanpun*, or it can be the first part of a geminate obstruent, as in the second syllables of the verbs *hasitteru* and *utatteru* in figures 17.1b and 17.1c.

As *sanpun* shows, a long syllable that is closed by the moraic nasal can be word final. By contrast, a long syllable that is closed by an obstruent must have a following syllable to provide the second C position for the necessarily geminate consonant. This constraint is one of the motivations for positing prosodic constituents above the syllable as well as below. That is, the place and manner autosegments for a geminate consonant necessarily associate to a sequence of C nodes that is medial to a *prosodic word* (abbreviated ω).

(a) voiced, accented

ja ma no ŋa o joi de rɯ

[d]

Ya'mano-ga oyo'ideru.
'Yamano is swimming.'

(b) voiceless, accented

kʰ a ʃ i no ŋa ha ʃ(i)t te rɯ

[ʃ] [h] [ʃt:]

Ka'shino-ga hashi'tteru.
'Kashino is running.'

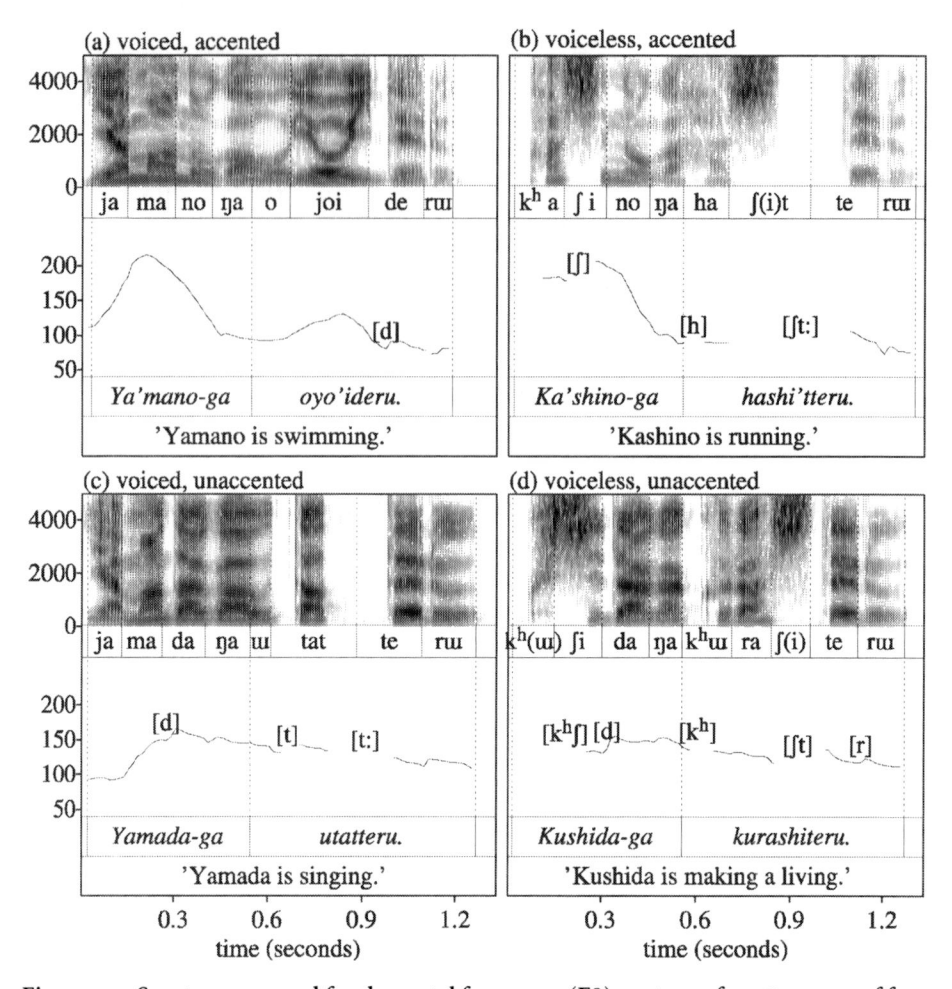

(c) voiced, unaccented

ja ma da ŋa ɯ tat te rɯ

[d] [t] [t:]

Yamada-ga utatteru.
'Yamada is singing.'

(d) voiceless, unaccented

kʰ(ɯ) ʃi da ŋa kʰɯ ra ʃ(i) te rɯ

[kʰʃ][d] [kʰ] [ʃt] [r]

Kushida-ga kurashiteru.
'Kushida is making a living.'

Figure 17.1 Spectrograms and fundamental frequency (F0) contours for utterances of four sentences with the structure [proper noun-NOM]$_{NP}$ [V (cont.)]$_{VP}$: (a) and (b) contain two accented words, and (c) and (d) contain two unaccented words.

To recap, then, the hierarchy of prosodic constituents in the phonological description of an utterance is analogous to the hierarchy of syntactic constituents in its syntactic description. By this analogy, the prosodic constraint that each syllable must have a V (vowel) category autosegment positioned to be its head is comparable to the syntactic constraint that a verb phrase must have a V (verb) category word positioned to be its head. It is in this sense that we say that the inventory of segments for a language is analogous to the lexis of the language. One argument in favor of this analogy is that the prosodic category of a segment such as [i] is inherently ambiguous in the same way that the syntactic category of a word such as *happyoo* is inherently ambiguous. That is, *happyoo* can be parsed either as the verb 'to announce, present' or as the noun 'announcement, presentation' in different morphosyntactic contexts. Similarly, the palatal constriction that gives rise to the low first formant and high second formant on either side of the medial [o] in the word *oyoideru* in figure 17.1 can be parsed either as a C (written 'y') in the syllable onset or as a V (written 'i') in the

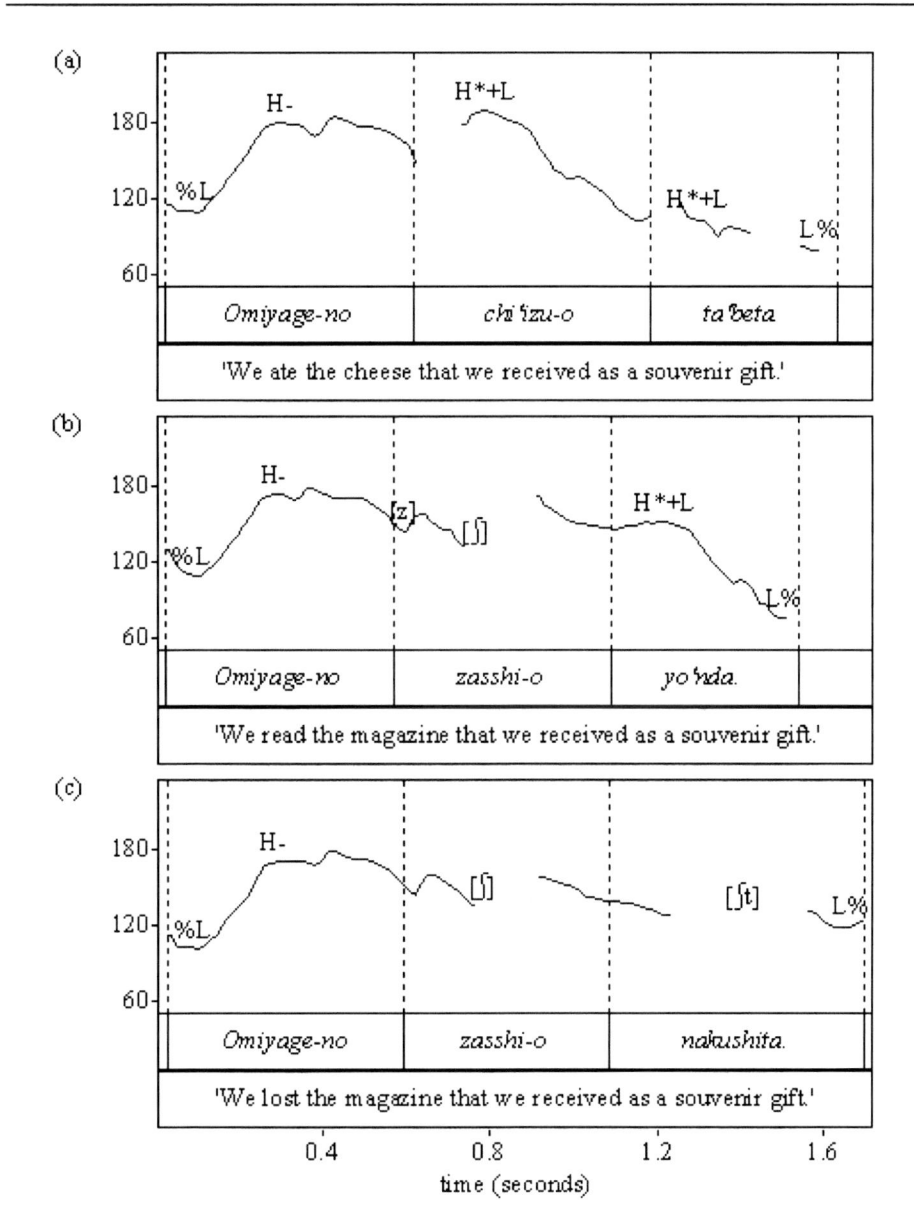

Figure 17.2 Annotated fundamental frequency contours for utterances of three sentences with the structure [[ ]ɴᴘ [[Noun-ɢᴇɴ Noun-ᴀᴄᴄ]ɴᴘ Verb-ᴘᴀsᴛ]ᴠᴘ] containing (a) two accented words, (b) one accented word, and (c) no accented words.

second mora of the syllable. A second argument in favor of this analogy is the way that empty structural positions are interpreted. That is, the implicit but unrealized subject noun phrase in sentences shown in figure 17.2 can be recovered from the syntactic parse of the rest of the sentence.

Similarly, the implicit head vowel in the second syllable of *hashitteru* in figure 17.1b and third syllable of *kurashiteru* in figure 17.1d can be recovered from the prosodic parse of the syllable structure even though there is no interval containing the usual acoustic traces of the vowel manner specification in the signal. These two tokens of the segment are "devoiced" and so cannot show the vowel formant values that cue the explicit [i] in *oyoideru*. Nonetheless, the listener parses the presence of some implicit head V for the second syllable of *hashitteru* and third syllable of *kurashiteru* from the fact that [ʃt:] and [ʃt] are not grammatical sequences of segments for any position in a prosodic word of the language. A good grasp of how listeners resolve prosodic ambiguities and of how they recover the intended autosegmental features of an implicit prosodic node in phonological ellipsis is critical for understanding the ways in which phonological structures above the word are manipulated to mark discourse prominence.

In introducing the prosodic constituents mora, syllable, and prosodic word in this section, we have defined them primarily in terms of the distribution of place and manner autosegments for consonants and vowels. In describing what listeners do to parse the prosodic categories of ambiguous segments or to recover elided segments, we have made passing reference to their phonetic interpretation, using the spectrograms in figure 17.1 as a convenient representation of the place and manner autosegments. We use the fundamental frequency (Fo) contours that are displayed below the spectrograms as a convenient phonetic representation of another type of autosegment that is critical for understanding prosodic structures above the word.

17.2.2 Tone Features and Prosodic Constituents above the Word

In addition to word-internal constituents such as the syllable, Japanese also has larger constituents above the word: various types of *prosodic phrases*. The X-JToBI model describes two levels of prosodic phrasing: the *accentual phrase* (AP) and the *intonation phrase* (IP). When our speaker produced the fluent utterances of the sentences in figures 17.1a and 17.1b, he grouped the prosodic words in each utterance into two APs, which in turn were grouped together to form a single IP for the utterance as a whole. To define these two larger groupings, we must refer to the distribution of another type of autosegment besides the place and manner autosegments that defined the C and V nodes of the prosodic tree. This third autosegmental tier is the string of *low (L)* and *high (H) tones* that correspond to the target pitch values that the speaker produces at different prosodic positions in the utterance.

The Fo contours below the spectrograms in figure 17.1 are a convenient phonetic representation of these target pitch values, and we have annotated each of them for some of the C and V autosegmental targets that also affect the pitch pattern in ways that can make Fo contours difficult for the uninitiated to read. In particular, there is a discontinuity in the Fo representation at each interval where the [−voice] autosegment is in effect. For example, there is a break in the Fo contour during the [ʃ] of *Kashino* and during the [h] and the [ʃt:] sequence in the first three syllables of *hashitteru* in figure 17.1b. Also, [+voice] consonants, such as the [d] and [r] in *oyoideiru* in figure 17.1a, can cause sharp dips in the pitch, because the speed of opening and closing of the glottis depends in part on the difference in air pressure below and above the glottis, which in turn depends on a steady venting of air through the mouth. Experienced readers of Fo contours automatically parse these effects as cues to the consonant or vowel segments rather than cues to the tones and see that the tone sequences in utterances figures 17.1a and 17.1b are essentially identical. There is a high tone target near the beginning of the subject NP, then a sudden fall to a low tone target, then a rise to a second high target on the second syllable of the VP, followed by another fall to a low target. The pitch rise at the beginning of the VP, which is especially apparent in figure 17.1a, marks the boundary between the first and the second AP.

In the previous section, we described how constriction targets can be called by their metrical functions as well as by their actual content, so that a close palatal constriction is symbolized differently depending on whether it marks a syllable boundary (C = [y]) or a syllable head (V = [i]). All tone targets, too, can be called by their metrical functions as well as by their pitch levels. For example, in the X-JToBI model, the low target at the AP boundary between the NP and the VP in figures 17.1a and 17.1b is analyzed as a *boundary tone*, which is aligned to the phrase edge. Following the usual AM conventions for indicating the demarcative prosodic function directly in the symbol for the category, this boundary tone is symbolized as [L%] in an X-JToBI tagging of the utterance. Given that the start of the utterance as a whole is also necessarily the start of a new AP, there is another instance of this low boundary tone marking the beginning of these two utterances as well as the beginning of the utterances in figures 17.1c and 17.1d. Following common practice in the AM literature, the X-JToBI conventions tag this boundary tone as [%L], using the function marker as a prefix to indicate that this boundary tone marks an initial boundary after a silent pause. Of course, this utterance-initial [%L] target is explicitly realized only when the text of the phrase begins with a sequence of [+voice] consonant and vowel autosegments on which the Fo can be realized, as in figures 17.1a and 17.1c. However, even when the phrase begins with a [–voice] segment, as in figures 17.1b and 17.1d, the [%L] can be recovered from the prosodic parse in the same way that the implicit [i] in the second syllable of *hashitteru* is recovered in figure 17.1b. In both figures 17.1a and 17.1c, the explicit low tone defines the start of a rise in Fo. The high tone target that defines the end of this rise is also explicitly realized in figures 17.1b and 17.1d, providing part of the context for positing an elided [%L]. In figures 17.1a and 17.1b, this high tone is the first tone target in a [H*+L] falling sequence that is specified in the lexicon, whereas in figures 17.1c and 17.1d it is an AP-level *phrasal tone*, symbolized with [H–]. These tone sequences and their metrical affiliations are shown in (1a,b) for the utterances in figures 17.1a and 17.1c.[1]

(1) Metrical structure and associated tone targets for (a) *Ya'mano-ga | oyo'ideru* (see figure 17.1a), (b) *Yamada-ga uttateru* (see figure 17.1c), and (c) *Ya'mano-wa ‖ oyo'ideru* (see figure 17.3a, black line).

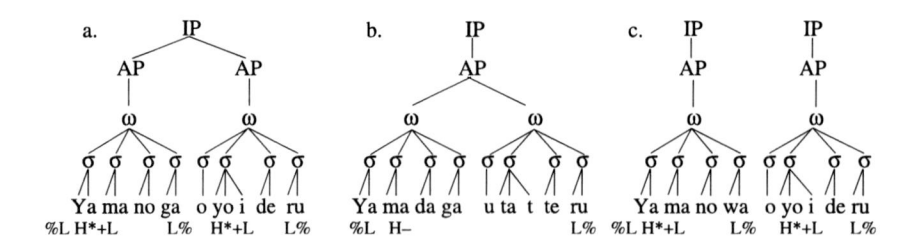

a.
```
       IP                          
      /  \                         
    AP    AP                       
    |      |                       
    ω      ω                       
  /|||\\  /|\                     
  σσσσσ  σσσ                       
 Ya ma no ga  o yo i de ru         
 %L H*+L      L%  H*+L    L%       
```

b.
```
       IP                          
      /  \                         
    AP    AP                       
    |      |                       
    ω      ω                       
  /|||\\  /|\                     
  σσσσσ  σσσ                       
 Ya ma da ga  u ta t te ru         
 %L H–             L%              
```

c.
```
    IP              IP             
    |               |              
    AP              AP             
    |               |              
    ω               ω              
  /|||\\          /|\              
  σσσσσ          σσσ               
 Ya ma no wa     o yo i de ru      
 %L H*+L    L%   H*+L    L%        
```

Each of the utterances in figure 17.1 constitutes a single IP, and the second [L%] boundary tone at the end of the utterance marks the final boundary of this IP as well as the final boundary of the second AP. By contrast, the utterance of *Ya'mano-wa oyo'ideru* in figure 17.3a (black line) is two IPs, so that the medial [L%] boundary tone here marks an IP boundary as well as an AP boundary. (The phonetic markers to the strength of this medial disjuncture include the noticeable phrase-final lengthening on the *-wa* as well as other less well-documented hiatus markers, such as a possible change in voice quality or glottal stop. However, they do not include a silent pause, so there is no separate initial [%L] boundary tone marking the beginning of the second IP.) There are many other tone sequences besides simple [L%] that can mark the end of a prosodic phrase, giving rise to a variety of boundary pitch movements (BPMs) with contrasting pragmatic functions.

We discuss the inventory of BPMs that can mark the end of a phrase in the next section, but first we must describe one more element that can occur in the tone sequence for some APs. This other AP-level element is the *akusento-kaku*, a sequence of tones that is tagged in Japanese ToBI as [H*+L]. This tone sequence is what results in the steep fall in each AP in figure 17.1a and the first AP in figure 17.1b. The APs *Ya'mano-ga* and *Ka'shino-ga* contrast with *Yamada-ga* and *Kushida-ga* in that each of the former has an *akusento-kaku* on its first syllable. The APs *oyo'ideru* and *hashi'tteru* similarly contrast with *utatteru* and *kurashiteru* in that each of the former has an *akusento-kaku* on its second syllable, and there would be a steep fall after the second syllable in *hashi'tteru* in figure 17.1b if the vowel in this syllable were not effectively deleted. That is, the listener parses the implicit high target for a [H*+L] from the surrounding pitch dynamics and from the relationship between the low-tone pitch targets on the first and the third syllables, even though the syllable bearing the high tone of the *akusento-kaku* is completely voiceless.

This term *akusento-kaku* is usually rendered in English as 'pitch accent' or 'accent', but we introduce it first by the Japanese term to try to decouple this use in translation from the way these two English terms are used in AM models of several other well-studied languages. In descriptions of English, for example, *accent* refers to any of a number of prominence-lending pragmatic morphemes that can be associated with the metrically strongest syllables in the most prominent content words of an utterance. In English, the location of these prominence-lending morphemes is determined by prosodic constraints such as OBLIGATORYHEAD (the principle that the intonation contour for each intonational phrase must contain at least one pitch accent associated to the metrically strongest prosodic position; see Hyman 2005) in

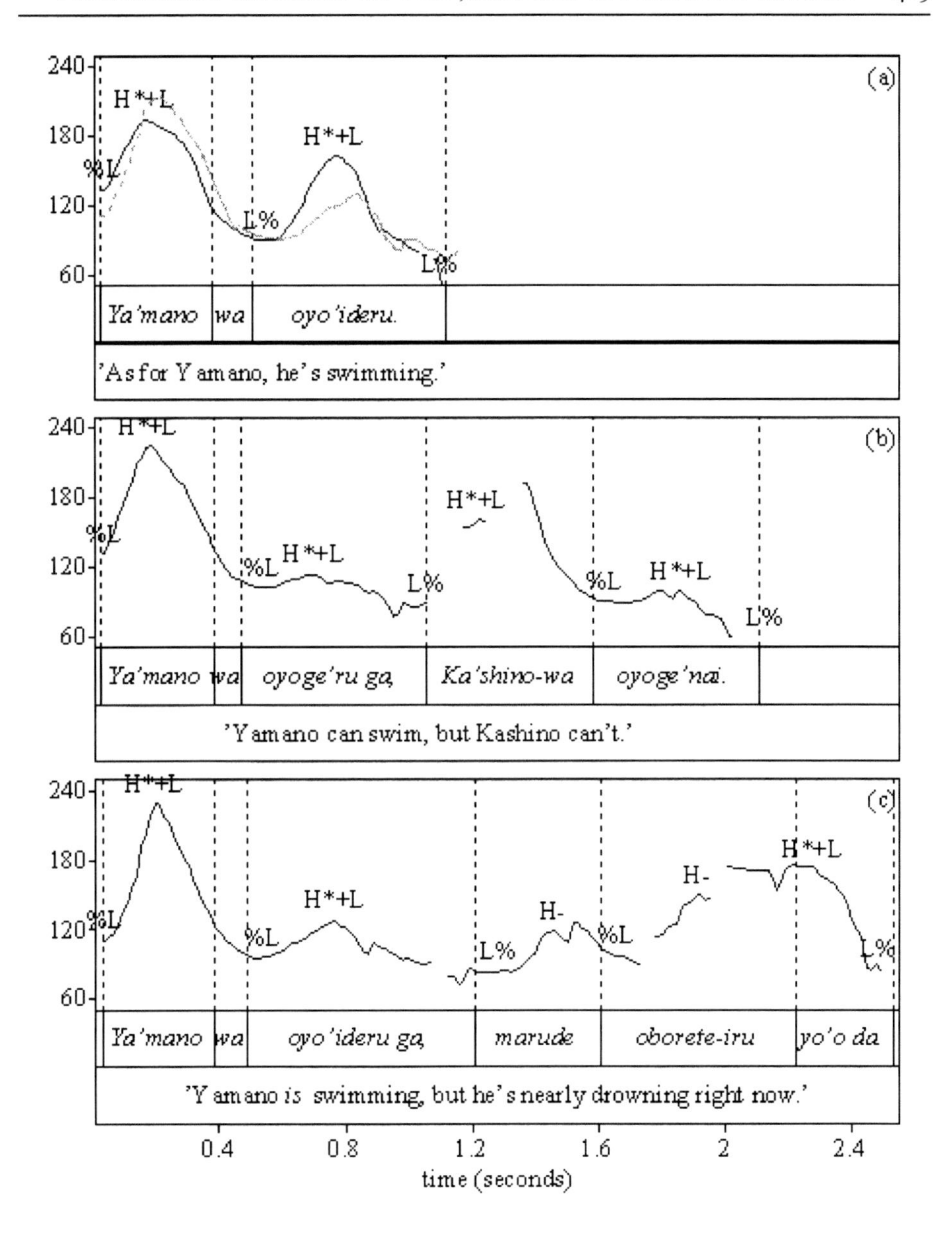

Figure 17.3 F0 contours for utterances of four sentences illustrating different pitch range relationships between Ya'mano-wa ... (or Ya'mano-ga ...) and the following verb phrase. The gray dashed line in (a) is a copy of the F0 contour of the utterance Ya'mano-ga oyo'ideru in figure 17.1a.

interaction with the information structure of the utterance in its discourse context. For example, a native speaker of English may choose to place a particular rising-falling configuration of accents on each of the nouns and verbs in the sentences in (2) to invoke the relevant contrast sets for each person and each activity.

(2) [context: Who's doing what?]
YaMAno is SWIMming. KaSHIma is RUNning. YaMAda's just standing there SINGing to 'em.

When speakers of English begin to learn Japanese, they may interpret the rises and falls in figure 17.1a and 17.1b in terms of such head-marking tonal morphemes in their native language. But this is a misparsing of the prosodic function of the tone shapes in these two Japanese utterances. Although the steep fall in *Ya'mano* in figure 17.1a is because this noun has a pitch accent on the first syllable, that fact is a property of the word itself, regardless of the context in which it is uttered. The specification of a [H*+L] fall at this point is part of the phonological contrast between accented *Ya'mano* and unaccented *Yamada*.

Japanese is like conservative varieties of Basque in having a lexical contrast between words specified for an accentual fall and words without this specification. (See Hualde 1991 and Hualde et al. 2002 for descriptions of the conservative Basque system and of the influence of contact with Spanish in other varieties.) Tokyo Japanese is crucially different from Basque, however, in that this lexical specification completely constrains the distribution of [H*+L] sequences in the surface intonation pattern. That is, in Basque, an unaccented word must be grouped together with a following accented word, and if a sentence contains only lexically unaccented words, an accent is inserted somewhere—either in the last argument before the sentence-final verb or earlier if there is narrow focus on an earlier constituent (see Ito 2002a). By contrast, there is no postlexical insertion of accent in Japanese. When a Japanese sentence contains no lexically accented words, the intonation contour of an utterance of that sentence does not contain any accents, whatever the focus pattern. Instead, it is composed only of the same tones as the contour in figure 17.1c (see also (3b)); there are the rises for the [%L H-] or [L% H-] sequences that mark the beginning of every AP, and there may be additional boundary tones marking the end of some phrases, but there are no other tones. Any fall in pitch within an AP is not the sharp localized fall of the accent [H*+L] but some more or less gradual interpolation between the high pitch target for the phrasal high and some following low tone. When these words are all grouped together into one long AP, as in figure 17.2c, this gradually falling Fo can describe a fairly long stretch of the contour from the high target at the end of the rise for the initial [%L H-] to the IP-level boundary [L%] at the end.

Note that this account of the long gradual fall in figure 17.2c assumes underspecification of tones relative to potential tone-bearing units. That is, none of the morae between the demarcative rise in *omiage* and the boundary tone at the end of the utterance is described as having an associated tone target of any kind. This differs from older accounts within the Autosegmental Phonology framework, such as Haraguchi (1977), who specifies a [H] tone target for each of the ten sonorant morae after the demarcative rise from the first to the second V in *omiage*. In such older accounts, the description of the fall that is actually observed over this purported sequence of ten [H] tone targets is relegated to *declination*—an "extra-grammatical" or "paralinguistic" manipulation of global pitch trends. Pierrehumbert and Beckman (1988) argue for their underspecified AM account (which X-JToBI follows in this regard) on the basis of slope measurements for unaccented APs containing varying numbers of syllables. In their data, the slope of the fall is inversely correlated with its length, just as predicted in an account that models the fall as an interpolation from the [H–] phrase tone to some later low target. In this AM account, then, the fall in figure 17.2c is attributed to the transition between different target values assigned to the [H–] and the [L%], just as the slightly rising plateau-like interval in the first AP in figure 17.2a is attributed to a transition between only slightly different target values for the phrasal [H–] at the beginning and the higher tone target of the [H*+L] accentual fall at the syllable that is lexically associated to the *akusento-kaku*.

The Fo contour for figure 17.2a also illustrates another phenomenon that has been treated differently in at least one older account in the Autosegmental Phonology framework. The [H*] target at the accent in *ta'beta* is considerably lower than that in *chi'izu*. The same relationship holds between the accent on the VP and the accent on the preceding NP in figures 17.1a and 17.1b. McCawley (1968) accounts for this relationship by positing a *mid (M) tone* for Japanese—that is, a tone target intermediate between [H] and [L] such as the [M] tone necessary to describe the lexical tone contrasts on monosyllabic words in Yoruba and Cantonese. In the AM account, by contrast, the lowering of the tone target on the verbs in figures 17.1a, 17.1b, and 17.2a is attributed instead to the component of the grammar that specifies parameters of the backdrop *pitch range* for each AP and for each IP.

Pierrehumbert and Beckman (1988) argue for the AM treatment on the grounds that there are many more intermediate levels than just one. For example, the medial AP-level [L%] boundary tone in figure 17.1a (see also example (1a)) is certainly lower than either the preceding or the following accent peak. Yet it is higher than an IP-level [L%] boundary tone at the end of the utterance. This can be seen by contrasting the AP-level [L%] to the utterance-final [L%] in that example or by contrasting the lower IP-level [L%] after *oyoge'ru-ga* in utterance figure 17.3b to the merely AP-level [L%] after the following *Ka'shino-wa*. This difference between the truly low target for the [L] at an IP boundary versus the intermediate [L] at a mere AP boundary is a fairly reliable cue to the level of the disjuncture. It seems to be the same kind of boundary strengthening effect noted for consonant features in many languages by researchers such Pierrehumbert and Talkin (1992), Fougeron and Keating (1997), and Jun (1998). Other types of systematic difference among tones are illustrated in the Fo contours of the two example sentences that are overlaid in figure 17.4.

One difference in figure 17.4 is contained just within the *Akai ya'ne-no* phrase (gray line). Here the high target for the phrasal [H–] is lower than the high for the following accent peak, and this is true for all three speakers. The same relationship also accounts for the rise in pitch over the plateau-like interval in the *Omiyage-no chi'izu-o* phrase in figure 17.2a. We have also seen flat or slightly falling shapes for

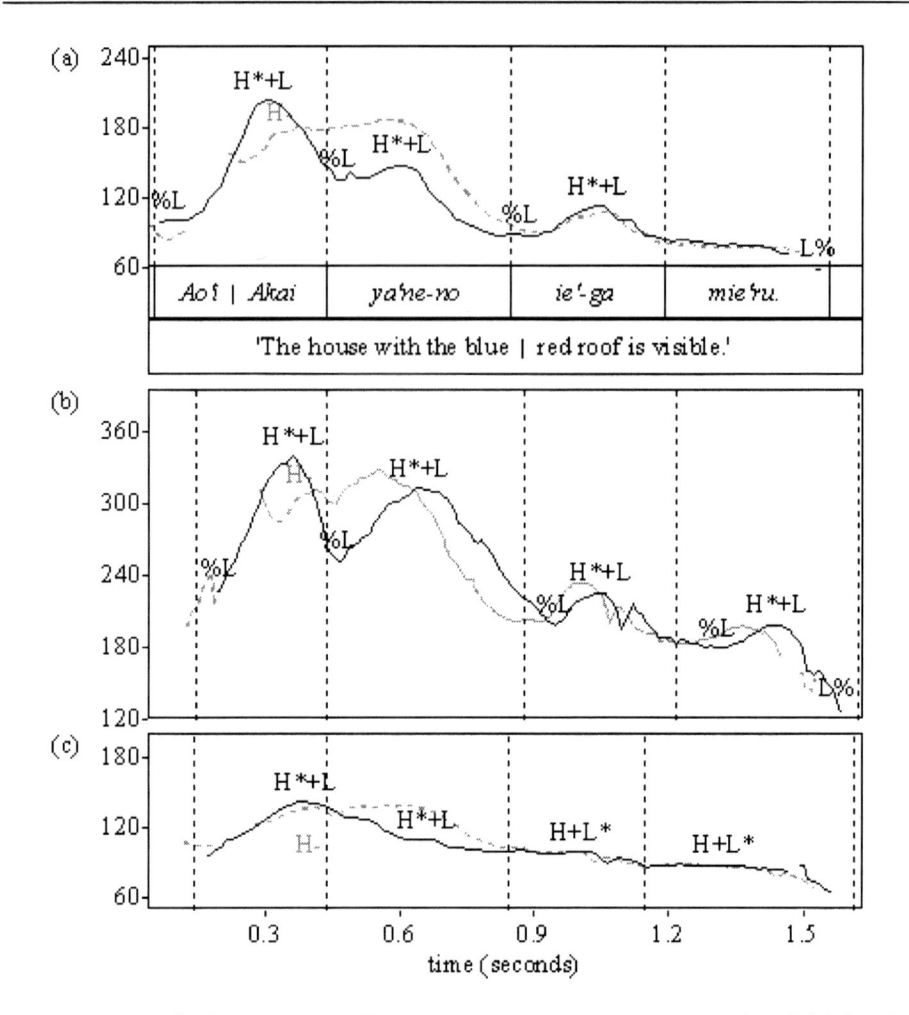

Figure 17.4 Overlaid F0 contours for utterances of two sentences produced (a) by the same male speaker who produced all of the utterances shown in earlier examples, (b) by a female speaker, and (c) by a different male speaker. In all three panels, the black line is for the *Ao'i*... sentence and the grey line is for the *Akai*... sentence.

longer accented phrases, such as the one in figure 17.2b. In read speech, however, a small rise seems typical for short phrases such as the *Akai ya'ne-no* phrase. That is, if [H–] is typically lower than the high target of [H*+L], then we can explain the difference in peak heights between unaccented *Yamada-ga* in figure 17.1c and accented *Ya'mano-ga* in figure 17.1a and between comparable minimal pairs in prior experiments by many researchers, including Pierrehumbert and Beckman (1988). This difference may be related to the same dissimilative *pre-L raising* seen in many other languages, including Yoruba (Laniran and Clements 2003), Thai (Gandour, Potisuk, and Dechongkit 1994), and Taiwanese (Peng 1997).

Another systematic difference seen in figure 17.4 is between the *ya'ne-no* phrase in the two overlaid utterances. The accent peak on *ya'ne* is lower after accented *ao'i* than it is after unaccented *akai*, as predicted by McCawley's rule lowering [H] to [M] in this context. However, each of the subsequent accent peaks in both sentences also is lower than its immediately preceding accent peak. Moreover, in the female speaker's utterances in figure 17.4b, where the medial [L%] AP-boundary tones are all clearly visible as local Fo minima, there is the same successive lowering of Fo values across the two or three utterance-medial AP boundaries.

Which of these intermediate levels should be singled out as the target level [M]? The X-JToBI model follows Pierrehumbert and Beckman (1988) in calling none of them [M]. Instead, all tone levels in Japanese are either [H] or [L], with the intermediate Fo values attributed to another type of phonological representation than the categorical contrast between these two tones—namely, a representation of backdrop reference pitch levels. For example, beginning with Poser (1984), all accounts in the AM framework model the systematically lower value for the [H] tone in *ya'ne* after the accented adjective in figure 17.4 in terms of *downstep*, defined as a compression of the pitch range that begins at the *akusento-kaku* and affects all tone targets up to the following IP boundary. Other current formal models of Japanese intonation patterns account for some of the systematic Fo target differences between and within utterances in subtly different ways from the account in the X-JToBI model. However, despite their differences, all current formal models of the Japanese intonation system share one property that distinguishes them from older Autosegmental Phonology accounts such as McCawley 1968 or Haraguchi 1977. All provide some way of representing the kind of continuous variation discussed in these examples directly in the grammar. Understanding this aspect of the AM framework model and other compatible models is critical for understanding one of the basic mechanisms for focus marking in the language. We expand on this aspect in the next section.

17.2.3 The Relationship between Tone Features and Pitch Range Features

Pierrehumbert and Beckman (1988) describe an intonation synthesis program that models the differences in Fo value among the various [H] or [L] targets in terms of *prominence* relationships at two different levels of specification. One level involves *tone scaling* within the local pitch range. For example, in figure 17.3b the more prominent IP-level [L%] target after the *oyoge'ru-ga* is scaled lower in the pitch range than the merely AP-level [L%] targets at the ends of the preceding and following phrases. Similarly, the more prominent [H] target of the accent is scaled higher in the pitch range than the phrasal [H–], as described above. In the synthesis program, these two local prominence relationships are specified in terms of two constants indicating tone-scaling ratios. The first constant positions an IP-final [L%] proportionally closer to the *bottom-line* value for the local pitch range, and the second one positions any accent [H*] target proportionally closer to the *topline* for the local pitch range. Such variation in tone-scaling changes the target position within the pitch range, but leaves the pitch range intact.

By contrast, other prominence relationships are modeled by varying the pitch range. The synthesis program provides for a paradigmatic choice of hertz values for the bottomline and for the topline of the pitch range of each IP. It also provides for the paradigmatic choice of an "AP prominence" factor—a ratio value that determines the topline for each AP relative to the pitch range of the IP that dominates it. For example, the accent peak on /Ya'mano-wa/ in figure 17.3a (black line) is lower than the accent peak on /Ya'mano-ga/ in figure 17.1a (reproduced as the gray line in figure 17.3a), because the topic IP /Ya'mano-wa/ is not in focus relative to the following predicate. In the synthesis program, this relationship is generated by specifying a lower top-line value for the first IP /Ya'mano-wa/ in figure 17.3a (black line). In a similar way, the accent peak on the *Akai ya'ne-no* phrase is very much higher than the peaks on *ie'* and *mie'ru* in all three speakers' renditions of this sentence in figure 17.4, because the initial AP is produced in a pitch range that is somewhat expanded relative to a more neutral reading. This reflects the focus structure of the sentence in the kinds of discourse contexts that the speakers could imagine for it. The distinctive roof color identifies which house it is that is visible. In the synthesis program, this is specified by an AP prominence ratio greater than 1.0 so that the topline for the first AP is above the topline for the IP as a whole.

The discourse-level considerations just described are not the only ones at play in determining the top-line value for an AP. There is also the general phonological constraint that AP-level high tone targets are lower in APs that occur after an accented AP within the same IP. This constraint is reflected in the lower value for the accent peak on *oyo'ideru* in figure 17.1a, where the subject and predicate are grouped together into one IP, relative to the accent peak on *oyo'ideru* in figure 17.3a (black line), where the predicate stands alone in an independent IP. The same relationship can be seen also on *ya'ne* in *Ao'i ya'ne-no* as compared to the accent peak in the *Akai ya'ne-no* phrase in figure 17.4. In the synthesis program, these differences are modeled by a *downstep* ratio that proportionally reduces the distance of the IP topline above the bottomline immediately after each accent [H*] target. The very much lower values of the peaks on *ie'-ga* and *mi'eru* in figure 17.4 then reflect the combined effects of focus subordination and of downstep.

The types of prominence relationships that are modeled in Pierrehumbert and Beckman's synthesis program are also modeled in a comparably direct way in Hiroya Fujisaki's model that was first described in Fujisaki and Sudo 1971 and that has been adopted in an impressive body of later studies that became the basis for the intonation synthesis modules in several leading Japanese text-to-speech and concept-to-speech systems (e.g., Fujisaki and Hirose 1993; Fujisaki et al. 1994; Hirai, Higuchi, and Sagisaka 1997; Kiriyama, Hirose, and Minematsu 2002). In the Fujisaki framework, the prominence relationship among different intonation phrases is modeled by specifying different amplitudes for their *phrase commands*. The phrase command is a local pulse aligned near the beginning of the phrase and then convolved with a decaying declination function. The prominence relationship among different APs, in contrast, is modeled by the specification of different amplitudes for the *accent commands*. The accent command is a square wave that generates the rise at the beginning of each AP and the subsequent steep fall after the accent peak in an accented AP. The differences between the X-JToBI AM framework model and Fujisaki's model primarily involve the treatment of unaccented phrases. The accent command in Fujisaki's model implies a [H] target at the end of an unaccented AP. In other respects the two frameworks provide comparable accounts of the many intermediate Fo target levels observed within and across utterances. The different frameworks are comparable enough that observations couched in one set of synthesis parameters can be translated readily into the parameters of the other model. That is, this kind of formal analysis-by-synthesis yields data that can be compared across frameworks in a way that is not possible with the informal pretheoretic observations reported in studies such as Selkirk and Tateishi 1991, which assumes a direct and deterministic mapping between syntactic and prosodic structures instead of building an independent formal model of the prosodic structure on its own terms. Both synthesis models also provide an explicit representation of continuous variation in the alignment of tone targets relative to the consonant and vowel segments of the associated text. This explicit representation of tone-text alignment is critical for describing the contrasting boundary pitch movements at the ends of intonational phrases, which we describe in the next section.

17.2.4 Boundary Pitch Movements

The preceding two sections have discussed the relevant metrical structure at both the AP and IP levels, as well as the tonal autosegments that mark the lower level of the AP and the pitch range compression that is triggered by the accent tones and affects all following tones until a new pitch range is chosen for the following IP. The literature in English focuses almost exclusively on these aspects of the Japanese intonation system, and all have been encoded even in the earlier J_ToBI conventions (Venditti 1997). By contrast, the last major element of Japanese intonation—the inventory of rises and more complicated tonal events that are licensed to occur after a phrase-final [L%] boundary tone—is rarely given more than passing mention.

In the X-JToBI conventions, these events are called *boundary pitch movements* (BPMs). A BPM occurs when the AP-level boundary [L%] is followed by one or more other tone targets, including at least one [H], to create a simple rise, a concave rise, a rise-fall, or some even more complicated Fo movement. There is a longstanding consensus that BPMs are pragmatic morphemes that are licensed to occur at the end of a phrase to contribute to the pragmatic interpretation of the phrase (see Kindaichi 1951, Ohishi 1959, Kawakami 1963, Miyaji 1963, Kori 1989b, Fujisaki and Hirose 1993, Muranaka and Hara 1994, Venditti, Maeda, and van Santen 1998, Katagiri 1999, among many others). Despite this primordial characterization of their general function, however, we do not yet have either an exhaustive inventory of BPMs or an exact description of the contrasting discourse meanings that they convey. In this section, we discuss the inventory of BPM categories in the X-JToBI scheme, which were used to tag all 178,000+ phrase boundaries in the forty-five-hour Core portion of the CSJ (henceforth CSJCore), yielding the counts in table

Table 17.1 Distribution of phrase-final tones in CSJCore

	L% only	L% + H%	L% + HL%	L% + LH%	L% + HLH%	Total
APS[a]	56,736	19,647	3,041	125	1	79,550
SPS[b]	64,546	11,148	6,997	259	9	82,959
D[c]	7,152	1,705	565	34	4	9,460
R[d]	5,118	1,636	33	1	0	6,788
Total	133,552	34,136	10,636	419	14	178,757
%	74.7%	19.1%	5.9%	0.2%	0%	100%

[a] APS (Academic Presentation Speech) refers to CSJ monologues collected from live academic presentations.
[b] SPS (Simulated Public Speaking) refers to monologues collected from lay subjects who were asked to give short presentations about everyday topics.
[c] D refers to dialogue recordings.
[d] R refers to read speech of (i) passages from popular science books or (ii) "reproduced" transcriptions of the APS/SPS spontaneous speech (see Maekawa 2003 for details).

17.1. We compare this list of BPMs with the inventory proposed by Kawakami in his insightful 1963 paper on phrase-final rises.

As table 17.1 shows, many prosodic phrases in the CSJCore end simply in [L%], without any additional boundary pitch events. This is true also of all of the prosodic phrases in our read example utterances in figures 17.2–17.4 and figure 17.5a. However, phrases ending in other boundary configurations are not rare even in fairly scripted spontaneous speech. For example, nearly a quarter of the phrases in the academic presentations (APS) in the CSJCore are tagged with some kind of BPM after the [L%].

The most common BPM tag in the CSJCore is [H%]. This corresponds to the shape that Kawakami (1963) termed the *futsuu no jooshoochoo* 'normal rise'. The pitch rises sharply from the onset of the final syllable of the phrase, as shown in figure 17.5b. The [H%] BPM should not be confused with the superficially similar 'question rise' illustrated in figure 17.5d. Its function is instead more closely related to that of [HL%], another BPM with which it also shares an alignment pattern for the [H] tone target. In the [HL%] BPM, as in [H%], the F0 rises sharply at the onset of the final syllable of the phrase, before it falls again. The final syllable is usually lengthened as well, as in the example utterance in figure 17.5c.

In each of the examples in figure 17.5, the BPM occurs on a sentence-final pragmatic particle *ne*. Katagiri (1999) describes *ne* as occurring only in dialogue, where it indicates lack of commitment to the proposition just uttered (in contrast to *yo*, which indicates the speaker's acceptance of the proposition into the mutual belief space). Katagiri also describes how this core meaning of *ne* interacts with the meaning of a rising versus a falling phrase-final intonation pattern to induce a variety of conversational implicatures, such as confirmation question, polite assertion, and the invoking of external authority. It is important to note, however, that Katagiri does not distinguish between the two types of rising BPMs illustrated

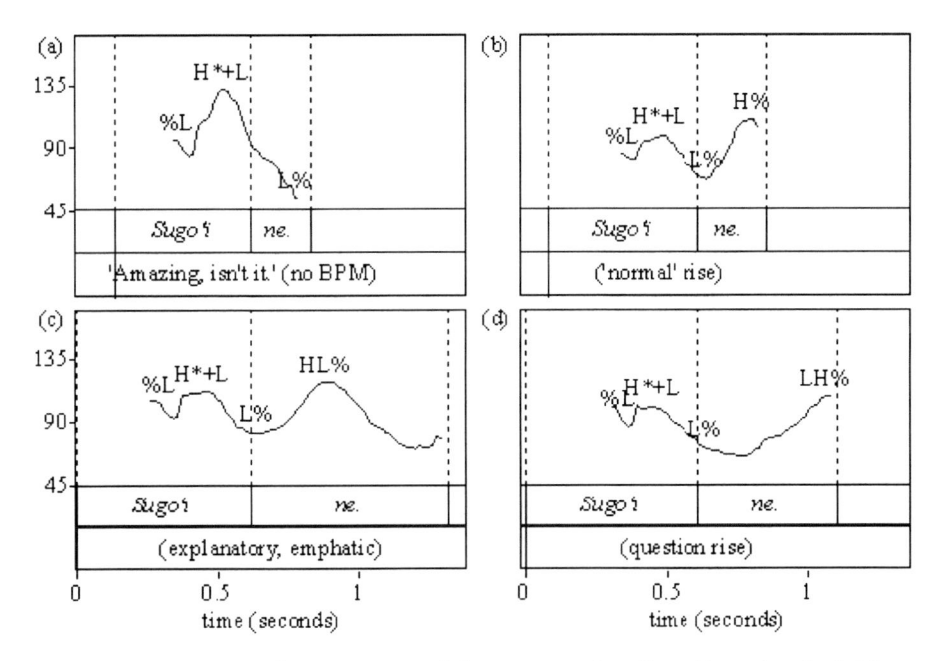

Figure 17.5 F0 contours for utterances of the sentence *Sugo'i ne* 'Amazing, isn't it' pronounced with four different final boundary-tone configurations.

in figure 17.5b versus 17.5d. Thus, it is possible that some of the meaning contrasts he shows are associated with tonal differences.

Katagiri is not alone in his failure to distinguish more than one rising BPM. Indeed, in the literature in English, this is the rule rather than the exception. For example, Pierrehumbert and Beckman (1988) also recognize only one rising BPM, which they analyze as a [H%] boundary tone. Moreover, they elicit this rise only in interrogative uses of the sentence-final particles *ka* and *no*. The occurrence of a rising BPM in association with an utterance-final interrogative *ka* or *no* marks a very salient, easily grasped speech act, so it is not surprising that all researchers have recognized at least one rising BPM in at least this one discourse context.

Pierrehumbert and Beckman also follow McCawley (1968), Haraguchi (1977), and Poser (1984) in assuming that this rise occurs only in sentence-final position. Based on this (mistaken) assumption, they posit a prosodic constituent above the IP (termed the *utterance*) as the domain that licenses the [H%] target. However, as figure 17.6a shows, the BPM that is tagged as [H%] in X-JToBI readily occurs sentence-medially in spontaneous speech (see also Nagahara 1994 and Nagahara and Iwasaki 1994 for a similar insight). Often the phrase-final syllable on which [H%] is realized is a postposition or case particle, although this need not be the case. For example, there are three instances of [H%] in figure 17.6a, but only one of these is associated to a case particle. Moreover, as the counts in table 17.1 show, this BPM occurs frequently in all genres represented in CSJCore. That is, unlike the particles *ne* and *yo*, the simple rise BPM is by no means limited to dialogue.

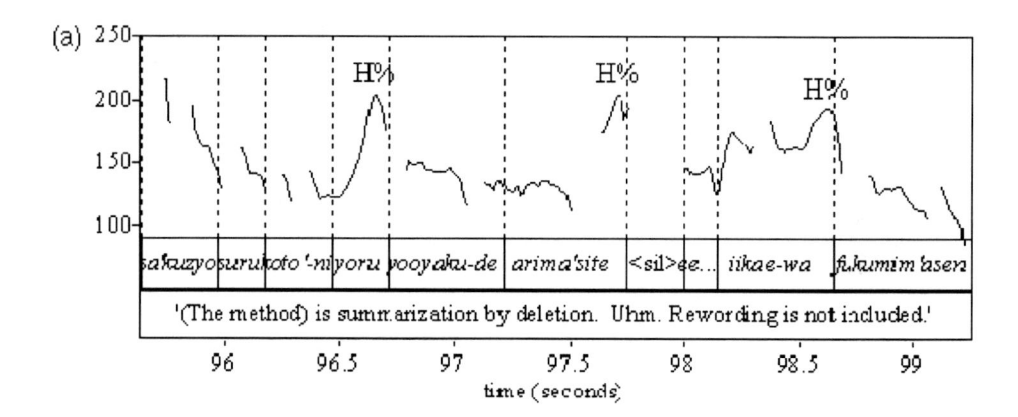

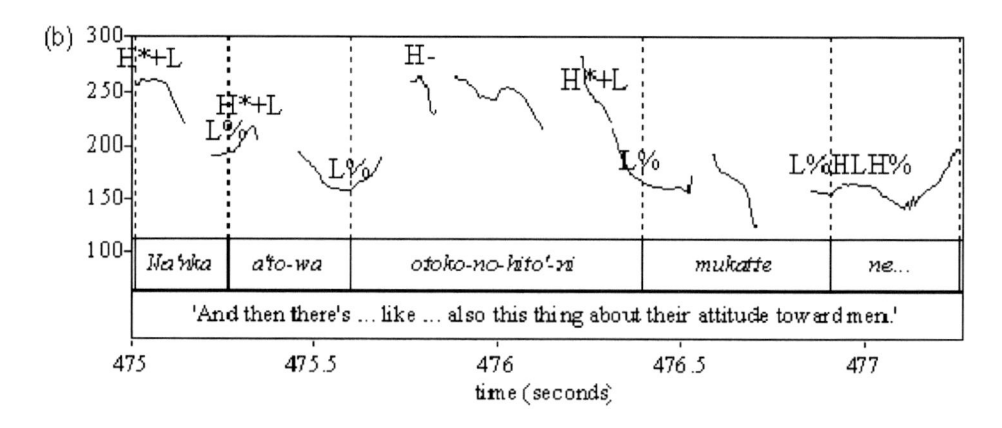

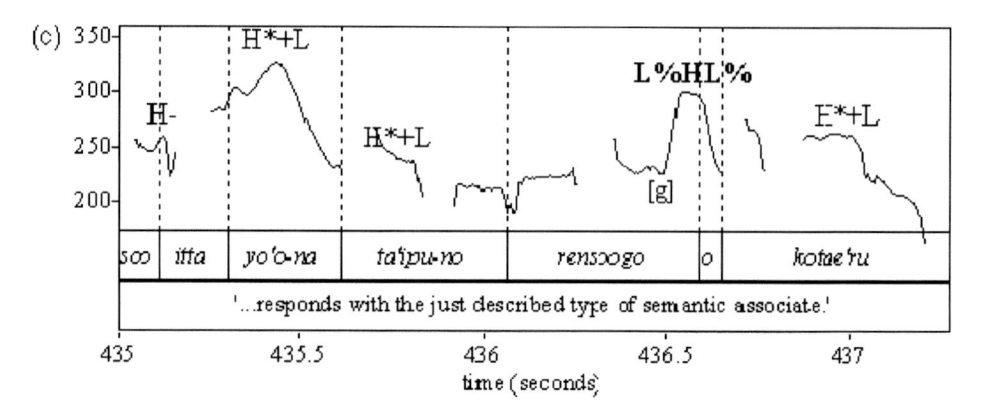

Figure 17.6 F0 contours for three utterances from the CSJCore. (a) An example of H% marking sequential phrases. (Tags for the accent tones and AP-initial rise tones are suppressed to highlight the [H%] BPM.) (b) An example of the HLH% boundary pitch movement (from a conversation between two young women about how Chinese women are different). (c) An example of the HL% PNLP: underlined extract of <AME> to ittara <AMAI> toka *soo itta yo'o-na ta'ipu-no rensoogo^-o kotae'ru* ... 'When presented with <CANDY>, the subject *responds with* <SWEET> or *some such associate of this type* ...' from a talk on processes of auditory lexical access of words that have near homophones differing minimally in lexical accentuation, such as *ame* 'candy' and *a'me* 'rain'.

In the (mostly non-English) literature that does distinguish at least two different rising BPMs, the function of the rise that is tagged as [H%] in X-JToBI is described as one of imparting prominence to the constituent to which it associates (see Ohishi 1959; Kori 1989b, 1997; Venditti, Maeda, and van Santen 1998; Taniguchi and Maruyama 2001; Oshima, 2007; among many others). This function contrasts with the function of the question rise in figure 17.5d, and it relates [H%] instead to [HL%], the rise-fall BPM illustrated in figure 17.5c. The rise-fall BPM in figure 17.5c is not included in Kawakami's (1963) inventory, but it is among the shapes examined by Venditti and her colleagues in a perception experiment (Venditti, Maeda, and van Santen 1998) matched with an extensive set of acoustic measurements (Maeda and Venditti 1998). In the perception study, Venditti, Maeda, and van Santen (1998) asked listeners to rate each stimulus on several semantic scales. They observed that listeners perceive [HL%] to be highly 'explanatory' and 'emphatic'. That is, Japanese listeners expect speakers to use [HL%] in contexts where they are explaining some point to their interlocutor and want to focus attention on a particular phrase in this explanation. Although it is not as frequent as [H%] and is markedly rare in read speech, [HL%] occurs at 4–8 percent of the phrase boundaries in the different genres of spontaneous speech in the CSJCore.

The next most frequent BPM in the CSJCore is much rarer, occurring at only 0.2 percent of phrase boundaries. This is the [LH%] rise illustrated in figure 17.5d. This BPM may occur sentence finally and is observed most often at the ends of utterances expressing questions. As noted already, this BPM is superficially similar in form to [H%] in that the Fo rises on the last syllable of the phrase. However, unlike with [H%], where the onset of the rise aligns with the onset of the final syllable, the rise of [LH%] occurs later within that syllable, making the overall shape of [L% LH%] more "scooped" or "concave" than that of [L% H%]. In some cases, especially in cases expressing incredulity, the final syllable is lengthened as well. In the Venditti, Maeda, and van Santen (1998) perception study, stimuli carrying [LH%] were perceived as 'seeking confirmation' from the interlocutor, and those that also had a lengthened final syllable yielded a high 'disbelief' rating (i.e., incredulity questions).

The X-JToBI [LH%] category corresponds to two different rise shapes in Kawakami (1963), who describes simple information-seeking questions such as *ka'eru?* or *ka'eru no?* 'Are you returning?' as having a *futsuu no jooshoochoo* 'normal rise' and distinguishes this shape from interrogatives indicating 'deep' questioning, which he describes as having a *hanmon no jooshoochoo* 'return rise'. In their acoustic analysis of BPM contrasts, Venditti, Maeda, and van Santen (1998) show that both the alignment and overall Fo curve shape categorically distinguish all questions from prominence-lending rises: in both information-seeking and incredulity questions ([LH%]), the rise onset occurs later in the syllable and the rise shape is more concave than in the prominence-lending rise ([H%]). By contrast, the phonetic distinction between the two question types is fuzzier. The duration of the final syllable varies continuously from the shortest most clearly information-seeking question (e.g., *ka'eru no?*) to the most drawn-out, clearest examples of an incredulity question (e.g., *ka'eru no?!!*). Additionally, the location of the rise onset (and other points during the rise) is correlated with the varying durations of the C and V autosegments on which the rise is realized. Given these results, we now understand Kawakami's *futsuu no jooshoochoo* and *hanmon no jooshoochoo* to be descriptions of the extreme endpoints of a continuum that includes many intermediate degrees of emphatic lengthening. That is, the gradient nature of the relationship between the phonetic dimensions and the continuum of contrasting degrees of incredulity suggests an analysis akin to the one that Hirschberg and Ward (1992) propose for the uncertainty versus incredulity interpretations of the English fall-rise contour.

The rarest BPM distinguished by X-JToBI is [HLH%], a very complex shape in which the F0 rises, then falls, then rises again. This BPM also is not included in Kawakami's inventory of rises. It seems characteristic particularly of child-directed speech, where it can give a wheedling or cajoling quality to the utterance to which it attaches. The counts in table 17.1 show that [HLH%] occurs a total of only 14 times on the 178,000+ boundaries of the CSJCore, one of which is shown in figure 17.6b. This is likely because the speaking genres that CSJ includes are for the most part not the types in which [HLH%] readily occurs; we would expect to count more instances of [HLH%] in interactions between mothers and their young children or in conversations between young female friends.

In addition to the BPM tags in table 17.1, the X-JToBI conventions provide a number of diacritics that mark distinctions within categories. Several of these could well be phonologically distinct tonal sequences. They correspond to categories that Kawakami (1963) discusses (e.g., 'floating rise', 'hooked rise') that do not seem to have any kind of gradient relationship between the phonetic dimensions of contrast and a continuum of pragmatic interpretation. However, research on these distinctions is even less well-developed than research on the differences between the two types of [LH%]. Moreover, the functions that have been suggested for them are not directly relevant to the theme of this chapter. Therefore, the only X-JToBI diacritic that we mention here is for an F0 rise that Kawakami does not mention as a distinct BPM type.

The shape of this rise is convex, like that of the [H%] BPM, with the [L%] target that begins the rise aligned early in the syllable to which it associates, and it has been described by Ohishi (1959), Kori (1989b, 1997), and others as having a similar prominence-lending function. This rise contrasts with the [H%] BPM, however, in that it occurs on the penultimate syllable of the phrase rather than the last. In the X-JToBI conventions, this earlier rise is termed the PNLP (for *penultimate non-lexical prominence*). Because the F0 typically also falls immediately after the PNLP to a [L] target at the following phrase boundary, the X-JToBI convention is to mark the PNLP using the [HL%] rise-fall BPM label on the tones tier, with an additional tag ('PNLP') on the comments tier. A total of 1,162 cases of PNLP were tagged in CSJCore (62.7 percent in APS, 33.7 percent in SPS, 1.9 percent in dialogue, and 1.6 percent in read speech). In the example in figure 17.6c, the PNLP tagged rise-fall is indicated in bold.

17.3 THE PROSODIC MARKING OF PROMINENCE

Having provided an overview description of the Japanese intonation system, we can now turn to the various ways in which intonation patterns are manipulated in the marking of focal prominence in the language. Given that this is an area of research where the literature has been muddled considerably by drawing analogies to pretheoretical intuitions about English focus-marking mechanisms, it is useful to begin by describing one way in which focal prominence is *not* marked in Japanese.

17.3.1 Distinguishing Accent from *Akusento*

Much of the theoretical literature on focus marking in English, German, and Dutch invokes a structural property that is variously called *accent*, *nuclear pitch accent*, *sentence stress*, or *nuclear stress*. As this jumble of terms suggests, focus marking in these languages involves a complex interplay of prominence markers at several levels of the prosodic hierarchy. We cannot do justice here to the richness of these systems, however, and instead we discuss just one example from English that we hope expresses as clearly as possible what we mean when we say that standard Japanese has no analog to the notion "accent" when it is used as a synonym for "nuclear stress" in these Germanic languages. Especially, we must emphasize that the notion "accent" in that sense is neither a formal nor a functional analog to 'accent' as a translation of *akusento-kaku*.

In section 17.2.2, we alluded to a common cross-language misparsing of the *akusento-kaku* in words such as *Ya'mano*, *oyo'ideru*, and *hashi'tteru* in figures 17.1a and 17.1b. The utterances in figure 17.7 illustrate how the English intonation system contributes to this misparsing. In figure 17.7a the first syllable of *running* is associated to the nuclear pitch accent in the intonation contour. By nuclear pitch accent, we mean a configuration of tones that marks the word (or some larger constituent) as the focus of the utterance and simultaneously invites the listener to make some inference about the pragmatic relationship between the focused constituent and the shared model of the discourse context. In figure 17.7a, this configuration is the fall in pitch defined by the transition from the [H*] pitch accent on the first syllable of *running* to the following [L−] phrase accent. In figure 17.7b, the second syllable of the (English) word *Yamano* is associated to the same kind of fall that makes *running* focally prominent in figure 17.7a.

The tone labels in figure 17.7 follow the MAE_ToBI tagging conventions described by Beckman, Hirschberg, and Shattuck-Hufnagel (2005). Other AM models of English offer different analyses of the falling pitch that is aligned earlier in figure 17.7b as compared with figure 17.7a. For example, Gussenhoven (2004) labels the fall as [H*+L], because he disputes the relevance of the notion "phrase accent" for English. Despite these differences across frameworks, however, there is

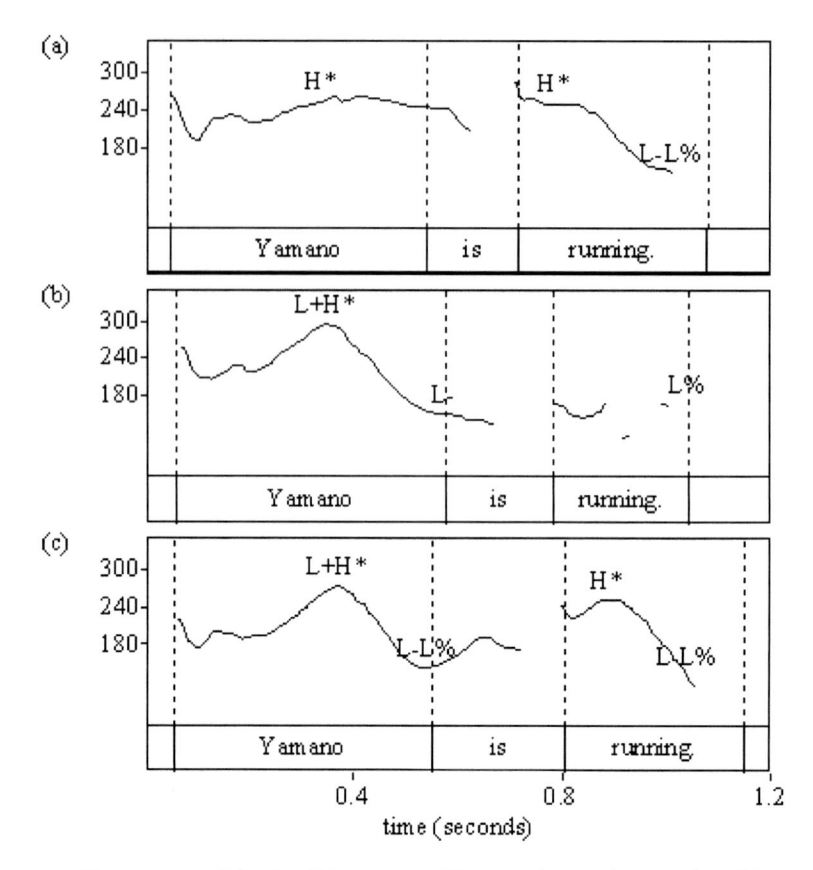

Figure 17.7 F0 contours of the English sentence *Yamano is running.* produced in response to (a) *What's happening in the next leg of the triathlon relay?* (b) *Who's doing this leg?* and (c) *Who's doing what?*

a broad consensus about the focus-marking function of the fall and about its culminative role. That is, any complete, well-formed intonation contour of English has exactly one nuclear pitch accent per intonation phrase. In figure 17.7c, then, the sentence is divided into two intonation phrases so that both *Yamano* and *running* can be associated to a nuclear pitch accent. That is, the restructuring of the sentence into two intonation phrases in figure 17.7c preserves the culminative distribution of nuclear pitch accents, with the result that there is exactly one word in each IP that is marked as bearing the one obligatory pitch accent in the intonation contour for the IP (what Liberman and Prince [1977] termed the "designated terminal element" of the phrase).

A noteworthy property of the English prosodic system is that this culminative distribution of nuclear pitch accents relative to IP boundaries in connected speech mirrors the culminative distribution of potential association sites for the nuclear pitch accent in polysyllabic words in the lexicon. In the words *Yamáno* and *rúnning* in figure 17.7, as in *rélay, dóing, átom, atómic, rétail, ráttle, legislátion,* and many other polysyllabic words of English, this potential association site is the penultimate syllable. In *átomize, ráttlesnake,* and *législature,* it is the first syllable. The terms *primary stress* and *lexical stress* refer to this potential for association to the nuclear pitch accent. As Hyman (2005) and many others before him have pointed out, the obligatory designation of exactly one primary stress per word imparts a sense of wordhood. Thus, compound words such as *ráttlesnake* and *láw degree* can be distinguished from phrases such as *ráttle it óff* and *láw and órder* because of the Compound Stress Rule—a morphological process whereby all but one of the primary stresses in a compound word lose the potential to associate to accent. Also, function words such as *the*, *of*, and *but* (which associate to pitch accents only in unusual circumstances) are commonly understood to be prosodically cliticized onto a neighboring content word. This link between the culminative distribution of primary stresses in words in the lexicon and the culminative distribution of nuclear pitch accents in the intonation phrases of a discourse gives rise to the terms *sentence stress* and *nuclear stress* to designate the stressed syllable in the word that associates to the nuclear pitch accent in an IP.

Another noteworthy property of the English intonation system is that association to the nuclear pitch accent is often accompanied by an exaggeration of other phonetic markers of prominence that together constitute the formal properties that define the *stress foot*, a lower-level constituent in the English prosodic hierarchy. These include, for example, (a) the aspiration of the foot-initial /t/ in *atomic* and *retail* as opposed to the lenited pronunciations typical of the foot-medial /t/ in *atom* and *rattler*, and (b) the constrained distribution of reduced/elided vowels that yields the morphological alternation between a full long /ɑ/ in the foot-initial *stressed* syllable of *atómic* and the reduced short /ə/ or deleted vowel (making the [m] syllabic) in the corresponding *unstressed* syllable in *átom*. Thus, the aspiration of foot-initial voiceless stops can be exaggerated when the word is accented (e.g., Docherty 1992, among many others), whereas foot-medial /t/ can be weakened further and even deleted in unaccented contexts in running speech (Raymond, Dautricourt, and Hume 2006). Similarly, the morphological alternation between full versus reduced/deleted vowels in related forms such as *atomic* and *atom* is echoed by the optional prosodic alternation between disyllabic pronunciations of words such as *rattler* ([ræʔ.lər]) in fast, unaccented contexts, and trisyllabic pronunciations ([ræ.rə.lər] or even [ræ.tʌ.lər]) when the stressed syllables in these words are associated with accents in the intonation contour (as noted by Beckman 1996a, among many others). Such segmental prominence ("stress proper") at the foot level is linked to the prosodic marking of focus in English because lexical stress constrains where pitch accents can and cannot go: any pitch accent in the intonation contour must associate to the head of a stress foot. This is the source of the unequivocally syllabic "strong" variants of words such as *of*, *the*, and *but* in contexts where they receive a pitch accent.

It is important to keep in mind that these links between syllable stress (in the lexicon) and pitch accent (in the intonation system) are particular to English and the handful of other languages that are like English. The prosodic organization of Japanese words and intonation phrases is quite different from that of English, and researchers should not be misled by the superficial phonetic resemblances that lead native speakers of Japanese to misparse the distribution of nuclear pitch accents in

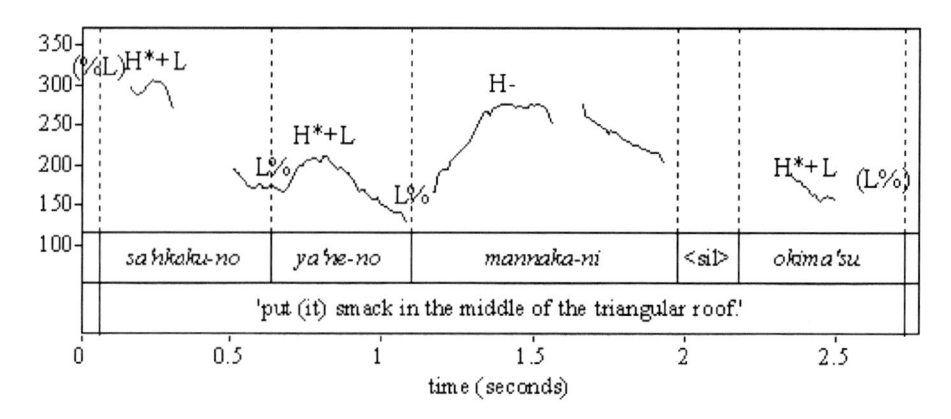

Figure 17.8 F0 contour of an utterance from a spontaneous narrative, illustrating a very prominent but unaccented focal constituent.

an utterance such as figure 17.7c in terms of the distribution of *akusento-kaku* in an utterance such as figure 17.1a, and vice versa.

The differences can be summarized most succinctly by contrasting the applicability of the notion "stress" in describing the two prosodic systems. In descriptions of English, this term is an indispensable shorthand way of capturing the many profound implicational dependencies among categorical markers of segmental prominence at the foot level and categorical markers of tonal prominence at the IP level. In Japanese, by contrast, there are no such fundamental links between segmental prominence and tonal prominence, and the term "stress" is at best a somewhat misleading translation of technical terms for pragmatic functions such as *kyoochoo* (better translated as 'emphasis' or 'focal prominence'). For example, where vowel lenition in English is constrained to occur in weak unaccented syllables, vowel lenition readily occurs in accented syllables in Japanese even in very deliberate read speech. The deletion of the [i] in the accented second syllable of *hasi'tteru* in figure 17.1b is by no means anomalous, as can be seen by the counts that Maekawa and Kikuchi (2005) report in all of the different genres in the CSJ. Also, where the typically unaccented (and lexically unstressed) pronunciation of function words in English is often described in terms of the notion "clitic"—that is, the prosodic grouping of function words onto adjacent content words in running speech—many function words in Japanese, such as *ma'de* 'until', *yo'ri* 'from', *su'ra* 'even', and *no'mi* 'only', are lexically accented, and although these words are almost always realized as clitics (i.e., produced without the [L% H–] rise that would demarcate them from the preceding noun phrase), the accented syllable nonetheless is often produced with an associated F0 fall for the *akusento-kaku*, as noted by Sagisaka and Sato (1983) and Kubozono (1993), among others. (See Maekawa and Igarashi 2006 for counts in the CSJ.) Conversely, content words that are lexically unaccented (i.e., lexically marked as having no possible association to an *akusento-kaku*) do not surface with an associated pitch accent even under focus. This fact is illustrated by the utterance in figure 17.8, in which the focally prominent word *mannaka* 'smack in the middle' is lexically unaccented and surfaces without any accent, whereas the following verb *okima'su* is lexically accented and surfaces with an accent but with none of the intonational hallmarks that make the preceding locative phrase the focus of the sentence. We turn to these hallmarks in the next section.

17.3.2 Phrasal Pitch Range and Focal Prominence

It has been widely noted in the literature that Japanese uses local pitch range expansion to mark focal prominence (see Kindaichi 1951; Kawakami 1957; Fujisaki and Hirose 1984; Fujisaki and Kawai 1988, 1994; Poser 1984; Pierrehumbert and Beckman 1988; Kori 1989a, 1989b, 1997; Takeda and Ichikawa 1990; Maekawa 1997; Nagao and Amano 2000; Ito 2002a, among others). Figures 17.3a and 17.8 illustrate this. In figure 17.3a, the F0 contour for an utterance of *Ya'mano-wa oyo'ideru* is overlaid on the F0 contour of an utterance of *Ya'mano-ga oyo'ideru*. The rendition of the *Ya'mano-wa*... sentence (black line) invokes a garden-variety "thematic" interpretation of *wa* (see Kuno 1973; Heycock, this volume), which makes the following verb the focal constituent in the utterance. By contrast, the rendition of the *Ya'mano-ga*... sentence (gray line) is an "out-of-the-blue" broad-focus utterance. In keeping with these contrasting focus patterns, the pitch range is expanded on *oyo'ideru* in the *Ya'mano-wa*... sentence relative to that on the same word in the *Ya'mano-ga*... sentence. Conversely, the pitch range on *Ya'mano-ga*... is expanded relative to that on *Ya'mano-wa*..., marking the subject as part of the focus constituent, which is the whole sentence in the broad-focus case. Because both *Ya'mano* and *oyo'ideru* are lexically accented, this pitch range expansion is most readily observed around the [H] tone of the [H*+L] *akusento-kaku*, which shows both a more extreme rise from the preceding [%L] or [L%] boundary tone and a more extreme fall to the [L] of the *akusento-kaku*. The utterance in figure 17.8, by contrast, shows that a word need not be accented to be a target of pitch range expansion.

This utterance is from a spontaneous monologue narrative that Venditti and Swerts (1996) elicit using a puzzle task in which the speaker is asked to describe the moves chosen to build a house from colored pieces of paper. In the just-completed move, the speaker places a triangular piece for the roof (*sa'nkaku-no ya'ne*), and in the utterance just before figure 17.8 in the monologue, she states that she will next place a pink rectangular piece for a window. In figure 17.8, then, she describes where exactly on the roof she will put the window piece. She produces prosodic prominence on the locative phrase *mannaka-ni* 'smack in the middle', which is the focal constituent. Note that this focused phrase is unaccented. That is, it does not contain the sharp fall in F0 that is present in APs containing words that are lexically specified as accented. Nonetheless, it is clearly marked for focal prominence by the expanded local pitch range. As noted above, this is a key difference from prominence marking in English, where a pitch accent is inserted on a rhythmically strong syllable postlexically to cue the pragmatic function of focal prominence. English speakers also employ pitch range expansion to mark focus, but it is localized to the tone targets of the nuclear pitch accent. Japanese is different in that accents cannot be inserted in phrases that do not contain lexically accented words. Therefore, when unaccented phrases such as *mannaka-ni* in figure 17.8 receive focal prominence, the local pitch range expansion must target tones other than the [H*+L] of the *akusento-kaku*. Specifically, the pitch range expansion is most easily observed on the [%L H–] boundary-marking sequence at the beginning of the focused unaccented AP.

This kind of dramatic rise at the beginning of the focus constituent is often termed *reset* or *Fo reset*. In both unaccented and accented phrases, the percept of reset can be enhanced in a gradient way by a contrast effect, as Maekawa (1997) notes in an experimental analysis of Fo heights of all phrases in an utterance containing a focused constituent. He shows that the pitch range of the prefocal phrase varies in inverse relationship to the degree of focal emphasis; more extreme pitch range expansion on the focused phrase is accompanied by more extreme pitch range compression on the immediately preceding phrase. Ito (2002a) similarly observes that the Fo values of prefocal peaks are lower than those in a baseline (broad focus) condition.

One topic of lively discussion in the early AM literature on Japanese is the exact extent of the local pitch range expansion after reset. This debate centers on the notion of the "domain" of pitch range specification and the "restructuring" of the prosodic constituent hierarchy that would license a local pitch range expansion such as that observed on *mannaka-ni* in figure 17.8. In Fujisaki's synthesis system (Fujisaki and Sudo 1971, Fujisaki and Hirose 1984), as in other models from that era when the paradigmatic specification of continuous variation in pitch range was first incorporated directly into the phonological formalism, there are two ways in which the extreme rise in Fo at the beginning of *mannaka* in this utterance can be formalized. First, it can be generated by specifying an unexpectedly large amplitude for the accent command on *mannaka-ni*.[2] (In the Pierrehumbert and Beckman (1988) synthesis model, this corresponds to the specification of an AP prominence ratio value that is much higher than 1.0 for the *mannaka-ni* phrase.) Second, it can be generated by inserting an unexpected new phrase command with an especially large amplitude around the beginning of *mannaka-ni*. (In the Pierrehumbert and Beckman model, this corresponds to an unexpected IP boundary after *ya'ne-no*, with an unusually high top-line value for the new IP that begins at *mannaka-ni*.)

To try to decide between these two alternative accounts (i.e., a local AP prominence or an IP break), Pierrehumbert and Beckman (1988) analyze utterances containing adjective-noun sequences such as *uma'i mame'-wa* 'tasty beans-TOP' that differ minimally by which word receives a corrective narrow focus, comparing these utterances with baseline utterances with broad focus on the noun phrase as a whole. In one analysis, they have a fluent speaker of Japanese listen to each utterance and tag the perceived degree of disjuncture between the two words. In this test, focused nouns are usually perceived as being set off from the preceding adjective by an IP boundary. Sometimes this percept could be attributed to a visible pause or glottalization. Another analysis exploits the fact that application of downstep is blocked across an IP boundary: Pierrehumbert and Beckman use materials that systematically vary the adjective between accented *uma'i* 'tasty' and unaccented *amai* 'sweet', and they observe whether downstep has applied by comparing the peak Fo in the following focused noun in the accented context versus the unaccented context. They find that the Fo height of the focused noun is *not* significantly lower when following an accented word. They interpret this nonapplication of downstep as further evidence indicating that an IP boundary is inserted immediately preceding a focused phrase. In other words, they conclude that focus marking involves the second of the two mechanisms described above—that is, the insertion of an unexpected high-amplitude phrase command in the Fujisaki model, or insertion of an IP boundary in the Pierrehumbert and Beckman model.

Kubozono (1993, 2007), by contrast, argues for the first of the two mechanisms, which corresponds to the unexpectedly large accent command in the Fujisaki model (or a local AP prominence in the Pierrehumbert and Beckman model). He shows summary statistics suggesting that downstep is not always blocked and thus concludes that late narrow focus within an adjective-noun sequence (or any other syntactic constituent that normally is produced as one IP) does not involve a restructuring of the prosodic hierarchy. Rather, the focused AP is produced with a "metrical boost" realized on the [H] tone targets. We return to this point in section 17.4.2 after describing other aspects of focus marking that also have been described in terms of restructuring, albeit at a lower level of the prosodic hierarchy.

17.3.3 Prosodic Subordination after Focal Prominence

Another older observation reconfirmed by Pierrehumbert and Beckman's study is that focal prominence has measurable effects on following material as well as on the focused constituent itself. That is, putting focal prominence on a word in an utterance induces some kind of prosodic subordination of all following words in the intonation phrase. For example, in the utterance in figure 17.8, the Fo on the verb *okima'su* is much lower than the [H–] target in the preceding *mannaka*. In figure 17.3b, similarly, the accent peak on the verb *oyoge'ru* is very much lower than the accent peak on the preceding *Ya'mano-wa*, in keeping with the "contrastive" interpretation of the *wa* in this utterance. That is, the degree of pitch range reduction on the verb in this utterance is more than can be accounted for simply by downstep, as can be gauged by comparing the peak Fo on *oyoge'ru* in figure 17.3b with the *oyo'ideru* in the broad-focus utterance of *Ya'mano-ga oyo'ideru* in figure 17.3a (gray line).

This postfocal prosodic subordination is realized in various ways that can be modeled in terms of more or less elaborate manipulations of the prosodic structure. In the simplest case, the only feature that is affected is the pitch range; there is an extreme pitch range reduction on all words in the postfocal region, but all tone targets are realized in the Fo contour. An example of such a realization is the small but observable rise-fall of the [L% H*+L L%] on *oyoge'ru* in figure 17.3b. In these cases, the demarcative rise from the AP-level [L%] to a following [H] target (the phrasal [H–] or the [H*] of an early accent) is preserved on the postfocal constituent, although the manifestation of this rise can be very subtle because of the substantially reduced range.

Quite often, however, the AP-initial rise is *not* realized after a focused word. Pierrehumbert and Beckman (1988) describe this later type of postfocal prosodic subordination as the process of *dephrasing*, which they define as a total deletion of the [L% H–] demarcative AP-initial rise and (in cases where this deletion would yield two *akusento-kaku* within the resulting merged AP) deletion of all but the first [H*+L] accent fall. That is, they posit a restructuring under focus that not only inserts a new IP boundary to set off the beginning of the focused constituent but also erases any following AP boundary within the IP. They relate this restructuring to the morphological processes that determine the accent patterns of compound words.

Pierrehumbert and Beckman illustrate dephrasing with figures of utterances that place narrow focus on the adjective in their target adjective-noun sequences. The figures show an extreme Fo rise marking the beginning of the adjective but no Fo rise at the beginning of the following noun. The lexical accents of the component words interact with dephrasing to yield three distinct contours. When the adjective is accented, the purported dephrasing is realized as a very steep fall at the *akusento-kaku*, followed by a gradual fall located in the lower part of the speaker's pitch range. This combination of steep fall followed by gradual fall resembles the Fo contour on the *chi'izu-o ta'beta* portion of figure 17.2a. Notice there is no Fo rise onto *ta'beta* in this case. When the adjective is unaccented, in contrast, dephrasing results in a more or less gradual decline in the upper part of the pitch range. In an unaccented adjective + accented noun sequence (e.g., AMAI *mame'* in Pierrehumbert and Beckman's materials[3]), such dephrasing resembles the gradually declining interpolation between the phrase-initial [H–] and the [H*+L] on the verb shown in figure 17.2b. In the unaccented adjective + unaccented noun sequence (e.g., AMAI *ame*), the shape resembles the interpolation between the initial [H–] and the utterance-final [L%] shown in figure 17.2c. Pierrehumbert and Beckman interpret all three of these patterns as indicating a prosodic restructuring that groups the postfocal noun into the same AP as the focused adjective. They identify this dephrasing with the morphological process of prosodic cliticization that distinguishes auxiliary verbs such as *iru* and *mi'ru* from their full clause counterparts, making the single AP *yo'nde-mi'ru* 'try reading' distinct from the two AP sequence *yo'nde mi'ru* 'read and then see' (as described in Poser 1984, for example).

Later work by Kori (1997) gives further support for this account and also clarifies the exact nature of the prosodic restructuring. Specifically, Kori's examples show that postfocal prosodic subordination effectively deletes the [L% H–] sequence that normally marks the boundary between two AP, but it need not delete the tone targets of the subsequent *akusento-kaku* when this dephrasing occurs within a sequence of two or more accented words. Kori describes cases of prosodic subordination after a focused accented word where postfocal accents are in fact maintained, noting they are prosodically weakened due to the fact that they (a) are realized in a reduced pitch range and (b) are lacking the phrase-initial rise. This is shown by the "shoulder" of the postfocal accent on *ikima'shita* 'went' in figure 17.9a. In contrast, Kori notes that prosodic subordination after unaccented focused words is realized differently, although it can be modeled in terms of the very same process of dephrasing at the AP level. That is, after an unaccented focused word, the deletion of the AP-initial [L% H–] rise before any postfocal word results in the Fo remaining relatively high in the speaker's range, as illustrated in figure 17.9b. As Kori points out, despite the striking superficial difference between low Fo after an accented focused word and higher Fo after an unaccented focused word, there is a common underlying prosodic restructuring. As he puts it, "At first glance, the behavior under focus seems to differ depending on the accentuation, but actually you can think of both of these realizations as 'weakening the autonomy of postfocal words'" (Kori 1997:178). That is, prosodic subordination can be accomplished by dephrasing (deletion of the demarcative [L% H–] rise) in both accentual contexts.

To understand the significance of examples such as figure 17.9a, where a focused accented word is followed by another accented word within the same AP, recall that Pierrehumbert and Beckman (1988) follow Fujisaki and Kawai (1988)

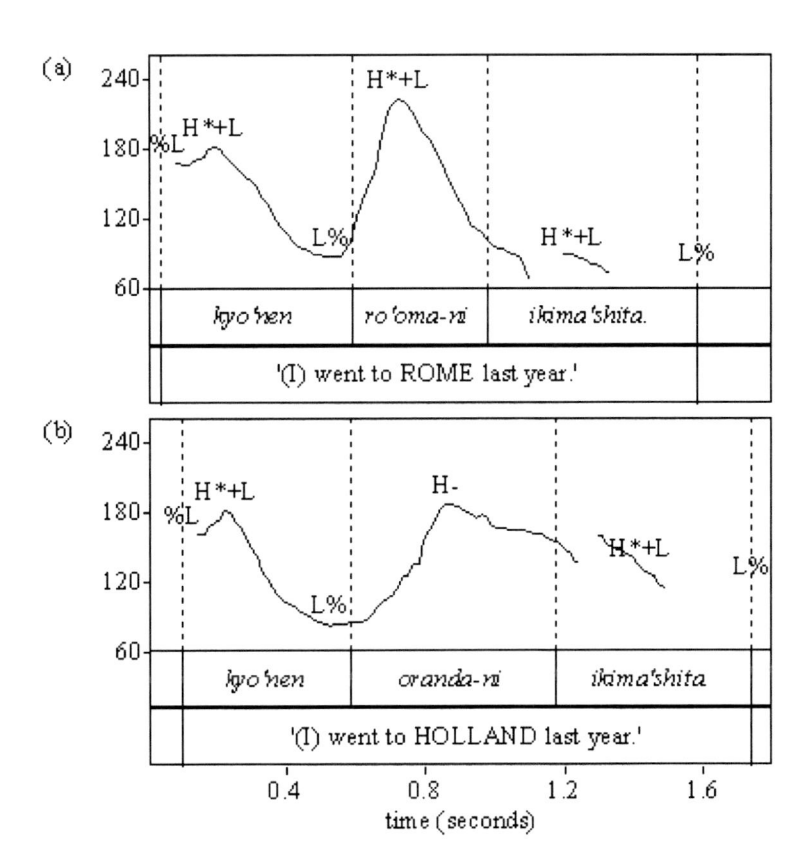

Figure 17.9 F0 contours of utterances illustrating postfocal prosodic subordination after an early narrow focus on (a) an accented word versus (b) an unaccented word.

and others in assuming that dephrasing deletes the tones of the second *akusento-kaku* as well as the demarcative tones at the AP boundary itself. Under this account, the culminative distribution of accents in compound words (as described by McCawley 1968 and Kubozono 1993, among many others) is mirrored in the culminative distribution of accents in the postlexical process of dephrasing for focus marking. Of course, in Fujisaki's model this linkage between dephrasing and accent deletion is unavoidable, given that the square wave of the accent command generates both the phrase-initial rise and the later fall at the accented syllable. In the AM framework, by contrast, there is no necessary coupling between the demarcative rise and the accent fall. This means that dephrasing can delete the [L% H−] sequence that marks the boundary between two accented words *without* deleting [H*+L] in the second word. Thus, as noted previously, function words such as *yo'ri* and *su'ra* can be cliticized onto the preceding content word and still surface with the lexically specified fall at the accent.[4] A related process of subordination of following accents seems to be involved in the contrast that Poser (1984) notes between *yo'nde-mi'ru* 'try reading' (where the auxiliary verb is cliticized onto the main verb) and *yo'nde mi'ru* 'read and see' (where the two verbs form separate APs). Because he assumes a full specification account, Poser describes this contrast in terms of a prosodic grouping that necessarily involves a complete deletion of all [H] tone targets in the auxiliary verb *mi'ru*, making the auxiliary reading lose its accent to be *yo'nde-miru*. However, Maekawa's (1994) statistical analysis of Fo slopes in postfocal *yo'nde-mi'ru* versus *yo'nde-iru* 'is reading' shows that this account is not tenable. That is, the contrast between accented *mi'ru* and unaccented *iru* is preserved even for the auxiliary verb readings of these two verbs. And, as figure 17.9a shows, narrow focus on the first word in a sequence of accented words can be realized by a prosodic subordination of postfocal material that drastically lowers the [H*] target without completely eliminating the accent fall in the second word.

Note that by this account (in contrast to Pierrehumbert and Beckman's original formulation), dephrasing after the focus constituent is a "postlexical" intonational process that is qualitatively different from the morphological processes that determine the distribution of accents in compound words. As described at length by McCawley (1968), Poser (1984), and Kubozono (1993), among many others, when two accented words are conjoined in compound word formation, the output is a word with at most one accent (e.g., *sha'kai* 'society' + *se'ido* 'system' → *shakaise'ido* 'social system').[5] By contrast, by the account of postfocal prosodic subordination presented here, when two or more accented words are conjoined by the deletion of the boundary-marking rise, the output is a single AP that can contain two or even more *akusento-kaku*. Note, too, that although his account is somewhat different from the one presented here, Kubozono also differentiates the morphological processes that enforce a culminative distribution of accents in compound word formation from the postlexical grouping of words into phrases to reflect the syntactic organization of sentences in a discourse. He reserves the term *accentual phrase* for the output of the compound accentuation rules and terms the postlexical prosodic grouping the *minor phrase*. Although Kubozono does not discuss post-focus subordination in these terms, we can say that his "accentual phrase formation" is roughly analogous to the English Compound Stress Rule in the same way that his "minor phrase formation" is roughly analogous to the application of the Nuclear Stress Rule to larger constituents such as noun phrases in the older literature on the syntax-prosody mapping in English. This recalls the analogy that Pierrehumbert and Beckman (1988) make between postfocal dephrasing in Japanese and deaccenting in English—that is, the constraint in the English intonation system against the occurrence of any further pitch accents within an IP after a word that bears the nuclear pitch accent. These analogies serve to highlight both the profound formal differences and the deeper functional similarities between the two intonation systems. Where Japanese uses prosodic grouping to mark prosodic subordination, English uses the culminative distribution of stress markers such as association to a nuclear pitch accent. Nonetheless, in both languages, there is a formal relationship between the mechanisms that mark morphological subordination in compound word formation and higher-level subordination of postfocal material within the IP. We return to this point in section 17.4.3.

17.3.4 Prominence-lending Boundary Pitch Movements

In the two previous sections we described how speakers can use prosody to cue focal prominence in Japanese (a) by inserting an IP boundary and manipulating the pitch range before and after that boundary to make for a dramatic reset at the beginning of the focus constituent, and (b) by processes of prosodic subordination after the focus constituent that include the deletion of the rise at the beginning of following APs as well as an extreme pitch range compression that can reduce subsequent accent peaks to the same level as the [L] target of the first [H*+L] when the focus constituent itself is lexically accented. We now turn to a different kind of restructuring to cue focus whereby the speaker sets off the focus constituent from adjacent material on *both* sides. That is, in addition to the reset that marks the beginning of the focused word, there is some salient marking of the end of the focus constituent to separate it prosodically also from following material. One way that speakers can mark the end of the focus constituent is by inserting a silent pause. When this pause is inserted after an unaccented word, it simply interrupts the interpolation from the phrasal [H–] to the next tone target in an attention-getting way. In figure 17.8, for example, the downward-sloping interpolation from the [H–] in *mannaka-ni* toward the lowered [H*+L] in *okima'su* suddenly stops for 200 ms before resuming again at the level that it would have reached if the two words had been separated instead by a filled pause. Another way of marking the end of the focal constituent to set it off from following material is by producing a BPM. As noted earlier, two of the four BPMs that are tagged as tonally distinct categories in the X-JToBI scheme—namely, [H%] and [HL%]—have been linked to a prominence-lending function. Both of these are illustrated in figure 17.10, and we describe each of them in turn.

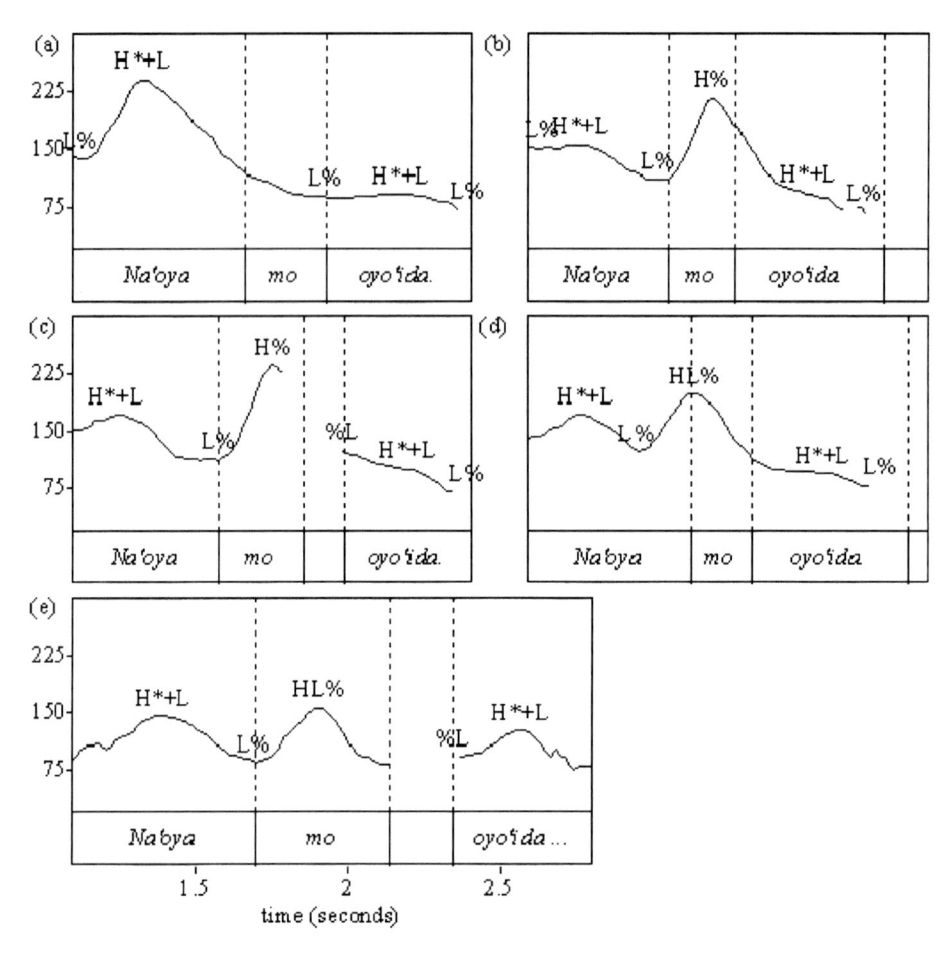

Figure 17.10 F0 contours of the underlined portion of *Kinoo, NA'OYA-mo oyo'ida* 'NAOYA also swam yesterday', illustrating five different ways of marking the focal prominence on Na'oya-mo.

17.3.4.1 The prominence-lending rise

The [H%] prominence-lending rise (PLR) is the BPM most commonly associated with a prominence-lending function. For example, focal prominence can be marked on the phrase *Na'oya-mo* 'Naoya-also' in the sentence *Kinoo Na'oya-mo oyo'ida* 'NAOYA also swam yesterday' by inserting an intonation phrase break before *Na'oya* accompanied by a large pitch reset, as described above and shown in figure 17.10a, or by putting a PLR at the end of the focused phrase, as shown in figures 17.10b and 17.10c. This second mechanism is noted by Ohishi (1959), Kawakami (1963), Miyaji (1963), Kori (1989b, 1997), Muranaka and Hara (1994), and Venditti (1997), among others, and more recently has been investigated experimentally by Venditti, Maeda, and van Santen (1998), Taniguchi and Maruyama (2001), Maruyama and Taniguchi (2002), Oshima (2007), and Mesbur (2005).

Figure 17.10a shows the use of expanded pitch range to cue focal prominence on *Na'oya-mo* 'Naoya-also'. Note the prosodic subordination of the following verb *oyo'ida* 'swam', similar to figure 17.9a. Figures 17.10b–e illustrate the use of the various BPMs to cue this same function: (b) shows [H%] marking *Na'oya-mo*, with no pause following; (c) shows [H%] with a pause following; and (d) gives an example of the penultimate non-lexical prominence (PNLP), which we discuss later. These three examples show prosodic subordination of the verb after the BPM, similar to figure 17.10a. The final contour figure 17.10e gives an example of the [HL%] 'explanatory' BPM, which was also illustrated in figure 17.5c.

Given that the PLR often occurs on phrases ending with a particle or postposition, many accounts of its form and function use terms such as "prominent particles," which might be misinterpreted as suggesting that the particle itself is the focus constituent. The [H%] does make the final syllable in a phrase stand out in the intonation contour, and its occurrence on a phrase-final particle can mark narrow focus on the particle itself, as in Ohishi's (1959) example of metalinguistic contrast in (3a).[6] More typically, however, the focus constituent is the entire phrase ending with the particle that is aligned with the PLR, as in Ohishi's example in (3b). This fact has been pointed out by a number of scholars, including Ohishi himself, who says: "When prominence is placed on a particle, the thing that is focused is not just the particle, but it is the word that that particle is affiliated or packaged with" (Ohishi 1959:95). Maruyama and Taniguchi (2002:18) also highlight this point: "Prominence on particles prosodically marks the right edge of the phrase which includes the focused element, and has the function of prosodically indicating the focus structure of an utterance which may not be represented by its syntax."

A further point to make is that whereas [H%] can occur on a particle, it need not do so, as is shown by the examples from various authors in (3d–f) and by the contour in figure 17.6a. Indeed, it appears that the only constraint on prominence-lending BPM placement (besides the need to be at or near the constituent edge) is that a prominence-lending BPM cannot occur sentence finally.[7] In this position, focal prominence can only be cued by reset—that is, by having a phrase boundary before the focus constituent where there can be a pronounced pitch-range expansion relative to prior material.

This constraint against marking focus on utterance-final phrases with PLR complements the constraints on marking focus by the mechanisms identified in the previous section. That is, on utterance-initial words, it is difficult to mark focus by inserting an IP boundary and expanding the pitch range, because the beginning of an utterance must be the beginning of a new IP in any case, and because there is no preceding material to produce in a relatively reduced pitch range to contrastively enhance the phrase-initial rise.[8] This functional motivation for the constraint is reflected in Ohishi's (1959) discussion of two of his examples, given here as (3b,c). Specifically, he suggests that although local pitch range expansion can indicate narrow focus on *a'ni* 'older brother' in (3c), it is impossible to use pitch-range expansion to focus the entire noun phrase *watashi-no a'ni* 'my older brother'. However, the speaker can still mark that phrase as the focus constituent by producing a [H%] PLR on the final syllable, as in (3b).

Another related point is that some speakers find it difficult to cue focus by expanding the range of an unaccented phrase, without setting off the focus constituent somehow from following material. That is, it is generally acknowledged among Japanese researchers (with suggestive instrumental support in an experimental study by Ito [2002a]) that it is difficult to expand the range of an unaccented phrase to mark focus. However, other experimental studies by Kori (1989a) and Pierrehumbert and Beckman (1988) have observed pitch range expansion on unaccented APs, and figure 17.8 shows that it can occur in spontaneous speech, too. The feeling of awkwardness probably originates in the lesser salience of the AP-initial boundary rise when there is no downstep to reduce the Fo values of the [L%] and any following [H*+L]. In such cases, the use of the [H%] PLR is a likely alternative to inserting a pause in the middle of the AP, as in figure 17.8.

(3) a. A. *Gakkoo-no*↑ *tooro'nkai?* (Ohishi 1959)
 'Did you say it's a debate ABOUT the school?'
 B. *Iya, gakkoo-de*↑ *yatta n de'su.*
 'No, it's that they held it AT the school.'
 b. *Watashi-no a'ni-wa*↑ *otonashi'i.*
 'MY OLDER BROTHER is shy.'
 c. *Watashi-no A'NI-wa otonashi'i.* [with pitch range reset on *a'ni-wa*]
 'My older BROTHER is shy.'
 d. *San-senchi-gu'rai akete*↑ *shita-ni okima'su.* (Venditti 1997)
 'I will OPEN UP ABOUT 3 CM and put it below there.'
 e. [Context: 'Is it the Mr. Yamada who lives in Miyajima?]
 Iie. Ao'mori-ni sunde-iru↑ *Yamada-san de'su.*
 (Maruyama and Taniguchi 2002)
 'No. (It's) the Mr. Yamada who LIVES IN AOMORI'
 f. *Ka'zuya-wa bi'iru-o sa'nbai*↑ *chuumon shima'shita.* (Oshima 2007)
 'Kazuya ordered THREE BOTTLES of beer.'

Using PLR to mark focal prominence is optional, just as pitch range expansion on the focal constituent is optional. In fact, Kori (1997) states that the only obligatory prosodic marker of prominence is the postfocal prosodic subordination discussed in section 17.3.3. In a naturalness-rating perception study, Maruyama and Taniguchi (2002) find that [H%] does indeed cue focus but that [H%] alone is not sufficient when the postfocal region is not prosodically subordinated as well. That is, whereas their intonation contour with PLR followed by a compressed pitch range (their pattern B) is judged by listeners as a highly natural way of focusing that phrase, the contour with PLR and no compression of the following pitch range (their pattern D) is judged as unnatural. They conclude, as Kori does, that postfocal prosodic subordination is crucial for cueing focus naturally.[9]

That said, postfocal pitch-range compression does not occur in all cases where apparently focal material is set off from following phrases by the insertion of [H%]. The utterance in figure 17.6a illustrates this point, representing a very deliberate speaking style that is common in monologue narratives such as the academic talks and prepared presentations in the CSJ; the speaker produces a string of phrases each deliberately set off (and given a kind of focal prominence) by [H%], with no obvious postfocal subordination. This use of [H%] to set off each phrase as a separate focal constituent is reminiscent of the short intonation phrases and frequent use of [L+H*] nuclear pitch accents in American radio and television news broadcast style, where prosody is used to break up the densely information-packed paragraphs typical of news stories. That is, examples such as figure 17.6a may point to another function of [H%] in discourse—a use that shares the foregrounding function of PLR in (3) but without the concomitant backgrounding of all material outside of the focus constituent. In the information-packed paragraphs of this kind of narrative monologue, the [H%] helps speakers and listeners chunk information in the speech stream. This "Here, parse this!" function is alluded to in Muranaka and Hara's (1994:396) descriptions of the PLR on particles as "making clear the syntactic structure" or "uttered with higher Fo when the preceding noun phrase is long, [indicating] the end of the phrase."

17.3.4.2 *The rise-fall BPM and PNLP*

The [HL%] BPM is also said to have a prominence-lending function, and some of the remarks just made about when and why a speaker chooses to mark focus with PLR also apply to the rise-fall. In the discourse in (4), for example, speaker B uses [HL%] to put prominence on *ano'hito* 'that person'. At the same time, however, [HL%] also expresses the speaker's irritation at B's misunderstanding. In their perception study using ratings on various semantic scales, Venditti, Maeda, and van Santen (1998) find that listeners perceive [HL%] as highly 'emphatic' (*kyoochoo shite iru*) and 'explanatory' (*joohoo-o setsumei shite iru*)—that is, the rise-fall BPM imparts a very strong sense of the speaker forcefully explaining some point to the listener. In fact, [HL%] is rated higher on these two scales than [H%] is. However, in this study listeners do not rate [HL%] as indicating the speaker's irritation, as it seems to do in the context in (4).

(4) A: (talking to B) *Ana'ta-ga Yamada-san de'su ka?*   Are you Mr. Yamada?
    B: *Iie, watashi-wa Yoshida de'su.*   No, I'm Yoshida.
    C: *Soshite watashi-ga*↑ *Yamada de'su.* (H%)   And **I** am Yamada.
    A: (talking to B) *Wakarima'shita.*   I understand.
       Ana'ta-ga Yamada-san de'su.   You are Mr. Yamada.
    B: *Iie, ano'hito-ga*^ *yamada-san na'n de'su.*(HL%)   No, THAT PERSON is Mr. Yamada.

The chunking function described for [H%] and illustrated in figure 17.6a is also characteristic of the rise-fall BPM; in many utterances in the CSJ presentation speech narratives, [HL%] sets off nearly every phrase in an especially deliberate way. This use of the rise-fall BPM seems especially common in dialogues among young speakers, especially young girls. In fact, some speakers use [HL%] so frequently that it seems to lose any local focalizing function and becomes more of a marker of the speech style and of the speaker's social identity in choosing the style. That is, the rise-fall BPM in these speakers and this style may be like the frequent use of the English high-rise contour by the younger speakers of American English that McLemore (1991) describes, where the frequency of use effectively weakens the meaning of this contour that is described by Hirschberg and Ward (1995), among others, and makes it instead a marker of solidarity (with the speaker's fellow sorority members, in the case of McLemore's study).

As noted earlier, X-JToBI uses the [HL%] sequence of the rise-fall BPM to mark another distinct prominence-lending shape—namely, the *penultimate non-lexical prominence*, or PNLP, illustrated in figure 17.6c. In that utterance, the rise is localized on the penultimate syllable of the phrase *soo itta yo'o-na ta'ipu no rensoogo-o* 'the aforementioned type of semantic associate' (indicated here by underlining). The PNLP puts narrow focus on the newly introduced term *rensoogo* 'semantic associate', which is being defined in this appositional use of *no*.

We describe the PNLP together with the rise-fall BPM in this subsection because it is tagged in the CSJCore using the [HL%] tone label (in conjunction with the PNLP comment label). However, this choice of the rise-fall BPM label in the tagging conventions should not be interpreted as indicating a commitment to the implied phonological analysis on the part of any of the researchers who developed the X-JToBI tagging conventions. Rather, the [HL%] tag was chosen as a quick-and-dirty first approximation to the superficially similar rise-fall shape that PNLP typically shows. For example, in figure 17.6c, the F0 falls over the duration of the accusative case particle *o* onto the first syllable of the following phrase, the verb *kotae'ru* 'respond'. However, there is an alternative account available for this fall. Given that the beginning of the phrase immediately following a medial PLR [H%] (like the beginning of a phrase after a silent pause) is marked by an initial [%L] boundary tone, the F0 fall after a PNLP could be the transition to this independently motivated [%L] target. The PNLP rise, then, could be a leftward-displaced instance of the PLR [H%].

This alternative account is appealing to us, because the PNLP is often cited in the literature (e.g., Ohishi 1959; Kori 1989b, 1997) as a variant of the "prominent particle" phenomenon we attribute to the PLR [H%]. Moreover, our impression from the instances that we have seen is that the PNLP is more similar to [H%] than it is to [HL%] in both form and function. Compare, for example, the slope of the [L% H%] rise in figure 17.10b with that of the PNLP in figure 17.10d. Additionally, the typical lengthening of the syllable that is aligned with the [HL%] (as seen in figure 17.10e) is not present in cases of either PNLP or [H%]. However, differentiating between these two (and several other more controversial) alternative accounts is a research question in its own right. Moreover, it is a question that requires more extensive corpus work than would have been possible before the development of resources such as the CSJ. We return to this point again briefly in section 17.4.4.

17.4 Ambiguities of the Prosodic Parse

At various points in our description of focus-marking mechanisms in section 17.3 we alluded to points of disagreement or potential disagreement among linguists currently working on Japanese intonational phonology. Many of these are points where the phonetic evidence that might differentiate between competing prosodic parses is inherently lacking or ambiguous. In this section, we briefly describe four of these points.

17.4.1 Postfocal Dephrasing

In section 17.3.3, we described the prosodic subordination of postfocal material in terms of the notion "dephrasing," which we defined as the deletion (or non-realization) of the [L% H–] sequence that marks the beginning of every well-formed accentual phrase. By this definition, the junctural cues are definitive. When no [L% H–] sequence is realized between two accents and there are no segmental cues to support an AP boundary in the absence of this tonal cue, dephrasing has occurred. When two accented words are phrased together into a single AP, both accent falls can be realized, although the second is typically reduced in prominence, so that its [H*] target is at the same Fo level or a somewhat lower level than the [L] target of the first accent, as in *ta'beta* in figure 17.2a and *ikima'shita* in figure 17.9a.

Note that by this account, for sequences of accented words, the line between dephrasing and extreme pitch-range compression is a fuzzy one, particularly when there is only one or two syllables separating the two accents. The Fo contour over the sequence of words *yo'o-na ta'ipu* in figure 17.6c illustrates this source of ambiguity in the prosodic parse. The inflection point at the beginning of the small rise to the accent peak on *ta'ipu* could be parsed as the [L] of the accent on *yo'o-na* or as a [L%] boundary tone at the word boundary. The X-JToBI transcriber must pay close attention to subtle cues such as the length of the word-final vowel in *yo'o-na* to distinguish between these two parses. This means that there are many different degrees of clarity to the phrasal disjuncture between two accented APs. Moreover, this continuum of degrees of perceived disjuncture is in a gradient relationship to the many different degrees of subordination that are also possible. The postfocal dephrasing evident in figure 17.9a, then, is toward one end of a continuum that includes (at the other end) the much less compressed pitch range of the following verb phrases relative to the *Ya'mano-wa* and *Ka'shino-wa* phrases in figure 17.3b.

By our account, in other words, sequences of two accented words are vulnerable to the kind of prosodic parsing ambiguity Beckman (1996b) describes, because the Fo pattern in the middle of a sequence of two accents within a single AP is phonetically very similar to the rise that marks the boundary between two APs. By contrast, sequences of two unaccented words are not phonetically susceptible to this type of misparsing of the intended prosodic structure, because a rise at the boundary between two unaccented words can only be parsed as [L% H–]. Of course, sequences of unaccented words are vulnerable to the opposite misparsing, because the [L%] is not subject to downstep and because (other things being equal) the phrasal [H–] is scaled lower in the pitch range than the peak in the accent [H*+L]. These two facts together mean that the demarcative rise is much smaller for sequences of two unaccented words as compared with sequences of two accented words for the same degree of prosodic subordination of the second word, so that listeners may misinterpret an intended sequence of two unaccented APs as having undergone postlexical dephrasing.

Note that this account of dephrasing as one endpoint of a continuum of subordination differs from the more categorical distinction assumed in some other accounts of postfocal subordination. That is, there is a broad consensus in the AM literature that dephrasing does occur. However, many other phonologists have assumed a slightly different account of dephrasing that does not go as far as our definition in differentiating the postlexical intonational process from the morphological processes that account for the accent patterns of compound words. Specifically, in most previous accounts other than Kori 1997, the output of postlexical dephrasing is assumed to preserve the (almost perfectly) culminative distribution of *akusento-kaku* in the lexicon. When two accented words are phrased together into a single AP, these accounts say, the second *akusento-kaku* must be deleted along with the demarcative rise.[10] In applying these models in analyses of actual utterances, then, the presence of a second [H*+L] fall in a sequence of two accented words is interpreted as unequivocal evidence that there is an intervening AP boundary even when the second peak is reduced to a target level at or even below the level of the inflection point for the [L] of the first accent. By these other accounts, then, the fall on *ta'beta* in figure 17.2a must indicate an AP break after the object NP, making the prosodic structure of this utterance different from that in the syntactically identical sentences in figures 17.2b and 17.2c. Moreover, the different shapes in the postfocal region in figures 17.9a versus 17.9b are interpreted as indicating different focus-marking mechanisms depending on the lexical accentuation of the word in focus.

For example, Sugahara (2002) observes what she takes to be evidence of an effect of lexical accentuation in determining prosodic phrasing in the postfocal region. That is, like Kori (1997), she describes a pattern of no AP-initial rise and continuous gradual fall on postfocal (contextually "given") words in unaccented sequences and a contrasting pattern with a "bumpier" transition when the focal word and the following word are accented. To account for this difference, she posits a dependency between accentual phrasing and lexical accentuation status. That is, she notes that postfocal material is not subject to dephrasing when it is contextually "new" information or at the left edge of a major syntactic constituent (XP), as might be expected if accentual phrasing tends to reflect both the discourse context and the syntactic structure of an utterance, but she also concludes that postfocal material is not subject to dephrasing when it is lexically accented. This is a somewhat surprising effect of the lexical tone pattern if we assume the strictly modular division of classical generative phonology between the phonological grammar that generates phonological structures and the phonetic processes that implement them.

Other researchers also have observed apparent interactions of dephrasing with lexical accentuation. Most notably, Ito and her colleagues (Ito, Speer, and Beckman 2003; Ito and Speer 2006) document such an interaction in spontaneous narratives, where the contrast between "given" and "new" information arises naturally from the nonlinguistic task that naive subjects were asked to perform. We can be confident, therefore, that it is not an artifact of eliciting the contrasting information structures in the laboratory using contrived dialogue scripts. More extensive corpus work, in conjunction with analysis-by-synthesis methods, needs to be done before we can say whether the apparent interaction can be explained away by the different, complementary phonetic susceptibilities to ambiguity in the parsing of tonal cues to disjuncture in accented-accented sequences as compared to unaccented-unaccented sequences.

17.4.2 Prosodic Restructuring or Local Boost?

In section 17.3.2, we described pitch range expansion under focal prominence in terms of a prosodic restructuring, such that an IP boundary is inserted before the focal constituent. As Kubozono (1989, 1993, 2007) and others have pointed out, however, there is an alternative account available, because the reset at the beginning of the focus constituent is potentially ambiguous: it could signal the start of a new IP, or it may be a more local boost that raises the topline of the current AP only, without affecting the prosodic organization of the utterance at the IP level.

To determine locations of IP boundaries, researchers sometimes compare the height of the target peak to that of the previous one: if the target is the same height or higher than the previous peak, they assume that there is an IP boundary between the two phrases. Kubozono (2007) refers to this as the "syntagmatic approach." Beckman and Pierrehumbert (1992) suggest that, as a research methodology, this approach is circular; typical peak height relationships can vary to contrast two categorically different levels of prosodic disjuncture (as in the contrast between IP and AP in the Japanese prosodic hierarchy), but peak height relationships can also vary in a continuous, iconic way to reflect discourse structure, including many different degrees of relative foregrounding versus backgrounding of constituents. They therefore suggest that the only way to definitively determine whether an IP boundary exists between two phrases is to systematically vary the accentuation of the first phrase and observe the downstep effects (if any) on the second phrase. Kubozono (2007) refers to this as the "paradigmatic approach" and he, too, suggests that it is a better method for deciding whether an IP boundary has been inserted before a focus constituent.

Using this paradigmatic approach, Pierrehumbert and Beckman (1988) find no significant effect of previous accentuation on focused peaks in their data. Specifically, although they find a small (albeit insignificant) mean difference for the peak height value in a focused word depending on the accent of a preceding word, a scatterplot showing the peak height relationship for each token in the data set suggests that this is due to variability in the phrasing, with a few tokens showing a dramatic syntagmatic reduction after accent, and all the others showing reset. This pattern leads them to propose that focal prominence typically introduces an IP break before the focused element. This proposal has been widely adopted in subsequent analyses of focus-related effects on phrasing in Japanese (Nagahara 1994, Ito 2002a, among others).

In contrast to Pierrehumbert and Beckman's findings, Kubozono (2007) finds a significant difference in mean values for Fo peaks in focused *wh*-phrases such as the *na'ni-o* 'what-ACC' in (5). Here, the accentuation of the two phrases preceding the target word *na'ni* is systematically varied, yielding a somewhat lower average peak value on *na'ni* in (5a) relative to the mean in (5b) for five of seven speakers. This small difference in mean values appears even though the pitch range of the *wh*-word appears to be expanded under focus in every token. Following his earlier work on local pitch range expansion at major syntactic boundaries (see Kubozono 1989, 1993), Kubozono posits a local Fo "boost" that occurs on focused phrases without undoing the effects of downstep from preceding accents, as would be predicted if reset were associated with an unexpected IP boundary just before the target word. Kubozono concludes that pitch range expansion for focus marking can occur without the prosodic restructuring posited by Pierrehumbert and Beckman.

(5) a. accented   accented   accented   (focus)
Ana'ta-wa Ao'mori-de Na'oko-to na'ni-o mima'shita ka?
you-TOP Aomori-LOC Naoko-with what-ACC saw-Q
'What did you see with Naoko in Aomori?'
b. accented   unaccented   unaccented   (focus)
Ana'ta-wa Oomori-de Naomi-to na'ni-o mima'shita ka?
you-TOP Oomori-LOC Naomi-with what-ACC saw-Q
'What did you see with Naomi in Oomori?'

How can we account for the discrepancies between these two studies? Kubozono points to one possible source of the difference in results—namely, a difference between his materials and the materials used in most other experiments, including Pierrehumbert and Beckman's. Kubozono examines *wh*-phrases, which are (under most accounts of focus in questions) natural targets of focal prominence.[11] By contrast, most other laboratory studies of focus use scripted dialogues that are designed to prompt the readers to perform a contrastive or even corrective focal prominence. For example, the materials in Pierrehumbert and Beckman 1988 use the "contrastive *wa*" construction illustrated in figure 17.3b. As Prince (1981) and many others have pointed out, the discourse phenomena that have been termed "focus" are no more homogeneous than the prominence-lending mechanisms that languages use to mark focus. Perhaps the differentiation of the contrastive use of *wa* from the ordinary thematic use of *wa* requires a more dramatic setting off of the focus constituent than does the "inherent" focus of the *wh*-word.

Another important point that emerges from comparing these studies is that the potential for misparsing the degree of prosodic disjuncture before a focus constituent interacts with the interpretation of focal prominence, and this interaction depends on the lexical accentuation in a way that is reminiscent of the ambiguities regarding dephrasing after the focus constituent discussed in section 17.4.1. That is, when preceding material is unaccented, the listener can directly compare the Fo before and after the [L% H–] rise to gauge the degree of relative pitch range expansion on the focal constituent—as in Kubozono's syntagmatic approach—and the speaker can induce the percept of focal prominence even with a fairly small reset at the beginning of the focused element. When the preceding material is accented, however, the listener must gauge the intended pitch-range relationship against the backdrop of Bayesian expectations regarding downstep—taking a necessarily paradigmatic approach by evaluating the reset relative to an internal representation of the typical effects of being after an accented word within the same IP versus being after an accented word across an IP boundary.

We suspect that this difference between the two cases is what gives rise to another interaction with lexical accentuation that Kawakami (1957) observes. He points out that after an accented word, pitch range expansion for focus marking must at least mimic the effect of blocking the downstep, creating syntagmatic cues that suggest an IP boundary, as in (6a). After an unaccented word, however, the speaker can put focal prominence on a word simply by producing the AP-initial rise within a syntactic constituent that is typically produced as one AP, as in (6b).

(6) a. *Ka're-no* ‖ ANE *desu.*   (Kawakami 1957)
    '(She)'s his OLDER SISTER.'
    b. *Watashi-no* | *ane desu.*
    '(She)'s my OLDER SISTER.'

Thus, just as the more extreme degrees of subordination of postfocal material leads to an ambiguity of parsing at the AP level in a sequence of two accented phrases, more extreme degrees of emphasis on the focal material leads to an ambiguity of parsing at the IP level. Moreover, this phonetic ambiguity at the IP level depends on the lexical tone pattern in a way that suggests that the components of the grammar that determine the prosodic structure of an utterance are not rigidly encapsulated away from the phonetic processes that implement that structure.

17.4.3 Scaling of High Tones within the AP

In section 17.4.1, we defined dephrasing as a postlexical process that differs from the morphological processes involved in compound-word formation by targeting the cues to the AP boundary alone, without deleting one of the accents when two accented words are conjoined. We suggested that this difference between the two processes may help to explain an otherwise puzzling dependency between dephrasing and the lexical accentuation of the focused and postfocal constituents. If we are correct in saying that the conjoining of two morphemes into a compound word differs prosodically from the conjoining of two words into a single AP, then we might also expect different behavior in cases of metalinguistic contrast on one of the elements in a compound word, as in (7).

(7) a. OTOGI-ba'nashi jana'kute, MUKASHI-ba'nashi da yo. (Gussenhoven 2004)
'It's not a NURSERY tale, but a LEGEND (Lit. OLDENTIMES-tale, with -ba'nashi from -hanashi').'
b. Mukashi MONOGA'TARI jana'kute, mukashi-BA'NASHI da yo.
'It's not an old-time STORY, but a LEGEND (Lit. oldentimes-TALE).'
c. Watashi-ga mi'tai no wa EIGA jana'kute, MUKASHI-BA'NASHI da yo.
'What I want to see is not a FILM, but a LEGEND (Lit. OLDENTIMES-TALE).'
d. Ho'n-DANA de'wa nakute ho'n-BAKO de'su. (Kawakami 1957)
'It's not a bookSHELF, it's a book-BIN.'
e. Koogyoo-DA'IGAKU da' ka koogyoo-GA'KKOO da' ka...
'Whether it's an industrial COLLEGE, or an industrial SCHOOL...'

The sentences in (7a–c) are based on work by Gussenhoven (2004), who cites Mariko Sugahara (pers. comm., 2000) as saying that the two elements of a compound word cannot be focused separately. More specifically, he says that a compound word such as *mukashi-ba'nashi* 'legend' (from *mukashi* 'oldentimes' plus a sandhi form of *hanashi'* 'tale') in (7a–c) cannot be divided into two APs to have different pitch ranges to express the difference between narrow focus on *mukashi* in (7a) and narrow focus on *hanashi'* in (7b), and he shows F0 contours of elicited utterances of (7a–c) that "are all basically the same" (Gussenhoven 2004:205). His figure suggests two further pieces of evidence for the purported prosodic indivisibility of the compound word: (a) the initial consonant in the second morpheme is [b] rather than the underlying [h], showing that the morphological process of *rendaku* ("sequential voicing") has applied, and (b) the location of the accent fall in the F0 contour reflects the compound accent pattern rather than the underlying final accent of *hanashi'* 'tale'.

By contrast, Kawakami (1957) says that corrective focal prominence on the second element in compound words such as *ho'n-dana* versus *ho'n-bako* in (7d) and *koogyoo-da'igaku* versus *koogyoo-ga'kkoo* in (7e) can be expressed by having the same kind of AP-initial rise in the middle of the compound word that he observes in sequences of words such as (6b). At the same time, he points out that even when this prominence-lending AP-initial rise occurs, the forms show the other prosodic hallmarks of being compound words. Specifically, *rendaku* applies to both the underlying *tana* 'shelf' and *hako* 'box' in (7d), and the compound accent pattern applies to put an *akusento-kaku* on the first syllable of *daigaku* 'college' and *gakkoo* 'school' (both of which are unaccented as simplex forms) in (7e).

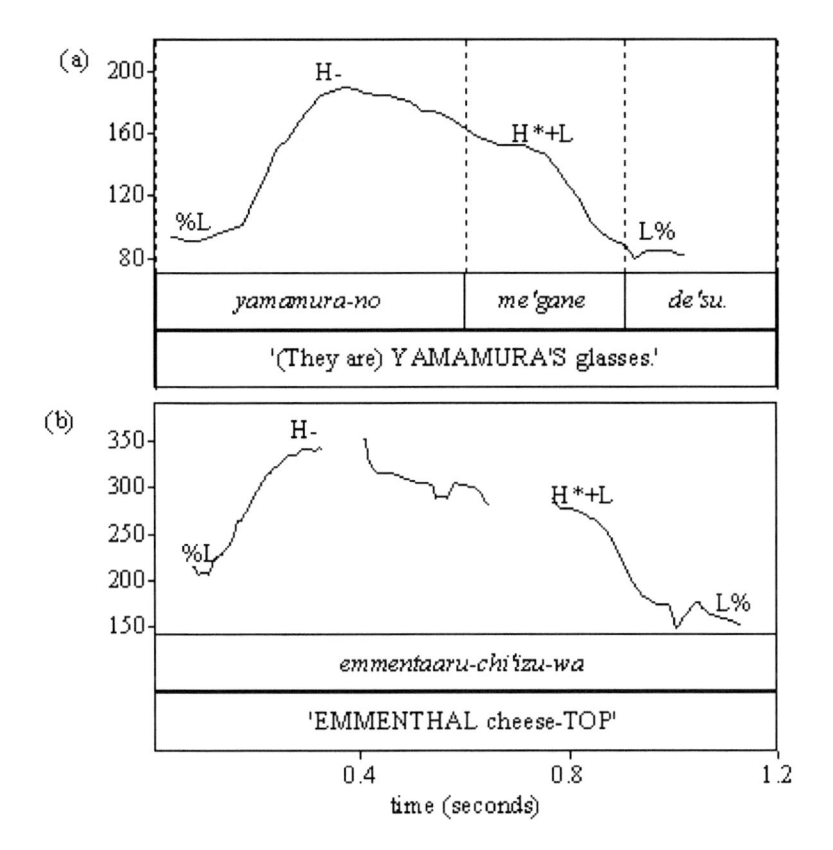

Figure 17.11 F0 contours for two utterances with early narrow focus. The utterance in (a) is in response to *Are those Suzuki's glasses?* The utterance in (b) is from one of the recipe narratives in Venditti 2000. The context describes why Emmenthal cheese (as opposed to other types of cheeses) has qualities that make it perfect for use in fondue.

The conflicting cues to the nature of the word-internal juncture that Kawakami describes for examples (7d,e) is reminiscent of the conflicting cues to the lexical status of the initial morpheme in English words such as *illiterate* and *impolite* when corrective focus associates the nuclear pitch accent to the prefix, as in (8).

(8) He's NOT polite. In fact, he's downright IMpolite.

Hay (2003) shows that native speakers find it easier to accent the prefix in such contexts of corrective focus when the derived form has low token frequency relative to that of the bare stem form, which makes the prefixed form more decomposable into its component morphemes. We suspect that similar considerations are at play in the apparent discrepancy between Gussenhoven's description of the impossibility of inserting an AP boundary to place focal prominence on the second element of *mukashi-ba'nashi* in (7b) and Kawakami's description of the focalizing AP-initial rise at the beginning of the second part of *ho'n-BAKO* in (7d).

At the same time, it is important to point out that Gussenhoven's identification of a common source of difficulty for expressing the narrow focus in (7a,b) assumes that focus marking on the first element of a compound should be the mirror image of focus marking on the second element. There is no logical necessity to this assumption. As we noted in section 17.3, there are complementary constraints on the availability of different focus-marking mechanisms at different positions in an utterance. Prosodic restructuring to begin the focus constituent with an unexpected IP boundary and reset is not a possible way to express narrow focus on an utterance-initial word, whereas postfocal dephrasing is not a possible way to express narrow focus on an utterance-final word. Analogously, the production of unexpected tonal cues to an AP boundary that Kawakami describes for (7d,e) should not be able to express the early narrow focus of (7a) as distinct from the whole-word focus of (7c), and if there is an analog to postfocal dephrasing, we might expect it to be constrained to occur on nonfinal elements of a compound word. The utterance in figure 17.11 suggests a possible analog to postfocal dephrasing within a compound word form, so long as it is accented and shows the late accent placement that is a typical output of the compound accentuation rules.

We mentioned in section 17.2.2 that the [H*] target of the accent is inherently scaled higher in the local pitch range for the AP than is the phrasal [H–]. In section 17.4.1, we discussed the implications of this difference for the interpretation of rises in the middle of sequences of accented words where the second accent is early in the word. Here we discuss another implication of this relationship of [H–] < [H*]. When an AP groups together an unaccented word with a following accented word, this difference in inherent tone scaling often results in an upward-sloping interpolation from the initial [H–] to the following accent [H*]. This is the pattern over the initial AP *Akai ya'ne* 'red roof' in all three panels of figure 17.4 and in the first two words *Omiyage-no chi'izu* 'souvenir cheese' in figure 17.2a. The productions of *mukashi-ba'nashi* that Gussenhoven shows for the three focus patterns in (7a–c) also have this [H–] < [H*] tone-scaling relationship, and he follows most earlier AM accounts in interpreting this as evidence that focal prominence on a word can only be marked by changing the pitch range specification for the AP containing the word as a whole, without affecting the inherent tone-scaling relationship of [H–] < [H*] within the phrase. As Pierrehumbert and Beckman (1988:108) put it, "focus is a property of the AP as a whole, and is therefore reflected in the realization of the accent H as well as the phrasal H."

Figure 17.8 already shows that this may be an oversimplification. The [H–] target on the focused *mannaka-ni* is very much higher that the [H*] target at the following accent in *okima'su*. Figures 17.9b and 17.11a show that this unexpected relationship of [H–] >> [H*] can be produced to mark narrow focus on the first element in an AP even when there is no silent pause interrupting the interpolation from the [H–] to the [H*], as is the case in figure 17.8. Figure 17.11b shows that this unexpected relationship of [H–] >> [H*] can even be produced in a compound word. That is, because the sequence *emmentaaru-chi'izu* is marked as a morphologically conjoined sequence by the compound accentuation pattern (*emmenta'aru* being underlyingly accented), the downsloping pattern in figure 17.11b is comparable to the patterns that Kawakami observes in (7d,e)—an instance where focal prominence is marked on just one of the elements in a compound, by reversing the expected relationship between tones and the prosodic structures that they mark. Examples such as (7d,e) and figure 17.11b thus exemplify another way in which the prosodic parse can be ambiguous; the segmental cues and compound accentuation pattern tell the listener that these forms are very closely conjoined morphologically, but the postlexical AP-boundary tones in (7d,e) and the independent scaling of the two [H] targets that allows for the [H–] >> [H*] relationship in figure 17.11b tell the listener that the two subelements of the compound form are independent enough that the second or the first of them can be marked separately as the focus constituent.

17.4.4 Prominence-lending Edge Markers

A final point of potential ambiguity that we briefly address here concerns the phonological analysis of prominence-lending pitch movements. At first glance, the rise-fall F0 movements located on or near the particle *mo* for the [L%H%] sequence in figure 17.10b, the PNLP in 17.10d, and the [L%HL%] in 17.10e are all strikingly similar in shape to the [%L H*+L] sequence for the AP-initial rise and lexical accent on the first syllable of *Na'oya* in figure 17.10a. This surface similarity has prompted some researchers to wonder whether the movements in figures 17.10b–e are in fact pitch accents (as opposed to boundary tones), and that is, in fact, how some researchers model them. Fujisaki and Hirose (1993), for example, generate all of these rises (including the more scooped question rise) by inserting an extra accent command. Oshima (2007) similarly argues that all particles are underlyingly accented, not just bimoraic ones such as *ma'de* and *su'ra*. This allows him to analyze the rise-fall shape on the particle *mo* in figures 17.10b–e as the resurfacing of the accent tones under narrow focus. That is, Oshima would interpret the PLR and other prominence-lending BPM in these examples as an exaggeration of an underlying [H*+L] fall on MO, marking the particle as the focus constituent.

The X-JToBI analysis that we adopt is different. Although the contour on *mo* in figures 17.10b–e does superficially resemble the shape around the lexical accent on the first syllable of *Na'oya* in figure 17.10a, we do not consider these BPMs to be the realization of an underlying accent on the monomoraic particle *mo*. This X-JToBI analysis is supported by Mesbur's (2005) experimental observation that multimoraic particles that have lexically specified accent on some nonfinal mora (e.g., *gu'rai* 'about, as much as') can be uttered with *both* the rise-fall of the lexical accent *and* a final [H%] PLR under focus, as in (9).

(9) Omame gu'rai↑ eiyoo no a'ru mono wa na'i n da kara.
'(You'd better eat them) since there's nothing with as much nutrition as beans.'

That is, examples such as figure 17.10a show that prominence can be marked on a lexically accented word simply by expanding the local pitch range so as to increase the [H*] target. If it were the case that one simply expands the pitch range of an underlying accent to make the particle prominent, as in Oshima's (2007) account, then we would expect speakers to do the same for GURAI. The fact that speakers can preserve the lexical accent in *gu'rai* while putting an additional [H%] rise at the end of the phrase suggests that the PLR is a phenomenon separate from the lexical accent.

At the same time, we can see clearly why Oshima (2007) and Fujisaki and Hirose (1993) were attracted to this account of prominence-lending BPMs as accents instead of as boundary tones. And an analysis that equates the prominence-lending properties of these BPMs with focalizing mechanisms that expand the accent fall in figure 17.10a is especially attractive for the BPM that X-JToBI calls PNLP (penultimate non-lexical prominence). The rise-fall movement of PNLP is transcribed as a [HL%] boundary tone, even though it is not realized at the phrase edge, as is the canonical 'explanatory' [HL%] (with which it shares its X-JToBI label) and the [H%] PLR (with which it is allied in alignment and duration characteristics). Thus, PNLP is inherently ambiguous. It looks and acts like the [H%] boundary tone of the PLR, but it violates our expectation that the phonetic realization of a boundary-marking tonal morpheme should be localized at the edge to which it is phonologically affiliated.

However, other languages have similarly ambiguous tones that can be analyzed as boundary-marking events despite their dislocation from the phrase edge. Compare, for example, the behavior of English phrase accents, which are associated with the phrase edge but spread leftward to fill up the space between the nuclear accent and the phrase edge. (The [L–] tones labeled in each panel of figure 17.7 are an example of such phrase accents.) Grice, Ladd, and Arvaniti (2000) review a number of languages that have prominence-marking tones with such an ambiguous or dual affiliation, including Greek and Hungarian. The prominence-lending function of the [H%] and [HL%] in figures 17.10b–d already suggests an affinity between these boundary tones and the phrase accents of languages such as English, Greek, and Hungarian. This prominence-marking function makes them susceptible to a diachronic reanalysis such as the one that may have given rise to the possibility of postlexical insertion of accents in Basque. The PNLP shares with the phrase accents of languages such as English, Greek, and Hungarian an even more inherently ambiguous parse because of its displacement from the edge to which it is phonologically associated. It will be interesting to see whether this displacement is the harbinger of a sound change that will make Tokyo Japanese more similar to Basque.

17.5 THEORETICAL IMPLICATIONS

We began this chapter by reviewing aspects of the Japanese intonation system that are especially relevant for understanding the interplay between information structure and prosodic organization. We then reviewed the literature that describes the ways in which prosody is used by the language to mark focal prominence on constituents in running speech. The literature shows that there is a rich variety of prominence-marking mechanisms even when morphosyntactic mechanisms such as scrambling are ignored.

In reviewing this literature, we have tried to highlight points of consensus that emerge from comparing how a particular phenomenon or particular set of phenomena is treated in models that make different assumptions about such aspects of the intonation system as whether the [H–] tone at the beginning of an accentual phrase is an independent target from the [H*] tone at the accent fall. When different models make analogous generalizations about older observations leading to similar predictions about future observations, this makes us confident that the generalizations are robust.

One generalization that emerges from comparing treatments across frameworks in this way is that pitch range specification plays an integral role in the intonational phonology. That is, as we saw in section 17.4.2, it is possible to disagree about whether the reset that marks the beginning of the focus constituent in examples such as (5) involves the insertion of an unexpected IP boundary or a boost to the pitch range after a mere AP boundary. But there is no disagreement that speakers have a flexibly continuous control of the pitch range on either side of this boundary and that they can use this control to produce a continuum of degrees of reset to indicate different relationships of foregrounding the focus constituent against the background of reduced pitch range on the preceding constituent. Moreover, although the exact details of the analysis differ across different frameworks, there is strong agreement that this continuous control of pitch range interacts with the control of categorical contrasts in lexical tone specification to produce superficially different patterns, as shown in figure 17.9. Nonetheless, listeners can parse this variation in terms of their expectations about how words and syntactic phrases will be reflected in the prosodic organization of an utterance to recover the intended focus pattern.

A closely related (and overarching) generalization concerns the importance of prosodic grouping and the role of constituent edges in the marking of focal prominence. The exaggerated reset in utterances such as figure 17.8 targets the beginning of the focus constituent, as does the unexpected AP boundary in examples such as (6b), whereas the prominence-lending boundary pitch movements discussed in section 17.3.4 target the end of the focus constituent. This focus on edges contrasts to the importance of head positions in the English intonation system. That is, prominence-marking in Japanese, unlike prominence-marking in English, does not target any such position as the syllable with primary stress in the focused word or the "designated terminal element" of the intonation phrase.

Despite this profound formal difference between the two languages, however, there is still a similarity concerning the associated types of phonetic properties that mark some constituents as more prominent and others as less prominent. For example, just as pitch range is manipulated to produce a more extreme rise to mark the beginning of a focused word in Japanese, pitch range is expanded to produce a more extreme rise or fall around the culminative pitch accent associated to the syllable that is the obligatory head of a focused word in English. If we understand the phonology-phonetics interface as being a counterpart to the syntax-semantics interface at the other end of the grammar, then this speaks to a deeper similarity in the ways in which the grammatical patterns are interpreted. However, this deeper "semantic" similarity can only be described accurately once the analysis moves beyond the fixation on more superficial similarities that lead to the cross-language misparsings described in section 17.3.1. That is, one has to first analyze each language on its own terms (and not just look at surface similarities) before one can see how the two languages are fundamentally the same.

Moreover, once each prosodic system is analyzed fully in its own terms, another related deeper similarity emerges. In each language, when there is no narrow focus within an utterance, some of the prominence markers are associated with constituents near the edge of the utterance. Looking at English first, we can say that the generalization about association to the obligatory head means that there must be a nuclear pitch accent somewhere in every well-formed IP. When there is no narrow focus, the nuclear pitch accent goes on the last content word (by the Nuclear Stress Rule). In Japanese, similarly, there has to be at least one IP-initial rise at the beginning of every well-formed utterance, and when there is no narrower focus prompting an IP break and reset later on, the rise from the utterance initial [%L] makes the immediately next [H] target (whether a phrasal [H–] or the [H] of a [H*+L]) the highest (most prominent) peak in the utterance. Thus, it is difficult to distinguish broad focus on the utterance as a whole from narrow focus on the relevant edge constituent in both languages, even though the edge is different—namely, last in English, first in Japanese.

This generalization across the two languages predicts that there should also be complementary patterns of *focus projection* within the VP in transitive clauses. That is, given that objects follow verbs in English, placing the nuclear pitch accent on the object NP should be ambiguous between narrow focus on the NP and broader focus on the VP, as indeed it is, as Gussenhoven (1983) and others have shown experimentally. Conversely, because objects come before verbs in Japanese, producing a prominent reset before the object and dephrasing the following verb should be ambiguous between narrow focus on the NP and broader focus on the VP, as indeed it is, as Ito (2002a,b) has shown experimentally.

Comparing across languages in this way also highlights important lacunae in our understanding of one or the other prosodic system. For example, Ito (2002a,b) tests her predictions about focus projection only with sequences of lexically accented object followed by lexically accented verb. Much previous work on English focus projection, comparably, had not examined the effects of varying aspects of the tune other than the location of the nuclear pitch accent, but more recent work shows, for example, that the broad focus reading of late nuclear accent placement is less readily available when the pitch accent on the object is [L+H*] rather than [H*] (e.g., Welby 2003). Are there comparable interactions in Japanese, such that focus projection is easier or more difficult in other types of sequences besides accented object followed by accented verb?

Comparing across models also highlights other substantial gaps in our knowledge. For example, one lesson to draw from the discrepancy between Kubozono's and Pierrehumbert and Beckman's results described in section 17.4.2 is that we need more work on the prosody-pragmatics interface, work that applies additional methods drawn from other fields such as sentence processing.

Another, equally important lesson that we glean from this comparison across frameworks is the reminder that phonological relationships such as the contrast between an IP boundary and a mere AP boundary are grammatical abstractions that native speakers acquire in the course of extensive exposure to a rich variety of language-specific cues. Some of these cues come from parsing the Fo contour in terms of tone targets and pitch range specifications. Others come from parsing the spectral patterns in terms of the dynamic flow of consonant constrictions and vowel resonance patterns. A frequently encountered congruence of cues from multiple sources in the signal induces a stronger abstraction, which allows adult native speakers to produce conflicting cues when necessary to convey the intended information structure, as in the *mannaka-ni okima'su* sequence in figure 17.8, where the Fo contour suggests that the adverbial phrase and the verb are grouped together into one AP, but the long pause suggests that an IP boundary separates them. The native listener, conversely, can accommodate to such conflicting cues to recover both the intended focus pattern and the syntactic grouping that the prosodic phrasing also cues. In a similar way, although *rendaku* and the compound accent pattern of *ho'n-dana* typically occur on sequences of morphemes that are grouped together into a single AP, the speaker can produce the tonal cues to an AP boundary to convey narrow focus on the *tana* and can do so without "undoing" the other prosodic cues to the morphological grouping. Moreover, the speaker can produce these conflicting cues in full expectation that the listener will recover both the intended information structure and the intended morphological grouping. The disagreements described in sections 17.4.1 and 17.4.2 come about because the same kind of statistical dependencies drive the various interactions between the preferred focus-marking mechanism and lexical accent pattern, making for inherent ambiguities. What this lesson means for the theoretical linguist, then, is that the next generation of models of intonational phonology needs to do better justice to these complex interactions among discrete contrasts (e.g., between accented and unaccented words) and continuous variation (e.g., more versus less extreme degrees of pitch range expansion or compression at the edges of focus constituents) and the ways that native speakers and listeners take advantage of the statistical dependencies among different patterns.

NOTES FOR CHAPTER 17

1. Following standard practice in the literature on Japanese phonology, we use an apostrophe following the vowel to mark the location of the *akusento-kaku* in the roman transliteration of any word that is lexically specified as containing a syllable that associates to this [H*+L] tone sequence. Also, we use | to indicate an AP boundary and || to indicate an IP boundary, when we need to highlight the distinction.

2. Recall that the Fujisaki model uses a square wave "accent command" to model *both* accented and unaccented phrases; in the unaccented case, the fall at end of the square wave is obscured either by a following accent command or by cessation of voicing for a following silent pause.

3. Following the usual conventions in the literature on focus marking, we sometimes adopt the shorthand notation of writing the focus constituent in small caps in lieu of explicating the context.

4. Kubozono follows Poser (1984) in calling this pattern "total downstep"; see pattern B in Kubozono 1993 (p. 104).

5. The exceptions to this culminative distribution involve a handful of productive prefixes such as *ju'n* 'quasi' and *mo'to* 'former' (the so-called Aoyagi prefixes (see Aoyagi 1969), which retain their accent in addition to the accent on the base noun, as in *mo'to-da'ijin* 'former minister'.

6. In text-only examples, we indicate a prominence-lending BPM by underlining the phrase-final syllable of the focus constituent, followed by the symbol ↑ (to represent the Fo rise that is realized on that syllable for [H%]) or ∧ (to represent the rise-fall shape for [HL%]). The symbol ∧ is also inserted after the penultimate syllable to represent a PNLP rise.

7. To clarify, [H%] can occur sentence finally, on sentence-final particles such as the *ne* in figure 17.5b, but this usage does not have a prominence-lending function and is not an example of PLR.

8. Compare the asymmetry in English between marking narrow focus on nonfinal constituents with an early nuclear accent versus the difficulty in marking narrow focus by nuclear pitch accent placement in utterance-final position (although it is possible to set off the final word with a preceding silence and by choosing L+H* as the nuclear accent so as to produce a steep rise onto the peak that is associated with the accented syllable).

9. Maekawa (1991) offers further evidence for this conclusion. He compares the prosodic patterns observed on the *wh*-question in (i) to that of the minimally different polarity question in (ii).

(i) Na'ni-ga mie'ru?   'What do you see?'
(ii) Na'ni-ka mie'ru?   'Do you see something?

Utterances of (i) typically have an expanded pitch range on *Na'ni*, with the predicate *mie'ru* being realized in a very reduced pitch range. By contrast, utterances of (ii) typically show a lower peak on *na'ni* and a prominent AP boundary or even a reset on the predicate. In a perception experiment using synthetic stimuli (where the /k/ vs. /g/ consonants are crucially replaced with white noise), Maekawa shows that listeners' judgments are influenced more by the degree of subordination of the predicate than by the height of the question word itself. That is, the percent of *wh*-question judgments increases as the Fo height of the predicate decreases, regardless of the height of the focused *wh*-word. This finding emphasizes the crucial importance of the postfocal region in the interpretation of focal prominence.

10. That is, even though AM accounts such as Pierrehumbert and Beckman's (1988) differ from Fujisaki's account (Fujisaki and Kawai 1988) in modeling the phrasal [H–] as an independent target from the [H*] of the accent fall, most previous AM accounts effectively model dephrasing as the formal equivalent of deletion of the whole accent command in the Fujisaki model.

11. See, for example, the contrast between *wh*-questions and *yes/no*-questions studied in Maekawa 1991.

REFERENCES

Aoyagi, Seizô. 1969. A demarcative pitch of some prefix-stem sequences in Japanese. *Onsei no Kenkyuu* 14:241–247.

Arisaka, Hideyo. 1941. Akusento no kata no honshitsu ni tsuite [On the nature of accent pattern]. *Gengo Kenkyuu* 7:83–92.

Arvaniti, Amalia, D. Robert Ladd, and Ineke Mennen. 1998. Stability of tonal alignment: The case of Greek prenuclear accents. *Journal of Phonetics* 26:3–25.

Beckman, Mary E. 1996a. When is a syllable not a syllable? In *Phonological structure and language processing: Cross-linguistic studies*, ed. Takashi Otake and Anne Cutler, 95–123. Berlin: Mouton de Gruyter.

Beckman, Mary E. 1996b. The parsing of prosody. *Language and Cognitive Processes* 11:17–67.

Beckman, Mary E., Julia Hirschberg, and Stefanie Shattuck-Hufnagel. 2005. The original ToBI system and the evolution of the ToBI framework. In *Prosodic typology: The phonology of intonation and phrasing*, ed. Sun-Ah Jun, 9–54. New York: Oxford University Press.

Beckman, Mary E., and Janet Pierrehumbert. 1992. Comments on chapters 13 and 14 [original title: Strategies and tactics for thinking about Fo variation]. In *Papers in laboratory phonology II: Segment, gesture, prosody*, ed. Gerard J. Docherty and D. Robert Ladd, 387–397. Cambridge: Cambridge University Press.

Bruce, Gösta. 1977. *Swedish word accents in sentence perspective*. Lund: Gleerup.

Docherty, Gerard J. 1992. *The timing of voicing in British English obstruents*. Dordrecht: Foris.

Firth, J. R. (John Rupert). 1957. *Papers in linguistics, 1934–1951*. London: Oxford University Press.

Fougeron, Cécile, and Patricia A. Keating. 1997. Articulatory strengthening at the edges of prosodic domains. *Journal of the Acoustical Society of America* 101:3728–3740.

Fujisaki, Hiroya, and Keikichi Hirose. 1984. Analysis of voice fundamental frequency contours for declarative sentences of Japanese. *Journal of the Acoustical Society of Japan (English)* 5(4):233–242.

Fujisaki, Hiroya, and Keikichi Hirose. 1993. Analysis and perception of intonation expressing paralinguistic information in spoken Japanese. *Lund Linguistics Working Papers* 41:254–257.

Fujisaki, Hiroya, and Hisashi Kawai. 1988. Realization of linguistic information in the voice fundamental frequency contour of the spoken Japanese. *Annual Bulletin of the Research Institute of Logopedics and Phoniatrics (RILP)* 22:183–191.

Fujisaki, Hiroya, Sumio Ohno, Masafumi Osame, Mayumi Sakata, and Keikichi Hirose. 1994. Prosodic characteristics of a spoken dialogue for information query. In *Pro-*

ceedings of the International Conference on Spoken Language Processing (ICSLP), 1103–1106. Tokyo: The Acoustical Society of Japan.

Fujisaki, Hiroya, and H. Sudo. 1971. Synthesis by rule of prosodic features of connected Japanese. In *Proceedings of the 7th International Congress on Acoustics (ICA)*, 133–136. Budapest: Akadémiai Kiadó.

Gandour, Jack, S. Potisuk, and S. Dechongkit. 1994. Tonal coarticulation in Thai. *Journal of Phonetics* 22:477–492.

Goldsmith, John A. 1979. *Autosegmental phonology*. New York: Garland.

Grice, Martine, D. Robert Ladd, and Amalia Arvaniti. 2000. On the place of phrase accents in intonational phonology. *Phonology* 17:143–185.

Gussenhoven, Carlos. 1983. Testing the reality of focus domains. *Language and Speech* 26:61–80.

Gussenhoven, Carlos. 2004. *The phonology of tone and intonation*. Cambridge: Cambridge University Press.

Haraguchi, Shôsuke. 1977. *The tone pattern of Japanese: An autosegmental theory of tonology*. Tokyo: Kaitakusha.

Hattori, Shiro. 1961. Prosodeme, syllable structure, and laryngeal phonemes. *Bulletin of the Summer Institute of Linguistics: Studies in Descriptive and Applied Linguistics* 1:1–27. Tokyo: International Christian University.

Hay, Jennifer. 2003. *Causes and consequences of word structure*. London: Routledge.

Hirai, Toshio, Norio Higuchi, and Yoshinori Sagisaka. 1997. Comparison of F0 control rules derived from multiple speech databases. In *Computing prosody: Computational models for processing spontaneous speech*, ed. Yoshinori Sagisaka, Nick Campbell, and Norio Higuchi, 211–223. Berlin: Springer-Verlag.

Hirschberg, Julia, and Gregory Ward. 1992. The influence of pitch range, duration, amplitude and spectral features on the interpretation of the rise-fall-rise intonation contour in English. *Journal of Phonetics* 20:241–251.

Hirschberg, Julia, and Gregory Ward. 1995. The interpretation of the high-rise question contour in English. *Journal of Pragmatics* 24:407–412.

Hualde, José Ignacio. 1991. *Basque phonology*. London: Routledge.

Hualde, José Ignacio, Gorka Elordieta, Iñaki Gaminde, and Rajka Smiljanić. 2002. From pitch-accent to stress-accent in Basque. In *Laboratory phonology 7*, ed. Carlos Gussenhoven and Natasha Warner, 547–584. Berlin: Mouton de Gruyter.

Hyman, Larry. 2001. Tone systems. In *Language typology and language universals: An international handbook (vol. 2)*, ed. Martin Haspelmath, Ekkehard König, Wulf Oesterreicher, and Wolfgang Raible, 1367–1380. Berlin: Walter de Gruyter.

Hyman, Larry. 2005. Word-prosodic typology. Paper presented at the Between Stress and Tone conference, Leiden, June.

Ito, Kiwako. 2002a. The interaction of focus and lexical pitch accent in speech production and dialogue comprehension: Evidence from Japanese and Basque. Doctoral dissertation, University of Illinois, Urbana-Champaign.

Ito, Kiwako. 2002b. Ambiguity in broad focus and narrow focus interpretation in Japanese. In *Proceedings of Speech Prosody*, ed. Bernard Bel and Isabelle Marlien, 411–414. Aix-en-Provence, France: Laboratoire Parole et Langage, Université de Provence.

Ito, Kiwako, and Shari R. Speer. 2006. Using interactive tasks to elicit natural dialogue. In *Methods in empirical prosody research*, ed. Stefan Sudhoff, Denisa Lenertova, Roland Meyer, Sandra Pappert, Petra Augurzky, Ina Mleinek, Nicole Richter, and Johannes Schliesser, 229–257. Berlin: Mouton de Gruyter.

Ito, Kiwako, Shari R. Speer, and Mary Beckman. 2003. The influence of given-new status and lexical accent on intonation in Japanese spontaneous speech. Poster presented at the 16th annual CUNY Conference on Human Sentence Processing, 34. Boston, March.

Jun, Sun-Ah. 1998. The accentual phrase in the Korean prosodic hierarchy. *Phonology* 15:189–226.

Jun, Sun-Ah. 2005. *Prosodic typology: The phonology of intonation and phrasing.* New York: Oxford University Press.

Katagiri, Yasuhiro. 1999. Dialogue functions of Japanese sentence-final particles. In *Proceedings of LP'98 (Linguistics and Phonetics'98)*, ed. Osamu Fujimura, Brian D. Joseph, and Bohumil Palek, 77–90. Charles University in Prague: The Karolinum Press.

Kawakami, Shin. 1957. Tookyoogo no takuritsu kyoochoo no onchoo [Tonal prominence in Tokyo Japanese]. Reprinted in 1995 in *Nihongo akusento ronshuu* [A collection of papers on Japanese accent], ed. Shin Kawakami, 76–91. Tokyo: Kyûko Shoin.

Kawakami, Shin. 1963. Bunmatsu nado no jooshoochoo ni tsuite [On phrase-final rises]. Reprinted in 1995 in *Nihongo akusento ronshuu* [A collection of papers on Japanese accent], ed. Shin Kawakami, 274–298. Tokyo: Kyûko Shoin.

Kindaichi, Haruhiko. 1951. Kotoba no senritsu [The melody of language]. *Kokugogaku* 5(2):37–59.

Kiriyama, Shinya, Keikichi Hirose, and Nobuaki Minematsu. 2002. Control of prosodic focuses for reply speech generation in a spoken dialogue system for information retrieval on academic documents. In *Proceedings of Speech Prosody*, ed. Bernard Bel and Isabelle Marlien, 431–434. Aix-en-Provence, France: Laboratoire Parole et Langage, Université de Provence.

Kokuritsu Kokugo Kenkyuujo [National Institute for Japanese Language (NIJL, formerly NRLI)]. 2006. *Nihongo hanashi kotoba koopasu no koochikuhoo* [Construction of the Corpus of Spontaneous Japanese]. NIJL report 124. Tokyo. http://www.kokken.go.jp/katsudo/seika/corpus/public/index.html.

Kori, Shiro. 1987. The tonal behavior of Osaka Japanese: An interim report. *Ohio State Working Papers in Linguistics (OSUWPL): Papers from the Linguistics Laboratory* 36:31–61.

Kori, Shiro. 1989a. Fookasu jitsugen ni okeru onsei no tsuyosa, jizokujikan, Fo no eikyoo [Acoustic manifestation of focus in Tokyo Japanese: The role of intensity, duration and Fo]. *Onsei Gengo* 3:29–38.

Kori, Shiro. 1989b. Kyooshoo to intoneeshon [Emphasis and intonation]. In *Nihongo no onsei/on'in (joo)* [Japanese phonetics/phonology (1)], vol. 2 of *Koza Nihongo to Nihongo Kyooiku*, ed. Miyoko Sugito, 316–342. Tokyo: Meiji Shoin.

Kori, Shiro. 1997. Nihongo no intoneeshon: kata to kinoo [Japanese intonation: Form and function]. In *Akusento, intoneeshon, rizumu to poozu* [Accent, intonation, rhythm, and pause], vol. 2 of *Nihongo Onsei*, ed. Tetsuya Kunihiro, 169–202. Tokyo: Sanseido.

Kubozono, Haruo. 1989. Syntactic and rhythmic effects on downstep in Japanese. *Phonology* 6:39–67.

Kubozono, Haruo. 1993. *The organization of Japanese prosody.* Tokyo: Kuroshio.

Kubozono, Haruo. 2007. Focus and intonation in Japanese: Does focus trigger pitch reset? In *Working papers of the SFB632: Interdisciplinary studies on information structure (ISIS)* 9, ed. Shinichiro Ishihara, 1–27. Potsdam, Germany: University of Potsdam.

Kuno, Susumu. 1973. *The structure of the Japanese language.* Cambridge, Mass: MIT Press.

Ladd, D. Robert. 1996. *Intonational phonology.* Cambridge: Cambridge University Press.

Langendoen, D. Terence. 1968. *The London school of linguistics: A study of the linguistic theories of B. Malinowski and J. R. Firth*. Cambridge, Mass: MIT Press.

Laniran, Yetunde, and G. N. Clements. 2003. Downstep and high tone raising: Interacting factors in Yoruba tone production. *Journal of Phonetics* 31(2):203–250.

Liberman, Mark, and Alan Prince. 1977. On stress and linguistic rhythm. *Linguistic Inquiry* 8(2):249–336.

Maeda, Kazuaki, and Jennifer J. Venditti. 1998. Phonetic investigation of boundary pitch movements in Japanese. In *Proceedings of the International Conference on Spoken Language Processing (ICSLP)*, 631–634. Rundle Mall, Australia: Casual Productions.

Maekawa, Kikuo. 1991. Perception of intonational characteristics of *wh* and non-*wh* questions in Tokyo Japanese. In *Proceedings of the International Congress of Phonetic Sciences (ICPhS)*, 4/5:202–205. Aix-en-Provence, France: Université de Provence.

Maekawa, Kikuo. 1994. Is there "dephrasing" of the accentual phrase in Japanese? *Ohio State University Working Papers in Linguistics* 44:146–165.

Maekawa, Kikuo. 1997. Effects of focus on duration and vowel formant frequency in Japanese. In *Computing prosody: Computational models for processing spontaneous speech*, ed. Yoshinori Sagisaka, Nick Campbell, and Norio Higuchi, 129–153. New York: Springer Verlag.

Maekawa, Kikuo. 2003. Corpus of Spontaneous Japanese: Its design and evaluation. In *Proceedings of the ISCA and IEEE Workshop on Spontaneous Speech Processing and Recognition (SSPR2003)*, 7–12. Tokyo.

Maekawa, Kikuo, and Yosuke Igarashi. 2006. 2-moora yuukaku joshi no inritsujoo no dokuritsusei: Nihongo hanashi kotoba koopasu no bunseki [Prosodic independence of bimoraic accented particles: Analysis of the Corpus of Spontaneous Japanese]. *Journal of the Phonetic Society of Japan* 10(2):33–42.

Maekawa, Kikuo, and Hideaki Kikuchi. 2005. Corpus-based analysis of vowel devoicing in spontaneous Japanese: An interim report. In *Voicing in Japanese*, ed. Jeroen van de Weijer, Kensuke Nanjo, and Tetsuo Nishihara, 205–228. Berlin: Mouton de Gruyter.

Maekawa, Kikuo, Hideaki Kikuchi, Yosuke Igarashi, and Jennifer J. Venditti. 2002. X-JToBI: An extended J_ToBI for spontaneous speech. In *Proceedings of the International Conference on Spoken Language Processing (ICSLP)*, 1545–1548. Boulder, Colo.: Center for Spoken Language Research.

Maruyama, Takehiko, and Miki Taniguchi. 2002. Bun no shooten koozoo to kyokushoteki takuritsu [Focus structure of sentences and local prominence]. *Kansai Linguistics Society* 22:18–28.

McCawley, James D. 1968. *The phonological component of a grammar of Japanese*. The Hague: Mouton.

McCawley, James D. 1970. Some tonal systems that come close to being pitch accent systems but don't quite make it. *Papers from the 6th Regional Meeting of the Chicago Linguistic Society (CLS)* 6:526–532.

McLemore, Cynthia Ann. 1991. The pragmatic interpretation of English intonation: Sorority speech. Doctoral dissertation, University of Texas, Austin.

Mesbur, James. 2005. Evidence for prominence-lending rise in focus phrases in Japanese. Ms., University of Pennsylvania, Philadelphia.

Miyaji, Yutaka. 1963. IV Intoneeshon [Intonation]. *Kokuritsu Kokugo Kenkyuujo* [National Institute for Japanese Language (NIJL, formerly NRLI)] *Report* 23, 178–208. Tokyo: Kokuritsu Kokugo Kenkuujo.

Muranaka, Toshiko, and Noriyo Hara. 1994. Features of prominent particles in Japanese discourse. In *Proceedings of the International Conference on Spoken Language Processing (ICSLP)*, 395–398. Tokyo: The Acoustical Society of Japan.

Nagahara, Hiroyuki. 1994. Phonological phrasing in Japanese. Doctoral dissertation, University of California, Los Angeles.

Nagahara, Hiroyuki, and Shoichi Iwasaki. 1994. Tail pitch movement and the intermediate phrase in Japanese. Paper presented at the Linguistic Society of America (LSA) annual meeting, Washington, D.C., January.

Nagao, Kyoko and Shigeaki Amano. 2000. A role of fundamental frequencies in the perception of emphasized words: Conference presentation abstract. *Journal of the Acoustical Society of America* 108(5):2465.

Nakanishi, Kimiko. 2007. Prosody and scope interpretations of the topic marker *wa* in Japanese. In *Topic and focus: Cross-linguistic perspectives on intonation and meaning*, ed. Chungmin Lee, Matthew Gordon, and Daniel Büring, 177–194. Dordrecht: Springer Verlag.

Ohishi, Shotaro. 1959. Purominensu ni tsuite: Tookyoogo no kansatsu ni motozuku oboegaki [Prominence: Observation of the Tokyo Dialect]. *Kotoba no kenkyuu* [Papers of the National Institute for Japanese Language], 87–102. Tokyo: Kokuritsu Kokugo Kenkuujo.

Oshima, David Y. 2007. Boundary tones or prominent particles? Variation in Japanese focus-marking contours. *Berkeley Linguistics Society (BLS)* 31:453–464.

Peng, Shu-hui. 1997. Production and perception of Taiwanese tones in different tonal and prosodic contexts. *Journal of Phonetics* 25:371–400.

Pierrehumbert, Janet B. 1980. The phonology and phonetics of English intonation. Doctoral dissertation, MIT, Cambridge, Mass.

Pierrehumbert, Janet B., and Mary E. Beckman. 1988. *Japanese tone structure*. Cambridge, Mass: MIT Press.

Pierrehumbert, Janet, and David Talkin. 1992. Lenition of /h/ and glottal stop. In *Papers in laboratory phonology II: Segment, gesture, prosody*, ed. Gerard J. Docherty and D. Robert Ladd, 90–116. Cambridge: Cambridge University Press.

Poser, William J. 1984. The phonetics and phonology of tone and intonation in Japanese. Doctoral dissertation, MIT, Cambridge, Mass.

Prince, Ellen F. 1981. Toward a taxonomy of given/new information. In *Radical pragmatics*, ed. Peter Cole, 223–255. San Diego, Calif.: Academic Press.

Raymond, William D., Robin Dautricourt, and Elizabeth Hume. 2006. Word-internal /t, d/ deletion in spontaneous speech: Modeling the effects of extra-linguistic, lexical, and phonological factors. *Language Variation and Change* 18:55–97.

Roberts, Craige. 1996. Information structure in discourse: Towards an integrated formal theory of pragmatics. *OSU Working Papers in Linguistics* 49:91–136.

Sagisaka, Yoshinori, and Hirokazu Sato. 1983. Secondary accent analysis in Japanese stem-affix concatenations. *Acoustical Society of Japan Transactions of the Committee on Speech Research* S83-05:31–37.

Selkirk, Elisabeth O., and Koichi Tateishi. 1991. Syntax and downstep in Japanese. In *Interdisciplinary approaches to language: Essays in honor of S.-Y. Kuroda*, ed. Carol Georgopoulos and Roberta Ishihara, 519–543. Dordrecht: Kluwer.

Sugahara, Mariko. 2002. Conditions on post-FOCUS dephrasing in Tokyo Japanese. In *Proceedings of Speech Prosody*, ed. Bernard Bel and Isabelle Marlien, 655–658. Aix-en-Provence, France: Laboratoire Parole et Langage, Université de Provence.

Takeda, Shoichi, and Akira Ichikawa. 1990. Analysis of prosodic features of prominence in spoken Japanese sentences. In *Proceedings of the International Conference on Spoken Language Processing (ICSLP)*, 493–496. Kobe, Japan: The Acoustical Society of Japan.

Taniguchi, Miki, and Takehiko Maruyama. 2001. Shooten koozoo to zyosi no takuritu [Focus structure and prominence of particles]. *Kansai Linguistics Society* 21:56–66.

Trubetskôi, Nikolâi Sergeevich. 1939. *Grundzüge der phonologie. (Travaux du Cercle linguistique de Prague No. 7.)* Prague: Cercle linguistique de Prague. (Trans. 1969, by Christiane A. M. Baltaxe as *Principles of Phonology*. Berkeley: University of California Press.)

Vallduví, Enric. 1992. *The informational component*. New York: Garland.

Venditti, Jennifer J. 1997. Japanese ToBI labelling Guidelines. *Ohio State University Working Papers in Linguistics* 50:127–162. (First distributed in 1995.)

Venditti, Jennifer J. 2000. Discourse structure and attentional salience effects on Japanese intonation. Doctoral dissertation, Ohio State University, Columbus.

Venditti, Jennifer J. 2005. The J_ToBI model of Japanese intonation. In *Prosodic typology: The phonology of intonation and phrasing*, ed. Sun-Ah Jun, 172–200. Oxford: Oxford University Press.

Venditti, Jennifer J., Kazuaki Maeda, and Jan P. H. van Santen. 1998. Modeling Japanese boundary pitch movements for speech synthesis. In *Proceedings of the 3rd ESCA Workshop on Speech Synthesis*, ed. Mike Edgington, 317–322. Jenolan Caves, Australia. New York: Institute of Electrical and Electronics Engineers.

Venditti, Jennifer J., and Marc Swerts. 1996. Intonational cues to discourse structure in Japanese. *Proceedings of the International Conference on Spoken Language Processing (ICSLP)* 2:725–728.

Welby, Pauline. 2003. Effects of pitch accent position, type, and status on focus projection. *Language and Speech* 46:53–82.

CHAPTER 18

THE STRUCTURE OF DP

AKIRA WATANABE

18.1 INTRODUCTION

The nature of functional categories is a controversial topic in the study of Japanese syntax. DP is no exception. It is well known that Japanese does not possess articles, definite or indefinite. It is premature, however, to jump from this simple observation to the conclusion that Japanese lacks DP altogether. Various properties of nominal expressions must be investigated before drawing a conclusion.

The opinion is divided concerning the issue of whether Japanese has DP. Tateishi (1989) posits D to accommodate the case particle. In Saito and Murasugi's (1990) analysis of ellipsis, the agreeing nature of D plays an important role. Fukui (1986), in contrast, takes the position that Japanese lacks DP. These authors, however, worked in the framework that posited only DP above NP. Since then, research on Romance, Germanic, and Semitic languages has led to postulation of further functional projections between DP and NP; see Bernstein 2001 and Longobardi 2001. In studies on Japanese, too, Kawashima (1994, 1998) and Kitahara (1993) make use of a NumP that comes between NP and DP to place the numeral-classifier combination at the position of its head. Thus, the issue is not limited to the presence or absence of DP. The internal structure of DP as a whole must be taken up.

18.2 Core Data

This chapter concentrates on two significant properties of nominal expressions in Japanese that set it apart from languages such as English. These properties turn out to provide interesting insights into the internal structure of DP.

First, in Japanese a numeral can occupy various positions in relation to the head noun and the case particle, as illustrated in (1).

(1) a. John-wa hon **san-satsu-o** katta.
    John-TOP book 3-CL-ACC bought
  b. John-wa **san-satsu**-no hon-**o** katta.
    John-TOP 3-CL-GEN book-ACC bought
  c. John-wa hon-**o** san-satsu katta.
    John-TOP book-ACC 3-CL bought
  'John bought three books.'

In English, however, the numeral appears in a fixed prenominal position. This contrast immediately raises the question about the source of the parametric difference between Japanese and languages such as English. Why does Japanese allow such diverse possibilities for numeral placement, whereas English does not?

One might wonder whether the numeral+classifier combination forms a constituent with the head noun in (1c), given that it appears after the case particle. No such question arises for (1a), where it is sandwiched between the head noun and the case particle, nor for (1b), where it is connected to the head noun (or NP) by a genitive-like linker *no*, as nonclausal prenominal elements generally are (Kitagawa and Ross 1982, Murasugi 1991). The constituency of (1c) has been controversial (see Fukui and Sakai 2003; Kamio 1983; Koizumi 1995, 2000; and Takano 2002), but Watanabe (2006a) presents a straightforward argument, observing that the same sequence acts as a constituent in the pseudopartitive construction, illustrated in (2).

(2) Roger-wa **donburi-ni** **yon-hai**-no gohan-o tabeta.
  Roger-TOP big.bowl-DAT 4-CL-GEN rice-ACC ate
  'Roger ate four big bowls of rice.'

Notice that exactly the same type of structure (noun+case+numeral+classifier) is used as the prenominal measure expression in (2). The dative phrase *donburi-ni* in (2) forms a constituent with the following numeral+classifier combination, which in turn is connected to the head noun with the linker *no*. It is impossible to break up the sequence of the dative phrase and the numeral+classifier combination, as shown by the complete ill-formedness of (3).

(3) *Roger-wa **yon-hai**-no gohan-o **donburi-ni** tabeta.

The mechanism that generates the measure expression of the form noun+case+numeral+classifier as a constituent guarantees that the numeral+classifier sequence in (1c) can also form a constituent with the preceding case-marked NP.

Interestingly, this noun+case+numeral+classifier sequence can occupy the same range of positions as the numeral, as shown in (4).[1]

(4) a. Roger-wa gohan **donburi(??-ni) yon-hai**-o tabeta.
 Roger-TOP rice big.bowl-DAT 4-CL-ACC ate
 b. Roger-wa **donburi(-ni) yon-hai**-no gohan-o tabeta.
 Roger-TOP big.bowl-DAT 4-CL-GEN rice-ACC ate
 c. Roger-wa gohan-o **donburi(-ni) yon-hai** tabeta.
 Roger-TOP rice-ACC big.bowl-DAT 4-CL ate
 'Roger ate four big bowls of rice.'

The diversity of possible positions is thus not limited to the numeral. Attributing the diversity of placement to the properties of the numeral alone, therefore, is a wrong direction to pursue, as noted by Kamio (1977).

An additional characteristic of the Japanese numeral system is that the numeral must be accompanied by a classifier. This appears to be an areal feature of East and Southeast Asia (Aikhenvald 2000, Simpson 2005). The treatment of numeral classifiers has come into the foreground of theoretical discussion since Chierchia's (1998a, 1998b) influential work, which connects the use of numeral classifiers with the absence of articles. The presence of a numeral classifier itself, however, is not related to the diversity of numeral placement possibilities (at least directly), given that languages such as Chinese do not exhibit such diversity despite the use of classifiers (see Li 1999 for some discussion of Chinese).

The second major characteristic of Japanese nominals is the indeterminate system. It has been well known since Kuroda 1965 that Japanese forms various quantificational expressions by adding a particle to a *wh*-phrase, as shown in (5).

(5)
	Interrogative	Existential	Neg-concord	Universal
Person	dare	dare-ka	dare-mo	dare-mo
Thing	nani	nani-ka	nani-mo	(nani-mo-kamo)
Place	doko	doko-ka	doko-mo	doko-mo
Time	itsu	itsu-ka	——	itsu-mo

The common *wh*-part is called the indeterminate. English has sporadic cases like *somewhere*, but the comparable system is absent. The question is what kind of principles enable Japanese to have an indeterminate system.

More data is introduced as the discussion unfolds. In addition to addressing analytical issues, which are presented next, this chapter also aims at putting together basic data on the syntax of quantifiers in Japanese in a more or less comprehensive way, because the past literature only gives a fragmentary picture. For the purposes of choosing among alternative accounts of the internal structure of nominal expressions, however, the minimal set given above suffices.

18.3 ANALYTICAL ISSUES

As to the treatment of numerals, the dominant view since Inoue 1978 has been that the various structural options for numerals in (1) should not be attributed to a unified underlying structure. The reason is that there are various differences, especially semantic, among the three kinds of expressions in (1). The nonuniform approach, however, has left it completely open why English and Japanese differ in the placement of numerals. No principled account of this parametric difference has been provided in the literature. This is a serious failure from the perspective of the principles-and-parameters approach.

Recently, Watanabe (2006a) put forth a concrete proposal that accounts for the diversity of numeral placement possibilities in Japanese, relying crucially on the presence of various functional projections between NP and DP to provide enough structural resources for a uniform treatment of (1a–c) as well as (4a–c). In fact, Watanabe's analysis is the only comprehensive one existing in the literature that covers the simple-looking data in (1) and (4) in a principled fashion. This proposal is reviewed in section 18.3.1.

Given that Inoue's (1978) major argument is invoked time and again (Kawashima 1998:fn. 2 and 28, and Nakanishi 2003, for example) to set aside the structure in (1b), it is important to revisit Inoue's arguments and observations to see what they really amount to. In fact, Haig's (1980) response nullifies their force, but subsequent researchers have either forgotten or overlooked this part of Haig's paper, leaving a vast empirical domain untouched as a result. Sections 18.3.2–18.3.4 are devoted to rectifying this situation.

The discussion of Inoue 1978 and Haig 1980 in section 18.3.2 leads us to the problem of partitive constructions, which forms the topic of section 18.3.3. Distribution of quantifiers other than the numeral is taken up in section 18.3.4 in relation to the problem of partitive constructions.

As stated at the beginning, the presence or absence of DP in Japanese has been a major issue. Section 18.3.5 turns to the question of how the treatment of numerals bears on the issue concerning D. Fukui and Takano's (2000) proposal, which does not posit DP, is taken up there. It is also shown that the indeterminate system provides an important insight into the nature of D in Japanese.

18.3.1 Articulated DP Structure and Placement of Numerals

18.3.1.1 *Massive remnant movement*

Watanabe (2006a) proposes that massive remnant movement within DP can relate the three structural options for the numeral in a straightforward way, assuming that Japanese nominals have the following layers of functional projections:

THE STRUCTURE OF DP 517

(6) [DP [QP [CaseP [#P NP #] Case] Q] D]

The # head is the locus of classifiers under this proposal. First, the derivation constructs the structure in (7a). After merger of the Case head with (7a), NP is raised to Spec,CaseP, as in (7b). This movement is obligatory. If nothing other than merger of higher functional heads takes place, (1a) is derived.

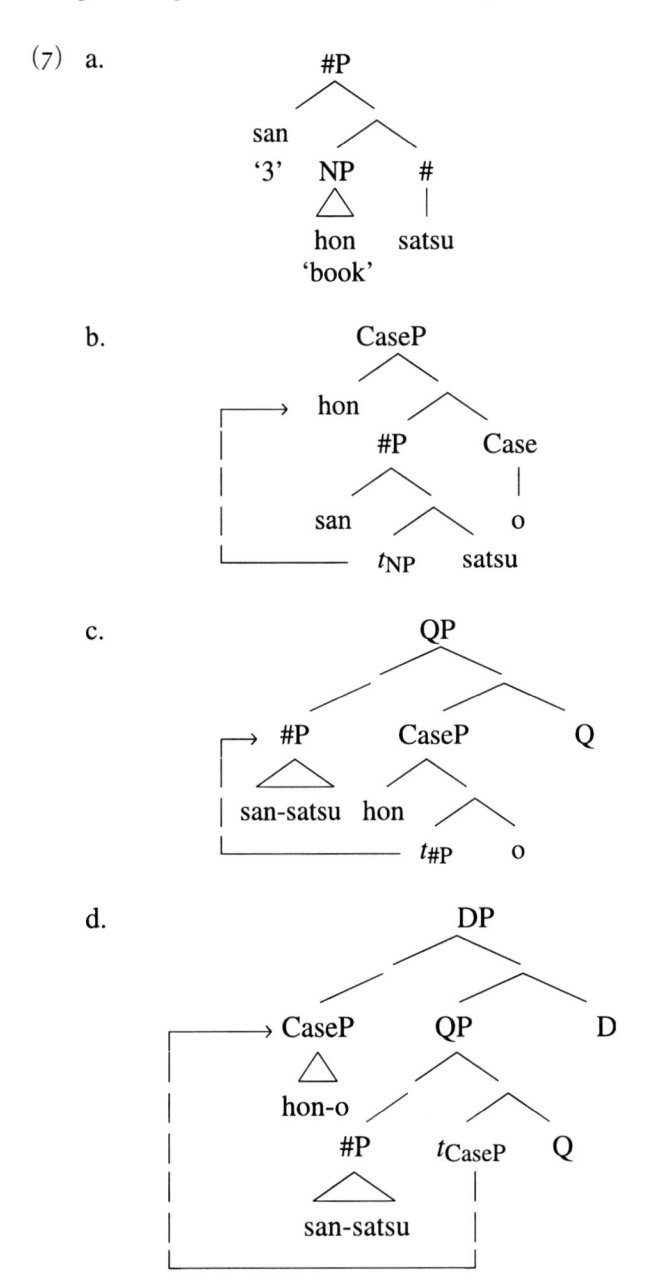

(7) a.

```
          #P
         /  \
       san   \
       '3'   NP    #
             /\    |
           hon   satsu
          'book'
```

b.

```
              CaseP
             /     \
   → hon          
   |          #P       Case
   |         /  \       |
   |       san   \      o
   |           tNP   satsu
   └────────────┘
```

c.

```
                    QP
                  /    \
    →  #P         CaseP        Q
    |  /\        /    \
    | san-satsu hon
    |              t#P    o
    └──────────────┘
```

d.

```
                    DP
                  /    \
      → CaseP          QP           D
      |  /\          /    \
      | hon-o
      |       #P      tCaseP    Q
      |      /\         |
      |  san-satsu
      └──────┘
```

If #P is raised to Spec,QP, which dominates CaseP, (7c) is formed, corresponding to (1b), with the linker *no* inserted through a morphological readjustment. Finally,

CaseP can be raised to Spec,DP as a next step, as in (7d), yielding (1c). These two movement steps are optional. Some more aspects of these movement operations are taken up in section 18.4.2.

One additional possibility not discussed in Watanabe 2006a is to move CaseP to Spec,DP without raising #P to Spec,QP, as in (8).

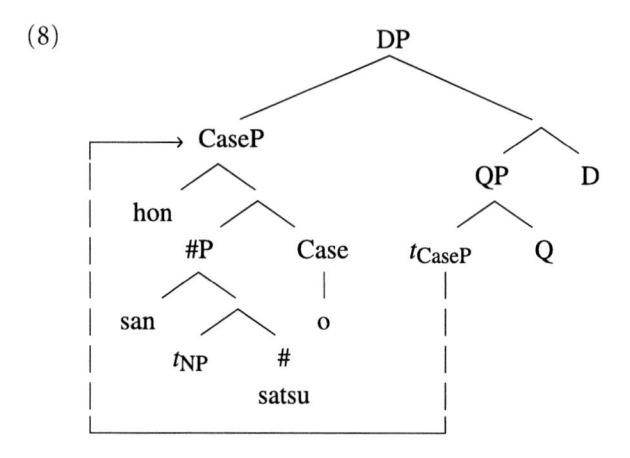

(8)

```
                         DP
                        /  \
         ┌────→ CaseP
         │      /  \
         │    hon    \          QP       D
         │         /  \        /  \
         │       #P    Case  tCaseP  Q
         │      /  \    │        │
         │    san   \   o        │
         │        /  \           │
         │      tNP   #          │
         │          satsu        │
         └───────────────────────┘
```

This derivation is possible, because raising of #P to Spec,QP is optional. The structure in (8) gives rise to the string corresponding to (1a). Example (1a) is thus structurally ambiguous under Watanabe's proposal.

Thus, the diversity of numeral placement possibilities in Japanese is reduced to the existence of optional phrasal movement within DP under the uniform approach. Given the standard view that the presence or absence of movement is a major source of parameterization, the fixed positioning of numerals in languages such as English follows from the absence of movement of the kind exemplified in (7).

The above analysis can accommodate the pseudopartitive construction in (4) as well. The relevant part of the derivation starts with the structure in (9a), which differs from (7a) in that the # head is phonologically null and that DP instead of a numeral occupies Spec,#P. The details of CaseP and #P inside this DP are given in (9b,c).

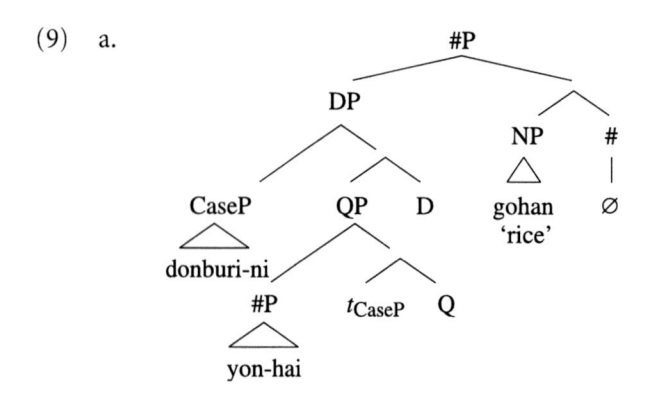

(9)   a.
```
                                    #P
                                   /  \
                        DP                 \
                       /  \                NP     #
                      /    \              /  \    │
                  CaseP    QP   D      gohan   Ø
                   /\      /\          'rice'
              donburi-ni  /  \
                        #P   tCaseP  Q
                        /\
                     yon-hai
```

b. [$_{\text{CaseP}}$ [$_{\text{NP}}$ donburi] $t_{\text{\#P}}$ [$_{\text{Case}}$ ni]]
          big.bowl   DAT
c. [$_{\text{\#P}}$ yon t_{NP} [$_\text{\#}$ hai]]
    4   CL

Notice that DP in Spec,#P in (9a) is structurally identical to (7d). The structure in (9a) undergoes the same set of derivational steps as (7) to give the three structures in (4). In other words, optional remnant movement gives rise to the same structural diversity for the pseudopartitive construction, too.

Adapting Tang's (1990) proposal for Chinese to Japanese, Kawashima (1994, 1998) and Kitahara (1993) place the numeral+classifier combination under Num as a complex head as in (10).

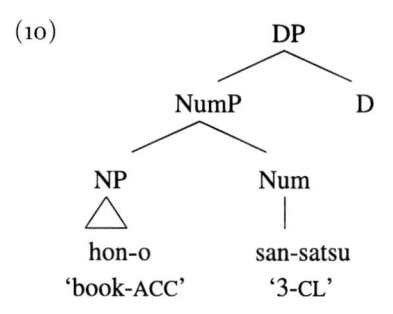

(10)

```
            DP
           /  \
        NumP   D
       /    \
     NP     Num
      △      |
    hon-o  san-satsu
  'book-ACC'  '3-CL'
```

This type of approach cannot be extended to accommodate the structural diversity of the pseudopartitive construction, because phrasal expressions such as *donburi-ni yon-hai* 'big.bowl-DAT 4 CL' cannot occupy a head position.[2] See also Simpson 2005 for additional arguments against putting the numeral+classifier combination under a single head from a cross-linguistic perspective. The parallelism between the pseudopartitive and the simple numeral supports the placement of the numeral in the specifier position. Furthermore, the structure in (10) is completely silent on the treatment of the cases where the numeral appears in a prenominal position (1b).[3]

Now, recall that there are semantic differences among the three structures in (1), which have been taken to constitute a prima facie argument against the uniform account of the structural diversity. Note, however, that the derived structures for the three kinds of nominal expressions in (1) are different from each other. The structural difference at the end of the derivation should be sufficient to guarantee semantic differences, given that derived structures are all that matters in semantic interpretation. Let us turn to one such semantic difference next.

18.3.1.2 *Justification for positing D: Specificity*

Kamio (1977) briefly mentions the observation that the structure exemplified by (1c) only allows the nonspecific reading. This intuition is most clearly brought out in the intensionality context, as shown in Watanabe 2006a. Consider (11).

(11) a. John-wa piano **ni-dai**-o kai-tagatta.
John-TOP piano 2-CL-ACC buy-wanted
b. John-wa **ni-dai**-no piano-o kai-tagatta.
c. John-wa piano-o **ni-dai** kai-tagatta.
'John wanted to buy two pianos.'

Examples (11a,b) are ambiguous between the reading where John wanted to buy two particular pianos and the nonspecific reading where John wanted two pianos but did not care which ones. Unlike (11a,b), however, (11c) lacks the reading where John wanted to buy two particular pianos.

It is worth mentioning at this point that the pseudopartitive construction exhibits an extreme case of nonspecificity. For (4) to be true, Roger does not need four bowls. A single bowl suffices. It is thus no coincidence that the measure expression in the pseudopartitive construction, which corresponds to the DP in Spec, #P in (9a), takes the form it does, given that this is exactly the form specifically tailored for the nonspecific interpretation.

Insofar as (non-)specificity is a property of D, it is reasonable to expect D to play a role in the formation of (11c). The uniform approach to the placement of numerals captures this insight by saying that movement of CaseP to Spec,DP takes place in the derivation of (11c). Under the current conception of movement, this movement is regarded as triggered by the properties of D, which ensure the nonspecific reading of this DP, a point that is taken up again in section 18.4.2.

There is another indication that the form exemplified by (1c) and (11c) forces the nonspecific reading. Harada (1976) notes that the NP-case-numeral-classifier order is incompatible with individual-level predicates, as illustrated in (12).

(12) a. Gakusei **san-nin**-ga eigo-ga umai.
students 3-CL-NOM English-NOM good
'Three students are good at English.'
b. **San-nin**-no gakusei-ga eigo-ga umai.
c. *?Gakusei-ga **san-nin** eigo-ga umai.

The deviance of (12c) can be explained by the restriction that prohibits individual-level predicates from taking a nonspecific subject (Diesing 1992), as suggested by Ishii (1991).[4]

To summarize, the fact that there is a semantic difference correlated with the different positioning of numerals does not necessarily present an obstacle to the uniform approach to the placement of numerals, which can accommodate the specificity difference in a principled fashion.

18.3.2 Inoue's (1978) Arguments and Observations Revisited

Next, let us take up Inoue's (1978) original arguments against the uniform treatment of the numeral placement and Haig's (1980) response. As noted before,

Inoue's arguments have been the obstacle to the uniform treatment of the numeral placement in the past, so they are worth examining in some detail.

Inoue's major argument consists in the observation that there is a semantic contrast between the following two examples, as indicated by the English translation:

(13) a. [Mae-o   hashitteita]   **ni-dai**-no kuruma-ga tsukamatta.
        front-ACC were.running 2-CL-GEN   car-NOM   got.caught
        'The two cars that were driving (ahead of us) got caught.'
     b. [Mae-o   hashitteita]   kuruma-ga **ni-dai** tsukamatta.
        front-ACC were.running car-NOM   2-CL   got.caught
        'Two of the cars that were driving (ahead of us) got caught.'

Inoue is careful enough to point out that this semantic difference typically arises when the presence of a relative clause turns the nominal into a definite expression. A related observation made by Inoue is that there are quantifiers that cannot appear prenominally but are acceptable after the case particle, as illustrated in (14).

(14) a. ***Hanbun**-no iawaseta   gakusei-ga   kougi-ni
        half-GEN   happened.to.be.there student-NOM protest-LOC
        sankashita.
        participated
     b. Iawaseta   gakusei-ga   **hanbun** kougi-ni   sankashita.
        happened.to.be.there student-NOM half   protest-LOC participated
        'Half of the students who happened to be there participated in the protest.'

The gist of Inoue's arguments is that these differences cannot be captured under the uniform approach.

Haig (1980) points out that both of Inoue's arguments should be subsumed under the general problem of partitives. Significantly, Inoue's observation that the semantic contrast illustrated in (13) is linked with definiteness finds an analogue in the English partitive construction, exemplified by the translation in (13b), which is most felicitous when the DP following *of* is definite, as shown in (15).

(15) a. some of the women
     b. *some of women

See Abbott 1996, Barker 1998, Hoeksema 1996, de Hoop 1997, Matthewson 2001, and the references cited there for the discussion of English partitives and complications related to this "partitive constraint."

There is another indication that the placement of the quantifier after the case particle induces the partitive interpretation. Sauerland and Yatsushiro (2004) observe that, whereas (16a) is not compatible with the scenario in which there is only one book, (16b) can be true under that scenario.

(16) a. John-wa   **hotondo**-no hon-o   yomi-oeta.
        John-TOP   most-GEN   book-ACC read-finished
        'John finished reading most of the books.'

b. John-wa   hon-o   **hotondo** yomi-oeta.
      John-TOP book-ACC   most   read-finished
      'John read most parts of the book(s).'

The interpretation of (16b) in question is known as mass partitive in the literature (Abbott 1996, Hoeksema 1996, Wilkinson 1996; see also Chierchia 1998a and Selkirk 1977). Some English examples from Hoeksema 1996 are given in (17).

(17) a. Most of the city is off-limits to foreigners.
      b. Some of him had stayed behind in his native Rumania.
      c. Half of every donation goes to administrative costs.

Mass partitives express part-of relations between an individual and its parts, or between a quantity of some substance and its subquantities. Abbott (1996) argues that mass partitives are partitives after all. The major reason is that mass partitives, just like ordinary partitives (15b), disallow embedding of bare plurals and mass nouns, as illustrated in (18).

(18) a. *most of brooms
      b. *some of milk

To conclude, when the partitive interpretation is singled out as a phenomenon to be treated separately, Inoue's arguments lose their force. She is right in singling out the partitive interpretation from the other readings of numeral quantifiers. But she goes too far when she denies the possibility of uniform treatment of numeral placement even for cases where the partitive interpretation is not found. Note that the partitive interpretation is absent in cases such as (11c), discussed in the previous subsection. If a semantic difference justifies positing a different structure, cases such as (13b) should be treated differently from cases such as (11c) by Inoue's own logic. Inoue (1978) simply draws a wrong line, as pointed out by Haig (1980).

One should not be misled by superficial similarity in form. In-depth analysis must be carried out to reach beyond simple observation. We have to turn next to the question of how the partitive interpretation arises in cases such as (13b).

18.3.3 Partitive Constructions

The question facing us now is whether the partitive interpretation should be attributed to the same structure as that of (1c) or is due to some other structure. Haig (1980) seems to be inclined to think that there is no need to posit a different structure. He points to the unambiguously partitive structure of the kind illustrated in (19) and states that the partitive interpretation requires the quantifier to follow the head noun.

(19) a. Mae-o   hashitteita   kuruma-no-#(uchi-no) **ni-dai**-ga
         front-ACC   were.running   car-GEN-out-of   two-CL-NOM

tsukamatta.[5]
got.caught
'Two of the cars which were driving ahead of us got caught.'
b. Iawaseta gakusei-no **hanbun**-ga kougi-ni
happened.to.be.there student-GEN half-NOM protest-LOC
sankashita.
participated
'Half of the students who happened to be there participated in the protest.'
c. John-wa sono hon-no **hotondo**-o yomi-oeta.
John-TOP that book-GEN most-ACC read-finished
'John read most parts of that book.'

Haig's view is that this generalization is sufficient to guarantee that the partitive interpretation is available when the quantifier follows the case particle.

Though the question is somewhat moot, there are several reasons to believe that a distinct structure needs to be posited for (13b), (14b), and (16b). First, the partitive interpretation is strongly linked to the definiteness of the nominals, as observed by Inoue. Partitive quantification works on this definite expression. If the DP structure in (6) is on the right track, it is reasonable to generate the quantifier in (13b), (14b), and (16b) outside the definite DP. The external generation of the quantifier allows us to capture the similarity between the English partitive construction and its Japanese counterpart, given that the English construction also generates the quantifier above the ordinary DP.

Second, the external generation of the quantifier makes it possible to account for Inoue's observation that the partitive interpretation also arises when there is an additional quantifier, as in (20).

(20) [Narande hashitteita **suu-dai**-no torakku-ga] **ni-san-dai**
lined.up were.running several-CL-GEN truck-NOM 2-3-CL
gaadoreeru-ni butsukatta.
guardrail-LOC struck
'Two or three of the several trucks that were driving abreast struck the guardrail.'

Given that the bracketed part in (20) is a full-fledged DP, it is no surprise that it contains a quantifier.[6] The impossibility of having multiple prenominal quantifiers, as in (21), is also an automatic consequence of the fact that the partitive construction does not involve prenominal quantifiers.

(21) *Ni-san-dai-no narande hashitteita **suu-dai**-no torakku-ga
2-3-CL-GEN lined.up were.running several-CL-GEN truck-NOM
gaadoreeru-ni butsukatta.
guardrail-LOC struck

It is also impossible to place the two quantifiers after the case particle as in (22).

(22) *[Narande hashitteita torakku-ga **suu-dai**] ni-san-dai
lined.up were.running truck-NOM several-CL 2-3-CL
gaadoreeru-ni butsukatta.
guardrail-LOC struck

The ill-formedness of (22) follows from the nonspecific reading forced on the bracketed DP.

Third, the structure exemplified in (19) is unambiguously partitive in interpretation. If cases such as (13b) and (1c) are taken to share the same structure that is compatible with the partitive and the nonpartitive interpretations, it is mysterious why the structure for (19) is used exclusively for the partitive reading. Haig's generalization that the partitive interpretation requires the quantifier to follow the head noun is too weak to differentiate between (1c)/(13b) and (19).

I would also like to point out that the partitive reading is not given for free. In other words, the placement of the quantifier after the case particle does not guarantee the possibility of the partitive interpretation, which is sensitive to idiosyncratic properties of individual quantifiers. The quantifier *takusan* 'many', for example, does not allow the partitive interpretation. Therefore, it cannot appear in the structures that force the partitive interpretation, as shown in (23).

(23) a. *John-wa toshoshitsu-ni aru go-roku-jus-satsu-no hon-o
John-TOP library.room-LOC are 5-6-10-CL-GEN book-ACC
takusan yonda.
many read
'John read many of the 50 to 60 books in the library.'
b. *John-wa toshoshitsu-ni aru go-roku-jus-satsu-no hon-no
John-TOP library.room-LOC are 5-6-10-CL-GEN book-GEN
takusan-o yonda.
many-ACC read

When the partitive interpretation is not forced, it can be placed after the case particle, as in (24).

(24) John-wa hon-o **takusan** yonda.
John-TOP book-ACC many read
'John read many books.'

Hotondo contrasts with *takusan* in this respect, as indicated by the acceptability of (25a,b).

(25) a. John-wa toshoshitsu-ni aru go-roku-jus-satsu-no hon-o
John-TOP library.room-LOC are 5-6-10-CL-GEN book-ACC
hotondo yonda.
most read
'John read most of the 50 to 60 books in the library room.'

b. John-wa   toshoshitsu-ni   aru go-roku-jus-satsu-no hon-no
   John-TOP   library.room-LOC   are 5-6-10-CL-GEN   book-GEN
   hotondo-o yonda.
   most-ACC read

We can pin down the special property of *takusan* by saying that it is a nonpresuppositional quantifier in the sense of Diesing 1992. The partitive reading presupposes that the restrictor of quantification is a nonempty set of individuals and therefore is incompatible with the nonpresuppositional nature of *takusan*.

Now, if nonspecificity (discussed in section 18.3.1.2) is an instance of nonpresuppositional quantification as claimed by Diesing, we need to posit a distinct structure for cases where the quantifier placed after the case particle produces the partitive interpretation, given that this reading is excluded by the structure that imposes the nonspecific reading. Thus, we have another reason for recognizing the structure that is specialized for the partitive reading.

To sum up, recognizing NP-case-numeral-classifier as a form of the partitive construction in Japanese helps explain a number of peculiarities exhibited by this form comparable to those of the English partitive construction.

18.3.4 Placement of Quantifiers Other Than Numerals and the Structure of Partitives

Given that the discussion extended to quantifiers other than numerals in the previous subsection, let us now consider their DP-internal distribution. It turns out that the placement of nonnumeral quantifiers has significant consequences for the structural analysis of partitive constructions.

Ishii (1991) observes that unlike numerals, *takusan* 'many, much' cannot appear between the head noun and the case particle, as shown in (26).

(26) a. *John-wa   hon   **takusan**-o katta.
        John-TOP book   many-ACC   bought
     b. John-wa   **takusan**-no hon-o   katta.
        John-TOP many-GEN   book-ACC bought
     c. John-wa   hon-o   **takusan** katta.
        John-TOP book-ACC many   bought
        'John bought many books.'

To account for this difference between numerals and *takusan*, Watanabe (2006a) proposes to place it in Spec,QP, as in (27), which corresponds to (26b).

(27)
```
                    DP
                 /      \
              QP          D
            /    \        |
        takusan   \       Ø
                CaseP   Q
                /   \
              hon    \
                  #P    Case
                 /  \
               tNP   #
```

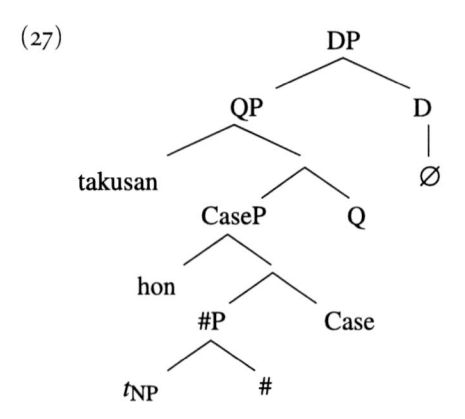

Example (26c) is generated once CaseP is raised to Spec,DP. As long as NP does not undergo movement to Spec,DP, the ill-formedness of (26a) is accounted for. It should be emphasized that positing the rich layers of functional projections enables us to account for the distributional difference between the numeral and the quantifier *takusan* in a straightforward way.[7]

Watanabe also notes that quantifiers such as *zen'in* 'all (human)', *zenbu* 'all (nonhuman)', and *subete* 'all' can come between the head noun and the case particle. Examples are given in (28).

(28) a. John-wa   seito-**zen'in**-o   atsumeta.
        John-TOP pupil-all-ACC   gathered
        'John gathered together all the pupils.'
     b. John-wa   nimotsu-**zenbu**-o ugokashita.
        John-TOP luggage-all-ACC   moved
        'John moved all the luggage.'
     c. Yotei-**subete**-ga   umaku   itta.
        plan-all-NOM   well   went
        'All the plans went well.'

Watanabe suggests that the quantifiers in (28) are all generated after the case particle in narrow syntax, as in (29), and placed between the head noun and the case particle through the operation of morphological merger used in distributed morphology (Embick and Noyer 2001, Halle and Marantz 1993).

(29)   John-wa   seito-o   zen'in atsumeta.
       John-TOP pupil-ACC   all   gathered
       'John gathered together all the pupils.'

The fact that *takusan* does not undergo morphological merger appears at first sight to be an idiosyncratic property. But once we recall from the previous subsection that *takusan* does not appear in the partitive structures, a generalization emerges: only the quantifiers in the partitive structure of the form NP-case-quantifier can undergo morphological merger. Indeed, other partitive quantifiers can appear between the head noun and the case particle, as in (30).

(30) a. John-wa   toshoshitsu-ni   aru go-roku-jus-satsu-no hon
       John-TOP   library.room-LOC   are 5-6-10-CL-GEN   book
       hotondo-o yonda.
       most-ACC read
       'John read most of the 50 to 60 books in the library room.'
   b. Iawaseta   gakusei **hanbun**-ga kougi-ni   sankashita.
      happened.to.be.there student half-NOM   protest-LOC participated
      'Half of the students who happened to be there participated in the protest.'

At this point, one can entertain an alternative to the morphological merger analysis. Examples (28) and (30) simply exemplify a third structure for the partitive. The fact that *takusan* cannot appear in this structure is a consequence of its nonpresuppositional nature. And once the options of partitive constructions are ruled out, the syntax of nonpartitive structures becomes directly observable, as illustrated in (26).

If the discussion so far is on the right track, Japanese turns out to have three types of partitive constructions, summarized in (31).

(31) a. nominal+*no*+quantifier+case
   b. nominal+quantifier+case
   c. nominal+case+quantifier

How can we account for that fact?

Now, we are entering an uncharted territory, but let us discuss proposals in the literature that attempted at least partially to cover the ground. For the type (31a) construction, Sauerland and Yatsushiro (2004) adapt Jackendoff's (1977) analysis of the English partitive construction and frame it in terms of the structure in (7b). More specifically, (19a), repeated here, is given the structural analysis indicated in (32), where the relative clause is omitted.

(19) a. [Mae-o   hashitteita]   kuruma-no-#(uchi-no) **ni-dai**-ga tsukamatta.
       front-ACC were.running car-GEN-out-of   2-CL-NOM   got.caught
       'Two of the cars which were driving (ahead of us) got caught.'

The higher N head, which takes another DP, is deleted as an instance of ellipsis when identical to the noun in DP2, as indicated by strikethrough.[8]

(32)

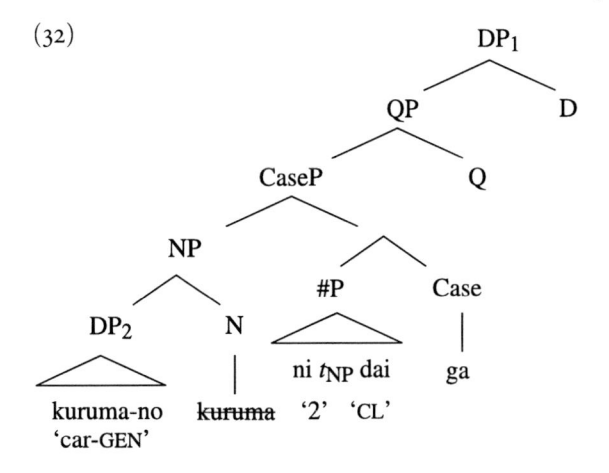

```
                              DP₁
                             /    \
                           QP      D
                          /   \
                      CaseP     Q
                     /     \
                   NP       \
                  /  \       #P      Case
                DP2   N     /  \      |
                /    |   ni t_NP dai  ga
           kuruma-no kuruma  '2' 'CL'
           'car-GEN'
```

Sauerland and Yatsushiro's structure can also be extended to the partitive construction characterized by the numeral+classifier sequence placed after the case particle—namely, type (31c)—if we assume that the higher Case head becomes phonologically null when the Case head of DP2 reflects the case assigned to DP1.

Interestingly, Nakanishi (2004:147) observes that cases such as (33) are unacceptable.

(33) *[Narande hashitteita **suu-dai**-no torakku **san-yon-dai**-ga]
 lined.up were.running several-CL-GEN truck 3-4-CL-NOM
 gaadoreeru-ni butsukatta.
 guardrail-LOC struck
 'Three or four of the several trucks that were driving abreast struck the guardrail.'

This means that the genitive-like linker *no* cannot be omitted from (32) when the Case head within DP2 does not reflect the case assigned from outside DP1. This account is natural under an analysis that assumes a higher N head, because the linker is obligatory when there is a nonclausal prenominal phrase (Kitagawa and Ross 1982).

Thus, Sauerland and Yatsushiro's proposal can handle the partitive constructions that feature numerals. There is a limitation, however: it cannot be extended to quantifiers other than numerals. Recall that nonnumeral quantifiers are generated in Spec,QP, a position too high to give the correct word order.

Kawashima (1994, 1998) proposes that the quantifier in the partitive constructions should be placed under the head that takes DP as its complement. It appears that this proposal can handle (31c), but not (31a,b), if the case particle is located within DP. Construction (31b) can also be accommodated if we resort to morphological merger, as noted above. This still leaves the postnominal linker *no* in (31a) unexplained. The real question, though, is whether placement under a single head is tenable. Recall from section 18.3.1 that it is problematic to place the numeral+classifier sequence under a head position. In the case of the partitives featuring nonnumeral quantifiers, too, there are expressions such as *hotondo subete* 'almost all' that look phrasal but can be used in all three of the structures in (31).

To conclude, there is much work to be done in the analysis of partitive constructions in Japanese. As in the case of the placement of the numeral+classifier sequence in nonpartitives, "diversity" seems to be the key word in the account of Japanese partitive constructions. We do not have a comprehensive account of them yet, but we should keep in mind that recognizing multiple partitive structures is an indispensable step to a proper understanding of quantifier placement in Japanese.[9] The nonpresuppositional quantifier *takusan* 'many', which is free from complications related to the partitive constructions, indicates that nonnumeral quantifiers are generated in a position higher than that reserved for numerals.

18.3.5 Presence or Absence of DP

Let us now focus on DP in Japanese, whose existence is an essential element in the uniform treatment of numeral placement reviewed in section 18.3.1.

18.3.5.1 DP and word order

The presence or absence of D has been controversial in the study of Japanese. It is a trivial observation that Japanese lacks articles of the kind found in languages like English.[10] It is another matter, however, to conclude that Japanese lacks D (or functional categories in general) altogether.

Fukui and Takano (2000) try to relate the head-final nature of the Japanese nominals and the use of classifiers by adopting the assumption that Japanese lacks D. Their proposal is based on the mechanism of linearization (34) put forward in Fukui and Takano 1998, which gives rise to the specifier-complement-head order if nothing special happens.

(34) Linearization
Applied to the structure Σ, Demerge yields $\{\alpha, \{\Sigma - \alpha\}\}$, α an X^{max} constituent of Σ, and Concatenate turns $\{\alpha, \{\Sigma - \alpha\}\}$ into $\alpha + (\Sigma - \alpha)$.

In languages such as English that have D, the head noun is raised into the domain of DP as X^{max} through agreement with D, producing the N-complement order. The numeral is hosted by the NumP, which has a formal feature that needs to be eliminated. This feature is eliminated by entering into an agreement relation with the head noun raised to the domain of D. Through this agreement relation, NumP is also raised to the domain of D, yielding the numeral-N-complement order. The resulting structure is illustrated in (35), where the formal features FF(Num) and FF(N) are adjoined to the D head as a result of agreement.

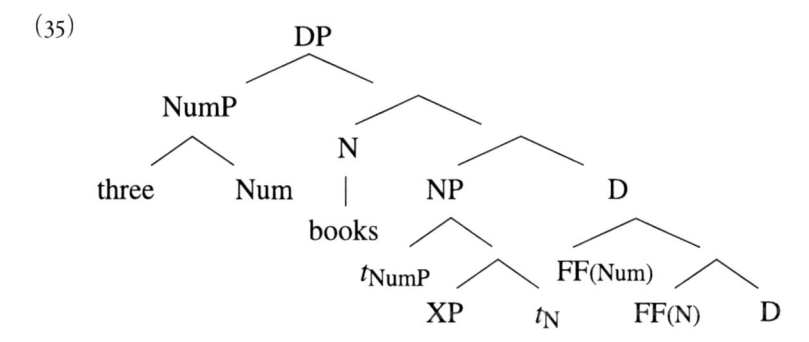

(35)
```
              DP
         /         \
      NumP          
     /    \         N
  three   Num       |        NP              D
                  books    /    \         /      \
                         tNumP          FF(Num)
                                XP   tN       FF(N)   D
```

In Japanese, however, the head noun stays in situ. The formal feature of NumP must be eliminated by means other than agreement. The only remaining possibility, Fukui and Takano claim, is morphological realization at Spell-Out, which happens to be a classifier; hence the head-final order and the existence of classifiers. The structure is given in (36), where *no* will be inserted right after NumP.

(36)
```
           NP
          /  \
       NumP   \
       /  \   XP  N
     san satsu    |
      3   CL     hon
                'book'
```

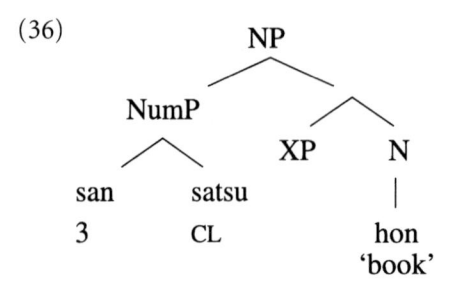

Fukui and Takano's proposal is intended to handle only the prenominal placement of the numeral, leaving (1a) and (1c) unaccounted for.

(1) a. John-wa hon **san-satsu-o** katta.
John-TOP book 3-CL-ACC bought
c. John-wa hon-o **san-satsu** katta.
John-TOP book-ACC 3-CL bought
'John bought three books.'

Fukui and Takano (1998) suggest the existence of KP on top of NP to host the case particle in Japanese. One might then entertain the possibility that the head noun is optionally raised into the domain of KP, giving rise to (37).

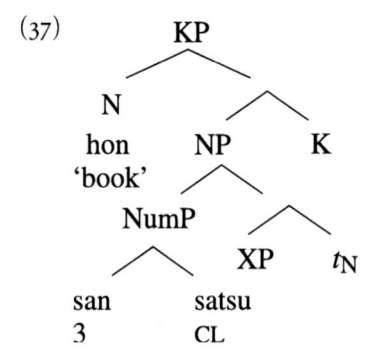

(37)
```
           KP
          /  \
         N    \
        hon   NP    K
       'book' / \
           NumP  \
           / \   XP  t_N
         san satsu
          3   CL
```

This movement would put the head noun in front of the numeral but give the wrong order with respect to the noun complement/modifier (XP in (37)), as shown in (38a).

(38) a. *John-wa hon san-satsu gengogaku(-no)-o katta.
John-TOP book 3-CL linguistics(-GEN)-ACC bought
b. John-wa gengogaku-no hon san-satsu-o katta.
John-TOP linguistics-GEN book 3-CL-ACC bought
'John bought three books on linguistics.'

The correct order is found in (38b). By now, it should be clear to the reader that the impoverished structure such as (36) or (37) leaves no room for accommodating apparent diversity of numeral placement in Japanese. Let me hasten to add that this problem is not specific to Fukui and Takano's proposal. Apart from Watanabe 2006a, there simply is no analysis in the literature that can account for (1) and (4) in a satisfactory way from the perspective of the principles-and-parameters approach.

The empirical generalization about the correlation of head-final order and classifiers that is supposed to support Fukui and Takano's analysis seems to be wrong, too, given classifier languages such as Thai and Vietnamese, where relative clauses and modifying adjectives follow the head noun (Simpson 2005). In other words, classifiers are not limited to head-final nominals. Thai and Vietnamese are not isolated exceptions. Persian, another classifier language, also displays the same word pattern as Thai and Vietnamese in the relevant respects (Ghomeshi 2003). Of course, one can entertain the possibility that in these languages, the head noun is raised to the domain of an intermediate functional projection, not of DP. But it remains to be demonstrated that an alternative analysis of this sort is indeed tenable. At present, there is no strong indication that the position of the head noun is correlated with the obligatory use of classifiers. Thus, the idea that Japanese lacks D does not receive support from classifiers or from the placement of the numeral.

18.3.5.2 *Indeterminates*

D plays an important role in another area of Japanese. Watanabe (1992) originally proposed that the quantificational particle attached to a *wh*-phrase occupies the D position. For space reasons, only the paradigm for *dare* 'who' is repeated here.

(39)   Interrogative Existential Neg-concord Universal
     Person   dare   dare-ka   dare-mo   dare-mo

Watanabe (2004a, 2004b, 2004c) proposes to analyze the relation between this particle and the *wh*-part (indeterminate) by means of agreement. This agreement relation is subject to the locality condition known as relativized minimality (Rizzi 1990) or the minimal link condition (Chomsky 1995), as demonstrated by Takahashi (2002), who observes the contrast between (40a) and (40b).[11]

(40)   a. [[**Dare**-o   hihanshita hito]-o   taihoshita keikan]-**mo**
           who-ACC criticized   person-ACC arrested   policeman-MO
           basserareta.
           was-punished
           'For every person x, the policeman who arrested a person who criticized x was punished.'
    b. *[[**Dare**-o   hihanshita dare-**ka**]-o   taihoshita keikan]-**mo**
           who-ACC criticized   who-KA-ACC arrested   policeman-MO
           basserareta.
           was-punished
           'For every person x, the policeman who arrested someone who criticized x was punished.'

Takahashi notes that the intervening particle *ka* in (40b) blocks the association of the indeterminate *dare-o* with the particle *mo*.[12] Takahashi proposes a head-movement analysis of the long-distance association of the particle with the indeterminate, which Watanabe rephrases in terms of agreement. Schematically, the relevant configuration is as shown in (41).

(41) [DP...[CP...[DP...[CP...indeterminate...]...D⁰]...]...D⁰]

Thus, the particle attached to an indeterminate is an instance of the agreeing D.[13]

Watanabe (2006a) observes that the quantificational particle also triggers movement of CaseP. Given the identification of the particle as heading DP, the movement in question is basically the same as that involved in the derivation of (1c). Thus, (42b) is derived by raising CaseP to Spec,DP from (42a), whose direct object has the structure in (43).[14]

(42) a. Sono purojekuto-wa **nan**-no seika-**mo** age-nakat-ta.
    that project-TOP what-GEN achievement-MO raise-NEG-PAST
  b. Sono purojekuto-wa seika-o **nani-mo** age-nakat-ta.
    that project-TOP achievement-ACC what-MO raise-NEG-PAST
    'That project didn't produce any result.'

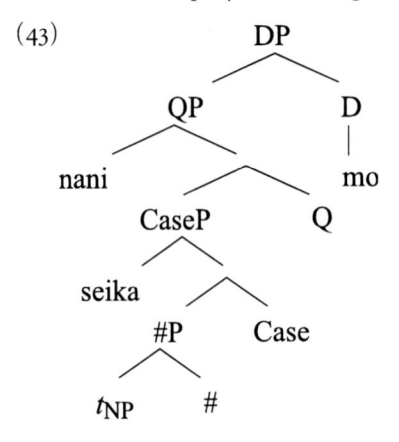

(43)
```
              DP
             /  \
           QP    D
          /  \   |
        nani  \  mo
             / \
          CaseP  Q
          /  \
       seika  \
             / \
           #P   Case
          /  \
        tNP   #
```

Now, Watanabe's (2004a, 2004b) cross-linguistic generalization is that those languages with a Japanese-type indeterminate system display phenomena that should be analyzed as movement of some constituent to Spec,DP, though the category of the raised constituent varies from one language to another. Crucially, English lacks phenomena of this sort, which means that the English D does not agree.[15] Watanabe further observes that those languages that have a Japanese-type indeterminate system either have no overt article at all or have a definite article quite unlike the English counterpart. The generalization can be summarized as follows:

(44) D-system Generalization

   The indeterminate system of the Japanese type cannot coexist with the article system of the English type.

According to this generalization, the absence of overt articles of the English type is a major characteristic of those languages whose D enters into an agreement relation with some DP-internal element. The indeterminate system of the Japanese type is another major feature of such languages. The article system of the English type, however, is an indication that D does not agree. The D-system generalization is taken up again in section 18.4.2.

18.4 IMPLICATIONS

The discussion in section 18.3 has various significant theoretical implications. Let me start with those related to the pseudopartitives. I turn to the problem of agreement in Japanese in section 18.4.2.

18.4.1 Nominal Denotations

Chierchia (1998a, 1998b) develops a theory of nominal denotations according to which NPs are mass in languages in which the numeral must be accompanied by a classifier. Chierchia uses Chinese to illustrate such a language, but the same analysis should apply to Japanese as well. I examine his theory in this subsection.

Chierchia proposes that languages differ in how NP is semantically mapped, encoding this difference in terms of the [±arg] and [±pred] features. In a [+arg, −pred] language, NP denotes a kind, so that it can appear as an argument without the help of an article. At the same time, the kind denotation is translated into a mass denotation in quantification by the 'up'-operator, so that languages of this type need a classifier as a counting unit when using a numeral. Apparently, Japanese fits this characterization.

Languages such as English, however, are [+arg, +pred], which means that NP can freely be predicative or argumental. Such languages have both count and mass nouns. At the same time, mass nouns as well as plural count nouns can appear as bare arguments due to the [+arg] value.

One of the considerations that are often taken to speak in favor of the idea that NPs are mass in languages such as Japanese is the analogy between classifiers and pseudopartitives. Chierchia (1998a) explicitly refers to *piles* and *stacks* in (45) as examples of classifiers.[16]

(45) a. two piles of wood
      b. two stacks of hay

This analogy, however, is misguided. Expressions such as *piles* and *stacks* in (45) are nouns after all. Note their plural morphology. Now, the Japanese pseudopartitive construction itself requires a classifier. Consider again (2), repeated here as (46).

(46) Roger-wa **donburi-ni** yon-hai-no gohan-o tabeta.
Roger-TOP big.bowl-DAT 4-CL-GEN rice-ACC ate
'Roger ate four big bowls of rice.'

The expression *donburi*, which is supposed to count the amount of rice, is accompanied by a classifier *hai*, which is used for things that are intended to serve food and drinks. The presence of this classifier is surprising under the analogy invoked by Chierchia and other researchers, because one is forced to say that a classifier is accompanied by another classifier. Once it is recognized that the counter in the pseudopartitive construction is a noun (or NP), however, everything falls into place. When a numeral is used together with a counter noun, it is expected that a classifier for this counter noun is required.

The uniform approach to the placement of numerals in Japanese, outlined in section 18.3.1, analyzes the classifier as nothing other than the # head responsible for number morphology. This number morphology is sensitive to the singular/plural distinction in languages such as English, but it takes the form of a classifier in languages such as Japanese. The obligatory use of a numeral classifier itself should not be taken to indicate that there is something special about nominal denotations.

18.4.2 Agreement Relations within DP

The minimalist perspective (Chomsky 1995 and subsequent work) forces us to think about the underlying agreement relation when we encounter instances of movement to specifier. In other words, movement of X to Spec,YP presupposes some agreement relation holding between X and Y. Agreement can also take place without overt visible displacement. If the uniform approach to the numeral placement reviewed in section 18.3.1 is on the right track, we are led to the hypothesis that the following agreement relations can be justified within the Japanese DP: those between NP and Case, between #P and Q, and between CaseP and D. Thus, Japanese provides an ideal model for investigating agreement relations within DP.

This is just the beginning. The next important task is to identify the features involved in these agreement relations. Watanabe's (2006a) suggestion for the relations between NP and Case and between CaseP and D is that Case features play a role, on the strength of the observation that there are languages such as German where both N and D inflect for case. Additionally, the feature for specificity (or presuppositional quantification) should also be involved in the relation between CaseP and D, given the discussion in section 18.3.1.2.

An obvious candidate for the relation between #P and Q is features related to number. Watanabe (2006a) adopts the [±singular] feature of Noyer (1997) and Harbour (2003) and the [±number] feature of Castillo (2001). The feature [−singular] is responsible for plural morphology in languages such as English. The feature [±number] is relevant for the mass/count distinction. As discussed in detail by Chierchia (1998a), quantifiers are sensitive to these distinctions. Although numeral classifiers in Japanese do not use different forms for singular and plural, it is reasonable to assume that the relevant features are located where the number information is found, given that they co-occur with a numeral.

At this point, comments are in order concerning the relation between these features and morphology. According to Chomsky's (1995:chap. 4) theory of formal features, interpretable features are sent to LF, not to PF. Only uninterpretable ones are morphologically realized on their way to PF. This is a natural hypothesis, given the division of labor between LF and PF. One thing that looks puzzling at first sight under this conception of features is the fact that nominal plural morphology contributes to meaning but is overtly realized in languages such as English. Plural meaning should not be pronounced on nouns. If, however, we can posit agreement between an interpretable number feature and its uninterpretable counterpart within DP, the latter will be sent to PF and can be realized morphophonologically. There is, then, nothing surprising about nominal plural morphology, as long as it is justified to assume an uninterpretable [±singular] feature on nouns. The [±singular] feature on the # head, however, is sent to LF and contributes to semantic interpretation. In this respect, agreement can be viewed as an essential element in the sound-meaning correspondence, to the extent that it pairs interpretable and uninterpretable features. This is a highly interesting conclusion from the minimalist perspective, because it suggests that agreement is a good design specification in the system that connects the PF and LF interfaces. It is a general observation about functional heads that they are often unpronounced. The existence of uninterpretable features that enter into an agreement relation with interpretable features of functional heads makes it possible for pieces of meaning to be connected to sound.

Chomsky's theory of features also provides an interesting perspective on the D-system generalization in (44) discussed in section 18.3.5.2. There, we see that the relation between an indeterminate and the associated quantificational particle displays the locality typical of agreement. The D-system generalization states that this type of the indeterminate system is incompatible with the article system of the English type. The suggestion made in Watanabe 2004a, 2004b is that the indeterminate system requires D to agree, whereas the article system of the English type embodies the nonagreeing D. One might wonder what it means to say that the ability of D to agree is parameterized. The system of features proposed by Chomsky (1995:chap. 4) enables us to give a very simple answer. Chomsky's theory distinguishes two kinds of features that reflect semantic properties: semantic features and interpretable formal features. The difference between the two is that the former does not participate in agreement whereas the latter does, although both contribute to semantic interpretation. Suppose that the quantificational features and the features of reference tracking such as definiteness and specificity are classified as formal in some languages (e.g., Japanese) but as semantic in others (e.g., English). If the Japanese-type indeterminate has an uninterpretable quantificational feature as proposed in Watanabe 2004c, it follows that languages such as English cannot possess an indeterminate system of the Japanese type. An expression containing such an indeterminate always fails to have the uninterpretable quantificational feature in question eliminated, which leads to a crashing derivation.[17]

Thus, the syntax of quantifiers and indeterminates in Japanese provides an exciting arena for exploring the general theory of features and agreement.

NOTES FOR CHAPTER 18

I would like to thank the audience at the Workshop of Linguistic Theory and the Japanese Language at the LSA Summer Institute in 2005 as well as Gennaro Chierchia, Ken Hiraiwa, Mamoru Saito, Andrew Simpson, and Daiko Takahashi for useful discussion. Thanks are also due to Shigeru Miyagawa, Mamoru Saito, and an anonymous reviewer for comments on earlier versions.

1. The appearance of the dative case particle is marginal in (4a) for a reason not well understood.

2. Modified numerals, illustrated in (i), are also problematic for the single-head analysis of the numeral+classifier combination, since *sukunakutomo go-dai* in (i) looks like a phrase.

(i) Kuruma   sukunakutomo   go-dai-ga   nusum-are-ta.
     car   at.least   five-CL-NOM   steal-PASS-PAST
     'At least five cars were stolen.'

See Watanabe 2006a on modified numerals.

An alternative worth pursuing is to put the classifier together with the numeral in Spec,#P, with the # head phonologically null. See Murasugi 1991, where the prenominal numeral+classifier combination is placed in Spec,QP and its interaction with nominal anaphora/ellipsis is discussed.

3. Terada (1990) also places the numeral+classifier combination as a complex head under Q in the structure [QP NP Q] for (1c). She claims that the relevant structure is NP rather than QP for both (1a) and (1b). She does not elaborate on the relation among the three structures, however.

4. Harada formulates the generalization in terms of stative versus eventive predicates. See also Nishigauchi and Uchibori 1991 and Tateishi 1989. Nakanishi (2004) provides an alternative account (though her major concern is the numeral+classifier sequence that is not adjacent to the nominal projection).

5. There seems to be a dialectal variation in the obligatoriness of *uchi-no*. Kawashima (1994:43–44) regards it as obligatory. My judgment concurs. There are speakers who do not require it, however; see Kubo 1996, for example.

6. Kamio (1983) observes that examples such as (20) become degraded when the relative clause is removed. See also Ishii 1998:fn. 7 for the relation between relative clauses and the partitive interpretation. These observations should be understood in terms of the definiteness requirement mentioned by Inoue.

7. It is interesting to note that the syntax of numerals must be treated somewhat differently from that of 'many' in Modern Hebrew as well. See Borer 2005 and Shlonsky 2004.

8. Sauerland and Yatsushiro's own proposal differs slightly in the category labels used. Note also that the treatment of the parenthesized item *uchi* still remains to be worked out under this analysis.

9. See Ishii 1998 and Kitagawa and Kuroda 1992 for other aspects of the partitive interpretation induced by so-called floating quantifiers. They do not consider the connection with the partitive constructions, though.

10. *Sono* 'that' is a demonstrative. Its difference from the definite article can be seen in the impossibility of **sono taiyou*, in contrast to the English *the sun*. The existence of a demonstrative itself does not justify positing D, given that it is generated in a relatively lower position within DP. See Bernstein 2001 and Brugè 2002 for recent discussion of demonstratives in general. See also Fukui 1986 for Japanese demonstratives.

11. For various cases of long-distance association of the indeterminate and the quantificational particle, see also Kishimoto 2001 and Nishigauchi 1990.

12. Note that the ill-formedness of (40b) is not caused by an alternative association with the particle *ka*. Such an association is impossible, as shown by the unacceptability of (ii).

(ii) *[**Dare**-o   hihanshita   dare-ka]-ga   basserareta.
       who-ACC   criticized   who-KA-NOM   was-punished
      'For some person x, someone who criticized x was punished.'

It is a task for future research to explain why (ii) is ill formed.

13. Watanabe (2004a, 2004b, 2004c) suggests that the locality violation found in head-internal relatives involves essentially the same configuration as (41) with an indefinite (instead of an indeterminate) associated with D, again pointing to the agreeing nature of D in Japanese. See also Watanabe 2006b for a summary discussion.

14. The shape and the position of the case particle are affected by morphological readjustment. See Watanabe 2006a:section 5.5 for details.

15. It is not obvious under the current conception of DP whether the prenominal genitive in English is located in Spec,DP. See Longobardi 2001.

16. Krifka (1995) also invokes the same analogy. Krifka's theory is different from Chierchia's in that even count nouns in English require a classifier, which happens to be covert. Borer's (2005) theory is fairly close to Krifka's in this respect. So is Muromatsu's (1998).

17. Or more precisely, the uninterpretable quantificational feature cannot exist in the English-type language, because such a feature must be formal by definition. Old English had an indeterminate system of the Japanese type, but it was lost subsequently. See Watanabe, in press.

REFERENCES

Abbott, Barbara. 1996. Doing without a partitive constraint. In *Partitives*, ed. Jacob Hoeksema, 25–56. Berlin: Mouton de Gruyter.
Aikhenvald, Alexandra Y. 2000. *Classifiers*. Oxford: Oxford University Press.
Barker, Chris. 1998. Partitives, double genitives, and anti-uniqueness. *Natural Language & Linguistic Theory* 16:679–717.

Bernstein, Judy. 2001. The DP hypothesis: Identifying clausal properties in the nominal domain. In *The handbook of contemporary syntactic theory*, ed. Mark Baltin and Chris Collins, 536–561. Oxford: Blackwell.

Borer, Hagit. 2005. *In name only*. Oxford: Oxford University Press.

Brugè, Laura. 2002. The positions of demonstratives in the extended nominal projection. In *Functional structure in DP and IP*, ed. Guglielmo Cinque, 15–53. Oxford: Oxford University Press.

Castillo, Juan Carlos. 2001. Thematic relations between nouns. Doctoral dissertation, University of Maryland, College Park.

Chierchia, Gennaro. 1998a. Plurality of mass nouns and the notion of "semantic parameter." In *Events and grammar*, ed. Susan Rothstein, 53–103. Dordrecht: Kluwer.

Chierchia, Gennaro. 1998b. Reference to kinds across languages. *Natural Language Semantics* 6:339–405.

Chomsky, Noam. 1995. *The Minimalist Program*. Cambridge, Mass.: MIT Press.

Diesing, Molly. 1992. *Indefinites*. Cambridge, Mass.: MIT Press.

Embick, David, and Rolf Noyer. 2001. Movement operations after syntax. *Linguistic Inquiry* 32:555–595.

Fukui, Naoki. 1986. A theory of category projection and its applications. Doctoral dissertation, MIT, Cambridge, MA.

Fukui, Naoki, and Hiromu Sakai. 2003. The visibility guideline for functional categories: Verb raising in Japanese and related issues. *Lingua* 113:321–375.

Fukui, Naoki, and Yuji Takano. 1998. Symmetry in syntax: Merge and Demerge. *Journal of East Asian Linguistics* 7:27–86.

Fukui, Naoki, and Yuji Takano. 2000. Nominal structure: An extension of the symmetry principle. In *The derivation of VO and OV*, ed. Peter Svenonius, 219–254. Amsterdam: John Benjamins.

Ghomeshi, Jila. 2003. Plural marking, indefiniteness, and the noun phrase. *Studia Linguistica* 57:47–74.

Haig, John. 1980. Some observations on quantifier floating in Japanese. *Linguistics* 18:1065–1083.

Halle, Morris, and Alec Marantz. 1993. Distributed morphology and pieces of inflection. In *The view from Building 20*, ed. Kenneth Hale and Samuel Jay Keyser, 111–176. Cambridge, Mass.: MIT Press.

Harada, Shin-Ichi. 1976. Quantifier float as a relational rule. *Metropolitan Linguistics* 1:44–49. (Reprinted 2000 in *Syntax and meaning: S. I. Harada collected works in linguistics*, ed. Naoki Fukui, 339–345. Tokyo: Taishukan.)

Harbour, Daniel. 2003. Elements of number theory. Doctoral dissertation, MIT, Cambridge, Mass.

Hoeksema, Jacob. 1996. Introduction. In *Partitives*, ed. Jacob Hoeksema, 1–24. Berlin: Mouton de Gruyter.

Hoop, Helen de. 1997. A semantic reanalysis of the partitive constraint. *Lingua* 103:151–174.

Inoue, Kazuko. 1978. *Nihongo-no bunpou kisoku* [Grammatical rules of Japanese]. Tokyo: Taishuukan.

Ishii, Yasuo. 1991. Operators and empty categories in Japanese. Doctoral dissertation, University of Connecticut, Storrs.

Ishii, Yasuo. 1998. Scrambling of weak NPs in Japanese. In *Japanese/Korean Linguistics* 8, ed. David J. Silva, 431–444. Stanford, Calif.: CSLI Publications.

Jackendoff, Ray. 1977. *X-bar syntax*. Cambridge, Mass.: MIT Press.

Kamio, Akira. 1977. Suuryoushi-no shintakkusu [Syntax of numeral quantifiers]. *Gengo* 6(8):83–91.
Kamio, Akira. 1983. Meishiku-no kouzou [Structure of NP]. In *Nihongo-no kihon kouzou* [Basic structures in Japanese], ed. Kazuko Inoue, 77–126. Tokyo: Sanseidou.
Kawashima, Ruriko. 1994. The structure of noun phrases and the interpretation of quantificational NPs in Japanese. Doctoral dissertation, Cornell University, Ithaca, N.Y.
Kawashima, Ruriko. 1998. The structure of extended nominal phrases: The scrambling of numerals, approximate numerals, and quantifiers in Japanese. *Journal of East Asian Linguistics* 7:1–26.
Kishimoto, Hideki. 2001. Binding of indeterminate pronouns and clause structure in Japanese. *Linguistic Inquiry* 32:597–633.
Kitagawa, Yoshihisa, and S.-Y. Kuroda. 1992. Passive in Japanese. Ms., University of Rochester and University of California, San Diego.
Kitagawa, Chisato, and Claudia N. G. Ross. 1982. Prenominal modification in Chinese and Japanese. *Linguistic Analysis* 9:19–53.
Kitahara, Hisatsugu. 1993. Numeral classifier phrases inside DP and the specificity effect. In *Japanese/Korean Linguistics* 3, ed. Soonja Choi, 171–186. Stanford, Calif.: CSLI Publications.
Koizumi, Masatoshi. 1995. Phrase structure in minimalist syntax. Doctoral dissertation, MIT, Cambridge, Mass.
Koizumi, Masatoshi. 2000. String vacuous overt verb raising. *Journal of East Asian Linguistics* 9:227–285.
Krifka, Manfred. 1995. Common nouns: A contrastive analysis of Chinese and English. In *The generic book*, ed. Gregory N. Carlson and Francis Jeffry Pelletier, 398–411. Chicago: University of Chicago Press.
Kubo, Miori. 1996. Some considerations on noun classes and numeral classifiers. In *Keio Studies in Theoretical Linguistics* 1, 89–124. Tokyo: Keio University.
Kuroda, S.-Y. 1965. Generative grammatical studies in the Japanese language. Doctoral dissertation, MIT, Cambridge, Mass.
Li, Yen-Hui Audrey. 1999. Plurality in a classifier language. *Journal of East Asian Linguistics* 8:75–99.
Longobardi, Giuseppe. 2001. The structure of DPs: Some principles, parameters, and problems. In *The handbook of contemporary syntactic theory*, ed. Mark Baltin and Chris Collins, 562–603. Oxford: Blackwell.
Matthewson, Lisa. 2001. Quantification and the nature of crosslinguistic variation. *Natural Language Semantics* 9:145–189.
Murasugi, Keiko. 1991. Noun phrases in Japanese and English: A study in syntax, learnability, and acquisition. Doctoral dissertation, University of Connecticut, Storrs.
Muromatsu, Keiko. 1998. On the syntax of classifiers. Doctoral dissertation, University of Maryland, College Park.
Nakanishi, Kimiko. 2003. Semantic properties of (non-)floating quantifiers and their syntactic implications. In *Japanese/Korean Linguistics* 12, ed. William McClure, 365–376. Stanford, Calif.: CSLI Publications.
Nakanishi, Kimiko. 2004. Domains of measurement: Formal properties of non-split/split quantifier constructions. Doctoral dissertation, University of Pennsylvania, Philadelphia.
Nishigauchi, Taisuke. 1990. *Quantification in the theory of grammar*. Dordrecht: Kluwer.
Nishigauchi, Taisuke, and Asako Uchibori. 1991. Japanese bare NPs and syntax-semantics correspondences in quantification. Ms., Osaka University, Toyonaka, Japan.

Noyer, Rolf. 1997. *Features, positions, and affixes in autonomous morphological structure.* New York: Garland.
Rizzi, Luigi. 1990. *Relativized minimality.* Cambridge, Mass.: MIT Press.
Saito, Mamoru, and Keiko Murasugi. 1990. N'-deletion in Japanese: A preliminary study. In *Japanese/Korean Linguistics* 1, ed. Hajime Hoji, 285–301. Stanford, Calif.: CSLI Publications.
Sauerland, Uli, and Kazuko Yatsushiro. 2004. A silent noun in partitives. In *Proceedings of NELS* 34, ed. Keir Moulton and Matthew Wolf, 101–112. Amherst, Mass.: GLSA Publications.
Selkirk, Elisabeth. 1977. Some remarks on noun phrase structure. In *Formal syntax*, ed. Peter W. Culicover, Thomas Wasow, and Adrian Akmajian, 285–316. New York: Academic Press.
Shlonsky, Ur. 2004. The form of Semitic noun phrases. *Lingua* 114:1465–1526.
Simpson, Andrew. 2005. Classifiers and DP structure in South East Asia. In *Handbook of comparative syntax*, ed. Guglielmo Cinque and Richard Kayne, 806–838. Oxford: Oxford University Press.
Takahashi, Daiko. 2002. Determiner raising and scope shift. *Linguistic Inquiry* 33:575–615.
Takano, Yuji. 2002. Surprising constituents. *Journal of East Asian Linguistics* 11:243–301.
Tang, Jane. 1990. A note on the DP analysis of Chinese noun phrase. *Linguistics* 28:337–354.
Tateishi, Koichi. 1989. Subjects, SPEC, and DP in Japanese. In *Proceedings of NELS* 19, ed. Juli Carter and Rose-Marie Déchaine, 405–418. Amherst, Mass.: GLSA Publications.
Terada, Michiko. 1990. Incorporation and argument structure in Japanese. Doctoral dissertation, University of Massachusetts, Amherst.
Watanabe, Akira. 1992. *Wh*-in-situ, Subjacency, and chain formation. MIT occasional papers in linguistics 2. Cambridge, Mass.: MIT Working Papers in Linguistics.
Watanabe, Akira. 2004a. Indeterminates and agreeing D. In *Generative grammar in a broader perspective*, ed. Hang-Jin Yoon, 405–429. Seoul: Hankook.
Watanabe, Akira. 2004b. Indeterminates and determiners. In *MIT Working Papers in Linguistics 46: Proceedings of the Workshop on Altaic Formal Linguistics* 1, ed. Aniko Csirmaz, Youngjoo Lee, and Mary Ann Walter, 390–405. Cambridge, Mass.: MIT Working Papers in Linguistics.
Watanabe, Akira. 2004c. Parametrization of quantificational determiners and head-internal relatives. *Language and Linguistics* 5:59–97.
Watanabe, Akira. 2006a. Functional projections of nominals in Japanese: Syntax of classifiers. *Natural Language & Linguistic Theory* 24:241–306.
Watanabe, Akira. 2006b. The pied-piper feature. In *Wh-movement: Moving on*, ed. Lisa Cheng and Norbert Corver, 47–70. Cambridge, Mass.: MIT Press.
Watanabe, Akira. In press. A parametric shift in the D-system in Early Middle English: Relativization, articles, adjectival inflection, and indeterminates. In *Historical syntax and linguistic theory*, ed. Paola Crisma, Chiara Gianolla, Christina Guardino, and Giuseppe Longobardi. Oxford: Oxford University Press.
Wilkinson, Karina. 1996. Bare plurals, plural pronouns, and the partitive constraint. In *Partitives*, ed. Jacob Hoeksema, 209–230. Berlin: Mouton de Gruyter.

Author Index

Abbott, Barbara, 521, 522, 537
Abney, Steven P., 222, 242
Aikawa, Takako, 18, 246, 281
Aikhenvald, Alexandra Y., 515, 537
Akiba, Sachie, 261, 262, 281
Akinaga, Kazue, 165, 173, 188, 189
Alderete, John, 95, 103
Alexiadou, Artemis, 46, 50, 343, 344
Altmann, Gerry T. M., 222, 223, 245
Amano, Shigeaki, 220, 242, 481, 511
Anagnostopoulou, Elena, 46, 50, 343, 344
Anand, Pranav, 151, 164
Andrews, Avery, 159, 162
Anttila, Arto, 85, 91, 92, 102, 103
Aoshima, Sachiko, 222, 224, 235, 236, 241, 242, 248, 249
Aoun, Joseph, 386, 390, 437, 451, 453
Aoyagi, Hiroshi, 12, 107, 113–115, 127–129, 132, 134, 138
Aoyagi, Seizô, 506, 507
Aoyama, Ikuko, 232, 242
Arad, Maya, 45, 50, 335, 336, 338, 344
Arikawa, Koji, 292, 296–297, 299, 303, 308, 313, 318
Arimoto, Masatake, 417, 420
Arisaka, Hideyo, 456, 507
Aronoff, Mark, 336, 343, 344
Arregi, Karlos, 368, 369, 382, 390
Arvaniti, Amalia, 502, 507, 508

Babyonyshev, Maria, 230, 240, 243, 279, 280
Baddeley, Alan, 219, 243
Baker, Carl L., 251, 281, 386, 390
Baker, Mark C., 37, 46, 50, 265, 281, 320, 326, 331, 344, 434, 448, 453, 454
Barker, Chris, 521, 537
Bauer, Laurie, 339, 344
Beck, Sigrid, 357, 369, 371, 390
Becker, Judith, 282
Beckman, Mary E., 8–9, 11, 15, 18, 187, 189, 456, 467–470, 473, 477, 479, 481–487, 493, 495–496, 500, 505, 507, 509, 511
Bedell, George, 192, 215
Berman, Stephen, 311, 316, 386–387, 390
Bernstein, Judy, 513, 537, 538
Best, Catherine T., 95, 103
Bever, Thomas G., 231, 237, 242, 243, 246

Bloom, Paul, 256, 281
Bobaljik, Jonathan David, 151–152, 158–159, 162, 303, 310, 316, 368, 369
Borer, Hagit, 9, 15, 267, 279, 281, 391, 455, 537, 538
Bošković, Željko, 6, 7, 16, 409–410, 413, 419, 420
Bradley, Dianne, 223, 239–240, 244, 249
Branigan, Holly P., 231, 248
Bresnan, Joan, 435, 454
Brodie, Belinda, 310, 317
Brody, Michael, 27, 50, 389, 390
Bruce, Gösta, 458, 507
Brugè, Laura, 537, 538
Büring, Daniel, 65, 80
Burzio, Luigi, 102, 103, 334, 431, 454

Cable, Seth, 351, 363, 367, 368, 369
Campbell, Lyle, 100, 103
Caplan, David, 219–220, 232, 243
Carlson, Greg, 122, 138
Carpenter, Patricia A., 218–219, 220, 243, 245
Carstens, Vicki, 342, 344
Castillo, Juan Carlos, 535, 538
Chang, Franklin, 237, 249
Charlkley, Mary Anne, 282
Chien, Yu-Chin, 161, 163, 278, 281
Chierchia, Gennaro, 406, 420, 515, 522, 533–535, 537, 538
Cho, Young-Mee Yu, 92, 103
Choe, Jae W., 350, 369, 378, 390
Choi, Hye-Won, 80, 82
Choi, Youngon, 246
Chomsky, Noam, 5, 6, 16, 27, 45, 50, 93, 103, 134, 136, 138, 194, 196, 197, 199, 200–202, 211, 213, 215, 221, 239, 243, 246, 251, 256, 266, 281, 292, 316, 320, 344, 379, 390, 395, 402, 410, 420, 439, 454, 531, 534, 535, 538
Chujo, Kazumitsu, 234, 243
Cinque, Guglielmo, 136, 138
Cipollone, Domenic, 25, 26, 50
Clahsen, Harald, 238, 247
Clancy, Patricia M., 257, 271, 277, 281
Clements, G. N., 468, 510
Cole, Peter, 351, 368, 369
Collins, Chris, 331, 344
Crain, Stephen, 229, 243, 252, 278, 281

Crocker, Matthew, 226, 249
Cuetos, Fernando, 231, 243

Daneman, Meredyth, 220, 243
Dautricourt, Robin, 479, 511
Dechongkit, S., 468, 508
Declerck, Renaat, 79, 80
Deguchi, Masanori, 366, 369, 389, 391
Demuth, Katherine, 279, 281
Den, Yasuharu, 221, 243
Diesing, Molly, 59–60, 80, 316, 520, 525, 538
Dikken, Marcel den, 67, 68, 80
Docherty, Gerard J., 479, 507
Doetjes, Jenny, 310, 313, 316
Doron, Edit, 62, 81, 418, 421
Downing, Pamela, 312, 316
Dowty, David, 155, 163, 307, 310, 314, 316, 317, 327, 344
Dubinsky, Stan, 23, 24, 50
Dupoux, Emmanuel, 94–95, 103, 105, 166, 189

Eberhard, Kathleen M., 249
Ekida, Fusae, 214, 216
Elbourne, Paul, 278, 281, 419, 421
Elordieta, Gorka, 508
Embick, David, 46, 50, 336, 343, 344, 345, 526, 538
Emonds, Joseph, 400, 421
Endo, Mika, 9, 19, 270, 285
Evans, Gareth, 399, 421
Everaert, Martin, 343, 344

Farmer, Ann K., 320–321, 345
Felser, Claudia, 238, 247
Feng, Gary, 246
Ferreira, Victor S., 237, 243
Fiengo, Robert, 65–66, 70, 74–75, 77, 78, 79, 80, 379, 389, 390, 391
Fintel, Kai von, 65, 81
Firth, John Rupert, 459, 501
Fitzpatrick, Justin, 303, 310, 313, 317
Fodor, Janet D., 221, 227, 229, 243, 244, 245
Fodor, Jerry A., 242, 243
Folli, Rafaella, 49, 50
Fong, Sandiway, 231, 246
Fortin, Catherine R., 46, 50
Fougeron, Cécile, 467, 507
Fox, Dana, 282
Fox, Danny, 7, 16, 279, 281, 419, 421
Fuji, Chisato, 246, 274–275, 280, 281, 283
Fujisaki, Hiroya, 456, 470–471, 481–483, 485–486, 501–502, 506, 507, 508
Fujita, Naoya, 301–302, 307–308, 317
Fukazawa, Haruka, 8, 16, 85, 91, 101, 103
Fukui, Misa, 183, 190

Fukui, Naoki, 7, 16, 19, 107, 118, 124–127, 134–136, 138, 192, 215, 263, 281, 284, 407, 421, 447, 454, 455, 513, 514, 516, 529–531, 537, 538
Fukushima, Kazuhiko, 125, 136, 138, 294, 295, 301, 312, 315, 317, 321, 324–325, 327–331, 333, 335–342, 343, 344, 345
Furukawa, Yukio, 321, 343, 345
Futagi, Yoko, 80, 81

Gamerschlag, Thomas, 321, 345
Gaminde, Iñaki, 508
Gandour, Jack, 468, 508
Ganger, Jennifer, 280
Garnsey, Susan M., 222, 243
Garrett, Merrill F., 242, 243
Geenhoven, Veerle van, 310, 317
Ghomeshi, Jila, 531, 538
Gibson, Edward, 221, 230–231, 235, 240, 243, 244, 246, 247
Giorgi, Alessandra, 444, 454
Gleitman, Lila R., 279, 281
Goldsmith, John A., 459, 508
Goodell, Elizabeth, 95, 103
Goro, Takuya, 261–262, 281
Gorrell, Paul, 226, 243
Green, John N., 413, 421
Grewendorf, Günther, 7, 16
Grice, Martine, 502, 508
Grimshaw, Jane, 155, 163, 325, 341, 345
Grodzinsky, Yosef, 155, 161, 163, 278, 279, 281
Groenendijk, Jeroen, 390, 391
Guasti, Maria Teresa, 265, 281
Gunji, Takao, 294, 296–297, 301, 307, 312, 317
Gussenhoven, Carlos, 94, 104, 457, 477, 498–500, 504, 508

Hagiwara, Hiroko, 232, 236, 242, 243, 245, 247
Haig, John H., 6, 16, 288, 297, 317, 430, 454, 516, 520–524, 538
Hagstrom, Paul, 355–357, 363, 367, 368, 369, 378, 384, 388, 389, 390, 391
Hale, Kenneth, 5–7, 10, 16, 36, 38–39, 41, 50, 206, 215, 253, 281
Halle, Morris, 37, 51, 93, 103, 133, 138, 320, 335, 345, 526, 538
Hamano, Shoko, 294, 302, 317
Hamblin, Charles, 353–354, 369, 379, 384–387, 390, 391
Han, Chung-hye, 80, 81
Hankamer, Jorge, 415–416, 420, 421
Hara, Noriyo, 471, 488, 491, 511
Hara, Yurie, 55, 56, 76, 81
Harada, Kazuko, 250, 281
Harada, Shin-Ichi, 7, 10, 16, 24, 51, 143, 144, 163, 192, 194, 210–211, 215, 223, 243, 290, 301, 317, 417, 421, 520, 536, 538

Haraguchi, Shôsuke, 8, 16, 167, 171, 189, 459, 466, 469, 473, 508
Harbour, Daniel, 535, 538
Harley, Heidi, 12, 39, 48, 49, 50, 51, 321, 343, 452, 454
Hasegawa, Nobuko, 10, 16, 221, 244, 311, 317, 321, 325–326, 245, 395, 421
Hashida, Koichi, 294, 296–297, 301, 307, 312, 317
Hashimoto, Tomoko, 24, 52, 257, 266, 272, 274, 275, 278–279, 280, 283
Hashimoto, Yumi, 185, 190
Haspelmath, Martin, 373, 391
Hattori, Shiro, 456, 508
Hay, Jennifer, 499, 508
Hayashibe, Hideo, 9, 16, 263, 281
Hayes, Bruce, 172–173, 189
Haywood, Sarah L., 222–223, 245
Heck, Fabian, 352, 364, 369, 389, 392
Heim, Irene, 63, 379, 386–387, 291, 432, 454
Hermon, Gabriella, 353, 345
Heycock, Caroline, 11, 12, 16, 56, 61–63, 65, 67–69, 79, 81, 457, 481
Higginbotham, James, 342, 345
Higgins, Francis Roger, 68, 81
Higuchi, Norio, 470, 508
Himeno, Masako, 322, 345
Hinds, John, 3–4, 16
Hirai, Toshio, 470, 508
Hiraiwa, Ken, 13, 159–160, 163, 192–194, 199–207, 214, 215, 364–365, 369
Hirose, Keikichi, 470–471, 481–482, 501–502, 507, 508, 509
Hirose, Yuki, 103, 189, 226–228, 231, 244
Hirotani, Masako, 366, 370, 389, 391
Hirschberg, Julia, 476, 477, 492, 507, 508
Hoeksema, Jacob, 310, 317, 521–522, 538
Hoekstra, Teun, 279, 281
Hoff, Jean, 322, 346
Hoji, Hajime, 5–7, 15, 16, 19, 56–57, 78, 81, 116–118, 134, 138, 204, 215, 253, 281, 284, 297, 317, 356–357, 370, 375, 391, 395, 397, 416, 421, 424–435, 440, 442–451, 452, 454
Holmberg, Anders, 107, 134, 138
Holmes, V. M., 230, 244
Hoop, Helen de, 521, 538
Hornstein, Norbert, 251, 282, 343, 345
Hoshi, Hiroto, 134, 138, 151, 157–158, 163, 271, 280, 282
Howard, Irwin, 3–4, 16
Hsiao, Franny, 231, 244
Hsu, Chun-Chieh, 231, 244
Hualde, José Ignacio, 189, 466, 508
Huang, C.-T. James, 254, 282, 348, 368, 370, 379, 388, 389, 391, 395, 396, 399–400, 414–415, 418, 421, 453, 454
Hume, Elizabeth, 479, 511
Hyams, Nina, 256, 279, 281, 282, 285
Hyman, Larry M., 187, 189, 456, 464, 479, 508

Ichikawa, Akira, 481, 512
Igarashi, Yosuke, 480, 510
Iguchi, Yoko, 224, 244
Iida, Masayo, 21, 25, 46, 47, 48, 51
Ikejiri, Kayo, 246
Inkelas, Sharon, 85, 91, 103
Inoue, Atsu, 221–223, 226, 227, 244, 245
Inoue, Kazuko, 5, 16, 144, 163, 192, 216, 290, 302, 317, 516, 520–523, 536, 538
Inoue, Masakatsu, 225, 232, 242, 243
Inui, Toshio, 219, 226, 240, 244
Ishii, Yasuo, 294, 296–300, 303, 312, 314, 317, 318, 451, 454, 520, 525, 536, 537, 538
Ishihara, Shinichiro, 136–137, 138, 366, 370, 389, 391
Ishizuka, Tomoko, 231, 244
Isobe, Miwa, 259–260, 270, 285, 449, 455
Ito, Junko, 8, 11, 16, 17, 84–85. 89, 91–93, 98, 102, 103, 104, 178, 189, 190,
Ito, Katsuhiko, 166, 189
Ito, Kiwako, 466, 481–482, 490, 495–496, 504, 508, 509
Ito, Takane, 321, 344, 345
Itoh, Kenji, 222, 223, 226, 233, 246, 247
Itoh, Kiwako, 243
Iwabuchi, Etsutaro, 257, 282
Iwasaki, Shoichi, 473, 511

Jackendoff, Ray, 66, 408, 421, 527, 538
Jackson, Eric, 46, 51
Jacobs, Haike, 94, 104
Jacobsen, Wesley M., 22–23, 29, 33, 36, 39–40, 49, 51
Jaeggli, Osvaldo, 413, 421
Jayaseelan, K. A., 386, 388, 390, 391
Jincho, Nobuyuki, 220, 244
Johnson, Mark, 222, 242
Jun, Sun-Ah, 457, 467, 509
Junker, Marie-Odile, 310, 317
Just, Marcel A., 218, 219–220, 230, 245

Kabuto, Yoshie, 255, 282
Kager, René, 102, 104
Kageyama, Taro, 134, 138, 143, 144, 157–158, 163, 321–327, 340, 342, 345
Kakehi, Kazuhiko, 103, 189, 233, 245
Kamide, Yuki, 222–224, 231–232, 245
Kamio, Akio, 292, 317
Kamio, Akira, 514, 515, 519, 536, 539
Kamp, Hans, 386, 391
Kanagawa Prefecture Social Studies Research Council, 96, 104
Kang, Yoonjung, 94, 100, 104
Kanno, Osamu, 247
Karimi, Simin, 7, 17, 49, 50
Karttunen, Lauri, 354, 370, 379, 391
Katagiri, Masumi, 294, 317

Katagiri, Yasuhiro, 471–473, 509
Katayama, Motoko, 95, 104, 188, 189
Kato, Sachiko, 24, 52, 157–158, 163, 280, 283
Kawahara, Jun-Ichiro, 249
Kawahara, Shigeto, 102, 104
Kawai, Hisashi, 481, 485, 507
Kawakami, Shin, 471–472, 475–476, 481, 488, 497, 498–501, 509
Kawamura, Tomoko, 7, 9, 17, 18, 263–264, 271, 283
Kawashima, Ruriko, 7, 17, 292, 312, 317, 513, 516, 519, 528, 536, 539
Kayne, Richard, 122, 138, 342, 345
Keating, Patricia A., 467, 507
Kenstowicz, Michael, 94–95, 104, 166, 189, 190
Kess, Joseph F., 217, 245
Keyser, Samuel Jay, 36, 38–39, 41, 50
Kibe, Nobuko, 185, 190
Kiguchi, Hirohisa, 219, 245
Kikuchi, Akira, 294, 313, 317, 413, 421
Kikuchi, Hideaki, 480, 410
Kim, Shin-Sook, 357, 369
Kim, Soowon, 14, 402, 405, 418, 421
Kim, Young-Joo, 278, 282
Kindaichi, Haruhiko, 471, 481, 509
King, Jonathan, 220, 230, 245
Kiparsky, Paul, 338, 345
Kiritani, Shigeru, 175, 191, 246
Kiriyama, Shinya, 470, 509
Kishimoto, Hideki, 12, 107, 129–132, 134, 139, 144–145, 149, 163, 355, 367, 368, 370, 400, 452, 454, 537, 539
Kiss, Katalin É., 74, 81
Kitagawa, Chisato, 514, 528, 539
Kitagawa, Yoshihisa, 21, 25, 27, 47, 51, 298, 307–308, 312, 314, 318, 321, 345, 366, 369, 370, 389, 391, 428–429, 445, 451, 452, 453, 454, 537, 539
Kitahara, Hisatsugu, 7, 17, 513, 519, 539
Kitahara, Mafuyu, 8, 16, 101, 103
Kluender, Robert, 222, 234–236, 249
Ko, Heejeong, 136, 297, 318, 369, 370, 388, 391, 413, 421
Kobayashi, Mari, 228, 248
Koizumi, Masatoshi, 12, 47, 52, 107, 111–113, 118–120, 122, 124–127, 134, 135, 136, 139, 148–151, 157–159, 162, 163, 219, 232, 234, 242, 245, 249, 400, 405, 421, 429–430, 445, 449, 451, 453, 454, 514, 539
Kokuritsu Kokugo Kenkyuujo (National Institute for Japanese Language [NIJL, formerly NRLI]), 458, 509
Komori, Mie, 248
Kondo, Tadahisa, 220, 222–223, 226, 233, 242, 245, 246
Konishi, Jyunji, 244
Koopman, Hilda, 342, 345
Kori, Shiro, 458, 471, 475, 476, 481, 484–485, 488, 490, 492, 494, 509
Kornfilt, Jaklin, 214, 216
Koshida, Ichiro, 247

Koso, Ayumi, 236, 245
Kratzer, Angelika, 45, 46, 51, 301, 318, 354, 374, 384, 387, 389, 391
Krifka, Manfred, 307, 318, 537, 539
Kroch, Anthony, 68, 81
Kubo, Miori, 280, 282, 536, 539
Kubozono, Haruo, 8–9, 11, 17, 95, 104, 166, 167–168, 170–173, 175, 178–185, 188, 190, 191, 480–483, 486, 495–497, 505, 506, 509
Kuno, Susumu, 3–5, 10–11, 17, 20, 22 24, 26–27, 51, 54–57, 60, 64, 69, 76, 78, 81, 127, 139, 141–143, 146–148, 163, 236, 245, 268–269, 282, 290, 303, 318, 320, 345, 416, 421, 457, 481, 509
Kuroda, S.-Y., 4–7, 10, 17, 20–25, 47, 49, 51, 55, 56–57, 60, 63–65, 70–73, 78, 79, 81, 141, 143, 146, 163, 280, 282, 288, 297–298, 307–308, 312, 314, 318, 320, 345, 373, 375, 386, 391, 395, 421, 426, 430, 449, 453, 454, 455, 515, 537, 539
Kurohashi, Sadao, 236, 245

LaCharité, Darlene, 94, 105, 166, 190
Ladd, D. Robert, 457–458, 502, 507, 508, 510
Langendoen, D. Terence, 459, 510
Laniran, Yetunde, 468, 510
Larson, Richard, 430–431, 439–440, 446, 448, 451, 455
Lasnik, Howard, 196, 197, 199, 216, 252, 280, 282, 379, 389, 391, 395, 420, 421, 432, 454
Law, Sam-Po, 231, 282
Lee, Kwee-Ock, 278, 282
Lee, Miseon, 221, 248
Lee, Sun-Hee, 240, 245
Lees, Robert B., 214, 216
Legate, Julie Anne, 278, 282
Leung, Man-Tak, 231, 245
Lewis, Richard, 240, 245
Li, Yafei, 320–321, 324–327, 342, 343, 345
Li, Yen-Hui Audrey, 312, 318, 386, 390, 437, 451, 453, 515, 539
Liberman, Mark, 478, 510
Lightfoot, David, 251, 282
Lillo-Martin, Diane, 256, 282
Lim, Hyungjung, 249
Lin, Chien-Jer, 231, 246
Lin, Jo-wang, 384, 386, 391
Lobeck, Anne, 408, 419, 421
Longobardi, Giuseppe, 513, 537, 539
Lotocky, Melanie, 243
Lust, Barbara, 10, 17

Machida, Nanako, 9, 17
MacWhinney, Brian, 242, 248, 263, 274, 282
Maeda, Kazuaki, 471, 475, 488, 491, 510, 512
Maekawa, Kikuo, 9, 11, 457–458, 472, 480–482, 486, 506, 507, 510
Maki, Hideki, 13, 149, 378, 391
Manning, Christopher, 21, 25, 46, 47–48, 51

Marantz, Alec, 28, 37, 39, 45–46, 49–50, 51, 52, 114, 133, 138, 139, 320, 334, 335, 336, 343, 344, 345, 346, 435, 437, 455
Maratsos, Michael, 267, 282
Maruyama, Takehiko, 475, 488–490, 510, 512
Mascaró, Joan, 102, 104
Matsuda, Yuki, 67, 79, 81
Matsumoto, Yo, 22, 48, 52, 280, 282, 321–322, 324–326, 336, 339, 340, 342, 343, 344, 346
Matsumoto-Sturt, Yoko, 231, 248
Matsuoka, Kazumi, 278, 282
Matsuoka, Mikinari, 433–434, 440, 442–444, 450, 452, 455
Matthewson, Lisa, 521, 539
May, Robert, 432, 454
Mazuka, Reiko, 10, 17, 217, 220–222, 226, 228, 233, 239, 244, 245, 246, 248
McCarthy, John J., 91, 93, 98, 104, 251, 281
McCawley, James D., 8, 17, 93, 104, 126–127, 139, 165–166, 168–169, 173–174, 176, 186, 190, 456, 467–469, 473, 486, 510
McCloskey, James, 290, 293, 310, 328, 418, 421
McClure, Madelena, 243
McClure, William, 65–66, 70, 74–75, 77, 78, 79, 80
McElree, Brian, 237, 243
McGinnis, Martha, 453, 455
McKee, Cecile, 252, 281
McLemore, Cynthia Ann, 492, 510
McNally, Louise, 63, 65–66, 78, 79, 81, 82
McRoberts, Gerald W., 95, 103
Mehler, Jacques, 103, 189
Mennen, Ineke, 507
Merchant, Jason, 310, 318
Mesbur, James, 488, 501, 510
Mester, Armin, 8, 11, 16, 17, 84–85, 89, 91–93, 98, 102, 103, 104, 178–179, 189, 190
Mihara, Ken-ichi, 294–295, 301, 303, 305–307, 315, 316, 318
Miller, George A., 220, 239, 246
Minai, Utako, 9, 17, 267, 269, 271, 282
Minematsu, Nobuaki, 470, 509
Misono, Yasuko, 225, 246
Mitchell, Don C., 222, 224, 231–232, 243, 245
Miyagawa, Shigeru, 6–7, 9, 13, 17, 18, 22–24, 27–28, 30–33, 35–36, 42–44, 47, 48, 49, 50, 52, 128–130, 132, 136–137, 139, 149, 159, 162, 164, 192–197, 199, 205, 210–211, 214, 216, 246, 269, 280, 283, 288–293, 296–297, 299, 302–303, 305, 308–309, 312–314, 318, 320, 343, 346, 400, 405, 415, 417, 422, 424, 426–429, 433, 435–447, 449–450, 451, 452, 453, 455
Miyaji, Yutaka, 471, 488, 510
Miyamoto, Edson T., 7, 9, 10, 13, 18, 219, 221–224, 226, 228, 231–236, 238, 240–241, 244, 245, 246, 247, 248, 269–270, 283, 449, 455
Miyamoto, Tadao, 217, 245
Miyamoto, Yoichi, 289, 318
Miyaoka, Yayoi, 249
Miyata, Susanne, 263, 269, 283

Morikawa, Hiromi, 278, 280, 283
Moriyama, Yoshiyuki, 402, 405, 407, 418, 422
Moro, Andrea, 68, 82
Müller, Gereon, 119–121, 139
Muraishi, Shozo, 257, 282
Muranaka, Toshiko, 471, 488, 491, 511
Muraoka, Satoru, 224, 247
Murasugi, Keiko, 7, 9, 13, 18, 24, 52, 204, 214, 216, 252, 254, 256–259, 263–264, 266, 271, 272, 274–275, 278–279, 280, 283, 408, 417, 418, 420, 422, 513–514, 536, 539, 540
Murata, Koji, 277, 283
Muromatsu, Keiko, 537, 538
Myers, Elizabeth, 243

Nagahara, Hiroyuki, 473, 496, 511
Nagano, Satoshi, 257, 278–279, 283
Nagao, Kyoko, 481, 511
Nagao, Makoto, 236, 245
Nagata, Hiroshi, 229, 238–239, 247
Naitoh, Kazuo, 246
Nakagome, Kazuyuki, 219, 240, 247
Nakai, Satoru, 192, 195, 216
Nakajima, Heizo, 247
Nakamura, Michiko, 221, 231–232, 234, 236, 240, 246, 247, 248
Nakanishi, Kimiko, 13, 56, 82, 300–302, 310–311, 313, 314, 315, 318, 457, 511, 516, 528, 536, 539
Nakano, Yoko, 238, 247
Nakatani, Kentaro, 229, 231, 249, 244, 247
Nakayama, Mineharu, 217, 232, 237–238, 240, 245, 247, 248, 264, 284
Namai, Kenichi, 342, 346
Namiki, Hiroshi, 220, 244
Nemoto, Naoko, 270, 284, 441, 455
Nevins, Andrew, 151, 164
Newmeyer, Frederick J., 343, 346
NHK (Japan Broadcasting Corp.), 102, 182, 183, 188, 190
Nicol, Janet L., 228, 248
Nishigauchi, Taisuke, 14, 157, 164, 294, 298, 301, 318, 319, 350, 357–358, 361–362, 364–365, 367, 370, 375–381, 386, 389, 390, 392, 536, 537, 539
Nishimura, Kohei, 98–99, 102, 104, 105
Nishio, Hiroko, 31, 52
Nishiyama, Kunio, 13, 47, 321, 324, 327–329, 331–335, 341–342, 343, 344, 346
Nishizaki, Yukiko, 248
Nishizawa, Sadahiko, 244
Niwa, Shinich, 246
Noguchi, Yasuki, 248
Noji, Junya, 274, 284
Nomura, Masashi, 152–154, 164
Noyer, Rolf, 49, 51, 343, 345, 526, 535, 538, 540

Ochi, Masao, 13, 18, 192–193, 197–199, 205–207, 209, 214, 216, 368, 370, 378, 387, 388, 392

Oehrle, Richard T., 52
Ogawa, Yoshiki, 344, 346
O'Grady, William, 221, 248
Ohishi, Shotaro, 471, 475–476, 488–490, 492, 511
Ohki, Mitsuru, 301, 319
Ohno, Sumio, 508
Ohno, Yutaka, 361–364, 370, 375, 381, 385, 392
Ohso, Mieko, 395, 422
Oishi, Hiroaki, 222, 248
Okada, Tomohisa, 244
Oku, Satoshi, 6, 14, 18, 403–405, 409–410, 413–415, 417, 418, 422
Okubo, Ai, 277, 284
Okutsu, Keiichiro, 290, 319
Ono, Hajime, 103, 104, 241, 248
O'Regan, J. K., 230, 244
Orgun, Orhan, 85, 91–92, 103, 105
Ortiz de Urbina, Jon, 351–352, 370, 382, 392
Osaka, Mariko, 220, 248
Osaka, Naoyuki, 248
Osame, Masafumi, 508
Oshima, David Y., 475, 488, 490, 501–502, 511
Oshima, Shin, 23, 52
Ota, Mitsuhiko, 8, 16, 101, 103
Otani, Kazuyo, 12, 14, 107–108, 110–111, 116–118, 134, 139, 396, 399–402, 414, 418, 422
Otsu, Yukio, 9, 18, 244, 253, 263–264, 277, 278, 280, 284

Pallier, Christophe, 103, 189
Paradis, Carole, 94, 105, 166, 190
Pater, Joe, 85, 87, 91–92, 105
Pearlmutter, Neal J., 243, 246
Peng, Shu-hui, 468, 511
Peperkamp, Sharon, 94–95, 105
Perlmutter, David M., 102, 105, 291, 319
Pesetsky, David, 280, 356, 370, 386, 389, 392, 452, 455
Phillips, Colin, 222, 224, 235–236, 241, 242, 248, 249, 279, 284
Pierce, Amy E., 266, 284
Pierrehumbert, Janet B., 8, 18, 87, 105, 456–458, 467– 470, 473, 481–487, 490, 495–496, 500, 505, 507, 511
Poeppel, David, 266, 284
Pollock, Jean-Yves, 134, 139, 400, 422
Portner, Paul, 63–66, 70, 78, 82
Poser, William J., 8, 18, 168, 173, 177, 190, 469, 473, 481, 484, 486, 506, 511
Potts, Christopher, 64, 82
Prince, Alan S., 91, 93, 98, 104, 183, 190, 478, 510
Prince, Ellen F., 496, 511
Pritchett, Bradley L., 221–222, 248
Pylkkänen, Liina, 32, 50, 52, 334, 346

Radford, Andrew, 265–267, 284
Ramchand, Gillian, 384, 392

Raymond, William D., 479, 511
Rayner, Keith, 218, 248
Reinhart, Tanya, 118, 139, 154–155, 161, 163, 164, 252, 278, 281, 284, 320, 346, 379, 386, 389, 391, 392
Rezac, Milan, 369, 370
Richards, Norvin, 14, 227, 352, 357–360, 364–365, 369, 370, 373, 376, 378–379, 381–383, 389, 392
Riemsdijk, Henk van, 352–353, 370, 379, 389, 392
Rizzi, Luigi, 5, 18, 265, 279, 284, 387, 392, 426, 455, 531, 540
Roberts, Craige, 65–66, 82, 457, 511
Roehrs, Dorian, 366, 369, 370
Romero, Maribel, 311, 318
Rosen, Sara Thomas, 155, 163
Ross, Claudia N. G., 514, 528, 539
Rullman, Hotze, 390
Russell, Kevin, 102, 105

Sabel, Joachim, 7, 16
Sadakane, Kumi, 47, 52
Sag, Ivan, 21, 25, 46, 47, 48, 51, 118, 139, 415–416, 420, 421
Sagisaka, Yoshinori, 470, 480, 508, 511
Saito, Mamoru, 5–7, 10, 15, 18, 19, 20, 29, 57, 82, 118–120, 134, 135, 139, 143, 151, 157, 162, 164, 192, 208, 214, 216, 223, 248, 250, 253, 263, 284, 292, 297, 312, 313, 319, 321, 324, 343, 346, 357–358, 370, 382, 388, 390, 392, 395, 397–398, 408–410, 413, 418, 419, 420, 421, 422, 447, 455, 513, 540
Sakai, Hiromu, 12, 107, 113–115, 118, 124–129, 132, 134, 135–136, 138, 139, 192, 216, 249, 514, 538
Sakai, Kuniyoshi L., 219, 248
Sakamoto, Tsutomu, 222, 224, 232, 239, 247, 248
Sakata, Mayumi, 508
Sano, Keiko, 9, 19, 263, 284
Sano, Masaki, 147, 164
Sano, Tetsuya, 9, 19, 231, 149, 270, 272, 279, 285
Santen, Jan P. H. van, 471, 475, 488, 491, 512
Sasaki, Yoshinori, 242, 248
Sato, Hirokazu, 480, 511
Sato, Kaori, 228, 248
Sauerland, Uli, 389, 392, 521, 527–528, 537, 540
Schlenker, Phillipe, 68, 82
Schwarzschild, Roger, 78, 82
Sedivy, Julie C., 249
Selkirk, Elisabeth O., 8, 19, 471, 511, 522, 540
Sells, Peter, 321, 342, 346
Sharvit, Yael, 389, 392
Shattuck-Hufnagel, Stefanie, 477, 507
Sheldon, Amy, 231, 248
Shibatani, Masayoshi, 5, 19, 20, 23, 52, 60, 65, 74, 77, 82, 142–143, 145, 147, 149, 162, 164, 168, 191, 192, 216, 290, 319, 417, 422, 438, 455
Shimojo, Mitsuaki, 80, 82

AUTHOR INDEX

Shimoyama, Junko, 14, 19, 349, 353–354, 358, 361–362, 365, 367, 368, 371, 374–375, 377, 381, 384–387, 389, 390, 391, 392, 393
Shinohara, Michie, 397–398, 417, 422
Shinohara, Shigeko, 95, 105, 170, 172, 180, 188, 191
Shirai, Yasuhiro, 217, 248
Shirose, Ayako, 175, 191
Shlonsky, Ur, 310, 319, 537, 540
Sibata, Takesi, 167, 184, 191
Siloni, Tal, 320, 346
Silverman, Daniel, 94, 105, 166, 191
Simpson, Andrew, 515, 519, 531, 540
Smiljanić, Rajka, 508
Smith, Jennifer L., 94, 96, 105, 366, 371
Smolensky, Paul, 94, 105, 183, 190
Snyder, William, 259–260, 279, 285, 427, 451, 455
Sohn, Hyang-Sook, 166, 189, 190
Sohn, Keun-Won, 120–122, 139
Soshi, Takahiro, 236, 245
Speer, Shari R., 495, 508, 509
Spivey-Knowlton, Michael J., 249
Sportiche, Dominique, 290, 293, 310, 319
Stechow, Arnim von, 14, 19, 361–365, 367, 371, 375, 378–381, 385, 389, 393
Steedman, Mark, 65–66, 78, 79, 82
Stokhof, Martin, 390, 391
Stowell, Timothy, 5, 19, 254, 259, 285
Stump, Gregory T., 34, 52
Sturt, Patrick, 226, 231, 248, 249
Sudo, H., 508
Sugahara, Mariko, 356, 366, 371, 494, 498, 511
Sugioka, Yoko, 321, 344, 345
Sugisaki, Koji, 7, 9, 13, 19, 254–255, 259–260, 262–263, 267, 269–271, 279, 285, 449, 455
Suzuki, Seiichi, 277, 285
Suzuki, Shogo, 388, 389, 393
Svenonius, Peter, 46, 52
Swerts, Marc, 512

Tada, Hiroaki, 147, 148, 159, 164, 270, 285
Tagashira, Yoshiko, 322, 346
Takahashi, Daiko, 6–7, 14, 16, 118, 361, 371, 375, 385, 393, 409–411, 413, 419, 420, 422, 531, 540
Takahashi, Shoichi, 222, 232–235, 238, 241, 247, 449, 455
Takami, Ken-ichi, 292–295, 303–305, 307, 312, 315, 319
Takano, Yasukuni, 312, 319
Takano, Yuji, 14, 48, 52, 107, 118, 120–124, 127, 134, 135, 136, 138, 139, 148, 151, 164, 293, 343, 428–432, 446–449, 451, 452, 453, 455, 514, 516, 529–531, 538, 540
Takayama, Tomoaki, 90, 105
Takazawa, Satoru, 247
Takeda, Shoichi, 481, 512
Takeuchi, Tatsuya, 248
Takezawa, Koichi, 142, 149, 162, 164, 223, 249, 253, 285
Talkin, David, 467, 511
Tamaoka, Katsuo, 234, 242, 245, 249
Tanaka, Hidekazu, 262, 286, 357, 368, 371, 378, 387, 393
Tanaka, Shigeki, 244
Tanaka, Shin'ichi, 173, 181, 191
Tancredi, Christopher, 390, 393
Tanenhaus, Michael K., 222, 249
Taniguchi, Miki, 475, 488–490, 510, 512
Tang, Jane, 519, 540
Tateishi, Koichi, 8, 19, 99–101, 105, 471, 511, 513, 536, 540
Terada, Michiko, 23, 52, 292, 300, 312, 319, 536, 540
Thornton, Rosalind, 155, 164, 252, 278, 279, 281, 286
Tokimoto, Shingo, 232, 249
Tomioka, Satoshi, 57, 62–64, 67, 69, 72, 76, 78, 82, 366, 369, 370, 397, 405–407, 409–410, 415, 418, 422
Tonoike, Shigeo, 162, 164
Torrego, Esther, 390, 393
Toyoshima, Takashi, 384, 387, 393
Tranel, Bernard, 102, 106
Travis, Lisa deMena, 46, 52, 445, 455
Trubetzkoy, Nikolai Sergeevich, 95, 106, 456, 512
Tsai, Wei-Tien Dylan, 350, 371, 386, 388, 393
Tsujimura, Natsuko, 15, 19
Tsujioka, Takae, 280, 283, 429, 433, 435–442, 444–447, 449–451, 452, 453, 455
Tsunoda, Tasaku, 144, 164

Uchibori, Asako, 13, 149, 301, 319, 536, 539
Ueda, Masanobu, 6, 19, 289, 319
Uehara, Keiko, 223, 239–240, 249
Ueno, Mieko, 222, 234–236, 249
Uetsuki, Miki, 232, 249
Ueyama, Ayumi, 126, 140, 442, 455
Uffmann, Christian, 166, 190
Ura, Hiroyuki, 149, 160, 162, 164, 192, 216
Uwano, Zendo, 168, 191

Vainikka, Anne, 265, 286
Valian, Virginia, 256, 286
Vallduví, Enric, 61, 63, 65, 67, 70, 74–76, 79, 80, 82, 457, 512
Venditti, Jennifer J., 9, 11, 225, 227, 249, 458, 471, 475, 481, 488, 490–491, 499, 510, 512
Vendler, Zeno, 152, 164
Vermeulen, R., 63, 78, 83
Vikner, Sten, 56, 83
Vilkuna, M., 74–76, 79, 80, 82
Volpe, Mark J., 23, 48, 49–50, 53, 321, 335–337, 343, 346

Ward, Gregory, 476, 492, 508
Washio, Ryuichi, 280, 286
Watanabe, Akira, 6, 14, 19, 47, 75, 80, 83, 122, 140, 192, 194, 199, 210, 213, 214, 216, 292, 302, 312, 319, 349, 356–357, 359, 361, 368, 371, 378, 382, 389, 393, 419, 514, 516, 518–519, 525–526, 530–532, 534–536, 537, 540
Watanabe, Eiju, 248
Waters, Gloria S., 219–220, 243
Weinberg, Amy, 222, 235–236, 241, 242
Welby, Pauline, 505, 512
Wexler, Kenneth, 9, 15, 17, 18, 19, 155, 161, 163, 164, 256, 262, 266–267, 278, 279, 280, 281, 282, 283, 284, 286
Whitman, John, 12, 14, 56, 83, 107–108, 110–111, 116–118, 134, 139, 356, 371, 396, 399–402, 405, 407, 414–415, 417, 418, 422
Wilkinson, Karina, 522, 540
Williams, Edwin, 109, 134, 140, 324, 341, 347, 389, 392, 399, 420, 422
Wold, Dag E., 390, 393
Woolley, Jacqueline D., 218, 245
Wurmbrand, Susi, 151–152, 158–159, 162

Xu, Liejiong, 396, 416, 422

Yabushita, Katsuhiko, 63–66, 70, 78, 82
Yamakoshi, Kyoko, 9, 19, 270, 285
Yamashina, Miyuki, 390, 393
Yamashita, Hideaki, 311, 319
Yamashita, Hiroko, 221, 225, 231, 232, 236–237, 243, 249
Yatabe, Shuichi, 312, 319
Yatsushiro, Kazuko, 148, 164, 375, 393, 429, 432–433, 440–442, 449, 452, 455, 521, 527–529, 537, 540
Yi, Li, 246
Yip, Moira, 94, 106
Yokoyama, Masayuki, 257, 278–279, 286
Yoshida, Masaya, 224, 231, 241, 248, 249
Yoshida, Tomoyuki, 387, 393
Yoshita, Hiromi, 237, 243
Yumoto, Yoko, 321–322, 347

Zenno, Yasushi, 23, 30, 33, 53
Zoll, Cheryl, 85, 91, 103

Subject Index

Accent: antepenultimate accent rule (*see* Loanword accent rules); commands, 470–471, 482–483, 486, 501, 506, 507; compound (*see* Compound accent rules); loanword (*see* Loanword accent rules); patterns, 11, 165–175, 177–179, 181–189, 484, 494, 498, 505; pitch (*see* Pitch accent); specification in the lexicon (*see* Lexical specification); verbs and adjectives, 11, 165–168, 172, 181–182, 186–187; word (*see* Word accent)
Accenting morphemes, 166, 174–176, 186
Accusative object, 13, 147–148, 150–151, 154–157, 162, 210–211, 223, 234, 324, 403, 443
A-chains, 9–10, 13, 267, 269–272, 279
Acquisition: of lexical items, 24, 166, 169, 171, 175–176, 272–275; of syntax, 8, 9–10, 13, 24, 250–286, 449
Adverb view of FNQs, 288, 294, 296, 302–303, 307–310, 313, 315
Adverbs of quantification, 311, 387
Affixal causatives, 20–28
Agree, 37, 159–160, 194, 200–204, 212, 214, 360, 364–365, 369. *See also* Multiple Agree
Agreement relations, 15, 162, 194, 200, 202, 206, 212, 265, 324, 529, 531–536
Akusento, 464, 467, 469, 477, 480–482, 484, 486, 494, 498, 506
Anaphora, 23, 65–67, 120–121, 143, 264, 268, 271, 396, 400–401, 405–406, 411, 415, 420, 432, 440, 536
Applicative heads 334, 340, 436–437, 439, 444–445
Attachment, high/low, 4, 13, 45–46, 230–232
A-movement, 119, 128–129, 196, 199, 210, 269–270, 279, 448–449
A'-movement, 42, 119–120, 196, 199, 264, 297, 313, 413, 448
Argument structure, 21, 26, 41, 44, 222, 273, 325–327, 334, 340, 341, 343
Articulators, 458
Autosegmental-Metrical framework, 12, 457–458
Autosegmental Phonology, 459, 466–467, 469

Basque 189, 160, 351–352, 354, 364, 366, 368, 373–374, 382, 466, 502
Binding, 24, 25, 36, 42, 57, 118, 120, 142–143, 146, 252, 278, 356, 358, 395, 425–426, 428–429, 431–434, 441, 443–444, 449, 451

Blocking effect, 33–35, 37–38, 40
Bound variables. *See* Variable binding
Boundary pitch movements (BPMs), 11, 464, 471–476, 487–489, 491–492, 501–503, 506
Boundary tone marking, 8, 463–464, 466–467, 469, 471, 473, 481, 492–493, 501–502
Brain responses in processing, 219, 449
Bulgarian, 359–360, 369
Burzio's Generalization, 334

Cantonese, 231, 456, 467
Case alternation. *See Ga/no* conversion
Case marking 13, 28, 148–151, 156–161, 162, 192–194, 197–199, 201–207, 210–213, 214, 215, 253–254, 257–258, 268–271, 278–279, 313, 334, 343, 432, 447, 449, 517–520, 526,528, 532, 534. *See also* Morphological case marking
Case Marker Drop (CMD) phenomenon, 253, 269, 278
Case Resistance Principle, 254
CaseP, 517–520, 526, 532, 534
Catalan, 456, 457
Causative construction, 12, 20–53, 131, 234, 239, 272, 274–275, 277, 280, 321, 435–436, 441; in acquisition studies, 24; inchoative alternations, 29–30, 38–40, 42–44, 48, 49. *See also* Affixal causatives. *See also* Lexical causatives. *See also* -*Sase*
C-command, 39, 42, 117–118, 121–122, 135, 150, 157–160, 195–196, 208–209, 250, 252, 264, 289, 313, 333, 357, 369, 387, 417, 425, 427, 453. *See also* Mutual c-command requirement
Center embedding, 13, 219, 226, 239–240
Chain Condition, 426–427, 429, 432–433, 440–442, 447, 449, 451, 453
CHILDES database, 263, 274, 280
Chinese 90, 149–150, 167, 231, 312, 324, 343, 384, 386, 396, 399–400, 413–415, 419, 515, 519, 533
Clause boundaries in processing, 13, 217, 223–225
Co-grammars, 91–92
Complex NP, 199, 259, 349, 351, 360, 375, 376, 378–379, 382–383, 386, 388, 389
Compound accent rule, 11, 165–166, 169, 182, 186
Compounding Parameter, 259–261

SUBJECT INDEX

Compounds: aspectual and psychological, 323–324; means/manner relation, 339; flexible argument, 331, 337, 340; V-*te*-V, 229; V-V (*see* V-V compounds)
Condition A, 431
Condition B, 155, 278, 395–396
Condition C, 6, 120, 252
Configurationality of languages, 7, 10, 14, 252–254, 178
Control, 21, 23–26, 30, 36, 42, 44, 156–158, 184, 239, 331, 333–334, 343, 416, 420, 441–442
Conversion of *ga/no*. *See Ga/no* conversion
Corpus of Spontaneous Japanese (CSJ), 458, 471–476, 480, 491–492
Covert movement 14, 134, 197–199, 207, 348, 350–352, 354, 356–358, 362, 364, 368, 369, 378–383, 389, 410, 419, 432, 451

Dagur, 206
Dative construction, 21, 23–24, 47, 118–120, 123–125, 132, 135, 142, 145–146, 160, 162, 210–211, 223, 229, 235, 239 241, 290, 324, 343, 423–424, 428–429, 431, 434–444, 452, 514, 536
Dephrasing, 484–487, 493–495, 497–498, 500, 504, 507
Determiner phrase (DP), 13, 14–15, 44, 59, 122, 127, 192–200, 206–210, 212, 312, 408, 410, 418–419, 436–439, 449, 452, 513–540
Discourse-level prosody, 12, 462, 465, 470–471, 473, 477, 479, 486, 491, 494, 495, 496
Dissimilation, 468
Distributed Morphology, 14, 36–38, 49, 320, 321, 335–336, 341–342, 526
Ditransitive constructions, 14, 35, 225–226, 232–234, 236–237, 270, 273, 333–334, 340, 423–455
Double-*o* Constraint, 223
Double object construction, 424, 428–429, 435, 437–438, 452
Downstep 469–470, 483, 490, 494–497, 506
DP structure, 418, 516–520, 523
D-system generalization, 533, 535
Dutch, 260, 313, 477

Ellipsis; NP, 14, 394–422, 513, 527, 536; phonological, 462; VP, 12, 108–109, 111, 116–118, 134
Elsewhere Condition, 37–46
Empathy marker (*kureru*), 228–229
English, 3, 5–6, 11, 15, 20, 21, 23, 34, 46, 49, 59–61, 66–68, 75–77, 78, 79, 80, 84, 87, 92, 94–97, 99–101, 107–109, 116–118, 121–122, 126, 131–134, 137, 152, 161, 172, 184, 187, 208, 213, 219, 222, 224, 229–231, 237, 241, 252–257, 259, 261–262, 265, 267–269, 273–274, 278, 290, 310–311, 323, 338, 348, 349, 366, 374, 378–379, 384, 386, 389, 394–397, 399, 404, 406–407, 410, 416, 418–419, 423–424, 430–432, 434–436, 439, 447, 449, 453, 456–459, 464–466, 473, 475–481, 487, 492, 499, 502–504, 506, 514–516, 518, 520–523, 525, 527, 529, 532–537
English Compound Stress Rule, 487
Event quantification, 301
Extended Projection Principle (EPP), 7, 128, 159–161, 210, 313, 439
Eye tracking, 218, 225, 233, 235

Fo reset, 482
Feature specification, 8, 37–38
Filler-gap dependencies, 229–231, 235–236, 238
Floating numeral quantifiers. *See* Quantifiers, floating numeral
fMRI. *See* Brain responses in processing
Focal prominence, 9, 11–12, 457, 477, 480–483, 487–491, 495–501, 503, 506
Focus, 12, 22, 58–63, 65–67, 69–71, 74–75, 77, 78, 79, 80, 112–115, 120–121, 135–136, 162, 428, 441, 452, 457, 469–471, 477–505, 506; projection, 59–61, 504–505
French, 95, 114, 213, 214, 239, 262, 266, 290, 313, 400
Functional categories 149–150, 408, 513, 529; in acquisition, 265–267, 272, 279

-*Ga*: conversion with -*no* (*see Ga/no* conversion); exhaustive and descriptive, 11, 55, 57–60, 70–71, 73, 78; information structure, 54–83
Ga/no conversion (GNC), 13, 192–216; optionality, 209, 211–212; transitivity restriction, 209–211
Genitive case, 13, 149, 162, 192–212, 214–215, 232, 254, 257–258, 278, 408, 429, 514, 528, 537. *See also No*
German, 75, 77, 262, 266, 310–311, 477, 532
Germanic languages, 11, 56, 78, 252, 262, 276, 513
Goal-theme order. *See* Theme-goal order
Goodall, Jane, 276, 280
Greek, 46, 502

Hamblin semantics, 384–385, 390
Head-driven Phrase Structure Grammar (HPSG), 25–26
Head-final languages, 49, 107, 221–222, 263, 342, 425, 529, 531
Hebrew, 45, 418
Honorification, 22, 48, 142–143, 323, 342, 343, 443–444, 452
Hungarian, 457, 502
Hyakurakan test, 220
Hybrid view of FNQs, 291–300, 309–310

Idioms, 23–24, 30–33, 36, 44–45, 48, 50, 132, 138, 338, 341–342, 439–440, 442
Ijo, 342

Imbabura Quechua. *See* Quechua
Implicit prosody. *See* Prosody, implicit
Inchoative construction, 29–30, 38–40, 42–44, 48, 49, 433–434, 443–444.
Inclusiveness Condition, 402
Incorporation, 27–28, 37, 320, 344
Indeterminate pronouns, 14, 372–393; and locality, 376–378, 380, 384–387, 390
Indexed Faithfulness, 91–94, 96, 98–99, 102
Indexed Markedness, 92–93
Information structure, 10–12, 54–83, 303–305, 465, 495, 503, 505
Interrogative construction, 14, 349, 353, 365, 367–368, 372–374, 376, 378–381, 384–386, 388, 390
Intervention effects 14, 202, 357, 359, 361, 368
Intonation systems, 456–512
Irish, 418
Island effects, 349–366, 378, 381–385, 390; adjunct, 349, 351, 388; complex NP, 349, 352, 383, 386, 389; *wh*-island 5, 349–350, 352–361, 366, 369, 376–378, 381–387, 389, 390
Italian, 5, 256, 262, 400
Ittai, 14, 349–350, 356, 359

J_ToBI labeling conventions, 457–458, 471

Ka, 14, 23, 135, 194–199, 201, 207–209, 241, 262, 354, 361–362, 366, 368, 373–377, 380, 385, 388, 389, 390, 473, 506, 515, 531, 537
Kagoshima Japanese, 168, 172, 184–185, 188
Korean, 48, 80, 100, 142, 240, 278, 375, 402
Kureru. *See* Empathy marker (*kureru*)

Last Resort, 7, 410–413, 419
Late Insertion, 12, 37, 39, 46, 133
Lenition. *See* Vowel lenition
Lexical class, 11, 84–106
Lexical causatives, 12, 22–25, 28–46, 48, 49–50, 277, 280
Lexical specification, 165–167, 171, 176, 466
Lexicalism, 320
Loanword accent rule, 11, 165–167, 169, 171, 187; antepenultimate rule, 168–173, 180–181, 186; Latin rule, 172–173
Loanword phonology, 8, 97, 166–167, 170, 187

MAE_ToBI labeling conventions, 477
Malayalam, 386, 388, 390
Maturation: of UG properties, 256, 265–272, 276; of A-chains, 9–10, 13, 267–271, 279
Memory, working. *See* Working memory
Minimal Link Condition, 352, 365, 434, 531
Mo: 'also'; universal, 375–378, 380–381, 385–388, 389

Morae, 167–172, 176–184, 186, 189, 469, 461, 466, 501
Morphological case marking, 28, 210–212, 214, 223–224
Morphology, 4, 8, 12, 13, 21, 27, 29, 33–34, 36–39, 43, 46, 48, 49, 113, 133, 194, 200–201, 214, 228–229, 239, 320–321, 324, 335–337, 341–342, 526, 534–535. *See also* Affixal causatives. *See also* Distributed Morphology. *See also* Rentai morphology
Morphology-syntax interface, 12
Multiple Agree, 159–160, 162, 202, 365
Multiple nominative, 61, 78, 239–240
Mutual c-command requirement, 290–292, 294–295, 297–300, 305, 312

Naze, 121–122, 135, 254–255, 349–350, 388, 389
Negation-disjunction expressions, 261
Negative evidence, 250, 277, 280
Negative polarity items (NPIs), 24, 28, 241, 373
No, 13, 149–150, 192–216, 257–259, 278–279, 473, 528–530. *See also Ga/no* conversion.
Nominal denotations, 533–534
Nominalization, 22–24, 34, 48, 49–50, 67, 136, 204–205, 214, 335, 337, 344
Nominative object, 12–13, 141–164
Noncompositionality, 33, 324, 335–337
NP ellipsis. *See* Ellipsis, NP
Nuclear pitch accent, 477–479, 481, 487, 491, 499, 504–505, 506
Nuclear Stress Rule, 487, 504
Null-argument parameter, 264–265
Null object, 12, 108, 110–111, 116–118, 134, 143, 394–401, 404–406, 414–415, 417, 418, 420
Null-subject parameter, 256
Numeral-classifier combinations, 513, 515, 520, 525, 528, 534–535, 536
Numeral quantifiers, floating. *See* Quantifiers, floating numeral

Object, nominative. *See* Nominative object
Optimality Theory, 8, 11, 85, 91
Otagai, 411, 426–427, 441–442, 449, 451, 452. *See also* Anaphora
Overgeneration, 257–259, 278–279

Parameter setting; delayed, 10, 256, 259, 261–262, 265, 267, 271, 278
Partitive constructions, 302, 307–308, 514, 516, 518–528, 533–534, 536, 537
Passives, 9, 46, 49, 145–146, 234, 237–238, 267–271, 280, 290–291, 312, 329, 417, 453
Penultimate non-lexical prominence (PNLP), 474, 476, 489, 491–492, 501–502, 506
Persian, 49, 531
Phrasal pitch range, 456, 481–483

Phrase commands in prosody, 470, 482–483
Phonology 8–9, 11–12, 84–106, 166–167, 170, 175, 187, 348–349, 367, 456–512. Se also Loanword phonology
Pied-piping, 14, 351–355, 357–359, 362--365, 367, 378–383, 389
Pitch accent, 8, 59, 187, 456, 464, 466, 477–481, 487, 491, 501, 504–505, 506. See also Akusento
Pitch range features, 469–471
Positive polarity items (PPIs), 261–262
Predicate raising. See Raising, predicate
Principle of Minimal Compliance, 360, 365, 389
Pro, 135, 142, 329, 418, 425, 442, 450
PRO, 239, 323, 333–334, 343
Probe, 159–160, 201–203, 214, 232, 360, 364–365, 369
Processing, 7, 10, 12–13, 217–249; incremental models, 221–224, 229, 234
Prominence-lending rise (PLR), 475, 488–492, 501–502, 506
Prominence marking, 458–512
Pronouns, indeterminate. See Indeterminate pronouns
Proper Binding Condition, 118
Prosodic phrases, 462, 464, 472
Prosodic subordination, 483–490, 493–494
Prosodic word, 459, 462
Prosody: commands (*see* Phrase commands, *see* Accent commands); effects with FNQs, 307–308; implicit, 227–228; word level, 456
Psycholinguistics. See Acquisition. See Processing

Quantificational particles, 372, 531–532, 535, 537. See also Indeterminate pronouns
Quantified phrase (QP), 398–399, 406, 442–443, 448, 517–518, 525, 528, 536
Quantifier Indexing Rule, 387
Quantifier stranding, 288–310
Quantifiers, floating numeral (FNQ), 13, 287–319, 437–438; aspectual delimitedness, 305–306, 316; distributional restrictions, 13, 288–289, 293–294, 302–303, 309; locality, 296–299; semantic restrictions, 300–302; pragmatic considerations, 303–305
Quechua, 199, 351–355, 364, 366–367, 368
Questions, wh-. See Wh-questions

Raising: predicate, 26–27; verb 12, 107–140
-*Rare*, 49, 145, 147, 152, 155, 157, 268–271, 280, 343
Reading experiments. See Eye tracking
Reconstruction, 7, 9, 14, 57, 119–120, 124, 151, 159, 196, 199, 264, 271, 362–363, 368, 379–383, 390, 400–402, 404, 406, 417, 425, 428, 431–432, 434, 447–449

Relative clauses, 10, 13, 149, 196–199, 201, 204–206, 210, 213, 217, 223–227, 230–233, 351, 375, 379, 389, 521, 527, 531, 536; attachment, 231–232; gap position, 230–231; parameter 259, 278, 27
Relativized Minimality, 387
Remnant movement, 119, 123, 363, 516, 519
Rendaku, 84, 188, 189, 338, 344, 498, 505
Rentai morphology, 193–194, 199–201, 203–204, 210, 213, 214–215
Reset. See Fo reset
Resultatives, 46, 259–261, 343
Rise-fall BPM, 471, 475–476, 483, 491–492, 501–502, 506

-*Sase*, 21–49, 274–275, 280
Scope, 13, 23–28, 36, 42, 44, 60, 64, 77, 79, 128–133, 137, 147–148, 150–161, 162, 194–199, 206–209, 241, 261, 309–310, 349–362, 366–366, 368, 376, 382–383, 385, 388, 389, 417, 425–429, 437, 451, 452; left-edge effect, 196–197, 207–209
Scrambling, 7–8, 9–10, 14, 112, 118–119, 121, 124, 126–129, 135, 162, 210, 217, 219, 222–223, 230, 232–239, 241–242, 263–264, 271, 292, 297, 309, 312, 313, 409–410, 413–415, 419, 424–450, 451, 453; reading times, 218–235; plausibility task, 234; antecedent reactivation and resolution, 237–239; acquisition, 263–264, 271. See also Filler-gap dependencies
Secondary predicates, 260, 289
Selectional requirements, 115, 158, 332, 338, 409–414, 419
Semantic interpretation of indeterminate pronouns, 378–387
Sentence processing. See Processing
Sinhala, 355–356
Sino-Japanese accent pattern, 8, 84, 86, 90, 102, 166–167, 172, 182, 458
Shuri Okinawan, 356
Sloppy interpretation, 108–111, 116–118, 134, 396, 400–401, 403–406, 413–415, 417. 418. See also Strict interpretation
Spanish, 231, 256, 260, 390, 413–415, 466
Specificity, 519–520, 525, 534, 536
Split quantifiers, 310
Split Topicalization, 310–311
Stranding view of FNQs, 288–300, 302–303, 307–310
Stress foot, 479
Strict interpretation, 108–110, 118, 417. See also Sloppy interpretation
Stricture gestures, 458
Subjacency, 5, 122, 132, 353, 364, 383, 389
Syntax-semantics interface, 367, 372, 378, 504
Synthesis systems in prosody, 469–471, 482, 495

Taiwanese, 468
Takusan, 200, 203, 524–528

TETU, 98–99, 102
Thai, 260, 468, 531
Thematic hierarchy, 430–431, 448
Theme-goal order, 425–426, 428–431, 433, 448–450
θ-roles, 241, 266, 271, 280, 325, 340, 343, 439, 444
Tlingit, 351–352, 354–355, 364, 366, 368
Tokyo Japanese accent system, 168–173, 175, 184–188, 366, 458, 466, 502
Tone marking. *See* Boundary tone marking
Tone scaling, 469, 500
Topic, 12–13, 54, 58, 61–72, 74–80, 136, 162, 225, 240, 264, 310–311, 315, 368, 457, 470
Toyama dialect, 204, 257–258
Truth-value judgment task, 252, 260, 262
Two-T hypothesis, 214

Unaccusatives, 9, 39, 48, 49, 59–60, 237, 269–270, 272–274, 290–291, 306, 325–327, 329, 332–337, 343
Unselective binding, 225, 356, 380

Variable binding 425, 428, 433, 443, 449, 451
Verb raising. *See* Raising, verb
Very Early Parameter-Setting, 9, 262
Vietnamese, 531
Vowel lenition, 480
VP-ellipsis. *See* Ellipsis, VP
V-V compounds, 13–14, 320–347; serial verb constructions, 326, 331, 339, 342, 343

-*Wa*: information structure, 10–12, 54–83; topic, 240; contrastive and thematic, 55–57, 74–77, 78, 483, 490, 496, 497; noncontrastive, 55–58, 63–66, 70, 74–77, 78. *See also* Topic
Weak crossover, 6, 428
Wh-movement, 6, 213, 254–255, 265, 348, 350–351, 358–359, 364, 366, 368, 378, 380, 382, 384, 389; covert, 350, 358, 364, 378, 382. *See also* Island effects, *wh*-island
Wh-questions, 6, 14, 121, 262–263, 348–371, 373–374, 376, 379, 385, 389, 506, 507; acquisition, 255; long-distance dependencies, 217, 220; in-situ *wh*-phrases, 14, 240–242, 255, 349–350, 352–359, 367, 368
Word accent, 11, 165–167, 188. *See also* Loanword accent rule
Working memory, 10, 217, 219–220, 222, 229–230

X-JToBI labeling conventions, 457, 462–463, 467, 469, 471, 473, 475–476, 487, 492–493, 501–502

Yoruba, 331, 342, 456, 467, 468

Zibun, 23, 108, 110–111, 116–117, 120–121, 143, 146, 238–239, 264, 268–269, 271, 274, 396–398, 400–406, 408–409, 412, 418, 419, 443–444, 452, 453. *See also* Anaphora